African American Music

African American Music: An Introduction is a collection of seventeen essays surveying major African American musical genres, both sacred and secular, from slavery to the present. With contributions by leading scholars in the field, the work brings together analyses of African American music based on ethnographic fieldwork, which privileges the voices of the music-makers themselves, woven into a richly textured mosaic of history and culture. At the same time, it incorporates musical treatments that bring clarity to the structural, melodic, and rhythmic characteristics that both distinguish and unify African American music.

The second edition has been substantially revised and updated, and includes new essays on African and African American musical continuities, African-derived instrument construction and performance practice, techno, and quartet traditions. Musical transcriptions, photographs, illustrations, and a new audio CD bring the music to life.

Mellonee V. Burnim is Professor of Ethnomusicology in the Department of Folklore and Ethnomusicology, Adjunct Professor of African American and African Diaspora Studies, and Director of the Archives of African American Music and Culture at Indiana University.

Portia K. Maultsby is Laura Boulton Professor Emerita of Ethnomusicology in the Department of Folklore and Ethnomusicology, and Adjunct Professor Emerita of African American and African Diaspora Studies at Indiana University.

African American Music

An Introduction

Second Edition

Edited by
Mellonee V. Burnim
Portia K. Maultsby

Routledge
Taylor & Francis Group

NEW YORK AND LONDON

Second edition published 2015
by Routledge
711 Third Avenue, New York, NY 10017

and by Routledge
2 Park Square, Milton Park, Abingdon, Oxon OX14 4RN

Routledge is an imprint of the Taylor & Francis Group, an informa business

Library of Congress Cataloging in Publication Data
African American music: an introduction/edited by Mellonee V.
Burnim, Portia K. Maultsby.—Second edition.
  pages cm
  Includes bibliographical references, discography, videography,
  and index.
  1. African Americans—Music—History and criticism.
  I. Burnim, Mellonee V. (Mellonee Victoria), 1950–, editor.
  II. Maultsby, Portia K., editor.
  ML3556.A34 2015
  780.89′96073—dc23
  2014010247

ISBN: 978-0-415-88180-7 (hbk)
ISBN: 978-0-415-88181-4 (pbk)
ISBN: 978-1-315-85767-1 (ebk)

Typeset in Scala
by Florence Production Ltd, Stoodleigh, Devon, UK

Senior Editor: Constance Ditzel
Assistant Editor: Denny Tek
Marketing Manager: Amy Langlais
Copy Editor: Sue Edwards
Cover Design: Jayne Varney
Project Manager: James Sowden
Text Design: Florence Production
Proofreader: Hamish Ironside

To our mentors:
Lois A. Anderson
David N. Baker
and in memory of Herman C. Hudson
for your guidance and support

Contents

Preface

At the time that we initially conceived of this book, our careers at Indiana University had already spanned well over twenty years as faculty in the Department of African American Studies. Each fall, in preparing for our classes, which traversed a broad spectrum of African American music traditions, we had struggled to amass a collection of readings suitable for our diverse student aggregate, who represented a wide range of majors, musical knowledge, and cultural perspectives. As ethnomusicologists, our pedagogical approach cast music as dynamic interplay and exchange among performers, composers, and audiences of various backgrounds, experiences, and sensibilities, across time and space. Few of the students we routinely encountered in our classes had formal music training, although the majority of them viewed music as a core of their individual and collective identities. Our constant challenge was to locate sources that met the diverse needs of our particular student demographic, and, at the same time, represented African Americans as conscious agents of their own musical and cultural development.

When Portia Maultsby initially began her teaching journey at Indiana University during the early 1970s, the scholarly study of African American music was in its infancy, as was the case for all subjects African American in the academy. The publication of Eileen Southern's ground-breaking volume *The Music of Black Americans: A History* in 1971 eloquently addressed the pressing need for African American music scholarship. Southern carefully documented key names, events, and significances—what happened when and to whom; the sheer magnitude of the history she foregrounded was compelling. But for ethnomusicologists, many seminal questions, particularly ones regarding socio-cultural and historical contexts and in-group perspectives, remained unanswered in this text. With our entrée into teaching at IU almost a decade after Southern's volume was initially released, the corpus of African American musical literature remained fraught with the uneven treatment of genres—an increasing body of publications on jazz and blues, for example, while religious music traditions, particularly gospel music, and popular music traditions, continued to be marginalized. Although important contributions to African American music scholarship continued to surface over time, the need for a single text that outlined the advent, growth, and development of major African American music genres, while also foregrounding the perspectives of African Americans themselves, remained elusive, even at the advent of the twenty-first century. Our decision to compile *African American Music: An Introduction* was prompted expressly by this need. This second edition represents our effort to expand the scope and utility of the original volume, and to provide additional components that will enhance the pedagogical experience for instructors and students alike.

NEW FEATURES

- Chronological explorations of seventeen genres of music created by Black Americans in the United States.
- Organization that follows the historic timeline placed after the Preface:

    — I. Antebellum Formations and Manifestations (1600s–);
    — II. Postbellum Period: Music in Transition (late 1800s–);
    — III. Music in Migration: Urban Voices (1900–);
    — IV. Post-Civil Rights and Beyond (1960s–).

- Pedagogical features for coursework in African American music:

    — projects at ends of chapters;
    — running glossary;
    — pictorial timeline;
    — photographs; and
    — musical transcriptions.

- Music tracks—40 listening selections.

NEW STRUCTURE

To better serve introductory courses in African American music or African American culture, this edition has been substantially streamlined and restructured in the following ways:

- Reduction in length. Because the breadth of the first edition far exceeded content that could be effectively covered in any single course on African American music, survey or otherwise, we have elected to divide the 707 pages that constituted the first edition into two separate volumes.

- Instead of the two major sections included in the original text, one devoted to genre chronologies, the other devoted to discussion of issues that crossed genre boundaries, this new edition includes only articles from Segment I, chronologies. The entire Issues segment has been removed.
- The creation of two separate volumes allows us to offer two different treatments of African American music—one diachronic, the other synchronic—which can function either independently or conjointly, in relation to course objectives.
- Also removed from the present volume are parts of three chapters (Chapters 4, 6, and 8), which originally appeared in Part I as interpretative commentaries designed to complement the chronologies on jazz, blues, and classical music.
- All essays in Part II, along with the commentaries to Chapters 4, 6, and 8 from the first edition will comprise a separate volume, entitled *Issues in African American Music*, slated for publication in the near future.

NEW CONTENT

Chapter 1, "The Translated African Cultural and Musical Past," introduced here for the first time, replaces the opening chapter on Intellectual History from the first edition. This new chapter examines the ways in which African musical and cultural practices have been preserved and translated into African American expressions in North America.

A new Chapter 2, "African American Instrument Construction and Music Making" by ethnomusicologist Ernest Brown, fills another void in our original collection. Brown explores the influence of African cultural memory on the ways that slaves constructed or modified existing instruments, as well as the unique approaches musicians of African descent employed in performing on musical instruments.

The original chapter "Religious Music" has been subdivided and expanded into separate entries (new Chapters 4 and 10) devoted to spirituals and gospel music— the two indigenous forms of African American religious music, which have historically served as a core of African American religious identity.

A new Chapter 5, "Quartets" by ethnomusicologist Joyce Jackson, traces the development of four-part, all-male a cappella vocal ensembles, beginning with the nineteenth-century religious traditions that later expanded to embrace secular derivatives as well.

Chapter 16, "Detroit Techno" by ethnomusicologist Denise Dalphond, is a completely new essay based on extensive, long-term ethnographic fieldwork. Dalphond traces the development of techno from its Detroit roots to its migration into transnational contexts, which resulted in its reconceptualization as a European rather than an African American genre.

Chapters on Ragtime, Rhythm and Blues, Funk, Disco and House, and Hip-Hop and Rap have been updated, revised, or expanded. Remaining chronologies from the original compilation that are included in this second edition reflect varying degrees of change.

We are pleased to include a 40-track CD, which places at your fingertips key musical examples discussed in the text. Each chronology is linked to at least one audio example on the accompanying CD, with the exception of two chapters (Art/Classical Music and Musical Theater) for which we were unable to secure the desired permissions. These audio examples allow the music to speak for itself in ways that words alone can never convey. Some are full-length tracks, while others are excerpts. In each of these instances, however, the audio segment included on the CD fully illustrates the musical concept referenced in the text.

ACKNOWLEDGMENTS

The expanded content and accompanying CD included with this second edition would not have been possible without the support of a superb cast of colleagues, editors, editorial assistants, friends, and family. We wish to express our most sincere thanks to those who are contributors to this volume for the first time, as well as to our colleagues who invested time, energy, and effort in revising their essays from the first edition. We wish especially to pay special tribute to our colleague Ernest Brown, who sadly succumbed to ill health during the compilation of this volume. His contribution to this work stands as a fitting testimony to his lifelong commitment to excellence in research and performance of musics of Africa and its diaspora.

The completion of this project is due, in large part, to our phenomenal and dedicated editorial assistants/managing editors, Susan Oehler and Rachel Hurley, who spent many hours poring over manuscripts. Susan, who assumed this role in the early stages, faithfully maintained communication with the authors, finalized initial submissions, renewed copyright permissions, and worked together with Joan Zaretti to develop discussion questions and projects. When Susan left the project to assume full-time employment, Rachel assumed this critical role, working tirelessly to bring the project to completion. We express our sincere gratitude to Rachel for her tenacity, attention to the smallest of details, and her willingness to go the extra mile, even when the hours grew long and tiring. Because of her meticulous work and commitment to excellence, this second edition of *African American Music: An Introduction* is so much the better.

The role we each played in the compilation of this volume was facilitated in critical ways by graduate assistants and staff of the Archives of African American Music and Culture (AAAMC) at Indiana University. Graduate student Christina Harrison assisted Portia by digitizing and editing recordings for the accompanying CD, and identifying and securing key library and archival sources. Brenda Nelson-Strauss, head of collections for AAAMC, supported our effort by locating missing dates and publishers for recordings, while Ronda Sewald, the AAAMC administrator and program coordinator, helped locate listening examples.

Portia's chapter, "The Translated African Cultural and Musical Past" benefited significantly from the critical insights of Kwasi Ampene, Ruth Stone, Austin Okigbo, and Clara Henderson. Similarly, discussions with Valerie Grim on key events in African American history contributed to the refinement and contextualization of musical developments in each of Portia's contributed chapters. Portia's interpretations of African American popular music continue to be enhanced by the insights of composer and record company producer Carl MaultsBy. Equally invaluable were her ongoing informal discussions of current trends and rising stars in popular music with graduate student Fredara Hadley, and friends Jeanelle Crouch and Paula Bryant, who self-identify as well-informed popular music advocates. While all of these contributors played meaningful roles in the formulation of the perspectives herein, the responsibility for the final content rests exclusively with us as both authors and editors.

We also wish to extend our gratitude to Mary Bacon, Vincent Green, Maxie Maultsby, Jr. Cinnamon Bowser, M.L. Hinnant, Nancy Allerhand, Francine Childs, Jamel Dotson, and to Mellonee's parents, Arzo and Ruby Burnim, who were always ready to hear and celebrate the latest progress report. We thank you for caring and providing those extra boosts of encouragement just when we needed them. And, of course, to our church families of Bethel AME and Fairview United Methodist—we can all claim the completion of this project as another manifestation of prayer.

Finally, we must acknowledge the unflagging support and *patience* we received from Routlege staff Constance Ditzel, senior music editor, and her assistant, Denny Tek. We will always be grateful to them for believing that this book would indeed come to fruition, and most of all, for bearing with us through the long journey.

Mellonee Burnim and Portia Maultsby
April 2014

CD Listening Examples

Track 23:   "Deep River." Paul Robeson.
Track 24:   "Let the Church Roll On." Southern University Quartet.
Track 25:   "Dusty Rag." "Perfessor" Bill Edwards.
Track 26:   "Crazy Blues." Mamie Smith and Her Jazz Hounds.
Track 27:   "Leave It There." Pace Jubilee Singers.
Track 28:   "Oh Happy Day." The Edwin Hawkins Singers.
Track 29:   "I Don't Feel Noways Tired." James Cleveland; Keith Pringle, soloist.
Track 30:   "Saturday Night Fish Fry." Louis Jordan and His Tympany Five.
Track 31:   "Shake, Rattle, & Roll." Joe Turner.
Track 32:   "Tutti Frutti." Little Richard.
Track 33:   "My Baby Loves Me." Martha & the Vandellas.
Track 34:   "We're a Winner." Curtis Mayfield/The Impressions.
Track 35:   "Dr. Feelgood (Love is a Serious Business)." Aretha Franklin.
Track 36:   "Stand!" Sly and the Family Stone.
Track 37:   "T.S.O.P." MFSB.
Track 38:   "Move Your Body." Marshall Jefferson.
Track 39:   "Roaming." Anthony "Shake" Shakir.
Track 40:   "Spoonin' Rap: A Drive Down the Street." Spoonie Gee.

African American Music Timeline

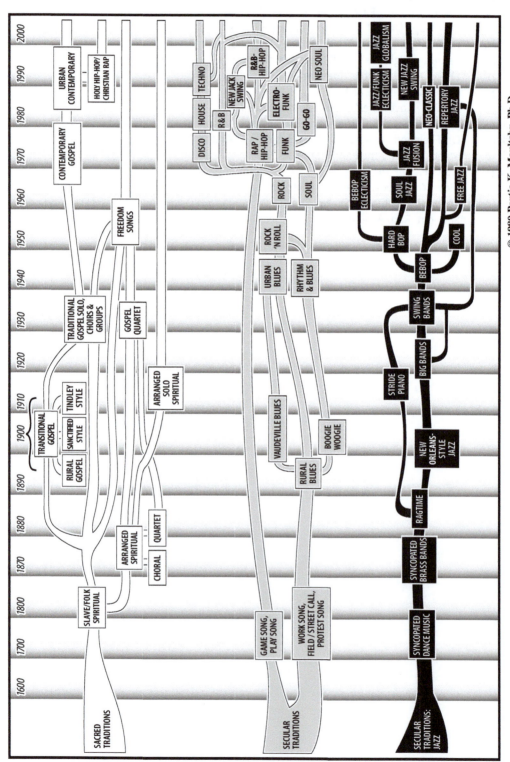

PART I

Antebellum Formations and Manifestations (1600s–)

CHAPTER 1

The Translated African Cultural and Musical Past

Portia K. Maultsby

> *If you build a town and there's no drummer in it, then it's not a town.*
> *If you build a town and there's no singer, then it's not a town.*
>
> (**Kpelle** proverb[1])

Kpelle
A people who live in Liberia, West Africa.

When African slaves began arriving in colonial America during the seventeenth century, they brought multiple cultural traditions that were foreign to European traders, slave captors, and slave holders. The languages they spoke, the religions and folklore they practiced, and the music and dances they performed for nearly three centuries in the United States suggest to a modern audience that the institution of slavery did not destroy the cultural legacy of slaves or erase the memories of an African past. In various contexts, slaves continued to practice African traditions in both original and modified forms. Captains of slave ships, in fact, facilitated the transmission of African cultural traditions during the Middle Passage. They brought African instruments—drums and the *banjar* (early form of the banjo)—aboard the ships and forced the slaves to play them, requiring singing and dancing to the music as an activity for exercise. Using a whip if necessary, the crew "danced the slaves" to reduce the rate of mortality during the Middle Passage. In the United States and through the eighteenth century, slaves continued to sing songs, perform dances, and play instruments of African origin.[2] They also reformulated customs and practices of European origin to conform to African aesthetic ideals. Novelist James Fenimore Cooper offers an account of an event held in 1757 near New York in his novel *Satanstoe*, published in 1845. He describes how slaves and free Blacks transformed the Dutch celebration, Pinkster,[3] into an African-styled festival:

> Nine tenths of the blacks in the city, and of the whole country within thirty or forty miles, indeed were collected in thousands in those fields, beating banjos, singing African songs ... It is true, there are not now, nor were there then, many blacks among us of African birth; but the traditions and usages of their original country were so far preserved as to produce a marked difference between this festival and one of European origin. Among other things, some were making music by beating on skins drawn over the ends of hollow logs, while others were dancing to it.[4]

Observers of slave celebrations and other social gatherings in South Carolina, New Orleans, and other geographical areas described similar African-style activities throughout the eighteenth and into the nineteenth century (see Chapters 2 and 3 for descriptions).[5]

Even though the United States' slave population was ethnically and linguistically diverse, written accounts of celebrations, ritual events, social gatherings, and other activities reveal that Africans and their African American descendants shared cultural customs and musical practices to some degree. Scholars historically have identified West Africa as the area from which slaves came to the United States. Contemporary scholarship on the slave trade, however, reveals that the majority of the slaves arrived from both West and Central Africa.[6] These areas were home to many different ethnic and linguistic groups, each having its own language, cultural, and musical traditions. Intentionally separated from others of their own ethnic group, the collective experience of Africans as slaves in the United States forged the merger of the separate and distinct cultural identities that had defined slaves prior to their capture and transport to the New World. This chapter examines the ways in which the African cultural and musical practices have been both preserved and translated into unique expressions in North America. It considers the role of music in community life, the production and interpretation of sound, and the concepts and principles that govern musical performance and experience.

MUSIC IN COMMUNITY LIFE

> *For many Kpelle people [Liberia], music performance is as much a part of a normal life as walking or talking or eating.*
> (Ruth Stone, *Music in West Africa* . . .[7])

> *They [negroes] sing at their work, at their homes, on the highway, and in the streets.*
> (Reverend C.F. Sturgis, Greensboro', Alabama, 1851[8])

Various authors have documented the centrality of music in African and African American community life.[9] Performed by both groups and individuals, music in traditional West and Central African contexts

Portia K. Maultsby

accompanies all major events, including royal functions, religious and **life cycle** rituals, community festivals, as well as occupational, recreational, and leisure activities. Music performances generally are organized as social events where community members become active participants. They join in by singing, dancing, clapping hands, stomping feet, shaking rattles, and so forth, thereby eliminating distinctions between "performers" and "audience." Such occasions, according to Ghanaian ethnomusicologist J.H. Kwabena Nketia, "provide at once an opportunity for sharing in creative experience, for participating in music as a form of community experience, and for using music as an avenue for the expression of group sentiments."[10]

Life cycles
Major events in life, such as birth, puberty, marriage, and death.

Many of the earliest, albeit sketchy, accounts of music in Africa document its role in the royal court, where kings maintained a large ensemble of professional musicians, who played for various occasions. Musicians announced the presence of royalty, assembled communities, led royal processionals, and provided entertainment for various political, celebratory, and social events. In 1067 a traveler through the kingdom of Ghana observed that the public appearance of the king "is announced by the beating of a kind of drum which they call *deba*, made of a long piece of hollowed wood. The people gather when they hear this sound."[11] A traveler in 1352 in Mali wrote:

> The sultan was preceded by his musicians, who carry gold and silver *gumbris* [two-stringed guitars[12]], and behind him come three hundred slaves . . . On reaching the *pempi* he stops and looks round the assembly . . . As he takes his seat, the drums, trumpets, and bugles are sounded.[13]

Other witnesses also describe the dances and instruments (horns, drums, lutes, xylophones, etc.) that accompanied the singing. In subsequent centuries, music and dance continued to be central to the activities of the royal court.

In North America, slaves living in New England preserved the concept of an authority figure by electing their own kings and governors on a holiday known as Negro Election Day (a.k.a. 'Lection Day). This yearly event, celebrated from the mid-eighteenth through the mid-nineteenth century, was an Africanization of the Colonial Election Day during which the New England White population elected their governors and other community leaders. On the Colonial Election Day, "shops and schools were closed, and town inhabitants, dressed in their finery, gathered in the marketplace." The holiday featured a parade and concluded with an evening feast.[14] Likewise, the festival associated with 'Lection Day also featured a parade with slaves dressed in elaborate outfits singing, dancing, and playing African and European instruments in a distinctly African style. The activities included games and the consumption of special foods and drinks.[15]

In addition to holidays, music accompanied all types of occupational activities both in Africa and the United States. Singing while working

1

"Hammer, Ring."

served to relieve boredom, pass the time, and regulate timing and speed of workers, especially those involved in collaborative work (see Track 1). Witnesses noted that drumming often accompanied the singing in Africa. A physician working in Sierra Leone, West Africa, from 1792 to 1796 wrote:

> When rowing in canoes . . . [the rowers] generally sing during the whole time, and one of the passengers accompanies the song with a small drum. One of the rowers sings a couplet, somewhat in a recitative voice, which is closed by a chorus in which they all join.[16]

The texts of such songs "frequently describe the passengers in a strain either of praise or of the pointed ridicule."[17] In the United States, slaves, as a collective and as individuals, also sang while working.

A passenger on a boat traveling the St. Johns River in Florida in 1835 observed:

> [T]he negroes struck up a song to which they kept time with their oars; and our speed increased as they went on . . . The words were rude enough, the music better, and both were well-adapted to the scene. A line was sung by a leader, then all joined in a short chorus; then came another solo line, and another short chorus.[18]

Former slave Frederick Douglass provides a perspective on the passenger's interpretation of the words as "rude." He explains that slaves mixed standard English "with other words of their own improvising— jargon to others, but full of meaning to themselves."[19] The slaves developed language practices that included the use of jargon, metaphors, and double entendre, which allowed them to freely express in both speech and song their feelings and worldview. The texts of work songs often related to the work performed as well as topics based on folklore, heroic figures, the local surroundings, and biblical themes, among others.

Slaves most often sang without traditional instrumental accompaniment, for loud instruments, especially drums, were prohibited in most southern states by the mid-1700s. Instruments that could be used effectively to communicate over long distances were viewed by slave-holders as potential threats to the system of slavery. Loud instruments could readily signal slave revolts and planned escapes to freedom. During the 1739 Stono Rebellion in Charleston, South Carolina, for example, slaves marched in military formation beating drums accompanied by cries of "Liberty"[20] (see Chapter 2).

Recreational and ritual events associated with adults and children revolved around music and dance. In his autobiography, former slave Charles Ball provides an account of a community gathering of slaves in South Carolina in 1837:

> [On Saturday night] our quarter knew but little quiet . . . singing, playing on the banjoe, and dancing, occupied nearly the whole community, until the break of day. Those who were too old to take any part in our active pleasures, beat time with their hands, or recited stories of former times . . . in Africa.[21]

Children of African descent in the United States and in Africa sang counting games and social games that involved hand clapping and dancing. These games aided children in developing motor skills and physical coordination, fostered group cooperation, and encouraged creativity. Traditional game songs, also known as play or play-party songs, derived their texts from various sources: the actions of the game itself, folktales, children's fantasies and experiences, and children's interpretations of local events and the world around them. These children's songs (see Track 2) were passed down orally through the generations (see Chapter 3).[22]

 2

"Who Are the Greatest?"

Music was a key element in all healing and religious rituals. In 1776 Abbé Proyart, a French missionary in Central Africa, witnessed a musical performance executed as a remedy for disease:

> [T]hey all enter in silence; but at the first signal which they give, the musical troop begin their performance; some are furnished with stringed instruments; others beat on the trunks of hollow trees, covered with skin, a sort of tabor.[23] All of them uniting their voices with the sound of the instruments, round the patient's bed, make a terrible uproar and din; which is often continued for several days and nights in succession.[24]

Music accompanied ceremonies associated with death among slaves in the United States. Describing the funeral procession of an old servant in 1861 in Charlotte County, Virginia, Mrs. Roger A. Pryor, wife of a Confederate officer, writes: "We had a long, warm walk behind hundreds of negroes, following the rude coffin in slave procession through the woods, singing antiphonally."[25] Similar accounts of funerals from throughout the South suggest that African cultural traditions shaped the character of these events, even into the twentieth century. Field reports compiled by the Georgia Writers' Project in the 1930s, for example, document the continuation of African customs: "The mourners beat the drum while on the way to the cemetery; after arriving they marched around the grave in a ring and beat the drum and shouted."[26] The functional dimension of music in community life represents only one aspect of the African musical continuum in the United States. In a comparative study on African and African American music, J.H. Kwabena Nketia concluded, "There are certainly areas in which African and Afro-American expressions shade into one another, either because of present day interaction or because of 'residual strains' which give an African quality to these expressions."[27] He identifies these residual strains as "a limited number of **structural characteristics** and **musical processes**,"[28] including call–response and polyrhythmic organization, for example, as well as the conceptualization, style of execution, and interpretation of performance.

Structural characteristics The form as well as rhythmic, melodic, and harmonic organization of music.

Musical processes The way music is created, performed, and experienced.

Ethnomusicologist Mellonee Burnim, in her study on Black gospel music, identifies three areas of aesthetic significance that govern performance in this genre: sound quality, mechanics of delivery, and style of delivery.[29] Embracing both musical processes as well as structural characteristics, Burnim's model is useful in identifying concepts of performance practice that transcend boundaries of genre. In other words, the areas of significance outlined in Burnim's work are applicable not only to gospel music but also to African American secular music genres as well as to genres formed in other historical periods, as I will illustrate below.

SOUND QUALITY (TIMBRE)

The non-African listener generally finds the [African] music strange, difficult, and unattractive.

(Francis Bebey, Cameroonian composer[30])

They accompany all their labour with a kind of monotonous song, at times breaking out into a yell, and then sinking into the same nasal drawl.

(Whitman Meade, describing stevedores in Savannah, Georgia, 1817[31])

When we came into the smoke-filled room [in Harlem], we could hear a tenor sax . . . honking one low note . . . Just as we sat down, the saxist switched to a very high note and kept screeching that one note.[32]

(Arnold Shaw, R&B historian[33])

Timbre
The quality of sound that distinguishes different voices or instruments from one another.

Sound quality, or **timbre**, is one of the primary elements in African and African American music that traditionally has been subjected to severe criticism from cultural outsiders. European travelers, missionaries, and other outsiders uniformly describe these vocal and instrumental timbres as "wild," "crude," "peculiar," "strange," "weird," and, more broadly, simply as "noise."[34] William Bosman, a Dutch trader, who lived on the coast of Guinea in the 1600s, describes the sound made by a horn. Detailing its construction, he writes, "[A]t the small end is a square Hole; at which by blowing they produce a sort of extravagant Noise." He also summarizes the quality of sound produced by beating drums using sticks or the bare hands as "dismal," "horrid," and "Noise,"[35] documenting his distaste for the aesthetic values that define this West African example. Cameroonian composer-performer Francis Bebey interprets the cultural meaning of African instrumental and vocal timbres that many Westerners delineate as "weird," "horrid," and "noise." Though his comments refer to African music in broad terms, his perspective represents the perceived synchrony he identifies as extending beyond a single region or ethnic group:

3
"Edom Sasraku."

4
"Inanga Bongerera."

5
"Dekuor."

The objective of African music is not necessarily to produce sounds agreeable to the ear, but to translate everyday experiences into living sound. In a musical environment whose constant purpose is to depict life, nature, or the supernatural, the musician wisely avoids using beauty as his or her criterion because no criterion could be more arbitrary.[36]

The varying timbres associated with African music are heard in the recordings (Tracks 3, 4 and 5) of ivory trumpets (Ghana), whispered singing

(Burundi), and group singing (Ghana). Accounts of encounters between Europeans and Africans during the period of the Atlantic slave trade reveal that musicians of African descent often produced musical timbres similar to those common in performances of African music that were, thus, unfamiliar to their Western captors.[37]

On the other side of the Atlantic Mary Boykin Chesnut observed a service conducted in 1861 by slaves on her plantation near Camden, South Carolina. Describing a prayer led by Jim Nelson, identified as a *"full-blooded African"* [emphasis added], she states: "He clapped his hands at the end of every sentence, and his voice rose to the pitch of a shrill shriek ... The Negroes sobbed and shouted ... most of them clapping their hands and responding in shrill tones: 'Yes, God!'" Laurence Oliphant, a British writer who toured the southern United States in 1856 also noticed that slaves "screamed rather than sung" certain words, especially biblical names, such as New Jerusalem.[38] The sounds were unlike any sounds Chesnut and Oliphant had ever heard. Alien to the Western ear and counter to the Western aesthetic ideal, many observers interpreted such sounds as "strange," "peculiar," "noise," and "weird."[39] (See Tracks 6 and 7.)

 6

"Talking 'Bout a Good Time."

The way in which varying timbres can shape the sound of a given song is illustrated in the performance of a hymn by a group of freedmen. The account is provided by Elizabeth Kilham, a teacher in the South in the 1860s just after the end of the Civil War. Witnessing a church service, she wrote:

 7

"Arwhoolie (Cornfield Holler)."

> During the singing of this hymn, the excitement, which had been gradually increasing with each change in the exercises, reached its height. Men stamped, groaned, shouted, [and] clapped their hands; women shrieked and sobbed ... wilder grew the excitement, louder the shrieks.[40]

In varying timbres from groans and shouts to percussive hand claps and foot stomps, the congregants were able to express their religious fervor and praise creatively and imaginatively without restriction. Similarly in 1863, Mississippian Belle Kearney describes an African American congregation singing a **"lined hymn"** as "one of those wild, weird negro airs, half chant and dirge, so full of demi-semi-quavers that only the improvisator-soul can divine it."[41] Kearney's strongly ethnocentric critique affirms the multiple variations of timbre that African Americans could employ during performance, while also revealing the strong distaste she had for expressions she considered as both "wild" and "weird," far from her ideal of the sacred.

Lined hymn
A style of hymn singing in which each line of text is sung or chanted first by the song leader and then echoed by the congregation.

Distinctive and contrasting timbres also characterize performances of jug and early jazz bands, and contemporary popular music such as Detroit techno. In jug bands, the combination of instruments such as banjo, guitar, jug, harmonica, and kazoo—which are uncommon in traditional Western ensembles—produce contrasting timbres and textures that conform to an African aesthetic ideal.[42] This instrumentation

8

"Viola Lee Blues."

9

"Potato Head Blues."

10

"Strings of Life."

3

"Edom Sasraku."

Slide or bottleneck
A playing technique in which a guitar player slides a metal bar or glass neck from a bottle across the strings to alter the timbre.

Leslie speaker
An amplifier that produces special sound effects via rotating sound waves in the speakers. Primarily associated with the Hammond organ.

is illustrated in "Viola Lee Blues" (1928) by Cannon's Jug Stompers (Track 8). Similarly, the collective improvisation style of early jazz bands, composed of a banjo, piano, clarinet, trumpet, trombone, and tuba, created contrasting timbres and textures, such as those heard in "Potato Head Blues" (1928) by Louis Armstrong and His Hot Seven (Track 9). In Detroit techno this African aesthetic ideal is embodied in the complex layering of varying rhythmic and melodic sounds generated by analog synthesizers and drum machines (and, later, computer-based digital instruments) that define the uniqueness of recordings such as "Strings of Life" (1987) by Rhythim is Rhythim (a.k.a. Derrick May) (Track 10).

In African and African-derived musical traditions, instrumentalists frequently imitate the voice. Because many languages in West and Central Africa are tonal, the relative pitch of the spoken word defines meaning. Described by Bebey, "a musical instrument 'speaks' the same language as does its player,"[43] which is illustrated in performances of historical songs. Often associated with the royal court, these songs chronicle the history of African kings with reference to their royal ancestry. Recounting such an event among the Akan, Ghanaian ethnomusicologist J.H. Kwabena Nketia explains that after the introductory ancestral references:

> The recitals are sung by two male singers. Breaks in the singing are filled in by talking drums, followed by talking trumpets, all of which play the "texts" that relate to the historical chant or praise the reigning monarch.[44]

Sharing Nketia's perspective, ethnomusicologist Kwasi Ampene elaborates, citing the praise poetry spoken by ivory trumpeters: "The trumpets 'speak' as opposed to playing melodic music. They are used in place of the human voice (surrogate speech)."[45] (See Track 3.) The talking drums are common in West Africa, and talking trumpets in West, Central, and East Africa. To produce vocal sounds, drummers alter the pitch of the hourglass-shaped drum by manipulating the tension strings that connect the two drum heads, while trumpet players vary embouchures, playing techniques, and fingerings.[46]

Similarly, African American performers make their instruments "talk" by producing a wide range of vocally inspired timbres using sound-altering devices such as mutes, **bottlenecks**, **Leslie speakers**, fuzz boxes, and synthesizers, and "by altering *traditional* [emphasis mine] embouchures, playing techniques and fingerings" associated with Western instruments.[47] Band leader and jazz musician James Reese Europe describes this process in detail:

> With the brass instruments we put in mutes and made a whirling motion with the tongue, at the same time blowing full pressure. With wind instruments we pinch the mouthpiece and blow hard. This produces the peculiar sound which you all know. To us it is not discordant. . . . Whenever possible they [band members] all embroider their parts in order to produce new, peculiar sounds.[48]

Europe's description reveals that African American musicians conceptualized timbre within the framework of their own aesthetic values and that they devised unconventional ways to produce "peculiar" sounds that White critics interpreted to be discordant. Examples of these vocal-inspired timbres in jazz are heard on Johnny Dunn's cornet solo on "You Need Some Lovin'" (1928) and Duke Ellington's performances of "Happy-Go-Lucky Local" (1946) and "C Jam Blues" (1958).[49]

Gospel and blues musicians produce similar timbres through the use of various devices and fingering techniques. Gospel singer-guitarist Blind Willie Johnson ("God Moves on the Water," 1929) and blues singer-guitarists Muddy Waters ("You Got to Take Sick and Die Some of These Days," 1941) and Homesick James ("Somebody Been Talkin'," 1968),[50] for example, slide a bottleneck or jackknife over the strings and bend them to alter the timbre, producing vocal sounds similar to moans, grunts, and screams, as well as those that imitate the vocal line (Track 11). Describing a performance practice of guitarist B.B. King that brings "his playing close to the spoken human voice," journalist Charles Sawyer observes King's "intermittent tendency to confine his figures to a narrow range of notes [that] give the tight melodic fragments more the aspect of inflected speech than the melody of song . . ."[51] King views his guitar as being more than an object, conceiving of it as a human voice. Similarly, gospel organists and funk keyboardists, guitarists, and bassists employ sound-altering electronic and synthesized devices to produce vocally inspired timbres, as illustrated in Walter Hawkins' "Goin' Up Yonder" (1975), Kirk Franklin's "The Altar" (2011), and Parliament's "Flash Light" (1977) (Track 12).[52]

 11
"God Moves on the Water."

 12
"Flash Light."

Within the context of African practice, Ruth Stone explains that instruments "are more than material objects. Rather, they often are considered quasi-human as they take on human features."[53] Not only do instruments imitate vocal timbres, they are given personal names as well. In Liberia, for example, musicians called a drum Goma, "a name given to women and meaning 'share with me.'" Similarly B.B. King calls his guitar Lucille, a name given to women. The human character of some instruments is further reflected in the carving of body parts on to the form as is the case with the Goma, which has "ears, body, waist, and feet."[54] The sonic and visual humanization of instruments reflects the conceptualization of instruments as extensions of human beings.

MECHANICS OF DELIVERY (TIME, TEXT, AND PITCH)

> *The leader improvises the words . . . and the whole then gives the chorus, which is repeated without change at every line, till the chorus concludes the stanza.*
>
> (Philip Gosse, observer of dock workers in Mobile, Alabama, 1859[55])

Mechanics of delivery The manipulation of variables of time, text, and pitch in African American musical performance practice.

Central to the gospel music aesthetic, according to Mellonee Burnim, is the "individual interpretation or personalization of the performance (most commonly referred to as improvisation)."[56] In their interpretation of songs, performers achieve variety by manipulating the time, text, and pitch. Time, Burnim explains, encompasses both the structural and rhythmic components of a song. As a structural element, artists can expand the length of songs by repeating words, phrases, and entire sections.[57] Methodist minister John F. Watson, who led camp meetings in the nineteenth century, observed that slaves "lengthened out [songs of their own composing] with long repetition [*sic*] *choruses* [original italics]."[58] The long choruses constitute a complete song, of which an unidentified witness in Macon, Georgia, in 1858 noted, "The words are generally very few, and repeated over and over again."[59] Such repetition also occurs in a two-part song structure known as call–response. Philip Gosse, an observer of dock workers in Mobile, Alabama, in 1859, outlines this structure: "The leader improvises the words ... and the whole then gives the chorus, which is repeated without change at every line, till the chorus concludes the stanza."[60] The response, or repetitive chorus, provides a stable foundation for the improvised lines of the soloist. As noted by J. Kinnard, who took passage on a boat rowed by slaves up the St. Johns River in Florida in 1835: "A line was sung by a leader, then all joined in a short chorus; then came another solo line, and another short chorus, followed by a longer chorus."[61] These descriptions illustrate that the call–response structure has multiple functions. It (1) encourages improvisation, (2) facilitates musical exchanges and cohesiveness among the participants, and (3) allows for songs to be lengthened and to continue indefinitely. These functions have been preserved in all forms of Black music in the United States for nearly five centuries (Tracks 1, 6, and 13).

"Hammer, Ring."

"Talking 'Bout a Good Time."

"Christian's Automobile."

Call–response
A song structure or performance practice in which a singer or instrumentalist makes a musical statement that is answered by another soloist, instrumentalist, or group. The statement and answer sometimes overlap. Also called antiphony and call-and-response.

Call–Response

Call–response is ubiquitous in early and contemporary accounts of African musical performance. Physician Thomas Winterbottom, for example, describes its use among men on a boat in Sierra Leone in the 1790s:

> One of the rowers sings a couplet, somewhat in a recitative voice, which is closed by a chorus in which they all join in. When there are several rowers the couplet is repeated by a second person, and concluded by a general chorus.[62]

Observing the Kpelle singing while working in rice fields in Totota, Liberia, two centuries later in 1970, ethnomusicologist Ruth Stone wrote: "The soloist began singing a part that is sung to the text: 'Oi-o-gbene-mei-o.' To this the chorus responded, 'Oi-o-gbene.' As the soloist continued she began improvising a new line every other time."[63] A similar call–response structure is heard in a song performed during a religious ritual in Ghana (Track 5).

The call–response structure remains fundamental to performances of twentieth- and twenty-first-century forms of African American music. In blues, for example, the guitar, the harmonica, or other instruments establish a dialogue with the singer, responding with short

"Dekuor."

Portia K. Maultsby

riffs or a mirror of the improvised line of the singer.[64] The gospel choir and instrumentalists respond to the creative vocalizing of the lead singer, especially when the song ascends to a climax and comes to a close.[65] The call–response structure also is used by jazz musicians to establish a base for musical change and tension as demonstrated by the Count Basie Orchestra:

> Basie's men played short, fierce riffs. Their riff patterns were not even melodic elements, they were just repetitive rhythmic figures set against each other in the sections of the band. Against this sharp, pulsing background, Basie set his soloist, and he or she had free rein.[66]

The repetitive rhythmic figures assigned to different sections in the band over which the soloist improvised added a level of tension that increased the intensity of the song.

Syncopation and Polyrhythms

Perhaps the most noticeable feature in African and African American music is its rhythmic complexity. In his study on African music, A.M. Jones concludes: "Rhythm is to the African what harmony is to the Europeans and it is the complex interweaving of contrasting rhythmic patterns that he finds his greatest aesthetic satisfaction."[67] An element of time, rhythm is organized in both linear and multi-linear forms. Musicians improvise around the basic pulse, accenting beats that anticipate, fall in between, or after the regular one, two, three, four beats per measure (often referred to as "off-beats"). From a European musical perspective, this "shifting of the 'normal' accents produc[ing] an uneven or irregular rhythm" is called **syncopation**.[68] Various accounts of Black music making during and after slavery mention the complexity of the rhythm. Sidney Lanier, a musician and writer who traveled throughout the South, discusses the uniqueness of these rhythms in his travelogue on Florida published in1875, referencing syncopation:

Syncopation
The shifting of accent from standard Western stressed beats to atypical stress points in the measure.

> Syncopations ... are characteristic of negro music. I have heard negroes change a well-known melody by adroitly syncopating it ... nothing illustrates the negro's natural gifts in the way of keeping a difficult tempo more clearly than his perfect execution of airs [folk songs] thus transformed from simple to complex accentuations.[69]

Lanier describes how Blacks transformed Euro-American "airs" (folk songs) into original compositions by manipulating time in ways that shifted the accents from the even or main beats of one, two, three, four common in European traditional music to the beats in between (Track 14).

Lanier's description of "negro" singing reveals how race and musical biases can inform the way difference is characterized. His assertion that the complex rhythmic treatment of melody is based on the "negro's natural gifts" fails to acknowledge that in Black music rhythm assumes a hierarchical position over melody. The "perfect execution" of rhythm

 14

"Maple Leaf Rag, 1916."

is based on a set of aesthetic values and rhythmic concepts that differ from those of European traditions. Value is placed on innovation—to reinterpret and personalize songs in accordance with Black aesthetic principles. The varying and complex treatment of rhythm is central to this process as exemplified in the construction of **polyrhythms**.[70]

Polyrhythm
Several contrasting rhythms played or sung simultaneously.

Polyrhythm, the layering of contrasting rhythms, is ubiquitous to sub-Saharan African instrumental ensembles made up of various percussive and melodic instruments. The instruments of various timbres are assigned different rhythmic patterns, some of which are repeated, without variation. When the song begins, each instrument generally enters at different times, a practice known as staggered entrances.[71] To illustrate, I describe a song played by Ga-Adangme musicians of Accra, Ghana, for social and recreational events (Track 15). The song of the *kpatsa* genre begins with a brief introduction played on the master drum (*kpanlogo*). The double bell (*gangkogui*) joins the *kpanlogo*, then takes over the phrase-length pattern, which is repeated throughout the song without variation. Known as the time line, this pattern provides the organizing structure for the layering and interweaving of contrasting rhythms. The next instruments to enter are a small slender drum (*kagan*) followed by a medium-size drum (*kidi*), each playing a different short repetitive rhythmic pattern. The master drum assumes the lead role, improvising on top of the layered rhythms throughout the song.[72] When singing is included in performances, the vocals provide yet another rhythmic and timbral layer. The song "Dekuor" (Track 5), performed during religious worship services of the Dagara people in northern Ghana, for example, begins with a repetitive phrase-length pattern played on the traditional xylophone known as the *gyil*. The next instruments to enter are a rattle, followed by a second *gyil* (assigned the time line), then the vocals and two drums (lead and supporting). A male leads the singing, alternating his improvised lines with responses of the mixed chorus. At different points in the song, female voices ululate, adding another timbral layer to the performance. The distinctive quality of the voices, combined with the contrasting timbres of the *gyil* and other instruments, produces sounds and textures that are counter to the European aesthetic ideal. Similarly, the layering of different rhythmic patterns that cross each other and accent the "off-beats" results in a rhythmic complexity uncommon in traditional European music.

15

Kpatsa.

5

"Dekuor."

In the United States, polyrhythmic structures also define rhythmic complexity in African American music, and they are prominent in children's social songs, jazz, funk, and gospel (Track 2). Jazz and funk musician Fred Wesley[73] describes this rhythmic structure in funk as "a syncopated bass line, a strong heavy back-beat from the drummer, a counter line from the guitar, the keyboard [and horn section]."[74] The bass guitar, functioning as the time line, interlocks with the drum pattern to establish the "groove"—a rhythmic feel, a rhythmic matrix, and aesthetic ideal.[75] The guitar, keyboard, and horn sections each are assigned

2

"Who Are the Greatest?"

contrasting repetitive short rhythms, which are layered and interwoven into each other, as well as on top of and into the groove. This description suggests that polyrhythms result from the combination of individual creativity and musical dialogue among musicians. This rhythmic structure is heard on the recordings of James Brown's band, the JBs ("Gimme Some More," 1971, and "Givin' Up Food For Funk," 1972); recordings of the funk groups Parliament ("Flashlight" 1978) (Track 12) and Roger ("So Ruff, So Tuff," 1981) (Track 16); and the jazz-fusion recordings of Herbie Hancock ("Watermelon Man," 1973, and "Doin' It," 1976).

"Flash Light."

"So Ruff, So Tuff."

In gospel music, the addition of voices adds yet another level of rhythmic complexity to songs. The short repetitive phrases sung by the chorus in response to the improvised lines of the lead singer are layered upon the instrumental patterns, generating a rhythmic tension and intensity as heard on "Old Landmark" (1972) by Aretha Franklin with James Cleveland & the Southern California Community Choir and "Blessing Me" (2004) by Bishop Larry Trotter. The songs discussed above move from the simple to the complex, as contrasting short instrumental lines or riffs or vocal refrain lines and those of the soloist are layered on to the rhythmic foundation or groove. This approach to song development characterizes performances of gospel **"shout songs"** as well as the **ring shouts** of slaves.

Shout songs
Emotionally charged gospel songs performed with heightened vocal delivery.

Although written descriptions of the ring shout do not include details of the singing, field recordings allow for analysis. The shout song "Good Lord (Run Old Jeremiah)" begins with call–response singing accompanied by a highly syncopated foot-stomped pattern that is repeated without variation. Added to this rhythmic foundation is a hand-clapped pattern, emphasizing beats two and four, which enters and leaves at different points throughout the song. As the song progresses toward a climax, the tempo and the intensity of the vocals, foot stomping, and hand clapping gradually increase. The song ends on the highest emotional and most rhythmically complex level. In other shout songs, such as "Reborn Again" and "Talking 'Bout a Good Time" (Track 6), the hand-clapped pattern on beats one, two, three, and four becomes highly syncopated and more complex with an increase in the tempo and vocal intensity.[76] Similar to performances of gospel music, these two examples illustrate how time "is further manipulated through the juxtaposition and layering of rhythms and through the effective use of tempo."[77]

Ring shout
A form of folk spiritual characterized by leader–chorus antiphonal singing, hand clapping, and other percussion, which incorporates highly stylized religious dance as participants move in a counterclockwise circle.

Text and Pitch

Text and pitch of songs are subject to manipulation as performers personalize their interpretations. An observer of slave singing in Macon, Georgia, in 1858 noted that "the words are generally very few, and repeated over and over again."[78] Hearing slaves sing as they rowed a boat up the St. Johns River in Florida in 1835, J. Kinnard, recalls:

"Talking 'Bout a Good Time."

7

"Arwhoolie (Cornfield Holler)."

 11

"God Moves on the Water."

 17

"Take My Hand, Precious Lord."

 12

"Flash Light."

 16

"So Ruff, So Tuff."

 18

"Sincerely."

 19

"Ezekiel Saw De Wheel."

Little regard is paid to rhyme, and hardly any to the number of syllables in a line; they condensed four or five into one foot [sic], or stretched out one to occupy the space that should have been filled with four or five; yet they never spoiled the tune. The elasticity of form is peculiar to the negro song.[79]

While the rowers condensed the text, they stretched out the line by embellishing a pitch over one syllable. In both early and contemporary forms of Black music expressions, performers also extend the length of notes at climactic points and they manipulate pitch by incorporating bends, slides, melismas, and other forms of embellishments (Tracks 7, 11, 17, 12, and 16).

As noted by Burnim, "Pitch is valued not as an absolute, but as an element of contrast."[80] This contrast also is achieved in both religious and secular performances of Black music by "juxtaposing voices of different ranges *or* [original italics] by highlighting the polar extremes of the single voice."[81] (See Tracks 18 and 19.) These features are common in all forms of African American music, from gospel ("Wholy Holy," 1972, by Aretha Franklin, and "His Blood Still Works," 2010, by Vashawn Mitchell) and funk ("Release Yourself," 1974, by Graham Central Station) to R&B ("You Bring Me Joy," 1987, by Anita Baker, "End of the Road," 1992, by Boyz II Men, and "Fallin'," 2001, by Alicia Keys).[82] Textual and melodic variation in the Black music performances is highly valued and expected. When artists successfully display their technical skills and understanding of the aesthetic values associated with performances of Black music, audiences express their approval both verbally and physically.

STYLE OF DELIVERY

Men and women, young and old alike [People of the Ituri Forest in Central Africa], contribute to the collective enjoyment [of daily occupations] by singing, clapping, stamping, and other rhythmic actions.
(Francis Bebey, Cameroonian composer[83])

The singing was accompanied by a certain ecstasy of motion, clapping of hands, tossing of heads, which continue without cessation about half an hour . . .
(Former slave, 1830s[84])

Style of delivery
The physical mode of presentation—how performers engage the body in movement and adornment during performance.

Accounts of African American music making for over four centuries describe instruments, musical sound, and how performers engage the body—the way music and movement are executed as a single act of expression. Fredrika Bremer, a Swedish traveler to the United States, wrote of a worship service she observed in Columbia, South Carolina, in 1850: "They sang . . . with all their souls and with all their bodies in unison; for their bodies wagged, their heads nodded, their feet stamped, their knees shook, their elbows and their hands beat time to the tune." Gospel singer Mahalia Jackson was very vocal about the need to use her hands, feet, and whole body while singing. Responding to criticism for doing so, she retorted, "Don't let the devil steal the beat from the Lord!

The Lord doesn't like for us to act dead. If you feel it, tap your feet a little—dance to the glory of the Lord."[85] Jackson's justification for her use of the entire body supports Burnim's observation that "performance in Black culture symbolizes vitality, a sense of aliveness" and that performers "must be overtly demonstrative if a Black audience is to be convinced." This use of the body also "reflects the Black perception of music as a unification of song and dance."[86]

In African cultures movement and its dance manifestations are intrinsic to music performance. Physician Thomas Winterbottom, who lived in Sierra Leone from 1792 to 1796, wrote, "Music ... is seldom listened to alone, but is generally used as an accompaniment to dance."[87] J.H. Kwabena Nketia explains that the social values of African societies encourage this form of physical engagement because it inspires group interaction and it "intensifies one's enjoyment of music through the feeling of increased involvement and the propulsion that articulating the beat by physical movement generates."[88] These same social values guide performances of African American artists, who employ various strategies to generate both physical and verbal forms of audience involvement. Soul singer Sam Moore of Sam and Dave recalls how he "would stop the band and get hand-clapping going in the audience [and] make them stand up."[89]

Soul singer James Brown used his voice and his entire body to engage his audience. While singing, he would clap his hands, stomp his feet, drop to his knees, and glide across the stage. Audience members would scream and holler, talk back, wave hands, jump out of their seats, and run down the aisles and on to the stage to dance with Brown.[90] Through an intense level of interaction Brown and his audience were united by a shared experience—one that reflected their social, cultural, and aesthetic expectations. Brown and other singers also generate audience response when they manipulate time, text, and/or pitch. During a performance of blues singer Bobby "Blue" Bland:

> [The] [w]omen sprinkled throughout the audience yell back at him, shaking their heads and waving their hands [in response to Bland's melisma] ... Suddenly the guitarist doubles the tempo and repeats a particularly funky phrase a few times accompanied by "oohs," "aahs," and "yeahs" from the audience.[91]

In addition to his voice, blues singer B.B. King uses his guitar to involve the audience. They respond to the guitar improvisations that mimic his voice by talking back to him with the phrases "I know what you're saying, B.B." or "Make her talk" (referring to his guitar, Lucille) and "Tell it like it is, B.B."[92] Such expressions are common to live and even recorded performances of Black music and they are signs that African Americans both recognize and celebrate the artist's ability to mimic or replicate vocal qualities on their instruments (see Chapter 2 for discussion on instruments).

When performers demonstrate their knowledge of the Black musical aesthetic, the responses of the audience can become so audible that they momentarily drown out the performer. The verbal responses of audiences are accompanied by hand clapping, foot stomping, head, shoulder, hand, and arm movements, and spontaneous dance. This type of audience participation is important to performers; it encourages them to explore the full range of aesthetic possibilities, and it is the single criterion by which Black artists determine whether they are meeting the aesthetic expectations of the audience. Songwriter-vocalist Smokey Robinson judges his concerts unsuccessful if the audience is "not involved in what's happening on stage."[93]

The significance of this level of involvement is summed up by J.H. Kwabena Nketia, who contends: "For the African [and by extension African American], the musical experience is by and large an emotional one: sounds, however beautiful, are meaningless if they do not offer this experience or contribute to the expressive quality of the performance."[94] That is, the display of emotions indicates that the musical performance has been experienced at the highest level of enjoyment.

CONCLUSIONS

As slaves, then as emancipated people consistently relegated to the racial margins of society in the United States since the seventeenth century, Africans and their descendants both preserved and translated African cultural and musical practices into unique expressions. In the North American context, music continued to play a central role in community life. Music accompanied various social, political, and ritualized events, and it functioned to unify people as a collective. These functions underline the approach to music making, which involves the participation of all—the collective—thus, eliminating distinctions between "performer" and "audience." African social practices and cultural values, therefore, shape the musical processes (i.e., the way music is created, performed, and experienced) and the structural characteristics (e.g., call–response and polyrhythms) that define the uniqueness of African American music.

The creative process in both African and African American traditions places value on improvisation, where performers bring their own interpretation to songs by producing unique and varying timbres and by manipulating time, text, and pitch in ways uncommon in European musical practices. Performers also convey a range of emotions through the way they engage the entire body—the face, hands, hips, and feet—during performance. When performers demonstrate their mastery of Black aesthetic principles, the audience expresses its approval, responding both aurally and physically, which heightens the interaction between performer and the participants and increases the intensity of the overall performance.

Even though changes have occurred in the African American musical tradition over time due to social upheavals, the adoption of new values, and advances in technology, it remains rooted in African cultural and musical traditions as evidenced by shared conceptual approaches to the music making process, structural features that define its uniqueness, and the role of music in daily life.

ACKNOWLEDGMENTS

This essay draws material from the previous publication by the author, "Africanisms in African-American Music" in *Africanisms in American Culture*, 2nd ed., edited by Joseph E. Holloway (Bloomington, IN: Indiana University Press, 2005).

QUESTIONS

1. Describe the role of music in African and African American communities. Give examples.

2. Describe the way music is created, performed, and experienced in African and African American communities.

3. Describe the ways in which the desired timbre in African and African American music differs from that of European-derived traditions.

4. Identify the two most common musical structures found in African and African American music. In what ways do they reflect the communal and interactive approach to making music?

PROJECTS

1. Compile an annotated discography of at least six examples of blues, jazz, gospel, soul, and hip-hop to illustrate the concepts of timbre outlined in this chapter.

2. Compile a discography of at least four African American musical genres (see Evolution of African American Music timeline on p. xvi) to illustrate the treatment of the musical structures outlined in this chapter.

3. Select three songs by White (American or British) country, pop, folk, and gospel artists that have been covered by African American artists and describe the ways in which the interpretations of the two versions are similar and different using the concepts of timbre and mechanics of delivery outlined in this chapter. Select three songs by African American blues, jazz, gospel, and R&B artists covered by White artists and describe the ways in which the performances of the two versions are similar and different.

NOTES

Please see the discography for information on resources for further listening.

1. Quoted in Stone 2005, 4.
2. Epstein 2003 (1977), 7–17.
3. Pinkster is derived from the Dutch word for Pentecost, a Christian holiday signifying the descent of the Holy Spirit upon Jesus's disciples. Originally Pinkster was a Dutch religious holiday that fell on the seventh Sunday after Easter. It also celebrated the change of season and the renewal of spring. Beginning in the seventeenth century, the Dutch settlers in the United States commemorated the holiday by attending church and visiting friends and family. By the early 1800s, the celebration had incorporated so much African culture—music, dance, and sports—that it was considered an African American holiday, which reached its peak between 1790 and 1810. For further details, see Southern 1983, 52, and "Pinkster Festival—18th Century Celebration of Spring," accessed August 22, 2013, http://figah.us/Pinkster_Festival.html.
4. Quoted in Epstein 2003 (1977), 67. For similar descriptions of Pinkster celebrations and other African-derived festivals see Southern 1997, 53–58, and Gellman 2006, 2–6.
5. Epstein 2003 (1977).
6. Holloway 2005, 18–38.
7. Stone 2005, 4.
8. Quoted in Epstein 2003 (1977), 224.
9. Acknowledging the diversity of African American communities, I refer to a limited number of communities that comprise the "critical mass"—the majority of Africans and African Americans who, within a specific time, place, and context, established and articulated shared codes and values to which they assigned cultural meaning.
10. Nketia 1974, 22.
11. Quoted in McCall 1998, 75.
12. Although *gumbris* are described here as "two-stringed guitars," a *gumbri* is best defined as a lute in the Sachs-Hornbostel classification scheme.
13. Quoted in Stone 2008b, 14. Brackets in original.
14. Kelly 1991, 2.
15. Gellman 2006, 3; Reidy 1978, 102–14; Southern 1997, 52–53.
16. Quoted in Epstein 2003 (1977), 6.
17. Ibid.
18. Quoted in Epstein 2003 (1977), 168.
19. Quoted in Epstein 2003 (1977), 179.
20. Wood 1996, 2580–81.
21. Quoted in Epstein 2003 (1977), 193. Brackets and ellipses in original. For a discussion of related events in Africa see Nketia 1974, 27–42.
22. See Jones and Lomax Hawes 1972 for a description of these songs.
23. "Tabor" in English refers to a small drum, called *tabour* in French (Randel 1999, 657).
24. Quoted in McCall 1998, 80–81.
25. Quoted in Epstein 2003 (1977), 236.
26. Quoted in Epstein 2003 (1977), 66.
27. Nketia 1973, 9.
28. Ibid. See Kubik 1998 for more information. Kubik's research documents intra-African musical exchanges and influences from antiquity through the twentieth century.
29. Burnim 1985, 154–65.
30. Bebey 1975, 1.
31. Quoted in Epstein 2003 (1977), 189.
32. These unusual timbres can be heard in Big Jay McNeely's "Nervous Man Nervous" (1953).
33. Shaw 1978, 169.
34. Epstein 2003 (1977), 29, 183, 287, 291–96.
35. Quoted in McCall 1998, 83.

36. Ibid.
37. Epstein 2003 (1977), 3–237.
38. Quoted in Epstein 2003 (1977), 225–26; Quoted in Epstein 2003 (1977), 228.
39. Epstein 2003 (1977), 2–3, 29, 281, 291–96.
40. Kilham 1967, 127–28.
41. Quoted in Epstein 2003 (1977), 214.
42. Wilson 1992, 327–38, refers to this aesthetic as the "heterogeneous sound ideal."
43. Bebey 1975, 119.
44. Nketia 1974, 198.
45. Kwasi Ampene, e-mail message to author, February 5, 2014. According to Ampene, the seven players in the ensemble are divided into four sections: *Seseɛ* (the sayer-leader); *Afre* (the callers); *Agyesoa* (the responders); and *Bɛɔsoɔ* (the reinforcer). Ampene explains that *edom* is the Twi word for "a huge crowd." A literal translation is "there might be several people in the community/village, town, or city but if you serve your people well, the ivory trumpets will praise you." The song, according to Ampene, is a form of advice for the King to "serve instead of rule" his people. Sasraku is the "name of an individual."
46. Bebey 1975, 68–78, 94–97.
47. Maultsby 2005, 334.
48. Europe 1999 (1919), 13.
49. "You Need Some Lovin'," *Jazz Odyssey*, Vol. 1, 1964, LP; "Happy-Go-Lucky Local," *Happy-Go-Lucky Local*, 1992, CD; and "C Jam Blues," *Blues in Orbit*, 2004, CD.
50. "You Got to Take Sick and Die Some of These Days," *The Complete Plantation Recordings*, 1993, CD; and "Somebody Been Talkin'," *Best Of Delta Blues*, 2013, MP3.
51. Sawyer 1980, 174.
52. "Goin' Up Yonder," *The Very Best of Walter Hawkins and the Hawkins Family*, 2005, CD; "The Altar," *Hello Fear*, 2011, CD; "Flash Light," *Parliament's Greatest Hits*, 1984, CD.
53. Stone 2005, 19.
54. Ibid.
55. Quoted in Epstein 2003 (1977), 165.
56. Burnim 1985, 162.
57. Ibid., 163.
58. Quoted in Epstein 2003 (1977), 218.
59. Quoted in Epstein 2003, 224–25.
60. Quoted in Epstein 2003 (1977), 165.
61. Quoted in Epstein 2003 (1977), 168.
62. Quoted in Epstein 2003 (1977), 6.
63. Stone 2005, 65
64. Evans 1982, 22–23, 25–26.
65. See the following recordings: Aretha Franklin, "Old Landmark," *Amazing Grace*, 1972, LP, released 1987, CD; and T.D. Jakes, *Still Friends?*, 2006, DVD.
66. Charters and Kunstadt 1962, 288.
67. Jones 1954, 26.
68. Chernoff 1979, 42.
69. Quoted in Epstein 2003 (1977), 294–95.
70. Quoted in Epstein 2003 (1977), 134.
71. Chernoff 1979, 47.
72. This song "Tchenhukumen" is found on *Musiques Dahoméennes*, OCR 17, 1963, LP.
73. Fred Wesley is a former musical director and arranger for soul and funk pioneer James Brown.
74. Fred Wesley, interview, "Lenny Hunts the Funk," *The South Bank Show*, ITV, January 12, 1992. *The South Bank Show* was a television arts magazine program produced between 1978 and 2010 in the UK by Crucial Films.
75. See Monson 1996, 26–27 and 66–69, for a discussion of groove as a rhythmic feel, a rhythmic matrix, and an aesthetic ideal in jazz.

76. For descriptions of the ring shout see Epstein 2003 (1977), 280–82; "Good Lord (Run Old Jeremiah)," performed by Austin Coleman with Joe Washington Brown & Group, *Negro Religious Field Recordings*, Vol. 1, 1994, CD; and Guy and Candie Carawan, field recording, 1967, "Reborn Again," performed by Benjamin Bligen and group, *Been In The Storm So Long*, 1990, CD.
77. Burnim 1985, 165.
78. Quoted in Epstein 2003 (1977), 224–25.
79. Quoted in Epstein 2003 (1977), 170.
80. Burnim 1985, 165.
81. Ibid., 163, 165.
82. Aretha Franklin, *Amazing Grace*, 1972, LP, rereleased 1987, CD; Vashawn Mitchell, *Triumphant*, 2010, CD; Graham Central Station, *Release Yourself*, 1997, CD; Anita Baker, *Rapture*, 1997, CD; Boyz II Men, single released as reissue on *Cooley-highharmony*, 1993, CD; Alicia Keys, *Songs In A Minor*, 2001, CD.
83. Bebey 1975, 18.
84. Quoted in Epstein 2003 (1977), 202. J.H. Nketia (1974, 209) explains that in African cultures, exaggerated bodily movements are common in the execution of dances. In Ghana, for example, basic movements include foot stamps, arm movements, leg gestures, and raised knees.
85. Levine 1977, 184.
86. Burnim 1985, 159–160.
87. Quoted in Epstein 2003 (1977), 6.
88. Nketia 1974, 207.
89. Sam Moore interview, with author, February 25, 1983.
90. White 2008 (1977), 230; Arbus 2008 (1966), 27. Part of the description comes from the author's observations of multiple James Brown shows over thirty years.
91. Keil 1966, 124, 139.
92. Sawyer 1980, 174.
93. Smokey Robinson, radio interview, WBLS, January 16, 1983. This paragraph also appeared in the previous publication by the author, Maultsby 2005, 337–38.
94. Nketia 1974, 206.

CHAPTER 2

African American Instrument Construction and Music Making

Ernest D. Brown Jr.

African Americans have a broad concept of what it means to make and play musical instruments. Historically, the concept of making musical instruments has been much more than the physical process of construction. Among African Americans, instrument making includes: (1) modifying existing musical instruments (or parts of them) physically or electronically; (2) using non-musical objects musically; (3) developing unique, highly specialized performance practices (ways of playing instruments); and (4) creating unique sounds through unusual instrument pairings. As a consequence of these varied approaches, the roles of musician and instrument maker merged, as was the case with such important historical figures as James Reese Europe and Duke Ellington, as well as such contemporary artists as Grand Master Flash, Roger and Zapp, and the Fat Boys, among others.

What often has been interpreted as unorthodox combinations of instruments or questionable timbral choices in African American musical practice is in actuality a manifestation of the creativity African Americans have employed to sustain themselves, spiritually and culturally, in the face of inadequate resources, racist oppression, and musical tools that simply were not designed to do what musicians of African descent needed and desired. Since their arrival in the North American colonies in 1619, African Americans have been compelled to "hit a straight lick with a crooked stick."[1] That is to say, African slaves navigated their status as chattel by developing and executing non-threatening or subversive strategies of resistance. This practice set the tone for complex cultural interactions, conflicts, and achievements that continue to define and distinguish African American and American cultural practices today. The necessity for African slaves (that is, the people who would become African Americans) to hit a straight lick with a crooked stick began on the slave ships when crews "**danced the slaves**" with a whip to prevent their human cargo from dying for lack of fresh air and exercise before they could be sold. It was common for slave ships to transport both European and African instruments to accompany this sinister practice.[2]

"Dancing the slaves" Method used on slave ships to exercise human cargo to reduce the rate of mortality during the Middle Passage.

From the time African slaves marched in chains through doors of no return to leave slave dungeons and board countless slave ships sailing for the Americas, these subjugated African people never yielded their power to express themselves in ways that affirmed their African-derived identities. It was this sense of "otherness" that produced a set of general principles for organizing musical sounds and dance. Depending upon changing circumstances, needs, and aspirations, this aesthetic framework has been realized in different ways. African Americans have adopted, adapted, reinterpreted, and realigned components of European, Euro-American, and African musics and musical instruments, as well as dances, to create unique traditions and practices with staying power over time.

AFRICAN INSTRUMENTS IN THE NEW WORLD

The West and Central African slave trade was dominated by the British, whose slaves were transported to colonies in the West Indies and United States. A drum housed in the British Museum provides evidence of the West African presence in colonial Virginia. A photograph of this instrument, an Akan drum made in Ghana, probably between 1730 and 1745, appears on the British Museum website, with the following caption:

> The drum is made of wood (*Cordia* and *Baphia* varieties, both native to Africa), vegetable fibre and deer-skin. It was collected by a Reverend Mr Clerk on behalf of Sir Hans Sloane, founder of the British Museum. Sir Hans Sloane entered the drum in his catalogue as a "drum made of a hollowed tree carved the top being brac'd wt. peggs & thongs wt. the bottom hollow from Virginia." It is one of the earliest known surviving African American objects.[3]

Drums such as this one, as well as other instruments, were highly valued in African contexts because they accompanied dance and other social activities, and served as a means for slaves to celebrate and affirm their shared cultural identities. A study of the musical practices of slaves, as well as the reactions of slave holders to these music making activities, broadens our understanding of the cultural importance of slave instruments in the United States during the colonial era.

Until 1776, it was common for British slave masters who owned and operated estates in both Virginia and the West Indies to travel with their

Ernest D. Brown Jr.

slaves between these regions.[4] Sir Hans Sloane reports that prior to the late 1680s slaves in Jamaica were allowed to use trumpets and drums of their own making at festivals.[5] Because of the association of these instruments with war in African contexts, however, slave masters later banned trumpets and drums in Jamaica, fearing their ability to incite rebellion.[6]

Slave holders in the United States, however, initially did not ban such instruments, and African-derived instruments did come to play an important role in the South Carolina Stono Rebellion of 1739. Historians have documented lengthy civil wars that took place in the kingdom of Kongo during the eighteenth century and the use of drums and loud horns for communication. Slaves from the kingdom of Kongo—which included coastal parts of modern-day countries Democratic Republic of the Congo, Republic of the Congo, Gabon, and Angola—figure prominently in the **Stono Rebellion**. Significant numbers of these slaves had military training, including in the use of firearms.[7] The Stono Rebellion has been described as follows:

> The rebels seized a store of firearms and marched off on a trail of destruction and killing, with two drums and banners flying, which attracted a large crowd of slaves. Having reached over sixty in number, they paused at a large field and "set to dancing, Singing and beating Drums to draw more Negroes to them."[8]

The Stono Rebellion was clearly more than a short-lived act of resistance. The slaves' conscious choice to utilize drums to accompany singing and dancing is indicative of the persistent depth of a continuing African consciousness among New World slaves, even in the face of life-threatening adversity. The use of instruments—drums in particular—which were highly valued in African contexts, served as a rallying battle cry that both celebrated and reinforced the rebels' collective sense of cultural identity.[9]

THE BODY AS INSTRUMENT

African Americans have been prolific in creating forms of music and dance by either transforming the body into a percussion instrument, performing percussively on melodic instruments, or performing melodically on percussion instruments. They have not only subverted efforts of Europeans and Euro-Americans to impose foreign cultural and musical values, they have asserted their identity as people of African descent who possess self-defined values and behave in ways that are culturally proscribed. At times, with no resources other than the human body and African-derived concepts of music making, New World Africans hit a straight lick with a crooked stick, creating such traditions as **pattin' juba**, the juba dance, and **hambone** during the period of slavery, and tap dance, step dance, and the human beat box—a form of vocal percussion and

Stono Rebellion
An eighteenth-century slave revolt, during which slaves danced and beat drums.

**Patting (pattin')
juba**
Rhythmic body percussion used by slaves to accompany singing or dancing.

Hambone
A form of rhythmic body percussion that involves slapping the hands against the thigh and hip bones.

singing that turned the voice into a new kind of instrument—in the twentieth century.

Hand clapping and the human voice are the most common African musical instruments, and pattin' juba has been described as an African American extension of the ubiquitous rhythmic hand clapping that accompanies singing and dancing in much of sub-Saharan Africa:

> The practice known as "patting juba" was an extension and elaboration of simple handclapping, raising it to the level of a self-contained accompaniment for dancing. It seems quite likely that the prohibition of drums in the colonies contributed to the development of this less threatening rhythmic device.[10]

The identification of this practice with African Americans is evident in the comments of Henry Bibb, born in Kentucky in 1815 to a slave mother, who "deplored the encouragement by the slaveholders of secular amusements, such as dancing, patting 'juber,' singing, and playing the banjo."[11] The musical synthesis of hand clapping, singing, and dancing is documented in Africa as early as 1621. Pattin' juba (Track 20) is first documented in the United States in the 1820s.[12]

20

"Juba."

Solomon Northup, a free Black musician who was kidnapped in New York and enslaved in Louisiana from 1841 to 1853, describes a performance of pattin' juba he witnessed outside New Orleans in 1853. During the Christmas holidays, Northup had been hired to provide an evening of fiddle accompaniment for Black versions of European society dances that were conceived as amusing entertainment for both slaves and their masters:

> [After the set dances were done] they set up a music peculiar to themselves. This is called "patting," accompanied by one of those unmeaning songs, composed rather for its adaptation to a certain tune or measure, than for the purpose of expressing any distinct idea. The patting is performed by striking the hands on the knees and then striking the hands together, then striking the right shoulder with one hand, and the left with the other—all the while keeping time with the feet and singing.[13]

Over half a century later, in 1913, African American classical composer, R. Nathaniel Dett, paid homage to pattin' juba in his *In the Bottoms Suite*, the fifth movement of which is titled "Dance Juba." Conceived as a work to be staged with a fiddler, dancers, and a juba patter, Dett's program notes for the piece reflect the lighthearted gaiety characteristic of pattin' juba performed in informal contexts:

> This is probably the most characteristic number of the suite, as it portrays more of the social life of the people. "Juba" is the stamping on the ground with the foot and following it with two staccato pats of the hands in two-four time. At least one-third of the dancers keep time in this way, while the others dance. Sometimes all will combine together in order to urge on a solo dancer to more frantic (and at the same time more fantastic) endeavors. The orchestra usually consists of a single "fiddler" perched high on a box or table; who forgetful of self in the rather hilarious excitement of the hour, does the impossible in the way of double-stopping and bowing.[14]

A counterpart to the pattin' juba tradition (variously referred to as juber, juba patting, or hand jive) is the tradition of hambone. Performed alone or in a group, according to Georgia Sea Islander Bessie Jones, hambone "may be done on one side of the body only, using the right hand and thigh; or on both sides at the same time in parallel motion."[15] The percussive body slapping typically accompanies a rhyming verse using complex syncopated rhythms. Rhythms are executed after each line of the poem is chanted.[16]

Indicative of the fact that these body "pattin'" traditions were conceptualized as instrumental music is the significance of both rhythm *and* pitch in their execution. Bessie Jones's *Step It Down* treatise establishes this point quite clearly:

> If you slap your thigh and then the back of your hand, you will notice that the second slap is higher in pitch than the first. Slap other parts of your body—chest, side, cheek, the top of your head—and you will discover a whole range of pitches can be sounded on your own anatomy.[17]

Both pattin' juba and hambone marked the ability of African American slaves to subvert the intended impact of the prohibition on drums in Colonial America beginning in the 1740s.[18] While the instrument itself was banned, it was not possible to ban or even completely squelch the spirit that fueled its existence. The drum continued to live in African American memory and imagination, and it continues to fuel and sustain African American music making in the twenty-first century. Excellent performances that illustrate these pattin' traditions are included in the documentary *The Human Hambone.*[19]

INSTRUMENT MAKING THROUGH PERFORMANCE

At times, African American approaches to playing musical instruments merge the role of musician and instrument maker. This process of instrument making through performance transforms non-percussion instruments into percussion instruments as a reflection of African American sound ideals. W.C. Handy, sometimes referred to as Father of the Blues, reports that his grandfather told him how slaves transformed the violin into a percussion instrument:

> [F]olks knew as well as we do when it was time for the music to get hot. They had their own way of bearing down. A boy would stand behind the fiddler with a pair of knitting needles in his hands. From this position the youngster would reach around the fiddler's left shoulder and beat on the strings in the manner of a snare drummer.[20]

It is significant that **fiddlesticks** were used when slaves wanted to play music that more strongly reflected musical ideals derived from Africa. The modification of an instrument through performance practice allowed slaves to creatively assert African aesthetic values, by layering secondary rhythmic patterns on an instrument typically conceived as melodic. The fiddlesticks' rhythms created a polyrhythmic texture that enhanced the

Fiddlesticks
Devices such as straws, sticks, or knitting needles used to tap out rhythms on the strings of a fiddle.

sense of rhythmic drive and excitement in the music, which Handy referred to as "hot."

A variant of fiddlesticks as rhythmic instrument is reported from South Carolina in 1862. A group of slaves dance to the music of a fiddler, who is accompanied by another person who drums on the floor with two sticks.[21] In another instance, in New Orleans before the Civil War, George Washington Cable reports seeing an "extra performer [who] sat on the ground behind the larger drum, at its open end, and 'beat upon the wooden sides of it with two sticks.'"[22] I have seen the practice in both West and Central Africa.[23]

In the early 1900s, James Reese Europe began composing and performing an innovative and controversial kind of symphonic music that relied in part on European classical elements, but also incorporated African and African American melodies, and radically reconfigured his orchestra:

> Although we have first violins, the place of the second violins with us is taken by mandolins and banjos. This gives that peculiar steady strumming accompaniment to our music which all people comment on . . . Then, for background, we employ ten pianos. . . . The result . . . is a background of chords which are essentially typical of Negro harmony. . . . [We] have developed a kind of symphony music that . . . lends itself to the playing of the peculiar compositions of our race.[24]

A fellow African American classical musician urged Europe to assimilate—to follow the dictates of existing models of classical music composition and performance, contending "[I]f we expect to do anything lasting from an artistic standpoint, we, too, must study the classics as a foundation for our work."[25] Europe was not persuaded by this advice, however, for his work engaged in a classic pattern of subverting such assimilationist pressure. Europe was also asserting aesthetic values that were reinforced and affirmed in African American culture. His "Castle House Rag" (1914), which utilizes mandolins and banjos (the latter an instrument of African origin) to create distinctive musical timbres and textures, is an illustrative example.

Similar to Europe's unconventional conceptualization of timbre and performance practice, blues musicians have a long history of instrument transformation and substitution. In the early twentieth century, the more durable and versatile harmonica, once viewed as a children's toy, replaced the African-derived panpipes.[26] In 1952, in an effort to be heard above the electric guitars, bass, and drums of Muddy Waters' Chicago blues band, Little Walter Jacobs transformed the harmonica, which had formerly been played acoustically, into the Mississippi saxophone,[27] by holding a microphone attached to a tube amplifier very close to his harmonica. At high volume, the harmonica was then able to stand its ground with the rest of the band. The harmonica's timbre was altered, creating an altogether new and completely different tone quality that had never before been heard. In addition, Jacobs cupped and fluttered his hands around the harmonica, varying its distance from his mouth to bend pitches and add to its vocal expressiveness.

For eighty years after its physical creation by Adophe Sax, the tenor saxophone was not viewed as a serious instrument; it was ignored by the classical musicians for whom it was intended. One man changed all of that—Coleman Hawkins, who claimed, "I made the tenor sax. There's nobody plays like me and I don't play like anybody else."[28] Hawkins made the tenor saxophone the symbol of jazz that it is today by using an unusually wide mouthpiece and a hard reed, giving the instrument a strong, unfettered voice-like tone quality—a sound ideal in many African and African American cultures. His 1926 solo on "The Stampede" revolutionized how the tenor saxophone was perceived.[29]

In addition to his creating a unique tonality for the saxophone, Hawkins also improvised upon it in a way that set standards of excellence that continue to be recognized and emulated by jazz musicians. Hawkins' most famous improvisation is on the tune, "Body and Soul" (1939), on which his distinctive tone quality is very clear. Hawkins' characteristic saxophone timbre closely corresponds to the vocal quality of singers such as Louis Armstrong, Tina Turner, and James Brown, whose voices were gripping and forceful. An African example of a comparably rich yet unconventional timbre, by Western standards, is that of the Zimbabwean **mbira**. Its buzzy tone quality results from combining the timbre of the plucked lamellae, or keys, with that of an attached secondary rattle, such as a bottle cap.[30]

Mbira
An African melodic instrument with varying numbers of plucked keys made of either metal or wood.

NEW TRENDS

Rap music has had the most far-reaching impact upon American culture of any art form in the past forty years. According to the jazz drummer Max Roach:

> The culture that's come from black folks is the most profound sound of the twentieth century. From Jelly Roll Morton to Scott Joplin right up to hip-hop, it's all in the same continuum. Hip-hop is related to what Louis Armstrong and Charlie Parker did because here was a group of young people who made something out of very little . . . [that has] affected the whole world in terms of rhythm, movement [break dancing], the spoken word [rap] and the visual arts [graffiti].[31]

This impact is all the more astounding because rap involves a radical redefinition of what it means to be a musician, a singer, or an instrument maker. Unlike musicians who have mastered a conventional musical instrument—guitar, piano, drums, or trumpet—rappers become musicians based upon their verbal creativity, vocal dexterity, and skill with a microphone. Rap **MC**s must be credited with creating the tradition of the **human beat box**, a form of vocal percussion and singing that turned the voice into a new kind of instrument. Where traditions of body percussion were spawned among African Americans during the period of slavery, the advent of hip-hop showcased the voice as percussion instrument.

Human beat box
A form of vocal percussion that mimics instrumental rhythmic patterns and timbres.

MC
Also spelled "emcee" (abbreviated from "master of ceremonies"); a rapper who performs in a hip-hop context (typically, to accompaniment by a DJ, an instrumental track, vocal percussion known as a "beat box," or a cappella).

Using the lips, tongue, throat, teeth—virtually every component of the vocal anatomy—hip-hop artists crafted contemporary sounds and rhythms to complement their contemporary rhymes. Examples that showcase the use of the voice as instrument—the human beat box—include the Fat Boys, Doug E. Fresh, and Biz Markie representing the era of old school hip-hop, and Rahzel, a new school rapper who has created a complex style of beat boxing that involves polyrhythm, melody, and sound effects.

Rap **DJs** went beyond the roles of radio or discothèque DJs, who played pre-recorded music for dancing or listening, and asserted their musicianship by creating new musical sounds while operating turntables and manipulating pre-recorded sounds through a sound system. Without being able to sing or play a conventional instrument, they advanced a new concept of music making and performance. Missy Mist's "Gettin' Bass" (1989) listed the equipment a DJ had to master in the late 1980s. DJs made turntables and sound systems, formerly tools for reproducing music, into musical instruments, tools for producing music. Music critic Nelson George agrees:

> My favorite thing is talking about the turntable. Turntables are something that have been around for a long, long time . . . even in disco they were mixing . . . It took hip-hop. It took people from the street to say, ok, I can take and do something else with this. It doesn't have to be just something I play records with. I can make it into an instrument itself.[32]

Furthermore, with its radical de-emphasis of melody and harmony and laser-like focus upon dance rhythm, buzzy texture (e.g., scratching), call-and-response form, audience engagement and participation, and improvisation (especially in the type of freestyling that has become popular since the 1990s[33]), rap has redefined music based on African-derived aesthetic values. Something similar happened in funk.

On his 1972 album, *Talking Book*, Stevie Wonder and his sound-engineer collaborators, Malcolm Cecil and Robert Margouleff, created a kind of funk using **TONTO** (The Original New Timbral Orchestra), an analog synthesizer that Cecil constructed. Although Wonder did not invent this synthesizer himself, he used his full artistic control of this recording session to hire collaborators to bring his musical vision to fruition. The result was the creation of a new virtual instrument, a clavinet sound that was played with a wah-wah pedal, which made "Superstition" from the *Talking Book* album a landmark hit that firmly established Stevie Wonder as a mature artist.

The **clavinet** is essentially an electronically amplified clavichord, an acoustic instrument popular from the late medieval through the classical periods of European art music. At the time, Wonder proudly described this new instrument as "a funky, dirty, stinky, *nasty* instrument."[34] Funk bass man Bootsy Collins praises the sound of "Superstition," noting that:

DJ
Short for "disc jockey"; a person who plays records in a dance club or on radio. In hip-hop, one who uses turntables to accompany rappers and break dancers or to perform as featured instrumentalist.

TONTO
The Original New Timbral Orchestra; a large multitimbral polyphonic analog synthesizer.

Clavinet
An electronic version of the clavichord, a medieval keyboard instrument.

Ernest D. Brown Jr.

Those were like fresh sounds. You could play the same thing on a piano or on the organ, but it ain't gon' give you that same edge, that same flavor, or it don't touch you the same way. So, yeah, he brought a whole 'nother dimension . . . [Bootsy imitates the clavinet] Oh Man! You talk about funk. Oh, he's in funk heaven right there . . . Ye-e-s Lawd! Yes, he's funky. He's most funky . . . Definitely funky. You cain't . . . I mean you know, you cain't cut that with a knife.[35]

Technically, Wonder's collaborators created a distinctive sound quality that had:

more mid-range punch and lower-range resonance than clavinet recordings by other artists [while retaining] . . . the sharp, upper-range attack that gives the clavinet its guitar-like character. [At the same time they created] two clavinet parts with similar timbres but different rhythms [which] were placed in different locations in the stereo mix. Because of the clavinet's sharp attack, it attracts attention from the middle of a full texture and is easy to follow with the ear. By combining two parts, the result is a noticeable interlocking effect that seems to have a single sound source but which greatly increases the kineticism of the part by bouncing rapidly throughout the stereo mix.[36]

CONCLUSIONS

Transported to a foreign land against their will, from the outset, African slaves were confronted with ways of life that challenged them physically, psychologically, and creatively. With music having been an integral part of African cultural identities, it was to continue to play a seminal role in the formation of New World African identities. When introduced to instruments and music making practices that did not reflect the preferred sound ideals reminiscent of home, slaves entered the playful, creative flow where the magic of music happens, where they found personal and collective expression and artistic fulfillment in response to the needs of their communities. By pursuing their cultural and aesthetic goals with the resources that were available, African Americans have creatively and imaginatively shaped and reshaped, defined and redefined themselves, their instruments, their music, and their music making as people of African descent in the Americas.

KEY NAMES

R. Nathaniel Dett	Little Walter Jacobs
James Reese Europe	Solomon Northup
W.C. Handy	Stevie Wonder
Coleman Hawkins	

QUESTIONS

1. Identify four principles or concepts of instrument construction or performance that have historically characterized African American music making.

2. Define the concept of "hitting a straight lick with a crooked stick," as it applies to African American cultural and musical practice.

3. What is the musical significance of the Stono Rebellion?

4. Identify three traditions of body percussion and explain how the practice emerged during slavery.

5. Cite three African American musicians who either transformed instruments from melodic to percussion or reconfigured traditional ensembles to assert African American aesthetic values.

PROJECTS

1. Compile an annotated discography of at least six examples representing different genres and time periods, which illustrate one of the four principles of African American instrument construction and music making outlined in the introduction to this chapter.

2. Create a videography of examples of pattin' juba, hambone, and human beat box and prepare a short paper that compares and contrasts these three traditions of body percussion.

NOTES

Please see the discography for information on resources for further listening.

We mourn the passing of Professor Ernest Brown prior to the completion of this essay, which was finalized by the editors.

This chapter is a revised version, a remix, of an earlier essay that discusses music and instrument making in African American cultures in the Western Hemisphere more generally. See Brown 1990a.

1. Hurston 1958, 95, quoted in Brown 1990a.
2. Epstein 1977, 7–8; Roberts 1998, 3; Segal 1995, 34.
3. The British Museum, "Akan Drum," Trustees of the British Museum, accessed June 20, 2011, www.britishmuseum.org/explore/highlights/highlight_objects/aoa/a/akan_drum.aspx.
4. Roberts 1998, 3.
5. Quoted in Epstein 1977, 59.
6. Epstein 1977, 58–59.
7. Thornton 1999a, 117.
8. Thornton 1999b, 116.
9. Harding 1983 (1981), 34–35.
10. Epstein 1977, 141.
11. Ibid., 141–42.
12. Ibid.
13. Northup 1853, 219.
14. Spencer 1982, 145.
15. Jones and Hawes 1972, 34.
16. Ibid.
17. Jones and Hawes 1972, 22.
18. Epstein 1977, 59.
19. *The Human Hambone*, 2005. This documentary surveys the use of the human body as a musical instrument throughout North America.

20. Handy 1941, 5.
21. Epstein 1977, 140.
22. Katz 1969, 34.
23. Based upon personal experience researching music in Zambia during the 1970s, where these rhythms are commonly beaten with a stick on the sides of drums of the Angolan immigrants (the Mbunda and Luvale peoples) in western Zambia. I have also encountered this practice in learning to play the xylophones of the Dagara people of northwestern Ghana.
24. James Reese Europe, "The Negro's Place in Music," *New York Evening Post*, March 12, 1914. Reprinted in Kimball and Bolcom 1973, 61.
25. Southern 1997, 293.
26. For an example of panpipe playing in blues, see Henry Thomas's "Fishin' Blues" (1928).
27. See Jacobs' "Juke" (1952).
28. McDonough 1979, 3.
29. Coleman Hawkins, "The Hawk Talks: Coleman Discusses Individuality and Some Young Musicians," *Downbeat*, September 19, 1956, 13, 50.
30. Beauler Dyoko and Cosmas Magaya are excellent performers of the Zimbabwean mbira. In performances, I have seen them playing the mbira within a resonator that has bottle caps attached. Bottle caps are also attached to the soundboard of the mbira.
31. Owen 1988, 60.
32. Nelson George, interview, accessed June 26, 2011, www.88hiphop.com (page no longer available).
33. *Freestyle: The Art of Rhyme*, 2002.
34. Horn 2000, 121.
35. Quoted in "Ain't It Funky Now," *Soul Deep*, season 1, episode 5, produced by William Naylor (Bristol: BBC, 2005), DVD.
36. Hughes 2003, 145.

CHAPTER 3

Secular Folk Music

Dena J. Epstein with contributions
from Rosita M. Sands

A cloud of myth has surrounded African American secular folk music: Blacks arrived in the New World culturally naked; African instruments could not have been transported to the New World, because the slaves could not bring anything with them; the slaves had no secular music; the banjo was invented by White musician Joel Walker Sweeney in the 1830s.

For many years, these myths were widely accepted and retold in the most respected reference books, ignoring the flourishing secular music among African Americans. The myth that the slaves had no secular music derived in part from the eighteenth-century evangelical belief that all secular music and dancing was sinful. Even the instruments associated with dancing, such as the banjo and fiddle, came to be considered disreputable. Then, when abolitionists began their protest against slavery, they stressed the sufferings of the slaves, in striking contrast to the picture of the happy, carefree slave presented by the minstrel theater. Frederick Douglass wrote in his autobiography:

> I have been utterly astonished, since I came to the North, to find persons who could speak of the singing among slaves, as evidence of their contentment and happiness. It is impossible to conceive of a greater mistake. Slaves sing most when they are most unhappy. The songs of the slave represent the sorrows of his heart.[1]

Slaves certainly were unhappy, but they had their moments of fleeting pleasure. Contemporary documents establish beyond question the continuous presence of secular music and dancing among African Americans from their introduction to mainland North America to the present, secular music that embodied distinguishing characteristics of African music. They also identified features that establish African American music as a part of an African cultural continuum.

Among the peoples of Africa, music was integrated into daily life, as a group activity, rather than as a performance before a passive audience. Music accompanied all kinds of group work, regulating the pace of work and lessening the monotony. Even individuals working alone often sang about their work. Festivities were accompanied by music and dancing. Derisive singing, even in reference to the king, was accepted as a means of expressing sentiments that were unacceptable as speech. All these aspects of African culture were easily adapted to life in the New World.

Characteristic elements of African music have been described by J.H. Kwabena Nketia as multipart rhythmic structures, repetitive choruses with a lead singer, the **call–response** style of alternating phrases juxtaposed or overlapping, and scales of four to seven steps, elements that reappeared in modified form in African American music.[2] The short, repeated phrases that accompanied vigorous dancing upset Europeans accustomed to sedate dances and regular rhythmic patterns. To them, African **polyrhythms** sounded like "noise"; many Europeans could not acknowledge a music that did not conform to their rules and scales.

Before the invention of sound recording, the only means of preserving music was a notational system devised for European music. Musicologists and folklorists who tried to notate African or African American music had to omit or modify its distinguishing characteristics: blue notes, rhythmic complexities, overlapping of leader and chorus, melodic embellishments, and distinctive approaches to timbre. At best, these notated versions approximate the music; at worst, they distort it. Nevertheless, contemporary descriptions of African American music are meaningful. They document its existence, describe its salient features as viewed first hand, and provide the basis for a continuing history.

Not all Europeans were repelled by African music. Richard Jobson, a British trader who visited Africa in 1620–21, soon after the first Africans were brought to Virginia, wrote: "There is without doubt, no people on the earth more naturally affected to the sound of musicke [sic] then [sic] these people [. . .] singing [. . .] extempore upon any occasion."[3] He also described drums and an instrument made from a gourd with a neck fastened to it and up to six strings. Surely, this was a prototype of the **banjo** (Track 21). Later travelers reported similar instruments that were to be transported to the New World, sometimes by slaving captains who tried to preserve the health of their cargos by compelling the captives to dance aboard ship. In the New World, the Africans constructed familiar instruments from local materials. The British Museum has had since 1753 an African-style drum made in Virginia from native wood with a deerskin head, materials not available in Africa, although the drum is described as "typical of the Ashanti of Ghana."[4]

Besides drums, other instruments frequently described as African included various kinds of rhythm instruments, a xylophone called the

Call–response
A song structure or performance practice in which a singer or instrumentalist makes a musical statement that is answered by another soloist, instrumentalist, or group. The statement and answer sometimes overlap. Also called antiphony and call-and-response.

Polyrhythm
Several contrasting rhythms played or sung simultaneously.

Banjo
Instrument of African origin, originally with one to six strings and a neck running parallel to a gourd body.

 21

"New Railroad."

balafo or *balaphon*, quills (a form of panpipes), horns, and the banjo. The banjo is found throughout the Caribbean and the North American mainland under various names: *banza, banjah, bandore, banjar,* and others.[5]

AFRICANS IN NORTH AMERICA

Although Africans arrived in Virginia in 1619, there are not many descriptions of African musical activity in North America before 1800. This is partially due to the slow growth in the African American population during this period. In the seventeenth and eighteenth centuries, the North American colonies were not nearly as profitable as those in the West Indies, where the population increased rapidly, and Africans were brought in vast numbers. As islands became overpopulated, planters and their workforces moved, sometimes to the mainland. In the West Indies, the music brought from Africa was able to survive and flourish for at least a century and a half, but on the mainland, where the Black population was relatively smaller, the music became acculturated more rapidly. This was particularly true of the English colonies.

Dancing and Drumming in the Seventeenth and Eighteenth Centuries

On the mainland in the seventeenth and eighteenth centuries, the dances of the Africans were usually confined to Sunday, their only day of rest, but the English clergy was bitterly opposed to this desecration of the Lord's Day and did its best to stop the dancing. Dancing was allowed on those holidays that the planters permitted. Traditionally, the Christmas holiday lasted until the New Year, and some planters allowed a holiday at Easter. The religious nature of these holidays did not rule out secular music and dancing, which became a central feature of the holiday celebrations.[6]

In 1739, the Reverend George Whitefield complained that the Africans were permitted to "openly prophane [*sic*] the Lord's Day with Dancing, Piping, and such like."[7] In the same year, an insurrection at Stono, South Carolina, was accompanied by singing, dancing, and beating drums, with the intention of attracting more Africans to join the rebellion. As a consequence, the beating of drums was forbidden by law in South Carolina, as it had been earlier in the West Indies. Yet despite this ban, which was rigorously enforced, drumming continued unseen by the authorities. Former slaves in Georgia who were interviewed in the 1930s by the Georgia Writers' Project described how to make drums from hollow trees and recalled dancing to drums, which must have been done in secret.

With drums so central to African music and dancing, substitutes had to be found. One was a less threatening but still rhythmic instrument described by Thomas Jefferson as "the Banjar, which they brought hither

Dena J. Epstein with Rosita M. Sands

Figure 3.1
"Lynchburg Negro Dance, August 18, 1853," in *Sketchbook of Landscapes in the State of Virginia* by Lewis Miller. Reproduced by permission of the Abby Aldrich Rockefeller Folk Art Museum, Colonial Williamsburg Foundation, Williamsburg, Virginia.

from Africa."[8] Other rhythmic support to dancing was provided by hand clapping, foot stomping, and a practice apparently unique to the United States, **"patting juba."** Patting juba (Track 20) was an extension of simple hand clapping, raising it to the level of a self-contained accompaniment to dancing. It was described as striking the hands on the knees, then striking the hands together, then striking the right shoulder with one hand, the left with the other—all the while keeping time with the feet and singing. The earliest reference to the practice dates from the 1820s, but by the 1830s serious attention was being paid to its rhythmic complexities. In 1880, the poet Sidney Lanier described patting juba as a "quite complex successions of rhythm, not hesitating to syncopate, to change the rhythmic accent for a moment, or to indulge in other highly specialized variations of the current rhythmus."[9]

A variation of patting involved the use of two sticks to beat time on the floor, either alone or with other instruments. A Christmas celebration at Eutaw Plantation in South Carolina during the Civil War had dancing accompanied by "two fiddlers, one man with bones, and another had sticks with which he kept time on the floor."[10]

The rate at which this dancing became acculturated is not known. Initially it must have been largely African, but gradually the European influence began to modify the steps. The rate of acculturation varied from colony to colony. In the northern colonies, some holidays originally observed by Whites gradually became associated with the Africans.

**Patting (pattin')
juba**
Rhythmic body percussion used by slaves to accompany singing or dancing.

 20

"Juba."

In Connecticut, Rhode Island, and Massachusetts, "'Lection Day," involving processions, feasting, dancing, and the election of a king, became known as Negro Election Day by the mid-eighteenth century. In New York and New Jersey, the holiday Pinkster, originating with the Dutch, was a comparable holiday to Negro Election Day. Both holidays were celebrated in open fields with much ceremony, from the middle third of the eighteenth century.[11]

In these colonies, slaves lived singly or in small groups and had little community life. Gradually, they created midyear festivals where they could enjoy their distinctive culture: drumming, dancing, and singing. Banjos, fiddles, and Guinea drums, made from logs covered with sheepskin, provided the music for the Guinea dance. As slaves were caught up in the performance, their behavior was reported as more African.

Although reports of African music and dancing in the southern colonies before 1800 were not common, still rarer were reports of the impact of African culture upon European music and dancing. In an era when many people were preoccupied with preserving elements of their European heritage in an alien, often hostile, environment, it is hardly surprising that they recorded very little of an influence that they could not publicly acknowledge.

Yet evidence has been found that these transplanted Europeans performed "Negro dances," not just occasionally but with some regularity ("usual" was the term found in contemporary accounts). One description of Virginia published in Dublin in 1776 stated: "Towards the close of an evening, when the company are pretty well tired with country dances, it is usual to dance jigs, ... borrowed ... from the Negroes."[12] Thomas Jefferson's brother, Randolph, was described by a former Monticello slave as a "mighty simple man; used to come out among Black people, play the fiddle and dance half the night."[13]

In Richmond before 1820, the courtly Black fiddler Simeon Gilliat performed at balls that began with a reel followed by contra dances, a congo (demonstrably an African term), a hornpipe, and a jig that would wind up the evening. This intermingling of cultures was embodied by Gilliat himself, who, after a career of performing at society balls, was painted playing the banjo for a group of children.

As late as 1876, Henry W. Ravenel of South Carolina reminisced about his youth (he was born in 1814):

> The jig was an African dance and a famous one in old times . . . For the jig the music would be changed. The fiddle would assume a low monotonous tone, the whole tune running on three or four notes only . . . the stick-knocker changed his time, and beat a softer and slower measure.[14]

La Calinda

In Louisiana and the surrounding territory, areas that had been settled by the Spanish and the French, developments were quite different.

Dena J. Epstein with Rosita M. Sands

Cultural and governmental ties were not to the other mainland colonies but to Spanish America and to the French West Indies. Louisiana had been settled almost one hundred years after Virginia, with its African population coming directly from Africa between 1719 and 1731. With a relatively homogeneous population, the distinctive character of New Orleans was established early. A Frenchman who had worked as a planter wrote in 1758 of the crowds of Africans who danced the *la calinda*, a dance widely reported in the French West Indies with its associated instrument, the *banza*.

La calinda had been described in Martinique by a French missionary, Jean Baptist Labat, as early as 1694. It was accompanied by two drums of unequal length, each with one open end, and one covered with skin. The drummers held them between their legs and played with four fingers of both hands. The larger drum provided the basic beat, and the smaller was played more quickly. Despite the good priest's disapproval, all the Africans danced the *calinda*: the old, the young, and even the children. It seemed as if they had danced it in the wombs of their mothers.

In the mid-eighteenth century, Diderot's *Encyclopédie* included special entries for *calinda* and *tamboula*, the name of one of the drums.[15] The dance was always accompanied by a guitar-like instrument with four strings, called a *banza*. Another Frenchman, Moreau de Saint-Méry, writing in 1797, was as convinced of the African origin of the dance and instruments as Labat had been.[16]

La calinda
African dance performed in the French West Indies and Louisiana in the eighteenth century.

Other Popular Dances

Although evangelical religion condemned secular music and dancing in the seaboard southern states, in New Orleans African-style dancing was permitted to flourish. Popular dances included the *chica*, the *bamboula*, the *coonjine* or *counjaille*, and the congo dance. Both the French and Spanish governments had permitted such dancing, and after the Louisiana Purchase in 1803, new "Ordinances of Police" specified that the mayor should appoint places for slaves to dance on Sundays. Travelers frequently described these dances at what is now called Congo Square, sometimes giving details of the steps and accompanying instruments.

In 1819, Benjamin Latrobe, the engineer who had supervised the rebuilding of the Capitol after the War of 1812, described what he saw on a Sunday afternoon:

> They were formed into circular groups . . . The music consisted of two drums and a stringed instrument . . . On the top of the finger board was the rude figure of a man in a sitting posture, & two pegs behind him to which the strings were fastened. The body was a calabash . . .
> A man sung an uncouth song . . . which I suppose was in some African language, for it was not French . . . The allowed amusements of Sunday have, it seems, perpetuated here those of Africa.[17]

Latrobe accompanied his account with sketches of the instruments, among the very few contemporary drawings of African instruments that have survived from the mainland.

Figure 3.2
Sketches of African instruments from a manuscript journal of Benjamin Henry Latrobe. Entry from February 21, 1819, New Orleans. Reproduced by permission of the Papers of Benjamin Henry Latrobe, The Maryland Historical Society, Baltimore, Maryland.

ACCULTURATION OF AFRICANS IN THE NEW WORLD

The gradual transformation of African culture into something that came to be called African American began almost as soon as the Africans landed in the New World. Speaking many different languages, they had to learn to communicate with each other and with their new masters.

Acculturation
The process of change that occurs when two different cultural groups come into prolonged contact.

Secular Folk Music

They had to adjust to new surroundings, new customs, new sounds, smells, and tastes. They observed the music and dances of these strange Europeans and gradually learned to combine them with the music and dance they had brought from Africa. The process by which this **acculturation** took place was described often in the West Indies but only once on

Dena J. Epstein with Rosita M. Sands

the mainland. John Pierpont, a tutor from Litchfield, Connecticut, wrote from Georgetown District, South Carolina, of a Christmas celebration in 1805 when acculturated slaves danced on the portico of the plantation house while native Africans "did not join in the dance with the others, but by themselves" clapped their hands and "distorted their frames."[18] This complex of two cultures, side by side, influencing each other in intangible ways, led gradually to the formation of an African American culture.

Acculturation proceeded at different rates in different colonies. African dancing took place in New Orleans in 1819 and later, while as early as 1694 a Black fiddler was playing for the dancing of Whites in Virginia. This incident was recorded in a legal action brought by a minister against his daughter's friends, who had profaned his house by introducing a fiddler in the owner's absence. The dancing had continued until Sunday morning after church services had begun.[19] This same fiddler also might have played for the dancing of his fellow slaves.

There also was considerable variety in the circumstances of slavery in the different colonies. Settled in 1690, Carolina had a Black majority by 1708, while the northern states had only a small, scattered Black population. Plantations in the southern colonies developed their distinctive society, very different from the more urban society in the North. While slavery flourished in the South with the introduction of the cotton gin after the Revolution, slavery in the northern states declined and gradually disappeared. As more and more Blacks were born in the New World, African festivals in the North diminished, and were replaced by processions and parades that demonstrated the dignity of the Black community. With the passage of time, dancing and singing by African Americans in the northern states tended to be enjoyed in private rather than in public festivals in open fields.

Fiddlers

Although the prejudice against dancing and fiddling was widespread throughout the South, many planters not only permitted the activities, but encouraged them. James H. Hammond, of South Carolina, penciled in his plantation manual: "Church members are privileged to dance on all holyday occasions, and the class leader or deacon who may report them shall be reprimanded or punished at the discretion of the master."[20] A more common attitude was expressed in the thirteenth annual report of the Association for the Religious Instruction of the Negroes in Liberty County, Georgia, in 1848: "With the negroes [sic] dancing is a dissipating, demoralizing amusement . . . [It is incompatible with] religion or good morals."[21] "A Mississippi Planter" wrote to *DeBow's Review* in 1851, "I have a good fiddler, and keep him well supplied with cat-gut, and I make it his duty to play for the negroes [sic] every Saturday night until 12 o'clock."[22] Some planters went so far as to provide music teachers for talented servants.

It was also customary for a planter to advertise in local newspapers if he had a slave fiddler of a good reputation whom others might wish to hire. Solomon Northup, a free Negro from upstate New York who was kidnapped and sold into slavery in Louisiana, benefited from his ability as a fiddler. His fiddle "introduced me to great houses— relieved me of many days' labor in the field—made me friends . . . gave me an honored seat at the yearly feasts."[23] These obscure musicians at times achieved what would have been a professional status if their earnings had remained in their own pockets. Many of them earned a reputation for excellence that extended for miles around.

A legal action filed in the Chancery Court of Louisville in 1844 attached the steamboat Pike "to recover damages for the unauthorized transportation . . . of three slaves, Reuben, Henry and George . . . from Louisville to Cincinnati, whence they escaped to Canada."[24] The three were described as well-trained musicians who for several years had been playing at balls and parties. Their owner had given them written permission to play in any part of the South, but of course he objected to their fleeing to Canada. The court found that the unusual privileges permitted them had rendered them restless under restraint and desirous of freedom. Damages were denied.

Children's Game Songs

References to and descriptions of African American ring games and "play games" appear in journals and other contemporary writings from this period, and many ex-slaves reported in Works Progress Administration (WPA) interviews that both children and adults enjoyed playing these games, many of which involved body movements of some sort. Children were frequent observers of the adults singing and dancing these games, a situation that served didactic purposes and undoubtedly influenced the type of play the children engaged in with their peers, where they often mimicked the postures and movements of the adults. When African American musicians played for recreational dances among their own people, the musical repertoire often included **play-party** songs. Many of these songs were based on melodies and lyrics that were similar to and sometimes almost indistinguishable from the songs of White pioneers, but modified with African approaches to rhythm and traditional performance practices.

An article published in The Journal of American Folk-lore in 1890 provides one of the earliest published descriptions of the manner in which African American children participated in "song-games" while at play.[25] The article is based on the recollections of a Virginia-born servant who described her own experiences playing game songs as a child sometime during the nineteenth century. The games are described as "played by as many children as possible in some open field or common, and generally towards the close of the day."[26] The time of day identified for this "play" activity is logical, given the fact that, during slavery, many children were

Play-party
A celebration for children and young adults that features games, singing, and dancing without instrumental accompaniment.

Dena J. Epstein with Rosita M. Sands

also expected to labor and the time available to them for amusements and recreation would be limited. The description also provides us with a glimpse into the manner in which the game songs (Track 2) were played during the nineteenth century: "A circle is formed with one or more in the centre, all the players singing, and as far as possible suiting the action of the body to the words."[27]

2
"Who Are the Greatest?"

While some of these elements are universally found in children's game songs, such as the use of circle formations and pantomime, African American children also incorporated stylized dance movements, formations, and forms, such as those associated with the French quadrille. Some of the songs required the children to partner each other, a practice that is foreign to African traditional music performance practices wherein men and women dance separately. Another influence from Anglo-American or European cultures is the appearance of the words "lily-white hand" in the lyrics of one of the songs, a phrase that is frequently found in many Scottish, English, and Irish ballads, as well as in their transplanted versions sung throughout the southern United States.

The traditional children's games that were collected after 1900 likely originated much earlier, such as "Green, Green Rocky Road," "Little Sally Walker," "Loobie Loo," and "Mary Mack." Before the invention of sound recording, these games were widely known to be played but little noticed. While some of these songs were certainly borrowed and adapted from Anglo song materials, many also demonstrated the same cultural underpinnings that were found in the music of African American adults, a trait that is also shared by children's game songs within African cultures.

Work Songs

In Africa, singing frequently accompanied group work wherever it took place, in the fields or on the water. This practice was easily transferred to the New World wherever people worked in groups. Singing coordinated their movements, lifted their spirits, enabled the slower workers to keep up, and warded off fatigue. Singing could accompany hoeing, planting, harvesting, picking cotton, grinding corn, cutting brush, laying railroad tracks, cutting wood, hauling fishing nets, or rowing (Track 1). Understandably, planters prized leaders with good, strong voices, commanding personalities, and a strong sense of rhythm.

1
"Hammer, Ring."

Along the coast, boat songs were frequently described by travelers and in memoirs by planters' wives and daughters. Crews of four to eight rowed boats in tidal rivers from one plantation to another or to the nearest city. The leader would sing a line, and the rowers would chime in with a refrain. The words were often improvised and were sometimes compliments to the passengers, sometimes merely unconnected words and phrases. Or they could be more somber: there were songs about separation from loved ones, abuse by one's captain, or longing for freedom. A good leader could speed the boat along, no matter how tired the crew might be.

Work and boat songs continued a tradition that had been common in Africa—integrating music into daily life. Often, the chorus began to sing before the leader had finished his call. Work songs could have religious words. When William Cullen Bryant visited a tobacco factory in Richmond in 1843, the workers sang, but his guide informed him that they sang only sacred music (probably spirituals). The guide commented, "They will sing nothing else."[28]

Still another widely reported occasion for song throughout the southern states was corn shucking. The planter would invite workers from neighboring plantations to come on a chosen day. Gangs of workers would march, singing, to the appointed place, choose sides, and name their leaders. Each team would strive to outdo the other, spurred on by the magnificent voices of their leaders, to which the crew would respond in chorus. This ceremony had some resemblance to the English harvest home and corn huskings in the North, but the musical competition and the improvised singing were peculiar to the South. When all the corn had been shucked and the winning team acclaimed, the feasting and dancing began. The planter's family and guests watched the fun from a distance, perhaps getting a foretaste of the minstrel theater then in its infancy, initiated by White men in the North as a caricature of African American music and dancing.

Other crops inspired similar harvest celebrations. In the West Indies, the cane song was reported. In middle Georgia, the Fourth of July signaled the end of the planting and cultivating season. All the tools were brought in from the fields and piled together. There followed a big celebration with much food, singing, and dancing. Cotton picking lent itself to group singing, "some wild, simple melodies" sung in a chorus, "so loud as to be heard from one plantation to another . . . for miles with musical echoes."[29] Flailing rice, grinding hominy, and braiding baskets all provided opportunities for singing, with the tempo adjusted to the task at hand.

Other opportunities for group singing were observed aboard sailing vessels. Hoisting sails, winding the capstan, and loading cargo needed song to coordinate the movements of the men. Mobile, Alabama, for example, became known as a shanty mart where sailors from different countries learned shanties from each other. Sailors from the West Indies were especially known for their prowess at singing shanties. Later, when steamboats replaced sailing vessels, especially on inland rivers, firemen worked in a virtual inferno below decks. In 1850, Fredrika Bremer witnessed firemen on the Mississippi: a man standing on a pile of firewood improvised a song, which was punctuated by the sound of wood being tossed to men below. They responded in chorus while hurling firewood into the boat's furnace.[30]

Work songs, however, did not need large groups. Plentiful reports exist of individuals participating in solo or solitary "work songs," such as the singing of lullabies. Weaving, spinning, shoe shining, cooking, and

Dena J. Epstein with Rosita M. Sands

other examples of common work activities that might have been engaged in by solo individuals were also frequently accompanied by singing.

Another type of folk music that was typically practiced by lone individuals, or sometimes by an individual interacting with others, was the **field holler or field cry**. These hollers and cries were generally described either by context, such as cotton field hollers or simply field hollers, or by the specific function that they served, such as "water calls." Eileen Southern cites a traveler's diary written in 1853, in which a moving description is presented of the field cries of several individual slaves:

> Suddenly one [slave] raised such a sound as I never heard before, a long, loud musical shout, rising and falling, and breaking into falsetto, his voice ringing through the woods in the clear, frosty night air, like a bugle call. As he finished, the melody was caught up by another, and then, another, and then, by several in chorus.[31]

Field holler or cry
Short, florid, improvised melody sung by an individual working in the fields.

Like work songs, field hollers (Track 7) served multiple purposes. A holler could convey a request or communicate a need. Cries were also emotional expressions, ways of communicating sadness, loneliness, fatigue, or any other of myriad human emotions.

7
"Arwhoolie (Cornfield Holler)."

The song form known as the "street cry" developed later and was improvised by street vendors in southern cities. Street cries were highly functional, serving the purpose of describing what the vendor was selling in terms calculated to attract or entice buyers. Although Charleston, South Carolina, and New Orleans have been especially noted for the skill of their street merchants in improvising distinctive cries, examples of street cries could be heard throughout the South. Samuel A. Floyd Jr., in the introduction to *The Power of Black Music*, makes reference to "a blind seller of boiled and 'parched' peanuts who peddled his wares by singing street cries and blues as he walked the streets of [Floyd's] neighborhood, in Lakeland, Florida, in the 1940s and very early 1950s."[32] Such scenes were common in Florida and other southern states during this period and even later, with vendors who rode bicycles through Black neighborhoods using cries to advertise fish for sale as well as vendors who traveled on foot using cries to sell boiled or roasted peanuts. One of the most well-known portrayals of vendors using street cries can be heard in George Gershwin's folk opera *Porgy and Bess*, which features the characters of Crab Man and Strawberry Woman peddling their goods in South Carolina.

Creole Songs

Quite distinct from the folk songs of the eastern seaboard were the French **Creole** songs of Louisiana. Many Blacks spoke French and enjoyed a Francophile culture. Of greater significance was the ease of manumission under the French and Spanish governments, which created a comparatively large free Afro-Creole population that was relatively prosperous but mingled freely with the slave population. Nowhere else in the United States did circumstances encourage such mingling.

Creole
In southwest Louisiana, historically a person of mixed French and African ancestry.

French-speaking Afro-Creole families enjoyed street parades, dancing, and even French opera. Although free Blacks were not accepted socially by the White population before the Civil War, their presence in business and trade was familiar and customary. Within their own community, the Creoles of color could move with assurance and pride. Afro-Creole musicians were taught by teachers from the French Opera orchestra, and their folk music was heavily influenced by French music with the addition of African elements, such as rhythm and call-and-response forms. Traditional Creole songs were known in the French Caribbean as well as on the mainland. Unfortunately, this music has been sorely neglected, and even less of it was collected in the nineteenth century than other forms of Black folk music, although seven songs were included in *Slave Songs of the United States*.[33]

Protest Songs

The African tradition of improvised derisive singing was easily adapted to the American scene. In September 1772, the *South Carolina Gazette* reported a "cabal of Negroes" near Charleston on a Saturday night, numbering about sixty people: "The entertainment was opened by the men copying (or *taking off*) the manners of their masters, and the women those of their mistresses, and relating some highly curious anecdotes, to the inexpressible diversion of that company."[34] When Europeans were present, the entertainment usually involved a more subtle satire, which permitted the expression of ideas that otherwise might have been severely punished.

Improvising satire, sometimes too subtle to be recognized, and making fun of the master and his family in ways that did not provoke offense were specialties of the African American improviser. Satiric verses could easily be inserted in work songs, whether boat songs or corn songs. In 1841, a song was described that criticized a preacher for ordering his men to work on Sunday to harvest a crop before a threat of rain, thus violating traditional work arrangements. The leader sang, "'Twas on a blessed Sabbath day, Here's a pretty preacher for you," to which the chorus responded, "It rain, boys, it rain."[35]

Fewer satirical songs than spirituals have been preserved. William Francis Allen, editor of the 1867 collection *Slave Songs of the United States*, commented, "We have succeeded in obtaining only a very few songs of this character" in the Sea Islands.[36] The singers may have been reluctant to sing satiric songs, for both religious reasons and self-protection. Even after the end of slavery, it was not wise to sing critical songs in the South.

More explicit comments on the conditions of slavery were sung, sometimes interpolated into religious songs. Harriet Tubman is said to have communicated her intentions to leave the plantation by singing a song of farewell as she walked about the quarters. "Go Down, Moses" was not a safe song to sing in the South, with its refrain of "Let my people go," but a song about the promised land might seem innocuous to the casual listener. The song "Follow the Drinking Gourd" gave instructions on how to use the stars to guide a runaway to the North and freedom. Even corn shucking songs might include verses of protest such as "Grind de meal, gimme de husk; Bake de bread, gimme de crust."

THE END OF THE NINETEENTH CENTURY

Despite the influence of the White European music by which it was surrounded, African American secular music retained characteristics associated with African music. No matter that most of the Africans had been born in the New World, that they now spoke English in some form, and that Africa was known to them only in stories and reminiscences—their music and dancing was immediately recognized by outsiders as non-European. Their skill at improvisation—at making up songs to fit the occasion, to regulate the work at hand, to compliment or to denigrate—was remarkable to observers.

Before the rise of recordings, the only way of preserving folk music was transcription in a notational system designed for European music. These transcriptions might be corroborated by descriptions written mostly by Europeans of unknown musical competence. In spite of the efforts of some clergymen to disparage secular folk music and dancing, African American secular folk music persisted as a familiar part of everyday work and play, musically very similar to African American sacred music. When the immensely popular minstrel theater caricatured African Americans, their secular music was brought into discredit, leaving the spiritual (also, at times, discredited) as the pre-eminent form of African American music. Nevertheless, secular music continued to flourish, growing in popularity as the nineteenth century drew to a close. Although many conservative Americans considered folk music uncultured, it remained widely popular among African Americans. With the development of ragtime, a distinctly American contribution to world music became popular worldwide. As the twentieth century progressed, the blues and jazz were even more influential in demonstrating the power of African American secular music throughout the world.

KEY NAMES

Simeon Gilliat

Solomon Northup

QUESTIONS

1. Identify at least three myths about African American music and culture that circulated widely during the antebellum period. To what extent were these myths perpetuated? What has been the long-term impact of these myths?

2. Identify three African musical practices preserved by slaves in the West Indies and the Americas. What circumstances allowed African slaves to continue these practices in the New World? What circumstances fostered changes in African musical and cultural identities?

3. Give at least four examples of antebellum secular genres. What role did these genres play in early African American culture?

4. Identify two instruments associated with dancing among slaves during the eighteenth century.

5. What evidence do the authors provide that suggests that the banjo is an instrument of African origin?

PROJECTS

1. Identify two African American banjo players, and search for examples of repertoire that they share. Compare differences in these recordings.

2. Compare two artworks from the colonial era that portray African American musical culture. Describe details that either reflect or contradict the prevailing European American view of African American music at the time. To what extent are these paintings useful for understanding the historical and cultural past?

3. Interview several people about their sense of music in the United States before the Civil War. What are their perceptions of African American music during this time? What is the basis of their views? How do their views compare to predominant views of the antebellum era? What are the implications of your findings?

NOTES

Please see the discography for information on resources for further listening.

1. Epstein 2003 (1977), 179.
2. Nketia 1974.
3. Epstein 2003 (1977), 4.
4. Ibid., 49.
5. Epstein 1975.
6. Burnim 2001, 624.
7. Epstein 2003 (1977), 39.
8. Ibid., 34.
9. Ibid., 142–43.
10. Ibid., 144.
11. White 1994.
12. Epstein 2003 (1977), 121.
13. Ibid., 122.
14. Ibid., 123.
15. *Encyclopédie, or Dictionnaire Raisonné Des Sciences* 1751–65, 2:474, 15:874.
16. Moreau de Saint-Méry 1797, 1:44.
17. Epstein 2003 (1977), 97.
18. Ibid., 84.
19. Ibid., 80.

Dena J. Epstein with Rosita M. Sands

20. Ibid., 212.
21. Ibid., 212–13.
22. Ibid., 154.
23. Ibid., 150.
24. Ibid., 152.
25. Clarke 1890.
26. Ibid., 288.
27. Ibid.
28. Epstein 2003 (1977), 164.
29. Ibid., 163.
30. Bremer 1853, 2: 174.
31. Southern 1997, 157.
32. Floyd 1995, 3.
33. Allen, Ware, and Garrison, 1867, 109–13.
34. Epstein 2003 (1977), 82.
35. Ibid., 173–74.
36. Allen *et al.* 1867, x.

CHAPTER 4

Spirituals

Mellonee V. Burnim

Spiritual
Religious music of
African Americans
during slavery.

Hymn
Metrical
compositions in
strophic form,
typically eight bars
of rhyming couplets,
loosely based on
biblical scripture.

Call–response
A song form that
characterized many
of the earliest
documented
spirituals; a song
structure or
performance practice
in which a singer or
instrumentalist
makes a musical
statement that
is answered by
another soloist,
instrumentalist,
or group. The
statement and
answer sometimes
overlap. Also called
antiphony and call-
and-response.

The earliest form of religious music to develop among African Americans in the United States is known as the spiritual. A music born of slavery, this genre symbolized the slave population's unique expression of Christian religious values and ideals tempered by the social, cultural, and physical experience of prolonged involuntary servitude. The **spiritual**, as it was described in early encounters, departed radically from the form and performance style associated with the **hymns** and psalms introduced to slaves by European missionaries. Spirituals were *not* hymns, as they were frequently referenced by observers, nor were they the errant attempts of an unlearned population to reproduce repertoire in the hymn style. The defining structure of the spiritual was **call–response**, a pattern of musical organization that was ubiquitous in the regions of West and Central Africa from which the slave population originated. Demonstrative behaviors such as hand clapping, body movement, and unbridaled displays of religious ecstasy were also commonplace markers of an African-inspired Christianity. Cultural memory played an important role in fashioning the spiritual as a uniquely American product designed to meet the very special needs, religious and cultural, of a disenfranchised people who refused to be defeated or destroyed by the experience of protracted human bondage. The birthing of the spiritual symbolized a spirit of freedom—the underlying conscious will of slaves to express themselves in ways that reflected who they were as a people living far from home in a distant land.

Slave accounts of the origin of spirituals consistently credit them as original or divinely inspired. Writing in 1862, Colonel Thomas Wentworth Higginson, commander of a Black Army regiment during the Civil War, documents this creative process, noting that:

> For all the songs, but especially for their own wild hymns [read spirituals] they constantly improvised simple verses, with the same odd mingling,—the little facts of to-day's march being interwoven with the depths of theological gloom, and the same jubilant chorus annexed to all; thus,—
>
> We're gwine to de Ferry,
>   De bell done ringing;
> Gwine to de landing,
>   De bell done ringing;
> Trust, believer,
>   O, de bell done ringing.[1]

Higginson's findings are consistent with those of J. Miller McKim who, also in 1862, asked a slave about the origins of the spiritual and got this response: "Dey make 'em, sah." The slave explained further that if something of note occurred during the day, the slaves sang about it that night at the "praise meeting." Recognizing the craft and skill involved in this process, the bondsman asserts: "Some's very good singers and know how; and dey work it in—work it in, you know, till they get it right; and dat's de way."[2]

It is impossible to determine the precise date of the origin of the spiritual. Testimonies of ex-slaves document this genre as the progeny of the Black collective rather than the individual composer. Poet James Weldon Johnson attributed their origin to unnamed "Black and Unknown Bards," the title of a poem he wrote in 1917. As a music created and transmitted via the oral tradition, the date of the origin of the spiritual can only be surmised from the earliest extant accounts of observers who documented their experiences of religious musics performed by Blacks.

Although the first Africans arrived in the North American colonies in 1619, the Christianizing mission did not begin in earnest until over one hundred years later. Prior to the first **Great Awakening**, which began around 1740,[3] the numbers of slaves converted to Christianity, a prerequisite for the birthing of the Negro spiritual, were few. Those minimal conversion efforts directed toward the slaves were largely thwarted either by (1) language barriers among the African-born population, (2) tacit resistance from slaves committed to maintaining their African religious identity, or (3) opposition from slave owners who perceived of Christianity and its doctrines of egalitarianism as counter to their socio-economic self-interest.[4] Even though the Church of England had formed the Society for the Propagation of the Gospel in Foreign Parts (SPG) in 1701 for the purpose of engaging in missionary activity in the British colonies, its efforts yielded rather insignificant results among the slave population.

Great Awakening
Period of religious revival that swept the American colonies in the mid-eighteenth century.

It was not until the first Great Awakening that significant numbers of slaves converted to Christianity. Utilizing a conversion strategy that emphasized personal experience, rather than instruction through catechism, as had been the case earlier, Blacks began to respond to the call to Christianity in numbers sizable enough to generate notice. Writing of his experience in Virginia in the 1700s, Presbyterian clergyman Samuel Davies described seeing one hundred or more Blacks at services he led, while Methodist Bishop Francis Asbury noted in his 1793 journal a South Carolina congregation of over five hundred, with "three hundred being black."[5]

Comparable accounts from the nineteenth century provide a glimpse of the actual character of Black participation in the frontier worship. According to Dena Epstein,[6] an 1819 depiction from White Methodist minister John Watson represents the first written account of the existence of a distinctive form of religious music among the North American slave population. Watson's publication, entitled *Methodist Error; or, Friendly Christian Advice to Those Methodists Who Indulge in Extravagant Religious Emotions and Bodily Exercises*, reads as follows:

> We have too a growing evil, in the practice of singing in our places of worship, *merry* airs, adapted from old *songs*, to hymns of our composing, often miserable as poetry and senseless as matter, and most frequently composed and sung by the illiterate *blacks* of the society ... The evil is only occasionally condemned, and the example has already visibly affected the religious manners of some whites.[7]

Although the music Watson refers to is not labeled as a spiritual, his comments clearly establish the existence of a well-defined body of repertoire among Blacks in the early decades of the nineteenth century, which they themselves had composed. Watson makes it clear that this distasteful music performed by Black Methodists was distinct from that of standard White practice, and that it was sufficiently pervasive and compelling to have influenced musical practice across the Black–White racial and cultural divide.

Epstein suggests that this maligned repertoire could well have "referred to what became known as Negro spirituals," although the term itself does not appear in print prior to the Civil War.[8] Epstein argues that the characteristics that defined this musical expression as unique likely existed for some time prior to Watson's observation and critique.[9] Certainly, significant numbers of Black Christians existed in the southern colonies by the end of the eighteenth century, and independent African American church bodies had already been established by that point as well.[10] Furthermore, the spirit of resistance to physical and cultural subjugation had been operative among the slave population from its earliest existence in the colonies. Viewed collectively, these contentions suggest a late eighteenth-century origin for the spiritual.

Performances of songs now identified as the spiritual emerged in auto-nomous contexts where Blacks were able to articulate a self-defined concept of music and worship. In the South, the **invisible church**—clandestine gatherings in spaces designated for purposes other than worship—was the spawning ground; in the North, it was the independent Black church. Whether in the ravine, gully, field, or living quarters, African American slaves fiercely guarded their religious privacy, not merely out of fear of reprisal, but out of their collective desire to express themselves in a way that was most meaningful to them. Although Black codes that prohibited the assembly of Blacks outside the presence of Whites were passed as early as the 1630s in Virginia, slaves nonetheless chose to risk life and limb to engage in autonomous Christian worship.[11] Former slave Alice Sewell recalls, "We used to slip off in de woods in de old slave days on Sunday evening way down in de swamps to sing and pray to our own liking."[12] Similarly, Fannie Moore recounts her experience of slavery, stating:

> Never have any church. If you go, you set in de back of de white folks' church. But de niggers slip off and pray and hold prayer-meetin' in de woods, den dey turn down a big wash pot and prop it up with a stick to drown out de sound of de singin'.[13]

Testimony from ex-slave Lucretia Alexander shows how Blacks sometimes merely tolerated White religious leadership, preferring instead to conduct worship in their own time and in their own way:

> The preacher came and . . . He'd just say, "Serve your masters. Don't steal your master's turkey [. . .] Don't steal your master's hawgs. Don't steal your master's meat. Do whatsomever your master tells you to do." Same old thing all the time. My father would have church in dwelling houses, and they had to whisper . . . Sometimes they would have church at his house. That would be when they would want a real meetin' with some real preachin' . . . They used to sing their songs in a whisper and pray in a whisper. That was a prayer-meeting from house to house once or twice—once or twice a week.[14]

The character of worship among Blacks in the invisible church was closely related to that of contemporary African American worship. There was prayer, communal singing, testifying, and sometimes, but not always, preaching. The most striking aspects of the worship were evident in the manner in which these elements were expressed. Prayer was extempor-aneous, typically moving from speech to song. Congregational participation, in the form of verbal affirmations, was not only accepted but expected, and highly valued. Singing involved everyone present and was accom-panied by hand clapping, body movement, and—if the spirit was particu-larly high—shouting[15] and religious dance, both peak forms of expressive behavior.

The following account by Sarah Fitzpatrick, an Alabama slave, reiterates the desire of Blacks to worship independently of Whites, and illustrates the expressive freedom that Blacks often found in doing so:

Invisible church
Sites where slaves worshipped in secret, often in defiance of laws that prohibited their assembly without White supervision.

Niggers commence ta wanna go to church by de'selves, even ef dey had ta meet in the white church. So white fo'ks have deir service in de mornin' an' "Niggers" have deirs in de evenin, a'ter dey clean up, wash de dishes, an' look a'ter everthing . . . Ya see "Niggers" lack to shout a whole lot an' wid de white fo'ks al' round 'em, dey couldn't shout jes lack dey want to.[16]

Ecstatic worship, in which participants expressed themselves through altered states, was commonplace in the invisible church. Under the influence of the Holy Spirit, congregants could be moved to scream, fall to the ground, run, cry, or dance. When worshippers were particularly engaged, services sometimes lasted far into the night, the length being determined only by the collective energy that fueled the group.[17]

Double entendre
Song text with double meanings.

While the scripture-inspired messages of spirituals were clearly religious, this fact did not preclude their being sung in non-religious contexts. Whether encouraged by slave owners to sing while working, or opting to do so of their own volition, the message of spirituals remained constant. God was aware of the slaves' daily suffering, and God was capable of delivering them in due time, just as he had done for Daniel, Moses, and Joshua of the Old Testament. Sometimes spirituals conveyed slaves' desire for freedom, as in the **double entendre** texts, which covertly encouraged the slave to flee:

Call: Run Mary, run! Oh—
          Tell Martha, run! Oh—
          Tell Mary, run, I say!
Response: You got a right to the tree of life.[18]

For slaves of African descent, belief in Christianity did not signal a loss of cultural identity or spiritual hope, as the inner workings of textual meaning and performance execution indicate.

PERFORMANCE PRACTICE

Folk spiritual
The earliest form of indigenous a cappella religious music created by African Americans during slavery.

Nineteenth-century descriptions of indigenous African American religious music provide a glimpse of the overall character of how this music was performed. The label **folk spiritual** is useful in distinguishing this genre as a product of the antebellum South. The descriptions included in *Slave Songs of the United States* (1867), a compilation of 136 songs, representing the first published collection of spirituals, is instructive. The compilers of this text establish uneqivocally that folk spirituals were sung neither in unison nor in harmony. "There is no singing in *parts* as we understand it and yet no two [persons] appear to be singing the same thing."[19] This heterophonic texture can be heard on recordings of spirituals made by Guy Carawan during the 1960s (Track 22).

22

"Jesus Knows All About My Troubles."

Even though tempos were known to vary, folk spirituals had a characteristic regular pulse, with the text viewed as subservient to rhythm. Based on his personal observations, *Slave Songs* editor William Francis Allen notes:

Mellonee V. Burnim

The negroes keep exquisite time in singing and do not suffer themselves to be daunted by any obstacle in the words. The most obstinate Scripture phrases or snatches from hymns they will force to do duty with any tune they please.[20]

As previously mentioned, the call–response or leader–chorus structure played a dominant role in antebellum spiritual performance practice. This structure juxtaposed short phrases sung by an individual with responses sung by the group. The constant repetition of the response allows and encourages everyone to participate, while variation is provided by the leader or soloist who is free to make textual, melodic, and rhythmic changes at will. In some instances the soloist or leader ends the call before the response begins; in others, overlapping call–response results when the solo lead continues after the group response begins. One account offers this description: "The leading singer starts the words of each verse, often improvising, and the others, who 'base' him, as it is called, strike in with the refrain, or even join in the solo, when the words are familiar."[21]

Call:	I don't feel weary and no ways tired.
Response:	O glory hallelujah.
Call:	Just let me in the kingdom while the world is all on fire.
Response:	O glory hallelujah.[22]

The call–response form is a strong marker of the pervasiveness of African cultural memory in the lived experiences of New World slaves. Erich von Hornbostel, an African music scholar who pioneered in the field of ethnomusicology, wrote in 1926:

Still there is one feature in American Negro songs which is not European but African, namely the form consisting of leading lines sung by a single voice, alternating with a refrain sung by a chorus. This form, it is true, occurs in European folksongs, but in African songs it is almost the only one used.[23]

Folk spirituals were typically accompanied only by hand claps and foot stomps, which complement the singing with a percussive timbral quality reminiscent of drumming. Bans on the use of loud musical instruments, especially drums, which could be used as signaling devices, did not succeed in eliminating the percussive dimension so highly valued in African music. Contemporary performances of spirituals by such groups as the McIntosh Shouters of the Georgia Sea Islands in which a broomstick is struck against a hardwood floor to replicate the sound of the drums, are undocumented in nineteenth-century accounts.[24]

THE ROLE OF DANCE

Blacks who engaged in the performance of religious music during slavery executed a type of spiritual that incorporated a stylized form of celebratory group circle dance. Referenced as the shout, **ring shout**, or "running spirchil"[25] this form of religious musical expression (Track 6) was characterized by members of the group who, after the singing was well established, formed a circle in the center of the performance space and

Ring shout
A form of folk spiritual characterized by leader–chorus antiphonal singing, hand clapping, and other percussion, which incorporates highly stylized religious dance as participants move in a counterclockwise circle.

 6

"Talking 'Bout a Good Time."

began moving in a counterclockwise shuffling motion. Shouts were performed both indoors and out, functioning most often as an expression of praise during worship, but they could also serve as a form of "amusement" having no "well defined intention of praise."[26]

Just as variation in performance occurred in the singing of spirituals, the execution of the shout varied from individual to individual and from region to region. In what has been referenced as the "drama shout," a person in the center lowers the body inch by inch to the knees, then down until the head touches the floor. The shouter then begins to slowly rise inch by inch.[27] Colonel Thomas Wentworth Higginson recalls observing his soldiers in camp, engaging in a "half pow-wow, half prayer-meeting which they know only as the shout," and practice "night after night."[28] Higginson notes that the men would "heel and toe tumultuously," "tremble and stagger," "stoop and rise," "whirl," and "caper sideways," all while "steadily circling like dervishes."[29] He also indicates that group members were known to acknowledge special "strokes of skill" with applause.[30]

Describing observations of Blacks performing shouts in the Port Royal Sea Islands in the aftermath of the Civil War, *Slave Songs* editors Allen, Ware, and Garrison commented that "Song and dance are alike extremely energetic, and often, the shout lasts into the middle of the night, the monotonous thud, thud of the feet prevents sleep within a half mile of the praise house."[31] The religious dance that characterized the shout was far removed from the style of music and worship that missionaries had taught the slaves. The significance of dance to this tradition points once again to the continuing impact of the African cultural past in shaping the religious identity of the slave community. In the minds of those engaged in the ritual behavior, their stylized movement was not to be confused with dance as expressed in secular contexts. "Dancing in the usual way is regarded with great horror by the people of Port Royal, but they enter with infinite zest into movements of the 'shout.'"[32] Despite references to the shout as barbaric, savage, heathenish, and other disparaging terms, slaves obstinately refused to abandon those musical practices that redefined Christianity in ways that were most meaningful to them.

Other elements observers detailed concerning the shout include: (1) a high degree of repetition; (2) the continuation of the songs for indefinite, yet often lengthy periods; (3) variation of tempo in different contexts; (4) robust, full-bodied vocal timbre; and (5) highly embellished melodic lines, with an abundance of "slides from one note to another and turns and cadences not in articulated notes."[33] A comparison of these features with those evident in recordings of shouts from the Sea Islands in the 1960s reveals these practices as still evident. Moreover, recordings also clearly establish a **polyrhythmic** foundation (another defining principle of West and Central African musics) undergirding the songs.[34]

The compilers of *Slave Songs* indicate that a shout could be sung "to any tune,"[35] suggesting that the repertoire of the shout was consonant

Polyrhythm
Several contrasting rhythms played or sung simultaneously.

Mellonee V. Burnim

with that of the spiritual. The shout was, therefore, first and foremost, defined by performance practice, or style of execution. It was not a genre that could be identified by form or text alone. The counterclockwise circle dance was its embodiment.

Various authors have pinpointed the existence of the ring shout in the southern states of South Carolina, North Carolina, Texas, Louisiana, Virginia, and Georgia.[36] While some writers have designated the shout as exclusive to the Baptist denomination, documentation clearly exists of the shout among Black Methodists as well.[37] Musicologist Eileen Southern contends the shout belonged to "no one denomination or region. It simply represented the survival of an African tradition in the New World."[38]

SHOUTS IN THE NORTH

The establishment of the independent African Methodist Episcopal (AME) congregation under the leadership of Richard Allen set the stage for the autonomy that fostered the growth of the spiritual in the North. After separating from St. George's in 1787, the White Methodist church where he had attended and preached in Philadelphia, Allen made a conscious choice to reject his formal affiliation with Methodism as a governing dominational body. The racial indignity Allen and Black members of St. George's had suffered in being relegated to balcony seats during their tenure at the church prompted their move toward denominational independence. Despite Allen's decision to distance himself administratively from the Methodist denomination, Allen and his followers nonetheless chose to continue to embrace Methodist doctrines and practice. Allen was quite satisfied with the "plain and simple gospel" of the Methodist church, which, in his view, well suited his congregation, because it was one that "the unlearned can understand and the learned are sure to understand."[39] Allen's selective identification with Methodism was further evident in his decision to reject the use of the standard Methodist hymnal in the worship of his newly found independent African American congregation, choosing instead to compile his own, which included songs he felt had greater appeal for Black people.

The research of Portia Maultsby, Eileen Southern, William Tallmadge, and J.R. Braithwaite details the innovations that characterized the songs in Allen's hymnal.[40] Texts were simplified, and refrain lines and choruses were routinely added. Southern suggests that Allen quite likely wrote some of the texts for his 1801 hymnal (the book contained no musical notation); for tunes, he probably composed some himself and used popular songs of the day as well.[41] Allen's goal was to generate congregational participation and assure freedom of worship for his members.[42] Non-Black observers of Allen's worship were frequently struck by the high level of congregational involvement in spirited singing. Not surprisingly, these early commentators also included those who registered their displeasure with the fully embodied, demonstrative song style, as did John Watson in 1819.[43]

Eileen Southern contends that John Watson's comments on the undesirable practices of Black Methodists actually referenced Richard Allen's congregation, the "dominant Black Methodists in the Philadelphia conference at the time."[44] Illustrating that the behaviors and practices of Blacks had prompted the ire of those at the highest level of Methodist church governance, Watson reveals that John Wesley, founder of the Methodist church, had expressed his displeasure with those who chose to reject the standard Methodist hymnal for questionable substitutes, as Allen had done. Watson reports that Wesley actually expelled three ministers "for singing '*poor, bald, flat, disjointed hymns*'" and "singing the same verse over and over again with all their might 30 or 40 times, 'to the utter discredit of all sober christianity' [*sic*]."[45] Watson's critique documents musical values and practices among Blacks in the North that are consonant with those associated with the singing of spirituals by Blacks in the South in the invisible church. The likelihood that the repertoire sung by those Black Methodists to whom Watson and Wesley refer consisted of hymns, as Watson's treatise suggests, is unlikely. Both the song texts and the aesthetic principles that affirmed musical and textual repetition—hand clapping, foot stomps, and body movement—clearly met with great disapproval from the White Methodist establishment. The songs were certainly not representative of repertoire or performance practice that was in widespread use among Methodist celebrants. It was especially disconcerting that Blacks were known to use secular melodies in composing sacred songs, a criticism that has often been directed toward gospel music since its inception in the early decades of the twentieth century. But Watson's greatest annoyance with the music of Blacks in the church was their incorporation of elements of dance in their songs:

> Here ought to be considered too, a most exceptionable error, which has the tolerance at least of the rulers of our camp meetings. In the *blacks'* quarter, the coloured people get together, and sing for hours together, short scraps of disjointed affirmations, pledges, or prayers, lengthened out with long repetition *choruses*. These are all sung in the merry chorus-manner of the southern harvest field, or husking-frolic method, of the slave blacks . . . With every word so sung, they have a sinking of one or other leg of the body alternately; producing an audible sound of the feet at every step, and as manifest as the steps of actual negro dancing in Virginia, &c. If some, in the meantime sit, they strike the sounds alternately on each thigh. What in the name of religion, can countenance or tolerate such gross perversions of true religion![46]

The practices that governed performance by these renegade Methodists were virtually identical to those of the folk spiritual or ring shout documented in *Slave Songs*.

Watson's attitude toward the folk spiritual was echoed by that of Daniel Alexander Payne, minister, historian, AME church bishop (1852–93), and founding president of Wilberforce University (1852–76).[47]

Commenting in his 1888 memoirs *Recollections of Seventy Years*, Payne likened the ring shout ritual to a "bush meeting"; the songs he labeled "cornfield ditties," and in his mind, those who engaged in the practice were simply "ignorant but well meaning." A product of Lutheran seminary training, Payne's views stood in stark contrast to those of local AME churches under his supervision who regarded the shout as the essence of religion. For lay persons Payne encountered, ring shouts were neither frivolous nor tangential to the Christian experience; to the contrary, they were considered necessary for conversion.[48] The following account of one of Payne's confrontations regarding this musical ritual serves to illustrate:

> After the sermon they formed a ring, and with coats off sung, clapped their hands and stamped their feet in a most ridiculous and heathenish way. I requested the pastor to go and stop their dancing. At his request they stopped their dancing and clapping of hands, but remained singing and rocking their bodies to and fro. This they did for about fifteen minutes. I then went, and taking their leader by the arm requested him to desist and to sit down and sing in a rational manner. I told him also that it was a heathenish way to worship and disgraceful to themselves, the race, and the Christian name. In that instance they broke up their ring but would not sit down, and walked sullenly away. After the sermon in the afternoon, having another opportunity of speaking alone to this young leader of the singing and clapping ring, he said: "Sinners won't get converted unless there is a ring." Said I: "You might sing till you fell down dead, and you would fail to convert a single sinner, because nothing but the Spirit of God and the word of God can convert sinners." He replied: "The Spirit of God works upon people in different ways. At camp-meeting there must be a ring here, a ring there, a ring over yonder, or sinners will not get converted." This was his idea, and it is also that of many others.[49]

Bishop Payne's efforts to make the ring shout "disgusting" and to teach the "right, fit, and proper way of serving God" were, for all practical purposes, an abysmal failure among the masses of his congregants.[50] Though himself an African American, Payne's view of appropriate music and behavior in worship was clearly aligned with those of John Watson and other members of the White Methodist elite. Born in Charleston, South Carolina, during slavery to parents who were free persons of color, Payne was privileged to receive formal educational training as a child. Before embarking on his ministerial career, he had pursued teaching as a profession, and even opened his own school, which served both slaves and free Blacks alike until a South Carolina law prohibiting the instruction of slaves was passed in 1835. As the first African American to attend Gettysburg Seminary in New York City, Payne's initial imperative was not ministry; instead, he was simply driven to improve his teaching excellence.[51]

Those congregrants Payne later encountered in his leadership position in the AME church were clearly no educational or social match for Payne. His role as a religious leader was profoundly informed by his commitment to the educational uplift of his people. His rejection of musical and ritual practices that bore no resemblance to the teachings he had received during his educational and theological journey is therefore both logical and reasonable. The ring shout was not a part of Payne's personal history or experience during his formative years. His voice of dissent regarding the genre points to the impact of the variable of class in the formation of African American identities during this period. Payne's virulent appraisal of African-derived worship practices reflected his social and educational distance from the majority of those he served in the AME church. As a man of relative privilege, having traveled to Europe and having even had personal encounters with President Lincoln during his distinguished career, Payne's desire to eliminate the ring shout from AME worship was simply an indication of his belief that African-derived religious practice was antithetical to rational, theological observance of Christianity.

THE ARRANGED SPIRITUAL

As a form of religious expression performed primarily in contexts free of White control, antebellum folk spirituals were outside the boundaries of consciousness for the vast majority of the White American public. With the advent of the Civil War came an influx of northern Whites to the South whose interactions with Blacks and their music prompted significant changes to the spirituals as well as changes to the overall American musical landscape. While the 1867 publication of *Slave Songs* was a post-Civil War event, the compilation generated little attention from either the scholarly, religious, or musical community. It was not until the spiritual was translated on to the concert stage, beginning in 1871, that its true meaning and significance began to resonate beyond the Black community.

Figure 4.1
Portrait of the Fisk Jubilee Singers, *c.*1871. Left to right: Minnie Tate, Green Evans, Isaac Dickerson, Jennie Jackson, Maggie Porter, Ella Sheppard, Thomas Rutling, Benjamin M. Holmes, and Eliza Walker. Photographs and Prints Division, Schomburg Center for Research in Black Culture, the New York Public Library, Astor, Lenox, and Tilden Foundations.

Fisk University was founded by the American Missionary Association in 1866, for the express purpose of educating newly emancipated slaves. From the start, the school struggled financially. Driven to address this need, the school treasurer, New York native and Union Army veteran George White, began to promote the novel idea of a traveling musical group that would "sing out of the people's pocket the money that must soon be obtained in some way for the university." An amateur musician, George White started this unprecedented, highly speculative venture with a group of eleven students, six female and five male, most of whom were former slaves, and one of whom was only fourteen years old.[52]

Embarking on a tour designed to follow the route of the Underground Railroad from Ohio through Pennsylvannia and up the Eastern Seaboard to New Jersey, Massachussetts, Washington, Maine, New Hampshire, Vermont, Connecticut, and New York, White's initial vision was to sing for audiences comprised largely of members of the American Missionary Association, the organization that had founded Fisk and multiple other schools for newly freed slaves in the aftermath of the Civil War. White launched the singing tours without the full blessing of the school administration, for never before had there been a similar undertaking. The prevailing image of the Black performer was that of the Black-faced minstrel, not of the serious musician with a repertoire of patriotic songs, spirituals, and other popular musics, which bore little resemblance to the stereotypes of Blacks that had graced the stages of America's public since the formal advent of minstrelsy in 1845.[53]

Originally known as the "Colored Christian Singers," White eventually chose the name Jubilee Singers "after the Old Testament 'year of the jubilee'—a favorite figure of speech into which the slaves put their prayers and hopes for Emancipation."[54] After a rather disappointing beginning, the Jubilee Singers had earned $20,000 in the first three months of the tour. By the end of the campaign in 1878, the ensemble had raised $150,000, enough to erect Jubilee Hall on the Fisk campus. Their audiences had expanded beyond African American worshipping communities in the United States to command performances before crowned heads of Europe.[55]

The repertoire of the Jubilee Singers was initially quite eclectic, consisting of the national anthem and other patriotic songs, such popular songs as "Old Folks At Home" and "Temperance Medley," as well as spirituals ("Go Down, Moses," "Keep Me From Sinking Down," and "Steal Away").[56] As their touring progressed, the program content shifted in response to public demand to feature spirituals more prominently.[57] Under the tutelage of George White, the spiritual performed by the Jubilee Singers assumed a character and purpose that differed radically from its folk antecedent. According to Black composer John Work III (1901–67), who taught at Fisk University:

> Mr. White decided on a style of singing the spiritual which eliminated every element that detracted from the pure emotion of the song . . . Finish, precision and sincerity

were demanded by this leader. While the program featured Spirituals, variety was given it by the use of numbers of classical standard. Mr. White strove for an art presentation.[58]

The folk spiritual, created as an expression of African American culture and religion, was now transferred to the concert stage. While the repertoire of these new arrangements was identical to that of the folk spiritual, this change in function—performing before paying transracial audiences—was accompanied by a change in performance practice. The hand clapping, foot stomping, and individual latitude in interpreting the melodic line that had characterized the folk spiritual were replaced by a degree of formality and reserve that distanced this new version from its predecessor. The aesthetic values that characterized George White's own musical identity were now being superimposed on to the Negro spiritual. As Louis Silveri argues, "Singing spirituals in the field was one thing, singing them to sophisticated audiences [read *White*] was something else."[59]

University and College Groups

Early recordings of spirituals by the Fisk University quartet[60] document the continuing presence of a cappella, syllabic singing, and the importance of call–response, although it was typically embedded within larger compositional forms. In J.B.T. Marsh's 1876 collection, *The Story of the Jubilee Singers*, the call–response structure features prominently, as had been the case in *Slave Songs* twenty-five years earlier. In Marsh's transcriptions, however, call–response is typically integrated into a larger verse–chorus structure, as indicated below. This two-part demarcation between verse and chorus is not evident in the 1867 collection, a further indication that, as a genre, the performance of the spiritual was not static:

Chorus

And I ain't got weary yet,
And I ain't got weary yet;
Been down in the valley so long,
And I ain't got weary yet.

Verse

Solo: Been praying for the sinner so long,
Chorus: And I ain't got weary yet;
Solo: Been praying for the sinner so long,
Chorus: And I ain't got weary yet.

Arranged/concert spiritual
The post-Civil War form of spirituals in a fixed, non-improvised form, which evolved in schools created to educate emancipated slaves.

Since the mid-1800s, spiritual texts have been represented in English dialect, reflecting the non-standard pronunciations, syntax, and even vocabulary that captured the imagination of students of the genre, yet eluded precise and accurate transcription. The dialect of the antebellum spiritual remains constant in the post-Civil War version. However, the vocal quality of the singers performing choral arrangements is generally more reflective of European-derived ideals of timbre, for performers of

Mellonee V. Burnim

arranged spirituals almost always have some degree of training in Western classical music vocal technique (Track 19). Whereas folk spirituals could be repeated for indefinite periods of time, the length of the arranged spiritual has become bound by the dictates of the printed score. **Heterophony** is replaced with clearly defined harmonic parts, and the element of dance is eliminated altogether.

 19
"Ezekiel Saw De Wheel."

Heterophony
The simultaneous rendering of slightly different versions of the same melody by two or more performers.

The Fisk campaign was an overwhelming success, quickly prompting the formation of similar groups at other fledgling Black colleges, beginning with Hampton and the Fairfield Normal Institute in South Carolina in 1872.[61] This arranged spiritual tradition has come to represent a core component of the repertoire sung by choirs at historically Black colleges and universities (HBCUs) across the nation, with generations of Black composers who established careers developing folk melodies for performance on the concert stage. Notable among many are John Work II (1873–1925) and John Work III (1901–68), William Dawson (1899–1990), R. Nathaniel Dett (1882–1943), and Undine Smith Moore (1904–89). As an unparalleled American art form, spirituals have been embraced in transcultural and global contexts, with performances, arrangements, and recordings from the continents of Africa and Europe, and their inclusion in standard and supplemental hymnals of the United Methodist, Episcopalian, Lutheran, and Catholic Churches, among others.[62]

The Negro spiritual has become a broadly accepted component of American sacred choral music literature, as evident from its inclusion in the standard hymnals of major religious denominations and the widespread availablity and performance of arrangements by non-Black composers. The spiritual has also been successfully translated on to the international stage in such contexts as Europe, Africa, and Australia.

HARRY T. BURLEIGH

In 1916, Harry T. Burleigh (1866–1949) became the first person to arrange the Negro spiritual for solo voice. Chosen from a pool of forty-nine candidates for the position of soloist for St. George's Episcopal Church in New York City in 1894, Burleigh experienced a continual need and desire to present new and fresh musical literature to the congregation he served for fifty-two years. Burleigh's *Jubilee Songs of the U.S.* (1916) included his "Deep River," the most well known of his first solo arrangements, which has become a standard part of the repertoire (Track 23). Distinguished from the choral arrangement by its use of piano accompaniment, the solo arrangement otherwise shares virtually identical aesthetic values with its choral counterpart.

 23
"Deep River."

Although the repertoire and aesthetic values of the solo arrangement of the spiritual are largely identical to those of its choral counterpart, the solo arrangement is typically performed with acoustic piano accompaniment rather than being sung a cappella. Contemporary settings for

Figure 4.2
Portrait of Harry T. Burleigh, Mishkin Studio, New York, May 1916. Photographs and Prints Division, Schomburg Center for Research in Black Culture, the New York Public Library, Astor, Lenox, and Tilden Foundations.

accompaniment by other instruments, including pipe organ, acoustic guitar, and orchestra, are indicative of how new interpretations of the genre continue to emerge.

Harry T. Burleigh is credited with starting the practice of closing recitals with a group of spirituals. The tradition has been sustained by other pioneering Black vocalists such as Roland Hayes (1887–1976), one of the world's leading concert tenors from the 1920s to the 1940s, who at one time was a member of the Fisk Jubilee Singers,[63] and Marian Anderson (1902–93) (Figure 4.3), who, in 1955, was the first African American to sing at the Metropolitan Opera. Anderson is also well known for her historic public encounter with the social and political injustice toward African Americans that plagued American society during the 1930s. Repeated efforts to book a concert for Marian Anderson in Constitution Hall in the nation's capitol in 1939 were unsuccessful. Policies instituted by the Daughters of the American Revolution (DAR), the body that governed use of the hall, prohibited Blacks from performing there. Anderson was unwittingly thrust into the center of a national controversy, which culminated with First Lady Eleanor Roosevelt's withdrawal of her membership from DAR and subsequent support of a

Figure 4.3
Marian Anderson and
Franz Rupp, October
1961. Photo by John
G. Ross; Marian
Anderson Collection,
Rare Book and
Manuscript Library,
University of
Pennsylvania.

substitute concert for Marian Anderson at Lincoln Memorial on Easter
Sunday of the same year. A crowd of over seventy-five thousand attended,
with high-level dignitaries strategically seated for visibility. On that
occasion, Anderson's repertoire included "America," "Ave Maria," and
an entire set of Negro spirituals, of which "Nobody Knows the Trouble
I've Seen" was an encore.[64]

The person credited as the first to sing a concert comprised entirely
of Negro spirituals is the renowned bass-baritone Paul Robeson (1898–
1976). With a stellar academic career as a Phi Beta Kappa graduate of
Rutgers and Columbia Law School valedictorian in 1923, Robeson was
equally gifted as an athlete, being named an All American football player
at Rutgers. His career trajectory led him to excel as an actor on stage and
in film, becoming noted in particular for his role in Jerome Kern and
Oscar Hammerstein's *Showboat*, through which he made the ever popular
song "Old Man River" famous.[65]

As a performer of spirituals, Robeson's profile is distinguished in
several ways. First, although most African American artists who
pioneered in the performance of the spiritual held extensive training in
Western European classical music, Robeson's formal academic training
was in fields other than music. Second, Robeson, more than any other
before or after him, centered his performance of spirituals in a political
ideology that challenged oppression worldwide. For example, Robeson's
rendition of "Old Man River" underwent several textual transformations
over time. The opening lyrics, which referred to Blacks as "darkies," were
modified to reflect a spirit of resistance: "There's an old man called the
Mississippi, That's the ol' man I don't like to be."[66]

Contrasting with most celebrated performers of the solo arranged
spiritual, Robeson was known as an outspoken critic of racism and
oppression in the United States, making him an eventual target of the
House Un-American Activities Committee during the late 1940s. As a
consequence of his encounter with this body, Robeson's passport was

eventually revoked for eight years by the State Department, and he was ostracized by members of the White American public that had formerly revered him. During the height of his political infamy, African American churches became the mainstay of his concert appearances.[67] His recording *Paul Robeson in Live Performance* (1971) includes spirituals performed at "Mother [AME] Zion" Church in New York City in 1958 after his passport was returned and his concert career had been re-established. Robeson commented at that event:

> As I have said many times, any struggles I have been engaged in, whatever I do, it's been that my grandnephews and my grandchildren—that your children—somewhere —we all, of all races, all creeds can walk this American earth in unity.[68]

The solo arranged spiritual continues to hold a place of pride and prominence in contemporary African American worship, particularly in congregations with significant numbers of members who hold college degrees from HBCUs. The solo arranged spiritual also remains a mainstay of the repertoire of such renowned African American operatic singers as Camilla Williams (Anderson's protégé), the first African American to hold an extended contract with a professional opera company in the United States, Leontyne Price, Jessye Norman, and Kathleen Battle, the latter two featuring spirituals in their 1990 PBS telecast from Carnegie Hall.

ARRANGED SPIRITUAL CONTINUUM

Slave Songs of the United States is particularly valuable for its docu-mentation of songs collected from slaves themselves, several of which have twentieth-century correspondences. In other words, the *Slave Songs* collection establishes the fact that religious repertoire from the nineteenth century has been selectively translated into contemporary arrangements for ensemble, solo, and choir alike. One such example is "Roll Jordan Roll," number 1 in the collection, described as the most popular of all the songs cited, having been previously published in 1862 by Lucy McKim.[69] Other titles from the collection that have become a part of the standard repertoire of spirituals include: "No Man Can Hinder Me," "Michael Row the Boat Ashore," "We Will Walk Through the Valley," "Nobody Knows the Trouble I've Had," "Jacob's Ladder," and "The Old Ship of Zion." Careful review of these seemingly familiar songs reveals that the nineteenth-century versions are frequently radically different from their twentieth-century counterparts. "Roll Jordan Roll" of 1867, for example, reflects neither the melody nor the text as commonly cited in present-day collections or heard on recordings. *Slave Songs'* "Roll Jordan Roll" begins with the verse:

> My brudder sittin' on the tree of life
> An' he yearde when Jordan Roll
> Roll Jordan Roll, Jordan Roll, Jordan Roll.

In contrast, in 1909, the Fisk University Jubilee Singers recorded a radically different version of the same spirititual, which begins with the chorus rather than the verse. The latter version is representative of current practice:

Chorus 2×: Roll Jordan Roll, Roll Jordan Roll
I want to go to heaven when I die.
To hear Jordan Roll.

Verse: O sister you ought to been there
Yes, my Lord.
A sitting in the kingdom
To hear Jordan Roll.

In similar fashion, the 1867 title "Nobody Knows the Trouble I've Had" is now more generally known as "Nobody Knows the Trouble I've Seen." Its rather indelicate verse "I pick de berry and I suck de juice," cited in the *Slave Songs*, has not been retained in modern usage.

The biblical basis of the spiritual is confirmed in *Slave Songs* with the frequent references to Old Testament characters from Daniel to Paul and Silas to Moses, all of whom overcame seemingly insurmountable odds, just as the slaves sought to do in their struggle against human bondage. Viewed as a whole, the 1867 collection reflects a concept of God as personal and integral to everyday life. God was neither distant nor abstract, and, contrary to popular thought, neither were slave song texts devoted exclusively, or even primarily, with concerns of the afterlife. "No Man Can Hinder Me," number 14 in *Slave Songs*, serves as an example:

Walk in kind Savior
    No man can hinder me.
Walk in sweet Jesus
    No man can hinder me.

The recurring response, although embedded in the language of Christianity, is a forthright statement of the belief in individual and collective power to overcome and conquer any human threat. By welcoming God's oversight and companionship, the believer is shielded from harm.[70]

Similarly, the 1867 version of "O Daniel" castigates the insincere Christian and then, in the chorus, affirms God as a deliverer, not only for figures of the Old Testament such as Daniel, but for the slave as well:

Verse: You call yourself a church member
You hold your hand so high
You praise God with your glitt'ring tongue
But you leave all your heart behind.

Chorus: O my Lord delivered Daniel
O Daniel, O Daniel
O My Lord delivered Daniel,
Why not deliver me too?

Yet a third example, "Many Thousand Go," reveals the unveiled disdain slaves held for bondage, as they anticipate the institution's demise:

> No more peck o' corn for me
>> No more, no more
> No more peck o' corn for me
>> Many thousand go.

Subsequent verses proclaim "no more driver's lash" and "no more mistress' call." The unequivocal indictments of slavery evident in such passages as these ensured that they were not sung publicly. These song texts represented subversive acts of resistance punishable by death.

The spiritual text "We'll soon be free," with the refrain "when the Lord calls us home," led Blacks in South Carolina to be thrown into jail at the outbreak of the Civil War. A young man in Thomas Wentworth Higginson's regiment speculated that "Dey tink de Lord mean fuh say de Yankees."[71]

The Negro spiritual as it was originally conceived was a richly textured mosaic of Christian belief intertwined with African-derived cultural values. To perform the spiritual was to embrace the individual and collective identity of persons of African descent in the New World. Even when they conveyed subliminal messages understood only by the initiated, or members of the group, to sing the spiritual was to wage systematic warfare on the institutiton that imposed the chains of bondage. To sing the spiritual was to be free.

CONCLUSIONS

As a musical genre, the spiritual has functioned historically as both religious and cultural expression for its creators. Cultivated on American soil, the spiritual was yet the embodiment of an African cultural past. But, as African Americans have confronted seminal moments in their collective lived experiences in the United States, the spiritual has evolved to reflect those historical and cultural shifts. Present-day representations of the spiritual do not precisely replicate their eighteenth- and nineteenth-century counterparts, nor has the earliest recorded repertoire been maintained without continuous scrutiny and purging. Those spirituals that remain—"There Is a Balm in Gilead," "My Lord What a Mourning," "Didn't My Lord Deliver Daniel," and "Swing Low Sweet Chariot," to name but a few—have stood the test of time because of their intrinsic beauty and their enduring power to speak to the hearts of men and women across boundaries of time and space.

KEY NAMES

Richard Allen	Daniel Alexander Payne
Marian Anderson	Paul Robeson
Harry T. Burleigh	*Slave Songs of the United States*
Fisk Jubilee Singers	John Watson

QUESTIONS

1. When, where, and how did the folk spiritual develop? What are its key characteristics? In what context did the arranged spiritual emerge and what were its distinguishing characteristics? In what ways are these two forms alike? How do they differ?

2. Describe the character of worship services among Blacks in autonomous settings in the rural South during slavery. What aspects of the service were valued? How did these cultural values translate into song performance?

3. What is a ring shout? What are its key elements? Explain how the ring shout is an expression of both religious and cultural identity.

4. The growth of the spiritual in the North was fostered by the African Methodist Episcopal (AME) church. In what ways did Richard Allen's leadership impact the development of spirituals among his congregants? What is the significance of the accounts of Black religious song in the early nineteenth century written by John Watson and Daniel Alexander Payne?

5. Compare and contrast the repertoire, performers, and performance contexts for folk and arranged spirituals. What factors contributed to the distinctions you identify?

PROJECTS

1. Attend a worship service at a predominantly African American church of your choice and write an observation paper about the character of the worship service. Describe those values operative in this service that are consistent with or divergent from worship in the invisible church or Richard Allen's church.

2. Many of the songs collected in *Slave Songs of the United States* have become standard repertoire in various denominations. Referencing a hymnal from a Christian denomination of your choice, list the spirituals included in the collection, noting correspondences, if any, that exist with *Slave Songs*. Note how the spirituals are identified and how their origin is credited.

3. Listen to at least three different versions of a spiritual of your choice. In what ways are these recordings similar or distinct? Identify those characteristics that define your examples as either a folk or arranged spiritual. Prepare a short biographical sketch of the performers in each recording, highlighting, in particular, the extent to which they engage spirituals as an expression of African American religious and cultural values.

4. Performances of arranged spirituals are an important component of the repertoire of choirs at historically Black colleges and universities (HBCUs). How has the Fisk Jubilee ensemble changed over the years? In what ways

has it remained the same? Research the history of an HBCU choir other than Fisk University. When was this choir started and to what extent has it maintained the tradition of arranged spirituals over the years?

NOTES

Please see the discography for information on resources for further listening.

An abbreviated version of this chapter appears as "Spirituals, African American," in *Continuum Encyclopedia of Popular Music of the World, Vol. 8, Genres: North America*, edited by John Shepherd and David Horn (New York: Continuum, 2012).

1. Higginson 1962 (1869), 134.
2. Allen, Ware, and Garrison 1995 (1867), xviii.
3. Raboteau 1980 (1978), 128.
4. Ibid., 98–121.
5. Quoted in Epstein 1977, 104–06.
6. Ibid., 219.
7. Watson 1983 (1819), 62–63.
8. Epstein 1977, 219.
9. Ibid., 232.
10. Albert Raboteau (1980 (1978), 131) documents that by 1797 Black Methodist membership stood at 12,215, or almost one-fourth of the total membership, while Black Baptist membership in 1793 was between 17,000 and 18,000, also approximately one-fourth of the total membership. The founding date attributed to the African Methodist Episcopal Church (the group which scholar Eileen Southern contends Watson references in his 1819 commentary) is 1787 (Lincoln and Mamiya 1990, 50).
11. Harding 1983 (1981), 27.
12. Yetman 1970, 263.
13. Ibid., 229.
14. Raboteau 1980 (1978), 214. Ellipses Raboteau's; bracketed ellipses mine.
15. The term "shouting" represented an altered state not to be confused with the danced form of the spiritual referred to as the "ring shout."
16. Raboteau 1980 (1978), 225–26.
17. Ibid., 221.
18. Sung by the Seniorlites of Johns Island, South Carolina, on *Wade in the Water*, Vol. 2, no. 4, Smithsonian Folkways Series SF 40076, 1994.
19. Allen *et al.* 1995 (1867), v.
20. Ibid., iv.
21. Ibid., v.
22. Ibid., 70.
23. Quoted in Epstein 1977, 56–57.
24. Rosenbaum 1998, 31.
25. Allen *et al.* 1995 (1867), xv.
26. Ibid., xiii.
27. Southern 1974, 63.
28. Higginson 1962 (1869), 17.
29. Ibid.
30. Ibid.
31. Allen *et al.* 1995 (1867), xiv.
32. Ibid.
33. Ibid., vi.
34. See *Been in the Storm So Long*. Recorded by Guy Carawan, Folkways Records, FS 3842, 1967.
35. Allen *et al.* 1995 (1867), xv.

Mellonee V. Burnim

36. See Stuckey 1987, 68–69; Bremer 1983 (1853), 103–15; Allen *et al.* 1995 (1867), xxiii; and Rosenbaum 1998, 31.

37. Higginson 1962 (1869), 17, describes Methodist participation in the shout, while Allen *et al.* 1995 (1867), xv, reference Baptist involvement.

38. Southern 1997, 183.

39. Wesley 1969 (1935), 72.

40. Maultsby 1975, 401–20; Southern 1997, 75–80; Tallmadge 1968, 219–38; Braithwaite 1987 (1801) ix–xlvii.

41. Southern 1997, 77.

42. See Maultsby 1975, 413; Southern 1997, 75.

43. Watson 1983 (1819), 62.

44. Southern 1983, 62.

45. Watson 1983 (1819), 63.

46. Ibid.

47. Strobert 2001.

48. Payne 1983 (1888), 69.

49. Ibid.

50. Ibid.

51. Strobert 2001.

52. Marsh 1876, 17, 22.

53. Ibid., 31, 36.

54. Ibid., 27.

55. Ibid., 53, 76; Ward 2000, 211.

56. Marsh 1971 (1876), 32, 53; Silveri 1988, 106–07.

57. Ward 2000, 160.

58. Work 1940, 15.

59. Silveri 1988, 107.

60. *Fisk University Jubilee Singers, Vol. 1, 1909–1911*, Document Records DOCD-5533, 1997.

61. Southern 1997, 229.

62. See Lovell 1972, 402–580.

63. Helm 1942, 92.

64. Keiler 2002, 188–213.

65. Robeson 1981, 35–37.

66. Ibid., 37.

67. Ibid., 197–98.

68. *Paul Robeson in Live Performance*, Columbia M30424, 1971.

69. Allen *et al.* 1995 (1867), ii, 1.

70. The response "No man can hinder me" has been sustained in the spiritual repertoire, in large part through the ever popular Hall Johnson arrangement "Ride On King Jesus" for solo voice included in his 1949 collection. A highly popular gospel arrangement of "Ride On King Jesus" with the refrain "No man cannot hinder me" is included on the album *Victory Shall Be Mine* by the Wilmington Chester Mass Choir (Sweet Rain, 1990).

71. Higginson 1962 (1869), 217.

PART II

Postbellum Period

Music in Transition (Late 1800s–)

CHAPTER 5

Quartets
Jubilee to Gospel

Joyce Marie Jackson

INTRODUCTION

The African American **quartet** tradition is an artistic form with a unique history and aesthetic expression that originated in the mid-1800s, as an outgrowth of the African American university singing movement. The early African American sacred a cappella vocal groups were originally known as jubilee quartets because of the nature of their repertoire and characteristics of their performance style.[1] These groups, which most often consisted of men, developed a unique style of singing that, in the twentieth century, evolved as a sub-genre of gospel music. The quartet tradition is a synthesis of African American and Western practices, containing distinctive elements and sonic qualities that express cultural values and aesthetics of the African American community.[2]

In Western art music, the term "quartet" is usually considered to be either a musical group consisting of four members or a musical composition for four voices or instruments. Historically, within the context of African American music, a quartet was defined as a vocal ensemble that consisted of a minimum of four voices and a maximum of six voices singing four-part harmony arrangements in either an a cappella style or with limited instrumentation (i.e., guitar, bass, and drums). The definition of an African American quartet is not determined by the size of the group, as is the case in the European tradition, but rather by the number of designated harmony parts.

In many areas of the United States, sacred quartet singing still remains vibrant and dynamic with a large community following. Even

> **Quartet**
> In Western music, a musical composition or ensemble of four voices or instruments.

though many quartets traditionally grew from and remained at the periphery of the Black church, they have continuously provided the basic conceptual and behavioral framework for Black musical religious ensembles of today. Based on my analysis of audio recordings and long-term ethnographic and archival research on the African American quartet tradition, this performance genre can be sub-divided historically into: (1) the jubilee period, 1880–1929, (2) the transitional period, 1930–45, and (3) the gospel period, 1946–69.[3] Stylistic overlap exists within this periodization because existing styles can continue as new ones emerge amid socio-cultural, economic, political, and educational change.

JUBILEE PERIOD (1880–1929)

University Jubilee Quartet

Jubilee
Nineteenth-century genre with sacred or secular narrative texts, sung in moderate or fast tempo.

The university singing movement emerged after the American Civil War when the Freedman's Bureau and such benevolent groups as the American Missionary Association established educational institutions in the North and South for newly emancipated slaves. The majority of these schools are located in the South, and many—such as Atlanta University (now Clark Atlanta University) in Georgia; Hampton Institute (now Hampton University) in Virginia; Southern University in Baton Rouge, Louisiana; and Fisk University in Nashville, Tennessee—are still thriving institutions.

The American Missionary Association founded Fisk University in 1866, and its immediate challenge was to obtain funds for new buildings, equipment, and instructors. When the university was on the verge of bankruptcy and closing in 1870, George L. White, the university's treasurer and choir director, sought to address the financial problem by publicizing and promoting the institution. Although a somewhat speculative venture at the time, in 1871 he began touring with a mixed singing ensemble of nine students, most of whom were former slaves. Under his direction, this company—later named the Fisk Jubilee Singers— undertook a number of concert tours throughout the United States, expanding to Europe beginning in 1873.[4] On these tours, "a male quartet and a mixed quartet were extracted from the nine member ensemble to present various selections and medleys independently."[5] From 1916 to 1925, the school sometimes toured two fund-raising jubilee groups—a professional quartet and a student choir.[6] Male jubilee quartets became featured groups within the choir and some even replaced the mixed ensembles as the popularly favored group. The **jubilee quartet**, as it was known, reached a summit of activity during the late nineteenth and early twentieth centuries, when most Black colleges and normal and industrial schools organized musical groups to help support their mission.

Jubilee quartet
Male or female a cappella ensemble of four to six voices that performs formal arrangements of spirituals and jubilee songs in close four-part harmony, with emphasis on a percussive and rhythmic style of singing.

The earliest Fisk concerts initially consisted of a varied repertoire, but in later tours, spirituals dominated—a consequence of the overwhelmingly positive audience response (see discussion of spirituals in Chapter 4).

Income from the concerts helped to provide a financial cushion for the university, brought fame for the singers, and brought recognition of the spiritual as a distinct African American genre. The Fisk campaign became a prototype that would guide and influence musical groups from other historically Black colleges and universities.

The establishment of other university quartets, such as those sponsored by Hampton Institute; Southern University in Baton Rouge; Straight University (now Dillard University) in New Orleans, Louisiana; Morehouse College in Atlanta, Georgia; Tuskegee Institute in Alabama; Utica Institute in Mississippi; and Wilberforce University in Xenia, Ohio, represented strong musical forces that helped to reinforce the popularity of quartets both within the African American community and beyond. By the 1890s, the sacred quartet singing tradition had developed fully from its base in southern African American colleges. These university-affiliated jubilee quartets were the forerunners of the twentieth-century gospel quartet.

Traditionally, spiritual arrangements sung by jubilee quartets developed from a combination of three musical sources: harmonized Western-influenced ensemble singing of jubilee choirs, the African American barbershop quartet singing style, and call-and-response forms of African American folk spirituals and work songs. Usually the full group sings the chorus in harmony, and then a soloist sings the verse above repeated, harmonized, rhythmic phrases sung by the group. The emphasis was on well-blended ensemble singing with no instrumental accompaniment.

Quartet arrangements also retain elements from the traditional folk spiritual. For example, most university quartets perform in the a cappella style of the folk idiom and maintain harmonic simplicity by utilizing few chord changes. Most songs are **strophic**, in accordance with many folk spirituals, with the incorporation of either short or long phrase call-and-response. The utilization of call-and-response within the strophic form clearly demonstrates the synthesis of Western European and African-derived musical traditions. In essence, these quartet performances are a reflection of values grounded in the duality of African American identity (Track 24).

Strophic
Song form in which a single melody is repeated with a different set of lyrics for each stanza.

 24
"Let the Church Roll On."

Minstrel Jubilee Quartets

Along with the nineteenth-century university jubilee quartet, the minstrel quartet contributed to a musical style that provided part of the foundation of the twentieth-century Black community quartet. Minstrel shows, developed by and for Whites in the 1840s, were spurred by Northern curiosity about Southern Blacks and piqued by racial conflicts following the Civil War. Early minstrels used dances, songs, verbal dialogue, and performance routines that reflected the White racial imagination during that time period. Having initially been restricted from performing in White shows, African Americans responded by forming minstrel troops of their own. Companies with all-Black casts appeared as early as the mid-1850s, but did not become widely popular until the 1870s, during Reconstruction and after the Fisk Jubilee Singers had launched their initial campaign.[7]

During the 1870s, when minstrelsy was experiencing its greatest success, Black and White troops offered competing depictions of slave life. As a result, attention in Black shows was focused on religious practice, since earlier content was void of religious music.[8] The emergence of groups such as the Fisk Jubilee Singers provided the impetus for new religious material in minstrel shows. In response to public interest and in recognition of the acclaim associated with sacred folk songs presented by jubilee groups, enterprising African American minstrels introduced the spiritual repertoire to their shows. In 1875–76, this form of sacred expression had its first great impact on the Black minstrel show when Callender's Georgia Minstrels, a long-running Black troupe under White ownership and management, featured an ensemble performing jubilee songs.[9] This group and its repertoire sparked a renewed interest in plantation slave life, which had a tremendous effect on minstrelsy. From that time, Black minstrel troupes routinely included a religious singing group, and several of these troupes even added "jubilee" to their titles.[10]

In the latter part of the nineteenth century, every minstrel company and every vaudeville troupe, both Black and White, tended to feature an African American jubilee singing group. African American male quartets became highly desirable for commercial entertainment, singing not only jubilee songs or spirituals but also a mixture of popular tunes of the day, novelty (comedy) songs, and secular songs referencing plantation life. While minstrel quartets were based on the original Fisk University model, they expanded to meet popular entertainment demands. University jubilee groups provided the model for the use of close four-part harmony, the a cappella singing style, and sacred repertoire. The model for showmanship, humor, and entertainment, however, can be attributed directly to the minstrel tradition. Quartet singers also gained recognition, income, entertainment skills, and business acumen, which otherwise were unavailable to African American performers of the time. While winning the adoration of Black as well as White audiences, they successfully integrated into an entertainment world previously reserved exclusively for Whites.

Community-Based Jubilee Quartets

Both university and minstrel jubilee quartets had a significant influence on the development of community-based singing groups. The community-based jubilee quartets combined practices from both traditions, resulting in a set of aesthetic practices that, in many cases, still apply to quartet singing today. The organization of these community quartets depended on family, religious, occupational, and social group affiliations. Both teachers and students at African American educational institutions trained

Joyce Marie Jackson

many of the community quartets. Although some quartets were coached by a designated trainer within the group, others simply imitated groups heard on radio broadcasts and commercial recordings. Most community-based and minstrel quartets consisted of male singers who had no formal training in Western classical music.[11]

These typically male community quartets were the folk counterparts of the university quartets. They sang in numerous contexts, including church services, community functions, festivals, and road shows. Those community quartets that managed to gain professional status performed primarily as entertainment for profit in concert settings. Often they had a very large following among both Whites and Blacks.

The performance style of these first independent quartets was influenced by, but also departed from, the university quartet style. The university jubilee quartets presented spirituals as melodically conceived by enslaved African Americans and harmonically arranged by Europeans or by musicians formally trained in European classical music. In contrast, community-based quartet performance often contradicted rules that governed European musical theory and performance practice. These early community-based quartets developed a style of presentation that was culturally defined.

Quartets consisted of four singers during the jubilee period—first and second tenor, baritone, and bass. Although there was little emphasis on solo singing during this time, some quartets had members who sang falsetto leads and incorporated such expressive vocal devices as **blue notes**, **grace notes**, and **melismas**. Traditionally, all early community-based jubilee quartets sang in the a cappella style, focusing on a well-blended ensemble sound.

From the beginning, the bass voice, which provided the strong "bottom" or fullness to chords for which jubilee quartets were known, was prominent in community-based quartets. As the rhythm component of the ensemble, the bass singer also provided vocal interjections and solos during group rests. The four-part harmonies were very close, with contrary harmonic and rhythmic movement being characteristic of the bass vocal line. Chordal structures were basic triads, with an occasional use of flat thirds, fifths, and sevenths, all well blended. While harmonic and melodic simplicity remained intact, the prevailing rules on voicing, chord structure, and chord progression of the Western European tradition were not always operative.

Whereas university quartets employed a lyrical style of singing, in contrast, community quartets tended to concentrate on a percussive and rhythmic style. A classic example of the latter is the Heavenly Gospel Singers' arrangement of "Dip Your Finger in the Water" (Bluebird 6073, 1953), which uses such devices as **hocket**, **polyrhythms**, and syncopation to produce rhythmic variety.

All jubilee quartets specialized in singing harmonized spirituals and jubilee songs. Jubilee songs, the more popular of the two, were moderate

Blue note
A note, sounded or suggested, that falls between two adjacent notes in the standard Western division of octave, most often the third or seventh degrees in a scale.

Grace note
A short ornamental note performed as an embellishment before the principal pitch.

Melisma
A single syllable sung over several pitches.

Hocket
Interlocking patterns shared by two or more voices or instruments that produce a single melody.

Polyrhythm
Several contrasting rhythms played or sung simultaneously.

or fast tempo songs with verses, which recounted narratives based on either biblical or secular topics. For example, the "Atom Bomb" and other songs about World War II, as well as songs about union bosses, are neither sacred nor are they spirituals, but they are categorized as jubilees. Because many quartets performed in non-religious contexts, secular songs were also a part of the repertoire. Just as not all spirituals are jubilees, neither are all jubilees spirituals. Performance style and textual content distinguish the two. In both the community quartet and the university quartet, overlapping call–response, in which the soloist begins a phrase that the background members complete, is the predominant structure. The chorus usually features the entire group responding in harmony to the soloist's introductory call. Because emphasis is not on the soloist, improvisation from lead singers is minimal.

Since there were still vestiges of the formative university influence in this period, early community quartets typically wore performance attire of matching suits in conservative colors. In some cases well-polished professional groups wore tuxedos, especially when performing in formal contexts or before White audiences.

This early form of community Black quartet singing is represented by such groups as the Dinwiddie Colored Quartet from Virginia; the Heavenly Gospel Singers from South Carolina; and the Birmingham Jubilee Quartet from Alabama, all of whom were recorded around the turn of the twentieth century. They, along with other groups, began to make significant changes in quartet stylistic development after World War I.[12]

Shape-Note/Sacred Harp Quartets

Shape-note singing has sometimes been referred to as White spiritual and White gospel singing. Nevertheless, African American congregations in the South during the 1880s adapted the genre as an outgrowth of the New England singing school movement and the Great Awakening songs drawn from standard hymns, gospel hymns, spirituals, folk songs, and other forms of secular music. Sacred harp utilizes the four-shape notation of Little and Smith's *The Easy Instructor* (c.1800), in which each shape (triangle, circle, square, and diamond) represents a specific pitch of the scale. The term "fasola" singing, a common name for the four-shape system and style of music, is derived from the familiar *fa-sol-la* syllable sequence. In this system, the diatonic scale is represented by the sequence *fa-sol-la-fa-sol-la-mi-fa*. A similar system, which developed later and is associated with its own distinctive sound, uses seven shapes to render the scale *do-re-mi-fa-sol-la-ti-do*. In this seven-shape system, now considered the norm, the sequence *fa-sol-la* has the same two-whole-step structure no matter where in the scale it appears. Therefore, when any shape in the sequence is repeated (e.g., *FA-sol-la-FA-sol-la-mi-FA*), the resulting interval is either a fourth or a fifth, just as in the seven-shape system a repeated shape indicates an octave. So, in singing the songs there is a preponderance of fourths and fifths. Historically, this system served as a popular and effective way of teaching music literacy.[13]

Community quartets existed that were trained informally in shape-note or sacred harp singing schools, although this was not widespread among African Americans. In Louisiana and Mississippi, the tradition was prevalent only in the Mississippi Delta, which overlapped both states; however, there were also areas in Alabama, Tennessee, and Georgia where the tradition was vibrant. *The Colored Sacred Harp* (1934) by Judge Jackson is the only known collection of African American sacred harp compositions.[14]

Barbershop Community Quartets

Another antecedent of the jubilee and **gospel quartet** tradition that has permeated both Black and White communities is barbershop harmony singing. Jazz performers Jelly Roll Morton, Louis Armstrong, and blues musician W.C. Handy sang in early recreational quartets. Several well-known Black sacred and secular quartets were established in neighborhood barbershops, including the Mills Brothers, the New Orleans Humming Four, the Southern Stars, and the Golden Gate Jubilee Quartet. Recent scholarly work by Lynn Abbott (1992), Jim Henry (2001), and Gage Averill (2003) has demonstrated that the African American community has a much larger and more widespread barbershop quartet tradition than previously thought.[15]

Gospel quartet
Male or female ensemble of four to six voices singing close vocal harmonies, featuring melismatic lead singers and instrumental accompaniment of drums, guitar, and bass.

The barbershop quartet tradition was first observed among African Americans in the 1880s. During the following two decades, these quartets became well established and regularly headlined performances. They harmonized spirituals, folk songs, and popular songs of the era, recreationally, and various idiosyncrasies of the sound became long-standing in the community.[16]

White minstrel performers emulated African American barbershop quartets, and Black minstrel shows also included the style. Because recordings of the White groups singing the barbershop style proliferated, the majority community came to associate the sound with White quartets.[17] Gage Averill, in his work on American barbershop harmony, affirms this fact, stating, "Although not well known today, even among barbershop enthusiasts, these black harmony groups advanced close-harmony aesthetics in the late nineteenth century and were models for white recording quartets."[18]

TRANSITIONAL PERIOD (1930–45)

Between 1910 and 1920, over one million Blacks migrated from the South to the North in search of an opportunity to improve their economic and social condition.[19] Urbanization of the Black population in the North and South was accompanied by an increase in occupational, educational, religious, social, and economic opportunities. As the century progressed, many earlier university and community jubilee quartets began to transition to gospel repertoire and performance style. This transformation included lifting prior harmonic and vocal restraints, the increased prominence of the bass and solo voices (e.g., Isaac "Dick" Freeman of the Fairfield Four, Rufus F. Williams of the Ensley Jubilee Singers, William Bobo of the Dixie Hummingbirds and Roger Brooks of the Zion Harmonizers), and the addition of a fifth singer (e.g., the Humming Four of New Orleans and the Five Soul Stirrers from Houston), a rare practice in earlier quartet traditions. Minimal instrumental accompaniment and more varied repertoire also began to emerge.

While quartets who performed locally for church services and other activities in their own communities tended to continue singing folk spirituals and secular folk songs, as the years progressed, jubilee quartets gradually included gospel songs, which were gaining popularity in Black churches. Although they did not compose specifically for quartets, the works of Charles A. Tindley, Lucie Campbell, Thomas A. Dorsey, Theodore Frye, William Herbert Brewster, and other gospel pioneers tended to translate well for four-part harmony quartets.

Quartets that toured outside their home communities as professionals or semi-professionals sought to appeal to a variety of audiences, most of whom were African American but included mixed and exclusively White groups as well. Expansion of repertoire was necessary to please audiences in such varied contexts as cafés, house parties, company picnics, movie theaters, and nightclubs. Along with the Black religious songs—jubilees, spirituals, and gospels—quartet repertoire also included folk songs, patriotic songs, show tunes, and jazz pieces.

In the years between 1935 and 1939, when the Dixie Hummingbirds were performing for White audiences, it was customary for them to begin

> with at least one song that conformed to white expectations of what blacks ought to be singing before moving on to the rest of their show. The song they used as a "placater" was Stephen Foster's "Old Black Joe," . . . about an aged slave yearning for old times and friends long gone . . . The 1860 song's romanticized vision of slavery was especially popular with white audiences in the South. The Dixie Hummingbirds were aware that they were validating white stereotypes, but they viewed it as part of the price paid for the privilege of accessing wider audiences.[20]

Although "Old Black Joe" is a vestige of the minstrel tradition, it attests to the fact that the Dixie Hummingbirds adjusted their repertoire according to the racial identity of their audience. When they performed in front of African American audiences, they "moved the songs differently. Folks wanted old spiritual favorites like 'Swing Low, Sweet Chariot' and 'Ezekiel Saw the Wheel,' that kind of thing," says James Davis. "If you couldn't sing those, well then, you couldn't get over."[21]

Switch/swing/ double lead
Alternation of verses or phrases in a single song between two lead singers.

During the late 1930s, quartets expanded to five members instead of the usual four.[22] Adding a fifth singer to the quartet enabled two lead singers to alternate verses or phrases in a single song. This, known as **"swing lead," "switch lead,"** or **"double lead,"** was an innovation, which redefined the basic quartet concept of four voices. Either lead singer could sing an extended solo and there were still enough singers remaining for four-part background harmony. A similar device was the "**fifth lead**," essentially a baritone singing above the tenor line, using a falsetto voice. The falsetto voice was used increasingly as the quartet style progressed. Among the early pioneers of the swing and fifth lead concept were the Humming Four of New Orleans, who first added a fifth voice in 1936, and the Five Soul Stirrers from Houston.[23]

The role of the bass singer became more prominent during the transitional period because of his dual position as rhythm voice and second soloist. Bass singers provided the rhythmic movement known to most quartet veterans as the "**walking or pumping bass.**" It was also known as the "riffing" background.[24] Some outstanding quartet bass singers were Isaac "Dick" Freeman of the Fairfield Four, Rufus F. Williams of the Ensley Jubilee Singers, and Roger Brooks of the Zion Harmonizers.

In the 1940s, many quartets began to add guitar accompaniment in order to compete with contemporary trends, especially if they were touring or participating in quartet song battles. While quartets maintained the practice of overlapping call–response, lead singers began to assume a more prominent role on shouting songs, and as soloists, in general. These new developments were not the result of any grand design; it was more the influence of changes in worship that were becoming evident in African American churches.

Quartets continued to perform in the university and early community jubilee style on select repertoire. The reserved university and early

Fifth lead
Baritone singer who can double as falsetto lead in a gospel quartet.

Walking/pumping bass
Stepwise (walking) or intervallic (pumping) percussive, rhythmic foundation provided by bass singers in jubilee and gospel quartets.

Figure 5.1
The Fairfield Four as one of the featured performing quartets at the 1985 Smithsonian Festival of American Folklife. Left to right: Isaac "Dick" Freeman, William Waters, Rev. Lawrence Richardson, James Hill, Rev. Samuel McCrary (leader), and Louis McBride (front). Photo by Joyce Marie Jackson.

community jubilee style was sustained and incorporated as a distinct component of their expanded style and repertoire in which the soloist had a greater role.[25]

Song Battles

The dominance and popularity of quartets in African American communities prompted the establishment of song battles where quartets competed to win audience admiration, and trophies. In rare instances, winners of these competitions were awarded opportunities for radio broadcasts or recording contracts. These contests functioned to promote and maintain high standards of quartet musical performance, to define and validate Black cultural aesthetics and values, and, finally, to provide a forum for sharing collective expressive behavior in the community.[26]

Black newspapers such as the *Louisiana Weekly, Chicago Defender*, and the Cleveland *Call and Post* give early accounts of quartet contests and other types of community programs, which included quartets. The larger contests were publicized and sponsored by individuals who sought financial profit by programming the best groups and charging for admission. Rev. Sam McCrary, leader of the Fairfield Four of Nashville, recalls:

> They used to have the Big Ten [quartet contest]. They had all the quartets out of the east, west, north, and south, from the Golden Gates down to all the best groups traveling. For this annual Big Ten contest, quartets were selected according to their status in a particular region or state. The Golden Gate Jubilee Quartet, the Fairfield Four, the Dixie Hummingbirds, the Golden Gate Jubilaires, Soul Stirrers, Swanee Quintet, and the Flying Clouds of Detroit performed, all of whom were considered models of excellence in quartet performance.[27]

Quartet contests could be judged either by carefully selected individuals or by audience response. Contest rules were clearly formulated and defined by quartets and judges prior to each competition. The rules varied from time to time and from locale to locale; however, the categories on which the quartets were judged remained consistent from one event to another. Sherman Washington, leader of the Zion Harmonizers in New Orleans recalls: "They [quartets] would be judged by the harmony, the dressing, standing correct, voices, pronunciation, how you walk on the stage and stuff like that."[28] He notes also that: "They would go strictly by four-part harmony during that time back in '39 and the early '40s. Hooping, hollering, and running around dancing did not get it. You had to stand flat-footed and sing harmony, a cappella too."[29] While most of the groups in the 1920s and 1930s, whether community oriented or professional, still performed a cappella, use of body percussion—hand claps, thigh slaps, and foot taps—became an added feature. In "song battles" or quartet contests, these physical movements would actually be judged along with the harmony and enunciation.

Undoubtedly, in the contest as well as other performances, many pioneer community-based quartets of the early twentieth century pat-

Figure 5.2
Zion Harmonizers of New Orleans, LA. Clockwise from bottom left:
Henry Warrick, Louis Johnson, Nolan Washington, Sherman
Washington, Norris Lewis, and Howard Bowie, 1994. Photo by J.
Nash Porter. Courtesy of Joyce Marie Jackson.

terned their repertoire, singing styles, and song structures after the
quartets of southern Black colleges and universities. Leaders of these early
quartets trained their groups to imitate university quartets they heard
locally, as well as those featured on radio broadcasts and commercial
recordings. Therefore, several of the foundational performance concepts
as understood and practiced by independent quartets were based to some
extent on Western music precepts. However, it was the blending of
Western musical elements and African American performance practices
that molded the tradition into a distinctly Black phenomenon. Singers,
for example, marked rhythms with body movements, depending on the
song and context. As in the first period, context also dictated performance

attire. Quartets continued to wear identical dress suits or tuxedos, depending on the degree of formality of the performance.

THE GOSPEL PERIOD (1946–69)

Quartet music experienced tremendous change during the 1940s, most of which was due to the increasing commercial viability of gospel music. With the beginning of World War II came the end of the Depression, and with the end of the war came an increase in Black purchasing power. Groups who were recording saw higher-volume record sales as a result.

Although gospel music had been developed and established well before the 1940s, jubilee quartets came to be known as "gospel" quartets when they began to incorporate more performance practices characteristic of the gospel genre and repertoire. In searching for innovation, quartet trainers and other members were highly influenced by prominent gospel singers and instrumentalists. Even though quartets did not have an exclusively evangelical function, their dramatic improvisational delivery could nonetheless induce emotion-filled responses from congregations. Since the late 1940s, the quartet audience has been primarily African American Christians. Consequently, the earlier secular repertoire has been replaced with either gospel songs or gospel arrangements of spirituals and hymns.

Early jubilee quartets sang without instruments; in the 1940s, some gospel quartets added an unobtrusive acoustic guitar, which was later replaced with an electric guitar, backed by a rhythm section of drums and electric bass. Some quartets even experimented with using piano or organ, a practice influenced by gospel artists of the period. With this expanded instrumentation, more voices were added, although no more than six vocalists ever appeared simultaneously. As performances became more demanding vocally, it became the practice for some quartets to include enough performers to alternate soloists. One soloist could be designated to sing lead on the jubilee songs while another could be assigned to lead on the shouting songs. Typically, one or two members "sit out" on each song.

During this era, lead singers began to perform extended solo passages, incorporating vibrato, falsetto, shouting vocals, and timbre changes such as growls. Following the model of gospel soloists and preachers, lead singers in gospel quartets added improvised personal testimonies, which they sometimes referenced as "working sections," "working the audience," or "shouting the audience." These practices, which can be spirit induced, became standard with many gospel quartets as a showcase of the creativity and improvisational ability of the lead singer.

In 1946, the Golden Gate Quartet and several other groups started recording using a double bass.[30] The Pilgrim Jubilees' first recording session for Peacock in 1959 took place on the day their bass singer, Kenny

Madden, decided to quit the group. Willie Dixon, the blues musician, was in the studio, and they asked him to fill in with his double bass as they recorded the song "Stretch Out." Afterwards, Cleave Graham recalls, "it was one of the biggest hits we had. That's what really put us on the road for good."[31] What made the Pilgrim Jubilees' recording of "Stretch Out" unique was the prominent and aggressive role the double bass played in the arrangement and, more importantly, that the instrument replaced the bass vocalist.[32] The double bass and bass guitar began to take the place of the vocal bass and most present-day gospel quartets no longer have a true vocal bass.

The rigid concert stage decorum that characterized the jubilee period became passé after the early 1940s. Post-1940s quartets "walk and run the stage," fall on their knees, jump off stages, walk the aisles, gesture, pantomime, and whatever else they feel compelled or led by the Spirit to do. Classic examples of quartets who perform in the gospel style include the Five Blind Boys of Alabama and Mississippi, the Swan Silvertones, the Dixie Hummingbirds (Track 13), the Pilgrim Travelers, and Sam Cooke and the Soul Stirrers.

 13
"Christian's Automobile."

Quartet Trainers

Through all the quartet historical periods, the quartet trainer is a crucial link through which the musical and aesthetic elements of the tradition are transmitted. He is a focal point in the continuity, change, and creativity of the African American quartet tradition. While the trainer may or may not be a member of the group, in either case, he must have the ability to communicate effectively with quartet members. In order to achieve a culturally acceptable musical sound, the trainer takes the singers through a systematic and self-conscious process. He verbally communicates to members of the quartet by using in-group terminology and metaphor, and he teaches by rote or by using recorded examples of other quartets. Using these methods, music theory, aesthetics, and values are systematically articulated, and quartet singers learn how to perform in a style that is culturally accepted.

Many trainers prepared for this role by observing and participating in the tradition to develop mastery of its principles and nuances. Active involvement in the church or high school choir can serve as a point of entry for gaining the requisite musical knowledge to become a trainer. For example, Howard Bowie, trainer for the Zion Harmonizers in New Orleans, states:

> Well, I had a little musical background from high school, and I sang in the Booker T. Washington Senior High School Choir for about three years. And I was raised in the Baptist surroundings. And after I got out of school, I just developed a tone and ear for the gospel singing.[33]

Bowie developed his musical skill over the years and eventually became the trainer for the Zion Harmonizers.

Figure 5.3
Zion Travelers Spiritual Singers, Sunday morning radio broadcast at WIBR in Baton Rouge, LA, 1991. Left to right: James Harvey, Joel Harvey, Ado Dyson, Robert McKinnis, and Rev. Burnell James Offlee (leader). Photo by J. Nash Porter. Courtesy of Joyce Marie Jackson.

In addition to the coaching role, the trainer often serves as utility singer within the group, substituting for the background singer when one of them leads a song, or filling in when someone is absent. Rev. James Burnell Offlee, manager, lead singer, and trainer for the Zion Travelers Spiritual Singers of Baton Rouge, declares:

> I change up with them [vocal parts]. I sing tenor, baritone, bass. I sing all the voices in the quartet. Whichever one is a little bit short, I take it and fill in. If certain ones are leading, I fill in their background part.[34]

The mandatory musical skill for a trainer is having a "good ear," which implies having the ability to (1) conceive and teach harmony, (2) identify and assign vocal ranges, (3) create new song arrangements, and (4) accurately reproduce any vocal part in the quartet. Furthermore, the trainer should possess a strong sense of rhythm and tempo, knowledge of repertoire, and leadership ability, as well as mastery of the intricacies of the Black quartet aesthetic.[35] The role of the trainer is paramount in the maintenance of the Black quartet tradition. The trainer communicates traditional knowledge and enforces conformity to quartet musical behavior. In addition to validating the tradition, he also transmits musical style and standards of excellence. The trainer is the major vehicle or medium for the continuation of this dynamic cultural and musical expression.

THE COMMODIFICATION OF QUARTETS

In 1891, Columbia began recording the first African American group, the Standard Negro Quartette of Chicago, on cylinder. They continued recording until 1897 and two of these cylinders have actually been located.[36] Victor Record Company recorded the first Black sacred quartet on discs in 1902 (six single-sided discs of spirituals by the Dinwiddie

Colored Quartet). John Work III—quartet director, singer, and folklorist —arranged for the Fisk University Quartet to record for Victor in 1909 and 1911, and Natalie Curtis Berlin, an American musician, recorded the Hampton Institute Quartet on a cylinder phonograph between 1915 and 1917. Other larger record companies began recording sacred male quartets commercially in the early 1920s, the period when "race labels" discovered their market potential.[37] By the late 1920s, every "race label" featured one or more jubilee quartets and during the 1930s the majority of sacred "race" records featured quartets.

By the 1930s, radio broadcasts, commercial recordings, and touring further influenced the development and popularization of community quartets. Indeed, the launching of the **race series**, which targeted the Black community, and the increased number of live radio broadcasts, which often featured African American performers, further exposed quartet singers to an audience beyond local communities.

Women were also in the industry, although on a smaller scale. The first documented female quartet, the Wheat Street Female Quartet, was recorded in Atlanta in 1925, which may be the first actual recording of a female quartet. They recorded six sides for Columbia and OKeh in 1925 and 1926. The women may have been members of the Wheat Street Baptist Church in Atlanta, which was later known for featuring many gospel and quartet programs in the 1940s and 1950s.[38]

Race series
Special series of recordings issued between the 1920s and 1940s performed exclusively by African Americans and directed to an African American market.

Radio Broadcasting

The Southernaires, believed to be the first community-based African American religious quartet to broadcast on radio, performed on a Sunday morning NBC network show for over eleven years, starting in 1935. The university-affiliated Utica Institute Jubilee Quartet began broadcasting in 1927 on an NBC network in New York, resulting in their having the honor of being the first quartet to broadcast live.[39] In Roanoke, Virginia, the N&W [Norfolk and Western Railroad] Imperial Quartet was broadcasting as early as 1928 over the WDBJ radio station. The Silver Leaf Quartette of Norfolk and the Golden Crown Quartet were also beginning their featured programs in radio broadcasting around the same time.[40] During the 1930s, some radio stations began devoting a few hours a day to Black programming.[41]

During World War II, live radio broadcasting was the only aspect of quartet singing not affected by the war. Decreased production of automobiles, gasoline rationing, and a shortage of rubber for tires inhibited touring. A dispute between the musician's union and the record companies (1944 and 1945) and the shortage of shellac, essential to the production of vinyl discs, basically closed the entire industry.[42] Because of these restrictions, some groups sought out more radio jobs and began careers in broadcasting. According to Rev. Samuel McCrary, leader of the Fairfield Four, their group began broadcasting on WLAC for Sunway Vitamins in 1939 and continued until 1956.[43] During this same time, the

Four Harmony Kings (formed in West Virginia in 1938) began broad-casting on Sundays in Knoxville at WNOX; they changed their names to the Swan Silvertone Singers when the Swan Bread Company began sponsoring the show.[44] In Louisiana, the Soproco Spiritual Singers signed a contract in 1940 to broadcast for the Soproco Soap Company on WWL in New Orleans, and the Zion Harmonizers were sponsored by Schiro's Shoe Store. Some groups never acquired sponsorship, as was the case with the Zion Travelers Spiritual Singers from Baton Rouge, believed to hold the longest live radio broadcast history, having performed every Sunday morning for over fifty years at WIBR, a station whose standard programming targeted White country and western music listeners.[45]

Female quartets on radio included the Harps of Melody based in Memphis, who broadcast on WDIA during the 1950s, on WLOK in the 1960s, on KWAM in the 1970s, and on WSMS, the radio station of the University of Memphis, during the 1980s.[46]

Touring Circuits

The rise of gospel radio programming and the commercial recording industry in the first half of the twentieth century propelled quartet singing into a new era of popular culture. During the 1940s, quartet touring— a loosely structured circuit consisting of a network of relatives and other associates, singing organizations, and gospel promoters—reached its peak, further enhancing the popularity of the genre in both the United States and Europe. As a result of the proliferation of quartet tours, groups became very competitive.

What quartet members called a "touring circuit" made touring possible. This circuit or network consisted of a chain of quartets and individuals that formed a channel of communication in a particular territory or circuit. This network assisted quartets in arranging multiple city performance sites. In addition, the network helped locate housing accommodations, since, in the 1940s and 1950s, segregation still limited possibilities for public accommodations for African Americans.

As hundreds of quartets began traveling the country singing in churches, schools, public auditoriums, concert halls, fairs, and festivals, quartet singing changed dramatically. In order to maintain their viability, and ensure continued demand for their musical offerings, quartets began to compete among themselves and with other gospel performers for the public's attention. Versatility, therefore, became imperative. Performance styles and practices were modified drastically by many quartets to evoke maximum audience response and support. Many groups felt compelled to adapt popular musical trends, which facilitated the quartet crossover phenomena.[47]

Crossover Phenomena

Although quartets rapidly gained popularity in the 1930s and 1940s, during the 1950s interest in quartets began to wane. The **crossover** of sacred soloists into popular entertainment and the fact that entire groups sometimes switched to popular music were among the primary factors that led to the decline of quartets. The African American popular music style, rhythm and blues, was highly influenced by the sacred quartet style (see discussion of quartets in Chapter 12). Consequently, sacred singers who crossed over had minimal adjustments to make. Although most of the quartet crossovers occurred in the 1950s, this sacred/secular symbiosis has permeated the genre since its inception. One example of a quartet crossover to popular music in the 1930s is that of the famous Delta Rhythm Boys, who had previously been the Frederick Hall Jubilee Quartet of Dillard University.

Crossover quartet
A group that switched from the performance of sacred repertoire to secular.

By the 1950s, a market had emerged for Black popular music, which included both Black and White consumers. Often, members of the first rhythm and blues vocal groups were gospel performers who chose to shift to its secular counterpart. Many young rhythm and blues singers had been former lead singers of established gospel quartets. Listed among the ranks of the gospel artists who crossed over are Sam Cooke from the Highway QCs and the Soul Stirrers; Johnnie Taylor, also from the Soul Stirrers; Lou Rawls from the Pilgrim Travelers; Wilson Pickett from the Violinaires; Roscoe Robinson and Joe Henderson from the Fairfield Four; Brook Benton from the Bill Langford Quartet; David Ruffin from the Dixie Nightingales; Joe Hinton and O.V. Wright from the Spirit of Memphis; Ernie Kador of the Golden Chain Jubileers; and Johnny Adams of the Consolators.[48] In comparison to these crossover examples, for a period of time, the Humming Four from New Orleans, a sacred quartet with a twenty-year history, worked "both sides of the street." Identified as the Humming Four when singing sacred music, they were the Hawks as secular music artists. However, "many local churches closed their doors to the Humming Four just as they did to Sam Cooke and Rosetta Tharpe," when they began singing popular music.[49] The Christian community often frowned upon such musical transgressions.

This crossover from sacred to secular music often came as a result of prompting by record promoters and other recording company personnel. Clarence Fountain of the Five Blind Boys of Alabama remembers when they were urged to make the switch to secular music:

> We were there when Sam [Cooke] got his contract, because we were recording on the same label—Specialty Records. Sam got his deal going and we had a chance to go right along with Sam, because the man liked us and showed us the way. He said if you want to make some money, go into rock and roll. We wanted the money but we did not want to sing rock and roll. Because when you promised the Lord something, you got to stick with your promise . . . I always thought it was a bad thing to switch over in the middle of the stream when the Lord has been good to you. You have to stay in the power and presence of the Lord. So, that is why I did not sing rock and roll.[50]

Some industry executives continued to urge, and some even insisted, that a group make the transition as a condition for remaining with a company or label.

Other factors that contributed to the decline of quartet performances included the decrease in live radio broadcasts and commercial recordings; public disapproval of some performers' lifestyles; failure to adapt to current performance styles; and competition from emerging gospel groups, ensembles, and choirs. In essence, some of the very factors that had popularized quartets subsequently contributed to their decline.

New Directions

Even though gospel quartets have existed on the margins of the gospel tradition for several decades, they currently are being incorporated into musicals, as they were in the 1920s. In the 1980s, a gospel version of Sophocles' drama *Oedipus Rex* was produced under the title *The Gospel at Colonus*. It is a powerful dramatic work that combines features of Greek drama, such as protagonist and chorus, with gospel preaching and singing from soloists, quartets, and other groups. In the 1985 version of the production, released on video by Warner Reprise, two gospel quartets are featured: the Five Blind Boys of Alabama and J.J. Farley and the Original Soul Stirrers. They performed on Broadway for sixteen weeks, consequently boosting sales of their recordings.[51]

Since 1996, the quartet tradition has gained a new life beyond the borders of the United States. The Heavenly Light Quartet (HLQ), whose name derives from Swan Silvertones' *Heavenly Light, Shine On Me*, formed in April 1996 in Sydney, Australia. The group performs only material from Black gospel tradition, in their effort to "recreate this venerable quartet style," in a way that respects their forerunners, as "masters of time, articulation and harmony."[52] Having listened to this Australian group's music and interviewed its leader, I find that while they adhere closely to the musical arrangements, their objective is not to mimic or replicate the overall sound aesthetic of the African American quartet. In E. Patrick Johnson's study, "Performing Blackness Down Under: The Café of the Gate of Salvation" (2002), he examines the performance of Black American gospel music by all White, mostly atheist Australian gospel choirs. Johnson suggests:

> [A]n aversion to religion does not exclude persons from making personally meaningful connections to gospel music that sometimes resemble, sometimes contradict, and sometimes supersede gospel music's functions in the United States. Once signs— or, in this case, sounds—of "Blackness" are "let loose" in the world, they become the site at which cultures contest and struggle over meaning.[53]

The gospel quartet as a sign/sound of Blackness, has served a dynamic and transformative role, and has set the stage for other gospel groups in the past, present, and for future years to come.

CONCLUSIONS

Historically, the African American quartet is a result of the cross-fertilization of European and African American aesthetics and musical values. The styles of the African American quartet are cumulative and dynamic, reflecting the historical, socio-cultural, economic, educational, and religious influences experienced by African American people in community. While the quartet was heavily Europeanized in its initial phase, it gradually moved away from such an orientation and became heavily African American to meet the interests, needs, and aesthetics of the African American community.

The symbiotic relationship between African American sacred and secular music has been a primary factor in determining the image and identity of the quartet within the African American community. This relationship has plagued the quartet tradition since its inception, first because of the performance for profit modes of university, minstrel, and barbershop quartets, and later because of the crossover of quartet performers to secular music. Although the Black fundamentalist sacred community makes rigid distinctions between sacred and secular musical realms, the African American quartet tradition has historically transgressed these boundaries.

In the early twentieth century, the quartet evolved into a sub-genre of gospel music, and with its own history, performance style, and aesthetic expression that was distinct from those of gospel groups and choirs. During the second half of the twentieth century, however, quartet singing has increasingly exhibited performance practices and aesthetic values of gospel music.[54]

KEY NAMES

Sam Cooke	Georgia Minstrels
Dinwiddie Colored Quartet	Golden Gate Quartet
Dixie Hummingbirds	Pilgrim Travelers
Willie Dixon	Soul Stirrers
Fairfield Four	Wheat Street Female Quartet
Five Blind Boys	Zion Harmonizers

QUESTIONS

1. What was the relationship between jubilee quartets and mixed ensembles at universities? What were some of the challenges facing universities and how did quartets help fulfill some of those obligations? What were some of the benefits of the jubilee quartet to both the university and the quartet members?

2. How did the university jubilee quartet influence minstrel show performances? In what ways was the minstrel quartet different from the jubilee quartet?

3. What does the author mean when she states that the performance style of community-based quartets was "culturally defined"? Provide examples to support your argument.

4. What historical changes marked the transitional period from jubilee songs to gospel? What musical characteristics emerged during this period? How did audience and performance context play a role in repertoire modification?

5. How did "race labels," radio broadcasting, and touring contribute to the commodification of gospel music? What was the relationship between popular music and gospel quartets? What led to the decline of gospel quartets? How has the gospel quartet tradition begun to reappear in the United States and abroad?

PROJECTS

1. Listen to compositions by Charles A. Tindley, Lucie Campbell, and Thomas Dorsey and identify both a solo and quartet recording of the same song. Describe similarities and differences between the two.

2. What Sunday morning gospel radio or television shows are available in your area? Tune into one of these and create three different journal entries documenting (1) the repertoire, (2) performers, and (3) prevailing aesthetic values. To what extent are gospel quartets represented?

3. Listen to or view examples of Sam Cooke, Johnnie Taylor, Lou Rawls, or other artists whose careers embraced both sacred and secular music. In what ways do their vocal styles and aesthetic practices differ as they move from sacred to secular performance?

NOTES

Please see the discography for information on resources for further listening.

1. The term "jubilee" has various meanings depending on the context of its use and the period of history within which it is used. Jubilee has been used to designate special celebrations, spirited songs of freedom, and sacred or secular song narratives, as well as a performance style, and type of performance ensemble.

2. For an extensive treatment of African American quartets see Allen 1991, Jackson 1988 and 1996, and Lornell 1995. For detailed information on the biographies and careers of individual quartets see Young 2001 and Zolten 2003.

3. The evolutionary history and analysis of sacred Black quartet style is complex, and researchers have encountered many challenges in attempting to delineate different style periods. In Ricks 1977, quartets are grouped into a single all-encompassing jubilee style, even though multiple styles exist. Tallmadge 1981 divides quartet styles into five sub-genres, several of which overlap. While Boyer 1985 and Lornell 1983 both divide African American quartets into historical periods, neither provides explanation as to why the time intervals are chosen.

4. For a more detailed account of the Fisk Jubilee Singers see Lovell 1972, Marsh 1971 (1876), and Ward 2000.
5. Seroff 1981, 1, and Ward 2000, 92.
6. Richardson 1980, 81.
7. Lornell 1995, 10–11.
8. Toll 1974, 195, 198.
9. Ibid., 273.
10. Ibid., 283 and Lornell 1983.
11. See Jackson 1988 and 1996, for more on creation of quartets and the training process.
12. Examples of this early style include the Heavenly Gospel Singers' "Beautiful City" (1935) and the works of the Birmingham Jubilee Quartet heard on the albums *Birmingham Quartet Anthology* (1980) and *Jubilee to Gospel: A Selection of Commercially Recorded Black Religious Music, 1921–1953* (1996).
13. Goff 2002, 21–22.
14. Jackson 1992 (1934).
15. Abbott 1992, 289–326, and Henry 2001, 13–17. For a more detailed historical account and an examination of barbershop singing as an American institution, see Averill 2003.
16. Abbott 1992, 314–15.
17. Ibid., 292.
18. Averill 2003, 50–51.
19. US Bureau of the Census 1949: Series B48–71.
20. Zolten 2003, 29.
21. Quoted in Zolten 2003, 30.
22. Jackson 2004, 154–71.
23. Abbott, 1983b, 39; Rubman 1980, 87; Seroff 1983, 23.
24. Abbott, 1983b, 89.
25. Examples of traditional style include the Golden Gate Quartet's album *Travelin' Shoes* (1937–39) and the Swan Silvertones' album *My Rock/Love Lifted Me* (1952–53).
26. Jackson 2004.
27. Rev. Samuel McCrary (The Fairfield Four), interview with the author, Nashville, TN, July 18, 1985.
28. Sherman Washington (The Zion Harmonizers), interview with the author, New Orleans, LA, September 8, 1983.
29. Ibid., April 28, 2002.
30. Boyer 1985.
31. Young 2001, 79.
32. Ibid., 76, 77, 79.
33. Howard Bowie (The Zion Harmonizers), interview with author, New Orleans, LA, September 8, 1983.
34. Rev. Burnell James Offlee (The Zion Travelers Spiritual Singers), interview with author, Baton Rouge, LA, June 3, 1984.
35. Jackson 1988, 204.
36. Dixon, Godrich, and Rye 1997, 859–60.
37. Ibid., 215.
38. Funk 1987.
39. Lornell 1995, 20.
40. Williams-Jones 1975, 251; Rubman 1980, 39; Funk 1985, 24; and Lornell 1995, 21. The above authors disagree on the year that the Southernaires quartet began performing for NBC.
41. Rubman 1980, 36.
42. Lornell 1995, 25.
43. Rev. Samuel McCrary interview.
44. Rubman 1980, 88.
45. Rev. Burnell James Offlee, interview with the author, Baton Rouge, LA, September 15, 1983. The Zion Travelers Spiritual Singers celebrated their fiftieth year of broadcasting on WIBR in 1996.

46. Clara Anderson (The Harps of Melody), interview with author, Memphis, TN, July 20, 1985; Bowman 1998.

47. Abbott, 1983b, 42; Broughton 1985, 102; Maultsby 1981, 5; Seroff 1982, 20. For a more in-depth account on how gospel music influenced the secular sound of rhythm and blues see Goosman 2005.

48. Abbott, 1983a, n. p.

49. Clarence Fountain (The Five Blind Boys of Alabama), interview with author, New Orleans, LA, May 2, 2002.

50. For more information on regional recordings see Hayes and Laughton 1992 and Dixon *et al.* 1997. Also see Ray Funk's series of reissued recordings from various regions of the country: *A Cappella Gospel Singing*, Folklyric Records 9045, 1986; *The Golden Age of Gospel Singing*, Folklyric Records 9046, 1986; *Detroit Gospel*, Heritage HT 311, 1986; *Atlanta Gospel*, Heritage HT 312, 1940; Five Blind Boys of Alabama, *Five Blind Boys of Alabama*, Heritage HT 315, 1987; and Dixieaires, *Let Me Fly*, Heritage HT 317, 1987.

51. Clarence Fountain, interview 2002.

52. Liner notes from *The Heavenly Light Quartet* CD, 1996.

53. Johnson 2002, 99–119.

54. For an in-depth discussion of gospel music aesthetics, see Burnim, 1985, 148–69.

CHAPTER 6

Ragtime

Ingeborg Harer

INTRODUCTION

Ragtime came into existence long before the music was given a name. By the end of the 1890s, the term defined a performance style and practices applied to composing and playing popular song, dance, and instrumental music. An abundance of sheet music testifies to the multifold existence of this genre during this period of ragtime's widespread popularity from about 1896 to 1920.

But even during the ragtime era there was an uncertainty about the meaning of ragtime. Despite the divergent perspectives of contemporary observers, ragtime was uniformly defined as having African American musical roots. It is important to note that it was contemporary opinions and attitudes that determined the degree and quality of African American and/or European American musical elements. The genre of ragtime must be defined according to its duality between written music and oral tradition, between early jazz and classical music, and between African American and European American music. Researchers have established the inherent difficulty of attempting to extricate various cultural elements in ragtime. The essence of ragtime exists within these "blurred" cultural elements and practices.[1]

Historically, ragtime was variously conceived as song, dance, and syncopated instrumental music, even though the majority of sheet music available today is for piano. As part of the general marketing scheme, instrumental and vocal ragtime, **cakewalk**, and "**coon songs**" became synonymous in the public mind. Coon songs, typically performed by Whites (often in blackface) and Blacks in minstrel shows, portrayed denigrating and stereotypical lyrics sung in Negro dialect. African

Cakewalk
A dance that parodies White upper-class behavior, originally performed by African American slaves; the best performance was awarded a prize, usually a cake, from which the dance takes its name.

Coon song
Popular song style of the late nineteenth and early twentieth centuries that presented a stereotyped view of African Americans, often performed by White singers in blackface.

Americans were depicted as lazy, dishonest, violent, greedy, sexually promiscuous thieves and watermelon eaters. Minstrel performers who sang these songs also danced to the rhythms, basing their movements on the African-derived plantation dances of slaves, frequently described as "grotesque" by White observers.

Other slave dances such as the cakewalk were derived from those of slave masters. The cakewalk is described as a parody of White upper-class

Figure 6.1
"Good Enough!" by Rollin Howard (1871). Public domain. Historic American Sheet Music Collection, Rare Book, Manuscript, and Special Collections Library, Duke University, Durham, North Carolina.

behavior: dignified walking, bowing low, waving canes, doffing hats, and a high-kicking grand promenade. The setting for this dance was intrinsically competitive; according to ragtime scholar Edward Berlin, "the slave couple performing the most attractive steps and motions would 'take the cake.'"[2] Following its exhibition at the 1893 World's Fair in Chicago and a competition at Madison Square Garden, the audience for the cakewalk increased to mass proportions. From the late 1890s

Figure 6.1
continued

through the first decade of the twentieth century, the cakewalk became one of the most popular dances on the vaudeville stage and in the ballrooms of the United States and Europe.[3]

The term "cake walk" appears on piano music covers as early as in the 1870s, although the music does not yet show the typical cakewalk features. The sheet music cover of David Braham's "Walking for Dat Cake" (1877), however, clearly depicts African Americans dancing the cakewalk. Six years earlier, a Black couple is depicted performing the characteristic cakewalk steps on the cover of Rollin Howard's "Good Enough" (1871). This piece ends with an eight-bar "dance" that applies a simple syncopation pattern in the music, which indicates the evolution of cakewalk and, eventually, ragtime as a genre.[4]

Similarly, but quite differently from other contemporary observers, Will Marion Cook dates the origin of ragtime around 1888, based on African American performance traditions from the 1870s:

> As far back as 1875, Negroes in the questionable resorts along the Mississippi had commenced to evolve this musical figure, but at the World's Fair, Chicago [1892/93] "ragtime" got a running start, swept the Americas, then Europe, and today [1915] the craze has not diminished. Cause of Success: The public was tired of the sing song, same, monotonous, mother, sister, father, sentimental, songs. Ragtime offered unique rhythms, curious groupings of words, and melodies that gave the zest of unexpectedness.[5]

In their earliest stages, sheet music of coon songs, cakewalks and ragtime, for the most part, were musically indistinguishable. For commercial reasons, the titles "Cakewalk," "March," "Two Step," "Rag," and others were printed simultaneously on the title pages of the music. The images on sheet music covers often portrayed the lyrics or characters described in the text, varying from "neutral" images of flowers and trees to portraits of African Americans with big lips and bulging eyes dancing or eating watermelons. The latter images strongly reinforced existing stereotypes attractive to publishers and buyers as symbols of "authenticity" intended to support the perception that the music was indeed African American.[6]

The beginning of the twentieth century witnessed the emergence of a new kind of syncopated instrumental music. Later known as jazz, this music became popular in brothels and saloons, and on the vaudeville stage. During these transitional years initiating the jazz age, the terms "ragtime" and "jazz" were used synonymously, as were the verbs "jazzing" and "ragging." Ragtime is therefore more than an aside in the pre-history of jazz;[7] it is actually an inseparable part of it, as evident in the names of two early New Orleans jazz bands: Buddy Bolden's Ragtime Band and Jack Laine's Ragtime Band. Moreover, the term "rag" is used in the titles of the first jazz recordings by the Original Dixieland Jazz Band in 1917, including "Tiger Rag," "Sensational Rag," and "Reisenweber Rag."

The term "ragtime" remains somewhat elusive despite many attempts to explain it; **"rag"** is used both as a noun and as a verb. As a noun, it

Rag or ragging
The term applied to syncopated or embellished melodies during the ragtime era.

identifies a particular type of music. The noun "rag" may be linked to "handkerchief-flaunting in nineteenth-century folk dancing." In that case, "rag" is a synonym for handkerchief.[8] Another usage of the noun appears in 1899, when Rupert Hughes observed that "the negroes call their clog-dancing, 'ragging' and the dance a 'rag.'"[9] Although it becomes clear here that original African dancing was mixed with European (Irish) clog dancing, this source may be considered as key to the naming of the dance and music.[10] After all, the individual pieces of music were called "rags" rather than "ragtime."[11]

"To rag," as a verb, directs attention to the performative emphasis of ragtime. "To rag"—as many contemporary sources contend—means to syncopate a tune; at the same time ragging meant embellishing and decorating melodies. Rhythmic effects, particularly the shifting of accents (known as syncopation) were the main characteristics of ragging a tune. Any composition—songs, hymns, marches—could be played in ragtime. In the first decade of the twentieth century, ragging became a compositional technique applied to classical music, which resulted in the creation and marketing of many new works. Examples include: Aubrey Stauffer's "That Lovin' Traumerei" (1910), based on Robert Schumann's "Träumerei"; George L. Cobb's "Russian Rag" (1918), interpolating the world famous Prelude in C♯ Minor, op. 3 no. 2, by Rachmaninoff; Julius Lenzberg's "Hungarian Rag" (1913), based on Liszt's Hungarian Rhapsody no. 2 for Piano (1913); and Carleton L. Colby's "Misery Rag" (1914), a ragtime travesty on the famous "Miserere" from *Il Trovatore* by Verdi.

The concept of "ragging" preceded composed ragtime. Transforming music into a rag is, however, not the same as composing a rag. *Ben Harney's Ragtime Instructor* gives us an idea of how the "art" of ragging was conceived. Published in Chicago in 1897, it contains no real rag; rather, it provides instruction on how to play traditional tunes as ragtime. For Ben Harney (see below), who applied ragging to tunes of the folk tradition, ragtime was a "way of playing"; for Scott Joplin, Joseph Lamb, and Eubie Blake it was also a way of writing.[12] Joplin and his followers realized that the musical concepts applied in playing "in ragtime" could be used in original compositions. They gradually developed a sophisticated style of composing ragtime.

ORIGINS OF RAGTIME

Ragtime was created and popularized by itinerant African American musicians, many of whom did not read or write music. These musicians first developed ragtime as a playing style, disseminating this unnotated new music in brothels, saloons, bars, and other similar sites where Blacks found their first performing opportunities after the Civil War. The first audiences of ragtime, therefore, consisted of the player-composers themselves, the owners of the bars and brothels, the visitors (presumably affluent White men), and the prostitutes who worked there. Apart from these venues of low reputation, there were several other contexts within the contemporary entertainment business where ragtime was featured, such as vaudeville and the musical theater.[13]

One of the first musicians to publish a ragtime composition was Ben Harney, who claimed to be the inventor of the new style. His "You've Been a Good Old Wagon but You've Done Broke Down," published in 1895 with the assistance of John Biller, a professional musician, is one of the most important examples of early ragtime. Harney's song is a notated version of an African American banjo playing style, designed to teach the pianist how to play ragtime and how to rag a tune. Harney's publication documents the translation of ragtime from oral tradition to written score.[14] Without carrying the title "rag" or "ragtime" the song concludes with a "dance" consisting of forty bars, which displays the rhythmic pattern that came to identify ragtime. Harney's song also introduces "stop time," a rhythmic feature later used by Scott Joplin.[15]

Several important ragtime compositions were published in 1897. In January 1897, William Krell, a White bandmaster, published "Mississippi Rag." This piece, subtitled as "The First Rag-Time Two-Step Ever Written and First Played by Krell's Orchestra," was actually not a rag but a cakewalk. What followed were several other similar pieces called "rag-time," which corresponded to the musical features of cakewalk (simple syncopation) rather than those of ragtime (more complicated, intricate syncopation). Examples include Warren Beebe's "Rag Time March" and R.J. Hamilton's "The Rag Time Patrol." The first piano rag, Theodore H. Northrup's "Louisiana Rag Two-Step," was published in October 1897. It contained, for the first time, several types of syncopation, thus utilizing the rhythmic characteristic that most defines ragtime. Tom Turpin's "Harlem Rag," the first rag written by an African American composer, followed in December 1897. "Harlem Rag" is another example within the genre that depicts the transition from oral tradition to printed music; in this case, however, ragtime refers to Turpin's particular playing style rather than to pre-existing melodic material of the folk tradition. Because Turpin's composition was derived from actual performance, the musical practice, to some degree, became visible in the printed medium and could be adopted by others. In addition to defining the playing technique, Turpin revealed the melodic, harmonic, and rhythmic structures of ragtime within an overall musical form. For this reason "Harlem Rag" can be accurately labeled as a ragtime composition.

This chronology of ragtime as a written tradition might be misleading with regard to the actual emergence of ragtime as a distinct musical type. Many Blacks played ragtime before Krell's Orchestra added ragtime to its repertoire. Moreover, African American pianists did not initially consider translating their compositions for sale in print. Performing the music was financially attractive, because piano players in bars and saloons received tips. It was much more complicated to publish a rag, and for

African Americans it was generally more difficult to receive acknowledgment and payment in the publishing industry.[16] Some of them—for instance, Louis Chauvin—chose not to publish their compositions, because they had established reputations as performers rather than composers.

When ragtime shifted from oral to written tradition, it became known beyond its initial limited audience. The publishing of ragtime did not stop the improvised tradition, which continued to coexist and varied depending on who was playing (professionals or amateurs) and where (geographically and socioculturally) the specific playing style had evolved. The translation of playing styles into the printed medium resulted in quite different products as soon as White musicians wrote down what they thought they had heard. Because of their commercial interests and general unfamiliarity with ragtime as it was originally conceived, White musicians created a compositional and playing style distinct from that of African Americans. This style often reflected their own musical and aesthetic values and predispositions more than those of the original African American tradition. As the music developed and became more elaborate, playing became increasingly difficult. Thus, simplified versions of rags were published in the second decade of the twentieth century to meet the expectations of amateur players.

RAGTIME AS PRINTED MUSIC

As ragtime emerged from the culture of Black communities, leaving its indigenous contexts meant a gradual change from an orally transmitted music to printed sheet music. Transcribing, in many cases, meant a reduction of what was originally played; once notated, the music in its written form automatically concealed the variety and flexibility of playing styles as well as the improvisational moment originally inherent in the music. And it was often Whites who **transcribed** what African Americans played. Consequently, a commercially successful branch of the publishing business evolved.

Transcription
The process of notating musical performance.

Although transcriptions of ragtime performances definitely meant a very superficial translation to the printed medium, the publication of ragtime, nevertheless, had a significant impact, as Jeffrey Magee observes:

> The naming and printing of ragtime in the latter 1890s marks a crucial stage in the transformation of the music and made possible its broad impact on American culture. On one hand . . . the syncopated patterns that distinguish ragtime have their roots in African musical practices that came to America through the slave trade. On the other hand, there is a sense in which ragtime did not really exist until it was named and marketed as such.[17]

Musically, we might consider these representatives of popularized ragtime as translations of originally African American idioms into printed sheet music. These versions deviated widely from their authentic origins, but ironically became subject to the demands and needs of the majority of White middle- and upper-class piano players: rags that sounded good and were easy to play became bestsellers. Many of the White composer-arrangers producing these rags were employed by the publishing companies and did not have to search for publication opportunities.

Scott Joplin and his followers who had learned to read and write music developed skills that enabled them to create new impulses through the written medium. The sophisticated compositional style of ragtime developed and cultivated by Joplin, James Scott, and White composer Joseph Lamb for piano came to be called "**classic ragtime**," one reason why ragtime today is often exclusively associated with the piano.

Most Americans became acquainted with ragtime only after it appeared as printed music, which is why many authors describe ragtime as "composed" music, with little emphasis on ragtime as a performance art. Usually a ragtime piece was published in small numbers and sold a few dozen (sometimes a hundred) copies in the area where it was published. However, "Maple Leaf Rag" (1899) was the exception to this rule (Track 14).

The publication of "Maple Leaf Rag" and its tremendous success greatly increased Joplin's visibility and influence as well as that of publisher John Stark. Among all publishers Stark was the only one who committed himself to specializing in ragtime, which he promoted in announcements and in his catalogues. Previously, rags had only been listed as "new" on sheet music, and very often nothing else was done to enhance sales. Stark believed in ragtime and actively committed himself to advocating the value of ragtime as American music.

When Stark initially published "Maple Leaf Rag," Joplin received one penny per copy in **royalties**. By 1905, Stark was selling three thousand copies a month and "Maple Leaf Rag" had become the most popular and best-selling rag of all time. The incredible success of "Maple Leaf Rag"— a half-million copies were sold by 1909—inspired other music publishers to produce hundreds of rags.

Joplin assisted other ragtime pianists in publishing their compositions after his reputation as ragtime composer was well established. He recommended James Scott to Stark, who at Joplin's insistence issued Scott's "Frog Legs Rag" in 1906. It was to become Stark's second best-selling rag, and he went on to publish twenty-four additional rags by Scott. Joplin also suggested Marshall's "Lily Queen" to Joseph W. Stern Company in New York, which had published works by Blacks since the 1890s. It usually took some time for composers to get a rag published; this was true for White as well as for Black composers. Networks among composer-colleagues that existed across ethnic groups were also helpful in the publishing process. Joplin supported White composer Joseph Lamb after having been introduced to Lamb's composition "Sensation" at Stark's publishing company. At Joplin's request, Stark published "Sensation" in 1909, yet Joplin's name was imprinted on the title page in order to promote sales. Altogether, Lamb published twelve rags with Stark.

Classic ragtime
Notated or written compositions for piano, in four sections; associated with Scott Joplin and his contemporaries.

🔘 **14**

"Maple Leaf Rag, 1916."

Royalties
Payment made by a music publisher to a composer based on the number of printed or recorded copies sold. Also, payments made by record labels to artists and song publishers based on the number of records sold.

Ingeborg Harer

Although the majority of popular rags seem to have been written and published by White composer-arrangers, the question of whether this was an exploitation of the African American originators of the music cannot be answered simply. Current perspectives and definitions of "exploitation" differ greatly from those that were prevalent during the ragtime era. Standards for royalties and copyright did not apply to African Americans during this time period. It is obvious that African Americans were the originators of ragtime but did not reap commensurate benefits from their accomplishments. Scott Joplin serves as a classic example: although Joplin had a royalty contract with publisher John Stark for "Maple Leaf Rag," this arrangement did not apply to all of Joplin's compositions. In 1909, Stark informed Joplin that he would not pay him royalties on any new compositions. Consequently, Joplin's last rags were published by Seminary Music. Like Joplin, each composer had to negotiate royalties with publishing companies and often had to accept low rates, if granted any at all.[18]

PERFORMING RAGTIME

In some cases, the sheet music itself reveals the variety of performance in ragtime. Ernest Hogan's 1896 "All Coons Look Alike to Me" (Figure 6.2), one of the most successful but also infamous coon songs, documents the practice of highlighting the melody in ragtime. An optional arrangement of the song's chorus, subtitled as "Choice Chorus, with Negro 'Rag' accompaniment arr. by Max Hoffman," is presented on the last page of the sheet music. It proves to be the first application of the term "rag" and offers a piano version, in which the right hand plays the melody in ragtime, with the left hand providing accompaniment.

Other sheet music examples with optional arrangements in the rhythmic style of ragtime include "My Coal Black Lady: Symphony de Ethiopia" (1897) by W.T. Jefferson and "Take Me Back Babe: Symphony de Coon: Chorus Arranged in Rag Time" (1898) by Tim Barrett.

As the first major African American composer of rags, Tom Turpin was especially well known as an excellent performer.[19] Turpin lived in St. Louis from 1887, and in the early 1890s he began his career as saloon pianist in one of the most notorious sporting houses of St. Louis. In 1897, the year he published "Harlem Rag," Turpin opened his own business, Turpin's Saloon. Three years later, in 1900, his famous Rosebud Bar became the site where many ragtime pianists started their careers. The Rosebud Bar consisted of several rooms: barrooms, dining rooms, gambling rooms, and hotel rooms. Turpin played the piano in the wine room, where an upright piano was placed on wooden blocks so he could play while standing up. Tom Turpin fostered the careers of other Black piano players by enabling them to play and compose ragtime for his Rosebud Café (as Turpin's bar was also known). Among these promising pianists were Scott Hayden, Arthur Marshall, Joe Jordan, Louis Chauvin,

Figure 6.2
"All Coons Look Alike to Me" by Ernest Hogan, 1896. Public domain. Brown University Library.

Charlie Thompson, and Artie Matthews. They later gained reputations as ragtime figures, primarily of the Midwest, who developed their own individual styles. At his Rosebud Bar/Café, Turpin organized piano contests for the younger players who waited for a chance to earn their living as musicians. Many of the young men established their careers at Turpin's bar and eventually left St. Louis.[20] Turpin closed his bar in 1906, and in 1910 he opened the Eureka Club, where Arthur Marshall, Joplin's former student, became the house pianist.

Although Joplin was not the most outstanding ragtime piano player, he nonetheless formulated concrete guidelines for playing ragtime, particularly his own music. For his rag "Leola" (1905), he established playing rules that were printed on the sheet music: "Notice! Don't play

Ingeborg Harer

this piece fast. It is never right to play 'rag-time' fast. Author." Three years later, in 1908, he wrote his *School of Ragtime*, six exercises for amateur pianists. His guidelines for performance warned against "careless playing," which suggested his desire to mitigate against excessive liberties that had become commonplace in the tradition. Clearly, pioneering African American composer-performers acknowledged the existence of performance boundaries that they sought to reinforce in very systematic ways.

Louis Chauvin, called the "King of Ragtime Players," was known as the best pianist performing in St. Louis. He won the ragtime contest held during the St. Louis World's Fair in 1904 and was said to play completely from memory, unable to read musical notes. Sam Patterson describes Louis Chauvin's playing:

> When he would first sit down he always played the same Sousa march to limber up his fingers, but it was his own arrangement with double-time contrary motion in octaves like trombones and trumpets all up and down the keyboard . . . Turpin was great, but Chauvin could do things that Turpin couldn't touch. He had speed fingering and he tossed octaves overhead.[21]

The art of improvisation was central to the ragtime tradition as described by jazz pianist-composer James P. Johnson, who performed in many ragtime **"cutting contests"**:

Cutting contest
Informal competition among musicians, intended to identify the artist with the greatest creativity and skill.

> I played rags very accurately and brilliantly—running chromatic octaves and glissandos up and down with both hands. It made a terrific effect. I did double glissandos straight and backhand, glissandos in sixths and double tremolos. These would run other ticklers out of the place at cutting sessions. They wouldn't play after me. I would put these tricks in on the breaks and I could think of a trick a minute. I was playing a lot of piano then, traveling around and listening to every good player I could. I'd steal their breaks and style and practice them until I had them perfect.[22]

Tom Turpin, however, is perhaps the best example of a performer-composer, whose compositions show clear traces of his own improvisatory style. As a composer, Turpin thought like a performer, and "Harlem Rag," more than any other early rag, shows the amateur player how to put excitement into ragtime playing. Instead of the usual repeat-as-written markings at the ends of themes, "Harlem Rag" provides written-out repeats of its second, third, and fourth strains, each of which is trickier—and showier—than the original statement of the melody.[23]

Among the representatives of "classic ragtime," James Scott was probably the best piano player. His style of playing at approximately the age of fifteen was described as such:

> He sat at the keyboard with his left leg wrapped around a leg of the stool or bench and bounced up and down with the beat as he played, his short square fingers literally flying over the keys as he attempted to squeeze the greatest possible number of notes into the space of each beat. While thus occupied, he was lost to the world and the sordid environment around him, totally absorbed with the wonder of his music.[24]

During his lifetime, Scott Joplin participated in the classical musical tradition as both performer and composer. As a young man he was trained in the field of classical music, which is probably the basis for his preoccupation with this genre. Joplin composed several works for the theater and concert stages. His symphonies are lost, however, as is the score of his opera *A Guest of Honor*. Joplin was unsuccessful in getting his opera *Treemonisha* published by any established firm; he finally published it himself in 1911. Scott Joplin's great vision—his belief in education as the most important means for African Americans to achieve progress—is the main topic in this opera. Yet Joplin did not succeed in putting *Treemonisha* on stage, in spite of sincere attempts. David A. Jasen and Gene Jones speculate that Black as well as White producers might have rejected this work for various reasons:

> White producers dismissed out of hand the idea of an opera-length work by a black writer, simply because there was no commercial precedent for it. Black producers, preferring to show the progress of their race, would not stage a work that depicted the low estate of their people in Reconstruction Arkansas [where the opera is set]. Even the devotees of Joplin's rags would have had their doubts. *Treemonisha* is not a "ragtime opera"; it is as high-class as Joplin could make it.[25]

America was not ready yet for music without boundaries, for high and low classes, written and performed by African Americans.

Many of the ragtime pioneers were itinerant pianists for whom ragtime was their livelihood. It is evident that the ragtime player-composers were mutually influenced in their activities. Joplin stands apart from these pianists, because in the long run he himself gave up playing ragtime in favor of composing. He sought to elevate ragtime to the status of American art music and envisioned a music removed from the brothels and performed on the concert stage. Joplin conceived of ragtime as composed music, not merely a performed idiom. Because of his prodigious output, his contemporaries dubbed him "The King of Ragtime Writers." Joplin's publisher, John Stark, shared his vision of ragtime as an American art form. He articulated his view of "classic ragtime" in advertisements and brochures.

Stark moved his company from Sedalia to St. Louis in 1900 in order to be closer to the most active music scene. When he finally transferred his office to New York, he found a musical scene that was dominated by the commercial aims of **Tin Pan Alley** publishing. Stark rejected and distanced himself from the commercial standards of Tin Pan Alley publishers. He equated ragtime with the standard classical repertoire played in the homes of amateur musicians. Therefore, he chose to call his company "The House of Classic Rags" and, in describing the qualities of ragtime, he established links to European classical music. Stark was a prolific advertiser and persistently advocated for the excellence of "classic ragtime" as a distinct musical genre. At the same time, he sought to free

Tin Pan Alley
Composed styles of popular music reflecting the musical values of middle-class White America; published between 1880 and 1950, primarily by New York-based firms.

ragtime from its negative racial connotations. To this end, Stark transformed the marketing of rags by eliminating stereotypical images of African Americans on his sheet music covers. For example, the ragtime pieces he published bear names of plants and trees (Joplin's "Sun Flower Slow Drag" and "Weeping Willow"), or they refer to beauty or style (Joplin's "Elite Syncopations," 1902; and James Scott's "Grace and Beauty," 1909). Elegant young ladies playing the piano appear on many covers, no doubt identifying the music's potential clientele.

WOMEN IN RAGTIME

Sheet music publishing became a highly profitable industry at the beginning of the twentieth century, and ragtime was part of this commercial success. Playing the piano became very popular for amateurs, particularly for young White women, a fact that prompted piano sales, as well as sheet music sales, among middle-class families. Being able to play the piano and to sight-read became qualities that were to be useful for new jobs in music publishing-related industries. Sales clerks were employed in music shops and department stores to introduce customers to the newly published music for piano. Professional pianists and musicians were needed to transpose and arrange songs for professional performers, silent film accompaniments, and piano roll recordings. These new jobs were sometimes held by White women, as the piano was the most popular instrument to be played by women throughout the nineteenth century. In fact, learning to play the piano became a "trademark" of the typical middle-class education for girls. Considering the young women as "consumers" of ragtime, sheet music publishers targeted this group. Images on printed music, however, tended to portray African American and White women quite differently. While African American women were most often depicted in degrading, stereotypical roles, White women were generally portrayed positively as singers. Visually, the contrast is striking.

White women obviously were fascinated by ragtime, thus they were also tempted to start composing, usually as a hobby rather than for public recognition. The few amateur composers who published their own compositions often used a pseudonym or initials, hiding their identities. Most ragtime women were in their twenties when they composed rags, and many of them discontinued their musical activities after marriage.[26] Still, a representative number of the approximately three hundred ragtime women composers appear to have contributed to the history of the genre.[27] One of the most successful pre-1900 cakewalks was "Eli Green's Cake Walk" (1896), written by Sadie Koninsky.

A few years later, Adaline Shepherd's (1883–1950) "Pickles and Peppers" (1906) became very popular. Irene M. Giblin (1888–1974), who worked as a sales clerk introducing new sheet music to customers in department stores in St. Louis, published nine rags. Pauline Alpert

 25

"Dusty Rag."

(1900–88), a vaudeville performer, reached fame as a pianist, recording as many as ninety piano rolls for the piano roll company Duo-Art. Her piano playing was reportedly enthusiastic and fast. May Frances Aufderheide (1890–1972) grew up in Indianapolis and was supported by her father, who opened a publishing company to promote her ragtime compositions.[28] Aufderheide's "Dusty Rag" (1908) (Track 25) and "The Thriller" (1909) became very popular beyond Indianapolis.

According to ragtime author Rudi Blesh, her rags were performed by the early New Orleans jazz bands.[29] Aufderheide assisted in the publication efforts of other women such as Gladis Yelvington (1891–1957) and Julia Lee Niebergall (1886–1968) by convincing her father to publish their ragtime compositions. Despite the achievements of these and other women, they have largely been neglected by the scholarship on ragtime. In recent years, Nora Hulse has uncovered many details about ragtime women, notably identifying previously unknown White female ragtime composers.[30] Even though we may assume that Black women contributed to ragtime as performers and composers, sources that document their existence are elusive.[31] So far only one early rag and two rags of the later period composed by African American female pianists could be located by N. Hulse: Florence B. Roper's (1870–c.1910) "The Chief: Two Step" (1900); "The Crawfish Rag"(1919) by Viva Celeste Seals (1895–?); and "That Hateful Rag: Fox Trot" (1925) by Bertha Allen (1879–1978).[32] Not only did African American women have less access to ragtime piano playing, composing, and publishing than did White women, African American males were also more dominant than African American women. For example, the image on the sheet music "That Lovin' Traumerei" (1910) shows a Black male playing the piano while the Black woman is portrayed as the listener or singer. By the end of the ragtime era, a few Black women composers of classical music incorporated ragtime into some of their compositions, including "Negro Dance, op. 25, no. 1" (1921) by Nora Holt (1885 or 1890–1974), as well as Florence Beatrice Price's (1887–1953) "Cotton Dance, no. 31" (1931) and "Ticklin' Toes: Three Little Negro Dances" (1933).[33]

RAGTIME IN EUROPE

African American artists appeared in Europe as itinerant musician-singers from the eighteenth century onwards. As in the United States, ragtime was received with enthusiasm as well as with dismay as soon as it reached Europe around 1900. Because this new musical form had no "vocabulary" that observers or critics could use, White audiences described what they saw and heard in the same language they used for classical music. Because the repertoire and performance style differed radically from the established European canon, African American music and its performers were typically labeled "exotic," "eccentric," "grotesque," or "comical." The visual impression dominated the critiques, while the quality of the music itself was often ignored. Local newspaper commentaries frequently underscored the fun character of performances, using such telling headlines as "Original musical eccentrics Black & White."[34]

The Cakewalk

By the end of the nineteenth century, the cakewalk dance, rather than ragtime, seemed to have captivated European audiences. African American musicians frequently arrived in London, where they experienced fewer language barriers and from where they traveled further east (and north) as far as Paris, Berlin, Hamburg, Vienna, Budapest, and St. Petersburg.[35] While various American duos performed the cakewalk as a special attraction on vaudeville stages, it was also imitated by European performers and composers. The cakewalk became particularly popular on various European theater stages, including in ballets and operettas. Composer Franz Lehar's operettas contained cakewalks, which were also printed as piano sheet music.[36] One of the most important sources of information regarding the reception of the cakewalk in the German-speaking countries is an article printed in the *Illustrierte Zeitung Leipzig* in 1903.[37] It describes the impact of the cakewalk in Europe in great detail, including pictures of cakewalks on plantations and in ballrooms.[38]

The examination of theater, varieté, and circus programs reveals that cakewalk dancing was also introduced in Vienna in 1903.[39] Other writers in the local papers of middle Europe also refer to the new dance. Even *The New York Times* reports about the cakewalk in Vienna: "If the prognostication of the Paris correspondence of Die Zeit of Vienna comes true, the emphatic steps and nimble struttings of the 'cake walk' will soon absorb the attention of the Austrian capital."[40]

Newspaper articles and other sources documenting performances of the cakewalk by African Americans describe mainly the dances, and, consequently, the dance craze, rather than the accompanying music. As was the case with sheet music, the borderline between cakewalk and ragtime performance cannot be clearly drawn. Because the boundaries between the cakewalk and ragtime are blurred, references to these two genres have often been used interchangeably. We do not know with certainty what kind of music was played when the cakewalk was danced; however, the influence of these American dance traditions on European ballroom dance can hardly be overemphasized.

Will Marion Cook was among the first African Americans who introduced the cakewalk in Europe. In 1899, *Cook's Clorindy, or, The Origin of the Cakewalk*, the first show featuring African Americans and produced solely by African Americans, opened in London and was received with enthusiasm. The performances by Cook and other African Americans such as Arabella Fields, Lewis Douglas,[41] the Four Black Diamonds, the Louisiana Troupe, and others span the first two decades of the twentieth century. Some artists adapted their programs to European tastes.[42] For instance, Arabella Fields, whose career in Europe spanned more than thirty years, is known to have added Alpine songs and Austrian yodeling to her performances while touring Austria.[43]

The proliferation of cakewalk dancing and the favorable reception of African American artists and their music reflect the existence of a general positive attitude toward new influences from America. At the same time, negative appraisals of African American music and performers were also commonplace. While approval went hand in hand with a general fascination with American life and new developments, rejection was based on the fear that European culture might be threatened. Although some European musicians and music lovers were able to appreciate and recognize the distinctive characteristics of African American music, identifying the products as uniquely American, those who rejected

American influences felt ragtime would possibly have a destructive effect on Western art music.[44] In general, ragtime was not produced on piano rolls in Europe, because European White middle- and upper-class audiences would not accept African American popular music in their traditional bourgeois living rooms, where culture was strictly defined as European heritage.

Ragtime

Musicians visiting the United States sometimes brought African American ragtime as sheet music back to Europe; generally, though, it took one or two years until a piece of music arrived in Europe.[45] Soon, European composers began to imitate the new popular style of music associated with America. Although ragtime sheet music was produced in Europe, it came into existence under sociocultural conditions totally different from those in the United States. The social background that was the breeding ground for ragtime in the United States was totally lacking in Europe, as were the performers and variety of playing styles that were the lifeblood of ragtime. The classical ragtime composers such as Scott Joplin, James Scott, and Joseph Lamb were largely unknown outside the United States. What European composers thought was ragtime was far removed from the African American originals. African American musical elements were reinterpreted in accordance with traditional European musical values and practice.

European composers created their own versions (song, dance, instrumental music) of the new American idiom and German–Austrian publishing houses produced much sheet music at a time when there were no sound recordings. Therefore, these publications are the most important source for documenting the reception of ragtime and early jazz in Europe.[46] In German-speaking countries, it became common practice to translate the titles of original American cakewalks and rags into German. The German–Austrian Publishing House Ullstein (Berlin and Vienna), for example, edited a special issue titled "Amerika-Heft" as part of their magazine, *Musik für Alle: Monatsheft zur Pflege volkstümlicher Musik* ["Music for everybody: monthly paper for popular music"]. This publication also contains Kerry Mills' "Whistling Rufus," with the title translated into German.

We have no knowledge of specific ragtime playing styles that were transmitted, adopted, or developed by Europeans. Furthermore, there is no evidence of the existence of such practices as ragging a tune, nor do we have testimony of improvisation and variety in ragtime playing styles. Ragtime published in Europe was generally less syncopated, as was the case for the American pieces of music that became popular in Europe. Nevertheless, the impact of American piano and instrumental ragtime on European popular music is evident, even though ragtime as a distinct playing style did not exist in Europe. Although certain titles became extremely popular, these were not necessarily the same pieces of music

Figure 6.4
Kerry Mills' "Whistling Rufus." In "Amerika-Heft," *Musik für Alle: Monatsheft zur Pflege volkstümlicher Musik.*

that enjoyed popularity in the United States. In German-speaking countries, well-known favorites included "Whistling Rufus," "Temptation Rag," "Grizzly Bear," "Brooklyn Cakewalk," "Hiawatha," and "At a Georgia Camp Meeting."[47] Kerry Mills' "At a Georgia Camp Meeting," translated into German, became one of the most popular pieces in Germany and Austria, presumably contributing to the dissemination of cakewalk (music) in the German-speaking countries. It was also printed in the *Illustrierte Zeitung Leipzig* article already noted.

Although African American music was not always received with enthusiasm, European musicians, mainly composers working for the entertainment business (operetta, song), recognized its musical quality, rhythmic novelty, and its impact on traditional styles of composing. Among those who accepted the new American idiom, the percentage of European Jewish composers is comparatively high.[48] They apparently more readily adopted new music styles, seeking influences for innovation and success in the entertainment business.

Ragtime and Classical Music

From the beginning of the emergence of ragtime, there was interaction between ragtime and classical music. "Ragging the classics" was a feature characteristic of ragtime playing styles in the United States. The interaction between ragtime and classical music was reversed when composers of classical music discovered ragtime as a new, promising element of composition. European composers such as Claude Debussy, Paul Hindemith, Maurice Ravel, and Eric Satie incorporated ragtime elements in their compositions and thus contributed to the diversity of compositional styles in the early twentieth century.

Claude Debussy probably heard ragtime when John Philip Sousa and his band appeared in Paris in 1900. Debussy must have been attracted by the new sound of the African American idiom. As part of his suite *Children's Corner* (1908), he composed "Golliwog's Cakewalk," probably the best-known piano piece of this genre. Debussy also utilized ragtime in two later piano preludes: "Minstrels" (1910) and "General Lavine—Eccentric" (1913). Eric Satie dealt with ragtime in his ballet *Parade* (1917), while Igor Stravinsky wrote several works containing the ragtime idiom, such as "Ragtime for 11 Instruments" (1917–18), "Ragtime" (1918), and "Piano Rag Music" (1919).

RAGTIME REVIVAL

Although interest in ragtime had declined after the first decade of the twentieth century, there have been several revivals in various forms since the early 1940s. They include new recordings; reprinted sheet music; research and oral history projects; formation of ragtime societies and clubs; the publication of journals, newsletters, and books; live stage and television performances; and the use of ragtime as soundtracks for Hollywood films. The first revival occurred in the early 1940s when the San Francisco-based Lu Watters' Yerba Buena Jass Band recorded piano ragtime in the tradition of the 1920s jazz style. The band's recordings of Scott Joplin's "Maple Leaf Rag," Kerry Mills' "At a Georgia Camp Meeting," and George Botsford's "Black and White Rag" exposed the music to a broad audience, generated a renewed interest in the tradition, and inspired a new generation of ragtime performers. Other ragtime activities of the 1940s centered on the work of aficionados and scholars who began collecting oral histories and conducting research on the history of the tradition as well as the lives of the musicians. The research of Roy Carew (according to Berlin, Carew began publishing historical articles in 1943 in *Record Changer*), Alan Lomax (1950), and Rudi Blesh and Harriet Janis (1971; first edition published in 1950) culminated in historical and biographical publications.

Starting in the 1960s and to this day, various ragtime clubs and associations have played an important role in sustaining interest and perpetuating ragtime through performance. These clubs also organized ragtime festivals, and researched and published on the subject of ragtime history.[49] Many accomplished ragtime performers presented concerts, frequently using the lecture-demonstration format to discuss the music and its composers. Max Morath, who had published the anthology *100 Ragtime Classics* by 1963, and appeared regularly on television shows, was one of the leading figures of this ragtime revival.

By the 1970s, the formal study and performance of ragtime had spread beyond the clubs of aficionados into the academy where performers and scholars sought to celebrate ragtime as a form of America's "classical" music. Attention turned to Scott Joplin when pianist-musicologist Joshua Rifkin recorded the first of three albums of Joplin's ragtime compositions. Unlike other pianists, who took liberties in interpreting Joplin's rags, Rifkin performed the music as notated on the score, without any form of improvised embellishments. Although this concert-style approach generated some criticism, the interest in Joplin's music proliferated among intellectuals and resulted in the subsequent release of *The Collected Works of Scott Joplin* by the New York Public Library, the formation of the New England Conservatory Ragtime Ensemble, and the production of Joplin's opera *Treemonisha*. In 1972, the Atlanta Memorial Arts Center, in conjunction with an African American music workshop sponsored by Morehouse College, staged a production of Joplin's opera *Treemonisha*. Three years later, in 1975, the Houston Grand Opera produced a fully orchestrated and choreographed version of the opera, which was followed by a production in New York City at the Uris Theater on Broadway. In 1976, Scott Joplin was posthumously awarded a Pulitzer Prize, and *Treemonisha* has since been produced in Europe.

Overlapping these and other revivalist activities were the publications of scholarly works on the music and life of Joplin; these might have been motivated by Harold C. Schonberg, who, in a Sunday *New York Times* article in January 1971, advised: "Scholars, get busy on Scott Joplin." Since 1973, several scholarly works have been published on Joplin and ragtime in general, including those by Schafer and Riedel (1973), Terry Waldo (1976), Jasen and Tichenor (1978), Haskins and Benson (1978), Edward Berlin (2002 (1994)), Susan Curtis (1994), Tim Frew (1996), H. Loring White (2005), and Ray Argyle (2009), as well as various discographies, master's theses, and doctoral dissertations. Joplin became a household name in American popular culture in 1974 when his rags provided the soundtrack for the film *The Sting*. The film won several awards, including Best Musical Score, and the song "The Entertainer" was on the pop charts for most of the year.[50]

Reviving the works of a composer such as Joplin is only one facet of ragtime's revival. As early as the 1950s, a new generation of players and researchers came into existence and, with them, ragtime playing became popular once again among ragtime aficionados in America and elsewhere, which can be observed to this day. At this point, the circle closes; ragtime, as in the old days, is alive as a playing style.

KEY NAMES

Scott Joplin	James Scott
Joseph Lamb	John Stark
Max Morath	Tom Turpin

QUESTIONS

1. Describe the key stylistic characteristics of ragtime performance and composition. When and where did the earliest musical notions of ragtime develop?

2. What was Scott Joplin's vision for ragtime music, and what role did he play in its development? What social barriers did Joplin navigate in order to pursue his goals?

3. Define "classic ragtime," and assess the usefulness of the term in discussing the history of ragtime styles.

4. Give examples of ways in which ragtime performances impacted ragtime sheet music, and vice versa. How was the spread of ragtime impacted by its performance and availability on sheet music?

5. What is the difference between cakewalk and ragtime? How did the general responses of European audiences to each style compare to those of audiences in the United States?

PROJECTS

1. Listen to several different recordings of the "Maple Leaf Rag" by various pianists and ensembles over the decades, including Scott Joplin. What similarities and differences do you notice, and how does each compare with Joplin's?

2. View decorative covers of ragtime sheet music published between 1900 and 1925; select five to analyze closely as historical documents (images, text, dates, intended market, etc.). What does your study reveal about social attitudes toward African American music and culture?

3. Analyze sheet music for the "Maple Leaf Rag" as a model of a "classic ragtime" composition, using an edition with Scott Joplin's original notation, if possible. Compare five published rags by various composers to the model. In what ways do they follow or depart from the model?

NOTES

Please see the discography for further information on resources for further listening.

1. Harer 2007, 171–84; Harer 2006, 87–102.
2. Berlin 1980, 5–17, 32–7, 104; Southern 1997, 314–17; Floyd 1995, 67; Epstein 2003, 38–44; Harer 2007, 180–82.
3. Berlin 1980, 104.
4. Harer 2007, 181–82.

5. Lewis 1915. See also Harer 2007, 174.
6. Berlin 1980, 99–120, 147–49.
7. Ibid., 14–20; Jasen and Jones 2000, xxi, 296; Jasen and Jones 2002, 9.
8. Floyd 1995, 70.
9. Hughes 1899, 158.
10. For the meaning of ragtime dancing as social practice see Robinson 2009.
11. Hunkemöller 1998, 58–59.
12. Jasen and Jones 2000, xxix.
13. Jasen and Jones 1998, xxi–xxvi.
14. Tallmadge 1995, 173–82.
15. Tallmadge (ibid., 188–91) draws attention to an even earlier example of ragtime: Charles Gimble "Old Black Joe . . . Paraphrase de Concert," published in 1877, is a "translation" of African American playing style into the piano idiom.
16. Jasen and Jones 1998, 119–21.
17. Magee 1998, 389.
18. Berlin 2002 (1994), 186.
19. Jasen and Jones 2002, 1–9.
20. Ibid., 7.
21. Blesh and Janis 1971, 56–58.
22. Davin 1985, 174.
23. Jasen and Jones 2002, 4–5.
24. Vangilder 1976.
25. Jasen and Jones 2002, 27–28.
26. Lindemann and Eskin 1992; see also Lindemann 1985.
27. Morath 1985, 154–65.
28. For a description of the Aufderheide publishing company, see Jasen and Jones 2000, 153–57.
29. Blesh and Janis 1971, 221.
30. Hulse and Bostick 2002.
31. Some references to Black women in ragtime are included in Handy 1998.
32. Nora Hulse, personal correspondence, July/August 2010. I would like to thank Nora Hulse for providing these data and her latest research results for the present publication. For additional information about Black and White women in popular music, see also Vera Lee 2010, 80–109, "White Women in Popular Song (1900–1929): Blushing Roses of Tin Pan Alley" and "The African American Female (1900–1929): The Black Venus of the Blues."
33. Nora Hulse, personal correspondence, July/August 2010.
34. Harer 1998a, 186.
35. African musicians may be traced in Britain as early as in the eighteenth century. See Wright 1986, 14–24.
36. Lehár n.d.; Reiterer n.d.
37. *Illustrierte Zeitung Leipzig* 1903, 202–04.
38. See illustration in Harer 1998b.
39. Harer 1998a, 185.
40. "The Cake Walk in Vienna" 1903, 5.
41. Lotz 1997, 297–389. For performances in Austria see Harer 1998a, 185.
42. Pickering 2008, 159–83; Rainer Lotz (1997, 225–46) documented Arabella Fields' appearances in Europe.
43. Harer 1998a, 187.
44. Harer 1999.
45. Ritzel 1988, 503.
46. See list of rags published in Germany in Lotz 1989.
47. Lotz 1989, 102.
48. For a discussion of composers and lists of their works, see Cole 1977.
49. For more information on ragtime societies and their activities see the West Coast Ragtime Society, www.westcoastragtime.com.
50. Blesh and Janis 1971.

CHAPTER 7

Blues

David Evans

By the end of the first decade of the twentieth century, the term "blues" began to be applied to a new type of song emerging from Black communities in the southern United States. These songs were new and different both in their formal and musical characteristics and in the topics and attitudes they expressed in their lyrics. They are discussed in contemporary accounts of folklorists and other observers, and in later reminiscences of people who were involved in music at this time. The fact that blues songs seem to turn up everywhere in the Deep South and Midwest more or less simultaneously—in rural areas, small towns, and cities such as New Orleans, Memphis, and St. Louis—suggests that the form had been developing for a few years and probably allows us to place its origins in the 1890s.

HISTORICAL BACKGROUND AND CONTENT

The blues was not the only new musical development to emerge in the decades surrounding the turn of the century. Instead, it should be viewed as part of a wave of innovation in Black American music at this time that also saw the first stirrings of ragtime, jazz, gospel music, and barbershop-style vocal harmony. This occurred in conjunction with significant new developments in literature, theater, and the arts in general, as well as in Black political and religious life.

This creativity coincided with a hardening of White resistance to Black social and economic progress in the form of the **Jim Crow laws** and the institutionalization of racial segregation, disenfranchisement of Black

Jim Crow laws
Laws limiting African American freedoms and rights in US society, named for the minstrel character "Jim Crow."

voters, lynching and other forms of terrorism, and the loss of jobs to the swarm of new European immigrants. It was a time of the end of the American dream that had once seemed attainable for Black Americans following Emancipation. A new generation that had grown up to see the erosion of its parents' hard-won freedoms had to create new responses to its realization of the American situation. Earlier Black folk and popular music had consisted largely of folk and concert versions of spirituals, minstrel material, and instrumental dance music played on the fiddle and other instruments, as well as work songs and children's game songs. Many of the singers and musicians had some degree of White patronage. The new musical genres all exhibited in various ways a turning inward toward utilization of Black folk-musical resources; an adaptation of Western form, harmony, and instrumentation to characteristically Black style; and a greater reliance on Black audiences for monetary support and approval. With emphases on the performer, the creative composer, improvisation, soloing, and self-expression, the new music became more introspective, self-absorbed, individualistic, serious, and worldly at the very time that the majority of Whites were viewing all Blacks as an undifferentiated social caste with stereotyped mental and behavioral traits that cast them as ignorant, humorous, and carefree. The new types of music would challenge these stereotypes and lead the way in the Black struggle for freedom, justice, and equality throughout most of the twentieth century.

Of all the new types of Black music created at this time, the blues was the most self-contained. Throughout their history, blues songs have mainly been sung solo, although duet and quartet performances and background vocalizing are not unknown. The singers, especially males, usually play an instrument; in folk blues, this has generally been a guitar, piano, or harmonica. Many male folk blues singers have preferred to perform solo, as have some female singers, although most of the latter have been accompanied by a lone, usually male, pianist or guitarist. Even when other instruments are added, as is the case in most types of popularized blues, great emphasis is placed on individual expression and improvisation. Sometimes entire performances of the blues—lyrics, melodies, and instrumental work—are improvised, and although some performers are highly creative in this respect, many are also aided by a body of shared and familiar lyric and musical ideas and formulas that they recombine in constantly changing ways.

European and African Elements

Like most forms of Black American music created in the nineteenth and twentieth centuries, the blues combines elements from the European and African musical traditions. The European elements occur especially in the areas of form, harmony, and instrumentation. The use of a recurring multiphrase strophic form and basic I–IV–V harmonies in the instrumental accompaniment are clearly attributable to Western influence.

The major solo and ensemble instruments are all commercially manufactured items well known in Western music, although some secondary
instruments used occasionally in the blues, such as washboards, jugs,
kazoos, and homemade one-stringed zithers, are reinterpretations of
originally African instruments.

The uses to which the Western instruments are put in the blues,
however, would often not be described by European-trained musicians
as proper or legitimate in terms of Western music, and most of the
modifications in playing technique and resultant sound are attributable
to the influence of the African musical tradition. As will be noted below,
the Western elements of form and harmony are also frequently altered
in ways that can best be explained by reference to African patterns.
Beyond this, the African elements in the blues are found chiefly in the
area of style, particularly in the music's rhythmic, tonal, and timbral
flexibility. Although it makes enough reference to Western norms to
sound familiar to Western ears, it has essentially broken free from the
notions of strict duple or triple meters and rhythmic patterns, scales with
fixed intervals in multiples of one hundred cents (a semitone), and
idealized vocal and instrumental tone. Western musical aesthetics have,
of course, broadened over the course of the past century in the face of
this challenge.

Griot
West African music
specialist of a social
caste who serves as
a custodian of
cultural history.

The American blues tradition has often been likened to that of the
griots, a professional caste of musical entertainers found widely in the
West African savanna region, the region that contributed a significant
portion of the United States' Black population. Among the similarities
that have been pointed out are the degree of professionalism of both types
of performers, their often itinerant existence, their perceived low social
status, their preference for stringed instruments, the use of a declamatory
and melismatic singing style, and their songs of frank social commentary.
These similarities do, indeed, suggest an African savanna origin for
some elements in the blues, but it would be wrong to view blues
performers simply as biological or cultural descendants of *griots*. Most of
these characteristics can also be found elsewhere in Africa, elements from
other African geographical traditions can be detected in the blues, and
many of the typically African elements in the blues are simply pan-
African. There is also the space of most of the nineteenth century to be
accounted for between the arrival of the last *griots* in the United States
and the beginnings of the music known as the blues. Whatever specific
elements can be compared, and there are many, no complete counterpart
to the blues has yet been found in any specific African ethnic group or
musical genre.

Early Forms That Influenced the Blues

If the Old World sources of the blues are rather far in its historical
background, there were other, more recognizable, musical genres in
existence at the end of the nineteenth century that can be identified as

significant factors in the synthesis that resulted in the creation of the blues. The basic melodic resources of the blues seem to be largely derived from the field holler, a type of solo unaccompanied work song found in the rural South, characterized by great melodic, timbral, and rhythmic freedom and forceful delivery. To this one could add as influences the more individualized and improvisatory forms of religious vocal expression, such as moaning, chanted prayer, and preaching. Most blues singers throughout the twentieth century were exposed to both farm work and the church and had plenty of opportunity to listen to and participate in these vocal genres.

The harmonic and structural form of the blues comes mainly from the folk ballad. In the later decades of the nineteenth century, Black American singers had adapted this originally European narrative folk song genre, and by the 1890s they had begun to create original ballads about characters and subjects of interest within the Black community, often about individuals who stood outside the bounds of the law and of organized society (for example, "Stagolee," "Frankie and Albert," "Railroad Bill") or whose actions were in some way "bad" and bold (for example, "Casey Jones"). Many of these new ballads had instrumental accompaniments at fast tempos and used a three-line form consisting of a rhymed couplet plus a one-line refrain with the harmonies of each line beginning with the I, IV, and V chords, respectively. Instrumental accompaniment and the three-line form, which were Black American innovations and had not been characteristic of the European American ballad tradition, were adapted to the melodic material of the field holler and solo religious expression, and the outlaw content of many of the ballads undoubtedly contributed as well to the personal stance adopted by many blues singers. In the course of this adaptation, the rapid tempo of the ballads was generally slowed to accommodate the new types of couples dances, such as the "slow drag," which were becoming popular at this time and with which the blues would come to be associated. It is one of the great strengths and accomplishments of the blues that it managed to synthesize elements of songs associated with work and religion on the one hand and a carefree, worldly existence on the other.

CONTEXTS FOR BLUES PERFORMANCE

The geographical hearth area of the blues is the plantation country of the Deep South, stretching from the interior of Georgia to eastern Texas. Most blues singers were born and raised in this region. The music underwent a less intense, though still significant, development in Virginia and the Carolinas, and it was even less developed in the border states, southern mountain regions, and along the Atlantic and Gulf coasts. Within the large hearth area, certain regions, such as the Mississippi Delta and the river bottomlands of southeastern Texas, have proved especially important as places of innovation. Over the course of the twentieth century, artists from these and other regions of the hearth area migrated to cities both within the area and outside it, especially in the Midwest and California, bringing their rural styles with them and contributing to new urban musical syntheses. Over the years, the blues has exhibited musical and lyrical traces of its southern rural origins as well as evidence of the desire of many performers and audience members to escape those origins.

Although blues performance sometimes occurs as a solitary activity or in intimate settings such as courtship, it has always been most often found in situations where an audience is present. It exists as music for both listening and dancing, the two often occurring in the same context. In the rural South the most common setting was the house party or outdoor picnic. Another common institution, the juke house or juke joint, was a structure, often a residence, temporarily or permanently set up for music, dancing, drinking, eating, and other activities. In the towns, blues musicians would gather and perform at cafés and saloons, on sidewalks and street corners, in parks, in railroad and bus stations, and inside and in front of places of business. In the cities, the blues was sung in vaudeville theaters, saloons, cabarets, and at house parties, as well as in parks and on streets. Traveling tent and medicine shows and circus sideshows often hired blues performers, providing opportunities for local and sometimes extended travel. Most of these settings persisted in Black American communities until the end of the 1950s, but since then the main locations have been clubs and auditoriums. Concerts and festivals, both within and outside the Black community, have provided additional settings for blues music in recent years.

For the first two decades of the twentieth century, the blues was generally performed alongside other types of folk and popular music. Most blues performers born in the nineteenth century and the first few years of the twentieth had eclectic repertoires that might also include ragtime pieces, older social dance songs, ballads, versions of popular songs, and even spirituals. Those born after about 1905 increasingly came to identify themselves as blues singers and often concentrated on this genre exclusively. From the beginning, the blues was performed as a means of making money. Some of the rural musicians were farmers and sharecroppers, and some urban musicians held weekday jobs, performing blues only on weekends. Often they could make as much in music on a weekend as a person could make working all week at another job. Some used this weekend work to enable themselves and their families to live better. Others saw it as a way to make money for good times, and yet others saw it as a way to avoid more onerous types of work during the week. The latter often became itinerant professional performers, working circuits of house parties, juke joints, clubs, or theaters. Blind and other handicapped performers also joined their ranks, often becoming some of the outstanding virtuosos and creative figures in the blues. Because blues performers were often involved in an underworld of gamblers, bootleggers, pimps, and prostitutes, blues music and blues singers gained an unsavory reputation for much of the music's history. However, this reputation has steadily improved since the 1970s, as many of the older contexts for the music have faded out of existence.

DISTINCTIVE CHARACTERISTICS OF THE BLUES

Although many elements of the blues can be traced to antecedent musical forms, this genre was a distinct synthesis that has had an enormous impact on American and world music. Several characteristics of the blues were shocking and challenging to the norms of Western music and American popular music. They entered the larger musical world for the first time through the blues and have come to be associated with the blues ever since, although some are now commonplace throughout popular music. Four characteristics in particular have this special association with the blues: blues texts, the role of instruments, "blue notes," and blues forms.

Blues Texts

Blues lyrics are extremely frank and almost exclusively concerned with the self, though in relation to others. They are not only sung primarily in the first person, but when directed toward another person or about someone else, they deal with the interaction between the other person and the singer. Rather than telling stories in a chronological fashion, blues songs express feelings and emotions or describe actions based on them. These may be the real feelings and activities of the singer or those of a persona created by the singer—an exaggerated or dramatized self. The lyrics are realistic (as opposed to idealistic), non-sentimental, and serious (as opposed to light or frivolous). They may incorporate exaggeration or boasting, but these are to be taken as amplifications of essential truths. They may (and often do) contain humor, but this is usually as an expression of irony, cleverness, double or multiple meaning, or social commentary and criticism, not as an illustration of buffoonery or stupidity:

> You can read my letter now, you sure don't know my mind.
> You can read my letter now, you sure don't know my mind.
> When you think I'm lovin' you, I'm leavin' all the time.
>
> Let me be your rocker now until your straight chair come.
> Let me be your rocker now until your straight chair come.
> And I'll rock you easier than your straight chair ever done.
>
> Rube Lacy, "Ham Hound Crave" (1928)
>
> I woke up this mornin', and I looked up against the wall.
> I woke up this mornin', and I looked up against the wall.
> Roaches and the bedbugs playin' a game of ball.
>
> Score was twenty-nothin', the roaches was ahead.
> Score was twenty-nothin', the roaches was ahead.
> Roaches got to fightin' and kicked me out of bed.
>
> Furry Lewis, "Creeper's Blues" (1929)

This realism and seriousness, combined with the concentration on the self and a willingness to delve into sadness, deep feelings, emotions, and confessions, are probably responsible for the appellation *blues*, which became attached to this music at an early stage. Although just as many of the songs express optimism, confidence, success, and happiness, it is this melancholy or depressed side of the range of emotions that has given the genre its familiar name.

The songs deal with a full range of human feelings and describe the ups and downs of daily life. The most prominent subjects by far are love and sex. These are followed by travel; work, poverty, and unemployment; alcohol, drugs, gambling, and trouble with the law; sickness and death; magic and hoodoo (often in connection with these other themes); and current events from the singer's point of view or involvement. Many of these topics had rarely been discussed before in American popular song, except in a trivial, sentimental, idealized, or moralistic way. The highly secular content of the blues, its concentration on the self in the here and now, and its expression of certain emotions and subject matter that are beyond the bounds of polite society have caused it to be viewed by many both within and outside the African American community as low-down, self-centered, or even "the devil's music." On the other hand, a more positive view expressed by some intellectuals and some blues singers themselves stresses the existentialist quality of blues lyrics, their emphasis on self-reliance and self-sufficiency, and their often outstanding poetic quality.

The Role of Instruments

An instrument or group of instruments plays a necessary role in the construction and performance of the song itself, rather than serving simply as a more or less optional harmonic and rhythmic background to the vocal part. The instrumental part is, in fact, a second voice (sometimes several voices), punctuating and responding to the vocal lines. It is therefore an integral part of the piece itself. The role of instruments as voices is well known in most forms of African music and their New World derivatives, but seldom has the instrument had such a close conversational dialogue with the singing voice as it has in the blues. This sort of dialogue was certainly not common in nineteenth-century American popular song, but through its use in the blues and the influence of blues on other popular genres it has become commonplace.

Blue Notes

As the term itself suggests, the blues introduced the concept of the **blue note** into American music. This term is used rather loosely, but essentially it means a note, sounded or suggested, that falls between two adjacent notes in the standard Western division of the octave into twelve equal intervals. Blue notes are thus sometimes described as neutral pitches and can be notated by an upward- or downward-pointing arrow printed above

Blue note
A note, sounded or suggested, that falls between two adjacent notes in the standard Western division of the octave, most often the third or seventh degree in a scale.

a note, which functions in the same way as a sharp, flat, or natural sign. These arrows, however, are not such precise indicators of pitch, because the neutral note can fall anywhere within the space of 100 cents. Blue notes are especially common at the third and seventh degrees of the scale, but they can occur at other points as well, including even such a normally stable place as the fifth. In actual practice, blue notes can be far more than neutral pitches. In fact, a variety of pitches within a single neutral range might be used in a song, suggesting aural shadings. A blue note might be expressed as a slur, usually upward from the flat toward the natural, or as a wavering between flat and natural or two other points within the interval. It might also occur as the simultaneous sounding of the flat and natural pitches or simply their use at different times in a piece, suggesting tonal ambivalence or compromise. Finally, it might simply be expressed by the sounding of a flat where a natural would be expected.

Blue notes are easy enough to achieve with the voice, but they can also be played on many instruments by the use of special techniques to "**bend**" notes, for example pushing the strings on the neck of the guitar; special tonguing and blowing methods for the harmonica, woodwinds, and horns; glissandos on the slide trombone; and the **slide** or "**bottleneck**" technique on the guitar. The latter technique consists of sliding a knife, metal tube, or glass bottleneck along one or more strings of the guitar to produce a percussive, whining tone and varying pitch. It is adapted mainly from the playing of a children's one-stringed instrument of Central African origin. On fixed-pitch instruments such as the piano, blue notes can only be suggested by rapid alternation of adjacent notes, a flat grace note before a natural, or the simultaneous sounding of flat and natural in a chord or in the separate melodic lines played by the two hands. Pianists have been especially ingenious in turning this emblematic instrument of Western music into a blues vehicle.

Blue notes are found in most but not all blues, leading some to use the term "**blues scale**." There actually is no single scale for all blues. Many pieces are pentatonic, whereas others are hexatonic and heptatonic, if one views the shading within the interval of a semitone as variations of a single scale step. The term, however, is simply a convenient designation for a scale that differs from a typical Western major or minor one by containing blue notes. Such scales certainly existed in Black American folk music before the blues, but the blue notes in them were generally dismissed by musically literate observers as "wild" or "barbaric" sounds. The creation of the term "blue notes" helped greatly to give legitimacy to these sounds and make them seem less exotic. Blue notes are quite clearly an extension of African musical practices and sometimes additionally an attempt to come to terms with Western instruments whose keyboards, fret boards, valves, and fingering holes are not designed to enable the player to achieve them easily. Blue notes thus can be seen to represent symbolically both a tension between an African musical legacy and a superimposed Western system as well as a successful resolution of this

Bend
An instrumental technique used to slightly raise or lower pitch. For example, on guitar, the player pushes the string sideways against the fret.

Slide or bottleneck
A playing technique in which a guitar player slides a metal bar or glass neck from a bottle across the strings to alter the timbre.

Blues scale
The incorporation of the flat third, flat fifth, and flat seventh degrees in a scale.

tension. With respect to the African legacy, blue notes may be simply continuations of elements from African scales that employed intervals other than multiples of semitones (for example, the modes commonly found in the music of the African savanna), or they may be derived from African approaches to harmony in which singers often make slight adjustments to the pitches of notes in order to produce a richer harmonic blend. Whatever the case, blue notes have now become so familiar in American and world popular music that they are generally taken for granted and have lost their former exotic associations.

Blues forms

The majority of blues utilizes the **twelve-bar** AAB form or some variant or approximation of it. At its most basic, the stanza consists of a line of verse (A), the same line repeated, and a third line (B) that rhymes with the first two.

Usually the B line explains, amplifies, comments on, or contrasts with the A line, rather than following from it chronologically. Each line occupies only slightly more than the first half of a four-measure section, the other portion consisting of an instrumental response to the vocal, although the instrumental part is also heard during the singing and interacts with it. The first line usually begins with the suggestion of a tonic chord harmony, the second with the subdominant, and the third with the dominant, each of them resolving in the tonic chord by the time of the instrumental response. The third line usually passes through the subdominant on the way to the tonic figure. This harmonic pattern is essentially the same as that which was used to accompany many three-line folk ballads created at the end of the nineteenth century. The shorter vocal lines of the blues left spaces at the ends so that the accompaniment could also assume a responsorial role.

> **Twelve-bar blues**
> A stanza of three lines (AAB) of four measures each, the lines beginning respectively in the I, IV, and V chords and resolving in the I chord.

	C		C		C		C	

I'm going away, and I won't be back till fall.

	F		F		C		C	

I'm going away, and I won't be back till fall.

	G		F		C		C	

If my mind don't change, I won't be back at all.

Figure 7.1
A typical twelve-bar blues stanza in the key of C major, with measure divisions and implied harmonies.

This simple form can be altered in a number of ways. For example, a rhymed couplet can occupy the entire first four bars, which would normally be filled by the A line and its instrumental response. The last eight bars remain the same, occupied by two lines and their instrumental responses, but these now become a refrain repeated in every stanza. The harmonic scheme can also be varied through chord substitutions, the use of passing harmonies (all serving to make the piece more harmonically complex), or through simplification to two chords or only one (that is, a strictly modal piece without any suggestion of chord changes). The number of bars can also be shortened or lengthened from the standard twelve. Shortened, lengthened, and harmonically non-standardized blues are found mainly among solo performers from the Deep South, who have no need to adhere to a predetermined structure and are free to vary their blues spontaneously or according to their own harmonic notions. The twelve-bar AAB pattern with its standard harmonies, on the other hand, enables singers and musicians to work together effectively, molding their improvisations within a simple and familiar format. There are, in addition, eight-bar (two-line) and sixteen-bar (four-line) blues with their own typical harmonic patterns as well as variations, and there are some blues that are conceived in a more or less free-form manner without apparent reference to one of these standard patterns. The repetition of the A line, textually and often melodically, is a device typically found in much African music, whereas the use of a repeated multi-phrase form with harmonic changes is more typically European.

Another device that often occurs in the blues and that links it to the African tradition is the use of repeated short melodic-rhythmic phrases or **riffs**. A riff can be used both to extend the instrumental response to vocal lines and as a background in support of the vocal lines, serving as an identifying marker for an entire piece. Usually several different or variant riffs are used in a single blues where this concept occurs. The twelve-bar AAB form and the use of riffs entered the mainstream of American popular music through the blues and have now become so commonplace that they are seldom given special notice.

Many of these blues characteristics can be seen in the accompanying transcription of "Lonesome Home Blues," recorded by Tommy Johnson in 1929 (Figure 7.2). The guitar response following the first vocal line has been shortened to a single measure (measure 3), making this song an eleven-bar blues. Repeated riff variations occur in the guitar part in measures 2 and 3, 5 and 7, 7 and 10, and 7 and 11. The implied harmonies of the guitar part are the tonic chord (E) in measures 1–3, the subdominant chord (A) in measures 4–5, the tonic chord (E) in measures 6–7, the dominant seventh chord (B♭⁷) in measure 8, the subdominant chord (A) in measure 9, and the tonic chord (E) in measures 10–11. Blue notes (indicated by arrows) occur in the vocal line as a raised sixth (C♯) and a lowered third (G♯). In the guitar line they are achieved by bending strings and occur as a raised second (F♯) and a raised flat third (G).

Riff
A short, recurrent melodic-rhythmic phrase.

Figure 7.2
Stanza 2 of "Lonesome Home Blues" (Paramount 13000) by Tommy Johnson (vocal and guitar), recorded in Grafton, Wisconsin, March 1929, with measures numbered.

Even from the time of its folk music origins, the blues has been a commercial music in the sense that it has usually been performed with the expectation of some kind of monetary reward. It should not be surprising, then, that the blues almost immediately entered the world of popular entertainment and the mass media. By the end of the first decade of the twentieth century, almost every Black community in a city or a larger town, both in the South and elsewhere, had at least one vaudeville theater serving its entertainment needs. Traveling tent shows, minstrel shows, medicine shows, and circuses also brought entertainment to these communities as well as to many of the smaller towns that could not sustain a full-time theater. Thus, there were opportunities for support of an entire class of professional Black singers, musicians, dancers, and comedians, as well as composers and managers.

By 1910, there were reports of songs called blues being sung and played by vaudeville entertainers, and twelve-bar and other typical blues strains could be detected occasionally in published ragtime piano compositions. In 1912, five songs were copyrighted with the word *blues* in their titles, including W.C. Handy's "The Memphis Blues." Black-owned publishing houses, such as Handy's in Memphis and that of Clarence Williams in New Orleans, began turning out dozens of blues in the following years. A number of southern Black vaudeville singers became closely identified with this new music and rose to the status of stars, among them Gertrude "Ma" Rainey, Butler "String Beans" May, and Bessie Smith. They sang the published blues hits, their own compositions, and adaptations of folk material. Many of the vaudeville and sheet music creations that were called blues were actually popular songs or instrumental pieces in the ragtime style but incorporating one or more blues strains (for example, twelve-bar AAB) and blue notes. Blues were also commercially recorded at this time by vocalists and dance and jazz bands, all of them White, and many White songwriters published blues, indicating that the blues had achieved a national popularity and identity as a distinct new type of music.

Recordings

In 1920, vaudeville singer Mamie Smith became the first Black vocalist to record blues commercially, having hits with "That Thing Called Love" and "Crazy Blues" (Figure 7.3) (Track 26), both of them compositions of fellow vaudevillian Perry Bradford. Her success resulted in the recording of many other vaudeville blues stars during the 1920s, most of them women, accompanied by a small jazz combo. At first, the songs were generally the compositions of professional songwriters in the multistrain format of ragtime music, but with blue notes and the occasional twelve-bar AAB strain. Representative singers in this style, besides Mamie Smith, were Lucille Hegamin, Alberta Hunter, Trixie Smith, Lizzie Miles,

26
"Crazy Blues."

David Evans

Ethel Waters, and Edith Wilson. By 1923, however, a new wave of singers entered the studios, singing songs more often made up of variants of a single AAB strain and accompanied typically by a pianist, sometimes with one or two added jazz instruments. By this time, more of the songs were being composed by the singers themselves. Some of the more prolific and successful artists in this style were Bessie Smith, Ma Rainey, Ida Cox, Rosa Henderson, Clara Smith, Viola McCoy, Sippie Wallace, Sara Martin, Bertha "Chippie" Hill, and Victoria Spivey.

A few self-accompanied male vaudeville performers had recorded in the early and mid-1920s, such as Sylvester Weaver, Papa Charlie Jackson, and Lonnie Johnson, but in 1927 a wave of folk blues artists on record was launched by the recordings of Blind Lemon Jefferson.

Through the early 1930s, many recordings were made of solo guitar- or piano-accompanied blues singers, mostly male, presenting to a national audience the sounds typically heard at southern juke joints, **barrelhouses**, and urban rent parties. Some of the important singer-guitarists who followed Jefferson in this period were Blind Blake, Blind Willie McTell, Barbecue Bob, Sam Collins, Tommy Johnson, Charley Patton, Son House, Jim Jackson, Furry Lewis, Robert Wilkins, and Ramblin' Thomas; barrelhouse pianists included Clarence "Pine Top" Smith, Speckled Red, Charles "Cow Cow" Davenport, Charlie Spand, and Henry Brown. Guitar duos, such as those of Memphis Minnie and Kansas Joe (McCoy) or the

Barrelhouse
A wooden structure on logging and turpentine camps in forest areas of the rural South where laborers gathered to drink and gamble. Pianists played ragtime and blues. Term "barrelhouse" references the storage of alcohol in barrels.

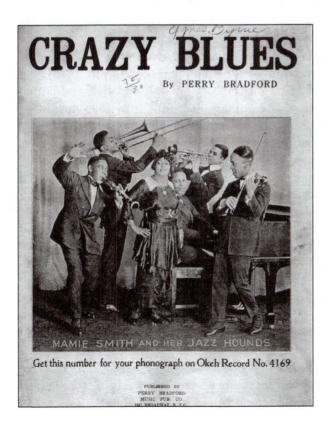

Figure 7.3
1920 sheet music cover of Perry Bradford's composition "Crazy Blues," advertising Mamie Smith's recording, the first recorded blues vocal by an African American singer. Sheet music courtesy Richard Raichelson, photo by David Evans.

Beale Street Sheiks (Frank Stokes and Dan Sane), and the combination of harmonica and guitar, as in the work of Bobbie Leecan and Robert Cooksey, were also popular at this time. So, too, was the combination of piano and guitar, first popularized in 1928 in the recordings of Leroy Carr and Scrapper Blackwell and those of Georgia Tom (Dorsey) and Tampa Red (Hudson Whitaker).

Blues musicians also formed larger groups, made up of various combinations of string, wind, and percussion instruments, known as jug bands, skiffle bands, juke bands, washboard bands, string bands, and hokum bands. Such groups sometimes included homemade instruments and household objects, such as the kazoo, jug, washboard, spoons, and washtub (or bucket) bass. These instruments were cheap, readily available, and often had an added humorous or novelty value. Most represented reinterpretations of African prototype instruments. Some of the better-known recording groups of this sort were the Memphis Jug Band, Cannon's Jug Stompers (Track 8), Whistler's Jug Band, the Mississippi Sheiks, and the Hokum Boys. All of these duos and small groups were especially prominent in urban centers of both the South and North, allowing rural migrants to find common ground in their solo performance styles, explore new musical directions, and compete with more established urban musicians.

"Viola Lee Blues."

The Great Depression effectively killed the institution of vaudeville and the blues style that was associated with it. As the recording industry began to recover in the early 1930s, Chicago became the primary center of blues recording activity, and the studios concentrated on stables of reliable stars who could sing, play their own accompaniment, help one another on records, and compose original songs to supply the increasing number of jukeboxes. This was a decade of consolidation and homogenization in the blues. The primary instruments of folk blues were brought into small ensembles (or made to suggest their sounds), as exemplified by the work of guitarists Big Bill Broonzy and Robert Johnson, pianist Roosevelt Sykes, and harmonica player John Lee "Sonny Boy" Williamson. Other stars of this period, who sometimes performed on one another's records, were Washboard Sam, Bumble Bee Slim, Jazz Gillum, Peetie Wheatstraw, Walter Davis, Curtis Jones, Johnnie Temple, Georgia White, Lil Johnson, Merline Johnson, Rosetta Howard, Lil Green, Bill Gaither, Blind Boy Fuller, Kokomo Arnold, and Arthur "Big Boy" Crudup.

Jump blues
An up-tempo blues style of the 1940s and 1950s characterized by boogie-woogie bass lines, shuffle rhythms, and prominent brass and reed sounds.

In 1937, the Harlem Hamfats, a seven-piece group based in Chicago and made up of Mississippi blues and New Orleans jazz musicians, pioneered a new type of blues combo sound that was a precursor of the modern blues band. Small combos continued to be popular into the 1940s, gradually adopting a louder and more rhythmic style known as **jump blues**.

Further jazz and pop influences were heard during this decade in the singing styles of such crooners as Cecil Gant, Charles Brown, and

David Evans

Ivory Joe Hunter, and shouters such as Wynonie Harris, Roy Brown, and Big Joe Turner. Female singers such as Dinah Washington, Ella Johnson, Nellie Lutcher, Julia Lee, Hadda Brooks, and Big Maybelle served as counterparts to the male crooners and shouters. These styles were especially prominent in urban centers of the Midwest and California, where many African Americans had migrated during and after World War II. Most of these artists sang other material besides blues, and their familiarity with popular and jazz styles enabled their blues to approach and enter the American popular musical mainstream.

Also coming to prominence in the late 1930s and 1940s was a piano blues style known as "**boogie-woogie**." The etymology of the term is uncertain, but it originally described a dance party or a place where such a party took place. Essentially, it is a type of rhythmic barrelhouse piano that features repeated bass figures, or riffs, often transposed to fit the tune's harmonic structure, over which the right hand plays lines that are to some degree improvised and often in a counterrhythm to the bass.

The boogie-woogie style originated among self-taught pianists in saloons and house parties, who substituted riff figures for the older ragtime-derived left-hand technique of alternating bass notes and chords to outline the tune's harmonic pattern. Boogie-woogie is attested from the 1910s and was recorded sporadically in the 1920s and more frequently from 1929 following the success of "Pine Top" Smith's "Pine Top's Boogie Woogie" (Figure 7.4). It entered spectacularly into the world of popular music through presentations at Carnegie Hall by Meade "Lux" Lewis, Albert Ammons, and Pete Johnson in 1938 and 1939. These artists, along with Jimmie Yancey, Camille Howard, and many others,

Boogie-woogie
Piano style popularized in the 1930s and 1940s that features repeated bass figures (riffs) against a syncopated improvised melody.

Figure 7.4
Piano bass (left-hand) figure of "Pine Top's Boogie Woogie" (Brunswick 80008) by Pine Top Smith, recorded in Chicago, December 29, 1928, notated in the treble clef, key of C. The riff of the first measure is simply transposed according to the standard harmonic pattern of the twelve-bar three-line blues.

popularized this style through the 1940s. It was often adapted by guitarists as well as swing bands and had a great influence on jazz, country and western, gospel, and the emerging rock and roll.

The Electric Guitar

From the earliest days, blues guitarists sought to increase their instrument's volume in order to be heard in noisy environments (saloons, house parties, street corners) and by larger audiences. They used metal strings and finger picks on acoustic guitars and eagerly embraced the new and louder steel-bodied guitars that were first manufactured in the 1920s. Some of the best-known blues recording artists began using electric guitars as early as the late 1930s. The electric guitar was an important factor in new blues sounds that came to prominence in the late 1940s and 1950s. The guitar's role in small combos was enhanced by the louder volume and new timbres of the electric instrument, played alongside the piano and the harmonica, which was now also played through a microphone and amplifier. Such recently arrived southern musicians as Muddy Waters (McKinley Morganfield), Howlin' Wolf, Little Walter, Jimmy Reed, and Elmore James pioneered in these small electric blues combos in Chicago and other cities during this period. At the same time, a new jazz-influenced hornlike lead style of playing, featuring extensive string bending, was being developed in the cities of the West Coast and South by guitarists Aaron "T-Bone" Walker, Lowell Fulson, Clarence "Gatemouth" Brown, Pee Wee Crayton, B.B. King, and others, working usually with larger bands containing horn sections. The electric guitar also gave new life to the tradition of solo guitar-accompanied folk blues, as exemplified in the music of artists Sam "Lightnin'" Hopkins and John Lee Hooker.

Soul Blues

During the 1950s and reaching full fruition in the 1970s, a melismatic, emotional, gospel-influenced singing style, known as soul blues, became popular, as one hears in the work of B.B. King, himself a pioneer in the modern lead guitar style. Soul blues can be viewed as a branch of the broader genre of **soul music**, and the term clearly highlights the influence of gospel singing style and suggests a deep emotionalism and sincerity in the singing. Indeed, a number of soul blues singers began their performing careers as gospel soloists or quartet singers. The style is especially common among urban blues singers from the South and upper Midwest, but it gained national popularity through recordings and tours. Other early soul blues singers were Bobby "Blue" Bland, Ray Charles, and James Brown. None of these artists, or those who followed them, restricted their singing only to blues material. This singing style, along with the introduction of the electric bass and organ toward the end of the 1950s, is perhaps the last major stylistic innovation in blues, whose popular contemporary sound is quite similar to what it was in the 1970s (Figure 7.5).

Soul music
Gospel-influenced African American popular music style that began to emerge in the late 1950s and became popular during the 1960s.

David Evans

EXPANSION OF THE BLUES AUDIENCE

It was during the 1970s, however, that large numbers of White Americans, as well as people overseas, began to take an interest in blues music. This interest included historical research, recording, sponsorship of concerts and tours, and participation in the performance of the music itself. White performers were not only attracted to the sound of the music but sometimes also viewed the blues as a vehicle for expressing rebelliousness against sexual, social, and political restraints. These artists varied in musical quality and in their abilities to absorb stylistic traits of African American originators, but in general they benefited from the easier sense of identification given to them by the new White audience as well as the generally more secure financial position of the White community and its dominance in the mass media. Some of the most prominent White blues artists have been John Hammond Jr. and Bonnie Raitt among solo performers; guitarist-singers Eric Clapton (British), Stevie Ray Vaughan, and Johnny Winter; harmonica player Charlie Musselwhite; and the Paul Butterfield Blues Band, Canned Heat, the Allman Brothers, and ZZ Top. This expansion of the blues constituency from its original Black American base has resulted in increased opportunities for performers as well as a revival of many older blues styles that had lost much of their popularity with the original audience. After approximately a century of survival in a kind of cultural, social, and musical underground, the blues has emerged to gain worldwide respect and recognition as a distinct and influential type of music.

In addition to having its own history and stylistic development, the blues has played an important role in most other major popular musical genres in the United States. This role can include the use of the twelve-bar three-line blues form, blue notes and blues scales, typical blues imagery and thematic material, typical blues instrumentation and instrumental techniques (e.g., slide guitar), and the general improvisational quality and tonal experimentation of the blues. The intrusion of the blues into ragtime in the first two decades of the twentieth century has already been mentioned. The tonal flexibility and improvisational performance style of the blues probably hastened the decline of ragtime itself. Blues tunes form a major part of the repertoire of early jazz, and one can hardly imagine jazz music at all without blue notes, improvisation, and many other qualities doubtless introduced mainly through the blues. The blues has continued to anchor a number of new jazz styles, most notably bebop. Country music had absorbed the blues form by the 1920s, its first major manifestation being the blue yodel as popularized by Jimmie Rodgers. Blues continued to be a major ingredient in the western swing and honky-tonk styles of the 1930s through the early 1950s and has made a comeback in contemporary country rock styles. Many early rock and roll performers of the 1950s, such as Elvis Presley, Carl Perkins, and Jerry Lee Lewis, had a background in country music, which they fused with newly acquired skills in the blues inspired by contemporary Black artists. Many Black performers of this time, in fact, made important contributions to rock and roll, such as Little Richard, Chuck Berry, Fats Domino, and Bo Diddley, performing music that was largely blues-based. Many rock styles of the 1970s, such as surf music, British rock, and psychedelic rock, made considerable use of blues repertoire and style, and the blues experienced a resurgence within rock in the 1990s. The blues also influenced gospel music through the increased use of blue notes and instrumentation, particularly the guitar. One of the leaders in introducing blues elements in the 1930s was gospel pioneer Thomas A. Dorsey, himself an ex-blues singer, pianist, and songwriter. Rap artists also have continued to sample blues riffs from earlier recordings. Finally, a number of important twentieth-century composers in the classical tradition, such as George Gershwin and William Grant Still, were greatly influenced by the blues. If one also considers the profound influence of the blues on the popular musics of Europe, Asia, Latin America, and Africa, the blues would have to be a strong candidate for being the most influential music of the twentieth century.

KEY NAMES

Paul Butterfield	Bessie Smith
W.C. Handy	Mamie Smith
B.B. King	Muddy Waters
Gertrude "Ma" Rainey	

QUESTIONS

1. Where and when did the blues develop? What African and European musical elements are evident in the blues?

2. Define the form and structure of the blues. Consider both musical and textual characteristics.

3. How was the blues first popularized? Identify the earliest documented performers of the blues and the contexts in which they performed.

4. Over time, how did changes in instrumentation and performance impact the evolution of the blues?

5. As the blues evolved historically, how did it shape other musical traditions? Provide examples from within the United States and beyond.

PROJECTS

1. Create an original diagram demonstrating how African American life influenced the blues and how the blues, in turn, influenced American culture at large.

2. Survey recordings of two different major blues performers, and identify at least six different textual themes among them. What does this thematic variety suggest about the scope of blues texts?

3. Review a documentary film about blues styles that emerged before the 1940s. Critique the content for musical and historical accuracy as well as the treatment of issues of race and culture.

4. Write a focused research paper that explores how issues of race, class, and/or gender have impacted the professional lives and careers of blues artists during and after the Jim Crow era.

5. Read at least three blues-influenced works by noted poets or other major literary figures. What characteristics of blues lyric forms, themes, or other aspects of blues music are evident?

CHAPTER 8

Art/Classical Music

Josephine R.B. Wright

A small number of classically trained African American composers worked professionally in the United States before the Civil War. Most lived above the Mason-Dixon line, but some resided in slave states. They received their formal instruction in music largely from immigrant European musicians who had settled in large metropolitan centers. Some learned from local practitioners or were self-taught. Generally, these early pioneers wrote short compositions based upon European American models (e.g., ballads, hymns, anthems, glees, marches, overtures); social dance music (e.g., waltzes, quadrilles, cotillions, mazurkas, polkas);[1] descriptive pieces for piano; or piano arrangements of patriotic songs, minstrel tunes, or popular operas. Their music featured straightforward tuneful melodies with simple diatonic harmonies.

Emancipation brought increased opportunities for professional training and exposure for Black composers. A small number studied after the Civil War at selected American colleges, universities, and music schools, where they received conservatory training that enabled them to write in larger musical forms such as opera, oratorio, cantata, symphony, or chamber music based upon classical models. By the end of the nineteenth century, musical nationalism (a movement that first emerged in Eastern Europe and spread to the United States by the dawn of the twentieth century) lured some Black composers to explore the use of African and African American musical idioms in Western art forms to affirm their cultural heritage.

The early twentieth century witnessed the emergence of several prominent conservatory-trained composers who taught at traditional

Black colleges and universities. A few won critical acclaim at home as well as abroad for their compositions, which ran the gamut of contemporary forms and styles. Their legacy was passed on to a younger generation of composers active during the 1960s and beyond, whose impact was felt throughout the academy and music industry, both in the United States and abroad, at the dawn of the twenty-first century.

BEFORE EMANCIPATION (1760s–1862)

A small group of Black composers flourished prior to Emancipation. Newport Gardner (1746–1826), from Rhode Island, has long been considered the earliest Black singing schoolmaster and composer. Brought from Africa to the American colonies in 1760, he was sold as a slave to Caleb Gardner, a prominent merchant of Newport. With assistance from his master's wife, Newport studied music briefly with Andrew Law, an itinerant composer, and he gained sufficient proficiency to teach others. In 1791, he won a lottery, which enabled him to purchase his freedom and open a singing school in Newport, where he taught Black as well as White students. He reportedly composed a choral composition, entitled "Promised Anthem" (c.1764), which has apparently been lost.[2]

During the **antebellum period**, Philadelphia, Pennsylvania, the nation's first capital, served as the cultural capital for Black America. It was host to the first generation of Black composers to compete successfully with White musicians, largely immigrants, for public patronage.[3] Despite racism, talented Black musicians flourished in the city. American audiences of the late eighteenth and early nineteenth centuries viewed professional musicians largely as purveyors of entertainment (i.e., as a servant class), rather than elevated cultural leaders in society, and race proved less of an inhibiting factor for the Black composer-musician at this time than it would in the post-Reconstruction era when judicial segregation of the races became the law of the land. Henry Raynor reminds readers that the pattern of music making in colonial America mirrored concert life in eighteenth-century England. During the eighteenth century, professional musicians in Europe were generally not embraced by members of genteel society as equals, inasmuch as they earned their livelihoods by giving concerts or working for patrons. Even when European musicians immigrated to the United States in large numbers after the Revolutionary War, Americans of the early nineteenth century experienced no social conflict in employing free Blacks or slaves to supply music for their functions.[4]

Among the leading Black composers of the Philadelphia school were Francis "Frank" Johnson (1792–1844), its acknowledged leader; James Hemmenway (1800–49); Isaac Hazzard (1804–c.1864); William Appo (c.1808–c.1877); and Aaron J.R. Connor (d. 1850). Johnson (Figure 8.1) was apparently born in the city.[5] A virtuoso on the keyed bugle, a music

Antebellum period
The period before the Civil War, when slavery was still the law of the land.

FRANK JOHNSON.

Published at the Arch St. Gallery of the Daguerreotype, Philadelphia.

PRINTED BY WAGNER & M'GUIGAN.

1846.

teacher, and a band director, he first came to public attention as a composer with the publication of his *A Set of New Cotillions* (1818). Between 1820 and 1844, he organized a dance orchestra and a smaller military band, and he toured widely with these ensembles along the eastern seaboard of the United States. He even ventured as far west as Missouri (then a slave state), performing much of the music he composed and arranged for White as well as Black functions.[6] From 1837 to 1838 he traveled to London, England, with band members Aaron J.R. Connor, Edward de Roland, William Appo, and Francis V. Seymour. He gave a series of concerts there, becoming the first American, Black or White, to tour Europe with such a group. Johnson published over two hundred compositions, mostly ballad songs, marches, and piano arrangements of social dances, and he left many compositions in manuscript. Several of his works have associations with Philadelphia: for example, "General Lafayette's Grand March" (1824), which was commissioned by city fathers in honor of the Revolutionary War hero's visit to the city, and the "Philadelphia Firemen's Cotillion" (*c.*1814–41), composed and respectfully dedicated to members of the Fire Association.

Although the association of Frank Johnson and James Hemmenway remains unclear, Hemmenway directed a band at Philadelphia's

Washington Hall, and he composed music, including his *The Fifth Set of Quadrilles* (1828) for the pianoforte; the "Philadelphia Serenading Grand March" (c.1826–30), arranged for the pianoforte with an accompaniment for the flute or violin; and the "Philadelphia Hop Waltz" (c.1815–41). Isaac Hazzard led another local ensemble in the 1830s and published several compositions for band, including the "Lucy Neale Quadrille" (1844), "Croton Waltz" (1844), and "Davis' Quickstep" (c.1844–47).[7]

William Appo, a member of Johnson's band, worked in New York City as early as the 1830s. He is remembered for two compositions: the anthem "Sing unto God," and "John Tyler's Lamentation," commissioned by the Utica (New York) Glee Club for the presidential campaign of 1844. The composer William Brady (d. 1854) was also active in New York City during the 1830s, as was the composer Aaron J.R. Connor, another member of Johnson's band who organized an instrumental ensemble during the late 1840s and performed in Philadelphia and Sarasota Springs, New York. Connor's ballad "My Cherished Hope, My Fondest Dream" appeared in the *Anglo-African Magazine* in 1859. And Peter O'Fake (1820–83), another composer and arranger, maintained a music studio in Newark, New Jersey, where he led a society orchestra in the 1840s and 1850s.[8]

Henry F. Williams (1813–1903) ran a music studio in Boston during the early 1840s. A composer of ballads, dance music, overtures, anthems, and marches, he arranged band music around this time for Patrick S. Gilmore, a local White conductor. After the death of Frank Johnson, Williams moved to Philadelphia and became the arranger for the reconstituted Johnson band. He is best known as a composer of such ballad songs as "Lauriett[e]" (1840), "Come, Love, and List Awhile" (1842), and "It Was by Chance We Met" (1866). His career lasted well past 1870.

Ohioans boasted of Justin Miner Holland, a classically trained guitarist, arranger, and composer (1819–87), who was born to free parents in Norfolk County, Virginia. After his parents died, he left the slave state in 1833 for Boston and the Chelsea area of Massachusetts, where he worked and studied music theory, flute, and guitar.[9] He reportedly attended the Preparatory Department of Oberlin Collegiate Institute (later Oberlin College) for one year (1841–42)[10] and later studied in Mexico during 1844. From 1845 to 1886 he resided in Cleveland, Ohio, where he maintained a studio and was active as a performer and teacher of classical guitar. During this period, he developed a national reputation as a composer and arranger for that instrument. According to Karl Merz, editor of *Brainard's Musical World* (the forerunner of *Etude* magazine), Holland collaborated professionally across interracial lines at a time when segregation was the norm throughout America.[11] Holland published two important guitar tutors, as well as numerous duets, solo compositions, and arrangements for the guitar.

Joseph William Postlewaite (c.1827–89), another free Black, directed several bands in St. Louis, Missouri, circa 1857–60, despite Missouri being a slave state. He wrote marches and popular social dance music of the period (e.g., waltzes, mazurkas, quadrilles, schottisches). Several of his compositions remained in print as late as 1870.[12]

Around 1857, Thomas Green Wiggins Bethune (a.k.a. "Blind Tom"), a prodigy slave, was promoted in Georgia as a concert pianist and composer by his owner, Col. James N. Bethune. Reportedly a savant, Blind Tom (1849–1908) actually received music instruction from the owner's wife and daughters, and tutors were hired to perform new repertoires of music for him and transcribe the musical compositions he created at the keyboard. During the Civil War he gave concerts to benefit wounded Confederate soldiers. After the war, the Bethune family retained legal custody of him on the pretext of managing his concert career, which extended through 1905. During these years, Blind Tom gave concerts widely throughout the United States, Canada, and Great Britain and earned large sums for his managers.[13] According to contemporary observers, he possessed an unusual ability to play from memory any composition after hearing it once. The repertoire of music he performed consisted primarily of nineteenth-century keyboard literature by European or American composers, piano transcriptions of popular operas, and works of his own composition. He reportedly composed more than one hundred keyboard pieces, primarily dances, marches, character pieces, and programmatic music in the romantic style of his era. One of his popular compositions was the descriptive "The Battle of Manassas" (1866).

Antebellum New Orleans produced several professional musicians among its free Black and Creoles-of-color community, including Victor-Eugène Macarty (1821–81), Edmond Dédé (1827–1903), the brothers Charles-Lucièn (c.1828–96) and Sidney Lambert (c.1838–c.1900/09), Samuel Snaër (1835–1900), and Basile Barès (1845–1902). Macarty, Snaër, and Barès worked primarily in the city. Macarty, an accomplished singer and pianist, performed at fashionable soirées and published *Fleurs de salon: 2 Favorite Polkas* (1854). Snaër played the organ at St. Mary's Catholic Church on Charles Street for many years. After the Civil War, he joined forces with Victor-Eugène Macarty and Basile Barès to organize a series of concerts at the Orleans Theater principally for Creoles of color. Snaër composed liturgical music as well as orchestral music and works for solo voice and piano. He conducted the New Orleans performance of Dédé's *Quasimodo Symphony* at the Orleans Theater on May 10, 1865.[14]

The Lamberts pursued professional careers outside the United States as pianists, composers, and music teachers. Charles-Lucièn studied in Paris in 1854 and emigrated in the 1860s to Brazil, where he opened a piano and music store and taught privately. Sidney likewise studied in Paris, where he settled and became a piano teacher and performer. Over one hundred compositions for keyboard are credited to the Lambert brothers in the Bibliothèque Nationale in Paris, primarily dances, variations, and descriptive pieces for piano.

Edmond Dédé similarly established his career in France. A gifted violinist, he attended the Paris Conservatory in 1857, becoming possibly the first Black from North America to be accepted by the institution. He studied violin there with Jean-Delphin Alard and composition with Jacques-François Halévy. Following completion of his studies at the conservatory, Dédé settled in Bordeaux, France, which had a sizeable Black population at that time. There he married a French woman named Sylvie Anna Leflet, and he directed several theatrical orchestras from circa 1860 to 1889. From 1891 to 1893 he settled in Paris and devoted himself to composing music. According to his biographer Marcus B. Christian, Dédé's dramatic aria, "Le serment de l'Arabe: Chant dramatique" (1865), was reportedly composed during a brief visit to Algeria.[15] Several of Dédé's compositions are housed in the Bibliothèque Nationale in Paris.[16]

POST-EMANCIPATION (1863–1900)

President Lincoln's **Emancipation Proclamation** in 1863, followed two years later by cessation of fighting between the Union and Confederate armies, spurred the US Congress to pass the nation's first Civil Rights Acts to protect the newly freed men and women; the Thirteenth, Fourteenth, and Fifteenth Amendments to the Constitution, passed between 1865 and 1870, extended federal protection to African Americans by abolishing slavery, granting citizenship to all Black Americans, and giving Black men the right to vote. Such legislation brought hope to many in the African American community that they might someday be assimilated into the greater American society. That optimism was reflected in the creative and performing arts by an unprecedented outpouring of musical erudition within Black America in the late nineteenth century, releasing a floodgate of pent-up hopes and desires for cultural parity with White America in the creative and performing arts.

Emancipation Proclamation
The official 1863 proclamation by President Lincoln, which freed slaves below the Mason-Dixon line.

Musicians born during the post-Emancipation era would exert considerable influence upon concert life in Black America during the first half of the twentieth century. A selected list of prominent composers of that generation includes Harry T. Burleigh (1866–1949), Will Marion Cook (1869–1944), Harry L. Freeman (1870–1954), J[ohn] Rosamond Johnson (1873–1954), Clarence Cameron White (1880–1960), R. Nathaniel Dett (1882–1943), Francis Hall Johnson (1888–1970), Florence Price (1888–1953), Eva Jessye (1895–1992), William Grant Still (1895–1978), Shirley Graham (1896–1977), Edward Boatner (1898–1981), William Levi Dawson (1899–1990), and John Wesley Work III (1901–67). All came of age in a segregated America. Yet each received advanced music education at reputable colleges, universities, or conservatories of music that prepared them for leadership roles. Burleigh studied, for example, at the now-defunct National Conservatory in New York (1892–96); Oberlin Conservatory claimed Cook (1884–88), White (1896–1901), Dett (BM, 1908), Still (1917, 1919), and Graham (BM, 1934; MM, 1935); the New England Conservatory nurtured J. Rosamond Johnson (1892–95) and Price (Diploma, 1906); Hall Johnson (no relation to J. Rosamond Johnson) graduated from the University of Pennsylvania (BA, 1910); Dawson attended the Horner Institute of Fine Arts in Kansas City, Missouri (BM, 1925), Boatner the Boston Conservatory of Music and Chicago College of Music (BM, 1932), and Work III the Institute of Musical Arts, now the Juilliard School of Music (1923–24) and Yale University (BM, 1933). A few even pursued additional training in Europe and/or obtained advanced graduate instruction in the United States.

Such academic training prepared this generation to assume more visible roles in the musical erudition and cultural uplift of Black America than their predecessors. More than half would hold teaching appointments at some point in their careers at traditional Black institutions, where they trained Black students before the end of judicial segregation of schools—e.g., Freeman taught at Wilberforce University (1902–04); Price at Shorter College (1906–10) and Clark College (1910–12); Dett at Lane College (1908–11), Lincoln University in Missouri (1911–13), Hampton Institute (1913–31), and Bennett College (1937–42); Jessye at Morgan State (1919–20); White at West Virginia State (1924–30) and later Hampton Institute (1932–35); Work III at Fisk University (1927–66); Dawson at Tuskegee Institute (1931–55); and Boatner at Samuel Huston College (c.1933). A few managed to sustain themselves largely through composing/arranging music, performing, or teaching music privately.

Many of these composers came under the influence of the musical nationalism espoused by the Czechoslovakian composer Antonin Dvořák. Philanthropist Jeannette Thurber recruited Dvořák to America as musical director of the National Conservatory of Music in New York City from 1892 to 1895. While in the States, he advocated building a national school of American music based upon use of slave plantation songs and the music of Native Americans. His *Symphony No. 9 ("From the New World")* was purportedly inspired by these influences.[17]

Another major influence was Afro-British composer Samuel Coleridge-Taylor (1875–1912), who advocated use of Black musical idioms in classical art forms to establish an American national school of composition. Early in his career, Coleridge-Taylor established a reputation in Great Britain as a composer and music director by conducting his compositions at the festivals in Bournemouth, Brighton, Gloucester, Kendal, and Westmorland. By the time of his death, he enjoyed a solid international reputation as a composer of more than one hundred and fifty compositions, including such extended choral works as the cantatas *Hiawatha's Wedding Feast* (1898) and *The Death of Minnehaha* (1899), symphonies, symphonic essays, and chamber music for solo instrument or voice. Exposures in London during the late 1890s to the Black American poet Paul Laurence Dunbar and to the Fisk Jubilee Singers in 1899 led Coleridge-Taylor to experiment with Negro music idioms in classical forms. Among his influential works in that vein were *African Romances* (1897), *African Suite* (1898), and *Twenty-four Negro Melodies Transcribed for the Piano* (1905). He made three concert tours of the United States (in 1904, 1906, and 1910), where he conducted his music and collaborated with African American musicians. His status as the most important composer of African ancestry at the turn of the century gave rise to several Samuel Coleridge-Taylor societies in the United States during the early 1900s and inspired many classically trained African American composers in the early part of that century.[18]

While a small number of African Americans pioneered in writing large-scale forms such as opera, symphony/symphonic essay, concerto, or sonata in the academic European tradition, most concentrated pragmatically upon composing choral music intended for performance by student singers at the traditional Black colleges and universities where they taught. These composers preferred the more conservative harmonic language of the post-romantic era than the modern, dissonant techniques of early twentieth-century music that distorted the melodic character of the Negro folk idioms the composers sought to employ.[19] According to William Grant Still, "Through experimentation, I discovered that Negro music tends to lose its identity when subjected to the avant-garde style of treatment."[20] (Still flirted briefly with atonal techniques during the early 1920s under the tutelage of Edgard Varèse before abandoning that idiom and returning to a more conservative harmonic language.)

Harry T. Burleigh surfaced as one of the first African American composers born after Emancipation to gain broad acceptance nationally in the United States. He excelled in writing solo art songs, composing more than three hundred works in this genre that were performed by such famous White concert singers of the early twentieth century as John McCormack, Ernestine Schumann-Heink, and Lucrezia Bori. Burleigh's major contribution to Black music history lay, however, in his transformation of the Negro spiritual from the choral tradition popularized by the Fisk Jubilee Singers to the solo art song tradition of the concert stage. Commencing with his arrangement of "Deep River" (1916), he published numerous arrangements of Negro spirituals for solo voice and piano (or orchestral accompaniment) that now enjoy a permanent place in American art song literature.

Burleigh in turn influenced younger contemporaries, associated with music of the **Harlem Renaissance** and beyond, who arranged Negro spirituals and African American folk songs as art songs. J. Rosamond Johnson pursued this course, for example, in the *Book of American Negro Spirituals* (1925) and his *Second Book of Negro Spirituals* (1926), co-edited with his brother, the writer James Weldon Johnson (1871–1938). The

Harlem Renaissance
A period of literary and artistic flowering by African American intellectuals based in Harlem during the 1920s.

Johnsons are best remembered today as the authors of "Lift Every Voice and Sing" (1900), the Negro national anthem (also known as the official song of the NAACP). During the early 1900s, the brothers joined forces with songwriter Robert "Bob" Cole (1868–1911) and became a successful group, producing several popular songs.[21] J. Rosamond Johnson also co-authored four Black musicals with Cole: *The Belle of Newport* (1900), *Humpty Dumpty* (1904), *In Newport* (1904), and *Shoo-Fly Regiment* (1905–07); he also wrote the operetta *Red Moon* (1908) with Joe Jordan. James later published *Rolling Along in Song* (1937), a chronological survey of Black folk song literature, as well as the *Album of Negro Spirituals* (1940). Edward Boatner earned a solid reputation for his art song arrangements of "Let Us Break Bread Together," "On Ma Journey," "Trampin'," and "Oh, What a Beautiful City." William Dawson, John Work III, Eva Jessye, Francis Hall Johnson, Florence Price, and William Grant Still likewise contributed substantively to this repertoire.

Clarence Cameron White, undoubtedly the most influential composer and propagandist of the Harlem Renaissance, drew inspiration for his musical nationalism through personal contact with Samuel Coleridge-Taylor during the composer's visit to the United States in 1904, as well as from private study with him in London in 1906 and from 1908 to 1910. White's best-known compositions were his works for the violin (e.g., *Bandanna Sketches*, 1918; *Cabin Memories*, 1921; and *Concert Paraphrases of Traditional Negro Melodies*, 1927–36), *String Quartet No. 1 in E Minor* (1931), the opera *Ouanga* (1932), and *Kutamba Rhapsody* for orchestra (1942). He was a founding member of the National Association of Negro Musicians (NANM), and he served as president of that organization from 1922 to 1924.

Henry L. Freeman, Will Marion Cook, J. Rosamond Johnson, and Shirley Graham made pioneering incursions into musical theater during the opening decades of the twentieth century. Freeman first attracted attention in 1892–93 with his opera *Epthelia*, and he composed twenty-four additional operas between 1897 and 1947.[22] He wrote his own librettos, basing many on Black themes, and he combined African American musical idioms with European forms in these works. Will Marion Cook, a gifted concert violinist, abandoned a solo concert career for the theater and wrote *Clorindy, or, the Origin of the Cakewalk* (1898), a ragtime operetta (libretto by Paul Laurence Dunbar) that introduced Black syncopated music on Broadway. Cook later collaborated on fifteen Black Broadway musicals, including *In Dahomey* (1902), *Bandana Land* (1908), *Darkydom* (1915), *Negro Nuances* (1924), and *Swing Along* (1929).

Canadian-born R. Nathaniel Dett sought to preserve the character of traditional Black music in the choral and keyboard music he composed, much in the way nationalist composers from Eastern Europe had treated indigenous folk music from their respective countries in the late

Josephine R.B. Wright

nineteenth century.[23] To that end, Dett wove Negro spirituals into the fabric of such works as his oratorio *The Chariot Jubilee* (1919), the motet "Don't Be Weary Traveler" (winner of Harvard University's Francis Boott Prize, 1920), the motet "Listen to the Lambs" (1923), and the oratorio *The Ordering of Moses: Biblical Folk Scenes* (1932). He edited two choral anthologies, *Religious Folksongs of the Negro as Sung at Hampton Institute* (1927) and *The Dett Collection of Negro Spirituals* (1936), and experimented with the use of vernacular Black folk music in the keyboard suites *Magnolia* (1912) and *In the Bottoms: Characteristic Suite* (1913).

Shirley Graham (1896–1977), later Mrs. W.E.B. DuBois, distinguished herself as the first African American female to gain national recognition as a composer and librettist of opera with her full-length musical drama *Tom-Tom* (1932), which she wrote during her Oberlin years.[24] This epic, three-act opera traced two centuries of Black music, from Africa, to southern slave plantations in North America, to syncopated music in Harlem during the early twentieth century. First performed on July 29, 1932, in Cleveland, Ohio, with Jules Bledsoe and Charlotte Murray in leading roles and a cast of about five hundred, *Tom-Tom* was possibly the earliest Black opera produced on a grandiose scale with professional performers.[25] Graham later supervised the Negro Unit of the WPA Federal Theater in Chicago between 1936 and 1938, designing and composing such musical scores as *Little Black Sambo* (1938), a children's opera, and *The Swing Mikado* (1938), a syncopated parody of Gilbert and Sullivan.

Francis Hall Johnson and Eva Jessye organized professional Black choirs and carried the concert choral tradition of the Negro spiritual into the radio, theater, and film industries during the 1920s and 1930s. Hall Johnson's choir performed, for example, in both the Broadway and film versions of *Green Pastures* (1930, 1935), for which he contributed twenty-two arrangements of Negro spirituals for chorus and two original compositions, "Hail! de King of Babylon" and "Hallelujah! King Jesus." He later published these pieces in an anthology entitled *The Green Pastures Spirituals* (1932), and he wrote the folk opera *Run, Little Chillun!* (1933).[26]

Jessye broke new ground as one of the first female conductors, Black or White, of a professional concert choir in the United States.[27] She directed her choir in performances over NBC and CBS radio during the early 1930s, and she also directed them in the first performances of Virgil Thomson's *Four Saints in Three Acts* (1934) and George Gershwin's *Porgy and Bess* (1935). Jessye composed three oratorios: *The Life of Christ in Negro Spirituals* (1931), *Paradise: Lost and Regained* (1934), and *The Chronicle of Job* (1936), in which she combined the use of Negro spirituals with narrative dialogue.[28]

Florence Price became the first African American woman to gain international recognition as a composer,[29] winning two Holstein awards in composition (1925, 1927) and two first prizes in the 1932 Rodman

Wanamaker Foundation Awards for her *Piano Sonata in E Minor* and her *Symphony No. 2 in E Minor*; the latter received its debut performance a year later with Frederick Stock and the Chicago Symphony. Her art songs were widely performed by such African American singers as Marian Anderson, Roland Hayes, and Leontyne Price.

William Grant Still (Figure 8.2), the "Dean of African American composers," charted new vistas for classically trained Black composers between the 1930s and 1960s.[30] Drawing upon his experience as a performer in theater orchestras, in the recording studio as musical director-arranger of the Black Swan label (the first major record company run exclusively by Blacks), and in jazz, Still brought intimate knowledge of vernacular Black music to the craft of art music composition. He was, as Eileen Southern has observed, the first African American composer to apply sounds of blues and jazz to symphonic music;[31] he accomplished this in his watershed work, the *Afro-American Symphony* (1930), which was first performed in 1931 by Howard Hanson and the Rochester Philharmonic. A versatile composer, Still wrote four additional symphonies, several symphonic essays, extended pieces for orchestra, chorus, or soloists (e.g., *And They Lynched Him on a Tree*, 1940; *Plain-Chant for America*, 1941; and *Lenox Avenue: Choreographic Street Scenes for Dancers*

Figure 8.2
William Grant Still.
Courtesy of William
Grant Still Music,
Flagstaff, Arizona.
All rights reserved.

Josephine R.B. Wright

or Narrator, 1936), art songs, solo instrumental music, chamber music, and seven operas. His *Troubled Island* (first performed in 1949 by the New York City Opera) was the first full-length opera by a Black composer mounted by a major American company. Still likewise pioneered in the media, writing soundtracks for the films *Lost Horizon* (1935), *Pennies from Heaven* (1936), and *Stormy Weather* (1943), as well as incidental music for the original *Perry Mason* television show (1954). His awards included fellowships from the Harmon (1928), Guggenheim (1934, 1935, 1938), and Rosenwald Foundations (1939–40), along with commissions from CBS, the New York World's Fair, the League of Composers, and leading orchestras.

THE MODERN AND POSTMODERN ERAS (1900–2012)

Dramatic social and political changes occurred in the United States in the twentieth century: two great wars; the Depression; the historic *Brown v. Board of Education of Topeka* (1954), which struck down judicial segregation of public schools; and the Civil Rights Movement of the 1960s, which prompted the US Congress to pass new legislation to protect the civil liberties of Blacks. Composers born in this new century reaped innumerable benefits from many of these transitions: in particular, easier accessibility to quality higher education, the ability to travel extensively and have their compositions performed and heard by audiences around the world, as well as the ability to have their music published and recorded. By the 1950s, membership of African American composers in such licensing organizations as ASCAP and BMI had risen, ensuring greater protection of their intellectual property rights. Some composers received commissions by major organizations to write works. Several established composers obtained professorships at major American universities or schools of music by the 1970s, 1980s, and 1990s: for example, Ulysses Kay (1917–95) at Lehman College of the City University of New York; George Walker (b. 1922) at Rutgers University; Hale Smith (1925–2009) at the University of Connecticut at Storrs; T.J. Anderson (b. 1928) at Tufts University; Frederick Tillis (b. 1930) at the University of Massachusetts at Amherst; David Baker (b. 1931) at Indiana University; Olly Wilson (b. 1937) at the University of California at Berkeley; Wendell Logan (1940–2010) at Oberlin College Conservatory; and Tania León (b. 1943) at Brooklyn College of the City University of New York. A few, such as Howard Swanson (1907–78), Julia Perry (1924–79), Arthur Cunningham (1928–97), Leslie Adams (b. 1932), and Alvin Singleton (b. 1940), would devote their energies primarily to composing music, sustaining themselves largely through commissions, grants, freelance work, or private teaching. With increased national exposure, many secured coveted awards and grants from government agencies and private foundations.

By mid-century, Ulysses Kay, Howard Swanson, Julia Perry, and George Walker were well on their way to achieving national prominence as leading neoclassical composers who employed eighteenth-century forms and concepts and modern neotonal harmonies. Kay, a pupil of Bernard Rogers and Howard Hanson at the Eastman School of Music (MM, 1940), and later Paul Hindemith (1941–42) and Otto Luening (1942–46), composed compositions with no overt hint of African American overtones. Kay wrote elegant, lyrical melodies, punctuated by dissonant neotonal polyphony, rich orchestration, and pulsating rhythms. A prolific composer, particularly gifted as a symphonist, he also composed chamber works, art songs, choral music, and operas. Among his masterpieces are *Markings* (1966), a symphonic essay dedicated to the memory of Dag Hammarskjöld, Secretary-General of the United Nations, and the film score for James Agee's documentary *The Quiet One* (1948).[32]

Howard Swanson, who graduated from the Cleveland Institute of Music (BM, 1937) and later studied with Nadia Boulanger at the American Academy in Fountainebleau, France (1938), consciously integrated African American idioms into the neoclassical forms he created. He attracted critical attention in 1949 when Marian Anderson (1902–93), the celebrated Black contralto, sang his art song "The Negro Speaks of Rivers" (text by Langston Hughes) at Carnegie Hall. His *Short Symphony* received its world premiere in 1951 under conductor Dmitri Mitropolous and the New York Philharmonic Orchestra, and it won the New York Music Critics' Award one year later. While not a prolific composer, Swanson produced three symphonies, a concerto for orchestra, miscellaneous chamber pieces, two piano sonatas, and several art songs that remain staples in modern twentieth-century American art song literature.[33]

Julia Perry emerged during the early 1950s as one of the foremost American female composers of her era.[34] An alumna of Westminster Choir College (BM, 1947; MM, 1948), she also studied in France with Nadia Boulanger at Fontainebleau and took private instruction from the serialist composer, Luigi Dallapiccola, in Florence, Italy. She completed ten symphonies, a string quartet, a viola concerto, and assorted chamber instrumental music, as well as four operas and music for solo voice and assorted instruments. Her best-known work is *Stabat Mater* for contralto and string orchestra (1951), which launched her career, and *Homunculus C.F.* for piano, harp, and percussion (1960).

George Walker, an alumnus of Oberlin College Conservatory (BM, 1941), Curtis Institute (1941–45), and the American Academy at Fountainebleau (1947), became the first African American to earn the DMA degree from the Eastman School of Music (1957), as well as the first to win the coveted Pulitzer Prize in music (1996). Walker has developed a distinctive style that combines neoclassical compositional techniques with jazz and African American sacred and vernacular music.

Josephine R.B. Wright

His extensive list of works includes compositions for full orchestra, chamber ensembles, chorus, solo instruments, and solo voice. Among his most frequently performed compositions are *Lyric for Strings* (1946, rev. 1990), *Sonata for Cello and Piano* (1957), *Concerto for Piano and Orchestra* (1976), *Cello Concerto* (1982), and four piano sonatas (1953–84). Walker's Pulitzer Prize-winning *Lilacs for Soprano or Tenor and Orchestra* (text by Walt Whitman), a work commissioned by the Boston Symphony Orchestra in celebration of the career of Black tenor Roland Hayes (1887–1976), received its first performance by that ensemble with conductor Seiji Ozawa and soprano Faye Robinson on February 1, 1996.

Hale Smith, Olly Wilson, and Alvin Singleton, on the other hand, have experimented with a wide range of avant-garde techniques. Smith, the elder statesman of the group,[35] graduated from the Cleveland Institute of Music (BM, 1950; MM, 1952) and worked during the late 1950s and 1960s as a jazz arranger before being appointed to the music faculty of the University of Connecticut (1970–84). *Contours for Orchestra* (1961), a work commissioned and first performed by the Louisville Orchestra, employs twelve-tone serial technique.

Olly Wilson, the Jerry and Evelyn Hemmings Chambers Professor Emeritus of Music at the University of California at Berkeley, holds degrees from Washington University (BM, 1959), the University of Illinois at Urbana-Champaign (MM, 1960), and the University of Iowa (PhD, 1964). In 1968, he won first prize in Dartmouth College's First International Electronic Music Competition for *Cetus*, a piece for electronic tape. Since the 1970s he has experimented with acoustic instruments and electronic sounds. The influence of jazz, traditional African American idioms, and West African music are pronounced in his compositions, especially in such pieces as *Akwan* for piano, electronic piano, and orchestra (1972); "Sometimes" for tenor and electronic sound (1976); and *A City Called Heaven* for chamber ensemble (1988).

Alvin Singleton emerged during the mid-1980s as a star among the avant-garde. After spending much of the 1970s in Europe, he returned to the United States and served residencies as a composer with the Atlanta Symphony Orchestra (1985–88), at Spelman College (1988–91), and with the Detroit Symphony Orchestra (1996–97). Singleton has experimented with tonal as well as post-tonal pitch classifications, sound-space structures, and minimalist techniques. In recent years he has concentrated on writing large-scale orchestral music; for example, *After Fallen Crumbs* and *Shadows* (1987), written for the Atlanta Symphony; *Sinfonia Diaspora* (1991), commissioned by the Oregon Symphony; *Durch Alles* (1992) for the Cleveland Orchestra; and *Umoja—Each One of Us Counts* (1996), for the Olympic Games Cultural Olympiad.

Classical music and jazz found a synthesis in what has been called "**Third Stream**" music (a term coined in 1957 by Gunther Schuller), which has come to dominate the works of David Baker, Wendell Logan,

Third Stream
Style that combines jazz improvisation with instrumentation and compositional forms associated with classical music.

and Frederick Tillis, each of whom brings extensive experience as a jazz improviser to the craft of writing composed art music.[36]

David Baker, chair of jazz studies at Indiana University (1966–2012), is a prolific writer of more than two thousand compositions, which range in style from jazz scores to such classical music forms as the cantata, oratorio, art song, choral music, symphony, solo sonata, chamber music, and symphonic essay. Baker has experimented with infusing jazz elements with modern compositional techniques, gospel, pop, and electronic music.[37] Among his important works are the cantata *Le Chat qui pêche* for orchestra, soprano, and jazz quartet (1974); his *Concerto for Cello and Chamber Orchestra* (1975), which was commissioned by cellist Janos Starker; *Singers of Songs/Weavers of Dreams: Homage to My Friends* for cello and seven percussion instruments (1980); the seven-part song cycle *Through This Vale of Tears* (1968), composed in memory of Martin Luther King Jr.; and the jazz-inspired *Shades of Blue* for orchestra (1993).

Frederick Tillis, a professor emeritus of the University of Massachusetts at Amherst, has blended traditional African, African American, and Southeast Asian music with jazz and contemporary Western art forms and compositional techniques. Among his representative compositions are *Freedom* for a cappella chorus and percussion (1968); *Niger Symphony* for chamber orchestra (1975); *Concerto for Trio Pro Vivo* (1980); *Spiritual Fantasies*, a series of eighteen works composed for various instruments (1980–98); *Kabuki Scenes* for brass quintet and timpani (1991); and the song cycle *In Celebration* (1993).

Wendell Logan, former director of African American music/jazz studies and head of the Division of Contemporary Music at Oberlin College Conservatory, incorporated sounds of the spirituals, blues, gospel, and jazz of his youth with modern classical forms and techniques. His compositions varied in style from tonal and atonal pitch class explorations to experimentations with multimedia, electronic, and aleatoric music. He was the recipient of several major commissions, including the Cleveland Chamber Symphony (1990), Columbia College–Chicago's Center for Black Music Research (1995), the San Francisco Contemporary Music Players (1999/2000), and the Fromm Music Foundation at Harvard University (2000). Examples of his music are the quasi-serial chamber piece *Proportions for Nine Players and Conductor* (1968); *Runagate, Runagate* (based on a poem of the same title by Robert Hayden, 1989/1991) for tenor and chamber/full orchestra, where the composer sought "to capture some of . . . [the] poems' inherent musical qualities: the frantic beat of the fleeing fugitives, the steady, rumbling beat of a train (symbolic of the Underground Railroad); the unmistakable melodic character . . . of lines from spirituals";[38] *Roots, Branches, Shapes, and Shades (of Green)*, a one-movement concerto for piano, chamber orchestra, and jazz trio that won the Cleveland Arts Prize in Music (1992); and *Doxology Opera: The Doxy Canticles* (text by Paul Carter Harrison, 2001), described by Logan as "an all-women's opera . . . having

Figure 8.3
Tania León. Photo by
Michael Provost,
courtesy Kaylor
Management, Inc.

to do with the disappearance of men from the earth. The women perform
a yearly ritual to procreate."[39]

Tania León (Figure 8.3), a Cuban American composer, has credited
choreographer-dancer Arthur Mitchell, director of the Dance Theater of
Harlem, as being her first mentor.[40] From 1969 to 1980, León served as
music director of the Arthur Mitchell Dance Company; in the mid-1980s
she worked in a similar capacity for the Alvin Ailey Dance Company.
Since 1985, she has taught composition and conducting at Brooklyn
College of the City University of New York, where she also directed the
orchestra. She has also held residencies at the Ravinia Festival (1991),
the Cleveland Institute of Music (1992), and the New York Philharmonic
(Revson Composer Fellow, 1993–96). León has rejected the application
of ethnic, racial, or gender labels to her work because she believes that
such labels limit the boundaries of an individual.[41] Yet her compositions draw heavily upon **syncretic** sounds of her native Cuba, where
Afro-Cuban, Yoruba, Congolese, and Creole Spanish cultures comingle.
Her list of works includes ballets, operas, works for solo voice or
instrument, chamber music, and orchestral compositions—for example,

Syncretism
Process of
hybridization that
occurs when
different cultures
come into sustained
contact.

Batá for orchestra (1985, rev. 1988); *A la par* for piano and percussion (1986); the song cycle *Pueblo mulatto* (text by Nicolás Guillèn, 1987), a set of three songs for soprano and chamber orchestra that depict the lives of impoverished Blacks in Cuba; *Indígena* for chamber orchestra (1991); and the chamber opera *Scourge of Hyacinths* (based on a play by South African author Wole Soyinka), which won the 1994 BMW Prize for the best new opera performed at the fourth Munich Biennale Festival.

Among the promising composers born after 1950 are Anthony Davis (b. 1951), Donal Fox (b. 1952), Lettie Alston (b. 1953), Jeffrey Mumford (b. 1955), Regina Harris Baiocchi (b. 1956), Gregory Walker (b. 1961), Michael Abels (b. 1962), Nkeiru Okoye (b. 1972), and Daniel Bernard Roumain (b. 1972).

Anthony Davis, a professor of improvisation and piano at the University of California at San Diego, is well situated in both jazz performance and classical music composition. Classical music lovers best know him as a composer of operas that received considerable press coverage in the late 1980s and 1990s: *X: The Life and Times of Malcolm X* (first performance by the New York City Opera in 1986); *Tania*, based on the 1974 kidnapping of heiress Patty Hearst by the Symbionese Liberation Army (first performed at the American Music Theater Festival in 1992); and *Amistad*, which recounts the story of the 1839 mutiny aboard a slave ship and the ensuing trial before the US Supreme Court that freed its human cargo (first performance by the Chicago Lyric Opera, 1997). As a composer, Davis defies rigid stylistic categorization. He embraces an intercultural approach to music and draws from many sources—traditional as well as contemporary African American popular music, avant-garde modern techniques, and the Javanese gamelan—as reflected, for example, in the opera *Tania*, where these elements are combined.[42]

Donal Fox, who is similarly at home in jazz and the classical music world, writes highly original scores that continue the tradition of "Third Stream" music in the postmodern era. *Refutation and Hypothesis I: A Treatise for Piano Solo* (1981), which established Fox's career as a composer, juxtaposes jazz and avant-garde classical music techniques with spontaneous shouts, body slaps, and cursing. In *Chamber Improvisation II* (1992) and *Chamber Improvisation IV* (1993), works commissioned respectively by the Dinosaur Annex and Boston Musica Viva, Fox prompts classically trained chamber instrumentalists to improvise upon the scores and cues.[43]

Lettie Alston, a pianist-composer, is an associate professor at Oakland University (Michigan) with degrees in composition from Wayne State University (MM, 1978) and the University of Michigan (DMA, 1983). In 2001, she won the ASCAPLUS Standard Award from ASCAP for producing *Keyboard Maniac*, a compact disc that featured performances of her music by local Detroit artists. The anthology contains thirteen works that display various styles of her keyboard compositional technique, ranging from the jazz-inspired *Sonata of the Day* and *Keyboard Maniac* (*Rhapsody No. 4*) for solo piano, to *Sweet Memories* and *Echoes from the Spirit* for two pianos, to *Diverse Imagery* and *The End Times* for assorted electronic instruments.

Jeffrey Mumford, a distinguished professor at Lorain County Community College, has received commissions from the McKim Fund of the Library of Congress (1986), the Fromm Music Foundation (1990, 1999), the Walter W. Namburg Foundation (1991), the National Symphony Orchestra (1995), Meet the Composer/Arts Endowment Commissioning Music USA Program (1996), and the Nancy Ruyle Dodge Charitable Trust (2001), among others. His *as the air softens in dusklight* (1994) won the 1994 National Black Arts Festival/Atlanta Symphony Orchestra Competition, and his compositions have been performed widely in the United States and Europe. His compositional style features long lyrical lines encased in layers of simultaneous movement. A prolific composer, representative works include *her eastern light amid a cavernous dusk* for wind quintet (1983–84, rev. 1987); *the focus of blue light* for violin and piano (1987–88); *a diffuse light that knows no particular hour* for violin, cello, piano, flute, and clarinet (1989–90, rev. 1993); and *a pond within the drifting dusk* for alto flute, cello, and harp (1986–87, rev. 1988).[44] Among his latter works are *eight aspects of appreciation* for violin and viola (1996, rev. 2000), *a landscape of interior resonances* for piano (2001), *amid the light of quickening memory* (2002), and *fanfare (good dial days) (w)e (c)elebrate (l)uminous (v)oices* (2002), written for classical Cleveland radio station WCLV FM's celebration of its fortieth anniversary on the air.

Nkeiru Okoye, a Nigerian American composer who currently teaches as an assistant professor at the State University of New York at New Paltz, holds degrees from Oberlin College Conservatory (BM, 1993) and Rutgers University (MM, 1996; PhD, 2000), where she studied with the late Nigerian-born composer Noel Da Costa (1929–2002).[45] Okoye has won several awards for her compositions, including an ASCAP Grant for Young Composers for *The Genesis* (1995), an atonal orchestral essay performed in 2001 at the St. Louis Festival of African and African American Music.

Regina Harris Baiocchi of Chicago was a finalist in the 1992 Detroit Symphony Orchestra/Unisys Corporation Symposium with her *Orchestral Suite*. Her *African Hands*, a concerto for orchestra and four African drums, received an ASCAP Special Awards Grant in 1996–97. She writes in a style that combines classical European forms and techniques with Black folk-derived idioms such as spirituals, work songs, blues, gospel, jazz, and traditional African songs. Much of her music remains unpublished, although an earlier *Etude* for piano (1978), a serial work, appears in the anthology *Black Women Composers: A Century of Piano Music, 1893–1900*.[46]

Over the last two decades, Michael Abels has garnered attention as a composer, particularly for *Global Warming* (1991), an orchestral essay that the Detroit Symphony first featured on its African American Symphony Composers Forum in 1992. It was also one of the first compositions by a Black composer programmed by the South African National Symphony after Nelson Mandela's election as that country's president in 1994. An eclectic work, this composition commingles elements of traditional Irish, African, and Middle Eastern music and creates a musical collage of "America's melting pot."[47]

Gregory Walker follows in the footsteps of his father, the composer George Walker, and has emerged as an innovative voice among the younger generation of avant-garde composers. He holds undergraduate degrees in both music and English from Indiana University, as well as advanced music degrees from the University of California at San Diego (MA, 1985) and the University of Colorado at Denver (DMA, 1992). He is currently a professor of music at the University of Colorado at Denver. Walker is a recipient of the American Academy of Arts and Letters' Charles Ives Fellowship (2000), an annual cash award offered to gifted composers in the middle of their careers, and of an ASCAPLUS award in the Concert Music Division (2006–07).[48] His compositional style employs elements of contemporary music and popular music, most notably in *Dream N. the Hood* for chamber orchestra and rapper (1994),[49] which was commissioned by the Colorado Symphony in commemoration of Martin Luther King Jr., and in *micro*phone for Amplified Orchestra* (1995), which was performed by the Detroit Symphony in 1998.

The Haitian American composer Daniel Bernard Roumain (a.k.a. DBR), another young innovator, combines contemporary classical music with modern jazz, hip-hop, rock, and the traditional musics of various cultures. An accomplished violinist and guitarist, he holds music degrees from Vanderbilt University (BM, 1993) and the University of Michigan at Ann Arbor (MM, 1995; DMA, 2000). DBR formerly chaired the Department of Music Composition and Theory at the Harlem School of the Arts, where he was also the resident composer. In addition, he served as music director of the Bill T. Jones/Arnie Zane Dance Company. He is a 2002 recipient of a Van Lier Fellow awarded by the organization Meet the Composer. Among his representative works are *Haitian Essay for Orchestra* (1992); *King* and *The X String Quartet* (1993), two string quartets dedicated to Martin Luther King Jr. and Malcom X, respectively; *Hip-Hop Essay for Orchestra* (1995); *Harlem Essay for Orchestra and Digital Audio Tape*, which was commissioned by the American Composers Orchestra and premiered by that organization in 2000 at Carnegie Hall; and *I, Composer* (2002), which combines classical music and hip-hop. Written for electric/acoustic violin, drum loops, percussion, synthesizers, and string quartet, *I, Composer* includes taped samples of conversations and spoken dialogue that reflect the urban African American experience.

SUMMARY

Black composers have contributed to the classical music landscape of the United States for approximately two hundred years. They have composed in a variety of styles and forms that defy a priori classifications. Appropriating in the early beginnings European forms and styles of the romantic era, composers born after Emancipation turned inward and drew upon Black folkloristic elements to create a Black national style of music. While some would experiment with a variety of modernist musical concepts by the mid-twentieth century, several influential composers incorporated the sounds of urban Black America in their compositions during the closing decades of that century, giving birth to a post-nationalist style of African American concert music.

KEY NAMES

Michael Abels

Lettie Alston

Regina Harris Baiocchi

David Baker

Thomas Green Wiggins Bethune
   (a.k.a. "Blind Tom")

Harry T. Burleigh

Anthony Davis

Edmond Dédé

R. Nathaniel Dett

Donal Fox

Newport Gardner

Shirley Graham

Eva Jessye

Francis Hall Johnson

Ulysses Kay

Tania León

Wendell Logan

Jeffrey Mumford

Nkeiru Okoye

Julia Perry

Florence Price

Daniel Bernard Roumain
   (a.k.a. DBR)

Alvin Singleton

Hale Smith

William Grant Still

Howard Swanson

Frederick Tillis

George Walker

Gregory Walker

Clarence Cameron White

Olly Wilson

QUESTIONS

1. Who were the major Black composers and musicians in major cities such as Philadelphia, Boston, and New York during the antebellum period? What factors contributed to their development as musicians?

2. How did the Emancipation Proclamation and the Civil Rights Act that followed impact the classical music of Black composers? What role did colleges and universities play in the composers' musical development?

3. Provide examples of composers who consciously incorporated African American musical idioms in their works and those who did not. What styles or characteristic features of African American vernacular musics did composers incorporate into their classical music compositions?

PROJECTS

1. Plan a concert or concert series by major Black composers. Identify the composers and repertoire. Provide a brief description of how you organized the concert and why.

2. Select one of the composers profiled in this chapter and research his or her life and musical works. Create a one-page summary of your research, which includes a short biography, timeline, training, key compositions and significant writings by or about the composer, which could serve as a program supplement for a concert featuring this musician.

NOTES

Please see the discography for information on resources for further listening.

Biographical information on some of the people discussed in this chapter is based on entries in Southern 1982, Floyd 1999, and Sadie and Tyrrell 2001.

1. See Floyd and Reisser 1980, 161.
2. See Southern 1982, 142–43, and 1983, 36.
3. Southern 1997 (1971), 107-14.
4. Raynor 1978, 163.
5. Charpié 1999.
6. Southern 1977, 3–29.
7. Southern 1971, 114.
8. Trotter 1968 (1878), 304–06.
9. Clemenson 1989, 1–17.
10. Ibid.
11. See Merz 1887, 204.
12. *Complete Catalogue of Sheet Music and Musical Works* 1973 (1871).
13. See Southall 1979, 1983.
14. Liner notes for *American Classics: Edmond Dédé*, Naxos 8.559038 (2000).
15. Ibid.
16. Ibid.
17. See Tibbetts 1993.
18. See Southern 1982; Sayers 1915; Thompson 1994; and Self 1995.
19. R. Nathaniel Dett spoke about this in 1920 in his Bowdoin Literary Prize Thesis at Harvard University, entitled "Negro Music"; see Spencer 1991, 33.
20. Still 1992 (1975), 226.
21. Davidson 1980.
22. Spencer 1991, 75–80.
23. Southern 1971, 369.
24. Horne 2000.
25. Perkins 1985, 6–17.
26. Carter 1975.
27. See also Black 1986.
28. Ibid.; see also Wilson 1989.

Josephine R.B. Wright

29. See Jackson 1977, 30–43; Green 1983; and Brown 1987.
30. See Arvey 1939 and 1984; Still, Dabrishus, and Quin, 1996; Haas 1972; and Still 1984.
31. Southern 1997, 433.
32. See Hayes 1971; Hadley 1972.
33. See Ennett 1973; Jackson 1973; and Porter 1983.
34. See Walker-Hill 2002, 93–140.
35. Breda 1975.
36. See Schuller 1986b, 114–33, for his statements on Third Stream.
37. See Baker, Belt, and Hudson 1978, 15–69.
38. Logan 1992, 41–46.
39. Quoted in "Fromm Music Foundation at Harvard Announces 2000 Commissions" 2001.
40. See Lundy 1988, 218–19.
41. Ibid., 219; Oteri 1999.
42. Oja 2002, 6.
43. Garelick 2002.
44. "Works and First Performances," on Jeffrey Mumford's official website, accessed August 11, 2012, www.jeffreymumford.com.
45. See entry in Hine and Thompson 1997.
46. Walker-Hill 1992.
47. See Collins 1997.
48. "At a Glance," University of Colorado Denver website, accessed August 11, 2012, www.catalog.ucdenver.com.
49. See Ryan 1997.

PART III

Music in Migration
Urban Voices (1900–)

CHAPTER 9

Jazz

Ingrid Monson

Jazz is widely regarded as the pinnacle of African American music in the twentieth century, distinguished by the originality of its improvisation, the virtuosity and erudition of its performers and composers, and its professionalism and artistry. Many of its practitioners regard jazz as "America's classical music," or "African American classical music," although this definition is sometimes contested. The respectability acquired by jazz in the late twentieth century stands in stark contrast to the denigrated status of the music and its practitioners earlier in the century. Several broader social forces have shaped the history of jazz and its changing cultural meaning in the twentieth century, including urbanization, racism, the advent of recording and broadcasting techn-ology, modernism as an aesthetic ideology, World Wars I and II, and the Civil Rights Movement. The musical hallmarks of jazz are improvisation, syncopation, a rhythmic propulsiveness known as swing, blues feeling, and harmonic complexity. Unlike most other African American musical genres, instrumental rather than vocal performance has been the most prestigious and influential.

JAZZ AND RAGTIME

Several genres contributed to the formation of jazz, including **ragtime**, blues, marches, African American religious music, European classical music, American popular song, and musical theater. It is important to remember that these genres overlapped considerably, as the close relationship between ragtime, musical theater, and jazz at the turn of the

Ragtime
Style of African American music popular at the turn of the twentieth century, characterized by a syncopated melody placed against a steady bass line.

Coon song
Popular song style of the late nineteenth and early twentieth centuries that presented a stereotyped view of African Americans, often performed by White singers in blackface.

twentieth century illustrates. Although ragtime is most often associated with the piano compositions of Scott Joplin (*c.*1867–1917), audiences of the 1890s associated ragtime with song, especially so-called **coon songs** featuring lyrics about Black Americans, many of which emerged from the thriving African American musical theater scene in New York. Among the most noted Black American musical theater composers and performers of the day were Ernest Hogan (1860–1909), Will Marion Cook (1869–1944), "Bob" Cole (1868–1911), the Johnson brothers (J. Rosamond, 1873–1954, and James Weldon, 1871–1938), Bert Williams (1874–1922), and George Walker (1873–1911).[1]

After the success of Ernest Hogan's "All Coons Look Alike to Me" (1896), which launched a fad for coon songs that lasted until World War I, many of the pioneers of mainstream American musical theater began composing ragtime songs, including George M. Cohan (1878–1942) and Irving Berlin (1888–1989). Images of African Americans in ragtime song were largely stereotypical—derived from the representational conventions of minstrelsy and vaudeville—and contributed to a debate over ragtime's merits within both the Black community and mainstream American society. White society objected to the popularity of this "lowbrow" art form, while Black elites objected to the denigrating racial images in the songs.

Although ragtime made its initial impact on the musical stage, instrumental ensembles including dance bands, brass bands, and concert bands soon incorporated it into their repertories. Piano versions of ragtime songs were also published and, in time, a distinctive piano repertory emerged whose chief composers were Scott Joplin, James Scott (1885–1938), and Joseph Lamb (1887–1960). Perhaps the most famous piano rag is Joplin's "Maple Leaf Rag" (1899), which was widely performed by pianists and instrumental ensembles. In addition, both sung and instrumental versions of ragtime songs were associated with popular dances of the day, including the two-step, the cakewalk, the turkey trot, and the Texas Tommy.[2] By 1913, ragtime figured prominently in a craze for social dancing that witnessed the rise to prominence of dancers Vernon and Irene Castle. The Castles chose James Reese Europe's Society Orchestra to accompany them at their dance club known as Castle House. This collaboration led to the first recording contract offered to a Black ensemble: Europe's recording of "Down Home Rag," made in December 1913. Europe (1880–1919) recorded four more pieces in February 1914, including his "Castle House Rag," which is based on the form of Scott Joplin's "Maple Leaf Rag."

The most common trait associated with ragtime is syncopation. To "rag" a piece was to syncopate its melody. Instrumental ragtime made extensive use of 2/4 meter and march form—sixteen-bar strains or themes organized into various patterns. The most common formal arrangement consisted of two themes in the tonic key (AB or ABA) followed by a "trio" section consisting of one or two themes in the subdominant (C or CD). March forms are widely found in early jazz. Musical innovations leading to the development of jazz as a distinctive genre occurred within instrumental ensembles that included ragtime as part of their repertoire, and New Orleans occupied a special place in this process.

New Orleans

Although the historical narrative of New Orleans as the point of origin for jazz has been supplanted by one that emphasizes the interplay of local, regional, and national musical trends in the development of jazz, there is no doubt that the city of New Orleans occupies a special place in the story of jazz. The presence in New Orleans of French, Spanish, **Creole**, and African American (free and slave) populations, as well as the influx of immigrants from Cuba and the Caribbean, created an unusually diverse mixture of cultural influences. Most pertinent to the story of jazz is the tripartite division of New Orleans into White, Black, and Creole social spheres. Creoles, who celebrated their French cultural ties whether their heritage included African blood or not, had until 1894 been treated as a separate social sphere distinct from English-speaking African Americans. Creoles of color (the so-called *gens de couleur*) under this social system were not considered to be Black.

> **Creole**
> In southwest Louisiana, historically a person of mixed French and African ancestry.

However, New Orleans joined the trend across the South toward rigid Jim Crow segregation by passing strict segregation legislation in 1894 that reclassified the *gens de couleur* as Black. Downtown Creole musicians, formerly welcome in White brass and string bands, now had greater incentive to make common cause with their uptown English-speaking African American musical neighbors. The emergence of jazz has often been explained as the meeting of the uptown African American brass and string band tradition of blues-drenched, aurally transmitted music, with the downtown Creole band tradition of instrumental virtuosity, musical literacy, and training in classical music. Like all capsule histories, this story simplifies a more complicated reality that includes Creole musicians who did not have great musical literacy and Black musicians who did.[3]

Among the Creole musicians most important to the development of jazz are pianist and composer Jelly Roll Morton (Ferdinand LeMothe, 1890–1941), clarinetist Barney Bigard (1906–80), trombonist Kid Ory (1890–1973), and clarinetist and saxophonist Sidney Bechet (1897–1959). The uptown musicians most central to the emergence of jazz are cornetists Buddy Bolden (1877–1931), Joe "King" Oliver (1885–1938), and Louis Armstrong (1901–71).

A band led by Buddy Bolden is often cited as the first jazz band. Bolden was known for his deep feeling for the blues, improvisational elaboration of melodies, and ability to play so loud that he could be heard across Lake Ponchartrain. Bolden's competition in New Orleans included both brass bands and string bands, which featured a variety of repertoire including marches, ragtime, and waltzes. His ensemble, which included clarinet, cornet, trombone, guitar, bass, and drums, played a role in establishing the standard instrumentation for New Orleans jazz. By the early part of the twentieth century, contemporary observers agreed that New Orleans jazz featured an improvisatory style, the blues feeling of uptown Black New Orleans, and new rhythmic interpretations that had transformed a basic march beat into the slow drag and up-tempo strut, two basic distinctions of New Orleans jazz style.[4]

Chicago

Most of the classic recordings documenting the sound of New Orleans jazz, including those of Joe "King" Oliver and Louis Armstrong, were made in or near Chicago. Although New Orleans musicians and bands had traveled widely across the United States on variety show circuits between 1907 and 1917, the migration of over fifty thousand African Americans during and after World War I established Chicago as a primary destination for New Orleans musicians.

Joe "King" Oliver arrived in Chicago in 1918 and stayed for the next three years. After a sojourn in California, Oliver returned to Chicago in 1922, booking his Creole Jazz Band along "The Stroll," a thriving nightlife district on South State Street that featured several African American-owned clubs, including the Deluxe Café, the Pekin, the Dreamland Café, and the Lincoln Gardens.[5] Louis Armstrong joined Oliver's band in 1923, and the two set the town on fire with their vibrant music.

Chicago's Southside clubs also became sites of racial boundary crossing in the 1920s, as interested young Whites came to enjoy and learn the music. These "blacks and tans" attracted many aspiring young White musicians, including saxophonist Bud Freeman (1906–91), trumpeter Jimmy McPartland (1907–91), clarinetist Frank Teschemacher (1906–32), and drummer Dave Tough (1907–48). In the early 1920s, Chicago tolerated greater racial mixing in such venues than New York or New Orleans. Nevertheless, racial boundary crossing in Chicago was not reciprocal, because Black musicians were not free to patronize White clubs on the Northside. Even though jazz was a cultural arena in which there was greater interracial interaction than in mainstream American society, Jim Crow segregation had an enormous effect on the circumstances of interracial contact. Whites in general had greater freedom to cross the color line than African Americans.[6]

Between 1925 and 1928 Louis Armstrong made a series of recordings for OKeh (organized by his wife and pianist Lil Hardin) known as the Hot Fives and Sevens. These are among Armstrong's most celebrated recordings and they virtually defined the expansive improvisational style that was to become the hallmark of early jazz. Armstrong moved away from melodic paraphrase to a more elaborate improvisation guided by the underlying harmonies rather than the melody alone. Armstrong's solo on "Potato Head Blues" (Figure 9.1; Track 9) offers an excellent example of his classic style. Note the expressive use of vibrato at the ends (and

 9

"Potato Head Blues."

♩=c.180

Figure 9.1
Louis Armstrong's solo on "Potato Head Blues" (1928).

sometimes beginnings) of phrases, Armstrong's use of arpeggiation (mm. 2, 6, 8, 22), and chromatic fills between chord tones (mm. 16–17).

Armstrong's bandmates in the Hot Fives included Lil Hardin, piano; Johnny Dodds, clarinet; Kid Ory, trombone; and Johnny St. Cyr, banjo (the last three were old friends from New Orleans). The Hot Sevens added John Thomas, trombone; Baby Dodds, drums; Pete Briggs, tuba; and Earl Hines, piano. Despite the fact that these recordings were made in Chicago and that there are many earlier recordings by other bands that include improvised solos, Armstrong's style set the standard for New Orleans jazz style. The Hot Fives and Sevens recordings also established Armstrong as a cultural hero, especially in African American communities, where his tremendous success contributed to a communal sense of pride.[7]

COMPOSERS, ENSEMBLES, AND BIG BANDS

Although the emergence of the improvising soloist is the hallmark of jazz, it is important to note that the development of the jazz ensemble (large and small) was also key. Indeed, a particular sound produced through distinctive rhythmic, harmonic, melodic, and timbral vocabularies of the ensemble are just as crucial in defining jazz as a genre. Among the early jazz composers and arrangers who contributed to this emerging sound were Jelly Roll Morton, Duke Ellington (1899–1974), Fletcher Henderson (1897–1952), and Don Redman (1900–64).

Jelly Roll Morton's 1926 recordings for Victor provide examples of the creative use of the ensemble in early jazz. Among the most highly regarded compositions from these sessions are "Black Bottom Stomp," "Grandpa's Spells," "The Chant," and "Smokehouse Blues." Unlike the Hot Fives recordings, which omitted bass and drums, on Morton's 1926 recordings the listener can hear one of the best rhythm sections in early jazz: Morton, piano; John Lindsey, bass; Andrew Hilaire, drums; and Johnny St. Cyr, banjo. In "Black Bottom Stomp," Morton and his band deploy a full range of early jazz time feels to provide contrast and excitement to the well-planned architectural shape of the performance. The A sections of the piece proceed with a two-beat feel in cut time (bass notes on 1 and 3). The B sections include examples of two-measure solo breaks, stop time (repetition of a short pattern as the sole accompaniment), and extended solos. One B section proceeds partly in a four-beat time feel played by the bass, a technique foreshadowing the classic walking bass line that became standard in jazz of the 1930s. This passage is also an example of **double time**, a section in which the rhythmic pulse of the piece is doubled for dramatic effect (although the actual length of the measure remains the same; in a 4/4 measure, switching from a bass line that is played on beats 1 and 3 to a walking bass on beats 1, 2, 3, and 4 appears to double the pace of the music). Morton's final chorus might also be said to foreshadow the ubiquitous "**shout chorus**" of swing band arrangements. Here Morton's ensemble uses a back beat feel (drum on 2 and 4) for a rousing final chorus featuring trumpet and trombone.[8]

In New York of the 1920s, Fletcher Henderson and Don Redman developed a **big band** sound by incorporating jazz soloists such as Louis Armstrong and Coleman Hawkins (1904–69) into a dance band of larger instrumentation than the typical New Orleans jazz ensemble. Henderson's band featured three trumpets, a trombone, three reeds, and a rhythm section. Henderson and Redman worked as a team, developing an arranging style that featured **call–response** between the brass and reed

---

Double time
A section in which the rhythmic pulse of a piece is doubled for dramatic effect (although the actual length of the measure remains the same).

Shout chorus
In swing music, a climactic section usually occurring near the end of the arrangement.

Big band jazz
A form that evolved from New Orleans-styled combos in the late 1920s, characterized by the use of written arrangements and featuring the brass and reed sections trading melodic phrases in a call–response style.

sections and the use of one instrumental choir as a background accompaniment (often featuring a **riff**) for the other. Redman also wrote ensemble sections in the style of improvised jazz solos. All these devices and techniques became staples of big band arranging in the 1930s.

The composer who developed the most unique style for jazz ensembles in the 1920s was undoubtedly Duke Ellington. Ellington's singular style combined the "sweet" (i.e., not blues-inflected) dance band style, the exuberant New Orleans and blues-inspired trumpet style of New Yorker Bubber Miley (1903–32), and Ellington's own stride and ragtime-based piano style. Miley pioneered the growling trumpet sound that became a trademark of Ellington's so-called **jungle sound**. To produce this sound, Miley used a pixie mute (a small straight mute) over which he fanned an ordinary rubber bathroom plunger; the growling effect could be additionally enhanced by gargling with the throat and/or simultaneously humming a pitch into the horn. Ellington's recordings of "East St. Louis Toodle-Oo" and "Black and Tan Fantasy" from 1926 and 1927 provide excellent examples of Miley's "talking" brass effect. Tricky Sam Nanton (1904–46) adapted this sound to the trombone, and thereafter mastery of the growl sound was an essential for brass players in the Ellington band.[9]

These new brass sounds were only one aspect of Ellington's interest in timbral variety and unusual orchestration. "Mood Indigo" (Figure 9.2), one of the composer's most famous ballads, features an opening trio of muted trumpet, muted trombone, and clarinet that is as easily identifiable by timbre as thematic content. The trumpet plays in a comfortable middle register, while the trombone plays in a higher tessitura and the clarinet in the low register, creating a combination of relaxation and tension in a beautifully harmonized passage. Ellington makes careful use of contrary motion, augmented ninth sonorities (with the nine in the bass), and chromatic voice leading to produce an unforgettable moment.

Although Ellington's musical effects are interesting from the vantage point of musical analysis, Billy Strayhorn (Ellington's compositional collaborator) argued that there is something more to Ellington's sound:

> Each member of his band is to him a distinctive tone color and set of emotions, which he mixes with others equally distinctive to produce a third thing, which I like to call the "Ellington Effect." Sometimes this mixing happens on paper and frequently right on the bandstand. I have often seen him exchange parts in the middle of a piece because the man and the part weren't the same character. Ellington's concern is with the individual musician and what happens when they put their musical characters together.[10]

In 1927, Duke Ellington got his first major break when he was hired at the Cotton Club, a Harlem nightclub catering to a Whites-only clientele and decorated in plantation motif. The Cotton Club featured shows combining music, exotic dancing (some performed in pseudo-African garb), and theatrical presentation. The Ellington orchestra, now expanded from six to eleven members, provided the wealthy White clientele the

Call–response
A song structure or performance practice in which a singer or instrumentalist makes a musical statement that is answered by another soloist, instrumentalist, or group. The statement and answer sometimes overlap. Also called antiphony and call-and-response.

Riff
A short, recurrent melodic-rhythmic phrase.

Jungle sound
Term referencing Africa, associated with unique instrumental timbres typical of Duke Ellington arrangements in the 1920s and 1930s.

Figure 9.2
"Mood Indigo"
(1938).

"primitive" ambience they were looking for, often through sophisticated musical means beyond their imagination. The club's regular radio broadcasts during Ellington's tenure (1927–31) brought the Ellington Effect into America's living rooms and made him into a national figure.[11]

BROADCASTING AND THE SWING ERA

Radio broadcasts from major hotels, clubs, and dance halls were crucial in establishing and maintaining the reputations of bands such as those led by Benny Goodman (1909–86), Tommy Dorsey (1905–56), Count Basie (1904–84), and Duke Ellington. There were two types of radio broadcasts: "sustaining programs" originating late at night from hotels and clubs and featuring a variety of bands, and "sponsored programs" for which a company such as Coca-Cola or Lucky Strike hired particular bands for long-term contracts. Access to these radio opportunities was racially structured, with White bands at an advantage in both types of engagements. White bands were more likely to be booked at hotels and clubs with radio broadcast capability because most had segregated booking policies. Even so, many Black bands were able to make appearances on sustaining programs from locations that did hire Black bands, such as the Cotton Club, the Savoy Ballroom, or Chicago's Grand Terrace. Sponsored programs were out of the question for Black bands. Not until the late 1940s was there an all-Black sponsored radio program (NBC's *King Cole Trio Time*), and even guest appearances on White programs by prominent Black musicians were rare.[12]

The segregation of the public arena caused interracial collaborations of various kinds to occur in less visible ways. Hiring arrangers from across the color line was one; recording (but not appearing) with a mixed ensemble was another. Fletcher Henderson's compositions and arrangements, which Benny Goodman bought in 1934, served as the principal component of his band's repertoire as it established its national profile. Goodman later hired African Americans Henderson and Jimmy Mundy as staff arrangers for the band and defied the performance color line by hiring Lionel Hampton and Charlie Christian. Teddy Wilson (1912–86) recorded with the Benny Goodman trio a year prior to his famous 1936 appearance with the bandleader at Chicago's Congress Hotel. Although a considerable amount of mixing had taken place in Black venues from the very beginning, mixing in a predominantly White setting made this event newsworthy.[13]

The ambivalent reception of Benny Goodman's title of "King of Swing," especially later in the twentieth century, stems from the racially structured aspects of his rise to prominence. Goodman's story serves to illustrate several themes in ongoing debates over the relationship between Black and White jazz. In late 1934, Goodman was offered a regular slot on NBC's *Let's Dance*, a program sponsored by the National Biscuit Company. In choosing Goodman, NBC overlooked many prominent Black bands including those of Duke Ellington, Earl Hines, and Jimmie Lunceford. Goodman's success on the show was fueled by Fletcher Henderson's compositions and arrangements, and many White audience members came to know the swing music of an African American composer through the medium of White performance. Consequently, to the broader White public, swing did not appear to be Black music. This perception was reinforced by Jim Crow barriers that kept African American bands from being heard through the same high-visibility broadcast channels. That Goodman as an individual took actions facilitating the employment of African Americans in mainstream White dance bands (generally in advance of other White bandleaders) cannot be denied; yet he was also a beneficiary of the racial status quo in the music industry.[14]

During and before World War II there were several successful all-women swing bands, among them the International Sweethearts of Rhythm, the Darlings of Rhythm, and Phil Spitalny's House of Charm. These ensembles offered many women the opportunity to perform professionally at a time when participation by women in both big bands and small groups was rare. Among the most highly regarded players were trumpeters Jean Ray Lee, Tiny Davis, and Thelma Lewis, and saxophonists Roz Cron and Josephine Boyd. A few women succeeded as instrumentalists during the swing years, including pianist and arranger Mary Lou Williams (1910–81), who worked with the Andy Kirk band, and vibraphonist Marjorie Hyams (1923–2012), who played with Woody Herman.[15]

Swing Music

The major big bands of the **swing** era served as important training grounds for younger musicians. Many improved their music-reading skills, understanding of harmony, ensemble skills, and (for some) composing and arranging skills, under the tutelage of more experienced musicians. One hallmark of swing music is the extensive use of riffs (short ostinato figures) as ensemble textures. Riffs were used in many ways, including (1) as melodies, (2) in call-and-response with another riff or an improvised passage, (3) as a continuous supporting texture underneath a soloist or written passage, and (4) in layers. Two shout choruses of Count Basie's "Sent for You Yesterday" (1938) illustrate these usages

Swing
Big band jazz style developed in the 1930s that emphasized horn riffs and a rhythmic drive derived from the boogie-woogie bass line.

Figure 9.3
Two shout choruses
of Count Basie's "Sent
for You Yesterday"
(1938).

Ingrid Monson

(Figure 9.3). In chorus seven, two riffs are presented in call-and-response between the brass and the reeds. The drums play the classic swing ride rhythm on the hi-hat and the bass plays a walking bass, four to the bar. In chorus eight, the reeds play a continuous supporting riff while the brass riff (functioning as the melody) continues in call-and-response with improvised drum breaks. Here the call-and-response of the brass and drums is layered against the continuous accompanying riff in the reeds. Shout choruses such as these were often used at the very end of a piece as a climax. The artful use of repetition, which served as a solid anchor for dancers, was one hallmark of swing style.

Many virtuosic soloists emerged in the 1930s, from small groups as well as big bands. Expanding on Armstrong's lead, musicians strove to extend the scope of solo improvisation. Among the most prominent soloists were Roy Eldridge (1911–89), trumpet; Lester Young (1909–59) and Coleman Hawkins, tenor saxophone; and Art Tatum (1909–56), piano. Vocalist Billie Holiday (1915–59), whose inventive paraphrases of melody and timing inspired many, including Lester Young, also became prominent in the late 1930s, recording with many alumni of the Count Basie orchestra.[16]

Bebop

With World War II came not only a new aesthetic in jazz, but a new attitude in African American communities as well. The Double V campaign (which called for victory over racism at home as well as victory for democracy in Europe) perhaps symbolized the transition best, as African Americans deemed fit to risk their lives in battle chafed at the glaring racial injustices at home. As Scott DeVeaux has noted, professional jazz musicians were a relatively privileged elite who worked in an industry that accorded greater personal freedom, mobility, and prosperity than most occupations available to Black Americans. The symbolic value of that hard-won success and freedom to the broader African American community was enormous.[17]

During the war years, musicians who had become frustrated with the limited possibilities for extended improvisation in big bands and dismayed by the dominance of White bands in the popular music market forged an ambitious improvisational style that came to be known as **bebop** (musicians first called it modern music). No longer content to be entertainers, the younger jazz musicians demanded to be taken seriously as artists. The heroes of this movement were Charlie Parker (1920–55), alto sax; Thelonious Monk (1917–82), piano; Dizzy Gillespie (1917–93), trumpet; Kenny Clarke (1914–85), drums; Max Roach (1924–2007), drums; and Bud Powell (1924–66), piano. The series of legendary jam sessions that are said to have created the style took place in Harlem at Minton and Monroe's Uptown House.[18]

Bebop
Combo jazz improvised style that evolved from big band swing in the 1940s, characterized by exceedingly fast tempos, with improvisational lines based on the harmonic structure rather than on the melody.

The musical innovations of bebop affected several dimensions of the music: instrumental virtuosity, harmony, phrasing, rhythmic feel, timbre, and tempo. Charlie Parker and Dizzy Gillespie reharmonized and/or wrote new melodies for standard jazz tunes— such as "Cherokee," "I Got Rhythm," and "What Is This Thing Called Love?"—increasing the harmonic rhythm and the tempo and improvising highly subdivided phrases that set a new standard for instrumental virtuosity in the music. Drummers Kenny Clarke and Max Roach, picking up where Count Basie's drummer Jo Jones left off, transferred the standard ride rhythm (Figure 9.4) from the hi-hat cymbals to the suspended-ride cymbal, altering both the timbral color of the time-keeping pattern and increasing its volume. They also began "breaking up the time" by inserting off-beat accents on the bass drum and snare, creating greater rhythmic variety and dialogue in the rhythm section accompaniment.[19]

Figure 9.4
The standard ride rhythm.

Charlie Parker's legendary solo on "KoKo" (based on the chord changes to "Cherokee") illustrates many of the signature features of bebop melodic style (Figure 9.5). Notice the long succession of up-tempo eighth notes (throughout), the use of chromatic approach notes often alternating with arpeggiation (Figure 9.5a), and the use of sequences (Figure 9.5b). Parker's particular penchant for interpolating complex figurations around skeletal melodies can be seen in his famous bridge to the second chorus of "KoKo," where a varied melody of "Tea for Two" serves to anchor a rapid series of arpeggiations (Figure 9.5c).

Parker was also widely admired for his varied accentuation of long successions of eighth notes in a manner that served to emphasize the most harmonically pleasing moments of the voice leading. Dizzy Gillespie's phrasing style was similar but made greater use of whole-tone scales and the fabled "flatted fifth" alteration of the dominant chord.

Among Parker's most celebrated recordings are "KoKo" (1945), "A Night in Tunisia" (1946), "Parker's Mood" (1948), and "Embraceable You" (1947). For Gillespie, the most admired recordings include several made with Charlie Parker—"Shaw 'Nuff" (1945), "Salt Peanuts" (1945), "Hot House" (1953)—as well as many under his own leadership, including "Woody 'n You" (1946), "A Night in Tunisia" (1946), "Manteca" (1947), "Cubana Be, Cubana Bop" (1947, a collaboration with George Russell and Chano Pozo), and "Con Alma" (1967).

Gillespie's trademark goatee and beret were widely emulated by fans of the new music, and by the late 1940s bebop had acquired a subcultural quality that shunned mainstream "squares." Bebop style included the use

Figure 9.5
Charlie Parker's legendary solo on "KoKo" (based on the chord changes to "Cherokee").

of "bop talk" (drawn from African American vernacular speech), a critique of the racial status quo, and the unfortunate fashionability of heroin. Charlie Parker's well-known addiction set the example, as many young musicians seemed to conclude that Parker achieved his genius because of, rather than in spite of, the drug. Many musicians suffered arrest, loss of their New York cabaret cards, jail time, or death in pursuit of a habit that was rumored to intensify one's hearing. Although the drug addictions of several prominent African American musicians (Charlie Parker, Miles Davis, Sonny Rollins) are more widely known, several prominent White musicians (Stan Getz, Chet Baker, Art Pepper) share similar stories.[20]

In contrast to Parker and Gillespie, Thelonious Monk's reputation stems more from the originality of his compositions than his virtuosity as a soloist. In 1947, Monk made a series of recordings for the Blue Note label that included many of his most famous compositions—"Thelonious," "Ruby My Dear," "'Round Midnight," "Well You Needn't," and "In Walked Bud" among them. Although greatly admired within the jazz world of the late 1940s (pianist Mary Lou Williams was among his earliest champions), Monk did not achieve broader prominence until the late 1950s and early 1960s. Monk's loss of his cabaret card in 1951 certainly contributed to his marginality, but perhaps a more important factor was the great difference between his aesthetic and that of mainstream bebop.[21] If Parker and Gillespie's music emphasized dazzling virtuosity, Monk's own soloing seemed to argue that less is more. A celebrated example of Monk's ability to say more with less is his Christmas Eve 1954 recording of "Bags' Groove" with Miles Davis. Over nine choruses of the blues, Monk uses spare means to build a compelling larger shape for the solo. The openings of the first three choruses illustrate one way in which Monk accomplishes this. Each chorus begins with a riff that is developed over twelve bars. Notice that the riff for the first

Figure 9.6
Opening of the first three choruses of "Bags' Groove" (1954).

chorus begins with eighth notes, the second with triplets, and the third with sixteenth notes. Monk's use of rhythmic displacement (shifting a figure's position within a bar) as a means of variation is apparent in the triplet and sixteenth-note passages in choruses 2 and 3.

Cool Jazz and Hard Bop

The improvisational style of Miles Davis (1926–91) also leaned toward an aesthetic of less is more. Davis's solo career was launched by the celebrated *Birth of the Cool* recordings made in 1949 and 1950. The *Birth of the Cool* project emerged from a think tank of composers and musicians who met in arranger Gil Evans's (1912–88) apartment in the late 1940s to explore musical ideas and theories with potential application to jazz composition. The aesthetic that emerged from the group emphasized coloristic timbral effects achieved through unusual pairings of instruments (trumpet and alto sax, French horn and trombone, tuba and baritone sax), vibratoless tone, and a seamless integration of written and improvised music, which often disguised the formal sectional boundaries of the music.[22]

Birth of the Cool was an explicitly interracial project that distinguished itself from many others of the period by being under the leadership of an African American artist. In the early 1950s, the jazz community tended to embrace a colorblind ideology in opposition to prevailing societal segregation. Miles Davis's statement that "music has no color: It's a raceless art. I don't care if a musician is green as long as he's talented," was typical of the way in which this ideology was publicly expressed.[23]

Later in the 1950s, the aesthetic of **cool jazz**—emphasizing lyrical melodic style and softer tonal colors—became coded as a "White" sound, contrasted with **hard bop**, which was coded as a "Black" sound. Art Blakey and the Jazz Messengers (the quintessential hard bop band) often served to define the hard bop alternative. Historians emphasize Blakey's and Horace Silver's active embrace of African American roots through the exuberant expressive resources of blues, gospel, and rhythm and blues. Notable examples of this style can be found on Art Blakey's *Moanin'* (1958).[24] Obscured by this simple opposition is that prominent White saxophonists associated with the cool (or West Coast) sound (Stan Getz, Lee Konitz, Paul Desmond) often modeled themselves on the lyrical

Cool jazz
1950s jazz style often associated with the West Coast, characterized by a relaxed feeling and light tone color and texture.

Hard bop
A combo jazz style of the 1950s that incorporated the phrasings and harmonies of blues, rhythm and blues, and gospel music.

Ingrid Monson

playing and laid-back swing of African American artists such as Lester Young and Johnny Hodges. Also ignored by this binary contrast is that one of the most prominent ensembles with a cool sound was the Modern Jazz Quartet, an African American group.

Pianist Dave Brubeck's (1920–2012) trios and quartets dominated the listeners' polls for a considerable portion of the 1950s. Like Benny Goodman, historical ambivalence toward Brubeck's towering success stems from the racially structured advantages that benefited the group. Brubeck's appearance on the cover of *Time* magazine in 1954, his popularity on White college campuses, and the comparative lack of attention to worthy African American musicians in the media all contributed to hard bop's emphasis on African American roots.[25]

THE CIVIL RIGHTS MOVEMENT

By the mid-1950s, the burgeoning Civil Rights Movement exerted pressure on musicians to do their part in supporting efforts to end Jim Crow. The Black community expected musicians to demonstrate their commitment to the larger cause of racial justice, and they publicly shamed those artists (such as Nat King Cole and Louis Armstrong) who continued to accept engagements in performance venues that segregated audiences. The issue of audience segregation was far more important to civil rights organizations than whether or not a particular band had mixed personnel. Southern White audiences, after all, had long been comfortable with Black and mixed entertainment as long as segregated seating remained. The activist climate emerging from the principal events of the Civil Rights Movement—the Montgomery bus boycott (1956), the desegregation of Little Rock's Central High School (1957), the independence of Ghana (1957), the student lunch counter sit-ins (1960), the Freedom Rides (1961), the campaign to desegregate Birmingham (1963), and the assassination of Malcolm X (1965)—had important consequences for jazz of the 1950s and 1960s.[26]

The jazz community reacted in various ways to civil rights events, including the performance of benefit concerts, the recording of albums with political themes, attributing political meaning to particular jazz aesthetics, the exploration of African and other non-Western musical and religious ideas, and engaging in highly charged dialogues about race and racism in the jazz industry. Among the most well-known works exemplifying these themes include Wilbur Harden's "Gold Coast" (1958), Max Roach's *We Insist! Freedom Now* (1960), Charles Mingus's "Original Faubus Fables" (1960), Randy Weston's *Uhuru Afrika* (1960), Art Blakey's *Freedom Rider* (1961), and John Coltrane's "Africa" (1961). The emergence of several of the most revered figures in jazz and the aesthetics they represent—among them Miles Davis, John Coltrane (1926–67), Charles Mingus (1922–79), and Ornette Coleman (1930–)— took place against this volatile historical backdrop.

Modal Jazz

Modal jazz
Music based on the repetition of one or two chords, or music based on modes (scales) instead of chord progressions.

Among the most important musical innovations between the Montgomery Bus Boycott (1956) and the Civil Rights Act (1964) was the development of **modal jazz**. Exemplified by Miles Davis's album *Kind of Blue* (1959), modal compositions reduced the number of harmonic changes, allowing soloists to improvise for an extended period of time over one or two chords. "So What?" (1959), which has become the prototypical modal composition, is an AABA tune comprised of two chord changes, one for the A section (Dm7) and one for the B section (E♭m7). Davis explored the use of the Dorian mode (DEFGABC) to harmonize these sonorities and construct melodies. The more open harmonic background, in addition, allowed soloists greater freedom to superimpose a wide variety of modes, scales, voicings, and melodic ideas over any particular sonority.[27]

The conceptual father of a modal approach to harmony in jazz is George Russell (1923–2009), whose books *Lydian Concept of Tonal Organization* (1953) and *Lydian Chromatic Concept of Tonal Organization* (1959) offered the improviser and composer a complex system of associating chords with scales organized by their degree of consonance or dissonance. Russell emphasized the multiple choices available to performers and was widely known in the jazz community for his expertise in modes and scales. Both Miles Davis and pianist Bill Evans (who appeared on *Kind of Blue*) were familiar with Russell's ideas. The "Lydian Concept," however, was intended as a more general approach to harmony that could be applied to harmonically dense as well as harmonically sparse musical settings.[28]

Modal jazz also came to imply a more open-ended approach to form and harmonic voicings. Instead of observing a chorus structure, jazz musicians explored pieces that allowed a soloist to play indefinitely over a recurring chord pattern or rhythmic vamp. The vamp to John Coltrane's "My Favorite Things" (1960), as played by pianist McCoy Tyner (1938–), provides one example (Figure 9.7). Notice the prominent use of fourths (perfect and augmented) in the structure of the chords. By the omission of certain tones (especially the tonic), these more open voicings served to articulate more than one harmony, a hallmark of modern jazz piano style. Charles Mingus's *Pithecanthropus Erectus* (1956) and Art Blakey's extended percussion solos on *Orgy in Rhythm* (1957) and *Holiday for Skins* (1958) provide additional examples of a more open-ended conception of form. Blakey's collaborations with Afro-Cuban musicians on these albums—including Sabu Martinez, Patato Valdez, and Ubaldo Nieto—took place at the time of Ghana's independence, when there was much discussion of Africa in the African American press.

In the early 1960s, John Coltrane shifted from a well-developed modern bebop style featuring harmonically dense compositions such as "Giant Steps" (1959) to an open-ended modal conception that actively explored not only African, but also Indian sources of musical and

Figure 9.7
The vamp to John Coltrane's "My Favorite Things" (1960), as played by pianist McCoy Tyner.

spiritual inspiration. Coltrane's legendary ensemble, featuring McCoy Tyner on piano, Elvin Jones (1927–2004) on drums, and Jimmy Garrison (1934–76) on bass (among others), developed the rhythmic as well as harmonic implications of open-ended modal approaches to improvisation, something that Miles Davis's quintet (1963–68) did also. Freed from the necessity of delineating frequently changing harmonies, bassists expanded their use of pedal points, pianists accompanied long sections with intricate vamps and riffs, and drummers played with greater rhythmic density and cross-rhythms than had been customary in earlier styles. Among the recordings exemplifying this sound are John Coltrane's *My Favorite Things* (1960), *Africa Brass* (1961), *India* (1961), *Crescent* (1963), and *A Love Supreme* (1964), and Miles Davis's *My Funny Valentine* (1964), *Miles in Berlin* (1964), and *Live at the Plugged Nickel* (1965).

Free Jazz

A major aesthetic controversy erupted in the jazz world in early 1960 when alto saxophonist Ornette Coleman emerged on the New York scene. Coleman's dissonant harmonic style and abandonment of chorus structures and fixed harmonic changes as a means of organizing improvisational flow was claimed by some as the *Shape of Jazz to Come* (1959) (the title of Coleman's first release after his arrival in New York); by others it was decried as the destruction of jazz, and by still others it was championed as a music of social critique. Over the next seven years, an aesthetic community of jazz musicians, committed to what was variously termed "**free jazz**," "The New Thing," or "avant-garde jazz" emerged on the New York scene. Among them were Coleman, Cecil Taylor (1929–), Albert Ayler (1936–70), Archie Shepp (1937–), Sun Ra (1914–93), and John Coltrane. Coltrane's turn toward free jazz gave considerable prestige to the burgeoning movement. The new approach also fostered the creation of collective musical organizations such as Chicago's Association for the Advancement of Creative Musicians (AACM, 1965) and, later, St. Louis's Black Artists Group (BAG, 1968).[29]

Free jazz
Style that began in the late 1950s and abandoned the practice of utilizing fixed harmonic and rhythmic patterns as the basis for improvisation.

Its advocates claimed free jazz as the left-wing of jazz expression—its musically adventurous means were taken as a sign of revolutionary social critique, spiritual awareness, and freedom. The political meanings attached to the genre must be viewed in dialogue with the riveting events of the Civil Rights Movement that took place during its emergence. Shortly after Ornette Coleman's New York debut in late 1959, the Greensboro lunch counter sit-ins occurred (February 1960), launching the most activist phase of the Civil Rights Movement. For many, the dissonance of the music was taken as a sign of social dissidence. For modernist-oriented jazz critics such as Gunther Schuller and Martin Williams, the appeal of free jazz lay in its parallel with the historical development of Western classical music.[30] Schuller stressed that musical rather than historical and cultural logic determined the organic evolution of jazz from simple to complex, from tonal music to avant-garde. Here, free jazz was of interest for its modern avant-garde aesthetic, rather than its political radicalism.

Among the greatest champions of free jazz as a political music was playwright, poet, and critic Amiri Baraka (b. LeRoi Jones, 1934–2014), whose *Blues People* viewed free jazz as the logical outcome of the Black musician's centuries of struggle with racism in America. *Blues People* was the first major book by an African American author to advocate for a sociological and culturally contextualized view of Black musical history. Among musicians, Archie Shepp publicly raised the issue of racism in the jazz industry, in outspoken pieces such as his 1965 "An Artist Speaks Bluntly." Max Roach raised comparable issues and shifted toward free jazz in the 1960s as well. Later, Frank Kofsky's *Black Nationalism and the Revolution in Music* (1970) took a political view of avant-garde jazz.[31]

For many avant-garde artists, however, the politics of free jazz expression were a byproduct of its spiritual implications. For Albert Ayler, John Coltrane, and Sun Ra, spiritual communion (a different kind of liberation) through avant-garde expression was a primary motivation for their expressive choices. Ayler's work drew heavily upon the African American gospel and folk traditions, turning familiar hymn melodies into abstract wails and pleas of deep emotional intensity. Both John Coltrane and Sun Ra were drawn to non-Western modes of spirituality. Both men were widely read in spiritual traditions from locations as far ranging as Africa, India, China, and West Asia (the Middle East). Sun Ra's aesthetic appealed to both ancient Egypt and outer space as metaphors for liberation and spiritual depth.[32]

Critics of free jazz failed to see "progress" in the atonality and indefinite time feels of the music. They viewed the avant-garde as a decline in the music, brought on by young musicians who "didn't do their homework" or pay their dues in the tradition. An observer for *Muhammad Speaks*, the organ of the Nation of Islam, even suggested that avant-gardists such as Coltrane were pandering to White critics.[33] Observers from the mid-1960s confirm that as the music became increasingly atonal and less danceable, many Black audience members defected to the immensely popular Motown and soul sounds, or to soul jazz—the classic organ trio or quartet sound popularized by Jimmy Smith (1925–2005), Stanley Turrentine (1934–2000), and Shirley Scott (1934–2002)—leaving a disproportionately White audience for free jazz.[34] (Historians generally agree that the separation of jazz from dance began during the bebop era, partially as a result of musical changes such as faster tempos and breaking the regularity of the beat with syncopated accents, and partially due to the desire to present jazz as an art music. Free jazz, which made greater use of out-of-time passages than main-stream jazz, simply took the separation from danceable musics further.) During the **Black Power** years of 1966–70, a tense dialogue between a militant African American radical intelligentsia and radical White audience members and musicians often took place through free jazz performances.[35]

THE 1970s

The release of Miles Davis's *Bitches Brew* in 1969 augured a new direction for jazz in the 1970s that combined an embrace of popular music styles with the freedom and open-ended improvisational ethos of modal and free jazz. Widely heralded for its creative synthesis of jazz improvisation, rock and roll, electric instruments, and textural experimentation, *Bitches Brew* explored straight eighth-note time feels, as well as many of the post-production techniques of popular music, including overdubbing and looping. Davis was especially inspired by guitarist Jimi Hendrix (1942–70), whose blistering guitar pyrotechnics dazzled the counter-cultural scene of the late 1960s. Although several jazz musicians, including Tony Williams and Charles Lloyd, had experimented with rock musicians and styles between 1966 and 1969, the popular success of *Bitches Brew* (it sold over half a million copies) and the prestige of Miles Davis ensured that experiments in fusing extended jazz impro-visation and rock music would be a continuing trend in jazz of the 1970s. Indeed, many of the most prominent **fusion** bands of the 1970s included alumni of Miles Davis's bands: John McLaughlin's (1942–) Mahavishnu Orchestra, Wayne Shorter (1933–) and Joe Zawinul's (1932–2007) group Weather Report, and Chick Corea's (1941–) Return to Forever. Although some critics have dismissed this trend as blatantly commercial, the music played by these groups, which included extended instrumental solos and experimental timbres and textures, sounded little like mainstream rock music.[36]

Miles Davis was also interested in soul and funk—especially the music of Sly and the Family Stone and James Brown—and explicitly sought to reach a younger African American audience for his music in the early 1970s. Davis's *A Tribute to Jack Johnson* (1970) and *On the Corner* (1972) both included bassist Michael Henderson (1951–), who had

Black Power Movement
A movement of the late 1960s and early 1970s that emphasized Black unity, Black pride, and self-determination.

Fusion
1970s jazz style that incorporated rhythms, harmonies, and melodic motives from popular forms, especially funk and rock.

considerable prior experience in Motown, soul, and funk. Henderson's funky bass lines defined a time feeling for these albums quite distant from that heard on *Bitches Brew*. The most successful album combining jazz with the sound of early 1970s soul and funk was Herbie Hancock's (1940–) *Headhunters* (1973), which featured a compelling interlocked combination of funk bass lines, rhythm guitar parts, and horn riffs over which extended instrumental solos were performed.[37]

Although the 1970s are often cast as the decade of fusion, it is important to remember that these same years produced new directions in both avant-garde and mainstream jazz. The Art Ensemble of Chicago (founded in 1969), composed of members of the AACM, developed an approach to free improvisation that emphasized compositional decisions and group interaction. The group's performances, which included costumes, body painting, African instruments, and an expanded palette of percussion instruments, were theatrical and playful like those of Sun Ra's Arkestra. Anthony Braxton's (1945–) stunning solo compositions and improvisations for alto saxophone, as well as his abstractly titled compositions for larger groups, established a new level of virtuosity and imagination in avant-garde improvisation. Other influential musicians and groups active in the 1970s include David Murray (1955–), the World Saxophone Quartet, Rahsaan Roland Kirk (1936–77), Steve Lacy (1943–2004), Lester Bowie (1953–99), Roscoe Mitchell (1940–) and Arthur Blythe (1940–).[38]

A growing internationalization of avant-garde jazz also took place in the 1970s. European audiences proved to be especially receptive to free jazz, and an indigenous European avant-garde inspired by the American jazz emerged, including such figures as German performers Albert Mangelsdorff (1928–2005) and the Global Unity Orchestra, and Dutch musician Willem Breuker (1944–2010).

In the late 1970s, tenor saxophonist Dexter Gordon's (1923–90) return to the United States from Denmark heralded a renewed interest in straight-ahead jazz. The careers of many musicians who had been active in the 1950s and 1960s as sidemen emerged as leaders of their own groups, such as Johnny Griffin (1928–2008) and Ron Carter (1937–). Both avant-garde and mainstream groups began to draw attention to jazz history in their musical projects. Anthony Braxton recorded *In the Tradition* (1974), which featured compositions such as Charlie Parker's "Ornithology"; Henry Threadgill (1944–) and his group Air featured the music of Scott Joplin and Jelly Roll Morton on an album entitled *Air Lore* (1979). Some players, such as Scott Hamilton and Warren Vaché, modeled their playing exclusively on swing-era soloists. The interest in jazz history among musicians, in other words, antedates the emergence of the historicism in the decade to follow.[39]

By the early 1980s, many young jazz musicians found greater inspiration in the golden age of modern jazz (from 1945 to 1965) than in contemporary offerings of fusion and avant-garde. Trumpeter Wynton Marsalis (1961–) made no secret of his disappointment in recent jazz and passionately advocated a return to basic jazz values (making the changes and swinging) through studying the classic recordings of jazz masters such as Louis Armstrong, Art Blakey, Miles Davis, John Coltrane, Thelonious Monk, and Duke Ellington. Marsalis's outspoken criticism of the jazz avant-garde and the most recent fusion efforts of Miles Davis polarized older jazz listeners, who cast Marsalis as an aesthetic conservative. Marsalis nevertheless inspired and nurtured a group of young musicians who later became known as the **Young Lions**. These include trumpeters Roy Hargrove (1969–) and Terence Blanchard (1962–), drummer Jeff "Tain" Watts (1960–), bassist Christian McBride (1972–), and pianists Marcus Roberts (1963–) and Cyrus Chestnut (1963–). Marsalis's prominent success in both jazz and classical music made him the ideal figure to actualize a longstanding dream: that someday jazz would be treated as equal in stature to classical music and accorded an institutional home. In 1988, the Jazz at Lincoln Center program, dedicated to advancing jazz through performance, education, and preservation, was launched with Marsalis as its artistic director. Marsalis organized the Lincoln Center Jazz Orchestra, and since the early 1990s Lincoln Center has offered a highly acclaimed series of jazz concerts and educational events, often devoted to the repertoire of towering jazz figures such as Duke Ellington.[40]

Young Lions/New Traditionalists 1980s movement led by Wynton Marsalis, designed to highlight the traditional jazz styles of the pre-1950s era.

Critics of Lincoln Center have cited the narrowness of Marsalis's programming decisions, his neglect of the avant-garde in jazz, and his failure to commission more adventurous jazz compositions, as well as finding fault with his tendency to feature his own works over those of others. If Marsalis's narrow definition of jazz from its origins to the mid-1960s can be seen as part of a modernist project emphasizing canon formation and high art ambitions, many of Lincoln Center's critics advocate a more experimental or avant-garde modernism that emphasizes striving toward the future rather than the past of the tradition. Some take a postmodern interest in including popular and global musics within their artistic practice. Many combine aspects of these two critical perspectives, including Don Byron (1958–), Steve Coleman (1956–), Geri Allen (1957–), George Lewis (1952–), and Anthony Brown (1953–).

Another criticism of Lincoln Center has come from critics who claim that White musicians have been overlooked in Lincoln Center's programming decisions. This is the latest chapter in a longer history of the charge of reverse racism, which has generally emerged at moments of Black political activism and Black advancement.[41] It is germane to note that Lincoln Center is the first major jazz institution to have African

American leadership at the top and that Wynton Marsalis's list of predominantly African American central figures in the jazz tradition is hardly unusual. After all, a broad consensus of jazz historians and audiences has created much the same list.[42]

In the 1990s, a growing interest in global and ethnic musics was evident in the work of contemporary jazz musicians. A particular emphasis on musics of the African diaspora, with special attention to Cuban and Caribbean musics, can be seen in the music of David Sanchez (1968–), Danilo Perez (1966–), and Paquito D'Rivera (1948–). Although jazz has drawn on Caribbean music throughout its history, the expectation that mainstream jazz musicians show basic competence in the clave-based musical patterns of Cuba—such as *montunos* and *tumbaos*—increased substantially in the 1990s. Cuban music, both secular and sacred, has been an especially prominent trend. Steve Coleman's *The Sign and the Seal* (1996), a recording made in Havana with the Cuban folkloric group AfroCuba de Matanzas, investigates the rhythms and melodies of **Santería**.[43] Don Byron's *You Are #6* (2001), which includes percussionist Milton Cardona, also explores some of the sacred rhythms of Santería and features an ensemble expert in the clave-based music of Cuba and Puerto Rico.

Santería (also **Lucumí**) African-derived syncretic religion that originated in Cuba.

Another prominent trend in the late 1980s and 1990s was the emergence of several musicians, ensembles, and a record label exploring the possibilities of combining Asian musics and jazz. Among the most prominent representatives of this trend are pianists Jon Jang and Vijay Iyer, percussionist Anthony Brown, and saxophonists Fred Ho and Francis Wong. Most have recorded on Asian Improv, a record label founded by Jang and Wong in 1987, which now offers a list of over thirty musicians.[44] Central to the vision of many performers is the connection between the political activism of the African American avant-garde of the 1960s and the anti-racism struggles of Asian American communities. The current generation of Asian American jazz musicians has consciously emphasized their great identification with African American political and cultural self-empowerment. Musically, the timbral palette of the jazz ensemble has been expanded by the incorporation of Japanese, Chinese, and other Asian instruments into ensembles such as Brown's Asian American Orchestra. The group's recording of Duke Ellington's *Far East Suite* (1999), which included the Chinese *sheng* as well as the West Asian *ney* and *karna*, received a Grammy nomination in 2000.

The turn of the new century has amplified debates over both the legacy and future of jazz. Although it is too soon to assign definitive labels to the new musical landscape, musicians and audiences seem to draw on four partially overlapping discourses in defining their aesthetic perspectives: traditionalist modernism, populism, global internationalism, and experimentalism. Jazz at Lincoln Center in this framework emphasizes traditionalist modernism; its central goals have been defining a core jazz tradition and creating an institutional place of honor for jazz that was unimaginable during the first two-thirds of the twentieth century. Populism, a perspective that does not wish to confine jazz to a sphere resembling Western art music, can be seen in the aesthetics of musicians who accept the incorporation of musical influences from hip-hop, funk, and other popular dance musics as legitimate aspects of the jazz tradition. Global internationalism emphasizes the incorporation of African diasporic and other global or ethnic musics into the vision of the future of jazz. Sounds and aesthetics may be drawn from global popular, folk, or art music traditions and may or may not be combined with an avant-garde approach to improvisational process.

One of the great open questions in the new century is the future of avant-garde experimentalism in jazz. Although Wynton Marsalis has often criticized the avant-garde jazz music of the 1960s for its dissonance and lack of (traditional) musical discipline, experimentalism in jazz has refused to die. Many musicians are simultaneously fluent in the improvisational language of mainstream modern jazz as well as the experimentalism of avant-garde innovators such as Ornette Coleman, John Coltrane, Anthony Braxton, and Steve Lacy. The use of digital technology in both experimental and populist contexts—from the interactive computer-aided improvisational music of George Lewis to the hip-hop sound of Russell Gunn (1971–)—suggests the increasing fluidity of the boundary between populism and experimentalism and the increasing importance of digital technology in music. Contemporary jazz musicians are often eclectically postmodern in their aesthetic projects, performing in traditional, classical, experimental, and global internationalist projects at different points of time. Whatever the future of jazz as a virtuosic improvised tradition, the reach of the music will likely be defined by the ongoing engaged debates among a wide variety of aesthetic and cultural constituencies.

KEY NAMES

Louis Armstrong	Dizzy Gillespie
Art Ensemble of Chicago	Benny Goodman
Count Basie	Fletcher Henderson
Buddy Bolden	Wynton Marsalis
Dave Brubeck	Thelonious Monk
Ornette Coleman	Jelly Roll Morton
John Coltrane	Joe "King" Oliver
Miles Davis	Charlie Parker
Duke Ellington	

QUESTIONS

1. New Orleans was one of the major centers of early jazz. What made this city and its musicians an ideal breeding ground for the new music?

2. Identify three performers who pioneered the development of the big band style and discuss their major contributions.

3. Identify new jazz styles that evolved following World War II. What changing conditions led to their development? Name key musicians associated with the development of these new styles.

4. What socio-cultural and political events shaped the development of free jazz? How did the jazz community react to this new musical style? What prompted these reactions?

5. What is "fusion" jazz? Describe how it evolved and what elements it borrowed from popular musical styles.

6. How has an emphasis on recordings as the only "reliable documents" in jazz history shaped the discussion of this genre? How is a performance changed through the process of recording and marketing?

PROJECTS

1. Choose a major jazz style/period (New Orleans, Chicago, big band, bebop, cool jazz, etc.). Write a history of the period when the music flourished, emphasizing relevant events in the African American community, as well as in the musical world. Relate how the style you've selected was influenced by and shaped its era.

2. Choose a style of jazz that has prompted social or political controversy. Develop an essay on the artists who inspired these controversies, and the strategies they employed to express their points of view. What do such controversies surrounding musical expression suggest about the role and significance of music in American society?

3. Choose three recordings of the same jazz "standard" representative of jazz styles from three different decades. Compare and contrast the recordings in terms of instrumentation, timbre, rhythm, phrasing, and overall style. How has each artist reinterpreted the original?

4. View one episode of Ken Burns' ten-part PBS documentary on jazz (*Jazz: A Film by Ken Burns*, 2000). What types of jazz does Burns explore in this episode? To what extent does Burns engage issues of race, gender, and class in his treatment? What messages about these issues does the film convey?

Ingrid Monson

NOTES

Please see the discography for information on resources for further listening.

1. The material for this section is drawn from Berlin 1980 and Badger 1995.
2. The Texas Tommy is an African American couple's dance mainstreamed in San Francisco in the first decade of the twentieth century. The dance consisted of a kick-step-hop-hop combination in 4/4 time. For more information, see "Texas Tommy," available at www.streetswing.com/histmain/z3tex1.htm.
3. Peretti 1992, 22–38.
4. Porter and Ullman 1993, 19–26. For more about Buddy Bolden, see Marquis 2005 and Barker 1998.
5. Kenney 1993, 3–34.
6. Ibid., 103–04.
7. Porter and Ullman 1993, 57–73; Collier 1983.
8. Schuller 1986a (1968), 155–65.
9. Tucker 1989.
10. Strayhorn 1993, 270.
11. For further information about Ellington's life and music, see Hasse 1993; Schuller 1986a (1968) and 1989; Tucker 1993.
12. Stowe 1994, 107–12.
13. Collier 1989, 133–36, 171–76.
14. Ibid., 128–29; Stowe 1994, 123–26.
15. For a definitive account of the women's swing bands, see Tucker 2000.
16. For further information on the swing era and its principal figures, see Schuller 1989; Nicholson 1995; O'Meally 1991; Daniels 2002; Büchmann-Møller 1990; Basie 1987.
17. DeVeaux 1997.
18. Perhaps the most vivid account of Minton's is in Ellison 1964, 199–212.
19. Guides to listening to bebop include Berliner 1994; Owens 1995; and Kernfeld 1995.
20. Accounts of the lives of Gillespie and Parker include Gillespie with Fraser 1979; Shipton 1999; Giddens 1987.
21. Gourse 1997, 85–87. Monk was arrested for possession of heroin in 1951. He was sitting in a car with Bud Powell, who was responsible for the presence of the heroin. Out of loyalty to Powell, Monk refused to inform the police that Powell was the drug user. The narcotics violation resulted in the loss of his cabaret card.
22. The classic account of the musical characteristics of the cool sound is found in Hodeir 1979 (1956), 116–36.
23. Davis with Troupe 1989, 117.
24. For further information on hard bop, see Rosenthal 1992.
25. For more on Brubeck and West Coast jazz, see Hall 1996 and Gioia 1992.
26. Monson 2007.
27. For a detailed account of the recording of *Kind of Blue*, see Kahn 2000.
28. Monson 1998, 149–68.
29. Major works on free jazz include Litweiler 1984; Spellman 1985; Jost 1994; Radano 1992 and 1993; Lewis 1996 and 1998.
30. Schuller 1986b, 18–25, 121.
31. Baraka 1999 (1963); Kofsky 1970; Shepp 1965.
32. Szwed 1997; Nisenson 1993.
33. "John Coltrane: Dealer in Discord" 1963, 21.
34. Szwed 1997, 256; Dan Morgenstern, interview with the author, June 20, 1995.
35. "Point of Contact: Discussion" 1966, 19–31, 110–11.
36. Keepnews 2000, 488–501.
37. Davis with Troupe 1989, 291–332; Szwed 2002, 287–349.
38. Keepnews 2000.
39. Ibid.
40. Crouch 1987; Conroy 1995; Hajdu 2003.
41. Teachout 1995.

42. The most canonized figures are presented in jazz history texts; compare Porter and Ullman 1993; Gridley 2009; and Tanner, Gerow, and Megill 2008.
43. For further information, see Murphy 1994.
44. Fred Ho, Francis Wong, and Jon Jang are of Chinese American background; Vijay Iyer is of Indian American (South Asian) heritage; Anthony Brown is of African American, Japanese, and Native American heritage. See the Asian Improv website, www.asianimprov.org.

CHAPTER 10

Gospel

Mellonee V. Burnim

Gospel music is the twentieth-century form of African American religious music that evolved in urban cities following the Great Migration of Blacks from the agrarian South in the period surrounding World Wars I and II. Although the musical foundation for this genre was laid in several different contexts in the first quarter of the twentieth century, it was not until the 1930s that the term "gospel music," as well as its repertoire and distinctive performance style, gained widespread usage among Blacks across denominational lines. It was during this decade that Thomas Dorsey, lauded as the "Father of Gospel Music," relinquished his career as an accomplished blues and jazz pianist-composer, and devoted himself entirely to the development and advancement of gospel music.[1]

Gospel music
Religious music of African Americans that emerged in urban centers during the early decades of the twentieth century.

From the start, the very concept of this new genre was problematic for some members of the African American religious community. Dorsey recalls ministers who objected to the reference to gospel as *music*, arguing that gospel could only be preached, not sung. Similarly, gospel has also been defined as "good news."[2] These views, of course, reduce gospel music to the embodiment of the message of the first four books of the New Testament, which ignores the actual musical features that characterize the genre. As gospel music has evolved, it has come to be understood as much more than mere text. Among African Americans, the term gospel music now references a specific body of composed repertoire, as well as a performance style that can be superimposed upon other genres, particularly spirituals and hymns.

The origin of gospel music has sometimes been considered the work of a single individual, the progeny of a single denomination, or the evolution of a single genre. Some writers have interpreted gospel music as an outgrowth of the hymn, which disregards the role of the indigenous **folk spiritual** in its formation. Other analyses of gospel music include studies that attribute its origins to the Pentecostal Church exclusively, discounting or, at the very least, minimizing the fact that key pioneers in its development, dissemination, and proliferation included members of Baptist, Methodist, Spiritualist, and other denominations. Still others view the gospel tradition as practiced by African Americans as a mere subset of a genre that includes both Black and White practices.[3]

In recognizing the seminal influence of blues in the musical imagination of gospel's founding father, Thomas Dorsey, some analysts have chosen to assign the label "gospel-blues" to this religious genre, even though that term has never been a part of the lexicon used by its historical or contemporary practitioners, and the designation undermines the definitively religious intent of the genre, despite its structural and aesthetic parallels with blues.[4]

While students of gospel music can argue the significance of specific artists, events, and geographic locales as having sparked its current widespread popularity and stature, in actuality, the development of gospel resulted from a complex intertwining of people, places, and processes that collectively generated a music representative of broadly shared African American musical values and cultural ideals.

THE GREAT MIGRATION

During the years 1920 through 1930, an estimated three million Blacks migrated from the rural South to the urban North. Prompted by the desire to establish a better way of life, both socially and economically, this transplanted population served as a key stimulus for the creation of the form of expression that was to become known as gospel music. As the new migrants began to engage in occupations other than those of the agrarian economy they had left behind, they continued to embrace values and behaviors that had characterized their way of life in the rural South. Foods that had been a regular part of their diet in the South were those they sought out in the urban North. Patterns of dress readily identifed recent arrivals, and their preferred worship styles were consistent with those characteristic of southern rural Black Baptists and Methodists, the two denominations to which the largest number of African Americans belonged. In some instances, congregations made the move north intact, as Rev. R.H. Harmon from Harrisburg, Mississippi, indicated to a *Chicago Defender* reporter upon his arrival to the city:

> I am working at my trade. I have saved enough to bring my wife and four children and some of my congregation [twenty-eight members]. We are here for keeps. They say we are fools to leave the warm country, and how our people are dying in the East. Well, I for one am glad they had the privilege of dying a natural death there. That is much better than the rope and torch. I will take my chance with the Northern winter.[5]

Folk spiritual
The earliest form of indigenous a cappella religious music created by African Americans during slavery.

Great Migration
The mass movement of southern African Americans to urban cities during the period surrounding World Wars I and II.

Mellonee V. Burnim

The one-room folk church of the rural South became the **storefront church** of the urban North—a key context for the emergence of gospel music. Whether in former retail shops such as grocery or dry good stores, in houses, garages, or abandoned theaters, southern migrants, typically from the lower socio-economic strata, often expressed a preference for worship in storefront churches. Their smaller size, averaging sixty members or less, permitted members to identify personally with the pastor and with other worshippers, something that larger churches could not offer.[6] In addition, worship in the storefront church was less formal, and more closely akin to the worship Black migrants had been accustomed to in the rural South.

The ethnographic research of sociologists St. Clair Drake and R.H. Cayton in Chicago during the 1930s documents the experience of a woman who had become a member of the largest church in the city upon her arrival seventeen years prior. Of the preaching, she commented that she "couldn't understand the pastor and the words he used." On the music, she remarked "I couldn't sing their way. The songs were proud-like. At my *little* [emphasis mine] church I enjoy the service."[7] These comments strongly indicate the urban newcomer's need to comprehend the sermon content if worship was to be meaningful. The reference to the music in the large church as "proud-like" suggests a degree of self-conscious formality in that setting that contrasted with the performance style she embraced. Her recourse was to affiliate with a small storefront church whose style of worhip was familiar and therefore comforting.

Arna Bontemps and Jack Conroy, whose research on Chicago was conducted as editorial supervisors of the Illinois Writers' Project of the Works Progress Administration (WPA), assessed the significance of the storefront church during the 1930s:

> [T]he most important thing about the storefront was that everybody participated. Untrained but powerful voices joined in hymns sung in such an unorthodox manner that they gave rise to a whole new body of *gospel music* [emphasis mine]. The preacher might be illiterate, but he spoke a homely, straight-from-the shoulder language understood by all.[8]

While spirited demonstrative worship uniformly characterized the worship of the small urban storefront churches, the majority of which were Holiness and Baptist, there were also Baptist and Methodist churches during the period of migratory transition with sanctuaries that seated over two thousand members, and were known as "**shouting churches**," or churches where the worship was highly energized and participants could experience altered states.[9] At the same time, there were also Holiness and Spiritualist churches with sizeable congregations housed in large buildings who celebrated worship in the emotive style most commonly associated with the storefront. One migrant shared her delight in the worship experience she had in a large Chicago church during the 1930s:

Storefront church
A retail business structure that has been converted into a worship site.

Shout
An ecstatic expression of worship through demonstrative behavior, often reflecting an altered state of being. Not to be confused with the "ring shout."

I am well and thankful to be in a city with no lynching and no beating . . . I got here just in time for one of the greatest revivals in the history of my life—over 500 joined the church. We had a holy-ghost shower. You know how I like to *run wild* [emphasis mine] at the services—it snows here and even the churches are crowded and we had to stand up last night.[10]

TRANSITIONAL GOSPEL MUSIC: HOLINESS-PENTECOSTAL STYLE

The music of the urban storefront church of the 1930s is most consistently described by its style of delivery or aesthetic features. Just as the preaching and worship services of these small bodies reflected the continuation of a worship style that had distinguished Black independent churches in the rural South, the music expression was also consistent. While the repertoire included Protestant hymns, and occasionally spirituals, most often a new genre, sometimes referenced as gospel hymns and other times derisively referred to as jazz hymns, became the hallmark of these congregations.[11] The use of musical instruments, most of which previously had been associated with secular musics and denied entry into the worship of the mainline Baptist and Methodist congregations, was a compelling marker of this new form of religious music expression. A 1929 issue of *Crisis* magazine, an official publication of the National Association of the Advancement of Colored People (NAACP), included this rather biased, yet noteworthy, account of storefront worship and its music:

> It is night. My errand brings me through a busy street of the Negro section in a city having a colored population of seven thousand. Suddenly I am arrested by bedlam which proceeds from the open transom of a store front whose show windows are smeared to intransparency. What issues forth is conglomeration itself—a syncopated rhythmic mess of a tune accompanied by strumming guitars and jingling tambourines and frequently punctuated by wild shrieks and stamping feet. Above the din occasionally emerge such words as "Jesus," and "God," "Hallelujah," "Glory," and then I realize that this frenzy is being perpetrated in the name of religion. A young man of my own race who has stopped in amazement turns to me half-quizzically and says, "What do you know about that? Jazzin' God."[12]

Among the Holiness and Pentecostal denominations, the boundaries of musical expression in the African American church expanded. Having severed his ties with the Baptist Church over the theological tenets of Holiness (a post-Civil War ecumenical movement led by Methodists), Charles H. Mason founded the Church of God in Christ (COGIC) in Little Rock, Arkansas, in 1897. COGIC was a completely new denomination, divinely inspired, according to Mason. Its members were viewed as "saved and sanctified saints." During the course of his study of the doctrine of baptism in the Holy Spirit, in 1907, Mason attended the famed 1906–08 Azuza Street Revival in Los Angeles, led by William Seymour, the man generally recognized among African Americans as the founder of Pentecostalism. During his five-week stay at Azuza, Mason **spoke in tongues** for the first time, the experience he had sought. Upon his return

Transitional gospel music
Forms of African American religious music that represent the bridge between the spiritual and its twentieth-century counterpart of traditional gospel music.

Speaking in tongues
Uttering words or phrases in charismatic worship, which are spoken in a language intelligible only through spiritual discernment. Also known as "glossolalia."

to Mississippi, Mason testified that what he had gained at Azuza Street propelled his Mississippi ministry to new heights, prompting, in particular, the rapid spread of his new denomination. Indicating the transforming power of his Azuza experience, Mason also noted, "The Spirit had taken full control of me and everything was new to me and to all the saints. The way that He did things was all new . . . He taught me how and what to sing, and all His songs were new."[13]

The music that defined storefront churches in Black Chicago in the 1920s clearly reflected a strong COGIC imprint, for ministers and evangelists who were also musicians, and would later become recording artists, were a part of the migrant population. The artistry of Texas-born, blind singer-pianist, COGIC evangelist Arizona Dranes (c.1905–c.1960) is captured on OKeh recordings from 1926 to 1928. Her percussive piano style is reminiscent of ragtime, although there has been no evidence to indicate that she had engaged in performance of secular music prior. Her singing style, as captured on such titles as "I'll Go Where You Want Me To Go" (1928) and "He Is My Story" (1928), is equally percussive, characterized by short phrases that, by their intensity, often seem almost shouted. Hers is not the voice of one trained in Western vocal production; it is, however, the voice of one who sings with unbridled fervor and spiritual conviction.[14]

While traveling in pursuit of her ministry, Dranes sometimes collaborated with the Tennessee native Rev. Ford Washington McGee, who in 1925 established a COGIC church, McGee's Temple, on the south side of Chicago, the area Drake and Cayton referred to as Bronzeville because of its concentrated population of African Americans. McGee recorded forty-six sides for Victor, the last of which was in 1930, with musical accompaniment including various combinations of piano, cornet, drums, bass, guitar, tambourine, violin, trombone, and trumpet.[15]

The repertoire recorded by Holiness or Pentecostal performers consisted of new compositions, which reflected the beliefs particular to members of their denomination, as well as standard Protestant hymns such as F.W. McGee's recording of "Rock of Ages," by Toplady and Hastings; spirituals such as "Were You There When They Crucified My Lord?," and songs that traversed denominational boundaries among African Americans, including "I Am On the Battlefield for My Lord," by Sylvana Bell and E.V. Banks, recorded in 1928 by Rev. D.C. Rice, a minister in the Apostolic Overcoming Holy Church of God.[16] **Call–response** was routinely incorporated into simple verse–chorus structures, and singers and instrumentalists alike performed in a highly repetitive, improvisational style unencumbered by the need to adhere to a musical score. While harmony does occur in the vocal parts, it is often intermittent, alternating with the heterophonic textures that had characterized the singing of folk spirituals. As scholars of Black religious music argue:

Call–response
A song structure or performance practice in which a singer or instrumentalist makes a musical statement that is answered by another soloist, instrumentalist, or group. The statement and answer sometimes overlap. Also called antiphony and call-and-response.

Black urban religious music, particularly in the newly formed Pentecostal denomination, differed little from the folk spiritual of the rural South, except for instrumental accompaniment. Both song types were based on the call–response structure; both required a demonstrative style of delivery, complete with handclapping and dancing in the spirit; and both were sung in heterophony.[17]

THOMAS DORSEY

The man who figured most prominently in the movement of this emergent form of Black gospel music from the margins to the mainstream was Thomas A. Dorsey (1899–1993), who was a 1916 migrant to Chicago from Georgia. Born in Villa Rica, near Atlanta, the son of an itinerant Baptist preacher, Dorsey grew up playing organ in church. As a boy, however, he also worked selling soda pop at a vaudeville theater in Atlanta, where he was regularly exposed to such blues performers as Ma Rainey and Bessie Smith. Captivated by the music he heard at the 81 Theater, Dorsey chose to cultivate his own musical gifts by learning to read music and apprenticing himself to pianists who played at the theater where he worked. By the time Dorsey was sixteen years old, he had built a reputation as the number one blues piano player for rent parties in the city, eventually acquiring the name Barrelhouse Tom, a disparaging term that, according to Dorsey, associated him with barrels of liquor. Later, in Chicago, he was also known as Georgia Tom.

Like other members of the migrant community, Dorsey's move to Chicago was prompted by a desire for a better life, for in Chicago he anticipated the elimination of indignities he had routinely encountered in the South. "You didn't have to get off the street nowhere here," he commented.[18] During his first five years in the city, Dorsey was not a member of *any* church, but his inspiring visit to the National Baptist

Figure 10.1
Thomas A. Dorsey in 1975 at the piano. Photo by Amy van Singel, courtesy BluEsoterica.com.

Mellonee V. Burnim

Convention held in Chicago in 1921 prefaced a change in his level of religious engagement. At the convention, Dorsey heard A.W. Nix sing "I Do, Don't You," a 1907 composition by Melville Miller and E.G. Excell, which prompted him to begin writing and performing gospel music. In that same year, Dorsey joined New Hope Baptist Church, became its director of music and also wrote his first gospel song—"If I Don't Get There,"[19] later published in *Gospel Pearls*, a collection of 163 songs compiled by the Sunday School Publishing board of the US National Baptist Convention.

Gospel Pearls' front matter indicates it was designed to address "an urgent demand for real inspiring and adaptable music in all of our Sunday Schools, Churches, Conventions, and other religious gatherings." Its contents included "Standard [*sic*] old songs, gathered with great care and especially adapted for soul-winning, as well as the very latest and popular works of the very best composers of sacred song, and a collection of Jubilee songs known as Spirituals."

Dorsey's "If I Don't Get There," presumably considered as a "recent composition," was in good company in *Gospel Pearls*, for the compilation included six works by Charles Albert Tindley, the charismatic minister of Tindley Temple Methodist Episcopal Church in Philadelphia, whom Dorsey later credited as a seminal influence on the development of his own compositional style in gospel music. In writing gospel music, Dorsey expressed the desire to "further what Tindley started."[20] In his pioneering 1960 dissertation on gospel music, ethnomusicologist George Robinson Ricks suggests further that the music of the newly formed Holiness and Pentecostal churches of Chicago was also Tindley inspired.[21]

TRANSITIONAL GOSPEL MUSIC: TINDLEY STYLE

Within the predominantly White Methodist Episcopal Church, Rev. C.A. Tindley (1851–1933) was a man of considerable stature. Known for his dynamic preaching, he built the membership of his church to over ten thousand during the 1920s. With a sanctuary that seated only 3,500 and a bevy of visitors, Black and White, who routinely flocked to the church, worship services were consistently filled to capacity, requiring that members arrive several hours early if they desired to be seated. One observer recalls:

> Thirty-five hundred could be seated; another fifteen hundred could stand around the walls, and *every Sunday morning*, rain or shine, by twenty after ten, if you weren't in, you didn't *get* in. Because the place would be packed—they'd even lock the doors.[22]

For Tindley, music was an essential component of dynamic worship, and he was known to punctuate his sermons with songs he had written as an enhancement.[23] Because Tindley had been influenced by the doctrines of the Methodist-led Holiness movement of the late nineteeth century (which preceded the advent of Holiness and Pentecostal denominations), it was commonplace for services at Tindley Temple to be filled with extemporaneous prayer, spirited congregational singing, and even shouting. In some instances services were even known to last all night:

> In the Methodist Episcopal Church at that time, he [Tindley] was not the traditional preacher. There could have very easily been a sign out here, Tindley Temple Baptist, Tindley Temple Pentecostal, and people would have believed that's what he was, just by the experience. So if you have an image of what a United Methodist Church is like, that is, I think the usual image is a staid, quiet, reserved, dignified, not too many amens . . . then Tindley Temple is just the opposite of that.[24]

According to Ralph Jones, Tindley's biographer, around 1922, the C.A. Tindley Gospel Chorus was formed, a group of ten singers and a pianist, who specialized in singing Tindley's compositions. Described as possessing a "robust, tenor voice," Tindley's son Elbert was one of the main soloists for the group: "At several worship services Elbert sang, and the effect was so strong that good, old Methodist shouting and cries of amen, praise the Lord, and hallelujah broke out." When performing solos, Elbert was known to toss his head and use his hands and body to "dramatize and emphasize his singing." The success of the chorus was evident by the fact that they eventually formed a professional double quartet that presented recitals around the country.[25]

The first of Tindley's compositions was published in 1901, only two years after Dorsey was born, and precisely twenty years before Dorsey published his first gospel composition. Among Tindley's total output of forty-six songs,[26] all of which were published by 1923, are his enduring works, "We'll Understand It Better By and By," "Stand by Me," and "The Storm Is Passing Over," all of which continue to be sung by African American congregations across denominational lines.[27] Some analysts contend that the most compelling dimension of Tindley's compositions (sometimes referred to as gospel hymns, often referenced simply as hymns) are his song texts. A man without formal education, Tindley also lacked training in reading and writing music, relying on several different "arrangers" to translate his musical ideas to the score.[28]

From a musical standpoint, the chords in Tindley's compositions broke no new ground, as the standard I, IV, V harmonies dominated his work.[29] Reflecting his preaching prowess, however, Tindley's song texts spoke with poignance to his congregation of hard-working menial laborers:[30]

> As he wrote the music . . . well brothers and sisters, he wrote from *experience*. Not only his experience, but the experience of others . . . He had a way of taking those things that were natural and sometimes material and translating them into that which was spiritual.[31]

27

"Leave It There."

Tindley's "Leave It There," published in 1916 (Track 27), is believed to have been written not long after his first unsuccessful bid for the office of bishop, a disappointment he shared with his congregation. The message of Tindley's composition conveys a spirit of triumph over adversity, content with which his members would surely identify. Furthermore, he structured his texts in a way that reflected the musical values that had characterized the folk spiritual tradition of the rural South. The refrain, "Take your burden to the Lord and leave it there," is repeated in both the verse and chorus, providing an element that could be easily recalled in congregational singing. Tindley sometimes taught his songs to his congregation during the actual service when he initially introduced them, and repeated text would most certainly facilitate rote learning.[32] In the chorus of "Leave It There" the refrain line alternates with lines of changing text, as in the call–response structure; in addition, Tindley skillfully incorporates call–response in the opening line of the chorus, providing yet another opportunity for full congregational participation. Anyone who hears one of Tindley's most popular songs performed in an engaged African American worship setting will agree with music theorist Horace Boyer's assessment that Tindley songs spring to life during performance,[33] as was true of spirituals sung by slaves, and of music sung in post-Civil War Black southern rural congregations and the early twentieth-century urban storefront.

When Thomas Dorsey entered the world of Black religious music in Chicago in 1921, he found a scene that was rich and engaging. While the numbers of storefront churches with their rural southern-based musical expression represented only a very small minority of church members among Blacks in the first third of the twentieth century, their distinct worship style was replicated to some degree in larger Chicago congregations—Methodist, Baptist, and Spiritualist. Furthermore, Dorsey was struck by the music he heard at the National Baptist Convention in Chicago in 1921, and he acknowledged that the work of C.A. Tindley in Philadelphia was having widespread impact among Black Christians nationwide:

> The name "gospels" was used around 1905–1906 when C. Albert Tindley was writing songs. I can remember . . . his "[We'll Understand It Better] By and By" . . . this song was a great hit around 1907 in the churches of the South. They had no pianos but the sisters in the "Amen Corner" would carry the rhythm by *patting their feet and clapping their hands* [emphasis mine].[34]

Despite Dorsey's exposure and engagement with these varied articulations of Black religious music, none of them captured his imagination in such a way to immediately lure him away from his career in blues and jazz. During the same year he published his first gospel song, Dorsey also joined the Whispering Syncopators, a jazz band that included Lionel Hampton on vibraphone. In 1924, Dorsey worked as music director for famed blues singer Gertrude Ma Rainey, writing songs for her, recording and leading the Wildcats Jazz Band, which provided her musical back-up.[35]

After his stint with Ma Rainey ended, Dorsey partnered with Florida-born bottleneck guitarist Tampa Red to produce over sixty recordings from 1928 to 1932. Their risqué 1928 Vocalian recording, "It's Tight Like That," became their biggest hit, even though they released a number of other double entendre titles, including "Pat That Bread," "You Got That Stuff," and "Where Did You Stay Last Night?" Sales of "It's Tight Like That" launched Dorsey into newfound notoriety and financial success. But no sooner than the first royalty check was deposited, his bank failed, a victim of the 1929 stock market crash and the impending Depression. Interpreting his misfortune as God's corrective hand, Dorsey turned once again to gospel music, with the National Baptist Convention serving as a point of entry.[36]

In 1930, Thomas Dorsey had the good fortune of having his composition "If You See My Savior" performed at the Jubilee Anniversary of the National Baptist Convention, held once again in Chicago. The significant role that music played in this annual event was evident by its one-thousand-voice mass choir and fifty-piece orchestra, both under the overarching leadership of Lucie Campbell, the powerful music director of the convention.[37] The repertoire of the convention included "Am I a Soldier of the Cross" by Isaac Watts, whose hymns had been popular among Blacks since slavery, and Tindley's "Take Your Burden to the Lord and Leave It There," both of which are included in *Gospel Pearls*. Dorsey's "If You See My Savior" was so well received that before the convention had ended, he had sold four thousand copies of his music.[38]

Over the next two years, Dorsey sustained and built upon his involvement with gospel music in Chicago, organizing choirs at Ebenezer and Pilgrim Baptist churches, respectively. At both churches, Dorsey was selected for this position by ministers who had migrated to Chicago from the South, one from Alabama, the other from Mississippi. Their interest in creating gospel choirs, in contrast to the existing "senior choirs," which sang anthems (read: classical music), was to introduce music into their worship that appealed to the migrant populations in their pews.[39] As the son of Rev. Austin of Pilgrim Baptist recalls:

> My dad was farsighted, I think. He could see times changing and people desiring another type of music. He said, "Dorsey's music's going to sweep the country. And I want it in Pilgrim Church!" And he tried it in his church. And when they started liking it, brother, it just went like wildfire, like a fire in your house. When the fire started, he didn't have a thing to do but just let the good times roll.[40]

According to Michael Harris, Dorsey's biographer, "over 100 people joined the Ebenezer chorus," using the few songs Dorsey had written at that point and other "traditional songs," among them "I Am on the Battlefield for My Lord," whose sixteen-bar AABA textual structure in the chorus was a defining feature in spirituals. The words "I am on the battlefield for my Lord" are repeated three times, with different text included only in the third line. Most instructive, however, was the style of delivery that Dorsey employed when performing. He would sometimes stand rather than sit at the piano, while Mississippi-born Theodore Frye, who worked closely with Dorsey as choir director and lead singer, was known to walk and "strut" during his performances, reflective of the performance aesthetics Dorsey had employed as a bluesman.[41] Dorsey readily acknowledged how his gospel style was influenced by his background in secular music:

> This rhythm I had, I brought with me to gospel songs. I was a blues singer, and I carried that with me into the gospel songs . . . I always had rhythm in my bones. I like the solid beat. I like the moaning groaning tone. I like the rock. You know how they rock and shout in the church. I like it . . . Black music calls for movement! It calls for feeling. Don't let it get away.[42]

TRANSITIONAL GOSPEL MUSIC: RURAL

Discussions of gospel music typically reference Thomas Dorsey's embrace and interchange of sacred and secular musics as a trend that he single-handedly fostered during gospel music's infancy. To the contrary, during the 1920s and 1930s, a style of religious music that was virtually identical, save for its text, to that of the rural blues tradition, was both performed and recorded by a number of Black artists. Often sung by solo blues singers with guitar or harmonica accompaniment, this early subgenre of gospel music was characterized by the minimal chord changes and variable rhythmic structures (adding or subtracting beats from measures) that typified rural blues around the turn of the twentieth century, and call–response between voice and instrument.

In some instances, performers of this rural gospel style were simply itinerant bluesmen and women who recorded religious music under pseudonyms. Texas-born guitarist Blind Lemon Jefferson (c.1897–1929), for example, recorded gospel under the name Deacon Bates. In other cases, artists recorded religious songs exclusively, as did Texas singer-guitarist Blind Willie Johnson (1902–c.1949) (Track 11).[43] Another highly skilled singer-guitarist, Rev. Gary Davis (1896–1972) of South Carolina, is lauded in the film series *Masters of the Country Blues*, as "one of the greatest traditional guitarists of the century."[44] Despite his popular success as a bluesman, particularly around Durham, North Carolina, Davis repudiated blues in the early 1930s and subsequently became an ordained Baptist minister, recording a series of gospel songs in 1935 considered "masterpieces." While Davis's vocal style on such songs as "If I Had My Way" is reminiscent of the shouting preacher and singers in the storefront church, his instrumental accompaniment on the steel guitar is indistinguishable from that of the rural blues.[45]

 11

"God Moves on the Water."

TRADITIONAL GOSPEL MUSIC

The path that Dorsey forged in blending his secular music experience with his new-found commitment to sacred music was not uncharted

Traditional gospel music
Black religious music that emerged in urban contexts during the 1930s; pervasive in present-day African American worship.

territory. Musicians of considerable stature engaged in similar pursuits, but in the realm of gospel music, the name Thomas Dorsey holds singular prominence. Perhaps Thomas Dorsey's most enduring achievement warranting his designation as "Father of Gospel Music" was his role in forging elements representative of each of the three forms of transitional gospel music—rural gospel, Tindley style, and Holiness-Pentecostal style—into a unitary thread. Dorsey's musical abilities prompted his partnership with other key figures interested in systematically developing a broad base of support for its performance. The growth of gospel music into a position of national prominence resulted from the creative imagination, shared vision, and collective enterprise of a core group of musical entrepreneurs.

Dorsey was drafted as founding president of the National Convention of Gospel Choirs and Choruses in 1933, an organization created for the purpose of promoting and disseminating this new genre. At the time, over twenty churches in Chicago had organized choirs devoted exclusively to singing gospel music, and twenty-four states had choruses. The leadership of the convention was an alliance of key proponents of gospel music in Chicago—southern migrants who understood that this music, which spoke so profoundly to their hearts and minds, would also be readily embraced by African Americans across the nation. Sallie Martin, of Rev. Clarence Cobbs's First Church of Deliverance Spiritualist Church, with its weekly radio broadcast; Theodore Frye, Baptist—Dorsey's partner in forging the success of gospel choruses at Pilgrim and at Ebenezer; Magnolia Lewis Butts, choir director at Metropolitan Community Church, a congregation formed after severing its ties with the African Methodist Episcopal Church; and Mississippi-born Willie Mae Ford Smith, a former African Methodist Episcopal Zion who became Pentecostal, were all a part of the core leadership.[46] The organization was ecumenical from the outset—an independent African American body singularly committed to advancing a music they themselves had created as a statement of their own unique religious and cultural identity.

Dorsey recalls that the public response to the formation of the National Convention of Gospel Choirs and Choruses was all they had expected and more. The degree of opposition the group initially faced reflected, to some degree, its tremendous appeal:

> There were some who were dubious, or wavered in opinion as to the success of the convention. A minister said to me there that week, this thing is starting off too big and with too much public notice and support, it can't last long. Another friend said to me, I don't think this kind of organization can hold out because gospel singing is new and the people as a whole who like the *better music* [emphasis mine] are not for it in our churches.[47]

With a unified network of local units, called choral unions, the National Convention of Gospel Choirs and Choruses grew from its initial nucleus of some two hundred to an international membership of more than three thousand in the 1990s.[48] Their week-long, annual gatherings,

Mellonee V. Burnim

held in major cities across the country, feature rehearsals, concerts, worship services, and classes on all aspects of gospel music production and performance. The Dorsey model spawned the growth of over a dozen comparable organizations, the largest of which is the James Cleveland Gospel Music Workshop of America, founded in Detroit (another important gospel music center), in 1969, which boasts annual attendance of more than twenty thousand.[49]

Without question, Dorsey's most famous song is "Take My Hand, Precious Lord," written in 1932 in the aftermath of the death of his wife and newborn son. The text is original, but Dorsey acknowledges that his tune is Maitland, commonly associated with the nineteenth-century hymn "Must Jesus Bear the Cross Alone," by Thomas Shepherd, a fact that is either unknown to most members of the gospel community or is of little consequence. Dorsey's use of this "borrowed" tune again points to the way that other genres contribute to gospel music repertoire. While gospel literature includes original compositions, melodies from existing hymns and spirituals also serve as primary source material. The written melodic line from the familiar "Must Jesus Bear the Cross Alone" used in "Take My Hand, Precious Lord" merely serves as a point of departure for the skillful gospel vocalist and accompanist, for inspired gospel singers are expected to embellish and interpret the melody in ways that reflect aesthetic values shared among all genres of African American music, sacred and secular.

"Take My Hand, Precious Lord" has been published in "twenty-six different languages and released on recordings in most European countries and Australia."[50] It is included in hymnals from the United Methodist Church, African Methodist Episcopal Church, National Baptist Convention, and the Church of God in Christ, among others. "Take My Hand, Precious Lord" (Track 17) was sung at the funeral of Martin Luther King Jr. by Mahalia Jackson, at the funeral of Mahalia Jackson by Aretha Franklin, and at the funeral of President Lyndon Baines Johnson by Leontyne Price.[51]

 17

"Take My Hand, Precious Lord."

Mahalia Jackson

Thomas Dorsey was not the only seminal gospel music pioneer for whom Chicago was the final destination in the mass migration of Blacks from points south. Mahalia Jackson (1912–72) arrived in 1928 from New Orleans. Like Dorsey, Jackson embraced both sacred and secular musics from childhood. Not only were hymns a part of her musical background, so were the blues. Affiliated with the Baptist Church, with its "foot-tapping and hand-clapping," Jackson's formative religious exposure also included the Pentecostal Church, whose music she loved. She recalled:

> I know now that a great influence in my life was the Sanctified or Holiness Churches we had in the South. I was always a Baptist, but there was a Sanctified Church right next door to our house in New Orleans . . . Those people had no choir and no organ. They used the drum, the cymbal, the tambourine, and the steel triangle. Everybody in there sang and they clapped and stomped their feet and sang with their whole bodies. They had a beat, a powerful beat, a rhythm we held on to from slavery days, and their music was so strong and expressive it used to bring the tears to my eyes.[52]

Although Jackson's Aunt Duke, who parented her in New Orleans after her mother's death, did not sanction her listening to "worldly" or secular music, Jackson immersed herself in her older cousin's blues collection whenever her aunt was not at home. Her favorite performer was Bessie Smith, whose vocal quality she greatly admired and admittedly sought to imitate: "I remember when I used to listen to Bessie Smith sing 'I Hate to See that Evening Sun Go Down,' I'd fix my mouth and try to make tones come out just like hers."[53] Jackson even speculates that, had her aunt not intervened, she might otherwise have been lured into the world of secular song. Yet, for Jackson, blues and gospel, although related sonically, were distanced from each other by the oppositional messages conveyed through their texts, as well as the kinds of inward responses they provoked. The textual message—that is, the intent—was of consequence. Although Jackson was influenced musically by the blues, her music was equally informed by spirituals and by hymns. She *never* collapsed the boundaries that distinguished sacred from secular and as she adamantly asserts below, she never considered either her repertoire or her performance as "gospel blues":

> People were always pestering me about becoming a blues singer. They'd tell me, "Girl, you could become a great blues singer." I'd answer, "What Negro *couldn't* become a blues singer!"
>
> I'll never give up my gospel songs for the blues. Blues are the songs of despair, but gospel songs are the songs of hope. When you sing them you are delivered of your burden. You have a feeling that there is a cure for what's wrong.
>
> It always gives me joy to sing gospel songs. I get to singing and I feel better right away. When you get through with the blues, you've got nothing to rest on. I tell people that the person who sings only the blues is like someone in a deep pit yelling for help, and I'm simply not in that position.[54]

Thomas Dorsey and Mahalia Jackson were affiliated with two different Baptist churches in Chicago during gospel music's formative years, yet their mutual devotion to the genre and their likeminded commitment to its performance fostered an early partnership between the two. Struck by the staunch opposition and criticism he faced from preachers and congregations of established Baptist and Methodist churches when he initially began promoting his compositions, Dorsey recounts:

> Gospel music was new and most people didn't understand. Some of the preachers used to call gospel music "sin" music. They related it to what they called worldly things—like jazz and blues and show business. Gospel music was different from approved hymns and spirituals. It had a beat.[55]

Referencing the centrality of rhythm to gospel performance style, Dorsey joined forces with Mahalia Jackson, to initiate an "audience development" strategy that bypassed the Black religious and musical establishment altogether by taking the music "to the streets":[56]

> There were many days and nights when Mahalia and I would be out there on the street corners . . . Mahalia would sing songs I'd composed, and I'd sell sheet music to folk for five and ten cents . . . We took gospel music all around the country too.[57]

Mellonee V. Burnim

While Dorsey rose to a position of prominence in gospel music as a composer, director, and promoter, Mahalia Jackson was first and foremost a singer, whose powerful and richly textured contralto voice and style of delivery captivated audiences all over the world through her recordings, radio and television appearances, and live performances. Soon after her arrival in Chicago, she became a member of the Johnson Singers, a mixed group of five young people from her church, Salem Baptist. Although she did not read music, *Gospel Pearls*, with its familiar hymns and spirituals, was her constant companion. Not all churches welcomed her brand of gospel, for her music was something people could "clap and rock by."[58] Jackson moved when she sang, using her face, hands, body, and feet to convey the message of a song. When she became totally enraptured with the spirit, her voice could express a quality closely akin to shouting.

At age seventeen, Jackson was once castigated from the pulpit by a minister who judged her "shouting, bouncing, and clapping" as inappropriate for worship. Sallie Martin, a Spiritualist, recalls that initially, "Most big churches . . . didn't receive her work," while other singers "looked down their noses at her." Jackson had only a fifth-grade education, and the high-spirited freedom she exuded in her singing was neither contrived nor consciously cultivated. It was, however, influenced by the practices she witnessed in the Pentecostal church situated next to her home in New Orleans. The criticism she received, for exhibiting behaviors that ran counter to the prescribed modes that signaled upward mobility for African Americans, only fueled her conviction to sing in ways that reflected her cultural heritage and her religious belief. Her retort was:

> I was born to sing gospel music. Nobody had to teach me. I was serving God . . . [T]here was a Psalm that said: "O clap your hands, all ye people! Shout unto the Lord with the voice of a trumpet!"[59] If it was undignified, it was what the Bible told me to do.[60]

In 1946, Jackson signed with Apollo Records. Even though her initial release was a commercial flop, in 1947 Apollo agreed to a second attempt—"Move On Up a Little Higher" by Black composer Rev. William Herbert Brewster of Memphis, which had already received favorable hearings at the National Baptist Convention. Released as a single, the length of "Move On Up a Little Higher" filled both sides of the 78-rpm record—Parts I and II. Within four weeks, fifty thousand records sold, with demand coming from the East and West Coasts and points in between. Ultimately, "Move On Up a Little Higher" sold two million records, raising Jackson's stature to meteoric proportions among African Americans.[61]

With her recording success, Jackson was soon swept with media coverage locally and nationally. Over the course of her career, her network television exposure included repeated appearances with Ed Sullivan, Bing Crosby, Dinah Shore, and Dave Garroway. In 1950, she appeared in the films *St. Louis Blues* and *Imitation of Life*, and in 1952 she launched her first of several European tours. For twenty weeks in 1954–55, Jackson had her own radio show on a CBS station in Chicago, and in 1955 she appeared regularly on the Chicago WBBM-TV program *In Town Tonight*. When John Kennedy was inaugurated in 1961, Mahalia Jackson sang "The Star Spangled Banner," and at the 1963 March on Washington, she stirred the crowd with her gospel version of the spiritual "I've Been Buked and I've Been Scorned."[62] Honored at her death in 1972 with two funerals, one in Chicago, the other in her hometown of New Orleans, Jackson was awarded a Grammy posthumously in 1976, in recognition of her distinguished recording career. Her repertoire included hymns and spirituals, which she reinterpreted through her gospel music performance lens, as well as original works by composers such as C.A. Tindley and Thomas Dorsey.

Roberta Martin

More than any other pioneer, over the course of her career, Mahalia Jackson came to represent the public face of gospel music. But the advancement of gospel music unquestionably resulted from the collective effort of multiple contributors in a number of different sites. The Roberta Martin Singers were founded in Chicago in 1933 by composer-pianist Roberta Martin (1907–69), who migrated with her family from Arkansas to Chicago. Honing her skills on piano with fifteen years of classical study and working as accompanist for a "junior choir" led by Thomas Dorsey and Theodore Frye during her youth, she is considered as a progenitor of the gospel piano style.[63]

Roberta Martin's publishing house, established in 1939, with its catalogue of 280 songs, was a major outlet for compositions by composer-pianist-director James Cleveland, as well her own works, among them "He Knows Just How Much We Can Bear" (1941), which became a gospel standard, and is included in the *New National Baptist Hymnal* and *Songs of Zion* (United Methodist), among others.[64] Beginning in the 1930s and remaining strong until the onset of decline prompted by increasing record sales and photocopying, Chicago was also home to gospel publishing ventures led by Lillian Bowles, Sallie Martin, Kenneth Morris, and Thomas Dorsey.[65]

Albertina Walker

In 1952, Albertina Walker (1929–2010) formed the all-female group known as the Caravans, so named because its members were located in distant points across the city. Over the years, the Caravans' stellar personnel included the prolific recording artist James Cleveland as pianist and Shirley Caesar; the latter's career, as did Walker's, spanned into the twenty-first century, and she still figures prominently on the gospel scene today.[66]

Mellonee V. Burnim

Clara Ward

Gospel trendsetters located in other major cities included the Ward Singers, founded in Philadelphia in 1934 and comprised initially of Gertrude Ward and her daughters Clara and Willa. Eventually expanding to include two additional female voices, the Ward Singers are credited with recording one of the first million-selling gospel records, "Surely God Is Able," by Memphis Baptist minister, William Herbert Brewster, around 1948–49.[67] They also gained considerable notoriety for their controversial decision to perform gospel music in Las Vegas casinos in 1962.[68]

Rosetta Tharpe

The career of the celebrated Rosetta Tharpe, whose self-accompaniment on guitar constituted her signature sound, was rooted in the Pentecostal Church, where her mother served as an evangelist. Tharpe is also remembered for her controversial collaborations with the jazz bands of Cab Calloway and Lucky Millinder during the 1930s and 1940s.[69]

CONTEMPORARY GOSPEL MUSIC

The release of the recording "Oh Happy Day" by the Edwin Hawkins Singers (Track 28) in 1969 ushered in the **contemporary gospel** era. Initially considered innovative because of its use of the Fender bass, bongos, and horns as accompaniment (which closely paralleled popular musics of the period), this recording represented the beginning of the development of a significant crossover market for gospel music. Sales of "Oh Happy Day" exceeded one million copies, well above the 100,000 units that the GospoCentric label had originally anticipated, and well above the sales figures typically generated by even the most popular of gospel music artists of the period.[70]

28

"Oh Happy Day."

"Oh Happy Day" was originally pressed in 1968 by the forty-six-member Church of God In Christ Northern California State Youth Choir. Conceived as a fundraising project, eight Edwin Hawkins arrangements were recorded with only two microphones in a single two-and-a-half-hour session in a church in Berkeley. The serendipitous exposure that "Oh Happy Day" received on underground radio, after having fallen inadvertently into the hands of an Oakland rock promoter, placed it on a trajectory that the performers had never envisioned.[71]

Contemporary gospel music
Post-1970 gospel that embraces elements of R&B, rock, funk, jazz, and other popular styles, usually performed by a small ensemble.

With the advent of the contemporary gospel music era, gospel moved beyond the protective confines of the Black church to become a music that knew neither denominational, racial, cultural, nor musical boundaries. Although striking in its musical distinctiveness when it was first released, "Oh Happy Day" now falls into the category of traditional gospel music as the sonic boundaries of the genre continue to expand.

Following the success of "Oh Happy Day," the trend-setting Hawkins family continued to be a major force in the gospel music industry, noted in *Billboard* as having produced four of the Top 40 gospel albums from

1973 to 1994. Walter Hawkins' *Love Alive* and *Love Alive II* were ranked as numbers 1 and 2 respectively on this list, while *Love Alive III* and *IV* were numbers 11 and 23. Other contemporary gospel artists among the Top 40 during this roughly twenty-year period include Milton Brunson and Andrae Crouch, each with four entries, and the Clark Sisters (*Is My Living In Vain*), John P. Kee & the New Life Community Choir (*We Walk By Faith*), Vanessa Bell Armstrong (*Chosen*), BeBe & CeCe Winans (*Different Lifestyles*), and Kirk Franklin (*Kirk Franklin and the Family*), each with one.[72]

 29

"I Don't Feel Noways Tired (Part I)."

While contemporary gospel artists are well represented on this Top 40 list, albums of traditional gospel artists are of equal consequence. Six entries, more than any other artist, are credited to James Cleveland, including his presentation of the Harold Smith Majestics' *Lord Help Me To Hold Out* (no. 3) and *I Don't Feel Noways Tired* (no. 28) (with the Salem Inspirational Choir) (Track 29). Three albums of Minister Shirley Caesar are cited—*Live In Chicago* (no. 8), *Jesus, I Love Calling Your Name* (no. 36) and *First Lady* (no. 38), and the Mississippi Mass Choir holds slots 3, 7, and 30.[73]

In 1993, almost twenty-five years after the "Oh Happy Day" phenomenon, a gospel release of comparable magnitude hit the charts. *Kirk Franklin and the Family* was one of the first products of the Black female-owned GospoCentric label, formed in the same year as Franklin's debut (see Figure 10.2).[74] Vicki Mack Lataillade, founder of GospoCentric, had worked with some of the biggest acts in the industry, including the Winans, a group of brothers from Detroit, Tramaine Hawkins, who began her career with the Edwin Hawkins Singers, and Take 6.[75]

After a rather lackluster debut, *Kirk Franklin and the Family* was carefully and strategically marketed to maximize airplay and exposure of the album in the mainstream. Defying the original GospoCentric projection of 100,000 units, *Kirk Franklin and the Family* eventually went platinum, signifying sales of over one million copies.[76] "Why We Sing," the major hit on the album, was winner of two Dove awards from the predominantly White Gospel Music Association, two Stellar awards, conferred by the Black gospel music industry, and the James Cleveland Gospel Music Workshop of America 1994 Excellence Award.[77]

Franklin's 1997 release, *God's Property*, included the crossover hit "Stomp," recorded with female rapper Cheryl "Salt" James of the rap duo Salt-N-Pepa. Although "Stomp" was named "Song of the Year" at the 1997 Stellar Awards, sponsored by the Black gospel music industry, in his acceptance speech, Franklin referenced the criticism he encountered from members of the African American Christian community regarding the close intersection between his sonic vision and that of secular musics of the day.[78]

Franklin's embrace of rap, hip-hop, and funk in his music is consistent with that of other contemporary gospel music groups, such as Take 6, whose sound is strongly rooted in jazz. As a multi-platinum-

Mellonee V. Burnim

Figure 10.2
Kirk Franklin performs
as musical guest on
*The Tonight Show with
Jay Leno*, Episode
1504, December 7,
1998. Photo by
Margaret Norton/
NBC/NBCU Photo
Bank via Getty
Images.

selling recording artist, Kirk Franklin has crossed over to rhythm and
blues charts as well as the Contemporary Christian chart, which reflects
a breakthrough into the White Christian market. Franklin's response to
those who criticize his musical affinities echoes that of his predecessors
in gospel music—Thomas Dorsey, Mahalia Jackson, and many others—
who faced similar indictments for their perceived drifts toward seculariza-
tion. This recurrent trope points to the tension that exists for artists whose
work, fueled by creativity, as well as religious belief, appeals to a fan base
that is far from homogeneous. As Franklin indicates, gospel music artists
typically see their work as more than musicianship, for historically the
work of gospel music and its musicians has been extricably linked to the
mission of the Christian church—saving souls.

GOSPEL MUSIC AESTHETICS

The performance of traditional gospel music reflects aesthetic values consonant with the performance of the folk spiritual sung by slaves. Although
specific composers are identifiable in gospel music, unlike spirituals,
which were communally composed, gospel music is nonetheless transmitted through the oral tradition. Historically, gospel performers were
known to add songs to their repertoires that they heard live, on the radio,
or on a recording, frequently oblivious to who the actual composer might
be. Gospel composers and publishers were aware of this intersection
between oral and written transmission, taking this fact into account as
they anticipated sheet music sales. In a 1956 interview, after his career
was well established, Thomas Dorsey commented: "Negroes don't
buy much music. A white chorus of one hundred voices will buy one
hundred copies of a song. A Negro chorus of the same size will buy two:
One for the director and one for the pianist."[79]

Timbre
The quality of sound that distinguishes different voices or instruments from one another.

Polyrhythm
Several contrasting rhythms played or sung simultaneously.

Melisma
A single syllable sung over several pitches.

As a music that comes to life during performance, traditional gospel resonates with fully embodied **timbres** emanating from the chest rather than the head, **polyrhythms** that include hand claps on beats two and four, and movement of the body on beats one and three in duple meter. The dance that so strongly identified the ring shout during slavery is reinvented; the circle is no longer present, but collective movement in synchrony to the music is a mainstay. Singing in harmony, gospel choirs and ensembles most commonly utilize only three parts (SAT—soprano, alto, tenor), which all move in parallel motion. But certainly a most distinguishing factor that characterizes gospel music performance is its **melismatic** treatment of text—singing several pitches to a single syllable. From Mahalia Jackson to such contemporary voices as Rance Allen, Vanessa Bell Armstrong, Daryl Coley, and Yolanda Adams, the melisma has become a trademark of gospel music performance.

The traditional gospel music that Thomas Dorsey, Mahalia Jackson, and other gospel pioneers promoted so fervently rose to a position of prominence in the worship of African Americans of virtually every denomination across the United States, and the international appeal of the genre is ever increasing. It is sung by solo and ensemble, choir and quartet, men and women, young and old, Black and White, Christian and non-Christian. In contrast to the simple accompaniment of piano and electric organ that characterized the early years of gospel, there are now no limits to the types of instruments used to complement the voice—from saxophone to synthesizer to symphony orchestra.

Unlike traditional gospel music, which is embraced by soloist, small ensemble, and mass choir, contemporary gospel music is typically performed by small ensembles. The predictability of traditional gospel music, with its easily memorized melodic lines and parallel motion in the vocal parts, is replaced with more complex forms and harmonies. Both the instrumental accompaniment and the vocal arrangements of contemporary gospel music are virtually indistinguishable from secular musics of the day.

The strong representation of both traditional and contemporary gospel artists in the *Billboard* Top 40 listing from 1973 to 1994 points to the continued coexistence of these two subgenres of gospel, with many artists laying claim to both on a single compact disc. Over one-half of the *Billboard* Top 40 listings of this period are produced by only six artists, who collectively represent the best of both traditional and gospel music. As gospel music continues its now global ascent—with increasing television and radio exposure (CNN; *Bobby Jones Gospel* and *Sunday Best* on BET; *Good Morning, America*; and *Arsenio*) and its international fan base across Europe, Africa, the Carribbean, and Australia—current chart-topping artists such as Yolanda Adams, Donnie McClurkin, Mary Mary, Richard Smallwood, Tye Tribbit, Smokie Norful, and a host of others have become household names.

Mellonee V. Burnim

CONCLUSIONS

Gospel music, from its beginning, was a conscious and willful expression of the desire of African Americans to articulate, embrace, and celebrate those beliefs, attitudes, and values that affirm and distinguish their cultural and religious identity in the United States. While the distinctiveness of different forms of gospel music reflects the collective adaptation of African Americans to an ever-changing sociocultural and political milieu, the continuities that exist among these forms are equally indicative of the existence of a self-defining core of cultural values that have persisted over time. Whereas new gospel music compositions are being added constantly to the repertoire, arrangements and reinterpretations of spirituals, hymns, and other forms also represent a vital component of the standard gospel literature. Their texts have such relevance that they cannot be discarded; they are simply revived and revitalized by being fused with a more contemporary sound.

KEY NAMES

James Cleveland	Sallie Martin
Thomas Dorsey	Bessie Smith
Kirk Franklin	Rosetta Tharpe
Edwin Hawkins	Albertina Walker
Mahalia Jackson	Clara Ward
Roberta Martin	

QUESTIONS

1. What factors precipitated the musical transformations among African Americans that led to the evolution of the music that came to be known as gospel music?

2. What key differences distinguish the creation of the spiritual from that of gospel music? In what ways are these two genres related, and how do they differ?

3. Identify the three styles of transitional gospel music, noting their distinguishing characteristics and seminal performers. What role did these styles have in the development of gospel music in its present form?

4. What were the similarities and differences between the folk spiritual of the rural South and Black urban religious music of the newly formed Pentecostal denomination in the first quarter of the twentieth century?

5. What are the implications of referencing gospel music as "gospel blues"? To what extent does this designation represent African American perspectives of gospel music?

6. What contributions warrant Thomas Dorsey's designation as "Father of Gospel Music" and what was his most noted composition? What prompted the opposition he faced when he began to promote his compositions?

7. Identify the recording that represents the advent of the contemporary gospel era. How is contemporary gospel music distinguished from traditional gospel? In what ways do recurrent critiques of contemporary gospel music reinscribe historical commentaries on spirituals and traditional gospel music?

PROJECTS

1. Watch the film *Say Amen, Somebody* (2000 (1982)) by Bruce Nieremburg. Identify three seminal figures featured in the documentary, and outline their key contributions to the development and proliferation of gospel music. What key issues do they raise concerning the challenges they faced as gospel music pioneers? How did they overcome these challenges?

2. Compare examples of early recordings of Bessie Smith and Mahalia Jackson. Identify the areas where Smith's influence on Jackson is most strongly evident to you. Justify your answer with specific musical passages.

3. Listen to three different versions of "Take My Hand, Precious Lord," or another well-known gospel song, that represent different historical periods and different performance styles. If possible, compare the recordings to a musical score of the selected example. Note in particular variation in form, instrumentation, and vocal textures and harmonization as a lens to understanding the creative process performers employ in defining their distinctive style and signature sound.

4. Observe an episode of *Sunday Best* or *Bobby Jones Gospel* on BET, and list the repertoire performed during the show as well as the original recording artists. Categorize each example as either traditional or contemporary gospel music, making sure you include a justification of your choices.

NOTES

Please see the discography for information on resources for further listening.

Segments of this chapter are reproduced with permission from the *Continuum Encyclopedia of Popular Music of the World, Vol. 8, Genres: North America*, edited by John Shepherd and David Horn (New York: Continuum, 2012).

1. Duckett 1974, 13; Boyer 1974, 21.
2. Duckett 1974, 5; Ricks 1960, 141.
3. In his book *The Sound of Light* (1990), Don Cusic weaves a narrative that moves fluidly between what he references as "White gospel" and "Black gospel," as if the divergent traditions emanate from an identical historical and musical origin and simply represent two different subgenres of gospel. In *The Gospel Sound* (1975 (1971), xxiii) Tony Heilbut contends that hymns are "the basis of gospel repertoire," while Horace Boyer

Mellonee V. Burnim

argues in *How Sweet the Sound* (1995, 57) that gospel music was "created in the Pentecostal/Holiness churches of the South."

4. Throughout his 1975 (1971) work *The Gospel Sound*, Tony Heilbut repeatedly uses the term "gospel blues," which he attributes in an undocumented quote to Rosetta Tharpe (188, 313, 315). The label has been subsequently advanced by Michael Harris in *The Rise of Gospel Blues*, 1992; Horace Boyer in "Gospel Blues: Origin and History," 1992b; and Phillip Bohlman in *Music in American Religious Experience*, 2006.
5. Bontemps and Conroy 1966 (1945), 167.
6. Ricks 1960, 122.
7. Drake and Cayton 1962 (1945), 634.
8. Bontemps and Conroy 1966 (1945), 173.
9. Drake and Cayton 1962 (1945), 673.
10. Bontemps and Conroy 1966 (1945), 173.
11. Drake and Cayton 1962 (1945), 622, 670.
12. Crawford 1929, 45.
13. Mason 1985, 294.
14. Recordings of Arizona Dranes are included on *Negro Religious Music, Vol. 1*, 1968, and *Folk Music in America, Vol. 1*, 1980.
15. Oliver 1984, 169–98; Kent 1970, 49–52.
16. Oliver 1984, 169–98; Wardlow 1969, 164–67.
17. Burnim and Maultsby 1987, 121.
18. O'Neal and O'Neal 1975, 19.
19. Harris 1992, 67–75; O'Neal and O'Neal 1975, 29.
20. Bontemps 1958 (1942), 313.
21. Ricks 1960, 133.
22. Reagon 1992c, 43–44; Jones 1982, 67.
23. Jones 1982, 38.
24. Reagon 1992c, 38.
25. Jones 1982, 88, 104.
26. Boyer 1992a, 63. See *Beams of Heaven: Hymns of Charles Albert Tindley* (2006) for a complete collection of Tindley compositions.
27. Boyer 1992a, 58, 63; Jones 1982, 124.
28. Boyer 1992a, 60.
29. Ibid., 60–63; Reagon 1992c, 46–48.
30. Jones 1982, 38.
31. Reagon 1992c, 47.
32. Jones 1982, 38.
33. Boyer 1992a, 57.
34. Quoted in Ricks 1960, 133.
35. Harris 1992, 91–93.
36. Ibid., 148.
37. See Burnim "Women in African American Music: Gospel" for further discussion of Lucie Campbell and her role in the National Baptist Convention.
38. Harris 1992, 178.
39. Ibid., 192–95; Drake and Cayton 1962 (1945), 676; Ricks 1960, 125, 137.
40. Harris 1992, 201.
41. Ibid., 194.
42. Dorsey 1973, 190–91.
43. Marschall 1968, 8–10; *Biography and Genealogy Master Index*.
44. *Masters of the Country Blues*, 2001, DVD.
45. Ibid.
46. Harris 1992, 188.
47. Quoted in Ricks 1960, 137.
48. Kenneth Moales (president, National Convention of Gospel Choirs and Choruses), interview by the author, Indianapolis, IN, 1993.
49. Ed Smith (executive director, Gospel Music Workshop of America), interview by the author, Cincinnati, OH, 1992.

50. S. Ricks 1960, 138.
51. Jackson with Wylie 1966, 215; Schwerin 1992, 181; "Leaders: Lyndon Johnson; 1908–1973," *Time*, February 5, 1973, www.time.com/time/magazine/article/0,9171,906808,00.html.
52. Jackson with Wylie 1966, 32.
53. Ibid., 36.
54. Ibid., 72.
55. Duckett 1974, 5.
56. Ibid., 6; Goreau 1975, 56.
57. Duckett 1974, 6.
58. Goreau 1975, 57.
59. Ps. 47:1 actually reads, "Shout unto God with the voice of *triumph*" (King James Version; emphasis mine), but the message is not altered by Mahalia's substitution of "trumpet."
60. Goreau 1975, 57, 60; Jackson with Wylie 1966, 63.
61. Goreau 1975, 116; Jackson with Wylie 1966, 67, 86.
62. Jackson with Wylie 1966, 198.
63. See Maultsby 1992, 31; Williams-Jones 1992, 257.
64. See Boyer 1992c; Williams-Jones 1992.
65. Reagon 1992b, 333; Ricks 1960, 135.
66. Albertina Walker, interview by the author, 1994.
67. Hayes 1973, 161.
68. Ward-Royster 1997, 99, 134.
69. Southern 1982, 372.
70. Collins 1994, 27.
71. "Edwin Hawkins Singers," 66–68.
72. "Top Gospel Albums," 246.
73. Ibid.
74. Borzillo 1995, 23.
75. Collins 1994, 27; Franklin with Black 1998, 154.
76. Collins 1994, 27.
77. Jones 1995, 65.
78. Kirk Franklin, acceptance speech at the 1997 Stellar Awards.
79. Ricks 1960, 143–44.

CHAPTER 11

Musical Theater

Thomas L. Riis

The participation of African Americans in musical theater in the Americas naturally developed along with the ideas of theater and music themselves. From the time of the arrival of the first Africans on the North American shore, surviving accounts unanimously agree that their musicality was vigorous, impressive, and frequently pre-eminent.[1] Theater, as an outgrowth of religious ritual and communal storytelling, is a worldwide phenomenon. But settlers of all races in the New World lacked both the interest and the capacity to import the extensive theatrical apparatus that had developed over centuries in Europe, Africa, and Asia. In a sense, theater had to be reinvented in the land that was to become the United States. This chapter will discuss the social, musical, and political factors that encouraged and shaped those developments: the translation of the universal impulse to act out stories into formal performance genres; the aesthetic attitudes that informed the actors and their audiences; and the musical styles that sustained the actions being portrayed. The customary venues and accouterments—masks, makeup, costumes, props—for plays and their thematic and symbolic content will also be discussed.

THE PRE-MINSTREL THEATER FROM THE REVOLUTION TO THE CIVIL WAR

After 1750, in the English-speaking theater on the Atlantic coast, African Americans were involved in formal, text-defined theatricals only to the degree permitted within a climate generally hostile to all secular forms of theater. For example, the conservative Puritan and Quaker leaders in the cities of Boston and Philadelphia, respectively, frowned on the stage, which in their view acted as a magnet for licentiousness and vice of all kinds. It would long remain the dominant American middle-class belief that actors and their business were only barely respectable in the best of venues. Class, occupational, and race prejudices fenced out all but the most sanitized stage vehicles from public view and record.

New York, Charleston, and New Orleans, on the other hand, took a somewhat more tolerant view. All three cities greeted foreign immigrants who brought with them the latest music, dance, and theatrical fashions from Africa, Europe, the West Indies, and South America during the 1700s. A Black presence is especially well attested by the early nineteenth-century accounts of social dances, pit bands, and community music making in New Orleans. Other cities evidently supported active coteries of Black theatrical musicians from time to time. Eileen Southern reports the existence of "Negro tunes" or "Negro jigs," which may have been included in the general repertoire of musical theater songs in the early years of the republic.[2]

Shakespearean actors habitually added extra songs and dances to their plays in the early nineteenth century, and the all-Black African Grove theater company in lower Manhattan was no exception when, in the early 1820s, it staged *Othello, Hamlet,* and *Richard III,* along with a variety of lighter entertainments and pieces by the African American playwright William Henry Brown. The African Grove on Mercer Street, though short-lived, deserves recognition because it not only featured Black actors in full productions, but also trained at least one individual who would later achieve professional status and renown: Ira Aldridge (1807–67). This theater arose in 1816 as a private venture, a tea garden that finally went public in 1821, thereby incurring the wrath of hostile authorities in New York and the jealousy of the principal competing White theater, The Park. The rich variety and evidently multiracial appeal of the African Grove, as well as its attractiveness for middle-class aspirants, was undermined by the Grove's enemies, and the theater was closed finally in 1829.[3]

In 1838, the Marigny Theater in New Orleans opened for the "free colored population" of the city, so that African Americans of means could enjoy French light comedies and musical shows but be spared the indignity of sitting in segregated theaters. (Both slaves and Whites were barred from the Marigny.) The theater remained open for only a few months but revealed potential patrons for sophisticated theater among the Creole citizens of New Orleans. The Theatre de la Renaissance, whose orchestra included members of the Negro Philharmonic Society, was opened in 1840 and offered full plays, comic pieces, and variety shows in the years following. Neither of these venues led to the production of new or independently created works, but they represent the passion and persistence with which the Black middle class sought cultural participation and validation.[4]

Thomas L. Riis

Because popular theatricals throughout history have delineated, lampooned, and translated contemporary life, African Americans were portrayed for the American public well before they had full control of the messages given out by actors or directors in formal works for the stage. (On the other hand, many White minstrels often claimed to depict accurately the lives of Blacks whom they observed around them.)

African American performers who likely served as models for White actors' comic parodies before the Civil War include a New Orleans street vendor and theater singer with the stage name Mr. Cornmeal (d. 1842) and peripatetic banjo virtuoso John "Picayune" Butler (d. 1864), "known from Cincinnati to New Orleans" for his remarkable skill. Butler's repertoire consisted of popular dance tunes of the day: waltzes, polkas, schottisches, and reels. Master Juba, the most common sobriquet for William Henry Lane (c.1825–52), riveted the attention of crowds in the wildly diverse working-class neighborhood of Five Points, New York City, during the early 1840s. (He also caught the attention of English novelist Charles Dickens, who celebrated his phenomenal dancing in his *American Notes*, 1842.) Lane later joined a White minstrel troupe, as did Thomas Dilworth (or Dilward), who took the title Japanese Tommy. Dilworth sang, danced, and fiddled with the leading minstrel companies of the 1850s and 1860s, including those led by George Christy, Dan Bryant, and Charles Hicks. However, his dwarfish height (no more than thirty-six inches) probably drew as much attention as his talents. It appears that he was able to perform onstage with White actors as well as Black without fearing for his safety. To promoters in those days, the value of such a "curiosity" who danced and played the fiddle seems to have overcome any qualms they might have had about racial mixing in public entertainments.[5]

The most famous of early nineteenth-century White actors who paved the way for the minstrel show—he did solo performances in **burnt-cork makeup**—was named Thomas Dartmouth Rice (1808–60). A teenage comic apprentice and mime during the 1820s, Rice found his greatest success performing the song "Jim Crow" during the 1830s. "Jim Crow" Rice (and his imitators) in his famous song bragged on and danced about the exploits of frontier characters, the adventurers and frontiersmen who inhabited the American Southwest (Kentucky and Louisiana, in those days). Hundreds of extant text verses suggest that the song-and-dance was infinitely adaptable and theatrical. The source of the ungainly eight-measure tune, first published in 1833, has never been firmly established, but it may well have come from Rice's observations of Blacks in Kentucky where he worked as a young man. Soon after it achieved the status of "hit," it was identified as a "Negro song."[6]

Burnt-cork/ blackface makeup
Makeup used by minstrel performers to blacken their faces in caricature of African Americans.

Minstrel show
Full-length theatrical entertainment featuring performers in blackface who performed songs, dances, and comic skits based on parodies and stereotypes of African American life and customs.

Individual entertainers such as Lane, Dilworth, and Rice were eclipsed when the minstrel show, a more musically elaborate kind of four-man team theatrical genre, emerged in the 1840s. Each member of a minstrel troupe in blackface makeup played a fiddle, a banjo, or some other African-inspired instrument (bone castanets, tambourine, etc.) and performed various songs, dances, and skits. Although earlier actors working in blackface had conveyed a wide spectrum of ideas, not all necessarily addressing race or the conditions of African Americans, the Virginia Minstrels, the Christy Minstrels, and other White minstrel teams from the 1840s alleged that they were faithfully mirroring the habits and customs of southern slaves or urban Blacks. Perhaps they were familiar with the activities in the popular Black dance halls, such as Almack's in New York or Philadelphia's Dandy Hall.[7]

The founders of this form were chiefly northern White men whose experience in circus acts had predisposed them to employ wild gestures, tattered costumes, bold makeup, and percussive sounds. The musical and dramatic content of the shows varied during the 1840s and 1850s, although they always featured the element of satire in lyrics and skits with music that appealed to those who favored loud, raucous, and rhythmically jaunty tunes. Short, rhythmically insistent patterns in the songs, vigorous body movements to accompany them, and dialogue that engaged the audience in social commentary were clearly derived from a general African style, if not a single specific practice, preserved within the African American community.

The minstrel show rarely used a fixed text, but generally adhered to a standard tripartite format, which by the 1850s had become more or less predictable: (1) an opening act comprised of an overture, songs, and song parodies; (2) a middle section (or "olio") filled with miscellaneous variety acts such as instrumental solos, ensembles, and dances; and (3) an elaborate concluding skit (later referred to as an "afterpiece"), which was frequently set on a southern plantation. The grand dance conclusion, a blackface finale, was known as the "walk-around," the most famous example of which bore the title "Dixie's Land," by Northerner Dan Emmett.[8] Emmett published over two dozen songs and was known to have been well acquainted with the African American musical family, the Snowdens, who lived near his home in Mount Vernon, Ohio.[9]

Large cities and small towns sustained the minstrels for decades. Minstrel performers generated huge amounts of music allied with nonsensical dialect poetry, which challenged more elite, genteel products (parlor songs) in their high spirits, irreverent attitudes, and running commentary on political issues of the day, joking about everything from the banking system to presidential candidates.[10] Eventually, the minstrels also took up more emotion-laden songs, such as B.R. Hanby's "Darling Nelly Gray," which told of the sad tale of a female slave sold far south of her Kentucky home.

Thomas L. Riis

Banjo and fiddle tunes, with characteristic syncopations, were popular for dancing. Prominent White performers, such as Joel Sweeney, undoubtedly learned many tunes from anonymous Blacks and presented them on the minstrel stage. Among the first generation of minstrel songs, most frequently performed were "Lucy Long," "Old Dan Tucker," "Blue Tail Fly" ("Jimmy Crack Corn"), "Buffalo Gals," "Dandy Jim from Caroline," and "Boatman's Dance," the last two with words supplied by Dan Emmett. "Turkey in the Straw" (formerly "Zip Coon") and Stephen Foster's "Oh Susannah," shorn of their dialect texts, continue to be passed on in the oral tradition up to the present.[11] The importance of the minstrel phenomenon cannot be overestimated because it was so widespread and long-lived. Many groups traveled across the country and abroad. Indeed, as the first original theatrical genre in America, it completely swept aside other earlier forms of pantomime and spoken plays with songs inserted.

African Americans first entered American popular theater in large numbers via the burgeoning of traveling minstrel troupes in the mid-1850s and in much vaster numbers following the Civil War.[12] This collective act seems ironic in the extreme to later generations who have no visual recollection of what oral culture-based entertainments were all about in the nineteenth century. But what seems to us a monolithic and repulsive racist format, especially in its requirement of blackface makeup, may have appeared to free Blacks who aspired to the stage more like an opportunity to subvert or amend the message of minstrelsy by substituting a new messenger. Latter-day African American minstrel Tom Fletcher (1873–1954) declared in his autobiography:

> All of us who were recruited to enter show business went into it with our eyes wide open. The objectives were, first, to make money to help educate our younger ones, and second, to try to break down the ill feeling that existed toward the colored people.[13]

African American minstrel performers still employed burnt-cork makeup—such was the power of this defining aspect of the new genre —but also sought in their gestures, tone, and words to contradict the claim of authenticity purveyed by their White counterparts. "What could be more authentic than a real Black person performing as a Black minstrel?" they asked, and by so doing made a space in which to demonstrate Black talent and to reinforce images of independence, intelligence, and Black family togetherness. Throughout their skits they campaigned in favor of Emancipation, the Union, and amicable relations between the races. Between 1865 and 1890 over one hundred African American minstrel troupes were formed and toured and continued to deny the messages of the White troupes.[14]

Also in the post-Civil War period more sentimental motifs came to dominate the minstrel song repertoire. While African American minstrel singers shared a musical repertoire with White minstrels, the best Black groups made a distinctly original contribution by incorporating plantation songs, dances, and original composed melodies. Despite his misgivings, the Black intellectual James Monroe Trotter (1842–92) voiced what was probably a widespread opinion at the peak of minstrelsy's popularity in the 1880s, when he noted that the Georgia Minstrels, a Black group, "presented so much that was really charming in a musical way as to almost compensate the sensitive auditor for what he ... suffered while witnessing that part of the performance devoted to caricature."[15]

Several standout performers of this generation were African Americans. The celebrated and prolific Black composer-singer James Bland (1854–1911), who wrote "Carry Me Back to Old Virginny" and "Oh, Dem Golden Slippers," favored innocuous dialect lyrics and pleasingly smooth "barbershop"-style tunes. Sam Lucas published his songs (on Irish themes as well as in Black dialect) independently and in collections by his White friend Charles White. Many other now-forgotten entertainers, such as Billy Kersands and Ernest Hogan (Figure 11.1), made substantial careers and participated in the companies led by Lew Johnson, Charles Callender, Sprague & Blodgett, J.H. Haverly, Richard & Pringle, W.S. Cleveland, and the Hunn Brothers.[16]

The talents of these men—males completely dominated the minstrel stage until the 1890s—were individual and hard to appreciate out of context. Usually, minstrels in this period were constrained from

Figure 11.1
Portrait of Ernest Hogan, September 8, 1906. Billy Rose Theater Collection, The New York Public Library for the Performing Arts, Astor, Lenox, and Tilden Foundations.

Thomas L. Riis

addressing political issues (such as peonage, lynching, or segregation) except by indirection. However, by the late nineteenth century, many were even rejecting the use of burnt cork and, by clever subversions of well-known jokes, creating a stage message with multiple meanings. By 1900, a militant young African American entertainer such as Robert "Bob" Cole could write, in effect, an anti-minstrel song called "No Coons Allowed!" and get away with performing it in front of an Anglo audience.[17]

Unfortunately, the original "Ethiopian delineators"—as the White troupes were euphemistically termed—had established a powerful image in habitually depicting African Americans as thoughtless, shuffling, superstitious, devious, and servile. Such oafish stereotypes persisted well into the twentieth century and are still perceptible on stage, in film, and on television. Ironically, as these old and tired images have been maintained, the originality of new African American song and dance—from jig-dancing to cakewalk, ragtime to swing jazz, rock and roll to hip-hop—has also figured strongly in all of America's most important theatrical venues, a process that sociologist Eric Lott has aptly described as a combination of "love and theft."[18]

INDEPENDENT BLACK STAGE COMPANIES OF THE LATE NINETEENTH CENTURY

The independent touring company was the principal way by which all Americans became familiar with musical theater during most of the nineteenth century. Although a few major cities had popular resident companies, the only way for most actors to make their living was to travel from place to place as part of the cast of a specific play or show. Theater owners and managers would periodically meet with booking agents in New York or another large city in their home region in order to fill their theater dockets for an entire season. Establishing a relationship with a booking agency relieved individual performers or company managers of heavy organizational and promotional burdens, just as theaters in cities connected by railroads were proliferating coast to coast after the Civil War. A handful of Black entertainers affiliated themselves with powerful agents located in the Northeast.

An early counterweight to the stock characters of minstrelsy was provided by a pair of California sisters named Anna and Emma Hyers, who, led by their enterprising father Sam, formed a touring concert company in 1871.[19] Subsequently, with the help of fellow singer-actors Sam Lucas and Wallace King, supportive playwrights Joseph Bradford and Pauline Hopkins, and the influential Boston-based Redpath Lyceum Bureau, they presented the first full-fledged musical plays in American history in which African Americans themselves comment on the plight of the slaves, the relief of Emancipation, and the challenges of Reconstruction without the disguises of minstrel comedy. Advertised variously as "operettas" and "musical dramas," these plays were created on the old ballad opera model, which employed familiar modern songs interspersed among sections of dialogue. Entirely lacking blackface makeup and farcical situations, they represent a huge step forward in African American self-portrayal.

In the headlines for their 1876–77 season circular, the Redpath agency proudly trumpeted "The Hyers Sisters' Combination [Company]/ The Centennial Sensation!/The Great Moral Musical Drama/entitled/ OUT OF BONDAGE . . . comprising all the Best Colored Artists in the World."[20] Their production toured the country and was well received by both Black and White audiences of all economic strata throughout the northern United States (coast to coast) and in lower Canada. They played in public auditoriums, schools, churches, and at least once in a prison, as well as in typical music or concert halls. Both *Out of Bondage* (sometimes called *Out of the Wilderness*) (1876) and a later show, *Peculiar Sam, or, The Underground Railroad* (1879), with various additions, interpolations, and revivals, enjoyed a place in the Hyers' touring repertoire until the sisters' official retirement in 1893.[21] The playwright and musical arranger of *Peculiar Sam*, a remarkable "musical drama in four acts," was an African American woman from Boston only twenty years of age at the time, Pauline Hopkins (1859–1930). Hopkins apparently wrote her work to feature the famous Black minstrel performer Sam Lucas in the un-stereotypical title role. The music for the show, like that for *Out of Bondage*, was selected from the popular repertoire of the time, which consisted of ballads, spirituals, and dances. Although they were well received by audiences, the works themselves were not taken up by other troupes once they were laid aside by the Hyers family, and they fell into obscurity until the 1990s.[22]

Other than minstrel shows, documentation of Black companies in the third and fourth quarters of the nineteenth century is extremely slim, but since hundreds of individuals experienced as minstrels, instrumentalists, jubilee, or opera singers existed, it is not unreasonable to guess that they at least occasionally formed small, local companies for the amusement of themselves and their neighbors.

Opera Theater

The conscious separation of comic and serious strains within musical theater was pronounced and clearly class-related in the late nineteenth century. American opera (as distinct from American recreations or imitations of European works) had come into its own. Operas by Mozart, Rossini, and Verdi, performed in their original languages, began to attract adherents across the social spectrum as the idea of a historical canon of theatricals came into being, and theaters were built that could accommodate the spectacular dreams of Victorian producers. African Americans made efforts to associate themselves with these lavish forms of entertainment through the creation of full-fledged operas at this time, and they attracted an audience within the African American community.

Although the commercial impact of these shows was negligible, the landmark works deserve recognition in order to illustrate the full range of Black participation long before Black performers would be allowed to sing in the New York Academy of Music or the Metropolitan Opera.

Virginia's Ball (1868) by John Thomas Douglass (1847–86), an accomplished violinist, is generally deemed to be the first opera by an African American composer.[23] Although the music—registered for copyright—is now lost, a first performance was noted as having taken place in New York in the year of its creation. Bostonian Louisa Melvin Delos Mars was the first African American woman to have an opera produced, *Leoni, the Gypsy Queen* (1889), in Providence, Rhode Island. She composed no fewer than five full-length musical dramas between 1889 and 1896.[24] The participation of educated middle-class women in amateur and church-sponsored operettas was also common by the end of the nineteenth century. Full-fledged African American divas, such as Marie Selika (c.1849–1937) and Sissieretta Jones (1869–1933), had significant careers as touring soloists at the same time. The latter, known as "the Black Patti" (a comparison to Adelina Patti, an eminent contemporary White soprano), sang as a virtuoso soloist at Madison Square Garden and the White House in 1892, as well as at the World's Columbian Exposition in Chicago the following year, but her theatrical career did not begin until she formed a traveling troupe in 1896. The songs that these women sang were typical of the concert solos of the day, including French and Italian operatic arias and parlor favorites such as "Home, Sweet Home" and "I Dream of Jeannie with the Light Brown Hair."[25]

America's greatest turn-of-the-century composer of "classical" (his term) piano music, Scott Joplin (c.1867–1917), tried his hand at stage works on at least three occasions. *Ragtime Dance* (1899), for dancers and singing narrator, was first mounted at Wood's Opera House in Sedalia, Missouri. *A Guest of Honor* (1902), an opera telling the story of Booker T. Washington's visit to President Theodore Roosevelt in the White House, set out on a brief tour during the summer of 1903. Unfortunately, all traces of the score and script are lost. Joplin published his final opera himself in 1911, but *Treemonisha*, which celebrated an inspired teacher's efforts to lead her people out of ignorance to prosperity and enlightenment, was almost entirely ignored, never enjoying a complete staged production in Joplin's lifetime. Despite Joplin's confidence in the work and his extensive efforts to bring it to public attention, its merit was only recognized much later, after revivals and recordings made in the 1970s. Joplin was posthumously awarded a Pulitzer Prize for this remarkable work in 1976.[26]

Black Revues and Musical Comedies, 1890–1930

Although the Hyers Sisters' shows had paved the way in the 1870s and 1880s, the principal entrance of African Americans into the commercial mainstream of secular non-minstrel theatricals occurred in the 1890s with a handful of plays including characteristic musical plantation scenes. Plays such as Turner Dazey's *In Old Kentucky*; Whalen and Martell's *The South Before the War*; *Darkest America*, managed by Al G. Fields; *Swanee River*, sponsored by Davis and Keogh; and the perennial favorite *Uncle Tom's Cabin*, George Aiken and George Howard's musical play based on Harriet Beecher Stowe's 1852 novel, benefited from expanding urban populations, well-organized road tours, and production syndicates seeking ever larger audiences. Also benefiting were the variety shows conceived and created by Sam Jack's Creole Burlesque Company, John Isham's concert companies, and Sissieretta Jones's ensemble, called the Black Patti Troubadours (at the conclusion of which she performed a medley of operatic arias from Gounod's *Faust* and Verdi's *Rigoletto*, among others). The directors and producers of most of these shows were White, although they were created mostly with Black actors for Black or mixed audiences.[27]

The appearance of many a short-lived show is noted in the pages of the trade papers of the 1890s, *Billboard* and *The New York Dramatic Mirror*, as well as the Black weekly from Indianapolis, *The Freeman*. The tendency of these shows towards **vaudeville**—that is, a series of separate acts—illustrates a general American taste for variety and episodic entertainments over narrative-rich continuous plays in popular venues. The next step on the road to full-fledged comedy or drama was the **revue**, a series of brief skits mixed with songs and dances. A single revue was performed by one small cast, whose individual members' roles changed with each skit. Occasionally, revues had a unifying theme related to the news or fashions of the day, but never a full-blown plot. Because this preference for vaudeville acts and revues also tended to support novelty and independent initiatives, Black acts were able to gain a foothold in theater while being barred for allegedly financial reasons from more complex production opportunities or more overtly anti-stereotypical shows.

From *A Trip to Coontown* to *Shuffle Along*

A sizable coterie of Black talent gathered in New York in the 1890s, and out of this vibrant pre-Harlem community Black **musical comedy** (that is, shows created, directed, acted, and accompanied by African American musicians) was born. "Bob" Cole and his partner Billy Johnson, veterans of earlier touring concert companies, put together up-tempo songs, comic dialogue within a modest narrative plot, and several talented young performers to create *A Trip to Coontown* (1897). The simultaneous emergence of ragtime piano pieces and songs—in a style universally recognized as African American—with shows such as *A Trip to Coontown* was a fortunate coincidence. By 1896, ragtime had invaded the stage at all levels—White and Black. Between 1897 and 1930, African Americans made over three hundred shows (by Bernard Peterson's count) composed

Vaudeville
Theatrical form consisting of a variety of unrelated performing acts, including actors, singers, dancers, acrobats, comedians, magicians, trained animals, and other specialty acts.

Revue
A series of brief skits mixed with songs and dances.

Musical comedy
A play with humorous content featuring songs that advance the storyline.

of ragtime or novelty tunes (later jazz) and comedic dialogue often embedded in the characteristic revue format.[28] The singing and dancing of Bert and Lottie Williams, George Walker, Aida Overton Walker, Ernest Hogan, "Bob" Cole, and the Johnson brothers (James Weldon and J. Rosamond) were the featured attractions of the first decade. Of this group, only Williams regularly used burnt cork. J. Leubrie Hill, in his productions collectively known as the *Darktown Follies*, inaugurated the next generation of shows (1911–15), where the dancing and choral singing were prized above all else. World War I band conductor James Reese Europe (1881–1919) began his career directing shows of this era.[29]

Without access to the elaborate stage apparatus and expensive trappings of full-blown operettas, the Black-cast shows of the early years of the century focused on the talents of individual star players, the propulsive energy of the dance with its complexities of movement, the seemingly spontaneous vernacular humor, and the overwhelming vocal power of massed choruses. The Black shows used at least two conservatory-trained musicians, Will Marion Cook and J. Rosamond Johnson, whose command of the new syncopated music, together with abundant conducting and arranging skills, glued together the inevitably disparate parts of productions.

Both Cook and Johnson were hit-tune writers in 1900 ("Darktown Is Out Tonight," "Under the Bamboo Tree") and their success enabled the stars who sang their tunes to be presented in well-constructed contemporary vehicles such as *In Dahomey* (1903), *Abyssinia* (1906), *The Shoo-Fly Regiment* (1907), *Bandana Land* (1908), and *The Red Moon* (1909).

Both Blacks and Whites saw and knew these shows—and sat in what were, of course, segregated houses. Most of the actors did not don blackface makeup, however, and so although the shows' plots and song lyrics can appear stereotypical (if not downright slanderous) to a modern viewer because of their broad comedy and pun-saturated dialogues, they represented an advance in some respects in their own day. Whereas a White-authored coon song of the 1890s, such as Charles Trevathen's "Bully Song," could and did fling images of rampant Black violence and mayhem at will (references to slashing razors and stolen chickens pervade the genre), the lyrics of "On Emancipation Day" by Paul Laurence Dunbar for Will Marion Cook's music in *In Dahomey*, filled with dialect though they were, proclaimed a kind of Black *joie de vivre* of which Whites might be envious:

> On Emancipation Day
> All you white folks clear de way . . .
> Coons dressed up lak masqueraders
> Porters armed like rude invaders
> When dey hear dem ragtime tunes
> White fo'ks try to pass for coons . . .

Figure 11.2

First page of "Swing Along!," an early twentieth-century song popular in both the United States and England. It was used by Will Marion Cook as the first big chorus in the musical *In Dahomey* (1903) during its London run and remained popular in revival into the 1920s. Courtesy David A. Jasen.

Figure 11.3

The beginnings of seven songs presented in *Bandana Land* (1908). This set of excerpts was intended as a kind of teaser on the back cover or advertising sheet to encourage the purchase of each song in full piano–vocal score. *Bandana Land* was one of Williams and Walker's most critically acclaimed shows. Courtesy David A. Jasen.

The shows were generic farces, but they nevertheless made a strong impression on all viewers alert to racial politics. Black men and women were placed, through the vehicle of the stage, in a commanding expressive position night after night, all over the country. Consequently, Bert Williams, Aida Overton Walker, and Ernest Hogan were among the most famous African Americans of their day. They were viewed as race leaders, not merely entertainers. The most astute critics of these performers observed their mastery of mime, remarkable comic timing, vital dancing, and distinctively animated presentation time after time. The overall impression left in the minds of the viewers after an extravaganza such as Williams and Walker's *Bandana Land* (1908)—with multiple sets, marvelous stage effects, and live animals—must have forcefully contradicted the recollections of tired and tawdry minstrel shows from a bygone era.[30]

The most prominent of the Black stars at the turn of the century was Bert Williams (1874–1922) (Figure 11.4). Many books have been written about him, and some of his signature routines have been preserved on recordings and film. His initial triumphs as a cakewalking comedian with his partner George Walker, his series of musical comedies from 1898 to 1908, and his subsequent emergence as the only Black member of the *Ziegfeld Follies* revue team place him in a class by himself. An expressive comic singer, slow-talking comedian, eccentric dancer, and mime extraordinaire, Williams was admired onstage and off by his White colleagues Eddie Cantor and W.C. Fields, as well as by artists further afield from musicals, such as playwright David Belasco and actor Eleanora Duse. Williams was an international star, probably the most famous African American of his day, with the sole exception of Booker T. Washington. But his fame was purchased at a price. He always used blackface, and insisted that he would be ineffective without it. Although he had been encouraged to branch out into straight plays and non-blackface scenes, he never sought out the proper vehicle in which to make this change. As a master of "the comic side of trouble," to use his phrase, he strongly identified with the archetype of the sad clown. His command of slow gesture and pathos, his ability to bring an audience to sympathetic tears and laughter at the same time, was achieved through considerable personal effort and professional struggle within a racist society that often refused to treat him with dignity once his makeup was removed. W.C. Fields famously called Bert Williams, "The funniest man I ever saw, and the saddest man I ever knew."[31]

After 1912, the first Black triumphs on Broadway were pushed aside as Harlem grew and downtown producers feared further competition and the visibility of up-and-coming Blacks. The premature deaths of Black Broadway business leaders (especially Ernest Hogan in 1909) led many leading entertainers to opt for traveling vaudeville or neighborhood-based shows in the larger cities. Black ownership of theaters and audiences

Figure 11.4
The popular vaudeville team of Bert Williams and George Walker, pictured on an early sheet music cover. Courtesy David A. Jasen.

around the country increased dramatically between 1910 and 1920, so, naturally, the number of places where a Black audience could see Black performers grew in many urban centers, especially in the South.[32]

In 1921, the Black musical comedy came back with a blockbuster, the tuneful and energetic hit *Shuffle Along*, featuring the remarkable talents of singer-lyricist Noble Sissle, pianist-composer Eubie Blake, and comedians Flournoy Miller and Aubrey Lyles, who wrote the play's script. The cast included a large number of fresh faces, many of whom later went on to stardom: Josephine Baker, Caterina Yarboro, Florence Mills, and Paul Robeson on stage and Hall Johnson, William Grant Still, and Leonard Jeter in the pit. Originally a 1907 Chicago show by Miller and Lyles, *Shuffle Along* required considerable updating to make it a Broadway vehicle. Fortunately, Eubie Blake's years of songwriting experience served the show well ("I'm Just Wild About Harry," "Love Will Find a Way," "Dixie Moon"). The result was an outstanding success that ran for over five hundred performances, toured for two years on the road, and spawned many imitators through the decade.[33]

THE IMPACT OF *SHUFFLE ALONG*

As with all great shows, the reasons for *Shuffle Along*'s success were multiple. The talent was young and dedicated, but the key players drew on considerable experience. The musical material was varied. From the lyrical and romantic to the upbeat and jazzy, it accompanied a veritable kaleidoscope of dances and stage movements. Blake provided flashy piano interludes. The personalities of the stars were alluring. Everything was executed with virtuosity and struck the audience as thoroughly modern. Faced with stringent economies, the production even managed to be credited as sensibly modest. The play was familiar and genuinely funny (although nothing in the way of dramatic substance was ever expected in Broadway comedies of its type). It was produced in a theater that was accessible to regular Broadway theatergoers (at Sixty-Third Street) and a substantial Black neighborhood on the west side of the city, if not quite in the heart of the theater district. Not unimportantly, influential critics loved it.

The stimulus provided by *Shuffle Along* and the economic boom of the 1920s saw even more Black employment in theatricals, especially song-and-dance revues. Tom Fletcher, a veteran entertainer, also claimed that "prohibition had closed all the bars in hotels and cabarets, and that made business in theaters jump."[34] The new shows combined old-fashioned motifs (plantation scenarios, sentimental Old South clichés, and shuffling characters out of minstrelsy) with novelty updates (urban scenes, themes of Black "uplift" and "improvement," glamorous female blues singers, and jazz bands). Broadway flourished in general, and shows with primarily Black creators and actors made a strong impression. White *Ziegfeld Follies* star Gilda Gray sang in 1922, "Every cafe now has the dancing coon / Pretty choc'late babies / Shake and shimmie everywhere . . . It's getting very dark on old Broadway."

The revue genre tended to dominate the scene because it allowed a succession of splashy specialty acts without hindrance from a plot. Revues also habitually featured popular dances and so highlighted the Black specialists in this area. James Reese Europe had devised the music for Vernon and Irene Castle's foxtrot step before World War I. After the war, it seemed the whole world was dance crazy. Comedians Miller and Lyles, assisted by Black choreographer Elida Webb, placed the show-stopping Charleston into *Runnin' Wild* in 1923. James Weldon Johnson, no stranger to the Black musical comedy stage, observed:

> [T]hey did not depend wholly upon their extraordinarily good jazz band for the accompaniment; they went straight back to [early] Negro music and had the major part of the chorus supplement the band by beating out the time with hand-clapping and foot patting. The effect was electrical. Such a demonstration of beating out complex rhythms had never before been seen on a stage in New York.[35]

Tap dance, Black bottom, acrobatic styles, and slow drags all made their way to popularity in the shows of the 1920s.

The show names alone tell much about the high-spirited effervescence of the works as well as their somewhat restricted dramatic palette: *Strut Miss Lizzie* (1922), *Plantation Revue* (1922), *Chocolate Dandies* (1924), *Lucky Sambo* (1925), *My Magnolia* (1926), and *Blackbirds of 1928*. These full-length shows were developed in order to showcase young and dynamic stars such as Florence Mills, Bill Robinson, or Snake Hips Tucker, but the jokes and skits tended to rely on old-fashioned dialect and "darkey" humor. The character of the shows indicates that while stereotyped roles and situations might be providing jobs for more Broadway professionals, the fading of minstrelsy as a genre had not dimmed its influence on successor forms.

The quality of the relatively new and inspired shows of the Will Marion Cook era (before 1910) and the creativity of individual Black dancers and vaudevillians in vaudeville (1910–20) were probably not surpassed in the 1920s. But at least there was a lot more to choose from, plus many more songs written by the likes of Shelton Brooks

("Darktown Strutters' Ball"), Joe Jordan ("Lovie Joe"), Chris Smith ("Ballin' the Jack"), W.C. Handy ("Memphis Blues"), and Fats Waller ("Ain't Misbehavin'").

Full-fledged dramatic vehicles with substantial music—what would later be termed "musical dramas," as opposed to dance revues or variety shows—are barely detectable in the historic record. This is partly because the phrase "serious musical" would have seemed self-contradictory before Kern's *Showboat* (1927). The moneyed investors who were willing to underwrite major Broadway musicals in the period mistrusted extreme novelty and would have been disinclined to support anything so out of the ordinary as a tragi-comedic musical with an African American cast. As a result, no such shows were produced.

During the 1920s and 1930s, the Black creative component varied among the shows with Black casts; arrangers and composers were both Black and White, and the financial benefits to African Americans were negligible because the principal producers and financial investors were White. Individual Black geniuses, such as eminent Broadway arranger and Gershwin mentor Will Vodery, are almost lost to history, but songwriters such as Fats Waller prospered.[36] Some chose to work behind the scenes. Others developed alternative careers playing jazz and singing the blues. But the producing dictators of the musical theater stage were not yet ready to admit African Americans into full and equal participation in management. African American singers and actors continued to train and gain experience by traveling the country doing their acts on vaudeville, most notably on the TOBA (Theater Owners' Booking Association) circuit, which provided entertainment for Black audiences in more than eighty theaters located from the Northeast to the Southwest, including the Deep South, between 1920 and 1932. At their height in the mid-1920s, TOBA houses were collectively entertaining as many as thirty thousand viewers per week, according to one estimate from the Chicago Defender.[37] This sounds impressive, but even in the best of situations, many African American show people felt that unfair conditions and abysmal salaries so dominated the scene that TOBA actually stood for "Tough on Black Actors."

EVOLVING IMAGES ON THE STAGE, FROM THE DEPRESSION TO THE CIVIL RIGHTS ERA, 1930–60

A desire for heightened realism and more-stringent production economies in the 1930s were reflected in the new Black shows of that decade. But many of the most familiar motifs, formats, and character stereotypes remained. Interest in vernacular dancing faded somewhat, partly because there was so much of it. An excessive amount of rather routine work disappointed audiences.[38] Massive choruses and long chorus lines became unaffordable as the Depression worsened.

The music on the stage combined old and new elements. Black intellectual Alain Locke in 1925 had called the spirituals "the most characteristic product of the race genius as yet in America," and so with this seal of approval it is no surprise to find pageants such as *The Green Pastures* (1930) trying to include such by-now familiar songs. In a somewhat more modern vein, *Brown Buddies* (1930) showed Bill Robinson and Adelaide Hall acting the romantic parts of the loyal soldier and sweet-tempered civilian entertainer, respectively, in a dynamic combination using the songs and dances of a number of popular Black composers (Joe Jordan, Millard Thomas, J. Rosamond Johnson, and Shelton Brooks). *Sugar Hill* (1931), subtitled "an Epoch of Negro Life in Harlem" and featuring music by premiere stride pianist James P. Johnson, attempted a social critique of the Black aristocracy and bore some resemblance to Elmer Rice's Pulitzer Prize-winning play of 1929, *Street Scene*.[39] Ethel Waters sang four songs, including an unvarnished plaint about lynching, in the innovative 1933 revue *As Thousands Cheer* (songs composed by Irving Berlin).

Two major musical works featuring Black performers, but with problematical scripts and contexts, represent the divisions and tensions within the entertainment industry of the 1930s: Marc Connelly's old-time "religious pageant" *The Green Pastures* (1930), which fantastically likened heaven to a carefree southern fish-fry and used spirituals sung by the professional Hall Johnson Choir; and George and Ira Gershwin's opera *Porgy and Bess* (1935). Because creative control was racially restricted in both instances (Connelly and Gershwin were White), these works continue to generate controversy. Both were also celebrated as masterpieces and garnered kudos from many respected critics. Black audiences were divided, but most agreed that the high-quality work of the performers was mitigated by the reliance on either inappropriate genre conventions (the Gershwin operatic style) or insultingly naive depictions that amounted to racist fantasy (Connelly's assumptions about Black religious practice and belief).

The Federal Theater Project (FTP) of the Works Progress Administration (1935–39) also provided some work for Blacks in musicals as well as straight plays in several American cities, but the Depression ensured that the numbers of employed actors would still be far lower than the peak decade of the 1920s. The array of genres represented did not vary from the earlier period, and musicals tended to be avoided. *Swing It* (1937), put together by R. Cecil McPherson (Cecil Mack), J. Milton Reddie, and Eubie Blake, and which reminded many critics of *Shuffle Along*, was derided as hopelessly hackneyed and old-fashioned.

Two plays with songs inserted that found favor in limited runs were the FTP's Seattle unit's productions of *Natural Man* (also known as *This Ole Hammer*) and *Walk Together Chillun* (1936), which ran for nineteen performances in Harlem's Lafayette Theater. *Natural Man*, at first conceived as a through-sung opera but soon modified to a "folk drama with music in eight episodes," featured an elaborate retelling of the John Henry story with several indomitable railroad workers and colorful supporting characters. An off-stage and acoustically amplified chorus sang songs in a wide range of styles, from folk songs to honky-tonk hits, including many traditional favorites such as "John Henry" itself and "Beale Street Blues."[40] *Natural Man* was among the most coherent of regional works to make it to the stage, with a month-long run from January to February 1937; it also enjoyed a brief revival in Harlem in 1941.

The Chicago "Negro unit" of the Federal Theater, directed by Shirley Graham DuBois, produced the most influential musical to come out of the WPA. A jazz version of the Gilbert and Sullivan operetta *The Mikado*, called *The Swing Mikado* (1939), was set on a mythical tropical island (rather than in an Anglicized Japan) complete with swaying palms, a backdrop to suggest ocean vistas, and scantily clad "natives." It featured a medley of the popular swing dances of its day but mostly used Sullivan's original music. After playing for over five months in the Midwest, the company was brought to New York, where it continued to draw full houses for sixty performances and then was parodied by an imitative Broadway extravaganza called *The Hot Mikado*, which bore little resemblance to the original but gave White producer Mike Todd a chance to showcase dance sensation and screen star Bill "Bojangles" Robinson dressed in gold from head to toe. *The Hot Mikado* made money and was filled with razzle-dazzle.[41]

A gradual trend toward the integration of isolated Black stars into White musicals and a growing allowance of more individualized Black characters is perceptible from the 1940s through the early 1960s, although there were exceptionally few all-Black shows and the amount of Black participation in the preproduction process was almost invisible. Indeed, Allen Woll refers to the wartime and postwar period as "the second period of exile" for Black musical theater. Although stories and themes of interest to African Americans and Black actors themselves were present in the work of Vernon Duke (*Cabin in the Sky*), Kurt Weill (*Lost in the Stars*), and Oscar Hammerstein II (*Carmen Jones*), because the creative forces behind the scenes did not include many African Americans, a link to the past was lost—or at least temporarily ignored. In addition, the powerful impact of Rodgers and Hammerstein's *Oklahoma!* (1943) heralded a new era. This famous team created a model that took as its ideal the complete integration of music, lyrics, and spoken dialogue, thus placing even more importance on the work of art before live production began. Rodgers and Hammerstein sought out and refashioned serious literary stories in an unprecedented way, and their shows, germinating from well-made books rather than star turns, dance extravaganzas, or independently composed songs, pushed other formats into the shadows after 1945. A 1952 revival of *Shuffle Along*, even with a certain amount of updating, was considered "painfully embarrassing" by Black and even some White critics.[42]

Continued discrimination, lack of institutional memory for the Black contribution to turn-of-the-century Broadway, the autonomy of Harlem's entertainment venues, and the rise of the Rodgers and Hammerstein format downtown all contributed to the dearth of professional Black musicals in New York. Hollywood provided some opportunities, but by and large the movies tended to imitate the racial attitudes already in place elsewhere and even exaggerate them on the big screen.

There were individual successes, of course. Juanita Hall sang in *South Pacific* (1949), Todd Duncan appeared in *Lost in the Stars* (1949), and *Mr. Wonderful* (1956) and *Golden Boy* (1964) featured Sammy Davis Jr. Harold Arlen's trilogy of shows on ethnic themes—*St. Louis Woman* (1946), *House of Flowers* (1954), and *Jamaica* (1957)—provided important Broadway showcases for dancers Harold and Fayard Nicholas and vocalists Pearl Bailey and Lena Horne, among others. All of these musicals—whether musical comedies or the more up-to-date musical dramas—were well received and sensitive to racial issues without being explicitly political.

Duke Ellington applied his musical genius to the revue genre with limited success. In 1941, *Jump for Joy* optimistically celebrated the demise of Uncle Tom stereotypes with such provocative numbers as "Sun-Tanned Tenth of the Nation," "I Got It Bad and That Ain't Good," and "Uncle Tom's Cabin is a Drive-in Now." It enjoyed a long run in Los Angeles where it originated but was not picked up widely elsewhere. He penned an updated version of *The Beggar's Opera*, called *Beggar's Holiday*, for a racially mixed cast in 1943, but then more or less abandoned Broadway genres until 1966 when he created the score for *Pousse-Cafe*, a stage makeover of the classic film *The Blue Angel*, set in New Orleans, which lasted all of three performances.[43]

Despite liberalizing trends and the easing of discrimination in the larger post-World War II society, racial barriers still tended to restrict the creative options for Black actors, musicians, and playwrights while reinforcing the tendency of White producers to rely on minstrel formulas in casting. Black men, women, and children continued to sing, play, and dance on the stage, but they did so largely in the makeup of comic servants, urban vagabonds, Caribbean exotics, and jungle savages.[44]

MUSICAL DRAMA AND MUSICAL COMEDY, 1960–2000

Black Power Movement
A movement of the late 1960s and early 1970s that emphasized Black unity, Black pride, and self-determination.

The emergence of the **Black Power Movement** in the 1960s and 1970s had critical cultural importance for musical theater because it fed an interest in reviving the core vitality that had pervaded African American theater before 1930. The civil rights struggle and the revolutionary ideology of the period added to the urgency of making a clear creative statement. The joys as well as the hardships of Black life began to be celebrated by such distinguished writers as Albert Murray and Ralph Ellison. In the popular press, expressions of the new "Afro-American

Thomas L. Riis

culture" multiplied. Black—but not "Negro"!— style was fashionable, and Americans of all races and ethnicities became aware of soul food, soul music, Afro hairdos, the language of the streetwise Black militants, the Black Muslims, the Black Panthers, and especially the figure of the galvanizing martyr Malcolm X, whose autobiography (published posthumously by Alex Haley) became a national bestseller in 1967.

During this heady and turbulent time, the comic conventions of the old-fashioned musical comedy, with hackneyed characters steeped in farce and pseudo-dialect speech, had little resonance. Ever since World War II, in fact, resistance toward broadly played blackface comedy had begun to harden, and the term **"Uncle Tom"** (understood to mean an acquiescent toady in the struggle against White racism) entered common usage. Energy aiming to build a new more soulful theater in general was abundant. Dozens of local theater companies sprang up, fired by the desire to represent the diverse talents of the larger community. Meanwhile, real-life political figures such as Adam Clayton Powell, Malcolm X, and Martin Luther King Jr. injected a new element of seriousness into race relations and perceptions. With the issues of racism and segregation on the front pages of every daily paper in America, Black actors, like the African American man or woman on the street, could no longer be seen by audiences as harmless clownish stereotypes.

Histories of Black musicians and actors from the previous decades were beginning to be written, inspiring a new generation conscious of the work of its forebears. The National Black Theater (NBT) of Harlem (1968–72) created works using African and West Indian rituals and dances, emphasized community involvement, eschewed the "star" system and external funding, and embraced the search for "roots" in Africa exemplified by Alex Haley's book of that title. Some organizations, such as the Negro Ensemble Theater (NET), avoided musicals in their repertories altogether but used music and jazz as a metaphor or background in straight plays. The satires of Douglas Turner Ward, *Day of Absence* and *Happy Ending*, suggested how fresh points of view could enliven Black theater. The Black folk arts, especially spirituals and sung sermons, were celebrated in such works as *Trumpets of the Lord* (1963), based on James Weldon Johnson's *God's Trombones* (1927), while Melvin Van Peebles' *Ain't Supposed to Die a Natural Death* (1971) and *Don't Play Us Cheap* (1972) provided sustained and invigorating dramatic contributions to this new theater. Its angry, confrontational dialogue anticipated by a generation the powerful speech rhythms of rap artists.[45]

Langston Hughes (1902–67), a Columbia University student during the glory days of Broadway in the Roaring Twenties, possessed a New Yorker's love of the musical stage as well as jazz. Still a young man, he emerged as a poet and legitimate dramatist, and his New York-produced plays *Mulatto* (1935) and *Don't You Want to Be Free* (1937) established him as an intellectual force to be reckoned with. His collaboration on the lyrics

Uncle Tom
A derogatory term for a Black person seen as supporting rather than challenging the racist power structure. The term is based on the empathetic title character of Harriet Beecher Stowe's 1852 novel, *Uncle Tom's Cabin*.

for Kurt Weill and Elmer Rice's innovative Broadway opera *Street Scene* (1947) confirmed his interest in the musical side of theater. An operatic version of *Mulatto* called *The Barrier* (musical score by Jan Meyerowitz) was authorized in 1950. In the previous year, Hughes had also begun to collaborate with William Grant Still to turn Hughes's play *Troubled Island* into an opera as well. Almost single-handedly, he set about the task of resuscitating the African American musical play in the 1950s and early 1960s by writing original lyrics and scripts and then engaging dedicated professional musicians, White and Black. He made a hit with *Simply Heavenly* (1957), based on his own play and novels that featured a lovable Harlem character named Jesse B. Semple, and two religiously themed plays: the Christmas pageant *Black Nativity* produced on Broadway in 1962 and *Tambourines to Glory* (1963). The latter was a "gospel song play" dominated by two dozen dynamic musical numbers and a choir directed by Clara Ward, all loosely held together by a plot about the formation of a Harlem storefront church.[46]

Gospel musical
A play with a theme loosely derived from biblical stories, featuring music that either imitated or was directly drawn from African American gospel traditions.

The success of these shows prepared the way for the enthusiastic reception accorded to later similar efforts by others: *The Prodigal Son* (1965), *A Hand at the Gate* (1966), *Your Arms Too Short to Box with God* (1976), and *The Gospel at Colonus* (1983). The musical style of these shows, while superficially similar to the religious folk pageants of the 1930s, was of course unburdened by the tendency of the 1930s shows to smooth out or restrain the dynamism of Black song through the use of more classical vocalism. The new **gospel musicals** supplemented or sometimes replaced the old forces with the hard-driven, rhythmically strong vernacular sound of authentic urban church groups or singers who had been raised in and were thoroughly acquainted with the style.

Except for Hughes and his collaborators, playwrights in the revolutionary mode of the 1960s—the figures who worked with such innovative companies as the National Black Theater—eschewed traditional Broadway music, with its almost unavoidable association with minstrel humor and insensitivity. Gospel and rock and roll, once they came to Broadway, however, would henceforward significantly enhance the prospects for a rebirth of Black musical theater in New York. It appeared that audiences also were ready for fresh material. The emergence of rock and roll as the principal style of popular music across the board—with its undeniable African American components—unfortunately paralleled ever mounting production costs and the decreasing number of new, original shows on Broadway.

The effects of inflation and recession in the early 1970s urged producers to back financially safe vehicles that reused tried-and-true materials or well-known classics. Nevertheless, the 1970s saw more participation of African Americans on Broadway than had occurred since the 1930s, with the musical contents often tending to be retrospective, nostalgic, and historical in shows such as *Me and Bessie* (1975), *Bubblin' Brown Sugar* (1976), *One Mo' Time* (1979), and *Eubie* (1979). The trend toward recycling familiar African American tunes was maintained in *Sophisticated Ladies* (1982), *Williams and Walker* (1986), and *Black and Blue* (1989). In a class apart, *Bring in da Noise/Bring in da Funk* (1996) transcended its dancing-show ancestors by creating a tour de force of rhythmic counterpoint realized on suspended pots, pans, and buckets, as well as the usual tap shoes. The original moves and sustained energy flowing from this show, glossed thinly with a historical veneer, electrified audiences in a lengthy cross-country tour after its New York success.

Some Black-cast musicals of these same decades began to draw on the proven efforts of Black playwrights, with such box office hits as *Purlie* (1970), based on Ossie Davis's *Purlie Victorious*, and *Raisin* (1973), taken from Lorraine Hansbury's *Raisin in the Sun*. Other less successful shows, such as *Doctor Jazz* (1975) and *The Tap Dance Kid* (1983), attempted to address the problems of modern Black performers.

Three major award-winning shows, *Ain't Misbehavin'* (1978, revived 1988), *Dreamgirls* (1981–85), and *Jelly's Last Jam* (1992), emphasize the point that legendary figures from African American popular musical history (Fats Waller, the Supremes, and Jelly Roll Morton, respectively) were more apt than other subjects in this era to inspire dynamic products with substantial box office appeal. As in the first decades of the original African American musicals (1897–1927), the elements that most attracted audiences to the revivalist shows of the 1970s–1990s were syncopated songs, dazzling dance routines, powerful choruses, and distinctive solo turns. But something had changed.

By the end of the twentieth century, most mainline commercial American popular music was preponderantly composed of historically Black elements—*and was acknowledged to be so*. More importantly, rock in some form had superseded pre-rock and roll idioms on the Broadway stage itself, not only in the wider market. Tin Pan Alley ballads (typically featuring a chorus of four rhymed text phrases in thirty-two bars of music), the reliable building blocks of musicals since the 1910s, now almost always had to share the bill with songs inspired by the blues, ragtime, jazz, gospel, soul, or rock.

Perhaps the most self-conscious recognition of the paramount importance of Black aesthetics in popular music (coupled with an intuition that Broadway was now ready to accept the fact) was the fantasy-parody *The Wiz* (1975, revived in 1984), which took the 1939 film classic *The Wizard of Oz* as a springboard for reinterpreting the Black experience in America. Scored by the skillful Charles Smalls, *The Wiz* ran for over 1,500 performances, received numerous Tony and Drama Desk awards, and succeeded with viewers despite the doubts of hostile early critics. It did so because it was far more than protest statement, revival, sequel, or imitative revue. Its vibrancy and unapologetic embrace of Black vernacular language—matched with a flamboyant visual production and superb choreography—drew on a variety of sources. Its musical style was modern and rhythmic to the core, and its hit song ("Ease On Down the Road") spoke directly to a wide audience of all races.

Thus, over the last two hundred years, African American musical theater has traversed many genres and types of expression, finding both success and opposition along the way. Emerging from traditional rituals and commercial entertainments, incorporating formal as well as improvisational styles, and combining farce with field holler, Black musicals are unified through time by a constant preoccupation with communal celebration. They tell about a group experience—the life of a people—as well as the joys and sorrows of individual persons. At their best, the shows of African Americans are celebrated for their inventive and especially distinctive music, skillful demonstrations of body movement, robust choral singing, and highly coordinated ensemble presentations. As they have in the past, graceful finesse and energetic execution will surely continue to enrich American musical theater through the twenty-first century.

KEY NAMES

Eubie Blake and Noble Sissle	Anna and Emma Hyers
James Bland	J. Rosamond Johnson
"Bob" Cole and Billy Johnson	Sissieretta Jones ("the Black Patti")
Will Marion Cook	Thomas Dartmouth Rice
Langston Hughes	Bert Williams

QUESTIONS

1. How did the minstrel show develop? Describe its form, major characters, and musical content. When and why did African Americans become minstrels? In what seminal ways did African American and White minstrel performances differ?

2. Discuss the historical and socio-cultural significance of the productions *A Trip to Coontown* and *Shuffle Along*. To what extent was the music of these shows of African American origin? Identify at least two African American stars who emerged from these productions and discuss the full extent of their influence on African American musical theater.

3. How did the production *Porgy and Bess* represent the socio-cultural and political climate of the era when it was initially produced? Name examples of subsequent musical productions that avoided the racial stereotypes that characterized *Porgy and Bess*.

PROJECTS

1. Research the history of the popular tunes "Old Dan Tucker," "Turkey in the Straw," or "Oh Susannah!" Who composed these tunes, and what messages, either overt and covert, do they convey? What are the implications of contemporary performances of such repertoire?

2. Listen to at least six recordings by Bert Williams, Paul Robeson, or Eubie Blake, noting the range of topics addressed in their repertoires. How would you describe their musical appeal? Their musical message?

3. Compare the soundtrack of *The Wiz* to that of original production *The Wizard of Oz*. How have the musical themes and performance style been altered to reflect African American musical and cultural values?

4. The musicals *Ain't Misbehavin'*, *Dreamgirls*, and *Jelly's Last Jam* focus on such legendary figures as Fats Waller, the Supremes, and Jelly Roll Morton. After listening to the soundtrack or viewing a film of one of these productions, answer the following questions: What aspects of these well-known entertainers are highlighted in the musicals? What aspects of their lives are ignored? How is music used in these productions to generate box office appeal?

NOTES

Please see the discography for information on resources for further listening.

1. Epstein 2003 (1977), 1–46, passim.
2. Southern 1997, 44, 68, 133.
3. Ibid., 116–21; Hay 1994, 6–11.
4. Kmen 1966, 235–36.
5. Southern 1997, 94–96.
6. Cockrell 1997, 75.
7. Southern 1997, 12–14.
8. Toll 1974, 54–57.
9. Sacks and Sacks 1993, 1–3, 160–65.
10. Mahar 1999, 59–63.
11. Ibid., 230.
12. Toll 1974, 275–80.
13. Fletcher 1954, xvii.
14. Toll 1974, 195–229 passim.
15. Trotter 1968 (1878), 274–82. Also cited in Riis 1989, 7.
16. Simond 1974 (1891), xvii–xxiv.
17. Riis 1992a, 15–22.
18. Lott 1993, 38.
19. The most complete discussion of the Hyers Sisters to be found appears in Southern 1994, xiii–xxii.
20. Ibid., xv.
21. Ibid., xxii–xxiii.
22. Ibid., xxiii, xxvi.
23. Southern 1997, 251.
24. Wright 1992b, 385, 87.
25. Graziano 2000, 568–69, 89–90.
26. Berlin 2001.

27. Woll 1989, 4–5; Riis 1989, 12–13, 20–24.
28. Peterson 1993, 393–406.
29. Badger 1995, 27–29.
30. Riis 1989, 117–22.
31. Charters 1970, 11.
32. Riis 1992b, 236–38.
33. The most complete documentary history of *Shuffle Along* can be found in Kimball and Bolcom 2000 (1973), 86–116.
34. Fletcher 1954, 311.
35. Malone 1996, 77.
36. Tucker 1996, 123–82.
37. Morgan and Barlow 1992, 84.
38. Malone 1996, 114.
39. Peterson 1993, 335–36.
40. Ibid., 246–47.
41. Ibid., 342–43.
42. Woll 1989, 209.
43. Bordman 1978, 647.
44. A rich discussion of stereotypes on stage and screen can be found in Bogle 1994.
45. Southern 1997, 561. See also Van Deburg 1992, 193–202, 276, 278.
46. Woll 1989, 229–48.

CHAPTER 12

Rhythm and Blues/R&B

Portia K. Maultsby

Rhythm and blues is a form of Black dance music that began to evolve during World War II (1939–45). Recorded primarily by small, regional independent record labels, its development is associated with demographic, economic, and social changes that occurred in American society from the 1940s through the 1960s. The term "rhythm and blues"[1] was used first as a marketing label to identify all types of secular music recorded by and for African Americans. Introduced by *Billboard* magazine in 1949 to replace the **race** music label (a term in use since 1920),[2] rhythm and blues encompassed all Black musical traditions, from rural and urban blues, boogie-woogie, swing, jazz combos and trios to vocal harmony groups, solo singers, and rhythm and blues combos. As a musical style, the term identified a hybrid musical genre that combined elements from jazz, blues, gospel music, and, later, pop.

Race records
Music industry term used from the 1920s through the 1940s to designate recordings produced by and marketed to African Americans.

SOCIAL CONTEXT

The emergence of rhythm and blues coincided with two major events associated with World War II—the military draft (established by the Selective Training and Service Act of 1940) and the **Second Great Migration** of African Americans (1940–70). The military draft led to a drastic reduction in males in America, which altered the nature of social interactions and the character of entertainment venues. Ballroom dancing, for example, waned in popularity and many jazz swing bands eventually broke up due to personnel instability. As a result, many ballrooms closed and smaller venues opened. Musicians, in turn, formed

Second Great Migration
The period between 1940 and 1970 during which five million Black southerners moved to the North and West.

Bebop
Combo jazz improvised style that evolved from big band swing in the 1940s, characterized by exceedingly fast tempos, with improvisational lines based on the harmonic structure rather than on the melody.

Rhythm and blues (R&B)
A form of Black dance music that evolved during the World War II era and the two decades that followed as a fusion of blues, big band swing, gospel, and pop elements.

Jim Crow laws
Laws limiting African American freedoms and rights in US society, named for the minstrel character "Jim Crow."

bands with fewer members and developed two distinct musical genres—**bebop** and **rhythm and blues**.

During World War II and the two decades that followed, an estimated 1,500,000 African Americans (nearly 15 percent of the southern African American population) migrated from the rural South to large industrial cities throughout the country.[3] They sought better economic and educational opportunities as well as escape from racial oppression and inequalities sanctioned by **Jim Crow laws**. Abandoning jobs as domestics, sharecroppers, tenant farmers, and general laborers, these migrants found high-paying jobs in wartime and other manufacturing industries. Life in cities, nevertheless, proved to be challenging. Restrictive covenants and agreements among real estate agents and lending institutions fostered the growth of segregated urban communities. Other venues sanctioned such discriminatory policies as featuring Black musicians as performers while denying the admission of African Americans as patrons.[4]

In every major city across the United States the racial marginalization of African Americans created conditions ripe for the establishment of a vibrant Black entertainment district. In urban contexts, the southern migrants transformed rural traditions into new and diverse regional musical styles.

Rhythm and Blues: A Diversity of Styles

Rhythm and blues is stylistically diverse, reflecting the emergence of regional styles in cities with significant African American populations, such as Los Angeles, Chicago, Detroit, New York City, Philadelphia, and Washington, DC. Musicians were among the millions who migrated from the rural South to these large industrial cities during and after World War II. Relying largely on transportation by rail, the directional path of migrants from specific locales fueled the development of regional rhythm and blues styles. The majority of the migrants to Los Angeles, for example, came from Louisiana, Texas, Arkansas, and Oklahoma. Their musical preference for the southwestern blues and territory jazz styles resonates in the rhythm and blues styles that evolved in Los Angeles. In contrast, the blues tradition of the Mississippi Delta dominated the early rhythm and blues sounds in Chicago, the city that became home for the majority of Blacks from Mississippi as well as a smaller number from Tennessee, Arkansas, and Alabama and far fewer from other southern states. The predominant vocal harmony sounds from gospel quartets of the Southeast traveled with migrants to the Northeast.[5] Regardless of the region or city, new sounds grounded in jazz, blues, and gospel came from the clubs, bars, lounges, theaters, churches, and street corners in African American communities. They reflected the factory sounds, street noises, and new amplified technologies of city living.

Live performances of rhythm and blues generated a demand for recordings. Although the major record companies[6] were the primary producers of Black music in the 1920s, they discontinued their involvement during the Depression (1929–1930s) and did not resume production after World War II.[7] Instead the majors recorded mainstream popular musics—big band jazz (most featured pop singers) and classical music—to target the growing suburban White middle-class consumer populace. This targeted focus created a musical void in the race record market, which inspired entrepreneurs to establish independent record labels. Many of these were jukebox operators and proprietors of nightclubs, record shops, and restaurants in African American communities, who were aware of the demand for recorded Black music.[8] The first successful labels were located in Los Angeles, New Jersey, New York, Cincinnati, Chicago, and Houston. As home to six independent labels in the 1940s, Los Angeles became the first major hub for the production of Black popular music that became known as rhythm and blues.[9]

REGIONAL STYLES: THE FIRST STREAM, 1940s THROUGH MID-1950s

Los Angeles: Excelsior/Exclusive, Modern, Aladdin, Specialty, and Imperial Records

Nearly 400,000 African Americans migrated to Los Angeles for work in the war-related industries (aircraft and ship building). The segregated South Central district, where the migrants lived, quickly became home to a plethora of clubs and bars that featured jazz, blues, and the evolving new musical genre, rhythm and blues.[10] Two related, yet distinct, rhythm and blues styles emerged in these venues—trios and combos.

Trios consisting of piano, guitar, and bass provided entertainment for small, intimate clubs or lounges, known as **after-hours clubs**.[11] Jazz pianist-singer Nat King Cole is credited as being the first to form a trio, the King Cole Trio (formed in 1937). Doubling as vocalist and pianist, Cole performed a diverse repertoire that included jazz, novelty songs, ballads, and blues.[12] By the mid-1940s, trios specializing in the blues quickly became favorites in after-hours clubs that attracted the Black working class. Johnny Moore's Three Blazers, which featured pianist-vocalist Charles Brown ("Blues at Sunrise," 1945, and "Drifting Blues," 1946), was a pioneer in developing the blues-oriented trio style. Brown later left the group and formed his own trio, further popularizing the trio style and blues repertoire ("Trouble Blues," 1949, and "Black Night," 1951).[13]

In the larger clubs, musicians gave shape to a rhythm and blues combo style. Bandleader Johnny Otis explains:

> [W]e [Otis, T-Bone Walker, Roy Milton, and Joe Liggins] began to develop something within something. It was a hybrid form that began to emerge. It surely wasn't big band; it wasn't swing; it wasn't country blues. It was what was to become known as rhythm and blues, a hybrid form that became an art form in itself. It was the foundation of rock and roll.[14]

After-hours clubs
Small, non-alcoholic venues where patrons gathered after the curfew of those licensed to sell alcoholic beverages.

Many of the pioneers of West Coast rhythm and blues styles were former members of **territory jazz bands** of the Southwest;[15] others were blues singers and instrumentalists from the rural Southwest. Adapting to life in the city and preserving the familiar sounds of the past, these musicians formed combos and built on the model established by Louis Jordan, who was living and performing in New York City at the time.

Arkansas-born Louis Jordan had been a vocalist and alto saxophonist with Chick Webb's swing band in New York City. In 1938, he formed his own combo of seven or eight musicians, a smaller group than Webb's big band of twelve to sixteen musicians. Jordan's up-tempo combo style, known as "jump blues," is rooted in the blues tradition. The "jump" or swing character results from the twelve-bar boogie-woogie bass foundation overlaid with shuffle rhythms (triplet quarter note followed by a triplet eighth note; see Figure 12.1B) and swing-style horn riff patterns (of syncopated three- and four-notes). Louis Jordan and His Tympany Five featured Jordan on lead vocals with group singing on refrain lines and a solo alto saxophone. The humorous song titles and lyrics about urban and rural Black life resonated with African Americans, especially the working class, who identified with songs such as "What's the Use of Getting Sober (When You Gonna Get Drunk Again)" (1942), "Caldonia" (1945), "Ain't Nobody Here But Us Chickens" (1946), and "Saturday Night Fish Fry" (1949) (Track 30).

 30

"Saturday Night Fish Fry."

Musicians on the West Coast further developed the hybrid jazz–blues–boogie-woogie style that Jordan and His Tympany Five had introduced and popularized. The West Coast combos built on Jordan's model by incorporating a distinctive Texas blues guitar, triplet piano figures, and horn arrangements reminiscent of territory bands. They also replaced the alto sax with a "honking" tenor saxophone style (blowing the same piercing low and high pitches repeatedly)[16] as the featured solo instrument.[17] Various manifestations of this up-tempo combo style are heard in Roy Milton & His Solid Senders' "Milton's Boogie" (1946), Roy Brown's "Good Rocking Tonight" (1947), and Big Jay McNeely & Band's "Deacon's Hop" (1949).[18] The repertoire of rhythm and blues combos, although dominated by up-tempo dance songs, includes blues ballads such as "R.M. Blues" (1946) by Roy Milton & His Solid Senders and "Empty Arms Blues" (1949) by Amos Milburn.

Chicago: Chess and Vee-Jay Records

In contrast to the trios and jump combos of the West Coast, an urban form of the Mississippi Delta blues style called "urban blues" (see discussion of the blues in Chapter 7) took root in the clubs and bars on Chicago's South Side. Of the nearly 800,000 southern migrants who resided in this area in 1950, the majority were from the Mississippi Delta. Upon arrival, they sought out friends and family and formed "village-like" communities. "Two blocks in Chicago," for example, were "made up largely of Mississippians from Holmes County. Social life revolved round

Figure 12.1

Part A gives the most common notation for the shuffle rhythm; the 12/8 notation in part B represents the triplet feel as it is generally played. Transcription by Carl MaultsBy.

the folks from downhome as counties and small towns were contracted and re-formed on Chicago's South Side." Local entrepreneurs established entertainment venues on the South Side, where the new arrivals congregated, consciously recreating the atmosphere of southern juke-joints in blues bars. Blues musicians reconstructed "home" by connecting the past with the present, playing familiar songs with an urban sensibility.[19]

In the crowded small bars, they sang about the good times and hardships of life in the rural South and life in the city, using amplified guitars and harmonicas. The Chicago blues aesthetic of the early years is heard in the styles of Sonny Boy Williamson's "Better Cut That Out" (1947), Howlin' Wolf's "How Many More Years" (1951), Muddy Waters' "Still a Fool" (1951), and Jimmy Reed's "Ain't That Lovin' You Baby" (1955). Although marketed as blues, these and other blues artists appeared on *Billboard*'s race music/rhythm and blues label charts.

To capitalize on the popularity of the blues, Leonard and Phil Chess formed Aristocrat Records in 1947 (it became Chess Records in 1950) to record local blues artists. They were owners of Macomba Lounge, one of Chicago's venues featuring blues and jazz musicians whose music was in demand. The Chess brothers hired Mississippi-born blues bassist Willie Dixon as musical director-songwriter-arranger (**Artists and Repertoire/A&R**) for the company. Five years later in 1952, the newly established Vee-Jay Records[20] added local blues musicians to its developing roster. The blues recordings of these and other independent labels combined with a vibrant blues bar scene to position Chicago to become the blues capital of the world in the 1950s and 1960s.

Cincinnati: King Records

In the mid-1940s Cincinnati, Ohio, became a major center for the production of rhythm and blues records. The Black population of 78,196 (15.5 percent of the city's total)[21] attracted the few remaining blues-oriented big bands, such as Buddy Johnson, Tiny Bradshaw, Lucky Millinder, Todd Rhodes, and Willie Bryant. The diverse repertoire of these bands included jump blues, blues ballads, novelty songs, and pop standards. Syd Nathan, who launched King Records to record hillbilly music in 1943, expanded into rhythm and blues in 1945.[22] His first recordings were by the blues singers and instrumentalists from big bands, including Bull Moose Jackson and His Band ("I Know Who Threw the Whiskey in the Well," 1945), Todd Rhodes ("Blues for the Red Boy," 1948), Wynonie Harris ("Drinkin' Wine, Spo-Dee-O-Dee," 1949), and Tiny Bradshaw and His Orchestra ("Well, Oh, Well," 1950).[23] Nathan, as did the Chess brothers and other White owners of independent labels, also selected his A&R staff from these swing bands. Henry Glover served in this capacity for King Records, supervising the recordings by both rhythm and blues and country music artists.

By the early 1950s, rhythm and blues had evolved as a distinctive musical genre, separated from jazz by its new treatments of elements from gospel music and blues. King Records contributed to this change through releases by artists anchored in the gospel tradition, such as the Dominoes ("Have Mercy Baby," 1952) and later James Brown ("Please, Please, Please," 1956, and "Try Me," 1958) on its subsidiary label Federal. At the same time, the blues provided the foundation for a range of rhythm and blues styles, including signature sounds for independent record labels as evident in the formulation of the "Atlantic Sound."

New York City: The Atlantic Sound

Atlantic Records was co-founded by Ahmet Ertegun with Herb Abramson in 1947. After their first releases of jazz artists generated disappointing sales, the owners turned to blues and rhythm and blues, whose primary consumers were southern Black adults. In 1950, 68 percent of all Black people lived in the South, and less than one in four (between 15 and 25 percent) of this population in rural areas.[24] While targeting the adult market, Ertegun and Abramson wanted to make inroads with the growing Black teenage market in the South. In 1951, Ertegun, Abramson, and Atlantic's Black musical director-songwriter-arranger, Jesse Stone

Figure 12.2
Jesse Stone, musical
director, songwriter,
and arranger for
Atlantic Records.
Courtesy Archives of
African American
Music and Culture,
Indiana University.

(Figure 12.2), traveled into the Deep South in search of talent and ideas for developing a commercial blues-oriented rhythm and blues sound.[25] Stone recalls:

> We figured a buying public was a dancing public, and the dancing public was mostly Black … What we needed to do was to go South and see what kind of music was being done there, and pattern something on the style and improve on it—whatever we could do to offer a dance type of music that the young people would like.[26]

They observed teenage dances in Mississippi, Georgia, and Louisiana, where Stone discovered that the blues, especially boogie-woogie, was popular among this group. The musicians were boogie-woogie guitarists and/or pianists. They performed without bass and drums, allowing the steps of the dancers to provide the rhythmic foundation. In Louisiana he noticed that the steps for a popular dance called the Louisiana shuffle derived from the rumba rhythm (see Figure 12.3).

For Stone, the boogie-woogie bass line "was too busy and didn't fit the dances kids were doing."[27] He concluded that if he wrote songs that

Figure 12.3
The rumba pattern.

Figure 12.4
Examples of the "Atlantic Sound," transcribed from a series of piano demonstrations by Jesse Stone: (a) Boogie-woogie bass line adapted by Jesse Stone in the creation of the "Atlantic Sound." (b) Atlantic Records' formulaic bass line, illustrated in Stone's rendition of the bass pattern for "5-10-15 Hours" (1952). (c) An alternate transcription of "5-10-15 Hours" that more accurately illustrates the triplet feel. Transcription by Carl MaultsBy.

simplified the boogie bass line to incorporate the rumba rhythm and streamlined the big band horn-styled arrangements common in popular music, they would sell.[28] This musical formula (see Figure 12.4), which often included a sing-along chorus, became known as the Atlantic Sound. Stone's musical strategy produced hits for many of Atlantic's artists—including Ruth Brown ("5-10-15 Hours," 1952), the Clovers ("One Mint Julep," 1952), and Joe Turner ("Shake, Rattle, & Roll," 1954)[29] (Track 31)—and established Atlantic as a major and competitive force in rhythm and blues, appealing to both adults and the emerging teenage consumers.

31

"Shake, Rattle, & Roll."

New York, New Jersey, Washington, DC, and Chicago: Vocal Harmony Groups

In virtually every African American urban neighborhood, males gathered for recreational singing in close harmony, a tradition that has its origins in the 1870s (see discussion of quartets in Chapter 5). By the twentieth century, according to researcher Lynn Abbott, barbershops and school-yards had become the rehearsal sites for these a cappella groups.[30] Beginning in the late-1930s, vocal harmony groups such as the Mills Brothers, Ink Spots, and Delta Rhythm Boys were broadcast on radio. They also sang with big bands, appeared in movies and performed on the Black theater circuit, appearing in such venues as the Apollo in Harlem, the Howard in Washington, DC, and the Regal in Chicago. Featuring a lead vocalist and supporting background singers, these groups performed a diverse repertoire of jazz, pop standards, folk, and jubilee songs. Other identifying features associated with the vocal harmony groups are (1) alternating lead vocals, (2) harmonizing choruses, (3) imitating instrumental timbres, and (4) contrasting timbres and vocal range. In the 1950s, following World War II, teenage groups formed in neighborhoods throughout the country, with a strong presence on the East Coast and in the Midwest, especially in New York, New Jersey, Washington, DC, and Chicago. They envisioned duplicating the success of their predecessors.

The Ravens, formed in New York City in 1945, provided the transition between pre- and post-World War II harmony groups. They ushered in a new era and introduced what became known as the "bird" groups (Crows, Cardinals, Larks, Flamingos, Orioles, Penguins, Swallows, Swans, Wrens). With their diverse repertoire, the Ravens modernized the harmony group sound by (1) establishing the blues form as a musical foundation, (2) introducing blues lyric themes, (3) incorporating blues elements in the jazz vocal stylings, and (4) institutionalizing the bass voice on lead vocals, a practice first popularized by the Delta Rhythm Boys gospel quartet. These characteristics are heard on "Bye Bye Baby Blues" (1948) and "Ricky's Blues" (1949).

Many of the postwar harmony groups can be divided into two stylistic categories—romantic and rhythmic. The romantic groups sang primarily ballads a cappella or with acoustic guitar accompaniment. Some later added drums and piano to increase their commercial appeal. The rhythmic groups specialized in up-tempo songs and were accompanied by rhythm and blues combos.[31]

The Orioles, formed in 1946 in Baltimore, popularized the romantic style. They are considered to be the first bona fide rhythm and blues vocal harmony group. Their songs captured the country's mood following the end of World War II:

> People wanted to become close. Their loved ones were coming back from the war . . . The theme was trying to get close to each other. You can't get close to nobody on the dance floor, jitterbugging, so ballads were the best medium . . . So it put you in a different frame of mind . . . to fall in love.[32]

Unlike the jazz-blues flavor of the Ravens, the group derived its harmonies from congregational singing heard in African American churches. Orioles member "Diz" Russell described their sound as "the bass on the bottom of chords, the baritone in the middle, and the first and floating tenor[33] on top, coming in and out and carrying the chord up and down."[34] The songs "It's Too Soon to Know" (1948) and "Crying in the Chapel" (1953) are illustrative of the romantic style, which subsequent rhythm and blues harmony groups adopted.

In contrast to the romantic groups, the rhythmic groups were aligned with both the blues and gospel quartet traditions. The blues structure and combo instrumentation combined with the call–response form, close harmonies, and vocal stylings of gospel music. The Clovers' "Don't You Know I Love You" (1951) and Billy Ward and His Dominoes' "Sixty Minute Man" (1951) and "Have Mercy, Baby" (1952) were among the first to popularize this style. In the early 1950s, singers from gospel quartets began switching to a more lucrative career in rhythm and blues; artists who made such career moves included Clyde McPhatter (from the Mount Lebanon Singers) of the Drifters ("Money Honey," 1953), Jackie Wilson (from Ever Ready Gospel Singers) of Billy Ward and His Dominoes ("Rags to Riches," 1953), and Sam Cooke (from the Soul Stirrers) as a solo singer ("You Send Me," 1957). Through the vocal harmony groups, the gospel sound slowly began to permeate the rhythm and blues tradition.

NEW REGIONAL SOUNDS: THE SECOND STREAM, MID-1950S THROUGH MID-1960S

By the mid-1950s, Black teenagers had become the primary consumer group for rhythm and blues. Record label owners targeted this demographic by signing artists with a fresh and youthful sound.[35] In New Orleans, A&R staff discovered piano players Fats Domino and Little Richard and, in Chicago, guitar players Chuck Berry and Bo Diddley. From Gary and Chicago came the doo-wop harmony groups the Spaniels and the Moonglows, respectively. Between 1954 and 1955, the collective innovations of these six artists changed the sound of rhythm and blues, reflecting new musical values, cultural sensibilities, experiences, and the ongoing fusion of blues and gospel elements.

The Sounds of New Orleans

A city of many cultures since the nineteenth century,[36] New Orleans was home to many musicians who created unique and eclectic musical styles that shaped the local sound of rhythm and blues.[37] Piano players dominated the New Orleans rhythm and blues scene in the early years. One of the most well-known players was Professor Longhair ("Mardi Gras in New Orleans," 1949),[38] whose style was highly rhythmic and incorporated triplet note figures played over the Cuban rumba rhythm. Dave Bartholomew (Figure 12.5)—Fats Domino's musical director, arranger, producer, and co-songwriter—used the rumba in his own rhythm and blues recordings ("Country Girl," 1949; Figure 12.6).[39] He also used this rhythm as the foundation for Fats Domino's recordings, on top of which Domino added the rolling fifth and octave figures (also associated with the Texas blues tradition) as well as triplets to develop a distinctive New Orleans rhythm and blues style ("Going Home," 1952; "Ain't That A Shame," 1955; and "Blueberry Hill," 1956).[40] Bartholomew doubled the rumba pattern in the horns and/or on the guitar to add depth to the sound. The Domino–Bartholomew innovations, along with those of Little Richard, modernized the sound of the West Coast "jump" combos.[41]

St Phillip
Publishing Co.
1616 No Galvez St.
New Orleans, La. 70119

Porter's Photo News

Figure 12.5
Dave Bartholomew, musical director, songwriter, and arranger-producer for Imperial, Specialty, and Aladdin Records. Courtesy Archives of African American Music and Culture, Indiana University.

Figure 12.6
Rumba rhythm from
Dave Bartholomew's
"Country Girl."

Horns

Bass

Originally from Macon, Georgia, Little Richard recorded in New Orleans. Like many early rhythm and blues artists, he wrote most of his songs and performed them in the clubs where they first became popular. In collaboration with producer-arranger and sometimes co-songwriter Bumps Blackwell, Richard recorded a series of hit songs. The first one, "Tutti Frutti" (1955), introduced a new rhythmic pattern to the rhythm and blues tradition (Track 32). Charles Connor, Little Richard's original drummer (Figure 12.7), explains:

> In rhythm and blues, you had a shuffle with a back-beat, but Little Richard wanted something different. He wanted something with more energy, but he didn't know how to describe the notes. So Richard brought me down to the train station in Macon, Georgia, in 1954 and he said, "Charles, listen to the choo-choo, choo-choo, choo-choo." I said, you probably want eighth notes or sixteenth notes. We went back to his house couple of days later . . . and we came up with that beat. Now, nobody had ever played that beat before.[42]

Figure 12.7
Charles Connor, original drummer for Little Richard. Courtesy Charles Connor and the Archives of African American Music and Culture, Indiana University.

Portia K. Maultsby

The *choo-choo* beat provided the rhythmic foundation for Little Richard's national and crossover hits, beginning with "Long Tall Sally" (1956) and "Lucille" (1957). Many "rock and roll" groups appropriated this beat, which became known in mainstream popular music as the "rock and roll" beat.

The Sounds of Chicago

In Chicago, Bo Diddley and Chuck Berry transformed the blues into a distinctive rhythm and blues style by featuring the guitar as the primary instrument. Diddley's rhythmic guitar style and rumba rhythms ("Bo Diddley" and "Pretty Thing," 1955) and Berry's more melodic yet spirited approach and novelty lyrics ("Maybellene," 1955, and "Roll Over Beethoven," 1956) appealed to the changing musical tastes and cultural values of America's youth, both Black and White.

Similarly, the rhythmic vocal innovations of the romantic harmony groups the Spaniels ("Goodnight, Sweetheart, Goodnight," 1954) and the Moonglows ("Sincerely," 1954, and "Most of All," 1955) ushered in a new vocal group sound that became known as "doo-wop" (Track 18). **Doo-wop** is described as a combination of vocables (syllables without meaning) treated rhythmically to add movement to romantic songs. These two groups traditionally sang without instrumental accompaniment. They created a rhythmic foundation by using the bass voice as an instrument to imitate the "walking" string bass associated with jazz.[43] The back-up singers incorporated variations of the repetitive "doo-doo-wop" phrase in their responses to the lead singer. Many of the doo-wop groups, especially the car groups, added combos to increase the rhythmic intensity of songs (the Cadillacs, "Speedo," 1955, and "Peek-A-Boo," 1958; the El Dorados, "At My Front Door," 1955; and Frankie Lymon and the Teenagers, "I Want You to Be My Girl," 1956). These and similar groups, such as the Coasters ("Searchin'" 1957), became known as doo-wop and rock and roll vocal harmony groups.[44]

 18
"Sincerely."

Doo-wop
Typically, a cappella vocal harmony groups that emphasized the rhythmic delivery of phrases consisting of vocables (syllables without lexical meaning) such as "doo-wop."

doo   doo   doo   doo   doo

doo   doo doo   doo doo doo   doo   doo doo doo doo doo doo

Figure 12.8
Examples of "doo-wop" phrases.

By the mid-1950s, the sound of rhythm and blues vocal harmony groups and combos had begun to cross racial boundaries. The proliferation of small independent labels that recorded this music provided product for jukebox distributors, small record stores, and radio stations. Although independent labels initially did not have access to national distribution, Black Pullman porters became the unofficial distributors. Working on trains that traveled from the West Coast to the Midwest and East Coast, Pullman porters transported and sold records in all major cities. Leon René, the African American co-founder (with his brother) of Excelsior (1942) and Exclusive (1944) Records in Los Angeles, explains:

> Because of the demand for "The Honeydripper" in the midwest, Pullman porters would take records to Chicago from Los Angeles and bootleg them at ten dollars a disc. In Chicago, Harry Rife had a record shop on the South Side next to the Regal Theatre, and R&B fans would line up for blocks to purchase "The Honeydripper" [1945] by Joe Liggins and "I'm Lost" [1944] by Nat "King" Cole.[45]

Radio became the major catalyst in the exposure of rhythm and blues, first on low-wattage (100–5,000 watts) radio stations that targeted local African American communities, then on 50,000-watt stations with national and international reach. White radio disc jockey Gene Nobles was the first to broadcast rhythm and blues on the powerful 50,000-watt radio station WLAC, a CBS-affiliate in Nashville, Tennessee. His program filled the late-evening slot after the conclusion of syndicated programming. Nobles' broadcast of rhythm and blues began in 1946 with the sponsorship of record retailer Randy Wood (Randy's Record Shop in Gallatin, Tennessee) and, later, Ernie Young (Ernie's Record Mart in Nashville). Both had a mail-order business selling blues, rhythm and blues, and gospel music, and mail orders indicate that WLAC's programs of rhythm and blues and gospel music reached listeners as far as Canada, Mexico, the Caribbean, North Africa, and other international regions via shortwave radio. Although Nobles' three-hour (10:00 p.m. to 1:00 a.m.) program brought national attention to rhythm and blues, his successor John Richbourg (known as John R.) was the most successful of the White rhythm and blues DJs. In the 1950s and 1960s, his 10:00 p.m. to 3:00 a.m. broadcast reached "an estimated 14 million people in thirty-eight states. Although the majority of his listeners were black, his white listeners also numbered in the millions."[46]

Al Benson of Chicago reportedly was the first African American disc jockey to broadcast blues and rhythm and blues. In 1946 he hosted a daily fifteen-minute program. By 1948, he was broadcasting over four Chicago stations for a total of ten hours daily. By 1952 an estimated 200 to 250 radio stations reached 90 percent of the Black population and gave airtime to African American programming during part or all of their broadcast hours.[47] In contrast, pop radio refused to play the records of African American artists. Ahmet Ertegun recalls:

They had a set of stock excuses: "Too loud"; "Too rough"; "Doesn't fit our format." They'd never say, "We don't play black artists." But then they'd turn around and play a record of the very same song that was a copy of our record, only it was by a white artist.[48]

Those recordings by white artists were known as "covers"—imitative and often sanitized versions of the newly released rhythm and blues songs. Well-known covers include the Crew Cuts' version of "Sh-Boom" by the Chords, Georgia Gibbs's "Dance with Me Henry (Wallflower)" by Etta James, and Pat Boone's performances of "Ain't that a Shame" by Fats Domino and "Tutti Frutti" by Little Richard.[49]

Cover Records

Between 1954 and 1955, **cover records** had become omnipresent on pop radio, but they became passé when White teenagers discovered the original rhythm and blues artists through late-night radio broadcasts. Rejecting mainstream values and the musical preferences of their parents, White teenagers sought to establish their own identity through music, dance, fashion, and style. African American culture served as the primary resource. As early as 1952, some jukebox operators and record stores located in White neighborhoods requested rhythm and blues records from the distributors of independent record labels. By the mid-1950s, such requests had become common in both the South and North.[50] The racially defined distribution practices of the music industry, however, prevented easy access to this music. Yet, the increasing number of White teenagers who ventured into Black neighborhoods to purchase this music prompted retail outlets and jukebox operators in White neighborhoods to stock rhythm and blues records. In an attempt to obscure the racial origins of rhythm and blues and the identity of its performers, the music trade press, pop radio, and record companies relabeled the music "**rock and roll.**"

The media credits Cleveland disc jockey Alan Freed as having coined the phrase to describe the music that he played on his radio program "Moondog Rock and Roll Party." Air-check tapes of Freed's broadcast on WJW in Cleveland from 1952 through March 1954,[51] however, reveal that the name "Moondog Rock and Roll Party" referred only to the name of the program rather than to the music:

> All right, the old Moondog is leaping out folks, and the old Moondog Rock and Roll Party on Tuesday night is just getting under the way. Gotta long way to go. Two and a half hours of your favorite *blues* and *rhythm* [sic] records show for all the gang in the Moondog kingdom from the Midwest to the East Coast . . . this is WJW, WJW-FM in Cleveland.[52]

Photographs of Freed's live shows staged in Cleveland—"Moondog Coronation Ball" and the "Biggest Rhythm and Blues Show"—show predominately Black audiences, suggesting that Freed's listening audience was also largely African American.[53]

In the summer of 1954, Freed moved his "Moondog Rock and Roll Party" from Cleveland to WINS in New York City. A year later his

Cover record
A recording made by a White artist that attempted to replicate or approximate the sound, arrangement, and content of an earlier Black hit, aimed at selling to the White teen market.

Rock and roll
1950s derivative of rhythm and blues, characterized by Black gospel and pop influences; created for consumption by Black and White teenagers.

popularity soared, as did the ratings of the radio station. As author John Jackson notes:

> *Billboard* and *Variety* suddenly began to refer to Freed as a "rock and roll" disc jockey, and several record companies—majors and independents alike—began describing rhythm and blues as "rock & roll" in their trade advertising, eager to capitalize on the music's growing popularity.[54]

Freed eventually responded to the pressure of mainstream society to rename rhythm and blues "rock and roll" and to identify himself as a rock and roll disc jockey:

> Yours truly Alan Freed the old King of the Rock and Roller. Still to come but all ready for another big night of rockin' and rollin'. Rock and roll like good to the big beat in popular music in America today. Let it go and we'll be here 'til nine o'clock reviewing the top twenty-five rock and roll favorites of the week. Welcome to Rock and Roll Party number one.[55]

Freed's ongoing reference to "blues and rhythm" as "rock and roll" contributed to the music industry's repackaging and promotion of Black music as rock and roll for the consumption of White teenagers.

Even though the mass media marketed Black musicians as rock and roll artists, these artists repeatedly identified their repertoire and musical style as rhythm and blues. In an on-camera interview for the video *Rock and Roll: The Early Days*, for example, someone asks Fats Domino "how rock and roll got started." He responds: "Well, what they call rock and roll now is really rhythm and blues. I've been playing it for fifteen years in New Orleans."[56] Similarly, Little Richard's original drummer Charles Connor described rock and roll as "rhythm and blues played with a fast beat."[57] Even though many African American artists continued to self-identify as rhythm and blues artists, in the 1950s the term "rock and roll" became institutionalized through Hollywood "rock and roll" films as well as the nationally televised dance show *American Bandstand*.

The films *Rock and Roll Revue* (1955), *Rock, Rock, Rock* (1956), and *Don't Knock the Rock* (1957) featured rhythm and blues artists.[58] Rock and roll films, rock and roll concerts, and *American Bandstand* gave rhythm and blues artists unprecedented national exposure.[59] This repositioning of artists from the racial margins to the center of American popular culture caused consternation among Whites, especially those in the South, who attributed the deteriorating values, unruly behavior, and rebellious spirit of White youth to the influences of rhythm and blues. In response to this music (i.e., rock and roll), the Citizens' Council of Greater New Orleans, Inc., formed coalitions with other segregationist groups to protest the promotion, sale, and radio broadcast of rhythm and blues. As part of the campaign to rid society of this "licentious jungle music," the Citizens' Council distributed flyers (Figure 12.9) and organized press conferences and public meetings to publicly express their opposition.[60]

Portia K. Maultsby

Figure 12.9
A flyer campaigning against "Negro Records," distributed by the Citizens' Council of Greater New Orleans, c.1950s. Courtesy Archives of African American Music and Culture, Indiana University.

The popularity of rhythm and blues among White teenagers occurred at a pivotal point in race relations in society. In the mid-1950s, the Supreme Court ruled the unconstitutionality of segregated public schools, southern Blacks launched the Civil Rights Movement, Senator Joseph R. McCarthy organized the anti-Communist campaign, and southern White citizens' councils mounted protests against school desegregation, race mixing, and the marketing of rock and roll (i.e., rhythm and blues) across racial boundaries.[61] Despite lawsuits and various forms of protests to rid the nation of rhythm and blues, the music remained popular among White youth. Eager to cross over on to pop radio and to expand the consumer market for rhythm and blues across racial, class, and generational boundaries, record labels applied new and noncontroversial strategies in the production of African American artists.[62]

Crossover Strategies and Formulas

Crossover
The process by which a recording released in a secondary market achieves hit status in the mainstream market.

Two of the most frequent **crossover** strategies of record labels were recording rhythm and blues artists singing country songs[63] (Wynonie Harris's "Bloodshot Eyes," 1951, originally recorded by Hank Penny) and pop standards (Dinah Washington's "Teach Me Tonight," 1954)[64] accompanied by big band and combo arrangements. The most successful crossover strategy, however, was the use of pop post-production techniques—adding string and pop vocal arrangements, the latter often sung by conservatory-trained professional singers (called "legit" singers in the industry)—in rhythm and blues recordings.[65] Among the first uses of pop post-production techniques were Mercury's productions of the Platters ("The Great Pretender," 1955, and "My Prayer," 1956) and Dinah Washington ("What a Difference a Day Makes," 1959), and Atlantic's recordings of Clyde McPhatter ("Long Lonely Nights," 1957) and LaVern Baker ("I Cried a Tear," 1958).

In the mid-1950s, Latin American rhythms and dances were becoming popular in America. Record companies began incorporating versions of these rhythms, especially the Brazilian *baion* (Figure 12.10) and the Cuban *habanera* rhythm (Figure 12.11) in rhythm and blues productions. Atlantic led the way, establishing the Brazilian *baion* as the rhythmic foundation for the Drifters' "There Goes My Baby" (1959) and "Up on the Roof" (1962), and Ben E. King's "Spanish Harlem" (1960), and appropriating the Cuban *habanera* rhythm on the Drifters' "This Magic Moment" (1960) and "On Broadway" (1963).[66] Author Charlie Gillett appropriately describes these crossover new pop-oriented productions of African American artists as "uptown rhythm and blues."[67]

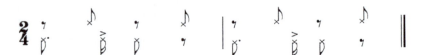

Figure 12.10
The Brazilian *baion* rhythm.

Figure 12.11
The Cuban *habanera* rhythm.

Portia K. Maultsby

While producing crossover hits, Atlantic and other labels continued to record songs that appealed to the Black poor and working-class adults, who preferred the traditional blues- and gospel-oriented rhythm and blues styles recorded by such artists as Joe Turner ("Corrina, Corrina," 1956), the Clovers ("Down in the Alley," 1957), Ray Charles ("The Right Time," 1958, and "What'd I Say," 1959), Etta James ("All I Could Do Was Cry," 1960), and LaVern Baker ("See See Rider," 1962).

The "uptown" production formula became standard to many recordings of rhythm and blues artists. Publishing firms hired mainly young White songwriter-producers[68] to write songs based on teenage experiences and fantasies. Musical arrangements incorporated "hook lines" (sing-along repetitive phrases), string arrangements, and adaptations of Brazilian rhythms. This formula launched the careers of many successful Black teenaged female vocal groups, including the Chantels ("Maybe," 1958), the Shirelles ("Will You Love Me Tomorrow," 1960), the Crystals ("He's a Rebel," 1962, and "Da Doo Ron Ron," 1963), the Chiffons ("He's So Fine," 1963), and the Ronettes ("Be My Baby," 1963). These groups crossed over into the mainstream and established the commercial viability of "girl groups."[69] At the same time, Motown Records was on the verge of changing the sound of these groups and their male counterparts. From the mid- to late 1960s, Motown was instrumental in shifting the 1950s crossover paradigm toward a culturally defined northern Black sound. Known as the "Motown Sound," it is rooted in the combo and northern styles of the 1950s. In the creation of the Motown Sound, Berry Gordy and his musical staff added a bebop flavor, removed some pop elements, and reworked others to conform to the Black aesthetic ideal. As the mainstream became acclimated to a Black sound through both diluted and original versions, their aesthetic preference for popular music began to change. By the end of the 1960s, the Motown Sound had crossed racial boundaries and become the "Sound of Young America."[70]

NEW REGIONAL SOUNDS: THE THIRD STREAM, 1960s THROUGH MID-1970s

Rhythm and Blues: The Motown Sound

Motown Records was founded in 1959 by Berry Gordy in Detroit, a city that boasted a vibrant musical scene featuring jazz, blues, rhythm and blues, vocal harmony, and gospel groups. The company was located in the heart of the Black community where "every local street-corner was occupied by trios, quartets, and quintets of kids teaching themselves the intricate harmonies they picked up off current hit records by the Platters, the Drifters, the Coasters, the Cleftones, the Flamingos" and "kids who played instruments were rare."[71] Gordy signed many of these aspiring artists. They soon would bring worldwide notoriety to the new "Sound

Motown
Record label created by Berry Gordy, named for its original location in Detroit, a.k.a. "Motor Town."

of Young America," performing in prestigious venues and before dignitaries throughout America and in Europe and Asia.

The 1950s combo, vocal harmony group, and uptown rhythm and blues traditions provided the model for Motown's early recordings (1959–63), Phase I of the company's development.[72] Motown's roster was diverse, encompassing solo singers, duos, combos, and vocal harmony groups. In the 1960s vocal harmony groups dominated the company's releases. The transition to a distinctive Motown Sound occurred between 1963 and 1964, the beginning of Phase II, when gospel and jazz and the reworking of pop elements became more pronounced in the recordings.[73]

Motown's artists and resident songwriter-producers were between the ages of eighteen and twenty-three. According to Mickey Stevenson:

> We were into young people's music . . . Writers are a reflection of the voice of people . . . so if you have a [young] writer, he is going to write about young love. He can't write about old love—he's never experienced it.[74]

Writing out of their youthful and urban experience, the song lyrics dealt with fantasies and feelings, in addition to young love.[75] The songwriters also structured their lyrics around catchy and memorable popular and classically derived melodies, to which they added vocal harmonies and call–response structures from Black gospel music. By the mid-1960s, this formula, which resonated with Black and White teenagers and young adults, catapulted Motown's artists into national and international prominence. Yet, the various racial/ethnic groups expressed preferences for particular artists—artists whose aesthetic qualities, such as vocal timbre, style, and overall group texture, mirrored their personal musical tastes.

Each vocal group had a distinct sound, largely due to the vocal timbre of the lead singer around whom songwriters tailored their songs. The thin, airy timbre and pop-oriented style of lead singer Diana Ross of the Supremes ("Where Did Our Love Go," 1964, and "Baby Love," 1964), for example, differed from the percussive quality and gospel-oriented style of Martha Reeves, lead singer for Martha & the Vandellas ("Dancing in the Street," 1964, and "My Baby Loves Me," 1966). The smooth and falsetto timbre of Smokey Robinson of the Miracles ("Tracks of My Tears," 1965) was in contrast to the raspy and percussive timbres of David Ruffin of the Temptations ("Ain't Too Proud to Beg," 1966).[76]

Although all of Motown's groups were popular among both African American and mainstream audiences, the Supremes were most popular among White audiences. Shelly Berger, manager of the Supremes and the Temptations estimated that the Supremes' concerts "were 70/30 white to black. And in a normal Temptations concert you would get 90/10 black to white."[77] The Supremes' vocal style, timbre, and texture were more akin to the aesthetic preferences of the mainstream, which made them highly marketable across racial lines. The Black gospel flavorings of the Temptations resonated more among African Americans.

During Phase II of Motown's development, the Funk Brothers, the company's integrated resident musicians, perfected the Motown Sound, which songwriter-producer Brian Holland contends:

> never varied much from the rhythm and blues base—the bass line, guitar feeling, and back beat—because Blacks always relate to the bass line and the beat most of all.[78] Even though the melodic orientation was kind of different, the foundation was still Black.[79]

Added to the swing jazz-styled walking and bebop-inspired bass lines were the tambourine, hand claps, a metallic ring from the guitar downstroke and back beat on beats two and four, or the bass drum, tambourine, and hand claps on all four beats. The Motown Sound is heard on tracks such as Marvin Gaye's "How Sweet It Is to Be Loved By You" (1965), Martha & the Vandellas' "(Love Is Like A) Heatwave" (1963), the Four Tops' "I Can't Help Myself" (1965), and the Temptations' "Ain't Too Proud to Beg" (1966). Teenagers across class, racial, and regional boundaries related to the music's infectious dance beat and other Black qualities that became commonplace in mainstream popular music.

Motown's musical arrangements applied new concepts to the use of strings in rhythm and blues that drew from Black aesthetic values.[80] Rather than employ strings to "sweeten" the songs, Motown's arrangements used strings as a timbral layer, in conjunction with syncopated horn lines, for a fuller sound; they also doubled the vocal, guitar, and bass lines, and played off the riffs of the rhythm section (Martha & the Vandellas, "My Baby Loves Me," 1966; Track 33).

 33

"My Baby Loves Me."

Even though some pop critics contend that the Motown Sound diluted Black aesthetic qualities for mainstream acceptance,[81] Shelly Berger counters:

> we *never*, we *never ever* produced a song or sang a song and said, "Um, this is the right thing to do at this time. White people will like this." We sang what we sang, you know. The writers wrote what they felt; they produced what they felt. And the audience bought into that because it was good; it was great.[82]

Gordy and his creative staff consciously produced music with commercial appeal without sacrificing the core musical values that defined a Black sound. But as cultural historian Suzanne Smith observes:

> In 1960 black popular music did not crossover to white audiences on the basis of its appeal alone. This transition involved an elaborate system of marketing the artists and behind-the-scenes deal making with distributors, disc jockeys, and record store owners.[83]

Discriminatory media policies, especially in the South, required creative crossover marketing strategies that included faceless album jackets and the hiring of Whites in sales, promotion, and management positions.[84] Gordy elevated the level of professionalism of Motown's acts by establishing the artist development unit, which included an image specialist, professional choreographer, and musical director. He successfully broke through racial barriers with performances of the groups and solo artists in prestigious venues such as the Palace in Las Vegas. Through this crossover success, Motown became a symbol of American popular culture, which contributed to the further browning of the American soundscape. In the late 1960s and early 1970s, this sound aesthetic became darker when the southern rhythm and blues combo style of Stax Records entered the mainstream.

Rhythm and Blues: Stax Records and the Memphis Sound

Stax Records was founded in Memphis in 1959 by bank teller and country musician Jim Stewart, who relocated his recording studio from his garage to an abandoned theater in the Black community. Stax's open door policy attracted a mixture of Black musicians from the neighborhood in addition to White country and rockabilly musicians who had worked with Stewart in his first location. A core of these instrumentalists jammed together and became Stax's resident studio band. This integrated group, which defied established social policies on race mixing in the South, formed as the Civil Rights Movement began gaining momentum across the South. Known as Booker T. & the MGs (Figure 12.12), they blended the blues, rhythm and blues, and rockabilly styles, which resulted in a unique southern sound. The addition of the horn section from the Mar-Keys (an integrated instrumental combo) to the MGs established the foundation for the "Memphis Sound" (1960–68), Phase I of the company's development.[85]

Figure 12.12
Booker T. & the MGs, house band for Stax Records. Courtesy BMI Archives.

Portia K. Maultsby

The Memphis Sound is best described as an urban sound with rural undercurrents. It is spontaneous, earthy, gritty, gutsy, and warm. The laid-back rhythm and blues–rockabilly stylings of Booker T. & the MGs, the syncopated horn riffs and sustained harmonies of the Mar-Keys, and the gospel and blues vocal stylings of solo singers captured the sensibilities of 1960s southern Black culture. Song lyrics encompassed the realities and contradictions of life in the segregated South—life experiences, adult relationships, and social issues.

Solo artists dominated Stax's roster. Many were between the ages of fifteen and twenty-two and wrote their own songs, often in clubs and in collaboration with the resident musicians. The company's first recordings were derived from rhythm and blues models popular in both the South and North. They include the instrumentals of the Mar-Keys ("Last Night," 1961) and Booker T. & the MGs ("Green Onions," 1962), the blues of Albert King ("Don't Throw Your Love on Me So Strong," 1961), and the uptown rhythm and blues of Carla Thomas ("Gee Whiz," 1960, and "A Love of My Own," 1961). Stax favored solo singers, whose vocal styles drew from the blues (Rufus Thomas, "Walking the Dog," 1963) and gospel (William Bell, "You Don't Miss Your Water," 1961, and Otis Redding, "These Arms of Mine," 1962).

As the rhythms and vocal stylings from gospel became more intense in the mid-1960s, the Memphis Sound became synonymous with "**soul**"—a by-product of the Black Power Movement. Otis Redding ("Respect," 1965, and recordings released posthumously after 1969), Sam & Dave ("Hold On! I'm Comin'," 1966, and "Soul Man," 1967),

Soul music
Gospel-influenced African American popular music style that began to emerge in the late 1950s and became popular during the 1960s.

Figure 12.13
Jim Stewart and Al Bell. Courtesy Deanie Parker photo collection/Stax Museum of American Soul Music.

and the Bar-Kays ("Soul Finger," 1967) were among the first artists to popularize the southern sound of soul (see discussion of soul in Chapter 13).

Until 1963, the Memphis Sound was largely unknown outside southern Black communities. In that year, Al Bell, a Black disc jockey in Washington, DC, began promoting the music on the East Coast. Bell (Figure 12.13) subsequently joined the Stax label in 1965 as its first National Director for Promotion, and two years later he became Vice President and Chief Operating Officer. In the latter role, Bell began diversifying and broadening the Memphis Sound while retaining its rhythm and blues and gospel foundation. During this period, he ushered in Phase II (1968–75) of the company's development. Bell expanded the staff of songwriter-producers[86] and arrangers and signed several new solo singers and vocal groups. Each artist had a distinctive soul style, which diversified and broadened the company's sound. The higher energy soul of Johnny Taylor ("Who's Making Love," 1968), supported by a rhythm and blues combo, differed from the smooth and laid-back style of Isaac Hayes ("By the Time I Get to Phoenix," 1969, and "Walk On By," 1969), accompanied by the funky, yet lush orchestral arrangement. The vocal groups were equally diverse. The dense texture and percussive timbre of the gender-mixed group Soul Children ("The Sweeter He Is," 1969) were in contrast with the lighter texture and airy timbre of the female trio the Emotions ("So I Can Love You," 1969). The Staple Singers ("Respect Yourself," 1971), a former family gospel group of five, brought a rural and folksy gospel sensibility to soul, while the male quintet Dramatics ("Whatcha See Is What You Get," 1971) from Detroit featured a northern flavor.[87] Under Bell's leadership, Stax became a national and international phenomenon.

RHYTHM AND BLUES: THE FOURTH STREAM, 1970s THROUGH 1980s

Rhythm and Blues: The 1970s

Rhythm and blues began to fade into the background as disco and funk dominated Black popular music production in the 1970s (see Chapters 14 and 15 on disco and funk). Rhythm and blues ballads, however, remained popular and provided an alternative to up-tempo dance music. The themes of love and personal relationships contrasted with the party lyrics of disco and funk, and the slow to moderate tempos of ballads established the mood for romance. Several vocal groups as well as solo artists specialized in these songs;[88] examples include the Dells ("Give Your Baby a Standing Ovation," 1973), the Stylistics ("You Make Me Feel Brand New," 1973), and the Manhattans ("Kiss and Say Goodbye," 1976).[89] Among well-known solo balladeers were Al Green ("Let's Stay Together," 1971), Tyrone Davis ("In the Mood," 1978), and Teddy Pendergrass ("Turn

Off the Lights," 1978). The 1970s also witnessed the rise of a new generation of teenaged rhythm and blues vocal groups who sang both ballads and up-tempo songs. With youth as their primary audience, the Jackson 5 ("I'll Be There," 1970 and "Dancing Machine," 1974) was the most popular of these groups. Later known as the Jacksons, they provided the model for subsequent teenaged groups such as New Edition ("Candy Girl," 1983).

Rhythm and Blues in Transition: The 1980s

Throughout the 1980s, the music industry and Black popular music were in a state of transition. Disco faded into obscurity, funk evolved into various hybrid forms, and electronic dance music and hip-hop began to influence new sounds in Black popular music. Simultaneously, the danceable rhythms and the **gospel-styled vocals** of 1970s Black disco artists[90] influenced the changing sound of mainstream popular music. These developments paralleled the growing new Black popular music demographic of White suburban and small-town teenagers as well as the post-disco crowd and the international community.

Even though disco had largely disappeared from the soundscape in the early 1980s, it firmly established a formulaic approach to the development of a Black **crossover aesthetic** (see the discussion of disco in Chapter 15). In the 1980s, this aesthetic became known as "Black pop." Productions of this music, especially ballads, were built around pop-styled orchestral arrangements and electronic technologies as illustrated in recordings of Lionel Richie ("Truly," 1982), Peabo Bryson ("If Ever You're in My Arms Again," 1984), and Whitney Houston ("Greatest Love Of All," 1985). Music critic Nelson George describes the impact of this crossover aesthetic as the "death of rhythm and blues."[91] This death results from the "soul" being drained from the rhythm and blues aesthetic.

Record companies marketed Black pop balladeers to Top 40 radio and promoted their rhythm and blues counterparts on **urban contemporary** radio. The aesthetic of the latter appealed more to Black listening audiences because of its soulful flavor and **groove** resulting from lyrical and melismatic vocals, a blend of melodic and percussive timbres, and polyrhythmic structures. This rhythm and blues aesthetic is heard in recordings of Freddie Jackson ("You Are My Lady," 1985), Anita Baker ("Sweet Love," 1986), Stephanie Mills ("I Feel Good All Over," 1987), Luther Vandross ("Here and Now," 1989), and Maze Featuring Frankie Beverly ("Can't Get Over You," 1989), among others. While the widespread popularity of these artists largely centered in African American communities, record labels released several interracial duets singing ballads in a Black style to target different demographics simultaneously. They include Michael Jackson and Paul McCartney ("The Girl is Mine," 1982), Patti LaBelle and Michael McDonald ("On My Own," 1986), and Aretha Franklin and George Michael ("I Knew You Were Waiting for Me," 1987).

Gospel-styled vocals
A melismatic vocal style that employs various timbres. Melodies incorporate slides, bends, moans, shouts, and other indicators of strong emotions.

Crossover aesthetic
Highly lyrical vocals with limited ornamentation, supported by lush orchestral arrangement and simple rhythmic foundation. Often strophic with hook line or verse-refrain structures.

Urban contemporary
A term coined in the mid-1970s to identify radio stations located in cities with sizable African American populations that played contemporary Black music, including rhythm and blues and electronic dance music, and, in later decades, early hip-hop and rhythm and blues/hip-hop hybrid styles. These stations were known as rhythm and blues radio in the 1950s and soul radio in the mid-1960s through the early 1970s.

Groove
Syncopated and repetitive rhythmic foundation established by the bass and drum.

Black artists began to reach new audiences two years after the launch of Music Television (MTV) in 1981. The exclusionary policies of MTV prevented the exposure of any Black artist until 1983, when the company aired three music videos[92] from Michael Jackson's eclectic album *Thriller* (1982)—a mix of rhythm and blues, funk-rock, and funk tracks. Because of Jackson's cross-cultural success, and his popularity among White audiences, the trade press labeled him the "King of Pop." This application of "pop" gives the term a new meaning. When first associated with Black artists,[93] pop identified those artists whose productions conformed to the aesthetic norms of mainstream popular music. Jackson's music, however, embodies the aesthetic of Black music. The "King of Pop" title suggests that a component of contemporary pop music is Black music.

MTV's programming became aesthetically darker after Jackson's success, which made possible the broadcast of music videos featuring other Black artists, including Prince ("Purple Rain," 1984). Four years later, in 1988, MTV added to the line-up the first nationally broadcast hip-hop show, *Yo! MTV Raps*.[94] The program featured hip-hop artists DJ Jazzy Jeff & the Fresh Prince ("Parents Just Don't Understand," 1988) and Eric B. & Rakim ("Follow the Leader," 1988) in the pilot episode.[95] This format change positioned hip-hop music, lifestyles, and values squarely at the center of American popular culture where White consumers embraced it and claimed it.

MTV became an important media outlet for the conglomerates that controlled the distribution of and the "purse strings" for the production of Black popular music. By the late 1980s, the multinationals were targeting the new generation of young adult and adult consumers. To exploit this market across racial, ethnic, and genre boundaries, these companies partnered with a new generation of African American independent songwriter-singer-producers.[96] Born in the late 1950s and 1960s, these musicians created contemporary rhythm and blues styles by combining their own musical innovations with elements from the genres popular during their formative years as teenagers and young adults. Songwriter-producers Jimmy Jam (b. 1959) and Terry Lewis (b. 1956), for example, drew from their roots in rhythm and blues and funk, and experimented with advanced technologies to create a unique synthesized funk-styled rhythm and blues popularized by Janet Jackson ("Nasty," 1986, and "Rhythm Nation," 1989).

Teddy Riley (b. 1966), songwriter-producer for the independent Uptown Records (formed in 1986 by rapper Andre Harrell, b. 1960), pioneered the new jack swing style that combined hip-hop beats and sound effects (e.g., scratching and backspinning) and a modified version of the jazz shuffle rhythm[97] with the traditional harmonic progressions and gospel vocal stylings of rhythm and blues. His first productions for the rhythm and blues singer Keith Sweat ("I Want Her," 1987) and his group, Guy ("Groove Me," 1988), popularized new jack swing.[98] Other songwriter-producers also capitalized on the popularity of this style among rhythm and blues audiences. Retaining the new jack groove, the team of Antonio "L.A." Reid (b. 1956) and Kenny "Babyface" Edmonds (b. 1958) added a rap and break section in between sung verses on their productions of Bobby Brown's "Don't Be Cruel" (1988) and his ballad "Roni" (1988).

Riley, Reid, and Edmonds provided the 1990s prototype for the cross-pollination of rhythm and blues and hip-hop that resulted in new crossover forms. Simultaneously, Jimmy Jam and Terry Lewis (Janet Jackson's *Control*, 1986), along with Prince (*1999*, 1982), established the model for electronic synthesized funk–R&B hybrids that later incorporated hip-hop elements. Both hybrid styles provided alternatives to the harder styles of hip-hop (e.g., gangsta rap) and electronic dance music, to which vocals had become secondary (see discussion of electronic dance music in Chapter 16). Within this context, hip-hop slowly gained acceptance on both urban contemporary and Top 40 radio. Initially, these playlists excluded hip-hop and electronic dance music.

Facilitated by MTV and Top 40 radio, Black music had become a major component of American popular music by 1990. Crossover audiences for Black music had grown to encompass White teenagers, young and mature adults from all walks of life, and internationals. Performers of this music were Black and White in addition to various other ethnicities. These developments resulted in Billboard's introduction of new labels to categorize and chart Black music. In 1990, the editors reinstated the label "R&B" to replace the "Black music" label, which had been in use since 1982. The editorial about this change reads: "[I]t is becoming less acceptable to identify music in racial terms." Furthermore:

> R&B as a label is less likely to create expectations about the race or ethnic origin of the music's creators. It should be made clear that Billboard never meant the term "black" to refer to the color of the artists making Black music.[99]

RHYTHM AND BLUES: THE FIFTH STREAM

R&B: 1990s into the New Millennium

Throughout the 1990s, the hybrid R&B productions of independent songwriter-producers launched the careers of many new artists. For example, in his work on Mary J. Blige's[100] debut CD, *What's the 411?* (1992), producer Sean Combs (a.k.a. "Puff Daddy," "Puffy," "P. Diddy," and "Diddy") evolved new jack swing into a new style he called "hip-hop soul." Old school hip-hop beats[101] provide the tracks for Blige's distinctive gospel-derived vocals and background harmonies associated with soul music. *What's the 411?* yielded three hit singles—the title track, "You Remind Me," and "Real Love"—thereby proving Blige worthy of her marketing title, "Queen of Hip-Hop Soul." Over the years, Blige has demonstrated her ability to remain current by incorporating contemporary elements into her recordings and featuring rappers, earning her

Spoken word style
Sung with the
rhythmic flow of the
spoken word.

continued success through the second decade of the millennium. For example, on "All That I Can Say," featuring Lauryn Hill (1999), Blige juxtaposes the **spoken word style** of delivery with lyrical and melismatic vocals, while on "Grown Woman" (2007) she raps alongside featured rapper Ludacris.

By the late 1990s, two production techniques were commonplace in R&B: (1) collaborations between rhythm and blues/soul singers and rappers; and (2) sampling choruses and refrain lines from 1970s and 1980s rhythm and blues/soul recordings.[102] Combs was in the forefront of popularizing a crossover formula based on these collaborations and samplings. He and Mase were featured rappers on "Mo Money Mo Problems" (1997) by Notorious B.I.G.; this track employs the popular crossover aesthetic by placing adjacent to and interweaving the sampled chorus from Diana Ross's "I'm Coming Out"(1980) into the rapped sections of the entire song. Similarly, Combs utilizes the crossover formula in his own music on tracks such as "Satisfy You" (1999), which features rhythm and blues singer R. Kelly and samples the 1987 single "Why You Treat Me So Bad" by Club Nouveau. Incorporating samples from rhythm and blues and funk and featuring rhythm and blues artists on hip-hop tracks established a musical balance between the different genres. This production strategy broadened the public's exposure to and receptivity of hip-hop during a period when the controversial gangsta rap dominated the tradition. It also proved an effective strategy for simultaneously targeting groups of consumers with different musical preferences. Digging deeper into the well of rhythm and blues, songwriter-producers discovered other styles to mine.

After disappearing from the charts in the 1980s, vocal harmony groups reappeared during the 1990s. Various songwriter-producers updated the 1950s and 1960s female vocal group sound by incorporating new musical trends such as rap and break sections (En Vogue, "Lies," 1990), and synthesized technologies and funk grooves (En Vogue, "You Don't Have to Worry," 1990). They also preserved the earlier vocal group aesthetic through stylistic imitation and cover recordings. En Vogue's vocal style and harmonies, for example, are in the tradition of the Jones Girls. Xscape's "Who Can I Run To?" (1995) is a cover of a 1979 Jones Girls track. Comparable female groups include the former gospel group SWV ("Weak," 1992).[103] Other songwriter-producers also added a hip-hop flavor to the female vocal group tradition by incorporating hip-hop vocal sound effects, beats, rapped sections, and a spoken word style of delivery. This R&B–hip-hop hybrid style was popularized by TLC ("Ain't 2 Proud 2 Beg," 1992), Xscape ("Just Kickin' It," 1993), and Destiny's Child ("Say My Name," 1999).[104] By the end of the 1990s and early 2000s, most female vocal groups had disbanded or taken a break to pursue solo careers or other professional opportunities.

Male vocal groups also contributed to the diversity of R&B in the 1990s and into the early 2000s. Like their female counterparts, they recorded slow, moderate, and up-tempo songs. Record companies, however, promoted the ballads of male vocal groups, for which they became known. Stylistically, these groups remained closely connected to the tradition of the 1960s/1970s male groups, whose vocal stylings, a cappella harmonies, and song interpretations drew from the gospel and jazz traditions.[105] "End of the Road" (1992) by Boyz II Men, for example, is performed in the style of the Manhattans' "Kiss and Say Goodbye" (1976).[106] At the same time, producers[107] of male vocal groups added a contemporary flavor to the 1970s ballad tradition by using synthesizers as the musical foundation for the vocals. This synthesized aesthetic is heard in the works of Mint Condition ("Breakin' My Heart [Pretty Brown Eyes]," 1991), Jodeci ("Come & Talk to Me," 1991), After 7 ("Till You Do Me Right," 1995), and Jagged Edge ("Promise," 2000). Unlike the productions of female vocal groups, the productions of male groups generally excluded hip-hop elements.

In the new millennium, however, collaborations between R&B and hip-hop artists became the norm, and the two traditions literally became one and the same. The inclusion of hip-hop beats, breaks, sound effects, mixes, and rap sections had become characteristics of R&B in the 1990s. In the 2000s R&B singers adopted the spoken word style of delivery associated with rappers, which they incorporated into their sung vocals. Artists known for blending the two vocal styles include Beyoncé ("Crazy in Love," featuring Jay-Z, 2003), Usher ("Confessions Part II," 2004), Mariah Carey ("Shake It Off," 2005, and "We Belong Together," 2005), Mary J. Blige ("The One," featuring Drake, 2009), and Trey Songz ("Say Aah," featuring Fabolous, 2010).

R&B artists also turned to earlier musical genres for creative inspiration. Beyoncé tapped into funk for polyrhythmic structures and the omnipresent horns riffs on "Crazy in Love," featuring Jay-Z (2003). Others experimented with synthesized percussive qualities and voice-altering effects, the latter created by the Auto-Tune and other devices. These features are heard on Chris Brown's "Kiss, Kiss," featuring T-Pain (2007); Mary J. Blige's "The One," featuring Drake (2009); Rihanna's "Only Girl in the World" (2010); and Kelly Rowland's "Kisses Down Low" (2013). Technological experimentations also led to collaborations with European producers of electronic dance music. Scottish DJ Calvin Harris, for example, produced and is featured on Rihanna's "We Found Love" (2011), and Italian DJ Benny Benassi produced and is featured on Chris Brown's "Beautiful People" (2011).

The eclectic sounds of R&B in the new millennium also borrowed from European classical music and other world traditions. For example, the signature sound of Alicia Keys is her classical piano style featuring **arpeggiated chords** and the classical-flavored string arrangements layered on to her melismatic gospel-styled vocals ("Fallin'," 2001).[108] Beyoncé in "Baby Boy" (2003) turns to other world traditions. The song features reggae artist Sean Paul and layers the East Indian sitar over hip-hop beats

Arpeggiated chord
A chord in which the notes are played in sequence or succession rather than simultaneously.

and synthesized tracks. As R&B artists continue to explore myriad musical possibilities, the resulting sound moves away from the R&B aesthetic toward that of contemporary mainstream pop with a rock sensibility (Alicia Keys' "Girl on Fire," 2012; Miguel's "Do You . . .," 2012; Rihanna's "Diamonds" and "Jump," 2013). Even though elements of hip-hop may be present, they often are dominated by synthesized pop arrangements and the extreme use of electronic vocal manipulation. This approach to production removes the "soulfulness" from songs.

While R&B artists have experimented and continue to explore the use of various musical styles and technologies, traditional R&B, soul, and funk remain influential in the musical development of many contemporary artists. Alicia Keys' use of a jazz-oriented R&B horn arrangement in "If I Ain't Got You" (2004), for example, echoes the 1960s era of soul. R. Kelly's "When a Woman Loves" (2010) evokes "To Be Loved" (1958) by Jackie Wilson and "When a Man Loves a Woman" (1966) by Percy Sledge. At the same time, artists from earlier decades have revived their careers, and in turn have influenced and collaborated with contemporary producers and artists. Charlie Wilson, of the funk group the Gap Band, made a successful comeback as a solo artist ("There Goes My Baby," 2008, and "You Are," 2010) and has collaborated with Snoop Lion (a.k.a. Snoop Dogg), Kanye West, Boyz II Men, and Mystikal, among others.[109]

Contemporary R&B producers and artists link the past with the present by remaining rooted in the earlier Black popular styles while extending, adapting, and realigning the concept of "tradition" to a changing music scene in the twenty-first century. In the process, they continue to broaden the aesthetic of Blackness, which has become synonymous with the mainstream popular culture and music as evidenced by the sale and placement of hip-hop and R&B/hip-hop forms on *Billboard*'s charts. According to sociologist Reebee Garofalo:

> On October 11, 2003, *Billboard* reported that, for the first time in the magazine's history, all ten of the top ten Hot 100 pop hits in the country were by Black artists, nine of them rappers, with Beyoncé at number one with "Baby Boy." Black dominance during this period was no fluke; it was a long-term trend. In 2004, every single recording to reach number one on the Hot 100 was by a Black artist. And in 2005, according to *Billboard*, rap and R&B/hip-hop accounted for nearly 25 percent of all album sales.[110]

In 2010, fourteen songs by Black artists placed in the Top 30 on *Billboard*'s end of the year "Top 100 Songs," four of which were in the top ten positions.[111]

SUMMARY

The terms "rhythm and blues" and "R&B" are marketing labels used to identify various styles of Black popular music produced during two different eras: the 1940s through the mid-1960s and 1990 through the present, respectively. The former is associated with regional styles created

Portia K. Maultsby

by musicians with backgrounds in swing bands, blues, and gospel music; the latter is created by those with backgrounds in rhythm and blues, funk, and hip-hop.

Rhythm and blues, often abbreviated as R&B during the 1940s, 1950s, and 1960s, was created and performed in juke joints, clubs, and bars, as well as on street corners and in parks in African American communities located in various regions of the country. The popularity of this music among African Americans led to the establishment of independent record labels that specialized in rhythm and blues. Although initially marketed exclusively to African American communities, the tradition of late-evening broadcasts of rhythm and blues on 50,000-watt radio stations beginning in 1946 catapulted the music across racial boundaries.

The increased exposure of Black music and its artists through rock and roll films and television dance shows resulted in the music's growing popularity among the nation's White youth, which occurred during a pivotal point in race relations in society—the beginning of the modern Civil Rights Movement. Segregationist groups, especially those in the South, opposed the availability of this music across racial boundaries, and they organized various campaigns to stop the production and sale of rhythm and blues. Despite these and other activities, rhythm and blues prevailed. By the mid-1970s, largely due to the cross-cultural popularity of the Motown Sound, artists such as Diana Ross, Smokey Robinson, the Four Tops, the Temptations, Stevie Wonder, Lionel Richie, and the Jackson 5 became household names among the masses. A decade later in the 1980s, several artists, including Michael Jackson, Prince, Janet Jackson, and Whitney Houston, became crossover superstars, which largely resulted from their exposure on MTV, pop radio, and in Hollywood films.

By the 1990s—five decades after the condemnation of rhythm and blues/rock and roll by mainstream society—Black popular music became the primary sound of American popular music. Renamed R&B by *Billboard* in 1990, rhythm and blues evolved into various contemporary hybrid styles. The producers of this music combined new technologies (e.g., computers, synthesizers, samplers, and the Auto-Tune) with current music trends and elements from past musical styles. Hip-hop replaced the foundational role of blues and gospel in rhythm and blues. Nevertheless, the producers of R&B continued to borrow elements from past traditions, which they reinterpreted through contemporary, yet Afro-centric, musical lenses. This approach to Black music production extended into the new millennium, positioning R&B as part of the Black musical continuum.

ACKNOWLEDGMENTS

The research for a study on the general topic of African American popular music, from which I drew for this essay, was conducted with the support of various institutions and foundations: a post-doctoral fellowship from the National Research Council and Ford Foundation (1984–85); residency as a fellow at the Center for Advanced Study in the Behavioral Sciences, Stanford, California (1999–2000), and financial support from the Andrew W. Mellon Foundation and the College of Arts and Sciences, Indiana University–Bloomington (1999–2000).

KEY NAMES

After 7	Berry Gordy
Dave Bartholomew	Holland–Dozier–Holland
Al Bell	The Ink Spots
Al Benson	The Jackson 5
Chuck Berry	Jimmy Jam and Terry Lewis
Beyoncé	Louis Jordan
Bumps Blackwell	Alicia Keys
Booker T. & the MGs	Little Richard
Boyz II Men	The Moonglows
Charles Brown	The Orioles
Nat King Cole	The Ravens
Sean Combs (a.k.a. "Puff Daddy," "Puffy," "P. Diddy," and "Diddy")	Antonio "L.A." Reid and Kenny "Babyface" Edmonds
	John Richbourg
Bo Diddley	Rihanna
Willie Dixon	Teddy Riley
Fats Domino	The Shirelles
The Drifters	The Spaniels
Alan Freed	Jesse Stone
The Funk Brothers	Billy Ward and His Dominoes
Henry Glover	

QUESTIONS

1. When was the term "rhythm and blues" first introduced by *Billboard*, what was its purpose, and why was it replaced in 1969?

2. Identify the historical events and describe the social conditions that contributed to the development of rhythm and blues as a musical style beginning in the mid- to late 1940s.

Portia K. Maultsby

3. Identify the various rhythm and blues styles/sounds. For each style/sound, identify the geographical region, key record labels (when applicable), the distinguishing musical features, and key musicians who pioneered and/or popularized the style/sound.

4. What were the key variables that contributed to the movement of African American popular music from the racial margins into the mainstream in the 1950s? What key artists figured into this process? What was the response from the mainstream?

5. Compare and contrast the development of the Motown Sound and the Memphis Sound, highlighting the social context and distinguishing musical features, as well as the pioneers/popularizers of each regional/company sound.

6. What were the key variables that contributed to the increase in widespread exposure and popularity of African American music across racial, ethnic, and national boundaries beginning in the 1980s? What key artists figured into this process?

7. Why did *Billboard* replace the term "rhythm and blues" with "R&B" to label African American popular music?

8. Compare and contrast the production and sound of R&B of the 1990s and beyond with those of rhythm and blues of the 1970s and 1980s.

PROJECTS

1. Trace the changing meaning(s) of these *Billboard* labels through their histories: race records, rhythm and blues, and R&B.

2. Write a comparative biography of two songwriter-producers, one from each of the following eras: 1940s through the 1970s and 1980s through the present. Compare and contrast their musical backgrounds, approach to musical productions (citing artists and songs), and contributions to the development of rhythm and blues/R&B.

3. Choose a major rhythm and blues style or period. Write a history of the time when the music flourished, emphasizing social and political issues in African American communities and in the broader American public. Also, discuss how the style represented musical trends of the current and past eras (or a reworking of them) as well as the innovations of the producer-songwriters and/or artists.

4. Trace the career and musical evolution of a rhythm and blues or R&B artist whose career spans three decades (e.g., Ray Charles, James Brown, Aretha Franklin, Isley Brothers, Patti LaBelle, Gladys Knight, Stevie Wonder, Smokey Robinson, Diana Ross, Lionel Richie, Curtis Mayfield, O'Jays, Prince, Michael Jackson, R. Kelly, Janet Jackson, Whitney Houston, or Mary J. Blige).

NOTES

Please see discography for information on resources for further listening.

1. Many authors have used the terms "rhythm and blues" and "R&B" interchangeably to identify Black popular music recorded from the 1940s through the late 1960s. In 1990, *Billboard* and record labels designated the "R&B" label to chart and market contemporary Black popular music, which differed stylistically from hip-hop. I use the term rhythm and blues to identify Black popular styles from the 1940s through the 1960s. I reserve the R&B label to identify contemporary rhythm and blues styles recorded from 1990 into the twenty-first century.
2. "Billboard's Black Charts," *Billboard*, February 25, 1989, 82.
3. Hine, Hine, and Harrold 2004, 393; Lemann 1991, 6–93.
4. Sugrue 1996, 36–177; Drake and Cayton 1993 (1945); Countryman 2006; and Shaw 1978.
5. See Jones 1980, 49, for a map of this migration pattern.
6. The major companies that dominated the production of Black music (called race music at the time) were Columbia, Paramount, RCA-Victor, and Decca.
7. Decca Records was the only major record company to resume production of Black music.
8. Shaw 1978, 180 and 195; Gart and Ames 1990, 3–12; PBS documentary *Record Row: The Cradle of Rhythm and Blues*, 1997.
9. The independent labels established in Los Angeles were: Excelsior (1942), Exclusive (1944), Modern (1945), Aladdin (1945), Specialty (1946), and Imperial (1949). The other cities and labels of significance were: New Jersey—Savoy (1942); New York—Apollo (1943), National (1944), and Atlantic (1947); Cincinnati—King (1944); Chicago—Mercury (1946), Chess (1947), and Vee-Jay (1952); Houston—Peacock (1949); and Memphis—Duke (1952).
10. Hine *et al.* 2004, 393; Otis 1993, 4; Eastman 1998, 79–103; Collins 1998, 213–37.
11. After-hours clubs were venues where people gathered after clubs that legally sold alcoholic beverages closed at 2:00 a.m., as required by state laws. These laws restricted sales in after-hours clubs to non-alcoholic beverages and "set-ups," buckets of ice and mixers. Patrons supplied their own alcoholic beverages.
12. Examples are: jazz-styled novelty ("Straighten Up and Fly Right," 1943), blues ("Easy Listening Blues," 1944), and ballads ("All for You," 1943). Cole later made inroads into White lounges, where his repertoire of jazz, ballads, and standards became identified as cocktail music, music performed primarily as background for conversation.
13. Other popularizers of the trio style were Tennessee-born Cecil Gant ("I Wonder," 1944, and "Another Day, Another Dollar," 1948), who was influenced by Nat King Cole, and Texas-born Ivory Joe Hunter ("Pretty Mama Blues," 1948), who earlier performed with Johnny Moore's Three Blazers. See Epstein 1999, 68–75; Eastman 1998, 85; Pavlow 1983, 15–21; and Shaw 1978, 89–104, for detailed discussion on trios.
14. Quoted in Shaw 1978, 161.
15. Territory bands had reputations in certain parts of the country. Many contributed to the development of jazz but were unknown outside of their territories because of limited commercial recordings. Such bands include those led by George E. Lee, Jesse Stone, Bennie Moten, and Walter Page (all four located in Kansas City), William McKinney (Detroit), Alphonse Trent (Dallas), Troy Floyd (San Antonio), and Milton Larkins (Houston).
16. Artists who adopted this combo style include: Joe Liggins ("The Honeydripper," 1945), Eddie Vinson ("Old Maid Boogie," 1947), Mabel Scott ("Elevator Boogie," 1948), Hal Singer ("Cornbread," 1948), Paul Williams ("The Huckle-Buck," 1949), Johnny Otis ("Head Hunter," 1949, and "Cupid's Boogie," featuring Little Esther, 1950), and Big Jay McNeely & Band ("Nervous Man Nervous," 1953).
17. Popularized by Illinois Jacquet in Lionel Hampton's remake of "Flying Home" (1942).

18. Other groups include: Wild Bill Moore ("We're Gonna Rock, We're Gonna Roll," 1947), T-Bone Walker ("T-Bone Shuffle," 1947), and Amos Milburn ("Chicken Shack Boogie," 1948).
19. Haralambos 1985 (1974), 30.
20. Vee-Jay was founded by African Americans Vivian Carter Bracken and husband James Bracken.
21. Trotter 1998, 124.
22. In 1945 Nathan founded Queen Records to record rhythm and blues. King and Queen Records merged in 1947 under King Records. For more about King Records, see "Syd Nathan's King Records," DK Peneny, www.history-of-rock.com/king_records.htm, last modified October 15, 2009.
23. Shaw 1978, 275–79; Trotter 1998, 124; Fox 2009, 1–41.
24. Hine *et al.* 2004, 392–93. In comparison, in 1940, 77 percent of all Black people lived in the South, a 19 percent decrease by 1950. Of the 77 percent, 41 percent of the total southern Black population lived in rural areas.
25. Ahmet Ertegun and Herb Abramson scouted for talent during their first trip through New Orleans, Mississippi, and Georgia in 1949. Accompanied by Jesse Stone on their second trip in 1951, they hoped to discover musical ideas for developing an original sound.
26. Jesse Stone, interview by the author, Jamaica, New York, November 30, 1982.
27. Ibid.
28. Ibid.
29. According to Charlie Gillett (1974, 97–99), the phrase "shake, rattle, and roll" is based on an expression Stone heard at poker games. Forming the chorus of the song, it is sung four times over eight bars, followed by four bars of a two-line response, constituting the concept of sing-along blues.
30. Abbott 1992, 289–323.
31. Jerry Holman and Albert "Diz" Russell, interview by the author, Washington, DC, September 27, 1984.
32. Ibid.
33. The concept of the floating tenor resulted from a technical challenge. According to Russell, the group's tenor Alexander Sharp could not maintain his part, "so he would sing an obbligato [elaborate melodic part] behind what was going on in the harmony. And this became central to the style of the Orioles."
34. Holman and Russell interview, 1984.
35. Broven 1978 (1974), 37.
36. These cultures include French, Spanish, African, Creole, Irish, German, American, and African American. In 1950, African Americans totaled 31.9 percent of the population and most resided in the segregated areas of Tremé, Central City, and the Lower Ninth Ward where many musicians honed their skills performing in brass bands and New Orleans-styled jazz in local venues.
37. Lichtenstein and Dankner 1993; Berry, Foose, and Jones 2009; Broven 1978 (1974); Aswell 2009; Sandmel 2012; "Largest US Cities by Population, 1850–2010," US Census Bureau, *World Almanac and Book of Facts 2012*, 613; "Largest US Metropolitan Areas by Population, 1990–2010," US Census Bureau, *World Almanac and Book of Facts 2012*, 612.
38. Hannusch 2001.
39. Dave Bartholomew, interview by the author, New Orleans, Louisiana, May 14, 1985.
40. Shaw 1978, 492.
41. Bartholomew interview, 1985. Other notable New Orleans rhythm and blues musicians include Smiley Lewis ("I Hear You Knocking," 1955), Bobby Marchan ("There's Something On Your Mind," 1960), Larry Williams ("Short Fat Fannie," 1957), Irma Thomas ("Wish Someone Would Care," 1964), the Dixie Cups ("People Say," 1964), Ernie K-Doe ("Mother-in-Law," 1961), Chris Kenner ("I Like It Like That," 1961), Lee Dorsey ("Ya Ya," 1961), and songwriter-producer Allen Toussaint.
42. Charles Connor, interview by the author, Los Angeles, California, November 10, 1990.

43. James "Pookie" Hudson, telephone interview by the author, Gary, Indiana, March 28, 1985.
44. The Coasters were a novelty group produced by the Jewish songwriting team Jerry Leiber and Mike Stoller, who grew up around African Americans. Their songs derived from tall tales, humorous stories that exaggerate events, which the Coasters delivered in playful vocal style accompanied by theatrical antics ("Down in Mexico," 1956, and "Young Blood," 1957). See Leiber and Stoller interview in Fox 1986, 169–72.
45. Quoted in Shaw 1978, 155.
46. Barlow 1999, 163.
47. Davis 2009, 23–24; Shaw 1978, 489; Barlow 1999, 93–153, 160–75.
48. Quoted in Shaw 1978, 397.
49. A comprehensive list of covers is found in Chapple and Garofalo 1977, 239–40.
50. Broven 1978 (1974), 37–38; Fox 1986, 128.
51. The aircheck of Alan Freed "The Moondog Show" originally was broadcast in March 1952 on WJW (Cleveland, Ohio) and is available as part of "Black Radio: Telling It Like It Was," SC 39, Archives of African American Music and Culture, Indiana University, Bloomington, and the online Alan Freed Archives, accessed August 13, 2012, www.alanfreed.com/wp/on-the-air-audio-2/#Airchecks.
52. Emphasis added. Alan Freed, broadcast on WJW in Cleveland, March 22, 1952. "Two and a half hours of your favorite blues . . .," Audio: WJW, AlanFreed.com, accessed February 5, 2013, www.alanfreed.com/wp/on-the-air-audio-2/audio-wjw/.
53. See photographs included in Freed's archives. AlanFreed.com, accessed February 5, 2013, www.alanfreed.com/wp/archives/archives-rocknroll-1951-1959/brooklyn-paramount/.
54. Jackson 1991, 88.
55. Alan Freed, broadcast on WINS, New York, 1995. "Part I," Audio: WINS—1955, AlanFreed.com, accessed February 5, 2013, www.alanfreed.com/wp/on-the-air-audio-2/audio-wins-1955/.
56. *Rock and Roll: The Early Days*, 1985, DVD.
57. Connor interview, 1990.
58. These artists included Joe Turner, Faye Adams, Ruth Brown, the Larks, Little Richard, Frankie Lymon and the Teenagers, Chuck Berry, and the Flamingos.
59. *American Bandstand* showcased Jackie Wilson, Chuck Berry, Chubby Checker, and Little Anthony and the Imperials.
60. *Rock and Roll: The Early Days*, 1985, DVD.
61. Jackson 1991, 72–87; Garofalo 2002, 169–74.
62. Maultsby 2001, 672.
63. Bull Moose Jackson's "Why Don't You Haul Off and Love Me" (1949) originally was recorded by Wayne Raney. Harris and Jackson were signed to King Records, one of the first labels to record covers of country artists by rhythm and blues artists and covers of rhythm and blues by country artists. Henry Glover, who supervised these recordings, told Arnold Shaw (1978, 278) that the rhythm and blues covers of country music were far more successful than the country covers of rhythm and blues.
64. Hank Penny and Ruth Hall wrote "Bloodshot Eyes." Hank Penny's country and western recording of 1949 peaked at number 2 on *Billboard*'s Country & Western charts in 1950. Wynonie Harris's version reached the number 6 position on the Rhythm and Blues charts. "Teach Me Tonight," written by Gene De Paul and Sammy Cahn, was published in 1953 and recorded by three pop artists in 1954. The most successful pop rendition was by the DeCastro Sisters, charting number 2 on *Billboard*'s Pop charts. Dinah Washington's version reached number 4 on the Rhythm and Blues charts and number 23 on the Pop charts.
65. The Mitch Miller Singers and the Robert DeCormier Singers were the professional background studio singers contracted to sing on most of the popular music recordings in the 1950s and 1960s.

Portia K. Maultsby

66. Atlantic Records songwriters-producers Jerry Leiber and Mike Stoller introduced and popularized these rhythms in rhythm and blues.
67. Gillett 1974, 189–223.
68. They included Carole King, Gerry Goffin, Barry Mann, Cynthia Weil, Ellie Greenwich, and Phil Spector, and African American Luther Dixon.
69. "Hit Makers: The Teens Who Stole Pop Music," on *Biography*, A&E Television Networks, 2001.
70. Early 1995, 79–92; Sykes 2006, 432.
71. Wilson 1986, 24–25.
72. These recordings include Barrett Strong's "Money (That's What I Want)" (1959), the Contours' "Do You Love Me" (1962), Marvin Gaye's "Can I Get a Witness" (1963) and "Pride and Joy" (1963), and Stevie Wonder's "Fingertips" (1963).
73. These characteristics are heard on Martha & the Vandellas' first hit "Come and Get These Memories" (1963) and "Dancing in the Streets" (1964), Mary Wells's "My Guy" (1964) and "You Beat Me to the Punch" (1962), and the Four Tops' "Baby I Need Your Loving" (1964).
74. Mickey Stevenson, interview by the author, April 20, 1983.
75. Motown's resident songwriters included Mickey Stevenson, Smokey Robinson, and the team of Eddie Holland, Lamont Dozier, and Brian Holland (known as H–D–H).
76. Brian Holland, interview by the author, April 29, 1983; and Stevenson interview, 1983.
77. Shelly Berger, interview by the author, March 15, 2011.
78. This foundation is best illustrated in Jr. Walker and the All Stars' "Shotgun" (1965) and "How Sweet It Is (To Be Loved By You)" (1966) and Martha & the Vandellas' "Nowhere to Run" (1965).
79. Holland interview, 1983.
80. Ibid.
81. Landau 1969, 298, and Bane 1992, 167–68.
82. Berger interview, 2011.
83. Smith 1999, 106.
84. Berger interview, 2011.
85. Bowman 1997, 3–48.
86. Stax's resident songwriters included Bettye Crutcher, Raymond Jackson, Carl Hampton, Homer Banks, Don Davis, and the team of Isaac Hayes and David Porter.
87. Deanie Parker, interview by the author, September 6, 1984; and Al Bell, interview by the author, May 26, 1983.
88. These artists also included up-tempo songs on their albums.
89. Other artists include the Chi-Lites ("A Letter To Myself," 1973), the Main Ingredient ("Just Don't Want To Be Lonely," 1973), the Spinners ("Sadie," 1975), the Dramatics ("Be My Girl," 1976), and the Delfonics ("Didn't I [Blow Your Mind This Time]," 1970).
90. They include Gloria Gaynor ("Never Can Say Goodbye," 1974, and "I Will Survive," 1978), Donna Summer ("Love to Love You Baby," 1975, "Last Dance," 1978, and "Bad Girls," 1979), Thelma Houston ("Don't Leave Me This Way," 1976), the Trammps ("Disco Inferno," 1976), and Chic ("Le Freak," 1978, and "Good Times," 1979).
91. George 1988, 147.
92. They were the funk-rock "Beat It," and the funk-derived tracks "Billie Jean" and "Thriller."
93. They include Nat King Cole ("I Don't Want to Be Hurt Anymore," 1964), and Johnny Mathis ("Stardust," 1975).
94. Despite high ratings, MTV terminated the show in 1995. On November 4, 1989, *Billboard* instituted the weekly "Hot Rap Singles" to chart the best-selling 12-inch rap singles. The name changed to "Hip-Hop" in the 1990s and it continues to coexist with the R&B charts.
95. Other artists to appear on the show were Run-D.M.C., Big Daddy Kane, LL Cool J, Slick Rick, N.W.A., and 2Pac.

96. They include Andre Harrell (Uptown Records/MCA Records, 1986), Antonio "L.A." Reid and Kenny "Babyface" Edmonds (LaFace Records/Arista Records, 1989), Marion "Suge" Knight and Andre "Dr. Dre" Young (Death Row Records/Interscope Records, 1991), Sean "Puffy" Combs (Bad Boy Records/Arista, 1993), and Jermaine Dupri (So So Def Records/Columbia Records, 1993). Most of these independent songwriter-producers had backgrounds in hip-hop. The exceptions were Reid and Edmonds, whose experience was in rhythm and blues and funk.

97. The process for modification was known as diminution, which involves collapsing the four-beat shuffle feel to two beats.

98. Hip-hop beats provide the rhythmic foundation for both songs. Sweat and Guy both utilize a vocal style that draws from the gospel tradition. "Groove Me" features close harmonies, phrasing, percussive timbres, call–response structures, and melismatic vocal style reminiscent of contemporary male gospel groups from the 1970s and early 1980s, such as the Winans ("The Question Is," 1981).

99. "Billboard Adopts R&B" 1990, 6, 35.

100. Mary J. Blige began her career singing hooks on Uptown Records' hip-hop productions such as Father MC's "I'll Do 4 U" (1990). "Puff Daddy" Combs began his career at Uptown as an intern and talent scout assigned to produce Blige.

101. These old-school beats are heard in "Gittin' Funky" (1988) by Kid 'N' Play, "Ain't No Half Steppin'" (1988) by Big Daddy Kane, and "Vapors" (1988) by Biz Markie.

102. Rapper MC Hammer was one of the first, if not the very first, to popularize the use of sampled sung choruses and refrain lines through an entire rap song. "Have You Seen Her" (1990) samples "Have You Seen Her" (1971) by the Chi-Lites.

103. En Vogue's recordings were written and produced by Denzil Foster and Thomas McElroy in collaboration with the group. Foster and McElroy formed the group in 1989; songwriter-producer Jermaine Dupri launched the successful career of Xscape. Working in collaboration with other songwriter-producers, a trend common in the music industry throughout the 1990s, he produced several hits for Xscape. Brian Alexander Morgan wrote and produced this and other hit songs on SWV's first album.

104. Dallas Austin and Lisa Lopes, the group's rapper, were the primary songwriters on TLC's debut album. Subsequent albums included other songwriter-producers in addition to Austin. Although Destiny's Child's song was produced by Rodney "Darkchild" Jerkins, it was written by the group along with several other songwriter-producers who contributed to the album.

105. These groups include the Chi-Lites, Dells, Delfonics, Dramatics, Main Ingredient, Manhattans, and Stylistics.

106. Both songs begin with spoken introduction by the baritone voice. The verse is sung by the lead vocalist, who is joined in harmony by the group on the chorus.

107. They include Kenneth "Babyface" Edmonds and L.A. Reid, Jimmy Jam and Terry Lewis, Sean "Puffy" Combs, and Jermaine Dupri.

108. R&B singer Ashanti also made extensive use of arpeggios in "The Way That I Love You (Main Version)" (2008).

109. Examples of similar collaborations include James Poyser and Ahmir "Questlove" Thompson of the Roots, who produced the soul legend Al Green's Lay It Down in 2008 and Questlove's work with soul legend Betty Wright on Betty Wright: The Movie in 2011.

110. An unpublished manuscript by sociologist Reebee Garofalo, 2011.

111. "Billboard Top 100 Songs of 2010—Year End Charts," bobborst.com, accessed December 22, 2013, www.bobborst.com/popculture/top-100-songs-of-the-year/ ?year=2010.

CHAPTER 13

Soul

Portia K. Maultsby

Soul music is a derivative of 1950s rhythm and blues[1] that evolved as a distinct genre in the mid-1960s and peaked in popularity in the mid-1970s. The soul sound results from the use of the rhythms, musical and formal structures, and vocal stylings from Black gospel music. These elements gradually dominated or replaced those of blues, jazz, and pop that prevailed in 1940s and 1950s rhythm and blues styles. The lyrics of soul retained the traditional topics of romance and social relationships common in rhythm and blues, and expanded topical coverage to include social and political commentary inspired by the Civil Rights and Black Power movements. Thus soul music is defined by both its lyric content and musical features.

Early soul styles paralleled the broad popularity of Black gospel music and coincided with the beginning of the **Modern Civil Rights Movement**, of which music was an integral component. The singers transformed the repertoire of spirituals, gospel music, and rhythm and blues into freedom songs during sit-ins, marches, and freedom rides. The result was the further blurring of the sacred/secular boundaries within these political contexts.[2]

In the mid-1960s, the **Black Power Movement** took root. It was spearheaded by college-age members of the Student Nonviolent Coordinating Committee (SNCC), who became increasingly disillusioned with the slow pace of social change promoted by its parent organization, Southern Christian Leadership Conference (SCLC). Many of SNCC's members rejected the nonviolent and integrationist approach advocated by traditional civil rights leaders. As an alternative, a core group of SNCC's membership embraced the Black Nationalist ideology of

Soul music
Gospel-influenced African American popular music style that began to emerge in the late 1950s and became popular during the 1960s.

Modern Civil Rights Movement
A movement beginning in the late 1940s and blossoming in the late 1950s to mid-1960s that pushed for equal rights for African Americans.

Black Power Movement
A movement of the late 1960s and early 1970s that emphasized Black unity, Black pride, and self-determination.

Malcolm X and the Nation of Islam, a concept that promoted Black solidarity, Black pride, self-determination, and self-empowerment. In 1966, they substituted the "Freedom Now" slogan with "Black Power." Soul music crystallized in this context.[3]

THE CONCEPT OF SOUL: A MANIFESTATION OF BLACK POWER

The concept of Black Power encompassed a broad social, political, economic, and cultural agenda. Kwame Ture (a.k.a. Stokely Carmichael), one of the founders of this movement, defined its fundamental principles as:

> the call for black people in this country to unite, to recognize their heritage, to build a sense of community. It is a call for black people to begin to define their own goals, to lead their own organizations and to support these organizations. It is a call to reject the racist institutions and values of this society.[4]

The call for Black Power evolved into a political movement to which Black people assigned cultural meanings they labeled "soul." In this context, the term "soul" became a signifier of "Blackness."

Soul first became a household word in African American communities during the inner-city uprisings (labeled "riots" by the media) of 1964 (Harlem), 1965 (Watts), and 1967 (Detroit and Newark). To prevent possible destruction and looting, Black businessmen identified their stores by displaying signs in the windows that read "soul brother." In 1965, Black disc jockeys across the country began identifying their Black-oriented stations as "soul radio," which influenced the national acceptance of this term.[5] The concept of soul, as noted by historian William L. Van Deburg:

> was closely related to black America's need for individual and group self-definition. During the Black Power era, the self-defining capabilities of soul were nowhere more evident than in the soul style that originated in and was authenticated by the urban black folk culture.[6]

Soul became associated with all forms of Black cultural production: music, dance, visual art, foodways, fashion (colorful bell-bottom slacks with three-inch cuffs, leather vests, wide-brimmed hats, platform shoes, and African-derived clothing and accessories), natural hair styles (Afros and African-derived crops and cornrows), non-verbal communication styles (rhythmic and complex hand shake greetings, a distinctive walk, and other inimitable body gestures). Soul also became associated with a unique language style of inner-city street talk and slang. Soul radio DJs broadly popularized and gave validity to this language style by superimposing phrases such as "ain't that the truth," "tell it like it is," "that's what's happening, baby," "show me where it's at," "you'd better believe it," and "dig it" over the music they played. In essence, soul signified the values and ideals of a new Black identity that underscored the concept of a "soul man," "soul brother," and "soul sister."

Portia K. Maultsby

The language of soul became further infused in African American culture through song titles such as "Woman's Got Soul" (1965) by Curtis Mayfield, "Memphis Soul Stew" (1967) by King Curtis, "Soul Man" (1967) by Sam and Dave, and "Soul Finger" (1967) by the Bar-Kays. Despite the earlier institutionalization of the term "soul" in Black America, the mass media did not give full recognition to its use until 1967 when *Billboard*, the leading trade music magazine, published the first issue of an annual series titled "The World of Soul" to document "the impact of Blues and R&B upon our musical culture."[7] In 1968, *Esquire* magazine published an article "An Introduction to Soul," and *Time* magazine featured Aretha Franklin on its cover as the subject of a lengthy article entitled "Lady Soul Singing It Like It Is."[8] In 1969, *Billboard* changed the name of its "Rhythm and Blues" charts to "Soul." This acceptance of the soul label by the mass media and music industry signified an initial victory for the Black Power Movement. White Americans had adopted a term first coined, sanctioned, and used by African Americans to describe themselves, their unique cultural productions, and their cultural institutions.

THE ARCHITECTS AND MUSICAL ROOTS OF SOUL

The pioneers of soul—Ray Charles, James Brown, and Sam Cooke—share common musical roots in Black gospel music, which inspired their transformation of rhythm and blues into the sound of soul. Although some of the early rhythm and blues vocal groups introduced a gospel quartet sound to Black popular music by substituting secular lyrics for religious ones (e.g., the Dominoes' "Have Mercy Baby," 1952). Ray Charles was the first to consistently incorporate a full range of components from Black church culture in rhythm and blues, from structure to harmony, rhythmic organization, and vocal style. These innovations forged the evolution of soul music as a distinctive musical genre in the 1960s.

Similar to the Dominoes, Charles's recording of "This Little Girl of Mine" (1955) represents a secular version of "This Little Light of Mine," achieved by simply changing the lyrics. In his original compositions, including "Come Back" (1955), "What Would I Do Without You" (1956), and "A Fool for You" (1955), as well as in his reinterpretation of the 1952 rhythm and blues hit by Sonny Thompson and Lula Reed "Drown in My Own Tears" (1956), Charles had replaced many blues-oriented rhythm and blues elements with those from Black gospel music. These songs are characterized by the use of 12/8 meter played with a 4/4, or **common meter**, feel; **call–response** structures; gospel harmonic progressions; and gospel vocal phrasing, inflections, and **melismas**. The gospel-inspired song "What'd I Say" (1959) represents an amalgam of blues and gospel.

Three years before Ray Charles released "What'd I Say," James Brown and the Famous Flames recorded the ballad "Please, Please, Please"

Common meter
4/4 time; sometimes superimposed over 12/8 meter or triplet background.

Call–response
A song structure or performance practice in which a singer or instrumentalist makes a musical statement that is answered by another soloist, instrumentalist, or group. The statement and answer sometimes overlap. Also called antiphony and call-and-response.

Melisma
A single syllable sung over several pitches.

(1956), a song written by Brown and Flames member Johnny Terry. The song is based on the repeated phrase "please, please, don't go," which Brown performs in an intense, percussive, and gospel-inflected vocal style similar to Clyde McPhatter, lead singer of the Dominoes, who had a major influence on Brown. Brown widely popularized this vocal style in rhythm and blues and in soul music. In the area of musical arrangements, however, his innovations in the transition from rhythm and blues to soul came gradually. According to Brown, this change reflected a new rhythmic conception—use of **polyrhythmic** structures, or the layering of different rhythmic patterns—as illustrated in "Papa's Got A Brand New Bag" (1965).[9]

In addition to Brown's polyrhythmic musical foundation, his studio singing style gradually became more intense with the interjection of vocables (syllables without lexical meaning), screams, and hollers ("I Got You [I Feel Good]," 1965; "It's a Man's Man's Man's World," 1966), which are a carryover from his stage performances (*James Brown Live at the Apollo*, 1962 and 1967).

A contrast to Brown's intense and percussive vocal aesthetic was the softer, lyrical, and melismatic style of Sam Cooke. Beginning his professional singing career as lead vocalist (1950–56) for the Soul Stirrers, a renowned Black gospel quartet, Cooke switched from gospel to rhythm and blues and recorded the hit "You Send Me" (1957) in a gospel-oriented style. This song became a crossover hit, reaching the number 1 position on *Billboard*'s "Rhythm and Blues" and "Pop" charts. Seven years later, Cooke recorded "A Change Is Gonna Come" (1964), in the year of the passage and signing of the Civil Rights Act and of Cooke's death. Many popular music scholars contend this song marks the transition from rhythm and blues to soul; it is performed in an unabashedly gospel style and its content may be interpreted as a reflection of Cooke's social consciousness and his expression of faith.

Throughout his career and as an admirer of Martin Luther King Jr., Cooke demonstrated his racial pride by challenging **Jim Crow laws** and de facto segregation, the latter outside of and within the complex of components—record labels, recording studios, publishing companies, etc.—that comprise the music industry. Cooke, for example, expressed his dismay at the injustices of the music industry by protesting the lack of African American musicians participating on his recording sessions, and by forming his own recording label (SAR) and publishing company (KAGS). Touring the South, he protested the Jim Crow laws by canceling performances at segregated venues and attempting to register at White motels. Residing in Los Angeles, Cooke experienced and challenged police harassment.[10]

Musician and close friend Harold Battiste described "A Change Is Gonna Come" as "the culmination of all their talk about race: one way to express how he was feeling about what he needed to do."[11] Cooke's social consciousness and musical paradigm, together with the musical

Polyrhythm
Several contrasting rhythms played or sung simultaneously.

Jim Crow laws
Laws limiting African American freedoms and rights in US society, named for the minstrel character "Jim Crow."

Portia K. Maultsby

innovations of Ray Charles and James Brown, provided the models for the new musical genre that later would be defined as soul.

SOUL LYRICS, CIVIL RIGHTS, AND BLACK POWER

The release of Sam Cooke's "A Change Is Gonna Come" coincided with the Impressions' recording "Keep On Pushing" (1964), which articulated the feelings and thoughts of lead vocalist-songwriter Curtis Mayfield (Figure 13.1) regarding racial injustices and the need for social change. The messages of several of Mayfield's songs emerged from his personal experiences of de facto segregation in Chicago, his commitment to the Civil Rights Movement, and the strong faith he developed growing up in the Traveling Souls Spiritualist Church pastored by his grandmother. He explains:

> As a young man I was writing songs like "Keep On Pushing" and "This Is My Country" and feeling all the love and all the things I observed politically. Of course with everything I saw on the streets as a young black kid, it wasn't hard during the later fifties and early sixties for me to write [in] my own heartfelt way of how I visualized things, how I thought things ought to be.[12]

Figure 13.1
Curtis Mayfield, January 1960. Photo by Michael Ochs Archives/Getty Images.

Many of Mayfield's songs embody the religious message of sermons, spirituals, and gospel music heard in the Black church. Acknowledging this influence, Mayfield implies that some of these songs were first written as gospel songs and required only minor changes in the lyrics:

> With "Keep On Pushing," all I needed to do was change "God gave me strength, and it don't make no sense not to keep on pushing" to "I've got my strength, and it don't make sense." I've got my strength. Nothing else needed to be changed.[13]

34

"We're a Winner."

Similarly "People Get Ready" (1965), a song covered by gospel singer Shirley Caesar, emerged from Mayfield's faith and his gospel vision. According to fans in attendance at a live concert in 1968, these songs, as well as "We're a Winner" (1967) (Track 34), "This Is My Country" (1968), and "Choice of Colors" (1969), gave inspiration. The popularity of Mayfield's songs among African Americans is evidenced by their top ten positions on the rhythm and blues charts.[14]

Despite the positive social messages, principles of faith, and the philosophy of Martin Luther King Jr. expressed in Mayfield's songs, some Black-oriented and many mainstream pop radio stations considered them to be too overtly political for broadcast. Group member Samuel Gooden recalled that the pop station WLS in Chicago, refused to play "We're a Winner" because the manager and DJs thought the Impressions had become too provocative and had labeled them "militant." Considering the era, Mayfield acknowledged that an inspiring message "wasn't really what radio was all about in those times."[15] Eddie Thomas, the group's manager, added the Impressions were "too early for our time . . . We wanted to equalize things."[16] However, as the Civil Rights Movement gained momentum beyond the southern states, and when Martin Luther King Jr. and Jesse Jackson adopted "Keep On Pushing" as a protest song, Black-oriented radio began to broadcast the social and political message of soul. Moreover, many Black DJs encouraged their listeners to hear the music politically.[17] Chuck Scruggs of KSOL in San Francisco explains:

> As a jock during that time I would take those message songs and add a line or two of editorial . . . something that would fit the title or the theme of the song . . . I didn't play a message song in isolation, and then go from that to something else that had no connection. I'd go from a message song like "Keep On Pushing" to, say, "Stand by Me." You see what I mean? I'd make the transition with words of hope for my listeners. You know—"Stand by me people 'cause we gotta keep on pushing for our freedom."[18]

Although Mayfield subscribed to the philosophy of Martin Luther King Jr., his lyrics also were inspired by the speeches of Black Power advocates H. Rap Brown and Stokely Carmichael, as well as those of local preachers and leaders. Mayfield's songs held relevance across the ideological divide and became central to the activities of both the Civil Rights and Black Power movements. One activist recalled: "I started out with civil rights and moved to Black Power. But wherever I was, Curtis's music was there."[19] Mayfield's songs and those of other soul singers that contained social and/or political messages became known as "message songs" and equated with the concept of soul.

Mayfield's candid views on racial issues, however, caused some concern among his production team, who anticipated a backlash from the Impressions' record company, ABC-Paramount Records. Sam Gooden and Fred Cash recall that Curtis had written "some real tough lyrics [on] 'We're a Winner' [1967] . . . One portion said: 'The Black boy done dried his eyes. There would be no more Uncle Tom. At last that blessed day has come and We're a Winner.'"[20] Mayfield's arranger anticipated that the label would not release the song with the original lines. For this reason, Mayfield reluctantly changed the lyrics, omitting the reference to Uncle Tom in the recording. Committed to being in *total* control of his artistry, Mayfield co-founded Curtom Records in 1968 with manager Eddie Thomas. He also purchased a sixteen-track recording studio. These acquisitions, according to Mayfield, "meant dignity, self-respect, [and] hopefully to move myself to another level."[21] When the Impressions' contract with ABC Records expired in 1968, Mayfield signed the group to Curtom Records.

By 1968, the Nationalist message of Black Power had begun to overshadow the integrationist ideology of the civil rights leaders; many soul singers became spokespersons for Black Power. Recording songs that were considered to be overtly militant and musically intense, James Brown (Figure 13.2) led the way. Songs such as "Say It Loud—I'm Black and I'm Proud" (1968), "I Don't Want Nobody to Give Me Nothing (Open Up the Door, I'll Get It Myself)" (1969), and "Get Up, Get Into It, and Get Involved" (1970) promoted the concept of Black pride, Black solidarity, and Black empowerment. Through the songs of Brown and other soul singers, Black America began to identify with and embrace these concepts. After Brown's performance of "Say It Loud" in Houston, Texas, less than two weeks after its release, his musical arranger Fred Wesley Jr. recalls:

> [T]o my amazement when James hit the stage and yelled out, "Say it loud," there must have been 15,000 people who answered back, "I'm black and I'm proud!"
> . . . [T]his record *was* very special. The message echoed the feelings of black people at that time. With the new civil rights bill and the new voting rights amendment now firmly in place, black people were ready for a theme song that inspired and inflamed that newfound spirit of pride and freedom.[22]

Within two months after its release, "Say It Loud" had sailed to the number 1 position on *Billboard*'s R&B charts and number 10 on the pop chart. Yet according to Brown:

> That song scared people too. Many white people didn't understand it . . . They thought I was saying kill the honky, and every time I did something else around the idea of black pride another top forty station quit playing my records.[23]

Even though Brown and Mayfield fell out of favor with White radio programmers and their small White following because of their "militant"

Figure 13.2
James Brown,
performing in
London, 1973.
Photo by Michael
Putland/Getty
Images.

message, they became heroes and role models in African American communities.

By 1971, the Black Nationalist message and the ethos of the Black Power Movement had influenced the content and musical arrangements that characterized the sound of soul. As observed by historian Brian Ward, "Black performers, writers, arrangers, deejays and music business entrepreneurs were all members of the larger black community and shared the general sense of intense frustration as the optimism of the early 1960s dwindled."[24] The passage of the 1964 Civil Rights Act and the Voting Rights Act in 1965 raised the expectations of African Americans regarding social, economic, and political change. Yet change came at a slow pace due to resistance of the broader society and the collapse of an industrial economy.[25] Other soul singers joined Curtis Mayfield and James Brown in campaigning for racial equality, social justice, and community empowerment through their songs. The Isley Brothers expounded on the need for "Freedom" (1970) while the Chi-Lites demanded that the government "(For God's Sake) Give More Power to the People" (1971); the O'Jays described betrayal in "Back Stabbers" (1972) and expounded on the effects of racism and greed in "For the Love of Money" (1973).

Simultaneously, the Staple Singers in "You've Got to Earn It" (1971) and "Respect Yourself" (1971) encouraged self-sufficiency and pride among African Americans.

Soul singers also criticized the "empty" speeches of politicians, as James Brown did in "Talkin' Loud and Saying Nothing" (1972). He explained that it:

> was aimed at the politicians who were running their mouths but had no knowledge of what life was like for a lot of people in this country. It was also aimed at some cats on their soapboxes ... who were telling the people one thing while manipulating their emotions for personal gain.[26]

Similarly, Brown directed "Funky President (People It's Bad)" (1974) toward President Gerald Ford, who replaced President Richard Nixon when he resigned on August 9, 1974. Brown recalls: "Every time he made a speech, it gave people the blues. He was a nice man, but he talked a lot and didn't say anything."[27] Stevie Wonder, in "You Haven't Done Nothin'" (1974), also critiques the empty promises of politicians.

Stevie Wonder was one of several Motown artists who recorded message songs that represented a shift in lyric content from the earlier teenage love songs that had defined the company's core repertoire. Motown's founder and president Berry Gordy explains: "As the new decade was beginning, the changes in society inspired changes in our music."[28] The Supremes sang about the hardships of having children in poverty in "Love Child" (1968), the Temptations reported on the cause and impact of drug use in "Cloud Nine" (1969), and Marvin Gaye's "What's Going On" (1971) and "Inner City Blues (Make Me Wanna Holler)" (1971) deplored the poverty that plagued inner-city communities, as did Stevie Wonder's "Living for the City" (1973). Addressing broader social issues, Gladys Knight & The Pips promoted racial harmony in "Friendship Train" (1969), Edwin Starr condemned the Vietnam War in "War" (1970), and the Temptations critiqued the status of society in "Ball of Confusion (That's What the World Is Today)" (1970). Similar to the songs of Curtis Mayfield, Stevie Wonder's "Jesus Children of America" (1973), "Higher Ground" (1973), and "Heaven Is 10 Zillion Light Years Away" (1974) articulated a spiritual vision for inner peace and racial harmony.

The themes of unity and respect advocated by the Civil Rights and Black Power movements also applied to personal relationships. Many soul singers, for example, offered advice for establishing rewarding relationships. Otis Redding suggested "Try a Little Tenderness" (1966) and, along with Aretha Franklin, demanded "Respect" (1965 and 1967, respectively). Al Green, in "Let's Stay Together" (1971), and Aretha Franklin, in "I Can't See Myself Leaving You" (1969), encouraged committed relationships. In Michael Haralambos's view, soul "expresses faith in love, hope for love, and the joy and happiness of love," rather than failed relationships, a theme frequently found in the blues.[29]

The sound of soul is characterized by a set of aesthetic features derived from the musical and preaching traditions of the Black folk church. Describing the relationship between these traditions, the late gospel music scholar and performer Pearl Williams-Jones observed:

> In seeking to communicate the gospel message, there is little difference between the gospel singer and gospel preacher in the approach to his subject. The same techniques are used by the preacher and the singer—the singer perhaps being considered the lyrical extension of the rhythmically rhetorical style of the preacher.[30]

Soul singers are best described as secular counterparts of gospel preachers, and, by extension, gospel singers. This singer–preacher linkage is illustrated in live performances of Aretha Franklin (Figure 13.3), as described by her brother Reverend Cecil Franklin:

> You listen to her and it's like being in church. She does with her voice exactly what a preacher does with his when he *moans* to a congregation. That moan strikes a responsive chord in the congregation and somebody answers back with their own moan, which means I know what you're moaning about because I feel the same way. So you have something sort of like a thread spinning out and touching and tieing [*sic*] everybody together in a shared experience just like the getting happy and shouting together in church.[31]

Figure 13.3
Aretha Franklin, performing live onstage at the New Victoria Theatre, United Kingdom, 1980. Photo by David Redfern/Redferns.

Portia K. Maultsby

Aretha's musical delivery also reflects the dramatic performance style of Black preachers, who employ a range of improvisatory devices—vocal inflections, varying timbres, word repetition, and phrase endings punctuated by "grunts," "shouts," and moans, etc.—to gradually build the intensity to a level that transforms the sermon into quasi-song. Preaching is, in this regard, similar in sound to the aesthetic of live performances of gospel and soul music; the latter is illustrated in the live recordings of Patti LaBelle, Natalie Cole, Gladys Knight & The Pips, and James Brown.

Both Black gospel music and the sound of soul encompass many vocal styles and **timbres**, ranging from the lyrical and tempered quality of Curtis Mayfield and Sam Cooke to the percussive and shouting approach of Aretha Franklin and James Brown. Artists employ a wide range of aesthetic devices to interpret songs that include alternating lyrical, percussive, and raspy timbres; varying between straight and vibrato tones; weaving moans, shouts, grunts, hollers, and screams into the melody; and juxtaposing unique vocal and instrumental **textures**. They also vary the pitch by contrasting voices of different ranges; shifting from high to low pitches; and incorporating "bends," "slides," melismas, and passing tones in the melody.[32] Black instrumentalists imitate these vocal sounds by altering traditional embouchures, playing techniques, and fingerings, and by adding devices to distort the traditional sounds of instruments. This African-derived sound aesthetic is in contrast to that associated with Western-European cultures.

Vocalists and instrumentalists combine the above improvisatory techniques with various rhythmic devices to build the intensity of songs. They extend the length of notes at climactic points by repeating words, phrases, or entire sections of songs, and by adding vocal or instrumental **cadenzas**.[33] Central to the improvisatory performance aesthetic of soul performers is the use of call–response structures, which facilitate musical exchanges between vocalists, instrumentalists, vocalists and instrumentalists, and performers and audience. These exchanges allow performers to display their creative abilities and technical skills and facilitate audience participation in the performance. When performers create and interpret songs within the aesthetic boundaries defined by Black people, the responses of audiences can become so audible that they momentarily drown out the performer. The verbal responses of audiences are accompanied by hand clapping, foot stomping, head, shoulder, hand, and arm movements, and spontaneous dance as illustrated at performances of Aretha Franklin (Track 35). Reviewing her concerts, music critic Charles Sanders wrote:

> At every show I wondered what it was—that very special thing she was always able to get going with an audience. Sometimes there were 16,000 people in a sports arena and Aretha would be working on stage, doing "Dr. Feelgood" and then "Spirit in the Dark," and it seemed that all 16,000 people would become involved in a kind of spiritual thing with her, sort of like what must have happened on the Day of Pentecost,

Timbre
The quality of sound that distinguishes different voices or instruments from one another.

Texture
The interaction among the vocal and instrumental lines in an ensemble.

Cadenza
An extended, sometimes improvised section in a vocal or instrumental performance, usually occurring at the end.

 35
"Dr. Feelgood."

and those people—all kinds: dudes, Sisters in Afros and those in blonde wigs, even church-looking people—would start moving with the music, and as Aretha took them higher and higher some of them would scream and jump up on their seats, and even men like 50 and 60 years old would run down to the stage and try to touch her.[34]

Similar to the audience's response to Aretha, audiences also engage in continuous verbal exchanges with performers. Sam Moore of the soul duo Sam and Dave explains:

When we performed, we had church. On Sundays the minister would preach and the people in the pews would holler back to him. This is what we started doing. I arranged the parts between Dave and me so that one of us became the preacher and would say "Come on, Dave" or "Come on, Sam." The audience would automatically shout "Come on, Sam" or "Sing, Dave" or "Yes, Sir." That was our style.[35]

In communicating with their audiences, Black performers also display an intensity of emotion and total physical involvement through use of the entire body. Sam Moore recalled: "We [Sam and Dave] would lose at least four and five pounds a night in sweat" from dancing and moving around so much. This kinetic activity extended to the accompanying musicians, who danced in synchronized steps while playing instruments.[36] This "unification of song and dance," as ethnomusicologist Mellonee Burnim described it in reference to gospel music,[37] is central to the aesthetic of soul and the broader Black popular tradition. Audience participation is important to performers—it encourages them to explore the full range of aesthetic possibilities, which increases the intensity of the performance, thereby generating continuous verbal and nonverbal feedback from the audience. This form of participation is the most important criterion by which soul singers determine whether they are meeting the aesthetic expectations of their audiences.

Live recordings capture the essence of the aesthetic of soul, which is illustrated on *James Brown Live at the Apollo* (1962), *James Brown Live at the Apollo* (1967), and *Aretha Live at Fillmore West* (1971). The soul aesthetic, however, is mitigated on studio recordings because of technical limitations of recording equipment of this period and the use of standard production concepts. Aware of these and other restrictions, Brown acknowledged that he "agreed to make his rhythms on the [studio] records a lot simpler" while "still going for that live-in-the-studio sound."[38] Similarly, a comparison of live and studio performances of Ray Charles and Aretha Franklin, among other soul performers, reveals major differences in the aesthetic. In live performances, the tempos are faster, rhythmic structures are more complex, word and pitch repetition are extensive, brassy horns are central to the musical arrangement, vamps are extended, the overall level of intensity is greater, and the music is continuous without breaks between most songs.

With few exceptions, between the mid- and late 1970s record companies began to limit or discontinue their production of soul music. Three major factors contributed to this decision: (1) the domination of the conglomerates in the distribution of Black music; (2) the expansion of the crossover market for Black music; and (3) the popularity of **disco** among the masses.

Throughout the 1970s, major companies bought the catalogues from the small independent labels specializing in Black music and the conglomerates began acquiring these companies. They also lured established soul music artists from the independent labels by offers of higher advances, recording budgets, and fees payable to artists as well as the promise for world-wide marketing and distribution. These expensive contracts, however, became a liability for many soul singers. To recover these expenses and realize a large profit, record labels pressured these artists to appeal to a broader audience market. They did so by transforming their soul aesthetic into a crossover sound through the use of a **pop production formula**. Journalist and culture critic Nelson George has labeled this process as the "Death of Rhythm and Blues."[39] Under the control of conglomerates, many well-established Black artists, including the proclaimed "Godfather of Soul," James Brown, became temporarily disempowered creatively.

Recording for the small, independent King Records from 1958 to 1971, Brown enjoyed considerable creative freedom. This arrangement eventually changed after he signed with Polydor in 1971, three years after Linn Broadcasting bought King Records as a subsidiary label. Brown explains:

> In the early years [beginning in 1971] with them I was hitting the singles charts in spite of the company. The songs were hits because I forced them through the company and made them hits myself. I was supposed to have creative control, but they started remixing my records. I mixed them, but when they came out they didn't sound like what I'd mixed. The company didn't want the funk in there too heavy. They'd take the feeling out of the record. They didn't want James Brown to be raw. Eventually, they destroyed my sound [around 1979]. . . .
>
> . . . In destroying my sound, Polydor had cost me my audience . . .
>
> They tried to take me over into disco by bringing in an outside producer, Brad Shapiro. I was against it from the first. Disco had no groove, it had no sophistication, it had nothing . . . I fought against doing it but finally gave in. They called the album *The Original Disco Man* [1979]. It wasn't disco all the way, but I was very unhappy with the result.[40]

In other words, James Brown was forced to relinquish artistic control over his productions and modify his soul and funk aesthetic to generate crossover sales. This strategy proved unsuccessful, as evidenced by Brown's failure to make the pop charts after 1975 and his low placements on the rhythm and blues charts beginning in 1978. Following the disappointing sales of *The Original Disco Man*, Brown and Polydor

Disco
Genre of 1970s dance music, derived from the abbreviation of discothèque, the main venue of consumption.

Pop production formula
Highly lyrical vocals without ornamentation, supported by lush orchestral arrangement and a simple rhythmic foundation; lyrics are often strophic with hook line or verse–refrain structures.

parted ways in 1980. With few exceptions, the crossover production aesthetic applied to established soul singers did not generate the anticipated results. Therefore, Polydor, CBS, Warner Brothers, and RCA, among others, chose not to renew the contracts of such artists as James Brown, Johnny Taylor, Bobby Womack, Tyrone Davis, Wilson Pickett, and Diana Ross.

Similarly, soul artists signed to independent labels experimented with the disco formula. Lamont Dozier, of Motown's Holland–Dozier–Holland songwriter-producer team, produced Aretha Franklin's *Sweet Passion* (1977) for Atlantic Records. This production did not meet the sale expectations of Atlantic. Her subsequent experimentations with disco under the direction of producer-performers Nile Rodgers and Bernard Edwards did not meet her own expectations. Reflecting on this period, Aretha recalled:

> I realized that my voice would have worked with disco tracks. But I was determined not to be labeled a disco artist. No matter how much the radio stations were shoving rhythm and blues [soul] back in the corner, I still believed and I believe today in the permanent value and staying power of soul music.[41]

Curtis Mayfield articulated a similar view after experimenting with disco elements between 1976 and 1979 on *Give, Get, Take and Have* (1976), *Never Say You Can't Survive* (1977), *Do It All Night* (1978), and *Heartbeat* (1979), the latter produced by Norman Harris, Bunny Sigler, and Ronald Tyson of Philadelphia International. These productions did not meet the success levels of Mayfield's earlier soul recordings, which led him to conclude: "Other people's styles could never express me the way I expressed myself. I learned from that that all my life the music only sold when I was being me, when I was just being Curtis."[42]

By the end of the 1970s, most of the 1960s soul performers had disappeared from the Top 40 charts and the popular musical soundscape. Moreover, the productions of the custom labels distributed by the conglomerates had begun to reflect new trends in Black popular music. Party themes replaced the social and political commentary, and the gospel elements that defined the unique character and spirit of soul eventually became less dominant. Synthesizers began replacing electric bass as well as acoustic instruments. These fundamental changes signaled the end of the soul era. Nevertheless, the soul aesthetic permeated the disco-soul sound of Sylvester and inspired the mellow gospel-flavored ballads of the post-disco era represented in the 1980s and 1990s soul-derived recordings marketed under the label R&B. Representative artists of the latter include Luther Vandross, Lionel Richie, Maze Featuring Frankie Beverly, Anita Baker, Freddie Jackson, the Isley Brothers, Keith Sweat, and R. Kelly.

Portia K. Maultsby

SECOND GENERATION OF SOUL SINGERS: THE 1990s AND INTO THE NEW MILLENNIUM

In the 1990s and into the new millennium, a new generation of performers invigorated the sound of soul (1960s–1970s). Although marketed as "**neo-soul**" singers, these artists more accurately are described as second-generation soul singers. They are torchbearers, carrying on a legacy of soul music. Singer Leela James (Figure 13.4), for example, refers to herself as "a combination of the old and the present. A lot of the old are the nuances in my voice, my vocal style. The present is the musical backing, the beats."[43] James's perspective, which reflects the views of other soul singers of the second generation, runs counter to the meaning of "neo" as "new, fresh, recent" according to *The Random House Dictionary of the English Language*.

Me'Shell NdegéOcello's *Plantation Lullabies* (1993) provided the prototype for the second generation of soul singers. This recording, anchored in the spoken word tradition, utilizes musical tracks derived from soul, funk, hip-hop, and jazz, with tempos ranging from slow to fast. Two years later with the release of D'Angelo's *Brown Sugar* (1995) followed by Erykah Badu's debut CD *Baduizm* (1997), soul music resurfaced as a popular genre. Similar to *Plantation Lullabies*, these two recordings combine the flavor of soul music and the spoken word of 1960s Black poets with elements of funk, jazz, R&B, and hip-hop. Each artist personalizes the recontextualization of the soul aesthetic and the

Neo-soul
A marketing term used to promote soul music created by the second generation of soul singers.

Figure 13.4
Leela James during *MBK Presents R&B Live at B.B. Kings—New York*. Photo by Johnny Nunez/ WireImage.

reformulation of content, which generates stylistic diversity in the tradition.

The emergence of 1990s soul parallels the rise of hip-hop and R&B as the two most popular forms of contemporary Black musical expression. Beginning in the late 1980s, Afrocentric/Black Nationalist and "gangsta" rap dominated the production of Black popular music. By the mid-1990s, however, soul re-emerged as an alternative to "gangsta" rap (which overshadowed the other hip-hop styles) and R&B. Many of the genre's popularizers were born in the 1970s to parents of the 1960s soul era. Their exposure to a broad range of Black musical expression (e.g., soul, jazz, classical, hip-hop, and rock) and the Black Nationalist leanings of the era provided inspiration for the worldviews and creative output of these artists.

Similar to hip-hop artists, the 1990s soul singers began their careers writing and reading poetry. As professional musicians, they wrote or cowrote and produced or coproduced many of their own songs, arranged and performed background vocals, and played acoustic and electric instruments (vs. synthesized and programmed electronic instrumentation) on their recordings. From the mid- to late 1990s these artists contributed to the continuing evolution of the genre. They established the spoken word in combination with jazz and the flavorings of soul as the core aesthetic. Characterized by slow and moderate tempos, this aesthetic is a subdued cross between speech and song, a rhythmic flow described as "lagging behind the beat"—a signature of Billie Holiday and an approach emulated by Dinah Washington and many jazz singers. The speech-derived aesthetic gives preference to a narrow pitch range and a syllabic-styled (one pitch per syllable) interpretation that juxtaposes percussive and melodic qualities. This approach is in contrast to the melismatic interpretation (several notes per syllable) characteristic of soul music. Erykah Badu's *Baduizm* (1997) and *Mama's Gun* (2000) illustrate the crystallization of a distinctive spoken word–jazz hybrid soul style that exploits a range of Black aesthetic qualities and improvisatory devices unique to jazz, including scat singing. Badu's style provided the model for soul singers of the twenty-first century, including Jill Scott (*Who Is Jill Scott?: Words and Sounds Vol. 1*, 2000).

Many neo-soul artists preserve the 1960s and 1970s spirit of soul using various approaches. D'Angelo's (*Brown Sugar*, 1995) smooth, mellow, and sultry vocals demonstrate an affinity to soul singers Smokey Robinson, Curtis Mayfield, and Al Green, whose styles inspired those of other male neo-soul singers such as Maxwell. In contrast to D'Angelo's speech-song delivery style, Maxwell (*Maxwell's Urban Hang Suite*, 1996) illustrates a more melodic approach, similar to that of Smokey Robinson, with a funk-oriented groove. Similarly, "Groove Theory," on their self-titled CD (1995), preserves the sensibility of 1970s soul reminiscent of the Emotions. Eric Benét (*A Day in the Life*, 1999), on the other hand, presents an eclectic mix of songs that combine the soul-oriented vocals of Maxwell and the jazz–spoken word approach of Erykah Badu.

Moving closer to the roots of soul, some neo-soul artists tapped directly into the gospel tradition (D'Angelo's "Higher," 1995; and Eric Benét's "Love the Hurt Away," 1999); others covered original recordings of soul (D'Angelo's "Cruisin'," 1995, originally recorded by Smokey Robinson; and Angie Stone's "Trouble Man," 1999, originally recorded by Marvin Gaye). They also sampled significant excerpts of 1970s soul recordings (Angie Stone's *Black Diamond*, 1999). For example, "Neither One of Us," recorded by Gladys Knight & The Pips, provides the instrumental track for Stone's original lyrics and melodies on "No More Rain (In This Cloud)"; and Earth, Wind & Fire's "Sun Goddess" does the same for "Visions." Stone's use of samples is intended to preserve the organic character of 1970s soul. Criticizing the recordings of what she calls "commercial soul," Stone contends that her representation of the genre is "not about watering down but using the roots of gospel and R&B."[44] Leela James, newcomer to the soul music scene in the new millennium, pays homage to soul singers Aretha Franklin, Chaka Khan, Gladys Knight, Tina Turner, Marvin Gaye, and Donny Hathaway in "Music" (2005). Perhaps the most noticeable marker of 1960s/1970s soul in the 1990s and into the twenty-first century is the instrumentation—drums, percussion, acoustic piano and guitar, Fender Rhodes and Wurlitzer pianos, Hammond B-3 organ, trumpet, trombone, and saxophone—on recordings (D'Angelo's "Higher," 1995; Erykah Badu's "Booty," 1997; Jill Scott's "It's Love," 2000; Eric Roberson's "Music," 2007; and Maxwell's "Cold," 2009).

The second generation of soul artists also embraced the 1960s ideology of a Black consciousness in various ways. Their CDs and song titles, as well as the lyrics, for example, draw from ethnic and cultural sources such as Angie Stone's *Black Diamond*, Me'Shell NdegéOcello's "Dred Loc" (1993), and Eric Benét's "Chocolate Legs" (2008). Maxwell describes his love interest as a "honeydosugachocolate dumpling" in "Sumthin' Sumthin'" (1996) and voices his preference for a lady with brown legs in "Suitelady (The Proposal Jam)" (1996). Jill Scott describes her man as being of a deep brown complexion in "Love Rain" (2000) and makes reference to soul food (black-eyed peas, collard greens, and sweet potatoes) in "It's Love" (2000), as does Leela James in "Soul Food" (2005).

The lyrics focus primarily on personal relationships. Unlike the demeaning and misogynistic representation of women that became commonplace in hip-hop in the 1990s, soul acknowledges the vulnerabilities and fears of both men and women in pursuit of rewarding and committed relationships (D'Angelo's "Lady" and "Alright," 1995; Eric Benét's "Spend My Life with You" and "Love the Hurt Away," 1999; Maxwell's "Sumthin' Sumthin'" and "Lonely's the Only Company," 1996; Erykah Badu's "Otherside of the Game," 1997, and "Bag Lady," 2000; Bilal's "Soul Sista," 2001; and Marsha Ambrosius's "Lose Myself," 2011).

Angie Stone describes the narratives of women as being about "all the ups and downs, the trials and tribulations, and the joys."[45] Women speak about these issues, as well as the social and political concerns of African Americans, with empowered and liberated voices. Me'Shell NdegéOcello's *Plantation Lullabies* (1993) references the 1960s struggle for racial equality in "I'm Diggin' You (Like an Old Soul Record)." She also addresses the negative effects of a capitalistic system on urban Black America in "Shoot'n Up and Gett'n High," and issues of Blackness and White standards of beauty in "Soul on Ice." Through their lyrics and musical features, the second generation of soul artists sought to preserve the African American musical legacy of earlier periods in contemporary expressions.

Changes in the Soul Aesthetic

Several artists continued to celebrate the legacy of 1960s/1970s soul in the new millennium. Eric Roberson and Leela James, for example, describe themselves as a "soul survivor" singing "back porch soul"[46] (2005). At the same time, the soul aesthetic became more eclectic with the incorporation of advanced technologies, production techniques and the dominance of musical elements from contemporary traditions. Synthesizers, computers, samplers, and other advanced technologies associated with electronic dance music, funk, and hip-hop, for example, replaced and/or were used in conjunction with acoustic and electric instruments characteristic of 1990s soul sound. The musical track for "Late Nights & Early Mornings" (2011) by Marsha Ambrosius, for example, blends the sounds of synthesized strings, an acoustic piano, and electronic drums with the sound effects produced by the **Auto-Tune**, a digital device used to manipulate vocal and instrumental timbres. Erykah Badu fully exploits the Auto-Tune technology in the P-Funk-influenced "Love" (2010). Furthermore, artists began producing entire projects on laptops using music software, as did Erykah Badu on *New Amerykah* (2008).[47]

The influence of funk and hip-hop on soul became more prominent in the twenty-first century. A new rhythmic foundation resulted from layering and juxtaposing funk grooves and hip-hop rhythms, incorporating hip-hop sound effects (beat box, scratching, mixing techniques, etc.), and adding rap sections that featured hip-hop artists. This new aesthetic characterizes Jill Scott's "Shame" (2011), featuring rapper Eve & the A Group, and "All Cried Out Redux" (2011), featuring Doug E. Fresh; and Eric Roberson's "Been in Love" (2007), featuring rapper Phonte from Little Brother. The funk style of Sly Stone and George Clinton surfaces in Maxwell ("Now/At the Party," 2001), Erykah Badu ("Amerykah Promise," 2008, and "Love," 2010) and Angie Stone ("Unexpected," 2009) (see Chapter 14 on funk).

The influence of hip-hop and funk on soul is further illustrated in the phonetic spelling and the combination of different words, respectively.

Auto-Tune
A digital device used to manipulate vocal and instrumental pitch. The synthesized vocoder preceded the Auto-Tune.

Portia K. Maultsby

Musiq Soulchild combines words and employs phonetic spellings to create song titles ("Musiqinthemagiq," "Iwannabe," "Womanopoly," and "Onmyradio"), as do Eric Roberson ("Iluvu2much" and "N2uF") and Erykah Badu ("New Amerykah"). Song lyrics continue to focus primarily on topics of personal relationships, although reference to social and political issues occurs in some recordings such as Angie Stone's "My People," featuring James Ingram (2007), and Erykah Badu's "Soldier" (2008) and "New Amerykah" (2008).

In the twenty-first century, soul artists continue to demonstrate their creativity and versatility while preserving the 1960s/1970s soul legacy. Even though they incorporate advanced technologies and contemporary musical trends in their productions, they continue to value the core aesthetic and traditional sound of 1960s soul as illustrated by Leela James ("Didn't I," 2005, and "Tell Me You Love Me," 2010), Ledisi ("Alright," 2007, and "Pieces of Me," 2011), Maxwell ("Cold," 2009), and Jill Scott ("I'm Not Afraid" and "Golden," both 2009). The organic quality of 1960s/1970s soul is achieved through cover recordings (Leela James, *Let's Do It Again*, 2009) and by featuring the original artists on recordings (Angie Stone, "Baby," featuring Betty Wright, and "My People," featuring James Ingram, both 2007).

Marketing Soul in the 1990s and Beyond

The term "neo-soul" was popularized by music industry executive Kedar Massenburg who used this label to market D'Angelo's *Brown Sugar* (1995) and Erykah Badu's debut CD *Baduizm* (1997).[48] By 2005, record labels and trade music magazines had begun to use the term indiscriminately, marketing R&B artists such as Faith Evans and Usher as neo-soul. This trend, along with a general dislike for labels, led many second-generation soul artists to reject the term. Desiring to be known simply as a soul singer, Jaguar Wright recorded *Divorcing Neo 2 Marry Soul* (2005). Marsha Ambrosius, former singer of British duo Floetry, took a more drastic step in demonstrating her disdain for the label by releasing the **mixtape** called *Neo-Soul is Dead: The Chronic Mixtape* (2008). The recording is laced with profanity and explicit lyrics sung over gangsta-rap samples from Dr. Dre's *The Chronic* (1992). Affirming their status simply as soul singers, Leela James refers to her music as "just raw soul" and Eric Roberson, a thirteen-year soul veteran, reiterates that he is a "Soul Survivor" (2007).

Mixtape
Informal collection of songs, often assembled by a DJ, sometimes recorded with a unique sonic stamp.

CONCLUSIONS

Soul music is an expression of a cultural identity and racial consciousness that reflects the preservation of values rooted in an African cultural legacy. According to DJ Jeffrey Troy:

> [Soul music] maintains a hell of a lot of importance because it is one of the very few things in this country that the black man can say is his. It's a part of his identification and very important for image making purposes.[49]

Emerging as a distinctive genre during the 1960s era of social unrest and the call for Black Power, soul music became the major vehicle for the promotion of a Black Nationalist agenda. Soul singers ascended as community icons, promoting concepts of Black solidarity, Black pride, and Black empowerment. Radio stations initially banned these recordings because of their overtly political messages. Nevertheless, soul became the most popular and influential form of Black musical expression in post-World War II America.

The 1960s/1970s soul sound is readily identified by its gospel roots, which blurred the perceived sacred/secular musical boundaries and provided a familiar sound that crossed all social classes and generations. The popularity of soul among the African American masses did not go unnoticed by the conglomerates that expanded into and began dominating this market in the 1970s. The involvement of major record labels in the production, marketing, and distribution of Black music occurred when disco emerged as a crossover formula. The popularity of disco among the masses influenced changes in the production of many soul singers. In some contexts, the aesthetic of soul gave way to crossover formulas that de-emphasized the core elements of a soul sound. In other settings, Black music productions blended disco elements with those of soul in ways that preserved and highlighted components of the soul aesthetic.

By the end of the 1970s, the 1960s sound of soul largely had disappeared from the popular musical soundscape. The spirit, character, and/or elements of soul, nevertheless, provided the foundation for the 1980s and 1990s forms of Black musical expression as well as those in the twenty-first century. Marketed under the labels "R&B" and "neo-soul," these genres illustrate how contemporary African American musical expressions represent a blending and reworking of past traditions within contemporary contexts. They also exemplify how the concept of soul remains relevant in the production of Black culture in the post-soul era.

ACKNOWLEDGMENTS

The research for a study on the general topic of African American popular music, from which I drew for this essay, was conducted with the support of various institutions and foundations: a post-doctoral fellowship from the National Research Council and Ford Foundation (1984–85); residency as a fellow at the Center for Advanced Study in the Behavioral Sciences, Stanford, California (1999–2000), and financial support from the Andrew W. Mellon Foundation and the College of Arts and Sciences, Indiana University–Bloomington (1999–2000).

KEY NAMES

Erykah Badu	Martin Luther King Jr.
James Brown	Curtis Mayfield
Ray Charles	Me'Shell NdegéOcello
Sam Cooke	Angie Stone
Aretha Franklin	The Staple Singers
Leela James	

QUESTIONS

1. Define soul music as both a cultural concept and a musical genre. How is soul music related to the Civil Rights and Black Power movements?

2. Listen to a YouTube performance or a live audio recording of "Dr. Feelgood" (soul) by Aretha Franklin and "Never Could Have Made It" (gospel) by Marvin Sapp, and identify the musical elements and performance practices common to both soul and gospel music.

3. Why did soul decline in popularity in the 1970s?

4. What elements of soul music were revived by the "neo-soul" artists of the 1990s?

PROJECTS

1. Choose a hit song by Ray Charles, Sam Cooke, or James Brown that exhibits features characteristic of gospel music. Identify at least four gospel-derived features and provide a rationale for your choices.

2. Select five soul songs and analyze them for the messages they convey regarding Black Power.

3. Compare recordings of soul and disco by a 1960s soul singer such as Aretha Franklin, Diana Ross, James Brown, or Johnny Taylor. What are the major differences between the recordings? Why did soul artists find it so hard to adapt to the disco style?

NOTES

Please see the discography for information on resources for further listening.

1. Many authors have used the terms "rhythm and blues" and "R&B" interchangeably to identify Black popular music recorded from the 1940s through the late 1960s. In 1990, *Billboard* and record labels designated the "R&B" label to chart and market contemporary Black popular music, which differed stylistically from hip-hop. I use the term rhythm and blues to identify Black popular styles from the 1940s through the 1960s. I reserve the R&B label to identify contemporary rhythm and blues styles recorded from 1990 into the twenty-first century.

2. Reagon 1987, 105–18.

3. Ward 1998; Van Deburg 1992; Hannerz 1969.

4. Ture and Hamilton 1992 (1967), 44.
5. Shaw 1970, 2.
6. Van Deburg 1992, 195.
7. Shaw 1970, 4.
8. See "An Introduction to Soul," *Esquire* 69 (April 1968): 79–90, and "Lady Soul Singing It Like It Is," *Time* (June 28, 1968): 62–66.
9. Brown with Tucker 1986, 149, 78–9, 121.
10. Guralnick 2005.
11. Quoted in Wolff with Crain, White, and Tenenbaum 1995, 292.
12. Quoted in Werner 2004, 67. Brackets in the original.
13. Ibid., 118–19.
14. Haralambos 1985 (1974), 117.
15. Fred Cash and Samuel Gooden, interview on *Movin' On Up: The Music and Message of Curtis Mayfield and The Impressions*, 2008, DVD.
16. Eddie Thomas, interview by Craig Werner, n.d.
17. Hirshey 1984, 251.
18. Quoted in Werner 2004, 68. Ellipses in the original.
19. Ibid., 66.
20. Cash and Gooden interview, 2008.
21. Mayfield, interview by Mike McAlpin for PBS documentary *Record Row: The Cradle of Rhythm and Blues*, 1997.
22. Wesley 2002, 109–10.
23. Bobby Byrd, interview by author, Nashville, Tennessee, August 8, 1984; Brown with Tucker 1986, 200, 202.
24. Ward 1998, 364.
25. Van Deburg 1992, 63–111; Horton and Horton, 2001, 323–39.
26. Quoted in Brown with Tucker 1986, 241.
27. Ibid., 242.
28. Gordy 1994, 293.
29. Haralambos 1985 (1974), 116.
30. Williams-Jones 1975, 381.
31. Quoted in Sanders 1971, 126.
32. Burnim 1985, 154–58.
33. Ibid., 162–65.
34. Sanders 1971, 126.
35. Interview by the author, Los Angeles, California, February 25, 1983.
36. Ibid.
37. Burnim 1985, 160.
38. Brown with Tucker 1986, 149, 157.
39. George 1988, 147–69.
40. Brown with Tucker 1986, 239–40, 253.
41. Quoted in Werner 2004, 219
42. Quoted in Werner 2004, 221.
43. Tarradell 2010.
44. Quoted in Neal 2003, 26, 27.
45. Stone 1999.
46. These phrases are found in Eric Roberson, "Music," from *Left* (2007), and Leela James, "I Know I've Been Changed Interlude," from *A Change is Gonna Come* (2005), respectively.
47. Arthur 2008.
48. Kedar Massenburg was the executive producer for both albums. See Cunningham (2010) for a detailed discussion of the origin and use of the term "neo-soul."
49. Quoted in Haralambos 1985 (1974), 131.

PART IV

Post-Civil Rights and Beyond (1960s–)

CHAPTER 14

Funk

Portia K. Maultsby

> *Funk is a Black thing. There is a need to express yourself as an African American. You need to be your own person.*
> (Danny Webster, guitarist and vocalist for Slave[1])

Funk is an urban form of dance music (also known as "party" music) that emerged in the late 1960s and became popular in the 1970s. Its creators were rhythm and blues and jazz musicians, who sang, played instruments, wrote, and often produced their own songs as self-contained groups. Funk borrows elements from a wide range of musical genres including rhythm and blues-styled horn arrangements, jazz-oriented solos, rock-oriented solos and guitar timbres, and vocal stylings associated with soul music. This hybrid musical aesthetic defies categorization, prompting music critics and others to label the early funk bands as "soul groups," "dance bands," "black rock," and "jazz-funk."[2] From the late 1960s to the early 1970s, soul music and the early funk styles overlapped as musical genres. The term "funk" captured both the complex, and often contradictory, feelings of optimism, ambivalence, disillusionment, and despair that accompanied the transition from a segregated to a post-civil rights society.[3] This range of emotions is reflected in diverse lyric themes—"party," social and political commentary, romance, and social relationships—which define the complex character of funk. As a musical style, funk reveals the resilience and creativity of African Americans under changing social and economic conditions.

DEFINING FUNK

Juba to Jive: A Dictionary of African-American Slang defines the word *lufunki* (of Central African origin), translated as "bad body odor," as the probable origin of the term "funk." Funk has been variously defined as "down-to-earth," "for real," "in touch with the essence of being human," or "an offensive or unpleasant smell or thing." The term alternately can be used to signify something "attractive or beautiful."[4] Initially interpreted as a dirty word, funk eventually became part of the African American vernacular, describing a feeling, attitude, philosophy, and behavior, as well as a musical and cultural style.

Hard bop
A combo jazz style of the 1950s that incorporated the phrasings and harmonies of blues, rhythm and blues, and gospel music.

The term "funky" was first used in a musical context in the 1950s as a way of describing the jazz style known as **hard bop**. Associated with musicians such as Horace Silver, Les McCann, Jimmy Smith, Lee Morgan, and Art Blakey, hard bop is characterized by heavy drum beats and straight eighth or sixteenth notes played on the hi-hat (a shift from the ride cymbal), bass lines with dark bluesy timbres, as well as gospel harmonies and melodic phrasings. This new sound inspired movement on the dance floor described by Black musicians and the Black working class as "earthy," "low-down," "dirty," or "nitty-gritty."[5] By the early 1970s, the term "funky" had become analogous with a distinctive musical style of rhythm and blues[6] and soul that later was to become known as funk.

THE ARCHITECTS OF FUNK

As a musical style, funk draws from the innovations of James Brown ("Godfather of Soul") and those of the rhythm and blues-rock-oriented group Sly and the Family Stone. Brown and Stone were musical revolutionaries who broke rules and crossed the boundaries of musical style and, in the process, redefined the direction of African American popular music. In the mid-1960s Brown transformed the sound of rhythm and blues by introducing a new rhythmic concept in "Papa's Got a Brand New Bag" (1965) that gave preference to beat one in a measure, played on the bass drum and bass guitar. The downbeat, which Brown

Polyrhythm
Several contrasting rhythms played or sung simultaneously.

called "The One,"[7] provided the anchor for the layering of different rhythmic-melodic lines or riffs assigned to the rhythm and horn sections, creating a **polyrhythmic** foundation. This percussive, high-energy dance rhythm became Brown's signature sound for subsequent recordings such as "Cold Sweat (Part I)" (1967), "There Was a Time" (1967), and "I Got the Feeling" (1968), which eventually evolved from the rhythm and blues–soul hybrid sound into funk (see discussion of soul in Chapter 13).

Sly and the Family Stone, an interracial, mixed-gender group from San Francisco, developed a funk style that borrowed technology common to rock music such as the wah-wah pedal, fuzz box, echo chamber, and vocal distorter, and incorporated a blues-rock guitar style ("Sex Machine,"

Portia K. Maultsby

1970). Larry Graham's revolutionary approach to playing the bass gave rhythm and blues and soul a new sound and a different kind of energy. Exploiting the instrument's rhythmic and timbral capabilities, Graham transformed the bass into a percussive instrument by pulling, plucking, thumping, and slapping the strings, techniques he developed while performing in clubs as a duo with his mother: "I started to thump the strings with my thumb to make up for not having a bass drum."[8] Graham's percussive playing style is evident in the 1969 recordings of "Hot Fun in the Summertime" and "Thank You (Falettinme Be Mice Elf Agin)." Scores of bass players adopted this technique, which eventually became commonplace in funk, jazz, and rock. The innovations of Graham and Stone were appealing to White audiences, who identified especially with the group's rock-funk aesthetic that some critics labeled psychedelic-funk. In contrast, James Brown's music attracted a predominately African American following. These two iconic figures became popular during the height of the **Black Power Movement** (which overlapped with the **Civil Rights Movement**), anti-Vietnam War, and hippie movements.

Brown and Stone symbolized change; their music captured the spirit of defiance and their lyric themes of social and political change challenged the status quo. The ideology of Black Power inspired Brown's creative impulse and the Civil Rights and counterculture movements had an equivalent impact on Sly Stone. Messages of Black pride and community empowerment permeate many of Brown's songs, including "Say It Loud, I'm Black and I'm Proud" (1968), "I Don't Want Nobody to Give Me Nothing (Open Up the Door I'll Get It Myself)" (1969), and "Get Up, Get into It, and Get Involved" (1970). In contrast, Stone's lyric themes of universal love and world peace transcended the ideological divide and agenda of the White counterculture movement. In "Everyday People" (1969) and "Stand!" (1969) (Track 36), Sly spoke out against social injustice and promoted concepts of universal harmony, encouraging all races to "Dance to the Music" (1968) because "I Want to Take You Higher" (1969).

Sly also juxtaposed his integrationist views with the ideology of Black Power. Revealing his political consciousness as an African American male in the United States, he candidly responded to society's racial views in songs such as "Don't Call Me Nigger, Whitey" (1969), "Thank You (Falettinme Be Mice Elf Agin)" (1969), and "Thank You for Talkin' to Me Africa" (1971). The release of *There's a Riot Goin' On* (1971) generated consternation among many of Sly's loyal fans. The hard-driving, psychedelic rock-funk orientation of Sly's earlier productions gave way to an introspective, laid-back blues-funk style while his themes of universal love and harmony transformed into a critique of society's racial attitudes. "With *Riot*," observed music critic Greil Marcus, "Sly gave his audience—particularly his White audience—exactly what they didn't want. What they wanted was an upper, not a portrait of what lay behind the big freaky Black superstar grin that decorated the cover of the album."[9]

Black Power Movement
A movement of the late 1960s and early 1970s that emphasized Black unity, Black pride, and self-determination.

Modern Civil Rights Movement
A movement beginning in the late 1940s and blossoming in the late 1950s to mid-1960s that pushed for equal rights for African Americans.

 36

"Stand!"

In other words, Sly's fans related largely to his music and stage persona, ignoring his identity as an African American male living in a racist society. Thus, *Riot* became a window into the inner world of Sly Stone, revealing how he negotiated the competing ideological perspectives of integration and nationalism. Such candid assessments of race relations and racial injustice were common in the recordings of the first generation of 1970s funk bands, as were the musical influences of both Sly Stone and James Brown.

FUNK LYRICS: CONTENT, MEANING, AND FUNCTION

Similar to other genres of African American music, funk lyrics are lenses into the experiences and worldviews of African Americans, who traditionally have used music to express their innermost feelings, preserve their identity, and record their history. Many funk musicians grew up in all-Black poor and working-class communities with whom they maintained social ties after becoming successful musicians. They drew from their experiences in these communities for lyric content, which provided commentary on urban life, romance, the 1960s Great Society legislation, deindustrialization, and the impact of changing economic conditions on African American communities. The growing numbers of the unemployed African American poor, for example, paralleled the recordings of funk groups who spoke out against economic and social injustice. Kool & the Gang asked "Who's Gonna Take the Weight" (1970) for the corruption, debt, and society's social problems? Similarly, a year later, War reminded society of the plight of the poor and the deteriorating conditions of ghettos in "Slipping into Darkness" (1971) and "The World Is a Ghetto" (1972).

By the late 1970s and throughout the 1980s, two recessions (1973–75) and (1980–82), the ongoing fiscal conservatism, and the cumulative impact of deindustrialization had increased the level of poverty in inner-city communities. Even though the Black middle class made considerable economic progress during this period, the anti-affirmative action movement, cultural misunderstandings, the lack of opportunities for advancement, and exclusionary practices in the workplace, nevertheless, generated frustration, anger, and resentment among members of this group. The optimism that once had prevailed transformed into disillusionment, and the unemployed abandoned all hope for improved conditions.[10] Responding to this changing mood, funk musicians wrote songs that encouraged African Americans from all socioeconomic classes to come together and "dance," "hang loose," "party," and be happy.

Party Themes, Social and Political Commentary

James Brown and Sly and the Family Stone first popularized the "party" theme in funk in the late 1960s. Kool & the Gang institutionalized this theme in "Funky Stuff" (1973) and "Jungle Boogie" (1973), as did

Portia K. Maultsby

Parliament in "Up for the Down Stroke" (1974). Funk soon became known as "happy music" and "party music," which Norman Beavers of Lakeside described as "a form of escapism from social problems."[11] For many African Americans, funk functioned as a temporary respite from the uncertainties and pressures of daily life. The recurrent chanted lyrics of "party," "dance, dance all night," "let yourself go," "give up the funk," and "release yourself" encouraged kinetic expressions (clapping hands, snapping fingers, stomping feet, and waving arms and hands), which, according to funk drummer Hamilton Bohannon, signified being happy. Bohannon observes:

> It takes a lot to be happy—it's hard being happy. If my music ["Foot Stompin' Music" (1975) and "Bohannon's Beat (Pt. 1)" (1975)] can make people move a little bit, bounce around a little and feel happy, it makes me really happy."[12]

In a similar vein, the Bar-Kays wrote "Shine" (1978) "to give people some hope and help" and Roger Troutman wrote "I Can Make You Dance" (1983), performed by Zapp, so people "could forget about their problems by dancing." Lakeside recreated past eras of adventure by metaphorically referencing the valor of historical characters such as Robin Hood on *Shot of Love* (1978), cowboys on *Rough Riders* (1979), pirates on *Fantastic Voyage* (1980), FBI agents on *Untouchables* (1983), and Arabian knights on *Your Wish is My Command* (1982), to help Black people "forget about the bad times."[13] Other bands who wrote party-funk songs with messages of encouragement include the Gap Band ("Shake," 1979) and Roger ("So Ruff, So Tuff," 1981) (Track 16).[14]

 16

"So Ruff, So Tuff."

P-Funk
Short for "pure funk," a style pioneered by George Clinton, whose lyrics promoted Black self-determination and liberation.

George Clinton, founder and lead singer of Parliament, took party-funk to another level when he combined party themes with those of Black nationalism advanced by the Black Power Movement to create a unique style known as **P-Funk** ("pure," "uncut funk"). Clinton's lyrics expressed the view that the movement toward an "integrated" society had resulted in the erosion of Black cultural values and the fragmentation of Black communities. To counter this trend, Clinton promoted two fundamental concepts: (1) self-liberation from the social and cultural restrictions of society; and (2) the creation of new social spaces in which African Americans could redefine themselves and find the funk ("Flash Light," 1977) to celebrate their Blackness as "One Nation Under a Groove" (1978). Clinton's nationalist views resonated with African Americans from all walks of life, especially those affiliated with multicultural institutions where they felt "pressured to give up their identities and to adapt to the surrounding white culture."[15] The lyrics of P-Funk encouraged Black people to liberate and empower themselves as a unified community.

The song "Chocolate City" (1975) from the album of the same title, which referenced Washington, DC, and other cities with predominantly Black populations, emphasizes the power of the Black vote, situating "Blacks in places where you don't conceive of them being."[16]

In "Chocolate City," Clinton alludes to the possibility of electing a Black President, with Aretha Franklin as First Lady, and Muhammad Ali, Reverend Ike, Richard Pryor, and Stevie Wonder as Cabinet members in the "Black House" (instead of the White House). In subsequent albums, he created stories that intertwined the party theme with social realities and fantasies featuring Black mythical heroes and villains.[17]

The albums *Mothership Connection* (1975) and *The Clones of Dr. Funkenstein* (1976) by Parliament situate African Americans in a spaceship on an imaginary planet, and *Motor Booty Affair* (1978) places them underwater. Using humor, metaphor, coded language, and creative word play such as "groovallegiance," "funkentelechy," "prosifunksti-cation," and "psychoalphadiscobetabioaquadoloop" in the critique of political and social issues, Clinton contends: "We try to not preach but we try to bring them [issues that impact African Americans negatively] up."[18] Clinton's blend of realism and intellectualism appealed to members of all Black social and economic classes, who were culturally liberated by his Black Nationalist message, which Rickey Vincent interprets through the lens of African cosmology (the concept of "oneness") and African religious systems (the transforming power of funk).[19]

African cosmology also inspired the lyric content of the 1970s funk bands, especially the songs of Earth, Wind & Fire, who promoted universal messages of love and peace. The group's leader and primary songwriter, Maurice White, describes himself as a spiritual and philosophical person who "is very conscious on a humanitarian level, and who really thinks about the creator, the stars, the moon and other planets, the universe as well as the existence of other planetary beings."[20] Referencing Egyptian cosmology specifically, White's lyric themes promote an awareness of self, of others, and the world as means of achieving universal peace, harmony, and love. "Keep Your Head to the Sky" (1973), "Shining Star" (1975), and "That's the Way of the World" (1975) by Earth, Wind & Fire are among the group's many recordings that embody White's philosophy.[21]

Male–Female Relationships and Encounters

Song lyrics that describe the trials and tribulations of male–female relationships are common in funk as illustrated in the Bar-Kays' "Too Hot to Stop" (1976) and "Hit and Run" (1981); the Gap Band's "Burn Rubber On Me (Why You Wanna Hurt Me)" (1981), "Early in the Morning" (1982), and "You Dropped a Bomb on Me" (1982); and Cameo's "Back and Forth" (1987).

The culture of the urban working class, the primary consumers of funk, also inspired lyric content about male–female encounters. The Ohio Players, for example, drew from the street culture of Dayton to create funk-ballads and up-tempo songs that personified the culture of the city's hustlers and "players." The players, who engaged in superficial relation-ships with several women simultaneously,[22] preferred women whose attire revealed the curvature of the body and whose sensuous movements matched those described in "Skin Tight" (1974). In contrast, "Jive Turkey" (1974) exposes the behavior of deceitful women. Other songs by the Ohio Players, such as "Fire" (1974), "Fopp" (1975), "Honey" (1975), "Sweet Sticky Thing" (1975), and "Angel" (1977), extol sexual pleasures using double entendre or coded language common in the blues tradition.[23]

Funk lyrics reflect the diversity of African American experiences and changing conditions in inner-city communities in years subsequent to the Civil Rights and Black Power movements. With the decline of traditional economic resources and recreational programs in the 1970s, drugs began to infiltrate urban communities. Many funk and other musicians were known to use drugs, a topic also reflected in their music, though it was masked through the use of double entendre. "Mothership Connection" (1975) by Parliament, "Riding High" (1977) by the Dayton group Faze-O, and "Mary Jane" (1978) by Rick James are such examples.

The messages of funk resonated with many African Americans as did its sound, which personified the sensibilities, cultural values, and aesthetic preferences of the Black working class. Because funk received minimal pop radio airplay, its popularity largely was limited to African American communities until the mid-1990s when it entered the mainstream through revival tours and broadcasts on classic R&B/soul radio stations. The funk aesthetic subsequently has become central to the soundscape of American popular culture.

THE EMERGENCE OF FUNK BANDS

In the late 1960s and into the 1970s, several jazz combos and rhythm and blues bands began to transform into funk bands across the country. By 1975, funk had crystallized as a distinctive musical genre characterized by aesthetic features in which rhythm assumes definitive hierarchical position over melody. The musical foundation centers on a **"groove"** defined by a polyrhythmic foundation layered on a syncopated bass line that locks with the bass drum pattern. This pattern often begins with a heavy "downbeat" on the first pulse (the "One") and an accented snare drum back-beat on the second and fourth pulse. The funk aesthetic is highly percussive; the bass functions as a melodic instrument; the harmonic progression is reduced to a minimum, often centering on one or two chords; and group singing often assumes prominence over lead vocals in the up-tempo songs.[24] Even though many fans associate funk with up-tempo party music exclusively, the genre includes ballads performed in a slow or moderate tempo as in Earth, Wind & Fire's "Reasons" (1975), the Gap Band's "Yearning for Your Love" (1980), the Bar-Kays' "Attitudes" (1977), and Cameo's "Sparkle" (1979).[25]

Although a set of aesthetic values defines funk broadly as a genre, such factors as new technologies, regional preferences, the musical background of performers, and current trends in popular music, influence diversity in the genre and the development of new styles. Defying

Groove
Syncopated and repetitive rhythmic foundation established by the bass and drum.

rigid musical categories, funk musicians fused and reformulated elements from jazz, blues, rhythm and blues, soul, rock, disco, and other genres in ways that produced various hybrid funk styles (e.g., jazz-funk, blues-funk, disco-funk, etc.).

The first funk bands to dominate the scene in the early 1970s were from all regions of the country—New Jersey (Kool & the Gang), Ohio (Ohio Players and the JBs), California (War, Tower of Power, and Santana), and Illinois (Earth, Wind & Fire). They were jazz, blues, and rhythm and blues musicians who established funk styles that were imitated by aspiring funk musicians. In Dayton, for example, the Ohio Players inspired the formation of approximately twenty teenage funk bands who covered the latest funk hits performing in talent shows, clubs, and entertainment venues in the community. Such experiences prepared these bands to open shows for, and back up, nationally renowned singers and to perform in the surrounding states while in high school.[26]

By the mid-1970s the Midwest (Ohio, Illinois, Indiana, and Michigan) and the South (Memphis, Tennessee) had become the major centers for the production of funk music. Between 1968 and 1999 thirteen funk groups from or associated with the small industrial city of Dayton, Ohio (without the presence of a record company) collectively produced 143 songs that landed on *Billboard*'s R&B/Soul single charts.[27] From Cincinnati hailed Bootsy's Rubber Band, the JBs (James Brown's back-up band), and the Isley Brothers, who successfully transformed from a rhythm and blues group into a soul/funk fusion band. In Detroit the former 1950s **doo-wop** singer, George Clinton, put a new spin on the sound and meaning of funk, building on the foundation established by James Brown and Sly Stone. Clinton established his sound, labeled P-Funk, in conjunction with Brown's musicians—Fred Wesley, Maceo Parker, William "Bootsy" Collins, and Phelps "Catfish" Collins—who left his band to join Clinton's organization. P-Funk preserves the signature sound of James Brown in the horn arrangements of Wesley, the saxophone solos of Parker, the percussive bass riffs of "Bootsy" Collins, and the guitar style of "Catfish" Collins. It also incorporates the rock timbres of Jimi Hendrix and Sly Stone. Expanding the traditional funk aesthetic, Clinton introduced a new approach to the treatment of tempo, texture, and timbre. P-Funk tempos range from slow to moderate while musical textures are sparse and light, resulting from the spacing of short, repetitive, and stratified melodic motifs of guitars and horns, as heard in Brides of Funkenstein's "Disco to Go" (1978).

A major feature of the P-Funk sound is the incorporation of varying timbral qualities produced by modern musical technologies. Employing Black aesthetic principles, keyboardist Bernie Worrell uses **synthesizers** to mimic the voice, bass, guitar, and horns, generating an array of timbres such as growls, slides, screeches, and unusual sound effects. Worrell's omnipresent synthesized strings add interesting colors and textures to chanted vocal lines and distorted bass lines, as well as the improvised

Doo-wop
Typically, a cappella vocal harmony groups that emphasized the rhythmic delivery of phrases consisting of vocables (syllables without lexical meaning) such as "doo-wop."

Synthesizer
Any electronic musical instrument that creates its sounds through digital means, allowing the performer to vary pitch, timbre, attack, decay, and other basic sound elements.

Portia K. Maultsby

call–response interplay between the rhythm and horn sections. Parliament's "Chocolate City" (1975) and "Flash Light" (1977) (Track 12) illustrate this technologically based P-Funk aesthetic.

⊙ **12**

"Flash Light."

Textural and timbral variety is commonly used in P-Funk as a device for mood change. It is achieved by superimposing a spoken voice (often electronically altered) over group singing, suddenly shifting from the group sound with full instrumentation to a "rap" section with sparse accompaniment and alternating melodic horn phrasings with percussive riffs. These features are evident in Parliament's "Mothership Connection" (1975), "Night of the Thumpasorus People" (1975), "Sir Nose D'Voidoffunk" (1977), and "Rumpofsteelskin" (1978).

George Clinton and his P-Funk aggregate (Figure 14.1) began to creatively exploit modern technology following Stevie Wonder's introduction of the clavinet and synthesizers in the albums *Talking Book* (1972) and *Innervisions* (1973). Funk recordings of the Commodores ("Machine Gun," 1974, and "Slippery When Wet," 1975), among other groups, employ these same innovations.

A unique funk style labeled "go-go" took root in and became the signature sound of Washington, DC, in the mid-1970s. This sound gained national traction with the release of Chuck Brown's "Bustin' Loose" in 1978. Live audience participation, in which the audience and performers spontaneously create and exchange phrases in an antiphonal style, is an essential component of the go-go tradition. A second distinctive feature of go-go is its use of Latin percussion instruments (congas, timbales, and cowbells) along with the drum kit to extend and connect different songs into a twenty- to ninety-minute performance. Musical variety results from the percussively played horn lines and extended horn

Figure 14.1
Pianist Bernie Worrell, guitarist Michael Hampton (in clown costume), Calvin Simon (in cape), Ray Davis (in vest), Fuzzy Haskins, Grady Taylor (fourth from right), and Garry Shider (right) of the funk band Parliament-Funkadelic perform onstage, *c.*1974. Photo by Michael Ochs Archives/Getty Images.

sections. Spike Lee brought national notoriety to go-go when he featured EU (Experience Unlimited) performing "Da' Butt" in his film *School Daze* (1988). Other go-go groups include Rare Essence, Little Benny and the Masters, Slim, and Redds and the Boys.[28]

TECHNOLOGY AND 1980s DISCO-FUNK FUSION

By 1980, major record companies had begun to dominate the production and marketing of Black music with the intent of broadening its consumer base. Recording company executives tacitly required Black groups to produce a more pop-oriented and homogenized sound for mass marketing. Thus, the use of **crossover** formulas became more common place among Black artists, which resulted in aesthetic changes in the "soul" of Black popular music, a concept that cultural critic Nelson George describes as "the death of rhythm and blues."[29] The trend toward crossover productions coincided with advancements in musical technology and the emergence of **disco** as a distinct electro-pop style, which led to shifts in the musical direction of many funk bands (see discussion in Chapter 15). Group-oriented singing gave way to lead vocals and, by the late 1970s, computers began replacing bass players because, in the view of Ohio Players' bassist Marshall Jones, the "beat was more infectious [and] computers could do things rhythmically that musicians actually can't do."[30] To remain competitive against the popularity of disco, many funk bands replaced bass and horn players with synthesizers and added disco rhythms to the funk groove.

The funk group Dayton, from Ohio, reached its maturity during the transitional period between disco and funk. They, like other funk bands, experienced difficulty in redefining their musical direction. Trumpet and keyboard player Chris Jones recalled: "There wasn't a whole lot of deep funk [i.e., 1970s funk aesthetic] with Dayton."[31] Dayton's use of advanced technology and disco's production techniques resulted in a disco-oriented sound with less obvious traditional funk roots. Similar to Heatwave's "Boogie Nights" (1977) and "The Groove Line" (1977), Dayton's sound was a funk–disco–jazz hybrid ("Eyes on You," 1980, and "The Sound of Music," 1983). Their biggest hit, "Hot Fun in the Summertime" (1982), however, was a pop interpretation (with disco overtones) of the funk song first recorded by Sly and the Family Stone in 1969.

Other funk groups also faced the dilemma of adjusting to changing trends in popular music. The first charted singles ("Ffun," 1977, and "Shake and Dance with Me," 1978) by the Vallejo, California-based group Con Funk Shun, for example, employed the traditional funk style that featured a prominent horn section and a strong polyrhythmic foundation. A year later, with the release of "Chase Me" from the album *Candy* (1979), the group began incorporating elements from other music genres. According to lead vocalist and synthesizer player Felton Pilate, "Disco was really happening and we tried to fuse funk and disco [on 'Candy']. Another song '(Let Me Put) Love on Your Mind' was experimental—rock guitar solos over a ballad kind of feeling."[32] In 1980, Con Funk Shun began experimenting with "pop" elements as noted in the promotional materials released by Mercury/PolyGram Records:

> "Too Tight," the first single from Con Funk Shun's newest album *Touch* marks a departure from their traditional funk trademark, and may have the distinction of helping to create a new musical category—"pop-funk."[33]

"Too Tight" peaked at number 8 on *Billboard*'s Rhythm and Blues and number 40 on the Pop singles charts. On subsequent recordings, Con Funk Shun released many songs with synthesizers, which replaced the horn section. Pilate explained:

> Most of the hits that are out now [1985] are just not saturated with horns anymore. I try to be a competitive writer and if I'm going to try to be commercial, then I got to pay attention to what's really happening.[34]

Despite Con Funk Shun's use of crossover formulas to appeal to a broad consumer market, the end result was only moderately successful. The album *Candy*, for example, reached the number 7 position on *Billboard*'s Rhythm and Blues charts and number 46 on the Pop charts; *Fever* (1983), which Pilate described as being more pop, claimed the number 105 spot on the Pop charts in comparison to number 12 on the Rhythm and Blues charts. These chart placements suggest that Con Funk Shun's "new" musical direction did not resonate decisively with any single market. Their songs retained some semblance of the rhythm and blues-funk aesthetic, which resonated more with African Americans than it did with the mainstream consumers of pop and disco.

Even though crossover formulas described in the promotional materials for Con Funk Shun's *Fever* de-emphasized the use of horns, other groups eliminated horns for economic and creative reasons. Record labels reduced production budgets and their support for national tours. Furthermore, audience preference shifted from a live to a synthesized aesthetic, in part, due to the popularity of disco. Despite attempts of record labels to broaden the consumer base for Black music, the audience for funk remained primarily African American.

While some funk bands used technology as a crossover device, others employed it to further develop the 1970s funk aesthetic as the foundation for contemporary funk styles. The Bar-Kays, for example, integrated synthesizers into the traditional funk instrumentation by arranging "horns as though they were an electronic instrument like synthesizers and mixed them in."[35] They also overlaid the electric bass with synthesized bass lines, which produced new textures and added depth to the music's foundation ("Hit and Run," 1981). When the group substituted synthesizers for horns, they retained the function and percussive quality of live horn, as on "Sexomatic" (1984) and "Freakshow on the Dance Floor" (1984). Midnight Star also incorporated synthesizers into the traditional

Vocoder/voice box
An electronic device
that is used to distort
natural vocal sounds.

16

"So Ruff, So Tuff."

funk instrumentation in "Freak-a-Zoid" (1983), "Wet My Whistle" (1983), and "No Parking on the Dance Floor" (1983).

Zapp and Roger (two groups comprised of overlapping members from the Troutman family) created a contemporary Dayton funk style by borrowing from the high-tech P-Funk aesthetic to produce strong dance rhythms and varied vocal and instrumental timbres. Roger Troutman also experimented with the **voice box** (also known as the **vocoder**) to "find new ways to express words in music" as illustrated in "More Bounce to the Ounce" (1980), "I Heard It through the Grapevine" (1981), "Dance Floor" (1982), and "So Ruff, So Tuff"[36] (Track 16). This innovation influenced the use of the vocoder to create a sci-fi aesthetic in Midnight Star's "Scientific Love" (1984) and "Body Snatchers" (1984).

The productions of the Minneapolis-based artists Prince and the Time also were heavily synthesized, yet their overall styles were distinct. Creating an eclectic repertoire of electro-funk in the albums *1999* (1982) and *Purple Rain* (1984), Prince incorporated elements of rhythm and blues and rock, as Sly and the Family Stone had done in the late 1960s and early 1970s. His rock rhythms and guitar aesthetic juxtaposed and blended with funk-derived rhythms in "Little Red Corvette" (1982) and "When Doves Cry" (1984), which appealed to broad audiences and generated several crossover Top 20 hits, two in number 1 positions on both *Billboard*'s R&B and Pop single charts. In contrast to Prince's electro R&B–rock aesthetic, the Time, a protégé of Prince, evolved a distinctive style of synthesized dance funk by employing gospel-inspired timbres reminiscent of Graham Central Station and high-tech sound effects in the albums *What Time Is It?* (1982) and *Ice Cream Castle* (1984).

Although the technological innovations of the 1980s funk musicians modernized the 1970s funk sound, hip-hop DJ Afrika Bambaataa established electro-funk as a distinctive funk style by using synthesizers and drum machines to incorporate funk beats in his eclectic mixes of music from various traditions. Afrika Bambaataa & the Soul Sonic Force's "Planet Rock" (1982), a reworking of Kraftwerk's space age or sci-fi aesthetic in "Trans-Europe Express" (1977), provided the model for Planet Patrol's "Play at Your Own Risk" (1982) and the Jonzun Crew's "Pack Jam" (1982). Electro-funk recordings and the recordings of established funk groups became integral to the soundtrack of hip-hop culture.

PERFORMANCE AESTHETIC: STAGE PRODUCTIONS OF FUNK

Stage productions (as well as the cover of album jackets) of funk centered on a musical concept and/or a unique group persona based on a philosophy, a way of being. The colorful, flashy, and customized coordinated costumes of musicians established a group's identity and helped to create an atmosphere for their musical renditions. The Ohio Players dressed in tuxedoes, furs, hats, and other fashionable "street" attire accented with diamond rings and other accessories, as well as customized sequined bellbottom jeans and jackets accented by white shoes to establish their persona as "players." The group adopted its name and image from Dayton's local "players," who dressed in the latest fashions, drove the newest cars, and projected a street image popularized in the Hollywood "blaxploitation" film *Superfly* (1972). This movie portrays the protagonist, Youngblood Priest, as a ladies' man who wore white suits and shoes, gold accessories, large hats with feathers, and oversized tie sticks, and drove an "El Dog" (Eldorado) with custom headlights. The cast of supporting characters were outfitted in colorful suits.

In contrast and influenced by cosmology, Earth, Wind & Fire became known for their space-age and futuristic aesthetic, dressing in shiny or sequined white- and bright-colored skin-tight and bellbottom pants, accessorized with decorative designs and platform shoes (Figure 14.2). Earth, Wind & Fire's persona, as well as the science fiction films *Close Encounters of the Third Kind* (1977) and *Star Wars* (1977), inspired the group Sun's name and yellow and white costumes accessorized with glitter, symbolizing the solar system. Childhood fantasies of adventure influenced Lakeside's characters and dress as warriors, cowboys, pirates, gangsters, FBI agents, horse jockeys, and Arabian knights, which came to life during live performances.

The funk musicians describe stage productions of funk as a form of theater.[37] Larry Blackmon, the leader of Cameo, explains:

> We go beyond the visual rhythm and blues groups in that we are all highly attuned to the art of showmanship. The way we emphasize emotions and moods, build momentum, utilize costumes and pace ourselves is very close to the traditional concept of theater.[38]

Stage presentations of funk became full-scale spectacles. The coordinated costumes and conservative lighting, sound, and visual effects associated

Figure 14.2
Earth, Wind & Fire, *c.*1970. Photo by Michael Ochs Archives/Getty Images.

with traditional rhythm and blues and soul groups gave way to flashy, individualistic, and sometimes outlandish costumes, elaborate stage props and lighting design, and audio and visual effects comparable to those of rock groups and Broadway musicals such as *The Wiz* (1975). The Ohio Players and Earth, Wind & Fire reportedly were the first funk bands to stage such theatrical productions, each reflecting its own group persona as well as the content of their song lyrics.[39]

The Ohio Players' live productions featured light shows, sounds effects, and expensive stage props. According to Keith Harrison of Dayton:

> The Players w[ere] the first group to use lasers. People never knew that. They had mirrors set up and used laser lights way back then and before productions became a big thing. The Players painted all their equipment white, which brought another brightness to the stage. They started adding the siren to "Fire" [1974]. On "Skin Tight" [1974], Marshall came out and blew a tuba. They were adding other things to try to make their stage production a little bigger because Earth, Wind & Fire was their biggest competitor when it came to stage production.[40]

Earth, Wind & Fire's productions, on the other hand, became known for their space-age and futuristic characterizations. Describing a performance of the group, Rickey Vincent recalls: "Stage props lifted the players to the rafters, spun the drum sets upside down, and beamed the band members out of cylinders on stage."[41]

Funk stage productions became even more elaborate when George Clinton mounted his 1976 P-Funk Earth Tour, a series of concerts performed by Parliament-Funkadelic that began in New Orleans. The tour was reportedly the most expensive production of any funk band, and Fred Wesley, composer-arranger-trombonist for James Brown, Bootsy's Rubber Band, and George Clinton's P-Funk Horns, describes it as an unprecedented extravaganza.[42] In addition to the $275,000 production budget provided by Neil Bogart, co-founder of Casablanca Records, Clinton's show required a weekly payroll of $75,000 (a handsome amount in 1976) for the entourage of eighty-eight instrumentalists, singers, and crew. It featured elaborate props and costumes designed to complement the **concept albums** in their repertoire.[43]

For example, the story of *Mothership Connection* (1975) unfolds around an imaginary planet. Clinton, as Dr. Funkenstein, and his crew return to Earth to bring back the funk—the aesthetic sensibility, social values, cultural traditions, and spiritual force—that, in earlier centuries, had sustained and empowered African Americans during slavery. Some members of the band assume the characters of a space alien with wings/fins, a clown, an Arab in faded purple, and an earthling in a floor-length, black velvet, gold-trimmed dashiki with white alligator-skin platform boots.

Stage props for the P-Funk Earth Tour were as elaborate as those used in European opera productions. They included a giant twelve-foot-high platform boot, a silver car, and a baby spaceship suspended by wire over the audience and rigged to fly from the back of the venue to join with the

Concept album
A collection of songs based on a theme that is reflected in the album's cover design and graphics.

Portia K. Maultsby

Figure 14.3
The Mothership of the funk band Parliament-Funkadelic lands onstage on June 4, 1977 at the Coliseum in Los Angeles, California. Photo by Michael Ochs Archives/Getty Images.

Mothership (Figure 14.3). Fred Wesley recalls: "The gargantuan Mothership hung out of sight over the stage … [appearing] to land … at the appropriate moment, delivering Dr. Funkenstein, who wore a white fur coat, white fur hat, and long, dark brown wig."[44] When the Mothership landed, a battery of synthesizers produced an array of sound effects accentuated by spectacular and colorful flashing lights, lasers, smoke machines, and other props.[45] P-Funk productions were mesmerizing and they led to a movement where audiences began "to adopt that P-Funk attitude and dress like P-Funk, act like P-Funk, and talk the P-Funk talk."[46] Thus, P-Funk was a concept that embodied a philosophy, attitude, culture, and musical style.

The Funk Continuum in Hip-Hop and R&B

Although most funk bands had begun to disappear from the popular soundscape by the mid-1980s, largely due to changes in the musical preferences of consumers, hip-hop DJs and computer programmers revived the funk aesthetic in the late 1980s by sampling the heavy funk beats, funky bass lines, guitar, keyboard, and horn riffs, and sung and spoken phrases. Reformulating these materials, hip-hop DJs created new musical tracks that brought the historical past into the present, reviving a 1960s Black consciousness in the process (see discussion of hip-hop and rap in Chapter 17). James Brown ("Funky Drummer," 1970; "The Payback," 1973; and "Get Up, Get into It, Get Involved," 1970), George

Clinton ("Atomic Dog," 1982; and "Flash Light," 1977), the Ohio Players ("Funky Worm," 1972), and Zapp and Roger ("More Bounce to the Ounce," 1980) became the most frequently sampled funk groups. Samples from these songs permeate all hip-hop styles, from party and novelty rap to Afro-centric and gangsta styles, as evident in the beats of Public Enemy ("Bring the Noise," 1988), Geto Boys ("Mind of a Lunatic," 1990), Ice Cube ("Jackin' for Beats," 1990), Digital Underground ("Doowutch-yalike," 1990), Snoop Doggy Dogg ("Serial Killa," 1993), Too Short ("Sample the Funk," 1995), X-Clan ("Xodus," 1992), Wu-Tang Clan ("Method Man," 1993), Mos Def ("Mathematics," 1999), Ludacris ("Two Miles an Hour," 2004), Nas ("Where Are They Now?" 2006), Black Milk ("Warning (Keep Bouncing)," 2010), and Erykah Badu (featuring Bilal and Lil Wayne) ("Jump Up in the Air and Stay There," 2010).

Funk's influence on hip-hop is manifested in various other ways. The P-Funk vocabulary inspired an original hip-hop lexicon as well as the use of humor (including cartoon and science fiction characters) as a strategy for "dropping science" (knowledge),[47] the mission of Five Percent rappers. Moreover, funk musicians have collaborated with rappers. Roger worked with 2Pac and Dr. Dre on "California Love," which received a Grammy nomination for Best Rap Song by a Duo or Group in 1996. Funk pioneers James Brown and George Clinton and P-Funk legend Bootsy Collins appear on audio and video recordings of hip-hop artists. Los Angeles producer and rapper Dr. Dre edited the footage of "The Landing of the Mothership" into his own video of "Let Me Ride" (1992).[48]

CONCLUSIONS

Funk is urban at its core, blending industrial-based and technological sounds with song lyrics about the realities of urban Black life. Funk is also multidimensional in function and meaning. Created as an urban form of dance or party music during an era of changing social and economic conditions, the lyrics of funk reflect both the optimism and disillusionment of African Americans in the struggle for racial equality. Even though the themes of "party" and "hang loose" permeate funk, those texts also embody nationalist messages that communicate a revolutionary spirit, an urban attitude of defiance, emblematic of the call for Black solidarity associated with the Black Power Movement of the late 1960s and early 1970s.

The funk aesthetic embodies the energy, sensibilities, and values of the African American working class. Yet, its audience included African Americans of all socio-economic strata, among them young Black professionals, who frequently migrated from their integrated neighborhoods to clubs in African American working-class communities where funk reigned supreme. Within African American communities, funk became an expression of cultural liberation and musical experimentation

—a rejection of mainstream values and norms. As funk guitarist and vocalist Danny Webster asserts, "Funk is a Black thing. There is a need to express yourself as an African American. You need to be your own person."[49]

ACKNOWLEDGMENTS

The research for a study on the general topic of African American popular music, from which I drew for this essay, was conducted with the support of various institutions and foundations: a post-doctoral fellowship from the National Research Council and Ford Foundation (1984–85); residency as a fellow at the Center for Advanced Study in the Behavioral Sciences, Stanford, California (1999–2000), and financial support from the Andrew W. Mellon Foundation and the College of Arts and Sciences, Indiana University–Bloomington (1999–2000). This essay draws some material from another publication, "Funk Music: An Expression of Black Life in Dayton, Ohio and the American Metropolis" in *The American Metropolis: Image and Inspiration*, edited by Hans Krabbendam, Marja Roholl, and Tity de Vries. Amsterdam: Vu University Press, 2001.

KEY NAMES

James Brown	Prince
George Clinton	Sly Stone
Earth, Wind & Fire	The Time
Kool & the Gang	Zapp and Roger
Ohio Players	

QUESTIONS

1. Define funk as both a musical genre and a cultural concept. Identify the pioneers of this genre and their contributions to its development.

2. Choose three funk groups and describe how the ideology of the Civil Rights and Black Power movements is exhibited in their recordings.

3. Compare and contrast the album/CD jackets and stage productions of Sly Stone, Earth, Wind & Fire, the Ohio Players, George Clinton, and Lakeside in terms of how they represent diversity in African American culture.

4. How did advancements in musical technologies impact funk music in the 1980s?

5. How has funk influenced later musical styles, specifically hip-hop in the 1990s and beyond?

PROJECTS

1. Investigate the formative musical careers, innovations, and legacies of two funk musicians, noting their involvement in varied musical styles. Create a diagram illustrating how funk music has influenced or been influenced by rhythm and blues, gospel, rock, soul, disco, and hip-hop.

2. Select five songs that represent key moments in the evolution of funk music, from its earliest days to its maturity, and explain your rationale for each choice. Describe distinctive changes in the lyrics, accompaniment, musical style, and other elements of these songs.

3. Compare images from a hit album and related tour by Parliament-Funkadelic with those of Earth, Wind & Fire (including any available video recordings). How does each group dramatically shape the musical themes of its album/tour, and what does this imply about the cultural meaning of funk music?

4. Identify five funk songs referenced by recent hip-hop recordings, either through sampling or borrowing lyrics and melodic ideas. Describe how the hip-hop songs incorporate aspects of each funk song, and discuss why the current artists may have referenced them.

NOTES

Please see the discography for information on resources for further listening.

1. Danny Webster, interview by author, Dayton, OH, August 18, 1997.
2. Vincent 1996, 15.
3. Jones 1977; Triandis 1976; Gill 1980.
4. Major 1994, 187–88.
5. David "Panama" Francis, interview by author, Orlando, FL, December 3, 1983; Vincent 1996, 3–4, 31–32.
6. Many authors have used the terms "rhythm and blues" and "R&B" interchangeably to identify Black popular music recorded from the 1940s through the late 1960s. In 1990, *Billboard* and record labels designated the "R&B" label to chart and market contemporary Black popular music, which differed stylistically from hip-hop. I use the term rhythm and blues to identify Black popular styles from the 1940s through the 1960s. I reserve the R&B label to identify contemporary rhythm and blues styles recorded from 1990 into the twenty-first century.
7. Vincent 1996, 37, 81
8. Quoted in Vincent 1996, 95.
9. Marcus 1975, 89.
10. Feagins and Sikes 1994; Moore and Wagstaff 1974; Davis and Watson 1982; Gill 1980; Trotter 1993, 80; Marable 2007, 59–111; Fine 1989.
11. Lakeside, interview by Karen Shearer Productions, Los Angeles, CA, January 28, 1982.
12. Hamilton Bohannon, interview by Mike Terry, Los Angeles, CA, September 28, 1978.
13. Lakeside interview, 1982.
14. Roger Troutman and Larry Troutman, interview by Karen Shearer Productions, Los Angeles, CA, August 8, 1982.
15. Feagins and Sikes 1994, 93–94.
16. George Clinton, interview by author and Charles Sykes, Bloomington, IN, March 5, 1995.
17. Ibid.

18. Ibid.
19. Vincent 1996, 258–59.
20. Maurice White (Earth, Wind & Fire), interview by Karen Shearer Productions, Los Angeles, CA, February 10, 1983.
21. Ibid.
22. Greg Webster, interview by Stephanie Shonekan, Dayton, OH, March 12, 1998.
23. James "Diamond" Williams, interview by author, Dayton, OH, August 19, 1997.
24. Some funk songs are constructed tightly, with an extended A section and a shorter "bridge" or B section that returns to the A section, as heard in James Brown's "Get Up (I Feel Like Being a) Sex Machine" (1970). Other songs employ free-form grooves consisting of improvised exchanges among musicians, as illustrated in the Ohio Players' "Pain" (1971) and "Jive Turkey" (1974).
25. Ballads performed in a slow or moderate tempo, employing a standard four-line verse–chorus structure or a variation thereof.
26. Charlie White, interview by author, Dayton, OH, August 19, 1997; Roger Troutman, interview by Karen Shearer Productions, Los Angeles, CA, August 4, 1983.
27. These groups are: Ohio Players (Westbound/Mercury), Roger (Warner/Reprise), Zapp (Warner/Reprise), Lakeside (Solar), Steve Arrington/Steve Arrington and the Hall of Fame (Atlantic), Slave (Cotillion/Atlantic), Heatwave (Epic), Sun (Liberty/Capitol), Dayton (Capitol), Shadow (Elektra), Faze-O (S.H.E./Atlantic), New Horizons (Columbia), Junie (Westbound/Columbia/Island), and Platypus (Casablanca).
28. Lornell and Stephenson 2009.
29. George 1988, 147–97.
30. Marshall Jones, interview by author, Dayton, OH, August 19, 1998.
31. Chris Jones, interview by author, Dayton, OH, August 18, 1997.
32. Felton Pilate (Con Funk Shun), interview by Karen Shearer Productions, Los Angeles, CA, June 7, 1985.
33. Con Funk Shun promotional materials, 1980, Karen Shearer Collection, 1935–1996, Archives of African American Music and Culture, Indiana University, Bloomington.
34. Ibid.
35. Harvey Henderson (Bar-Kays), interview by Karen Shearer Productions, Los Angeles, CA, July 17, 1984.
36. Roger Troutman, interview by Karen Shearer Productions, Los Angeles, CA, August 5, 1982.
37. Maurice White (Earth, Wind & Fire), interview by Karen Shearer Productions, Los Angeles, CA, January 20, 1981; George Clinton interview, 1995; Larry Blackmon (Cameo), interview by Karen Shearer Productions, Los Angeles, CA, December 1, 1986.
38. Larry Blackmon (Cameo), interview, 1986.
39. Keith Harrison, interview by author, Dayton, OH, August 19, 1997.
40. Ibid.
41. Vincent 1996, 188.
42. Wesley 2002, 205.
43. George Clinton, interview by Karen Shearer Productions, Los Angeles, July 1, 1983.
44. Wesley 2002, 205.
45. *The Mothership Connection* 1998, DVD.
46. Wesley 2002, 207.
47. The term "droppin' science" originally referred to a kind of wisdom expressed in rhymes. It originated with Five Percent rappers, who, as followers of the Nation of Islam, used a mathematical formula to interpret and present African American history as science. The phrase has been more broadly applied to rappers who critique traditional "scientific" studies as well as complex situations related to African American communities. The use of the term now extends beyond the Five Percent nation.
48. Vincent 1996, 313.
49. Danny Webster interview, 1997.

CHAPTER 15

Disco and House

Kai Fikentscher

Disco, the abbreviation of the French word *discothèque,* is a musical genre that emerged in underground dance venues in New York City in the 1970s. It was pioneered by disc jockeys (DJs) who initially entertained primarily African American, Latino, and gay dancers. Although the term originally defined a specific musical setting, disco evolved into a stylistic category that eventually included dance steps as well as fashion and hairstyles. The roots of disco can be located at the intersection between underground dance venues and gay sensibilities in New York City, beginning in the late 1960s.

After 1970, US-American popular dance music can be summarily viewed as the development of disco music, and disco's evolution, during the 1980s and 1990s, into three main categories of dance music: club, house, and hip-hop. These genres thus refer to related forms of twentieth-century American popular dance music. As such, they belong to a continuous history of American social dance that begins with formations such as the Charleston in the 1920s and to an even longer continuum of African American expressive culture.

In contrast to much rock and pop music, in which aspects of musicianship in performance are considered central and generally given priority, disco and post-disco dance music highlight the production process itself—exemplified in the roles of producers, recording engineers, and DJs. In contrast to the world of pop music (and, to an extent, of hip-hop), the central performers in disco and post-disco dance music are the DJ and the dancers rather than singers and musicians. In this performance environment, music is often as physical as it is audible, involving large sound systems, twin turntables, a mixer, and vinyl records in the DJ booth, and the human body as the chief musical instrument on the dance floor. Since the 1990s, digital equipment such as the vari-speed CD player and digital sound formats such as CD-R and MP3 have been used alongside or instead of their analog precursors.

DISCO: A PLACE TO DANCE

In New York City, the emergence of **disco** in the 1970s was the result of a fusion or overlap of three distinct types of social dance environment prevalent in the 1960s, all of which featured recorded music, with or without the presence of a **DJ**. One type was based on the European (originally French) concept of a discothèque. In Manhattan, this type of venue was typified by establishments such as Le Club, Arthur, El Morocco, and Cheetah, all conceptually derived from or modeled on the chic, socially exlusive, and often exotically decorated Parisian *boîte*, which, as Albert Goldman notes in his book *Disco*, had been brought to Park Avenue in New York by disco madam Regine Zylberberg.[1]

Goldman describes how the French concept of disco—based originally on the passionate relationship of Parisian jazz fans to their collections of jazz records, all subject to censorship under the German occupation of the French capital during World War II—was initally embraced by, and consciously styled and marketed for, small groups of rather well-off connoisseurs. Accordingly, the earliest label for this group to become associated with discothèques as exclusive sites was the "jet set." In the early 1960s, the cosmopolitan aspect of jet-set life led to a diffusion of this type of discothèque from Paris to places such as London and New York, cities proximate in terms of either geography or language. The clientele of these upscale venues showcased the latest dance trends based on R&B/rock and roll hits that often had eponymous names, such as "The Twist" by Chubby Checker, "Mashed Potato" by Dee Dee Sharp, "Monkey Time" by Major Lance, "The Jerk" by the Larks, and "The Watusi" by the Vibrations. Before crossing over to European discothèques, though, these dances, as well as the songs helping to promote them, were first popul-arized in African American dance environments.[2]

During the 1960s and into the 1970s, the character of discothèques gradually changed to accommodate various groups within urban society who differed significantly from those who frequented earlier disco-thèques. As outlets for music and dancing that expressed a rapidly changing popular culture, New York's discothèques of the late 1960s and early 1970s absorbed many of the social changes that affected Amer-ican society at large during that period. Chief among these changes, and important for the development of disco culture in the 1970s, was the formation of increasingly vocal segments of society that felt largely shut out of the processes of decision-making and power-brokering in the country. Among these were the young, ethnic minorities, women, and gays—urbanites who either felt, or actually had been, pushed to the margins of American society.

Disco
Genre of 1970s dance music, derived from the abbreviation of discothèque, the main venue of consumption.

DJ
Short for "disc jockey"; a person who plays records in a dance club or on radio.

Another prototype of a discothèque was exemplified by venues such as New York's Electric Circus, a psychedelic rock disco on St. Mark's Place in the East Village,[3] and Zodiac, where DJs such as Bobby "DJ" Guttadaro played an eclectic repertoire of rock (e.g., Led Zeppelin, Chicago, and Blood, Sweat & Tears), rhythm and blues (e.g., Rare Earth, Booker T. & the MGs, and the Supremes), and early forms of what, decades later, came to be marketed as "world music" (e.g., Santana, Osibisa, and Manu Dibango) to a crowd markedly younger and less affluent than the jet set. This audience included anti-establishment pre-Woodstock hippies, struggling poets, musicians, actors and other artists, and a mix of working-class Whites with some African Americans and Latinos.

The third type of proto-disco dance venue was comprised of neighborhood clubs or bars, both legal and illegal, that catered to gay men and/or women. Often these establishments served ethnically homogeneous urban enclaves, such as New York's Harlem or the Latino portions of Manhattan's Upper West Side and the Lower East Side. There, to the sounds provided by a jukebox or a DJ, older women or men (the latter sometimes in drag) often acted as initiators, and at times protectors, of younger gays into "the Life." Examples of this type of urbanized version of the rural juke joint in 1960s Manhattan were the Tabletop, which moved several times from its original uptown location on Third Avenue; Bosco's on Fifth Avenue; and André's on Eighth Avenue (all in Harlem). Others were located on the Upper West Side, such as the Candlelight and Piccadilly on Amsterdam Avenue, and in Greenwich Village, including the Stonewall Inn and the Snake Pit. After 1966, due mainly to a change in city government that led to a decrease in police harassment of gays, much of urban gay life emerged from the sociopolitical closet to become public and legal.[4] Still, gay bars continued to be subject to police raids throughout the 1960s. One of these raids involving the Stonewall Inn on Christopher Street turned into a battle between gays and police that ultimately became a turning point in the history of gay life in New York, important enough to be remembered as the "Stonewall Riots."

The degree to which the Stonewall Riots, on June 28, 1969, acted as a catalyst to synthesize these types of dance venues into one is a point of ongoing debate among historians. Still, despite much mythologizing in the gay press, many writers agree that "[a]fter Stonewall, . . . many lesbians and gays began to see social dancing not simply as a pastime but also as a powerful means of building a sense of communal gay and lesbian identity."[5] While there is no similar agreement on which was the first gay discothèque in New York, the first meeting of gays held to discuss the "sudden new defiance that seemed afoot among many homosexuals in New York City" after Stonewall took place on July 6, 1969, at the Electric Circus. A press release by the club's management that advertised the night said: "We'll be open to the general public as usual, but we're especially encouraging gay people to come—and we really hope that everyone will dance together and dig one another."[6]

By the fall of 1969, the Gay Activists Alliance started to hold gay dance parties in lower Manhattan on a regular basis, and the Gay Liberation Front (the second of these two important post-Stonewall organizations addressing gay issues in New York City) did the same beginning in the spring of 1971. By June 1971, the Gay Activists Alliance headquarters on Wooster Street in Soho—known as the Firehouse—had become "the most popular gay dance club in New York."[7] Initially, the DJs playing records at these parties were not professionals, but often recruited from among the organizers. Gay organizations in other North American cities such as Los Angeles and San Francisco quickly followed suit and imitated examples set in New York.

The fact that notions of gay identity, gay community, and a specifically gay agenda reverberated as long and strongly as they did throughout the 1970s is arguably due in large measure to Stonewall and its aftermath.[8] Anthony Thomas's assertion that "[a]lthough disco is most often associated with gay white men, the roots of the music actually go back to the small underground gay black clubs of New York"[9] is somewhat tempered by the agreement among many popular music historians who locate the roots of the disco phenomenon at the intersection between dance clubs and gay sensibilities.[10] Still, the notion of a gay community frequently did not extend beyond the issue of sexual orientation: "The fact that disco originated in black gay clubs did not stop white entrepreneurs from instituting racist door policies at many gay clubs."[11] Such policies, however, contributed to the establishment of interracial and predominately African American gay clubs. For example, the Paradise Garage recruited its initial membership in part from African Americans who had been turned away from Flamingo, one of the popular gay discos in New York during the mid-1970s.[12] However segregated some early discothèques were, though, the appeal of improvised social dancing to music programmed by a DJ eventually proved irresistible to America at large, spawning a new sector of the music industry that revolved exclusively around disco.

THE DISCO DJ

The first uniquely American discothèques were the offspring of dance parties at nightclubs, lofts, basements, and bars, held by and for a segment of urban society that—by default or choice—identified itself as being on the margins of mainstream society. This segment consisted largely of gays, but also included heterosexual African Americans, Latinos, and, to some degree, women, many of whom were musicians, poets, or visual artists. In this context, DJs introduced their audiences to music other than what was played on commercial radio. In contrast to radio programming where the focus was on individual records, the emphasis here was on individual DJ presentation style.

12-inch single
An extended-play 45-rpm record that accommodated remixed and rearranged versions of hit songs, permitting longer, uninterrupted dancing, especially for disco audiences.

Unlike pop and rock music of the day, disco tended to de-emphasize the individual artist as well as the individual song. Disco was instrumental in lengthening three-minute pop songs to extended versions as long as sixteen minutes, following the introduction of the **12-inch single** as a DJ-friendly format by DJ-producer Tom Moulton in 1975. As Carolyn Krasnow observes:

> the idea was to abandon the concept of discrete songs and instead have a continuous stream of sound organized around a relatively consistent rhythm. The ultimate test of a disco tune was whether it fit comfortably into a larger groove.[13]

In other words, instead of the recording artist, the dancer and the DJ were center stage. Pop music journalist Ken Tucker makes explicit the connection between the discothèque and the emergence of the DJ as artist-musician:

> These . . . discos offered the disc jockey as a species of pop artist. Through skill, timing, and taste, the disc jockey used two turntables to segue between records with compatible beats—the idea was to build and build the tension of the music until it "peaked," provoking screams of pleasure from the sweaty, exhausted, second-winded revelers on the dance floor. When combined with an array of lights pulsing and strobing to the rhythm of the music, a disco set overseen by a master disc jockey could be a hypnotic, ecstatic experience.[14]

Before disco, the DJ, whether employed in a bar or at a radio station, had been part of the service personnel, playing the songs requested by the crowd or the station manager. With disco, the DJ became a musical agent in his own right. This transformation took place in New York in the years preceding the disco boom and led to the establishment of concepts that have been commonplace in international club culture since: the edit, the **mix**, the remix, the instrumental, the break, the 12-inch single, and the combination of turntables and mixers into one instrument capable of musical expression.

Mix
(1) Verb: The recording studio term for combining and balancing instruments, vocals, and special effects in a sound recording.
(2) Noun: A seamless progression of pre-recorded songs.

The discothèque thus gave birth to the DJ as a new type of pop star. This star played a new instrument, consisting of twin turntables and a mixer, on a new stage. The DJ booth with its controls of sound and light —together with the dance floor addressed by a sound system putting forth non-stop, wall-to-wall sound—established the discothèque as a new performance environment. Using a repertoire of popular soul, funk, and Latin dance records (before 1975, only 45-rpm singles and 33-rpm album cuts were available), DJs began to create an uninterrupted flow of music at dance parties in nightclubs, lofts, and bars, following the example set by Brooklyn DJ Francis Grasso. Like many of the first generation of disco DJs in New York, Grasso was Italian American; veteran DJ Nicky Siano explains this circumstance with the fact that many dance establishments at that time had ties to the Mafia.

In 1970, at Sanctuary, a former German Baptist church on West 43rd Street in Manhattan, Francis Grasso played James Brown and Chicago Transit Authority, the Temptations and Led Zeppelin, Sly and the Family

Kai Fikentscher

Stone, Osibisa, Santana and Mitch Ryder & the Detroit Wheels. But he didn't just *play* these and other records—he mixed, sequenced, and programmed them, constructing a sonic sum bigger than the total of its parts. Largely due to his innovative way of presenting pre-recorded music in a seamless, uninterrupted manner, he became the first DJ who created an adoring fan base similar to that of a rock star.[15]

Grasso's innovation, later called *disco blending*, became a standard for generations of disc jockeys. The art of mixing and superimposing records to promote continuous dancing was picked up by downtown DJs such as Steve D'Aquisto, Michael Capello, Bobby Guttadaro, David Mancuso, Nicky Siano, and Walter Gibbons (the latter remixed the first commercially available 12-inch disco single, Double Exposure's "Ten Percent," on Salsoul Records in 1976), as well as by uptown DJs such as Pete DJ Jones, Kool DJ Herc, Grandmaster Flowers, Afrika Bambaataa, and Grandmaster Flash (who collectively helped lay the foundation of what was to become known as rap music).

AFRICAN AMERICAN ROOTS

Rhythm and blues historian Brian Ward suggests that disco was more than just a danceable form of music: "It was a time and place of leisure where an alternative, exciting, exotic and passionate lifestyle could be imagined, lived and enjoyed in the paradoxical peace of a high volume, high energy rhythmfest."[16] Disco dance parties were either private, members-only events, or events directed toward a more general clientele, largely by and for segments of urban society that identified as being on the margins of the American mainstream. Pop music aficionado Anthony Thomas identifies disco (along with club and house) as fundamentally African American music, a view confirmed by "ear witnesses" such as Jack Carroll, an Irish American who danced for years at New York venues known for their loyal gay clientele (Sanctuary in 1971, Flamingo in the mid-1970s, the Saint in 1984). In Carroll's view, the African American roots of disco are undeniable:

> In 1973, Black music with a strong heavy beat and a gospel-derived tone had almost totally eased out anything from the former decade. Songs had become longer than the old format, and stations like WBLS mixed these in without interruption for several songs in a row . . . At a point somewhere between 1973 and 1975, it was clear that a new era was arriving . . . in pop culture.[17]

Supporting this view of the African American roots of disco, Radcliffe Joe, *Billboard*'s dance editor during the emergence of disco, contends that "in 1974–75, the disco music scene was literally controlled by a handful of Black artists affiliated with a small group of specialized record labels led by Motown and Philadelphia International."[18]

Not surprisingly, there is no agreement as to what record should be considered the first disco record. Votes have been cast for Eddie Kendricks' "Girl You Need a Change of Mind," produced by Frank Wilson for Motown Records in early 1973. Another famous contender is Manu Dibango's "Soul Makossa." Originally released in 1972 as an import on the French Fiesta label, it was released domestically by Atlantic Records after WBLS DJ Frankie Crocker followed David Mancuso's example and played the song, originally exposed to dancers at Mancuso's Loft parties, to an enthusiastically responding radio audience. Before and after "Soul Makossa" entered the *Billboard* charts in 1973, it was both bootlegged and covered several times.

Although perhaps not the very first disco record, MFSB's now famous "Love Is the Message" (Philadelphia International, 1973) is arguably the most influential disco record of all time. Featuring a veritable orchestra of soul and funk musicians working out of Sigma Studios in Philadelphia, this anti-war tune helped define the lush sound that became known as the Sound of Philadelphia. An identifying feature of this sound, which later established the foundation for what became known as the disco beat, is the subdivided 4/4 meter played by drummer Earl Young on his kick drum and hi-hat, introduced on both "Love Is the Message" and its B-side, "T.S.O.P" (The Sound of Philadelphia, which became the theme song of the television show *Soul Train*) (Track 37), and central to the chorus in Harold Melvin & the Blue Notes' "Bad Luck" (1975).

 37
"T.S.O.P."

Using string and horn sections alongside a sizeable driving rhythm section, Philadelphia International's owners, Kenneth Gamble and Leon Huff, wrote and produced songs for the Trammps, the O'Jays, the Three Degrees, Double Exposure, Harold Melvin & the Blue Notes, and Teddy Pendergrass. In the process, they built a record company known for a sound (the so-called "Philly Sound") that drew the attention of young America as much as Berry Gordy's Motown Records, the inspiration for Philadelphia International, had done a decade earlier. Interestingly, Carl Bean's gay-liberation anthem "I Was Born This Way," released on Motown in 1978, was recorded at Philadelphia's Sigma Sounds, using MFSB musicians.

While at least three New York DJs claim to have "broken" (i.e., brought out of obscurity) disco, early disco records are largely significant because their popularity was initially built on club play, not radio exposure. Examples, besides "Soul Makossa" (1973), are Love Unlimited Orchestra's "Love's Theme" (1973), the Hues Corporation's "Rock the Boat" (1973), Carl Douglas's "Kung Fu Fighting" (1974), George McCrae's "Rock Your Baby" (1974), and B.T. Express's "Do It Till You're Satisfied" (1974), all of which rode to chart success after heavy club exposure, and before disco became a radio format.

As a consequence of this increasing popularity, DJs were given direct input into record production. For example, DJ David Todd developed the disco department at RCA Records after having familiarized R&B producer Van McCoy with a Latin dance called the Hustle, which resulted in an eponymous crossover hit for McCoy on the Original Sound record label in 1975.

THE DISCO INDUSTRY

With the appeal of discothèques such as the Sanctuary, Salvation, the Gallery, Le Jardin, the Loft, and Better Days, during the early 1970s New York City became the world's disco capital, with more than two hundred discothèques operating in Manhattan alone by the end of the decade. Following the success of disco-hits (a term introduced by *Billboard* in 1973 to differentiate them from radio hits) such as "Soul Makossa," "Rock the Boat," and "Rock Your Baby," radio stations such as WKTU changed to a disco format; disco records began to sell well enough to compete with rock and pop, and crowds jostled to get into Studio 54, arguably the most famous Manhattan discothèque of that period.

Between the early and mid-1970s, with the help of radio and television exposure across the United States and Europe, disco became one of the most popular sounds of the decade. Drawing on up-tempo rhythm and blues-based funk and soul music (for example, Booker T. & the MGs' "Melting Pot") and popular Latin repertoire (for example, Barrabas's "Checkmate"), disco's development in terms of both style and commerce increasingly involved electronic instruments (such as synthesizers and drum machines) and European producers (for example, Donna Summer's 1975 smash hit "I Feel Love," produced by Swiss producer Giorgio Moroder).

By 1973, disco was noted as a new trend in *Billboard* and *Rolling Stone* magazines. The next year, *Billboard* began printing DJ playlists, while New York radio station WPIX was the first to air a Saturday night "disco"/dance music show. Soon thereafter, WBLS integrated disco hits into its playlist and forced competing stations to follow suit.[19] Disco historian Brian Chin notes the role of television in popularizing this new genre:

> The TV show *Soul Train* provided immediate national exposure for records and instantly broadcast new dance styles all over the country. And disco-goers who didn't hear enough of the music on the radio, bought tens of thousands of records in the New York area alone, forcing labels to pay attention to records they'd been ignoring.[20] ... The year 1974 was the watershed for disco's above-ground emergence: a string of #1 pop hits put the industry on notice that clubs were discovering records that would make the whole country dance.[21]

The gay-oriented magazine *The Advocate* proclaimed 1975 as "the year of disco." Both RCA and Capitol Records now had disco departments, while Atlantic and Polydor Records developed disco-specific promotion techniques. In 1976, due to popular demand, the disco show on New York's WPIX went nightly. That year, *Billboard* hosted its first disco convention at the Roosevelt Hotel in Manhattan. Independent promotion companies devoted to disco product began to emerge in New York, as did West End Records and Casablanca Records, the latter releasing hugely popular records by the Village People and Donna Summer.

In 1975, disco music began to be issued in a new format, the 12-inch single. This "DJ-friendly" medium established the DJ as remixer who, through rearranging, editing, and eventually rerecording dance music versions for club play, became an important marketing tool for record companies eager to profit from the disco boom. In the process, discothèques became test labs for new dance music. Through DJ collectives known as "record pools," advance copies of a record were given to DJs before their commercial release to test audience responses on the dance floor. A famous example is the sixteen-minute version of Donna Summer's "Love to Love You Baby" (1975), crafted by Giorgio Moroder from an earlier six-minute prototype, which helped establish Summer's reputation as "Queen of Disco."

Disco's most profitable commercial venture was the November 1977 release of the film (and its best-selling soundtrack) *Saturday Night Fever*, produced by Robert Stigwood and featuring John Travolta and the music of a British/Australian pop trio, the Bee Gees. Many core disco aficionados dismissed the film and its soundtrack altogether as a cleverly executed business venture, a reflection perhaps of the fact that *Saturday Night Fever*, although filmed on location in Manhattan and Brooklyn and featuring local veteran DJ Monty Rock III, was by no means intended as a documentary of the local dance scene. Indeed, the film gives a skewed picture of disco dancing in musical, social, and sexual terms, since John Travolta's character and the Bee Gees are neither gay nor of African descent. Comparable to the dance crazes associated with 1930s swing and 1950s rock and roll (both African American dance/music styles that gained American mainstream acceptance only after their popularization by non-African American performers such as Benny Goodman and Elvis Presley, respectively), disco's popular success came at the price of obscuring its sociocultural origins. Nonetheless, *Saturday Night Fever* made a lasting impression on American audiences and confirmed New York's reputation as the capital of disco. By the mid-1970s, disco had become not only a multi-million dollar industry, but also the most prominent symbol of African American dance styles and of a newly defined sense of community among gays in the United States.

THE DISCO BACKLASH

The economic success of disco as America's most important mass sound of the 1970s helped to amplify the opprobrium of the mainstream rock/pop establishment, based to some degree on the association of disco with male homosexuality and ethnic minorities, but also on the fact that the music market became flooded with recordings of substandard quality. While some, notably British, rock musicians jumped on the economic disco bandwagon (for example, the Rolling Stones' "Miss You," 1978; Rod Stewart's "Do Ya Think I'm Sexy?," 1978; and Queen's "Another One Bites the Dust," 1980), some American rock fans joined efforts in organized attempts to combat disco fever.

On July 12, 1979, at a time when *Rolling Stone* magazine regularly published advertisements for "Disco Sucks" T-shirts, Chicago rock radio DJ Steve Dahl organized a public burning of hundreds of disco records inside Comiskey Park stadium to the chant of thousands: "Disco sucks!" In the words of disco producer Giorgio Moroder, however:

> disco killed itself . . . too many products, too many people, too many records jumping on this kind of music. A lot of bad records came out. I guess it was overkill. Everybody started to come out with disco and it became . . . what's the word? A cussword.[22]

In the early 1980s, the term "disco" rather quickly disappeared from media discourse and public life. The recording industry, chiefly through *Billboard* magazine, replaced disco with the more neutral term "dance music." Marketing subcategories include DOR (dance-oriented rock) and hi-NRG, a term used for up-tempo disco music of the early and mid-1980s that appealed mainly to non-African American gays, especially in Britain but also elsewhere in Europe and Asia.

CLUB MUSIC

While disco's original urban core clientele remained committed to disco, funk, and soul records, the attention of America's mainstream media and their audiences was increasingly caught by punk and new wave acts, and, from the mid-1980s onwards, by rap music. According to Brian Chin, "Disco had come full circle, from being ignored to being acknowledged to ignored by the industry again—all the while selling plenty of records to people who still liked to dance on weekends."[23]

Discothèques became increasingly referred to as clubs, and disco music was subsequently renamed **club**, underground music, or simply dance music. As an abbreviation, "club" eventually came to stand for the venue as much as the music, just as disco had before. The stylistic flexibility of this period is reflected in the eclectic repertoire of influential club DJs such as Afrika Bambaataa, who developed followings both in community centers in the Bronx and at the Mudd Club in downtown Manhattan. While his 1982 single "Planet Rock," a reworking of Kraftwerk's 1977 "Trans-Europe Express," enlarged audiences for rap and electro-funk, his downtown colleague Larry Levan (Figure 15.1), residing at the Paradise Garage, became the most influential club DJ in New York. With a wide-ranging repertoire, Levan was known to utilize everything from Philly-soul (e.g., "Doctor Love" by First Choice, 1977), to German electronic music (e.g., Manuel Göttsching's "E2-E4," 1984), to Caribbean pop (e.g., Eddy Grant's "Time Warp," 1982), to songs by

Club music
Music produced for and promoted at dance clubs during and after the disco era. DJs typically play a broad range of music, assembling material from various musical styles.

Figure 15.1
The late Larry Levan in the DJ booth at The Choice, New York City, 1989. Tina Paul, reproduced with permission.

the Who ("Eminence Front," 1982), the Clash ("Magnificent Dance," 1981), and Marianne Faithfull ("Why D'Ya Do It," 1979). Levan's musical eclecticism and his command of a superior sound system were contributing factors to the Paradise Garage being voted "Most Favorite Disco" at a record industry convention in 1979, making it an underground dance venue with a long-lived national and international reputation.

Levan was given the nickname "the father" by his disciples among New York's growing DJ circles. Club dancers in New York City, the erstwhile capital of disco, now distinguished between club music, party music (an early term for rap music), freestyle (a syncopated pop–dance hybrid aimed mainly at Latinos), electro-funk (programmed by both rap and club DJs such as Afrika Bambaataa and Jellybean Benitez), and house music (made popular first in Chicago by DJs such as Ron Hardy and Frankie Knuckles, Larry Levan's childhood friend).

HOUSE

House music
A style of electronic music originating in gay Black clubs in Chicago in the 1980s.

House music is generally viewed as the electronic offspring of disco music. As with disco and club music, the name refers to a location first and to stylistic traits second. House is originally the abbreviation of the Warehouse, an influential Chicago dance venue where a Bronx-bred DJ, Frankie Knuckles (Figure 15.2), took residence in 1977. Knuckles was referred to the Chicago club by his friend and mentor Larry Levan, who had declined an offer to relocate there from Paradise Garage in New York.

A second definition of "house" focuses on its production. Unlike disco, which was produced in professional recording studios, house

Figure 15.2
Frankie Knuckles at
the Dan Hartman
Memorial Party at
Sound Factory Bar,
New York City, May 5,
1994. Tina Paul,
reproduced with
permission.

music began as homespun music. This points to changes in music technology associated with the emerging home recording industry that blurred the line between the recording technology of the recording studio and the playback technology of the DJ booth. Accordingly, early house records often have a raw, amateurish sound. In addition, the singer, so central in much disco music, is often replaced with spoken words or dispensed with altogether.

Whereas the typical North American disco production involved studio musicians, studio technology, and professional production standards, house music pioneers such as Frankie Knuckles, Farley "Jackmaster" Funk, Chip E., Jesse Saunders, Steve "Silk" Hurley, DJ Pierre, Marshall Jefferson, and Larry Heard were influenced by the rapidly evolving home recording studio market with the analog synthesizer at its center. Corresponding musical influences were the synthesized sounds of American musician Patrick Cowley and of Italo Disco, but also music by other European musicians relying heavily on electronics, such as Kraftwerk, Manuel Göttsching, Telex, or Gary Numan. This emphasis on electronic technology and sounds that had recently become available and accessible with the establishment of MIDI standards and the affordability of home recording equipment (including synthesizers, samplers, drum machines, and sequencers) resulted in the recognizable sound of house music, characterized by the use of initially exclusively analog and, later, more costly digital electronic equipment. Larry Heard's "Can You Feel It?," Marshall Jefferson's "Move Your Body (The House Music Anthem)," (Track 38) and Master C & J's "Face It" (all released in 1986 on Chicago independent labels, the first two on Trax and the third on State Street) exemplify how the efficiency of Japanese music technology, combined

 38

"Move Your Body."

with a European "minimalist" approach set a new standard for US-American dance music production.

While early Chicago house records such as these evidence a relatively rough and unpolished sound conditioned by the do-it-yourself approach of their producers, home recording technology eventually helped house DJs to become producers, remixers, and recording artists in their own right. In the 1990s, Frankie Knuckles became one of the highest-paid remixers and one of the first DJs to receive a major label contract as a recording artist (with Virgin, a British label); in 1997, he received the first Grammy award for Best Remix, a newly established award category. In 2004, Chicago Mayor Richard M. Daley, along with the support of then-Senator Barack Obama, officially declared August 26 "Frankie Knuckles Day." The street where the Warehouse once stood became renamed "Frankie Knuckles Way."

Chicago clubs such as the Warehouse, the Powerplant, and the Music Box were as important to the initial exposure of house as were radio shows on WGCI and WBMX by the Hot Mix 5, a multi-ethnic disc jockey collective formed in 1981 by Kenny Jason and Farley Keith Williams (a.k.a. Farley "Jackmaster" Funk). Like their club-based colleagues Frankie Knuckles and Ron Hardy, these DJs mixed and produced music on 12-inch singles that were released by local independent recording companies, primarily Larry Sherman's Precision and Trax labels and Rocky Jones's DJ International company.

In the late 1980s, as house gradually branched out to other urban dance scenes, several subcategories emerged, including acid house, deep house, hip house, and, even later, garage and speed garage. The latter two terms, more current among British than American DJs and dancers, refer to the Paradise Garage, acknowledging the influence of New York club music produced after Paradise Garage closed in 1987. Since then, the economic center for house has shifted from the United States to London, where acid house, during the 1990s, turned into rave and **techno** music in the hands of British DJ/producers such as Jazzy M, Babyford, CJ Mackintosh, Paul Oakenfold, and Danny Rampling. Under the name "techno," European derivations of techno (a spin-off of Chicago house associated with African American DJs/producers working in Detroit; see Chapter 16) and British acid house have since become the soundscape in dance clubs across Europe and beyond. Because of its emphasis on instrumental timbres and textures, house music has been labeled the "current lingua franca" among European youth.[24] As a marketing term, house has fared less well than disco, with most music industry and media outlets preferring other names, such as "dance music" and "electronica." Derivations of house music (and of its Detroit-based cousin techno), such as garage, speedgarage, drum & bass, grime, Eurobeat, trance, minimal, electro, and tech-house, have also gained currency in the United States, but more so in Europe and Asia.

Techno
A form of dance music that emerged in Detroit in the early to mid-1980s that primarily features electronic instruments, including drum machines, multi-track mixers, computers, and samplers.

SUMMARY

The disco phenomenon of the 1970s is intimately tied to New York City as a geographic point that long has functioned as a center of the national music industry. In the most general sense, disco is the result of a meeting of African American cultural forms, chiefly music and dance, with an (initially) New York-specific social phenomenon now known as the gay community. By redefining urban spaces and institutions such as social clubs, bars, and discothèques, African American cultural content was poured into the vessel of a newly formulated sociopolitical agenda. This process was driven by a shared sense of marginalization among African Americans, Latinos, gays, and, to some extent, artists and women.

In hindsight, New York City turned out to be the laboratory for a relatively successful sociocultural experiment. What was pioneered in the Big Apple proved economically viable across the country and beyond, turning disco from an underground phenomenon into more than a national dance craze. Its eventual demise and reinvention as dance music and club music and, later, its transformation into rap and house music, point to the continuation of African American sensibilities in the development of American social dancing. These sensibilities make possible a conceptual link between the musical and presentational styles of 1970s artists such as LaBelle or Sylvester, of 1980s artists such as Michael Jackson or Madonna, and of new-millennium pop stars such as Timberland, Lady Gaga, or David Guetta.

KEY NAMES

Francis Grasso

Frankie Knuckles

Larry Levan

QUESTIONS

1. Describe the similarities and differences between disco and house music.

2. When and where did disco and house first develop? What was the role of race and gender in their evolution?

3. Although disco was shaped by those of various racial and ethnic backgrounds, this genre nonetheless reflects characteristics consonant with African American musical values and practice. Provide evidence that supports or contradicts this point of view.

4. What factors prompted the backlash against disco in the United States? What were the consequences of this negative response?

PROJECTS

1. Compare three recordings of disco produced by Philadelphia International in the 1970s with three European-produced recordings of Donna Summer, Village People, or Silver Convention. In what ways are these recordings similar yet distinct?

2. Write a critique of the film *Saturday Night Fever* (1977) that contrasts its depiction of disco music and dance with the fact-based history of the genre. What are the implications of your findings?

3. Compare a disco recording with a disco remix as house, hip-house, drum & bass, speedgarage, etc. What is the impact of technology on the production of both recording?

4. Research the history of an African American social dance style that has widely influenced twentieth-century America. How is this dance style similar to yet different from disco dancing?

NOTES

Please see the discography for information on resources for further listening.

1. Goldman 1978, 23–29.
2. Ibid., 29–40.
3. Joe 1980, 20; and Sukenick 1987, 165–66. Both authors discuss the Electric Circus and its role as an early form of discothèque.
4. Carroll 1994. Accessed from www.jessecc.com/index3.html, 2002 (site discontinued).
5. Hogan and Hudson 1998, 170.
6. Clendinen and Nagourney 1999, 25.
7. Ibid., 76.
8. Ibid.; see also Hughes 1994, 147–57.
9. Thomas 1995, 437–46.
10. Frith 1981, 128; Tucker 1986, 467–624; Straw 1990, 122; and Hughes 1994.
11. Hogan and Hudson 1998, 171. The authors also note one incident when members of the gay organization Black and White Men Together began holding weekly demonstrations outside the Ice Palace, a popular Manhattan disco, to protest the club's allegedly racist door policies (655).
12. Boykin 1996, 215.
13. Krasnow 1993, 41.
14. Tucker 1986, 524.
15. Generally, the American mainstream media were slow to recognize the DJ as a new type of pop star. *The New York Times*, for example, belatedly misidentified the hip-hop DJ as a new pop star in the early 1990s. See Dery 1991.
16. Ward 1998, 428.
17. Carroll 1994. See also Hughes 1994 for a discussion of the link of African American music to gay sensibilities.
18. Joe 1980, 21.
19. Chin 1999.
20. For example, in 1974 the Hues Corporation's "Rock the Boat" sold fifty thousand copies in New York City alone, due mainly to club exposure (Chin 1999).
21. Ibid.
22. As quoted in Haden-Guest 1997, 150. See also Braunstein 1998, 54–55, 58.
23. Chin 1999.
24. Gilroy 1993.

CHAPTER 16

Detroit Techno

Denise Dalphond

Techno is a form of electronic music produced using a wide range of analog electronic and computer-based digital instruments and software. It originated in Detroit in the early 1980s and is linked to a broader history of the city's funky, danceable electronic music culture.[1] Techno, **house**, and electro are the primary forms of electronic music in Detroit, and are not typically identified as African American on a national and global scale. Electronic music emerged among African Americans in Detroit during the 1970s and 1980s, grew immensely in popularity during the late 1980s in Europe, and partially transformed into a suburban, White **rave** culture in Detroit and the Midwest during the 1990s. In the 2000s, electronic music culture in Detroit thrives in ethnic and sonic diversity.

Detroit techno is characterized by percussive rhythms typically in common time (4/4) with tempos ranging from 120 to 150 beats per minute (bpm). There is an emphasis on polyrhythm, infusing a funkiness that is a distinctive quality of Detroit electronic music. Complex layering of rhythm patterns and emphasis on the back beat (or the second and fourth beats of each measure) is more typical of techno music produced by Detroit artists, and less commonly heard from European techno producers. These musical characteristics are typical of many forms of African American music. Detroit's musical history with Motown, disco, Black clubs, and Black radio ensures that musical aesthetics typically heard in African American music will undoubtedly be audible in techno.[2] Detroit techno is closely related to other forms of electronic music, such as Chicago house music, which is characterized by slightly slower tempos, a kick drum emphasizing each beat of the 4/4 meter (typically referred to as four-on-the-floor), and a greater propensity for melodies and female

Techno
A form of dance music that emerged in Detroit in the early to mid-1980s that primarily features electronic instruments, including drum machines, multi-track mixers, computers, and samplers.

House music
A style of electronic music originating in gay Black clubs in Chicago in the 1980s.

Rave
A large-scale, all-night party featuring electronic dance music, primarily house and techno.

vocals. However, the presence of melody is also common in Detroit techno. Vocals are less common in techno, but when utilized, they are more percussive, almost robotic, and generally male.

Cultural diversity and sonic eclecticism are foundational concepts in the ever-changing, complex culture of electronic music in Detroit. The early history of electronic music in Detroit, from the early 1970s to the early 1980s, is centered around African American, **bohemian**, middle-class, high-school, and college-age youth from primarily the Northwest neighborhoods of Detroit. This culture began from a foundation of local Black radio, disco music in the city, house parties, **cabaret** gatherings, and night clubs. Radio and dance clubs in Detroit in the 1970s brought a deep appreciation for musical eclecticism to Detroit listeners, a profound impact still felt today. Middle-class wealth gave these young women and men the comfort and confidence to look beyond Detroit with bohemian ideologies toward European disco music, known as Italo disco, and Italian fashion and language. They could actually acquire expensive Italian clothing and music, and use the language in the dance music culture they were creating and negotiating.[3] Some young entrepreneurs formed party promotion clubs, giving them names such as Giavante and Charivari, and would host parties in nightclubs and halls around Detroit. This youthful dance music culture rooted itself in Detroit, looking forward to decades of innovative, eclectic, and experimental electronic music production using analog electronic equipment and new wave, science-fiction ideologies.

In the early 1980s, the eclecticism heard on the radio and on the decks in dance clubs nurtured a vibrant culture founded on intellectual and philosophical approaches to music making and sharing. Also developing at this time was an independent creative aesthetic, and a strong emphasis on mentoring. It is around this time that Detroit electronic musicians began producing and releasing their own music on vinyl. Many also formed DJ crews in high school or when they returned from college in the summers, such as Deep Space and Direct Drive.[4] Electronic music of the early 1980s expanded from its early Detroit inceptions to a complex of exceedingly diverse musical and cultural influences. Electronic musicians in Detroit drew influences from electro-funk, early hip-hop, German **krautrock**, Japanese electronic music, American and British new wave music and electronic art music, dance music known as garage from New York City, and seemingly arbitrary songs such as "Rock Lobster" by the B-52s, which, according to DJ/producer Mike Banks, had the power to tame gang violence in Detroit: "You can't be too much of a tough guy while doing the rock lobster."[5]

The release of two tracks in 1981 mark the start of Detroit's electronic music history. The tracks "Alleys of Your Mind" by Cybotron (Juan Atkins and Richard Davis) and "Sharevari" by the group called A Number of Names (Sterling Jones, Paul Lesley, and Roderick Simpson) capture the experimental and innovative musical culture that had been developing in the late 1970s in Detroit. Cybotron reveals the percussive, electronic

Bohemian
A person who lives and acts without regard for conventional rules and practices.

Cabaret
In Detroit, a type of social gathering usually associated with a community of unionized workers or other socially specific group. DJs perform at these gatherings, and attendees dress in formal clothing, dance, eat, and drink.

Krautrock
Electronic music played by European groups of the 1980s, particularly German groups such as Kraftwerk, which featured heavy use of drum machines.

Denise Dalphond

funk that was influential to many musicians in Detroit and Chicago; and A Number of Names captures the Italo disco sounds and ideas stirring up Detroit. After these releases, Juan Atkins joined creative forces with Derrick May, Kevin Saunderson, and Eddie Fowlkes, now known as the founders of techno, to form notable record labels. Distribution networks in the mid- to late 1980s included artists themselves transporting records to Chicago by car, as well as independent distributors with national or global reach. With the establishment of Planet E Communications by Carl Craig in 1991 and Submerge Distribution by Mike Banks and Christa Weatherspoon in 1992, Detroit record labels gained consistent, reliable distribution. These groups' productions of diverse electronic sounds circulated around the world, and laid the path for many local musicians to produce and distribute music independently.

By the late 1980s, Detroit and Chicago had become important centers of African American electronic music production and partying.[6] During this period, electronic music quickly took hold in England and around Europe and became associated with raves. By 1990, Detroit's African American electronic music culture had paired with European rave culture to impact young, middle-class, suburban Whites in metropolitan Detroit, and also around the Midwest. This marked the beginning of a thriving, powerful rave scene in this region. An ethnically diverse community of entrepreneurial youth from Detroit and its suburbs hosted thousands of raves from the late 1980s through the 1990s in various clubs and halls, and in illegally obtained warehouses. Initially, excessive and widespread drug use was a characteristic of neither electronic music nor rave culture in Detroit. However, as raves grew in popularity in the Midwest, they became synonymous with drug use.

In some ways, the transition from an African American electronic music culture to a vibrant rave scene had a negative impact on Detroit's African American crews and crowds. Cornelius Harris, local musician, writer, and label manager for the Submerge recording and distribution company, discusses the strategic locations of raves during the late 1980s and 1990s in Detroit: "There was . . . this safari element to it where it was the sense that these were privileged white kids coming into the city to experience the dangerous Black folks."[7] However, Detroit's rave scene was not devoid of ethnic diversity. In the 1990s, African Americans continued to be consumers and entrepreneurs of electronic music, including rave culture. Many of Detroit's legendary Black DJs and producers played raves in Detroit and around the Midwest. While crowds at Detroit raves primarily consisted of White youth from outside the city, African American youth from Detroit and the suburbs, as well as Latino and Asian American young men and women, regularly frequented raves in and around Detroit. The legacy of diversity in Detroit electronic music continued through the 1990s and initiated a successful foundation for Black and White promoters, producers, and DJs, some of whom remain active in Detroit in the 2000s, producing music and parties.

During the 1990s, the older Black electronic music scene did not disappear. It was partially transformed into a more racially defined and politically voiced cultural context by seminal artists such as Theo Parrish (Figure 16.1) and Kenny Dixon Jr. Institutions such as Submerge,[8] a collection of local record labels as well as a distribution company that promotes awareness of political and social oppression through music, also played an important role in this transformation. The productions of

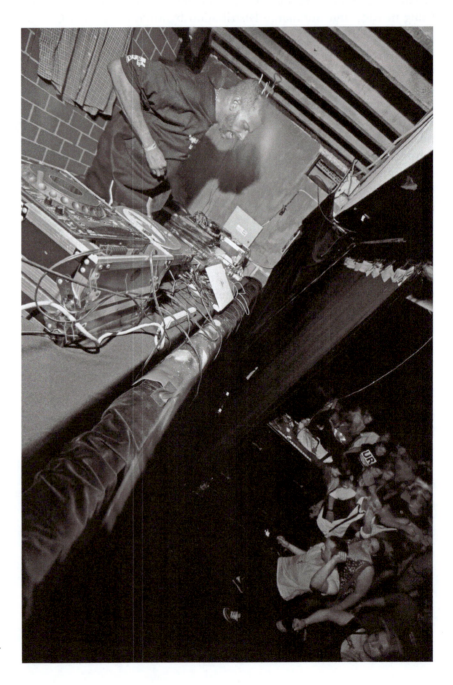

Figure 16.1
Theo Parrish.
Courtesy of James M.
Rotz.

Denise Dalphond

Parrish and Dixon Jr. emphasize African and African American culture in visual, verbal, and aural ways. Parrish has worn dreadlocks and Dixon often styles his hair in an afro; both include images of themselves and their African American and Native American family members on their vinyl record jackets and CD liner notes. Both artists explicitly and publicly contend that all music originated in Africa. Both employ complex polyrhythms and distorted sonic textures, and include sonic references to house and disco music of African Americans in their compositions and DJ sets. In the 1990s, there existed a simultaneous separation and permeable overlap between the older Detroit electronic music culture, and the younger rave culture.

In 2000, raves around the United States and Canada became a much smaller and more legitimized cultural practice due to controls imposed by municipalities and police. Detroit electronic music gradually left the previous decade of underground rave youth culture and entered a period of large-scale performances to international audiences in Detroit. The first Detroit Electronic Music Festival occurred in Hart Plaza on Memorial Day weekend in May 2000. DJ/producer Carl Craig led the first two years of this festival as Artistic Director. Also involved in the organization of the festival were people closely connected to Detroit's rave culture as event planners and promoters. The festival continues annually under different organizers and names, and continues to draw strong connections between Detroit's various electronic music scenes.[9] There is widespread debate on the success rate of these bridge-building efforts; however, there is enduring potential for musical and cultural "worlds to collide" each May in Detroit.[10]

The multi-sited and historic formations of electronic music culture in the city of Detroit aided the creation of a dynamic, Detroit-specific cultural expression. Detroit's electronic music culture is not stagnant; it is ever-changing and is contingent on time and space in a diverse array of forms. The negotiation of eclecticism in genre, and diversity in identity formation in both individual and collective contexts, are concepts that are essential to understanding Detroit and its electronic music culture.

DEFINITIONS AND INTERROGATING THE CONCEPT OF GENRE

Defining genres of music is always a tricky practice fraught with complexities and contingencies that simultaneously include and exclude related musical genres, or styles. Franco Fabbri defines musical genre as "a set of musical events (real or possible) whose course is governed by a definite set of socially accepted rules."[11] Other scholars have emphasized cultural context and contingency in the development and negotiation of musical genres.[12] These concepts of broadness and a connection to cultural practice and communication are central to an understanding of Detroit electronic music.

For many, electronic music is a type of music that defies definitions and categorization. Musicians in Detroit interpret and even reject genre in fascinating ways. Many Detroit DJs and producers are critical of the concept of genre as a restrictive, divisive, boundary-forming entity. Theo Parrish, producer and DJ, respects genres as useful historical references, but feels strongly that they do not effectively describe any type of contemporary DJ performance or production.[13] Mike Clark, producer and DJ, describes the similarities between techno and house music in the early days of electronic music in Detroit and Chicago:

> Even though [house and techno] were technically the same as far as sound usage, . . . it wasn't until later on when other people discovered what we were doing, they started generalizing these sounds and saying, okay, well, if Chicago made house, then this is what house sounds like. And if Detroit made techno, then this is what Detroit techno is supposed to sound like. Now technically, I'll say it again, it was the exact same thing.[14]

Carlos Souffront, often described as a DJ's DJ, a librarian of wax, explores the various trajectories of genre in Detroit:

> I just call it all techno . . . In Detroit . . . it was basically just house, techno, hip-hop, that's it, electro . . . Genre splitting has led to . . . some kind of cultural segregation, and some kind of sub-cultural segregation, . . . in some ways it was good, they can all celebrate music that turns them on, but in some ways it's bad because there's no space for everyone to come together and really kind of mix it up.[15]

The supposedly discrete boundaries that genres are built upon are eternally permeable and overlapping. Genre is primarily useful as an organizational category for music industries around the world. For artists and fans, genre often excludes and exasperates. At the same time, it is a primary tool that most people, whether fans, consumers, producers, writers, or music industry employees, use willingly to discuss, compare, and share music. Many times in my interviews with producers, DJs, promoters, and dancers in Detroit, my research consultant would explain the reasons why genre is a useless concept, and then we would inevitably begin to use genre categories when discussing another topic.

While resisting codification, this music is built on a foundation of specificity, categorization, and intensive cataloging of data. This conflicted philosophy of genre exists in concrete ways in Detroit. Extensive attention to detail and categorization is an essential element in electronic and dance music culture. Much like the stereotypically "masculine" ideologies and practices surrounding cars, comic books, or science fiction, intensive cataloging in the form of discographies, record collections, electronic production and performance equipment, and the varying ability to hold such extensive information in one's head available for immediate recall, are essential to electronic music cultures on both global and local scales. Erika Sherman, of the Detroit group Ectomorph, explains this tendency and her relationship to it as a woman:

I've always been into dude stuff, like computers and technology and gear . . . And I was definitely intimidated by the record store when I was younger the same way that when I was 8 I was intimidated by the comic book store, . . . they don't want to share anything with you . . . There's this tendency of men to be collectors . . . or having the dictionary kind of mentality about records and record collecting . . . I don't always know the names of everything because that's just not how I remember it. I remember what my records look like, and I remember what they sound like.[16]

Sherman, a highly competent and respected musician, demonstrates the contingency of genre on identity and personal creative tendencies. The boundaries are not precisely defined, nor are they consistently or universally negotiated.

Genre development has a strong history in Detroit's electronic music culture. Prior to the late 1980s, funky electronic music produced by Detroit artists was not called techno. If it was called anything, the common descriptive word was progressive. Key producers Juan Atkins, Derrick May, Kevin Saunderson, and Eddie Fowlkes in Detroit began using the term techno on occasion to describe the music they were creating in the mid-1980s. One piece in particular, "Strings of Life" by Rhythim is Rhythim (a.k.a. Derrick May), released in 1987, quickly became an anthem of Detroit techno, both in Detroit and internationally, in the late 1980s (Track 10). May's percussive and melodic use of string and keyboard sounds evident in "Strings of Life" was relatively new and exciting in electronic music at the time, and continues to be influential today.

 10

"Strings of Life."

The term techno and many other intellectual concepts that these early producers had in mind originated from futurist Alvin Toffler's book *The Third Wave*. In this work, Toffler constructs a concept of "techno rebels," which author Dan Sicko applies to producers and consumers of techno in Detroit. According to Sicko, this concept encompasses:

people who are cautious of new, powerful technologies and want to temper the breakneck pace of technological advancement . . . techno's underlying philosophy has less to do with futurism, as is commonly believed, than with the power of the individual and personal visions of Utopia.[17]

The precise moment that electronic music from Detroit, void of any marketable genre name, became techno came in the late 1980s when record collector Neil Rushton (described as a skilled hustler by a few Detroiters) visited Chicago and Detroit. He, with the help of Derrick May, compiled a collection of music by seminal Detroit electronic musicians. This CD, titled *Techno: The New Dance Sound of Detroit*, was released in 1988 in the United Kingdom. It was on this release that the word *techno* was officially affixed to electronic music in Detroit. With this compilation, a particular style of electronically produced music became explicitly associated with Detroit, allowing little room for variation. The music now labeled as Detroit techno produced in Detroit in the early 1980s, was associated with a stripped-down, mechanical, hard, cold, and fast, yet funky style of music. It was often compared to music that might be made by machines in a science-fiction fantasy. Often, listeners associated this music with being soulless or inhuman, computer or machine music.

Around this time, Chicago house music was also entering a codified, strictly defined realm of popularity. For some listeners, it had a more human, soulful, grounded sound, although, as clearly expressed by Mike Clark above, the distinctions between house and techno of the 1980s are minimal. The overlap and permeability of the genres of techno and house music are much more extensive than is commonly acknowledged. However, consumers, music critics, and record industry representatives, primarily from Europe, tended to categorize techno music and electronic music from Detroit in general as post-soul and, perhaps more pervasively, inhuman.[18] Techno became characterized by a machine-powered invisibility.

Detroit's history with cars and factories and, beginning in the late 1960s, with extreme poverty, debilitating racism, and a gradual exodus of White people and wealth, fuels this association with machines and invisibility. Race and class are inherently bound up with the reception of Detroit electronic music both outside and inside Detroit, perpetuating ideas of a city and culture so debilitated by extreme violence and poverty, and dominated by machines, that it could only truly exist in science fiction or fantasy. The Detroit that actually exists of the 1970s, 1980s, 1990s, and 2000s is an ever-changing complex of urban, suburban, and even rural environments, and is filled with people who care deeply about the civic well-being of the city and its residents.

BLACK CULTURE AND MUSICAL INSTITUTIONS IN DETROIT'S EARLY ELECTRONIC MUSIC CULTURE

The idea that a genre of music can belong to a particularly defined group of people is a complex element of Detroit's electronic music culture. The complexity arises with the acknowledgment that genre is an ephemeral concept maintained and negotiated by people. Genre is not simply an object in its own right that accomplishes divisions and categorization void of human control. Considering the ownership of a musical genre cannot simply mean scooping up a genre not typically framed as African American and relabeling it as such—contributing yet one more notch in the Black music canon. The complexity of this idea of ownership is staggering when considered in the context of Detroit. The population of Detroit proper according to the US census was 82 percent Black in 2000, and has been consistently majority Black for nearly half a century.[19]

The general consensus by Detroit producers and DJs is that the origins of techno, broadly defined, are in African American culture. The first people to make Detroit electronic music were Black, it was influenced by Detroit's version of Black radio, and it was celebrated by Black crowds at cabarets, gay and straight clubs, block parties, and basement parties in Black neighborhoods and homes, and at Black high-school dances and parties in and around Detroit. When asked whether he thought Detroit electronic music originated in African American culture, Mike Banks replied, "I don't recall any other people in Detroit during the late '70s and early '80s creating or dancing to this type of music other than Black people."[20] This historically and spatially specific point of origin for Detroit electronic music is widely accepted. However, when one looks further into the past or into the future from this brief time period, identity wreaks havoc on this simple image of a Black Detroit techno scene.

Urban, underground dance music scenes began to emerge during the early to mid-1970s in many American cities. Progressive music was the title given to electronic music in Detroit before techno, house, or electro existed as genre names. Progressive refers to funky, danceable, electronically produced music, with or without vocals, made for DJs and dance clubs, often for gay dance clubs. Detroit's Black underground dance music culture of the 1970s was primarily a thriving gay club scene for both men and women. At this time, disco and progressive music came through Detroit in the hands of Ken Collier, a legendary African American DJ who is famed for his nights at a club called Heaven.

Ken Collier and Heaven were significant to the early development of electronic music in Detroit. Collier, often described as a significant mentor to many Detroit DJs and producers, participated in a record pool for local DJs, and through that network he recommended and shared important music. He encouraged local DJs and budding producers in the 1970s and early 1980s to travel to New York City and Chicago to experience the music and intense energy of clubs such as the Paradise Garage in New York, and the Musicbox and The Warehouse in Chicago. Detroiters who benefited from his mentoring include Delano Smith, John Collins, Kelli Hand, Felton Howard, Alan Ester, Stacey "Hotwaxx" Hale, and Duane "In the Mix" Bradley.[21]

People who attended Heaven have described it as nothing they had ever seen, heard, or felt prior or since. The club was typically filled with Black gay men who would dance all night until daylight, competitively and aggressively, just for fun. The remarkably diverse and welcoming atmosphere of Heaven also included Black women, as well as Latino and White women and men, and anyone else who found their way there. A primary tenet in Detroit's music culture is a strong belief in the power and universality of music. According to this pervasive philosophy, music can communicate an eternal embrace to anyone, regardless of one's identity. This principle represented the ideology of underground dance music in the 1970s, and it characterizes contemporary Detroit as well. This is not to say that an idealized universal acceptance is always generated in Detroit, but the ideology is pervasive and meaningful.

In addition to Ken Collier and Heaven, a second significant element in the history of Detroit electronic music is radio. Charles "Electrifying Mojo" Johnson and Jeff Mills as the Wizard are significant figures in

Detroit radio of the late 1970s, 1980s, and early 1990s. As described by producer Todd Osborn, Mojo impacted Detroit with his multi-genre, eclectic approach to musical selection and sharing; and the Wizard impacted Detroit with his technically precise and impossibly fast mixing style.[22]

The Electrifying Mojo's radio shows on a variety of different stations in Detroit and Ann Arbor inspired millions of listeners in southeastern Michigan to enjoy music differently, and even to think about their lives and about Detroit differently. Mojo presented a vast range of musical styles to his listeners, playing anything from electro-funk, disco, pop, and hip-hop, to German electronic rock, classical music, rhythm and blues, and rock. Defying radio programming and formatting standards, Mojo transformed the concept of formats into his own "moodmats" based on his approach to radio and musical discovery.[23] While playing the introduction from The Midnight Funk Association, a segment of Mojo's radio program, Todd Osborn explains, "Mojo . . . to hear that stuff on the radio, it's like theater."[24] Using science fiction, fantasy, and political commentary on local and national social events, Mojo communicated with his listeners in powerful ways. He was the first radio DJ to play records by Detroit artists on the air, such as A Number of Names, Juan Atkins, Derrick May, and Kevin Saunderson. Mojo took an unusually eclectic approach to mixing and sharing music, pairing Prince with Beethoven, Kraftwerk, the B-52s, and Parliament. He remains the single most frequently referenced influence among Detroit DJs and producers.

Detroit radio's other figurehead was Jeff Mills as the Wizard. Wizard radio programs are legendary for extremely fast mixing, beat juggling, and scratching. His style was incredibly fast because of his innovative use of recording and playback equipment. Detroit DJ Felton Howard explained:

> [Jeff] would be in a record and before it had a chance to do anything, he would be out of it. So you had all these rhythms, constant . . . It's a bank of records, it's like maybe 5 records . . . in so fast of an order, that you don't know the difference . . . Jeff used to show up at parties with his records not even in the jackets. He'd just grab them, one to another. And Jeff could go through 50 records in 15 minutes . . . And he could keep the people's attention, because he had learned how to program music from the older guys. "I know how to get you and keep you. Okay, you like this record, I'm going to give you that much of that record, I'm going to give you that much of that record . . . and I'm going to keep you going all the way 'til the end of the night. And I can slip records in there that you don't even know, but before you get a chance to walk, I got you with another record."[25]

Mills approached radio DJing in a similar way. He would prepare some pre-recorded segments at home and play them on his radio show using a four-track recorder, while simultaneously using two or three turntables to mix records along with the pre-recorded segments.[26] For many years, listeners did not know Mills was using a four-track recorder and thought they were hearing records mixed only on two turntables. Using a variety of playback equipment allowed Mills to play a set on the air that sounded much faster than was humanly possible.

Ken Collier, Charles Johnson, and Jeff Mills provided the foundations of musical diversity and eclecticism that many Detroit musicians would carry with them and renegotiate in profound and lasting ways for decades to come. Collier provided regular spaces for diverse social groups to come together and party. Mojo and the Wizard imparted sonic eclecticism to complement that coming together.

DIVERSITY AND RAVES: DETROIT IN THE 1990s AND 2000s

Intimately linked to identity, race, and genre in Detroit is the local rave scene that began in the late 1980s, hit its peak in the mid-1990s, and slowly declined in popularity into the 2000s. Large-scale parties in a variety of spaces populated predominantly by young, White, suburban youth coexisted with the electronic music scene that had come before in Detroit. With the release of *Techno: The New Dance Sound of Detroit* in 1988 by Neil Rushton and Ten Records in the UK came the development of a spirited rave scene in England. Beginning in the late 1980s in Manchester, and later London, raves, also referred to as acid house parties, grew from crowds of a thousand to crowds of twenty-five thousand in warehouses and clubs.[27]

Acid house refers to the type of music played at these parties. It is a type of house music created by Chicago musicians using a Roland TR-303 drum machine, which is capable of producing the characteristic acid house "squelch" sound.[28] Most of the music played at acid house parties originated from African American and Latino electronic music producers in Chicago, Detroit, and New York City. It did not take long for youth in the United States to notice this British rave culture and attempt to reproduce it in their own communities. The British reinvention of Black American techno and house music quickly became a thriving part of youth culture in the United States as American club promoters and DJs in the Midwest, New York, and California began to host their own raves in 1989–90.

Richie Hawtin, a producer and DJ from Windsor, Ontario, Canada, across the river from Detroit, was a primary figure to introduce raves to Detroit. However, there were many other African American, Asian American, and White musicians and promoters who helped fill most Detroit weekends with large-scale electronic music events. People such as Terrence Parker, Buzz Goree, Kelli Hand, DJ Minx, Mike Huckaby (Figure 16.2), Claude Young, D. Wynn, and Anthony "Shake" Shakir, all African American producers from Detroit, enjoyed cult status as popular rave DJs, both in Detroit and around the Midwest.[29] "Roaming," released by Anthony "Shake" Shakir on a 12-inch titled *Tracks For My Father*, displays Shakir's unique skills with sampling, drum breaks, and breaking up and layering complex, percussive rhythms (Track 39). Shake, relatively

Figure 16.2
Mike Huckaby playing
the Detroit Electronic
Music Festival.
Courtesy of James M.
Rotz.

39

"Roaming."

underappreciated and unknown, is widely respected and revered by
Detroit electronic artists as a creative genius with sampling, drum breaks,
and complex rhythms. African American promoters such as Adriel
Thornton (Adriel Fantastique) and Buzz Goree hosted large-scale raves
in Detroit warehouses and clubs, featuring many of these DJs who were
significant to Detroit's African American electronic music history.

By the early 1990s, techno music and raving had become a cultural
experience practiced by primarily young, White, middle-class sub-
urbanites who were likely to go on to college. Crowds at Detroit raves,
while not as diverse as in the 1980s, maintained ethnic diversity with
smaller numbers of African American, Latino, and Asian American
youth. The primary demographic difference between Detroit's rave
culture of the 1990s and the electronic music culture of the 1980s was
racial identity. The faces at raves were much more likely to be Whites
who lived outside the boundaries of the city of Detroit.

Ethnic and racial diversity during this time period in Detroit also
can be explored in depth in the context of a collection of lofts at 1217
Griswold in downtown Detroit. The significance of these lofts to Detroit's
electronic music history rests with the residents who lived there from
about 1990 to 1995, the relationships formed there, and the parties that
were hosted there. Residents at 1217 during those years include John
"Bileebob" Williams, DJ/producer linked with Submerge and local writer/
documenter of Detroit's electronic music scene; Buzz Goree, DJ,
producer, and promoter known for his ability to throw lively parties that
consistently drew widely diverse crowds; Jason Huvaere, now the director
of Paxahau, the company that hosts the annual electronic music festival,
among other events; and Alan Bogel, founding member of VOOM, a key

organization in electronic music in Detroit in the 1990s. Regular visitors included Sam Foitas, another founding member of Paxahau; and Mike Huckaby, seminal DJ/producer and mentor to many through his years of work in the dance room at Record Time, a local record store, and currently as a teacher at YouthVille Detroit, a community center for Detroit youth. Additionally, producer/DJ Blake Baxter lived nearby and owned a record store across the street called Save the Vinyl. Residents of 1217 Griswold, primarily young men, came from diverse ethnic, racial, and class backgrounds. It is at this location and from these relationships that local musicians, entrepreneurs, and consumers continued to negotiate and maintain Detroit's electronic music culture in the 1990s and well into the 2000s.[30]

MASKS AND INVISIBILITY

From the 1970s to the present, as Detroit electronic musicians experienced increasing visibility and popularity around the world, there was a growing tendency among African Americans to conceal and protect their identities, and to elevate the music itself above individual personalities. Detroit radio had a profound effect on identity representation by Detroit musicians. In an interview in the spring of 2010, Detroit DJ/producer Kenny Dixon Jr. spoke at length about identity and image in Detroit electronic music; specifically about Detroit artists tending toward invisibility, or masked identities.[31] He first attributed this tendency to the Electrifying Mojo, who kept his identity hidden. Mojo performed on air and nothing more. He did no live appearances, shows, or parties:

> I never really took pictures. People don't know me facially, which is cool. It wasn't really about my face. I didn't want it to be. I decided that I wanted to be in the earshot of people talking wherever they were. I wanted to hear them. I wanted to get on a bus and hear what people are talking about. I wanted to walk in the crowd and feel the conversation. I wanted to take mental snapshots during the day and night and put them to music—the soundtrack to the images in my mind. The moment they know you, they look at you, they might tell you, they may not. You may have to figure it out. It's so easy being a voice on the radio, a face in the crowd, a figment of the imagination. You could get with a lot of people that you could not have gotten with before.[32]

Mojo's insistence on limited media attention and remaining a faceless voice in Detroit imparted a strong tendency toward privacy and identity protection through the use of literal and figurative masks. There are many electronic musicians in Detroit who have adapted this mask in a variety of creative ways. Some of these are Sherard Ingram (DJ Stingray); Lou Robinson (Trackmaster Lou) of Scan 7; Gerald Donald in his many groups, including Ectomorph, Dopplereffekt, and Drexciya; Kenny Dixon Jr. (Moodymann, Moody); and Mike Banks ("Mad" Mike Banks).

Kenny Dixon Jr. and other Detroit artists keep their identities hidden by masking their faces in performance, and participating very little in any kind of media representation. Dixon Jr. does excruciatingly infrequent interviews. He has been releasing music since the early 1990s, and has done only three interviews to date. His philosophy, like that of Mike Banks, is driven by a desire to share music without any associated personal image. These artists contend that music should be available for people to receive without any attachment to a human image. According to Banks, "We just went faceless, there was no reason for you to know what we look like, you just concentrate more on what the sound was."[33]

Adding to this understanding of invisibility, Kenny Dixon Jr. explained that his reluctance to share his identity, ideas, and experiences also hinges on his daily life growing up in Detroit. As a youth, Dixon Jr. recalls images of White people coming to turn off the gas and the White man coming to take his father to jail. The experience of growing up in Detroit, among a highly corrupt, largely White police force, with very few positive images of White Americans, led Dixon Jr. and many other African American Detroit residents to develop a general suspicion and mistrust of Whites.

Often the culturally established use of literal and figurative masks elicits strong responses from fans and other musicians, ranging from support and understanding to anger and resentment. This strong response often stems from a feeling of exclusion from the music, the artists, and Detroit. Because the artists are not open and embracing of the media world in an immediate and universal way, the response to this perceived distancing is the assumption that the mask is militant and aggressive, even racist—a tactic to keep out outsiders.

The misinterpretation of protection and privacy speaks to major misconceptions of the history of racial identity and racial prejudice in the United States. Detroit artists and fans are not engaged in a widespread campaign to exclude outsiders or to display arrogance and condescension as a general philosophy. Widespread appropriation of Black cultural expression is a commonplace, but rarely interrogated phenomenon. Producer/DJ Brenden M. Gillen explains, "Techno was not going to accept the previous paradigm of the Black man being exploited in music and being taken for a fool."[34] For this reason, many musicians felt a serious need to protect their creativity. In Detroit, this need for protection can be interpreted and negotiated as a need for privacy through invisibility. For many, a mask provides protection from exploitation. This practice of invisibility, paired with independent music production and distribution, and an insistence on placing the music ahead of the musician can be recognized as a strategy for cultural protection and for maintaining ownership over one's artistic creations.

Interestingly, the artists who keep their identities intimate and private in Detroit are those who make significant social and institutional contributions to the city and the people of Detroit. Kenny Dixon Jr. keeps his fame and success close to home, although he allowed himself increasing public visibility in 2010. He has publicly stated that he shares his financial successes with his community by not charging a fee to DJ in Detroit and by contributing in informal financial ways to his neighborhood residents. He also plays at fundraising events in Detroit, such as the annual Belle Isle House Music Picnic, which donates profits to and collects school supplies for area elementary schools. Dixon Jr. also mentors DJs and producers in Detroit. Described by Brendan M. Gillen, as a "capitalist anarchist,"[35] he participates willingly in the money-making aspects of music production, but does so free from formal institutional control.

Mike Banks is another Detroiter who makes fundamental contributions to Detroit on many levels. He mentors many Detroit musicians, assisting them in starting their own record labels through Submerge. He also helps them master and press their records, which he then distributes through his well-established, successful, and reliable global network. Submerge is an essential institution to Detroit's electronic musical culture and to the international presence of this music. Dedication to civic well-being in Detroit is evident among people of all levels of success with music, from those who support themselves completely via music production and performance, to local DJs with full-time day jobs and little to no income from musical releases. It extends to event promoters, management companies, and local fans in Detroit. American studies scholar, Carla Vecchiola, focuses on this issue of civic dedication in Detroit electronic music and in her dissertation explores "the principle commitments of the Detroit electronic music community including loyalty to the city of Detroit, commitment to community development, recognition for previously unappreciated achievements, and respect for the history of the electronic music community."[36]

Related to civic dedication in Detroit is a tendency of those associated with techno to operate independently of corporate guidance or control. Independence is rooted in all aspects of Detroit's cultural economy starting long before Berry Gordy's creation of Motown, and can be seen in contemporary storefronts citywide. There are many locally owned record stores in the Detroit metropolitan area, and also in the nearby towns of Ypsilanti and Ann Arbor.[37] National Sound Corporation (NSC) does mastering locally. Ron Murphy, NSC's owner and sole operator, who passed away in 2008, is a legend in Detroit's music history (Figure 16.3). He is responsible for mastering, with renowned skill, thousands of recordings by local artists since 1966. His lathe and other mastering equipment have been restored by Todd Osborn and Mike Banks at Submerge to ensure the continuing importance of vinyl record production in Detroit. Archer Records, where many electronic music releases from Detroit and outside of Detroit are pressed on to vinyl, is another local institution central to Detroit's electronic music culture. Finally, the city houses a large number of local, independent record labels.

Figure 16.3
Ron Murphy with
lathe. Courtesy of
Angie Linder.

Unfortunately, Detroit continues to be regarded as an empty, abandoned city riddled with violent crime and drug abuse, with little civic, political, economic, or cultural life. Visitors have explained that, even on the weekend of Detroit's Electronic Music Festival, when tens of thousands of people travel to Detroit from all over the world, it is possible to drive for miles and not see a single person. Buildings are empty, even skyscrapers are abandoned.[38] For fans of Detroit electronic music, these kinds of observations lead into a discussion about the creative inspiration that can be drawn from the barren, harsh landscape of Detroit, and the amazing music that stems from that backdrop. Detroit has a powerful history of musical abundance, extreme innovation, and prosperity prior to the mid-1960s. In the view of fans of Detroit electronic music, the city remains full of life, as well as cultural and civic activity.[39]

CONCLUSION

Essential to the exploration of electronic music as Black music are the concepts of social, cultural, and racial diversity, and sonic eclecticism. The relationships formed between people from many different racial, ethnic, class, and education backgrounds, as well as differing sexual orientations, formed a vibrant, complex culture that resulted in the creation and development of electronic music in Detroit, which has spread across the globe. The historical fabric of Detroit techno challenges the idea that this music is universal and void of any connection to race or other characteristics of identity. Electronic music has a significant grounding in African American culture beginning in the early 1970s and continuing

Denise Dalphond

into the twenty-first century. This foundation can be heard in the music, can be seen to varying degrees at parties, clubs, and festivals, and can be appreciated in the general historical lineage of electronic music.

KEY NAMES

Ken Collier	Electrifying Mojo
Deep Space	Derrick May
Direct Drive/Juan Atkins	The Wizard (Jeff Mills)

QUESTIONS

1. How are house, disco, and techno related? How are they distinct?
2. Identify the social, political, and demographic changes in Detroit that had the greatest impact on the development of techno from 1970 to 1999.
3. Identify local DJs whose radio broadcasts shaped the sound of Detroit techno. What specific contributions did each DJ make to the development of the genre?
4. How did techno spread into global contexts? In what ways did techno change as a consequence of its movement into Europe?

PROJECTS

1. Research online narratives of the history and artists of the Detroit Electronic Festival, including relevant images, and audio and/or video files. How has the festival evolved over time, and what is its impact on the local Detroit techno scene?
2. View a documentary film about electronic music that includes interviews with various innovators of the genre and explores the significance of Detroit in techno's development. Describe the forms of technology that these innovators used, and assess creative strategies they employed in their production.
3. Access simple synthesizers, drum machines, and a computer or recording studio to create a background track in the style of your chosen Detroit techno producer. Prepare an oral presentation about the making of your track that describes your process, notes any creative challenges you faced, and helps listeners identify the influences of Detroit on your production.

NOTES

Please see the discography for information on resources for further listening.

1. In my ethnographic research in Detroit on electronic music culture from 2008 to 2010, my consultants commonly refer to techno and house music as electronic music, rather than "electronic dance music." Although electronic dance music (EDM) and electronic

dance music culture (EDMC) are the more widely used terms in academic and popular literature, I use the term electronic music rather than electronic dance music when discussing Detroit. Carla Vecchiola (2006) discusses this issue in her dissertation on Detroit electronic music and civic dedication.

2. Burnim 1985. See also Maultsby 2005.

3. European disco music called Italo-disco was extremely influential in the late 1970s and early 1980s to many musicians of color in Chicago and Detroit. It was a style of disco produced by electronic musicians from Italy, Germany, the Netherlands, and other parts of Europe. See also Arnold 2009.

4. Deep Space membership included Juan Atkins, Derrick May, and Kevin Saunderson, and Direct Drive members included Todd Johnson, Mike Clark, Kevin Dysard, Al Ester, Darryle Shannon, and Dwayne Montgomery.

5. Quoted in Fisher 2007, 3.

6. The term "partying," in this chapter, refers to a cultural practice that encompasses the social and public ways in which electronic music is celebrated, listened to, and negotiated both in Detroit and around the world.

7. Cornelius Harris, panelist, *Roots of Techno*, October 21, 2006.

8. Submerge was founded in 1992 by Jeff Mills and Mike Banks.

9. Official names of the festival, in chronological order, are Detroit Electronic Music Festival (2000–02), Movement (2003–04), Fuse-In (2005), and Movement: Detroit's Electronic Music Festival (2006–10). The latter name has the potential to successfully continue well into the future.

10. Carlos Souffront, interview with the author, April 4, 2009.

11. Fabbri 1982, 1.

12. See also Holt 2007; Negus 1999; and Brackett 2002.

13. Theo Parrish, panelist, *Roots of Techno*, October 21, 2006.

14. Mike Clark, panelist, *Roots of Techno*, October 21, 2006.

15. Carlos Souffront, interview with the author, April 4, 2009.

16. Erika Sherman, interview with the author, December 5, 2009.

17. Sicko 2010, 12.

18. For an extensive exploration of the concept of post-soul in relation to Detroit techno and African American culture, see Albiez 2005. For general analysis of the concept of post-soul, as well as escapism and Afro-futurism, see Cosgrove 1995; Eshun 1998; George 1992; and Neal 2002 and 2003.

19. US Census Bureau. Accessed July 8, 2010, http://quickfacts.census.gov/qfd/states/26/2622000.html.

20. Mike Banks, interview with the author, November 30, 2009.

21. Felton Howard, interview with the author, May 31, 2008; Kelli Hand, interview with the author, June 1, 2008.

22. Todd Osborn, interview with the author, September 12, 2008.

23. Mojo created this term as a way to describe his approach to radio formatting.

24. Todd Osborn, interview with author, January 31, 2009.

25. Howard interview, 2008.

26. Osborn interview, 2008.

27. Reynolds 1999. See also Anderson 2009; Green 2005; Shapiro 2000; St. John 2009; Sylvan 2005; and Thornton 1996.

28. The first acid house track was "Acid Tracks" produced in 1987 by Chicago musicians Phuture, comprised of Nathan "DJ Pierre" Jones, Earl "Spanky" Smith Jr., and Herbert "Herb J" Jackson.

29. The Midwest in the context of raves and circuits of travel for DJs and partiers is widely defined to encompass urban, suburban, and rural sites in Michigan, Illinois, Wisconsin, Indiana, Ohio, Pennsylvania, Tennessee, Kentucky, Iowa, and Kansas.

30. Much of the information regarding 1217 Griswold comes from the assistance of John "Bileebob" Williams (interview with author, March 31, 2009, and Williams, 2010).

31. Moodymann 2010.

32. Patricola 2005, 50.

33. Quoted in Fisher 2007, 2.

34. Brendan M. Gillen, interview with author, July 22, 2009.
35. Ibid.
36. Vecchiola 2006, 50.
37. Record stores in metropolitan Detroit that consistently, or inconsistently, sell, or sold, music by local producers include Record Time, Melodies and Memories, Stormy Records, Detroit Threads, Somewhere In Detroit, Buy Rite Records, Vibes New and Rare Records, People's Records, Record Graveyard, Street Corner Records, and Record Collector. Additionally in Ann Arbor and Ypsilanti, Encore Recordings, Dubplate Pressure, School Kids Records, and School Kids Annex. Some of these stores are no longer open, but remain significant to the area's music history.
38. Dan Bean, interview with Mary Anne Hobbs, 2005. *The Detroit News* reported 95,000 people attended Movement: Detroit's Electronic Music Festival in 2010 (Nunez 2010).
39. Brubach 2010; Herron 1993; Hodges 2010; Saulny 2010; Tetzeli 2010.

CHAPTER 17

Hip-Hop and Rap

Dawn M. Norfleet

DJ
Short for "disc jockey"; a person who plays records in a dance club or on radio. In hip-hop, one who uses turntables to accompany rappers and break dancers or to perform as featured instrumentalist.

Rap
A popular African American dance musical style usually featuring an MC, who recites rhymed verses over an accompaniment created by a DJ or pre-recorded tracks.

Hip-hop is a creative expression, sensibility, and aesthetic that first emerged in largely African American, Afro-Caribbean, and Latino communities of the Bronx and then spread to Harlem and other boroughs of New York City in the early 1970s. It encompasses a wide range of performance expressions: aerosol art (graffiti); b-boying/girling (break dancing); **DJ**-ing, or the art of using turntables, vinyl records, and mixing units as musical instruments; and MC-ing (rapping), the art of verbal musical expression. The most celebrated component of hip-hop is **rap** music. This youth-oriented dance music emphasizes stylized verbal delivery of rhymed couplets, typically performed over pre-recorded accompaniment called "beats" or "tracks." By the 1990s, hip-hop had become an internationally recognized cultural phenomenon largely due to the popularity of rap music.

CULTURAL ROOTS

Rap draws from the cultural and verbal traditions of African Americans and other groups of African descent, especially Jamaican.[1] It borrows from the jive-talking style of African American radio personalities of the 1940s and 1950s, and the African-derived oral traditions of storytelling, boasting (self-aggrandizement), "toasting," and "playing the dozens" (competitive and recreational exchange of verbal insults). Jamaica had its own unique verbal tradition called "**toasting**," and, perhaps most significantly, a tradition of mobile disc jockey (DJ) units. Many of the hip-hop pioneers were Caribbean immigrants who brought musical practices from their native countries, such as the use of high volume levels and intense competition between DJs, and adjusted them to suit local African American tastes.

Jamaican migrants to the United States were already familiar with the music of African Americans through American soldiers stationed in Jamaica during World War II and through American radio broadcasts of swing, bebop, and **rhythm and blues**. African American dance music grew in popularity, particularly at blues dances, which took place in economically poor urban areas in the United States in the 1950s. Mobile DJs provided music for these social events that featured R&B records. DJs enlisted a paid crew of assistants, who took over the speaking roles, and drew loyal audiences.[2] Often, two DJs were booked to perform in the same space and competed for the attention and patronage of social dancers using large sound systems. Also called "sounds," these units consisted of turntables, powerful speakers, amplifiers, and a microphone. In battles of volume and carefully selected and ordered songs, DJs sought to elicit the maximum response from the dancers. The most prominent figures in the early era of the Jamaican mobile discothèques were Duke Reid and Sir Coxone.

Influenced by the style of African American radio personalities, the Jamaican DJ spoke "rhythmically over the music, [using] his voice as another instrument" on the microphone.[3] These addresses to the crowd, known as "**toasts**," complimented dancers and announced future events. Concurrent with the development of the Jamaican record industry in the 1950s, artists began to produce instrumental versions of popular songs, known as "**dubs**." In response to the growing popularity of toasting at social dances, these dubbed versions began to appear on the "B" sides of the vocal tracks. One of the most important figures of this tradition is U. Roy, the first to record in the dub style.[4]

Both Jamaican and North American mobile DJs were pioneers of the early rapping traditions in hip-hop. As the art of DJ-ing grew increasingly complex, African American DJs hired people to rap, who eventually acquired the title of **MC**, or master of ceremony. MCs revved the crowd and delivered information about upcoming social events. The African American tradition of toasting provided a major component for the emerging rapping tradition. Unlike the Jamaican musical practice of toasting, the African American toast was a spoken word tradition. In the 1960s and 1970s, the term "rapping" referred to the art of delivering skillful, verbal rhetoric intended to impress or persuade the listener. Popular R&B artists such as Isaac Hayes ("By the Time I Get to Phoenix," 1969), Barry White and Millie Jackson ("[If Loving You Is Wrong] I Don't Want to Be Right," 1974) and Diana Ross ("Ain't No Mountain High Enough," 1970) incorporated extended rapped sections in their songs.

This style became broadly popular through the 1970s-era "**blax-ploitation**" gangster films. Featuring largely African American casts,

Toast (African American)
Long verbal narrative, performed from memory and passed orally from generation to generation, that celebrated the feats of such cultural heroes as Staggolee and Signifying Monkey.

Toast (Jamaican)
A DJ rap that praised dancers and addressed topical concerns over an instrumental track.

Rhythm and blues (R&B)
A form of Black dance music that evolved during the World War II era and the two decades that followed as a fusion of blues, big band swing, gospel, and pop elements.

Dub
Jamaican-derived concept of creating instrumental versions of popular songs, over which DJs rap to audiences.

MC
Also spelled "emcee" (abbreviated from "master of ceremony"); a rapper who performs in a hip-hop context (typically, to accompaniment by a DJ, an instrumental track, vocal percussion known as a "beat box," or a cappella).

films such as *Superfly* (1972) and *Dolemite* (1975) utilized stereotypically street-oriented themes, which many considered exploitative of Black culture. One such example, *The Mack* (1973), celebrated the pimp's seductiveness: "To 'mack' meant to seduce a woman with talk, as did *rap* before it finally came to signify rhyming in rhythm."[5]

Rapping also encompassed spoken political and social commentary that characterized 1960s activists, such as H. "Rap" Brown (later known as Jamil Abdullah Al-Amin). Many well-known poets such as Nikki Giovanni ("Ego Tripping," 1971), Gil Scott Heron ("The Revolution Will Not Be Televised," 1974), the Last Poets ("Niggers are Scared of Revolution," 1971), and the Watts Prophets (Quincy Jones featuring the Watts Prophets, "Beautiful Black Girl," 1975) delivered their politically inspired and socially conscious poems over instrumental accompaniment during the 1960s and 1970s.

Socioeconomic conditions in parts of the Bronx and Harlem in the 1960s and 1970s profoundly shaped the aesthetics and activities of early hip-hop. Youth gangs proliferated and gang violence became common to daily life in the 1960s and early 1970s. Responding to these conditions, Bronx youths, particularly male, developed nonviolent but intensely competitive means of creative expressions. The first of these expressions primarily consisted of graffiti (which preceded hip-hop) and the competitive dance, later known as "**break dancing**," performed to music provided by the DJ.[6] Eventually, MC-ing was incorporated into what became known as "hip-hop culture"—a youth-focused expression that encompassed rapping, DJ-ing, clothes, attitude, graffiti, and African American urban language. Within two decades of its development, hip-hop became a powerful symbol of urban youth culture.

The primary mode of early rap musical expression was live performance. Rap shows and hip-hop events took place in parks, community centers, school gymnasiums, neighborhood clubs, and private basements. MCs established their reputations in these settings through battles between MC crews and through "freestyling," or rapped improvisation. Attendees passed along privately audiotaped shows and bought or shared locally pressed records. Tapes of rap music recordings were sold from the trunks of cars and briefcases for as much as fifteen dollars per cassette. These tapes, which were further duplicated and passed on, contributed to the popularity of such acts as the Cold Crush Brothers, the Funky 4 + 1, and Kool Moe Dee and the Treacherous Three beyond the boundaries of the New York City hip-hop community. As youths from the South visited relatives and friends in New York, and northern youths spent summers with southern relatives, they shared cassette tapes that had been reduplicated numerous times. Word of mouth and informal, person-to-person distribution were common means of popularizing artists for at least the next two decades.

"Blaxploitation" film
1970s film genre that featured stereotypical images of Black urban life.

Break dancing
Often acrobatic, early hip-hop dance, initially performed during the percussive "break" of a song, when the DJ performed extended instrumental sections suited to dancing. The dancers were known as "b-boys/girls."

Dawn M. Norfleet

1970s: The Era of the Hip-Hop DJs

DJs were the focal points in the early stages of hip-hop, providing the musical backdrop for the other forms of hip-hop expression. They served as the foundation and unifying element of hip-hop culture. In rap music, DJs were crucial in defining musical features that distinguished rapping from poetry recitation and other types of oral performance. Even though they provided music from pre-recorded discs, DJs used various strategies to incorporate the energy and feel of a live performance. Using complex technical maneuvers, hip-hop DJs (known as "turntablists" by the 1990s) transformed their phonographs, turntables, mixing units, and vinyl records into musical instruments. Although numerous DJs contributed to the development of turntablism, three Bronx DJs—Kool DJ Herc, Afrika Bambaataa, and Grandmaster Flash—are most frequently credited with the development of hip-hop as an all-encompassing cultural expression of music, graphic art, spoken word, and dance.

Having arrived in the west Bronx from Jamaica as an adolescent in the late 1960s, Kool DJ Herc brought his knowledge of and experience with the island's musical practices: Jamaican-style toasting, mobile DJ units, and high-energy competitions that established one's prowess. By 1973, he began providing music at social events in homes ("house parties"), public outdoor spaces ("block parties"), and community centers. By the **disco** era of the 1970s, he became known not only for his selection of records ranging from funk and R&B to Latin, but also for his method of playing the music. Using two turntables with identical records, he selected the most percussive or rhythmically appealing sections (the "breakdown") that often featured Latin instruments such as congas, timbales, and cowbells. Then he switched back and forth between the two turntables, placing the needle on the approximate spot where the section began. This resulted in an extended "break" section, to which the dancers responded energetically. Consequently, hip-hop dancing, or b-boying/girling, became known in popular culture as "break dancing."[7]

Kool Herc was also recognized for his sound system with its signature bass-heavy, massive speakers. His mobile unit had a reputation for overpowering competitors with its high volume capabilities. One such rival included fellow pioneer, Afrika Bambaataa. Although it was commonplace for DJs to rhyme over the microphone, Kool Herc was known more for his musical choices and sound system than for his rhyming ability. Later he hired assistants to form his unit, the Herculords or the Herculoids.[8] Just as in the earlier Jamaican mobile DJ party scene, battling for the attention of dancers became a feature of early hip-hop.

Afrika Bambaataa, also of Jamaican heritage, began as an informal student of Kool Herc's style and by the mid-1970s emerged as his mentor's competitor. He established his reputation as a DJ by mixing obscure and unusual records for his Bronx audiences, including rock, cartoon theme songs, and even excerpts from Western art music in his

Disco
Genre of 1970s dance music, derived from the abbreviation of discothèque, the main venue of consumption.

mix. Once the leader of a notorious gang in the 1970s, Bambaataa is credited with having redirected the gang's activity toward creative competition. Rather than violent confrontation, rival groups competed through b-boying/girling and graffiti writing. In 1973, he founded the Universal Zulu Nation, which promoted peaceful hip-hop expression. This organization helped establish the hip-hop aesthetic of competition through MC, DJ, and b-boy/girl battles. Decades later, in the twenty-first century, the Zulu Nation has remained active as an organization promoting hip-hop worldwide through its international chapters.

DJs who followed Kool Herc and Bambaataa became known for complex turntable maneuvers, techniques, and tricks that distinguished them from earlier stylistic trends. The Barbados-born, south Bronx resident Grandmaster Flash was one of several Bronx DJs who developed the act of turntable manipulations into a distinct musical practice. Flash combined his training in electronics with his interest in music to become one of the most influential figures in hip-hop. He introduced the electronic percussion system known as the "beat box," which eventually characterized the 1980s hip-hop sound, in which the sound of the beat box was reproduced orally. Later, influential artists such as Doug E. Fresh, Biz Markie, and Rahzel mastered the skill, known as "beat boxing."[9]

Scratching
Technique used by hip-hop DJs to create a percussive sound, produced by moving a very short section of a record back and forth under the record needle.

Cross-influence occurred among the DJs, as each established his reputation among local patrons through informal apprenticeship or by adapting practices learned from watching established DJs. Grandmaster Flash said that Grandwizard Theodore made **scratching** more percussive: "He had a way of rhythmically taking a scratch and making [it] sound musical."[10]

1979–85: Rap Music Enters the Mainstream

Although locally distributed recordings of rap predated commercial releases by several years, starting in the late 1970s numerous events thrust hip-hop into the consciousness of mainstream urban and nonurban America. Rap music's first commercial hit, "Rappers Delight," was recorded in 1979 by the New Jersey-based group, the Sugar Hill Gang, on Sugar Hill Records, an independent, Black-owned label headed by former R&B vocalist, Sylvia Robinson, and her husband Joe. The song used as its accompaniment a repeated four-bar musical phrase from Chic's disco hit, "Good Times," released earlier that year. A year later, the White "new wave" band Blondie helped broaden the audience for rap among mainstream listeners with its hit song, "Rapture."

Grandmaster Flash and the Furious Five's 1981 song, "The Adventures of Grandmaster Flash on the Wheels of Steel" was one of the earliest songs to feature the distinctive turntablist technique of scratching. The scratch is the percussive, whooping sound produced by manually moving a very short section of a record back and forth under the record needle. "Adventures" is also an example of a new type of recording that became

Dawn M. Norfleet

popular with hip-hop audiences, known as the "**mix**." The DJ often excised individual words or phrases from popular songs and included them in the mix. In "Adventures," Grandmaster Flash selects Blondie's phrase, "Flash is fast," which references himself—a common turntablist trick. In a mix, instead of playing the same sections of two identical records to extend the effect of a single phrase through repetition (a "**loop**"), the DJ overlaps sections of different songs for a collage effect. Voices of guest rappers and friends of the artists are recorded into the song to simulate the live "party" atmosphere. The earliest recordings of rap music often presented a rap artist rhyming over a live instrumental version of a popular song ("Rapper's Delight," 1979) or a combination of live and programmed instruments (Grandmaster Flash and the Furious Five, "The Message," 1982).

Similar to the Jamaican dub tracks, rappers formed new songs by adding their voices to the layer of live recorded instruments or to instrumental versions, which came to be known as "**remixes**." Bambaataa's group, the Soul Sonic Force, helped redefine the hip-hop aesthetic into one that placed a premium on electronically produced percussion and keyboards, steering rap music away from the live band and dance party sound that characterized its first phase.[11] Bambaataa's "Planet Rock" (1982) used a short, angular melodic phrase from "Trans-Europe Express" (1977) by the German proto-techno group, Kraftwerk (Figure 17.1). The new style of dance music that utilized programmable synthesizers and drums was called "electro funk"; it was popular among b-boys/girls, who now preferred the "electric boogie" and "pop locking" over the older break dancing. "Planet Rock" also laid the foundation for "sampling," the use of snippets of pre-recorded song material as the foundation of a new song or as a short thematic reference.

Sampling and other new **MIDI** (Musical Instrument Digital Interface) technology of the 1980s allowed for a faster and more convenient way to produce hip-hop music, prior to copyright laws that later restricted sample use. Sampling essentially accomplishes digitally what early hip-hop DJ-ing did manually; both processes use phrases of pre-recorded songs and sounds that the DJ creatively reassembles to form a new song. Samplers—electronic units that record phrases digitally—allow for the efficient recording of a loop. Bambaataa and Soul Sonic force were the first to use pre-recorded samples in their 1983 recording, "Looking for the Perfect Beat."

By the mid-1980s, digitally recorded phrases (samples) were used almost exclusively, taking the place of electro-funk's synthesized beats.

Mix
(1) Verb: To collage several songs, with the goal of maintaining a consistent, danceable rhythm. (2) Noun: A "new" song that the DJ (or producer) assembles from brief sections of current hits.

Loop
A short recorded phrase programmed to repeat indefinitely or for a designated length of time.

Remix
Typically, a popular song that has been reassembled by a turntablist DJ or producer, which is then recorded or presented during a DJ's performance. The vocals or recording are recorded or played over an entirely different track from the original, to achieve a contrasting groove and/or to extend the shelf life of a hit song.

Sampler
An electronic unit that records sound digitally, allowing for the recording of a phrase that can be "looped," or programmed to repeat for a desig-nated length of time.

Figure 17.1
Transcription from Afrika Bambaataa's "Planet Rock" (1982).[12]

"Funky Drummer," a 1970 recording by James Brown that featured the work of drummer Clyde Stubblefield, contains the most widely used sample beat.[13] Popular songs that used this drum loop included "Rebel Without a Pause" by Public Enemy (1987), "Straight Outta Compton" by N.W.A. (1988), and "Mama Said Knock You Out" by LL Cool J (1990).

Further thrusting the electronic hip-hop sound into the mainstream was "Rockit" (1983), featuring innovative jazz legend Herbie Hancock and popular Bronx DJ Grandmixer D.ST. Although "Rockit" featured scratching, the song was unusual by later hip-hop standards in that it was instrumental and featured no rapped vocals. The contemporary 1980s funk sound combined with Hancock's voice electronically altered to resemble a synthesizer became a hit with African American dance music audiences. "Rockit's" futuristic video won several 1984 MTV Video Music Awards and generated nationwide exposure for hip-hop. The electro-funk single was groundbreaking on several fronts. "Rockit" (1) was the first recorded collaboration between a jazz and hip-hop artist; (2) won a Grammy for Best R&B Instrumental Performance in 1983; (3) was the first hip-hop-influenced record to win a Grammy Award; and (4) had a music video that was one of the first works by a Black musician to be aired on MTV.

As the 1980s progressed, the DJ took a back seat in visibility and the live performance aspect of hip-hop diminished. According to author and critic S.H. Fernando, "[t]he era of the [DJ] peaked around 1978, and gradually the spotlight shifted to those controlling the microphone—the MCs."[14] The MC, typically male, now became the central figure in hip-hop, and was spokesperson for the entire hip-hop culture in the public mind.

Although the public face of hip-hop has been consistently male, women have been part of this tradition from its beginning. Some were part of mixed MC crews such as the Funky 4 + 1, while others were members of all-female crews such as Sequence and the Mercedes Ladies. In the mid-1980s, some female artists were popularized momentarily through "answer" songs, which ridiculed popular songs previously recorded by male acts. Examples include Roxanne Shante's "Roxanne's Revenge," responding to UTFO's 1984 hit song, "Roxanne, Roxanne" and Pebblee Poo's "Fly Guy," a response to the Boogie Boys' 1985 hit, "A Fly Girl." Although the women in these songs criticize the sexist lyrics of male acts, their artistic persona, nevertheless, was based on a male model. After several spinoffs from "Roxanne's Revenge," the most popular of the answer songs, the novelty soon wore off. Because the answer song rappers failed to establish a unique artistic identity, their careers did not survive the popularity of the initial songs.

Dawn M. Norfleet

1985–88: Hip-Hop Meets the Corporate World

Rap music in the mid- to late 1980s experienced a stylistic and economic shift as its distribution moved from local, predominately Black-owned labels such as Sugar Hill and Enjoy Records to international conglomerates with much larger markets. Rap's entry into the corporate world was largely due to the efforts of Russell Simmons and his then business partner, Rick Rubin. Simmons grew up in a middle-class section of Queens, New York. After seeing the market potential of hip-hop as a college student, he formed the hip-hop business, Rush Management. His first major client was Run-D.M.C., a hip-hop trio comprised of his brother Joseph "Run" Simmons, Darryl "D.M.C." McDaniels, and DJ Jam Master Jay. After releasing Run-D.M.C.'s album *King of Rock* (1985) on independent label Profile Records, Simmons formed a business partnership with Rubin, a young White New York University student, which resulted in the founding of Def Jam Records in 1984. Simmons managed business matters, while Rubin handled musical production and Artists and Repertoire (A&R). Def Jam's first act was a young teenaged rapper named LL Cool J ("Ladies Love Cool James") who recorded "I Need a Beat" in 1984.

Rubin's work with Def Jam artists was instrumental in establishing what came to be known as a more street-oriented, "harder" hip-hop sound that incorporated hard rock riffs, explosive timbres, relatively sparse instrumentation and aggressive accents as illustrated in Run-D.M.C.'s "My Adidas" (1986).[15] The subsequent huge national sales successes of the first Def Jam artists—LL Cool J and the Beastie Boys (a White act that fused rock and rap styles)—attracted the attention of a major record company, Columbia Records. Def Jam and Columbia struck a deal worth over $1 million whereby Columbia would press and distribute Def Jam artists. A negotiation of this magnitude was unprecedented in hip-hop at the time.[16]

In 1987, Def Jam released *Yo! Bum Rush the Show*, an album by a group from Long Island known as Public Enemy. The first overtly and consistently politically oriented group in hip-hop, they delivered fierce social criticism over equally aggressive musical tracks. Public Enemy helped form a lasting image of the young, African American, urban male as an intriguing figure to be admired or feared by the masses ("Fight the Power," 1990). The group's forceful image was further reinforced by powerful, often cacophonous, musical production by the team known as the Bomb Squad.

Unlike the tales of violence and sexual exploits common in what came to be known as "gangsta rap," Public Enemy's urban appeal was based on texts that encouraged political confrontation. The militant messages professed by the group, which referred to itself as the "epitome" of a "public enemy," appealed to the primarily Black hip-hop base for its perceived cultural authenticity.[17] Concurrently, the message of mainstream rebellion also appealed to the larger, more lucrative audiences of suburban White youth, whose parents perhaps once had their own mainstream model in Elvis Presley or bebop. Public Enemy's 1990 tour with heavy metal band Anthrax further developed a hip-hop fan base among the young, White, and rebellious.

In the late 1980s, Rubin left Def Jam to start his own company, Def American (later, American), which focused on alternative rock. Before Rubin's departure from Def Jam, he played a seminal role in exposing hip-hop to mainstream audiences by fusing hard rock and hip-hop. Run-D.M.C.'s *Raising Hell* (1986), for example, included a reinterpretation of "Walk This Way" by the popular 1970s rock group Aerosmith. The hip-hop version featured the original band singing the refrain with Run-D.M.C.'s rap. This fusion not only exposed hip-hop to Aerosmith's audience, it also helped to revive the band's career. The phenomenal success of the Def Jam groups from suburban Queens and Long Island propelled hip-hop and the concept of urban street culture even further into mainstream pop culture.

HIP-HOP DIVERSIFIES

From the mid-1980s to the mid-1990s, hip-hop experienced a growth spurt. This general period is sometimes considered to be hip-hop's "Golden Age" because of the many creative streams that began to emerge, particularly in the early 1990s—styles as diverse as the jazzy Digable Planets, the eclectic Arrested Development, the sophisticated De La Soul, and the rough-edged Wu-Tang Clan. **Classic**, **hardcore**, **pop**, and **alternative**[18] became recognized as distinct styles. "Classic hip-hop" artists included Naughty By Nature ("Uptown Anthem," 1992), A Tribe Called Quest ("Check the Rhyme," 1992), and Nas ("The World is Yours," 1994).[19] These groups, typically from the eastern regions, developed ways of combining compelling, street-themed storytelling, catchy radio- and crowd-friendly hooks, and strong production. Consequently, they sold well both in the hip-hop and mainstream markets. Classic hip-hop artists usually employed hardcore themes and explicit language, but also recorded "clean," or self-censored, versions of their songs or albums. The lyrics or subject matter in classic hip-hop was edgy enough for the act to appear to be "keeping it real" for its core audience, which referenced itself as the "hip-hop community," but not so edgy to prompt controversy or outright bans from commercial radio and video airplay.

The mid-1980s broadened the discourse and general representation of women in hip-hop, at the same time rap was expanding its parameters in general. Still, Black life and empowerment from a female perspective were just beginning to be explored. Historically, producers of rap music were typically male, who influenced artists' lyrical content and shaped their artistic personas. Missy Elliott was the first successful female artist to earn recognition as a songwriter, rapper, singer, and producer.

Classic rap
Rap with elements of hardcore and pop-rap affirmed by the core hip-hop audience and the mainstream.

Hardcore rap
A controversial hip-hop style characterized by hypermasculine images, exaggerated street themes, aggressive delivery, and often explicit language.

Pop-rap
Rap characterized by humorous, catchy, and upbeat lyrics with little controversial subject matter, which targets a mainstream audience.

Alternative rap
Hip-hop music that does not conform to commercial forms of rap, such as gangsta, hardcore, and pop-rap. Instead, alternative rap freely draws from other genres, uses a loose interpretation of the rhymed couplet tradition, and/or includes themes that are more blatantly political than those of commercial rap.

Dawn M. Norfleet

Figure 17.2
Photo of Lauryn Hill, *c*.1990. Photo by Larry Hulst/Michael Ochs Archives/Getty Images.

She gained notoriety with her debut album of R&B–hip-hop, *Supa Dupa Fly* (1997), which sold over one million units.

Fellow multifaceted artist Lauryn Hill (Figure 17.2) had already established herself as a respected MC and vocalist in the mid-1990s as the front woman for the popular alternative hip-hop band from New York City, the Fugees. However, Hill's first solo effort, *The Miseducation of Lauryn Hill* (1998), was a phenomenal success with sales of over eight million units, in addition to sales of several million copies of various singles. Of her nominations for ten 1998 Grammy Awards, she won five.[20] For the very first time, women in hip-hop achieved major success as respected artists, producers, and stars in the forefront, able to navigate the highly demanding hip-hop community and the unpredictable mainstream. Several women of diverse perspectives on issues ranging from politics to sex experienced some degree of success in the 1990s, including Yo-Yo, Da Brat, Bahamadia, Eve, Lil' Kim, and Foxy Brown.[21]

The Hardcore Movement

The term "hardcore" contains two key concepts essential in hip-hop, especially of the 1990s: "hardness" (denoting impenetrability, control, and coldness) and "core" (denoting centrality, authenticity, and essence). The metaphor of hardness is reflected in the names of rap artists such as Just-Ice, Ice-T, and Ice Cube. Additionally, hardness carries with it a common, mainstream association with male sexual prowess and, at the extreme, sexual domination. In the hip-hop value system, hardness represented the ideal for many urban Black males. As a multidimensional, hypermasculine symbol, hardness also provided a standard by which promoters distinguished their "new school" clients from the boasting and relatively simple party rhymes of their "old school" predecessors.[22]

At the center of this harder style loomed the issue of "authenticity," which became the primary concern of hip-hop in the 1990s, as reflected in the ubiquitous slang phrase, "keep it real." What was deemed real was defined by urban, African American, male, youth-oriented "street" values. According to cultural scholar Michael Eric Dyson, "[t]he question of black authenticity haunts the culture; within hip-hop it is especially vicious, with artists often adopting a stance as a thug or gangsta to prove their bona fides and their ability to represent the street."[23] When the lines blurred between fictional narratives of authenticity and real life, the result was often life altering or, at worst, deadly. Many popular hip-hop artists associated with the hardcore movement were arrested or served jail time during their careers.[24]

In the mainstream mind, these fictional narratives had too much potential to influence reality, especially in light of the Los Angeles Riots (a.k.a. "Rodney King Uprising"), which took place in reaction to the beating of Rodney King by Los Angeles Police in April 1992. Ice-T, widely criticized and censored for the recording "Cop Killer" (1992), provides an insider's perspective on interpreting hardcore lyrics:

> Hardcore rap is an acquired taste. You got to understand it . . . [W]e fade from reality to fiction to reality to outrageousness to totally serious in the middle of a sentence. And you got to say, "Oh, he's talking crazy there, oh, he meant that."[25]

In other words, the content of hardcore lyrics is not always an accurate portrayal of reality, nor is it intended as such.

Gangsta rap
A hardcore style popularized on the West Coast, beginning in the late 1980s, with street-oriented lyrics and delivery associated with gang culture.

Different styles of hardcore include: **gangsta**; sexually explicit; and "conscious," "message," or "edutainment" (a contraction of the words "educational" and "entertainment"). Conscious or message-oriented hardcore hip-hop does not always use profanity, nor rhyme about sexual prowess. Instead, the hardcore label is represented through a combination of powerful urban imagery, Afrocentric themes, and vocal delivery that could be booming as in the style of KRS-One of Boogie Down Productions ("South Bronx," 1986), or icy-smooth, as in Rakim from Eric B. and Rakim ("Microphone Fiend," 1988).

The verbal message of hardcore was often complemented by strongly percussive musical accompaniment to achieve its startling impact on listeners. An explosive rim shot occurring on the second and fourth beats, comparable to the sound of an audio-enhanced gunshot, replaced the traditional hand claps heard in R&B and earlier hip-hop. Rakim transformed the microphone into a metaphoric weapon: "magnum, murderin' MCs."[26] More often, however, other hardcore artists used a thematic cocktail of explicit lyrics combined with tales of sexual exploits, and violence against women, gays, police, "punks," and/or "sucka M.C.s," as heard in "Punks Jump Up to Get Beat Down" (Brand Nubian, 1992).

Dawn M. Norfleet

As rap music grew in popularity as a form of mainstream enter- tainment, so did the association between rap performances and violence. Hip-hop became a popular symbol of urban Black life to the wider American society, embodied by the young Black male—exotic, dangerous, and feared, yet simultaneously appealing and marketable. Despite successful record sales, rap artists had limited performance opportunities, due to venue owners' fear of potential violence. A December 1985 concert at Madison Square Garden in New York City, which included LL Cool J, Doug E. Fresh, and Kurtis Blow, received considerable negative media attention after a concert attendee was shot. Negative events associated with hip-hop performances were greatly publicized, while peaceful rap music concerts, philanthropic activities of rap artists (such as the "Stop the Violence" movement), and violence at White rock concerts were relatively underrepresented in the media.[27] According to music journalist Jon Pareles, "To much of the American mainstream, rap is an outlaw music that otherwise well-informed people vilify and fear."[28]

As streetwise, young Black males became symbols of Black culture for the White mainstream, women in much hardcore rap became symbols of male sexual conquest and domination.[29] The male-defined language of street culture and the strict gender-based hierarchy that often denigrated women in gangsta rap narratives was condemned by many as misogynistic.[30] Dr. Dre's debut recording, *The Chronic* (1992), for example, concludes with an unnamed track that features the refrain, "bitches ain't s—— but hoes and tricks," serving as a graphic example of the portrayal of women as sex objects.[31] Too Short ("Freaky Tales," 1989) and DJ Quik ("Sweet Black P——," 1991) also recorded songs with similar themes.

The negative portrayals of women, lyrics with explicitly sexual and/or violent content ubiquitous in the recordings of "gangsta rappers" drew criticism from members of the Black and White middle classes alike. The opposition to the lyrical content fostered alliances between such seemingly disparate groups as the former US "Drug Czar" William Bennett, the conservative Parents' Music Resource Center, and such Black community leaders as C. Delores Tucker and prominent New York minister Calvin Butts. The opposition to gangsta rap rallied to ban its sales and/or restrict its airplay. A powerful voice that supported the First Amendment rights of gangsta rappers to free expression was that of African American congresswoman Maxine Waters, who viewed rap music as a "new art form to describe [urban youth's] pains, fears and frustrations with us as adults."[32] What many of the opponents seemingly did not understand is that hardcore publicly depicted dialogues that had been taking place in Black communities decades before N.W.A., or "Niggaz with Attitude." Banning hardcore rap would not eliminate the conditions that had initially produced it.

Since masculinist hardcore images proliferated in hip-hop and came to dominate the hip-hop landscape in the early to mid-1990s, many record companies questioned the viability of female rappers, operating under the "conventional wisdom" that "female rappers don't sell." Hip-hop success was defined by what males valued. Monica Lynch, former president of popular hip-hop label, Tommy Boy Records, opined, "We've been finding from . . . focus groups that the perception of a female being virtuous and socially conscious is not an attractive quality to most men."[33] As the 1990s approached, veteran female rappers adjusted their styles accordingly.

In the early 1990s, MC Lyte adapted her message-oriented style heard in *Lyte as a Rock* (1988), to appeal to hardcore audiences in *Ain't No Other* (1993). KRS-One, a prominent hardcore advocate, lent MC Lyte street authenticity by assuring the listener that her album "will bring nothing but the lyrical terrorism and hardcore beats."[34] The album's first single, "Ruffneck," a homage to hardcore men, became MC Lyte's first gold hit and eventually sold over a million copies worldwide.

Queen Latifah, whose first album, *All Hail the Queen*, was recorded in 1989, took a different approach. She chose to address the hardcore issue directly, without changing her message. Her single, "U.N.I.T.Y.," from the *Black Reign* (1993) album, criticized the ubiquitous images of women as sexual objects. Rather than a didactic tirade against misogynistic men, her demand for respect and honor of urban womanhood came via a mid-tempo track that combined jazzy accompaniment and R&B-style singing. Her smoothly sung vocal chorus of "U.N.I.T.Y." contrasted with her confrontational question: "Who you callin' a bitch?"[35] In this song, she punches a man who touches her inappropriately, and "call[s] out [her] name,"[36] thereby achieving street justice. With *Black Reign*'s messages of female empowerment and its blend of rap and R&B-style singing (which proved to be a successful formula for later female artists such as Lauryn Hill and Missy Elliott), the album went gold. Both MC Lyte and Queen Latifah were among a handful of artists whose stylistic and professional adaptability were certainly factors in their ability to survive the turbulent waves of changing trends, including the highly pervasive hardcore aesthetic.

Classic and Pop-Rap

By the late 1980s, "pop" or commercial rap grew in popularity among mainstream audiences. Relative to hardcore and even classic rap (which, though popular, still looked to its hardcore audience for validation of authenticity), the lyrics and images of pop-rap artists were relatively benign, making them more acceptable to both Black and White middle-class audiences. Indeed, a mainstream-friendly version of hip-hop was the first recipient of the new rap music Grammy category awarded in 1988. Interestingly, the winner was not a New York act but a duo from Philadelphia: Jazzy Jeff and the Fresh Prince (Will Smith). The winning song, "Parents Just Don't Understand," was a humorous song far removed from street-oriented themes associated with hardcore hip-hop.

Dawn M. Norfleet

Please Hammer, Don't Hurt 'Em (1990) launched the pop-rap career of Oakland entertainer MC Hammer. His hit single "U Can't Touch This," which sampled funk artist Rick James's "Super Freak" (1981), focused on the catchy hooks, energetic dancing, and popularity of its base song, rather than lyrical content. Initially, MC Hammer and his music were readily embraced by the mainstream. Corporate America even capitalized on his commercial appeal by marketing an MC Hammer doll and cartoon program. However, the core contemporaneous hip-hop community, at this time, vilified artists who participated in this form of commercialization as inauthentic "sellouts." Despite two subsequent hit songs, MC Hammer's popularity faded by the mid-1990s. In later years, he would reappear in the public realm as a reality television star and televangelist.

White Texas-based rapper Vanilla Ice followed a similar stylistic formula combining image and catchy choruses as a pop-rap artist. As MC Hammer had done, he became a symbol of the precariousness of the pop-rap market, but for different reasons. After his hit single "Ice Ice Baby" (1990), he was criticized for lack of originality because the title and refrain of his hit song were identical to a popular chant used by an African American fraternity. Furthermore, both the hip-hop community and music critics condemned Vanilla Ice for falsely claiming authentic gangster roots, leading to his rapid downfall. Vanilla Ice faded into hip-hop obscurity and never regained commercial success.

"Pop-rappers" were in a very precarious position because they relied on two seemingly different audiences for commercial success: the hip-hop (urban Black-identifying) audience, seen as a marker of "authenticity" and the pop (mainstream White-identifying) audience, which represented an expanded consumer base. Because the hip-hop community of the 1990s was extremely territorial, it quickly rejected those who did not adhere to the accepted model, as depicted in EPMD's video for "Crossover" (1992). Factors, such as overexposure by the mainstream media, smiling in photographs, or appearances in certain types of commercials could be perceived as "selling out," or abandoning one's street alliances.

Negotiating the constantly shifting line of acceptability between mainstream R&B and hardcore hip-hop, such artists as Pete Rock and C.L. Smooth ("They Reminisce Over You," 1992) and Heavy D and the Boyz ("You Can't See What I Can See," 1992) recorded a hip-hop/R&B blend known as "**R&B rap**" in the early 1990s. This style was first perceived by hip-hop audiences as middle ground between hardcore and pop before becoming acceptable by the late 1990s, thanks to Sean "Diddy" Combs's production of the Notorious B.I.G. R&B rap utilized tracks with bass lines and keyboard chords, often with sung refrains. R&B hip-hop preferred highly melismatic, and more nasal vocal riffs to the full-throated gospel-styled singing of classic soul and 1970s R&B. An R&B antecedent was "new jack swing," a short-lived but influential style popularized by producers, Teddy Riley and the team of Jimmy Jam and Terry Lewis.

R&B rap
Hip-hop/R&B hybrid considered middle ground between hardcore and pop-rap; characterized by rapped verses, sung refrains, and harmonized choruses.

New jack swing, whose heyday was approximately 1987–91, contained distinctive, syncopated, swung rhythms in the snare sound of the Roland TR-808 drum machine. Male, typically tenor, singers included Keith Sweat ("I Want Her," 1987), Johnny Kemp ("Just Got Paid," 1988), and Bell Biv DeVoe ("Poison," 1990), who adopted hip-hop's prevailing "bad boy" image to appeal to the hip-hop audience. Although traditional R&B was considered to be "soft" or too feminine by the core hip-hop audience by the early 1990s, new jack swing laid the foundation for the next wave of what many listeners described as "hip-hop R&B," which included highly successful female acts, such as Mary J. Blige, Total, and TLC.[37]

REGIONAL STYLES

The late 1980s saw new cities emerge on the hip-hop map, such as Philadelphia, Los Angeles, and Oakland. Subsequently, distinct rap subgenres developed, influenced both by regional styles and local community preferences. Video programs capitalized on the growing popularity of hip-hop, and served as commercials for new artists, with shows such as *Yo! MTV Raps* (1988–95) and BET's *Rap City* (1989–2008). Music videos also placed regional artists on television sets across the country and throughout the world. The hip-hop landscape was changing, as more areas claimed a stake in defining it, and as communities nationwide had begun to develop and support their own, local hip-hop styles.

The West Coast

In the late 1980s, African American and Latino communities in California—communities of Oakland in the north and "South Central" Los Angeles, Compton, and Long Beach in the south—became important new bases for hip-hop culture. This region, known as the West Coast, was distinguished by its unique slang, accent, tempo, thematic emphasis, and local references. On the West Coast, the African American toasting tradition melded with themes influenced by Black gangster characters and films of the 1970s. These movies became popular with Black and Latino youth through the growing home video industry and cable television, which burgeoned in the 1980s. The influence of such films is visible in rap lyrics that often centered on themes of "hustling" (making money by any means—often illicitly). The result was a distinctive subgenre of hardcore known as "gangster/gangsta rap," which celebrated gang life, "pimping," and the street culture of Black urban males,[38] as exemplified in the music of N.W.A. (*Straight Outta Compton*, 1988), and Oakland's Too Short (*Life is . . . Too Short*, 1988). The hip-hop subgenre of gangsta rap was considered by many West Coast hip-hoppers as the authentic voice of urban California youth.

N.W.A. identified with Compton, a city in southeastern Los Angeles County, comprised of mainly working-class African Americans and people of Mexican descent. N.W.A. members included Eazy-E, Dr. Dre,

Ice Cube, DJ Yella, MC Ren, and the D.O.C., who replaced original member the Arabian Prince. The poem "Boyz N Tha Hood," written by Ice Cube in his high-school English class,[39] became a song recorded by the group and originally released as a single in 1986. The group garnered a strong local following in a manner similar to that of the early Bronx MCs: N.W.A. pressed records, passed along cassette tapes to friends, and sold them from cars and at flea markets. Eazy-E, a former drug dealer, formed Ruthless Records and then established a partnership with an older White music industry professional, Jerry Heller; together, they began "shopping" the group to record companies. Eventually, N.W.A. signed with the small independent label Priority Records.

Because of N.W.A.'s explicit lyrics, radio and music video stations refused to air their music. Still, the music was advertised through word of mouth, and its spread was comparable to the earlier westward migration of copied hip-hop tapes from the Bronx and Harlem. Rap recordings and notoriety of N.W.A. and other West Coast groups traveled eastward in the mid- to late 1980s, and caught the attention of mainstream and White listeners along the way. Despite the lack of support by traditional media—radio, video, and television—N.W.A.'s first full-length album, *Straight Outta Compton*, was released in 1988 and sold more than two million copies. *Straight Outta Compton* gained notoriety particularly due to the single, "F—— Tha Police," whose explicit lyrics critiqued the treatment of African Americans by the Los Angeles police department.[40]

As a by-product of the controversy, the song earned mainstream promotion from its detractors, including the FBI, who accused the group of advocating "violence against and disrespect for the law-enforcement officer."[41] One line from the song verbally confronts a police officer by challenging the lethal and legal authority that the badge and the gun represent; without them, the lyrics contend, the officer is just another "sucka . . . waiting to get shot."[42]

Rather than encouraging wanton violence against all police agencies, more accurately "F—— Tha Police" voiced anger felt by many African American males in Los Angeles. In an interview years later, Ice Cube reflected that "N.W.A. was simply coming from the heart, not trying to be rebellious or dark, just trying to do exciting music . . . [T]here was a lot of gang violence in our neighborhood, so that tension got onto the record."[43] Ice Cube noted the difference between the song's intent (to express views from the perspective of young Black men in south Los Angeles, vis-à-vis law enforcement) and its public perception (as anti-establishment and violent). Reality versus perception became increasingly polarized through the middle of the 1990s, as many rappers from coast to coast were striving to achieve and maintain a hardcore image.

The East Coast/West Coast Feud, 1990–97

From the early days of DJ units and MC crews battling each other in Bronx neighborhoods, hip-hop had been competitive, territorial, and even combative.[44] Hip-hop's growing diversity also spurred regional and stylistic rivalry into full-blown conflict. In California, gangsta rap was more popular than the message rap associated with the East Coast (mainly New York, New Jersey, and Philadelphia). By the 1990s, the popularity and record sales of the major West Coast acts had begun to eclipse nationwide sales and popularity of their New York counterparts.

In retaliation against the dislodging of New York as hip-hop's center, many East Coast artists, radio stations, and rap magazines publicly accused the West Coast acts of being "studio gangsters"—that is, rappers whose lyrics glorified a fictional gangster lifestyle. The West Coast accused the East of "playa [player] hating," or spiteful envy, and disrespecting West Coast contributions to the culture. This cross-regional bickering fueled the East–West rivalry, while the burgeoning, highly influential hip-hop media fanned the naturally combustive competitive flames that consumed hip-hop's two biggest icons.

By the early 1990s, Marion "Suge" Knight, founder of the notorious Death Row Records, had become the most powerful, if not infamous, hip-hop figure on the West Coast. One of the most prominent artists to join his roster was Tupac Shakur, who joined Death Row in 1995 after scoring several hit songs. Born in New York City, the son of Black Panther Afeni Shakur, "2Pac's" lyrics covered the spectrum of urban life and lore. His diverse themes explored the pitfalls and excesses of "thug life" in songs such as "Shorty Wanna Be a Thug" (1996), while telling poignant stories in "Brenda's Got a Baby" (1991) and "Dear Mama" (1995). Although he had a promising dual career in acting, it was the gangsta sobriquet and lifestyle of hardcore excesses that likely led to Tupac's violent death. Shakur accused popular Brooklyn artist and rival the Notorious B.I.G. (known popularly as "Biggie Smalls") and his producer, Sean Combs (a.k.a. "Puff Daddy," "Puffy," "P. Diddy," and "Diddy") of having arranged his first attempted murder. In hardcore braggadocio at its extreme, Shakur claimed to have had sexual relations with Biggie Smalls's wife, vocalist Faith Evans, in the song "Hit 'em Up" (1995),[45] adding even more fodder to the existing flames of regional rivalry.

The Notorious B.I.G. grew up in the Bedford–Stuyvesant section of Brooklyn, New York.[46] After dropping out of high school to pursue drug dealing, he eventually gave up "hustling" and joined with Combs, the ambitious founder of Bad Boy Entertainment, to pursue a career as a rap artist. Biggie Smalls was respected as a gifted urban storyteller and quickly became the symbol of 1990s New York-style hardcore, backed by Combs's slick R&B tracks. His first venture, the R&B/hip-hop-styled recording *Ready To Die* (1994), was a tremendous success. Because of his cleverly constructed tales of Brooklyn street life, many in the New York hip-hop community considered Biggie a hero. The hit single "Juicy" chronicled his youth in urban poverty and emergence into the material comforts of hip-hop stardom. Other singles on his album—"Ready to Die," "Me and My Bitch," and "Suicidal Thoughts"—presented the dark

Dawn M. Norfleet

side of street life; the album concludes with his character shooting himself.

Often suspected of being heightened by the media, the East Coast/ West Coast tension was later blamed, at least in part, for the murders of Shakur and Smalls. Tupac Shakur died September 7, 1996, at age twenty-five; barely six months later, Biggie Smalls/Notorious B.I.G. died March 9, 1997, at age twenty-four. While both camps blamed each other for the deaths, cultural critic Nelson George sees these two murders, unsolved as of 2011, as likely to "be remembered (rightly or wrongly) as the last tragic gasp of the infamous East Coast/West Coast conflict."[47]

Biggie Smalls's wide popularity not only elevated him to the status of hip-hop icon, it also helped to establish Brooklyn as New York's hip-hop center by the mid-1990s, replacing the Bronx and Queens. Only the first of Biggie Smalls's albums was released in his lifetime; ironically, one of his posthumous releases was a song titled "You're Nobody Till Someone Kills You" (1997). Smalls's and Shakur's deaths, and the mysterious circumstances that surrounded them, transformed these two promising young rap stars into the first rap martyrs, rendering them, literally, larger than life. In the minds of some, the cause worth dying for was "keeping it real." To others, it was a hardcore-style consequence of "believing the hype," or adopting highly inflated media messages as reality.

Despite the fierce regional conflicts, successful interregional collab- oration took place in the mid-1990s, and increased throughout the decade and beyond. Whether influenced by artists' desires to heal regional rifts, a keen eye for the huge marketing potential of cross-state collaborations facilitated by innovations in music and communication technology, or a combination of both, such activities became increasingly commonplace. Cross-influence occurred as a result. Former N.W.A. member Eazy-E produced the first releases by the Ohio-based group Bone Thugs-n-Harmony ("Thuggish Ruggish Bone," 1994) featuring slower tempos contrasting with faster, sixteenth-note rapping, foreshadowing later southern hip-hop styles. Producer J Dilla (also known as Jay Dee), originally from the respected Detroit group Slum Village, produced the Pharcyde's jazz-infused single "Runnin'" (1995) and other songs from the Los Angeles-based group's second album, *Labcabincalifornia*. Dr. Dre produced and mentored a young White rapper from Detroit named Eminem, who, in turn, discovered New York rapper 50 Cent.

The "Dirty South"

During the 1990s and into the twenty-first century, the hip-hop territory expanded to include the "Dirty South," a popular reference to areas such as Houston, New Orleans, Atlanta, Miami, and Virginia. The Dirty South "represented a seismic shift in the established geographical imaginary of rap music, centrally related to claims of authenticity and marketability."[48] Adopted from a 1995 song title by the Atlanta-based group, the Goodie

Mob, "The Dirty South" became increasingly influential on the national hip-hop scene, and an umbrella for a number of styles associated with specific cities. The first southern act to gain notoriety was the hardcore rap group from Houston, known as the Geto Boys. Their first hit, "My Mind is Playing Tricks on Me" (1991), is similar to West Coast gangsta rap in theme and style. The Geto Boys were among the rap groups targeted for their explicit and violent themes. In Miami, Luther Campbell and 2 Live Crew became the most controversial group with regard to lyrics. Their song, "Me So Horny" (1989), paired hardcore sexual lyrics with video images of scantily clad women dancing suggestively. These artists' use of explicit texts and titillating images earned them great notoriety in the early 1990s.[49] The musical style was known as "Miami bass," a fast-paced electronic style influenced by Afrika Bambaataa's 1980s electrofunk.

Other southern styles include "trap-music," New Orleans "bounce," Memphis "crunk," and "chopped and screwed" remixes that spread out from Houston's DJ Screw. Like his predecessors in the Bronx, DJ Screw garnered a following from his unique adaptation of **mixtapes**, which he called "screw tapes." These recordings "presented a technological reworking of rap songs [that] involved playing the song at half-speed (producing an extra-deep bass and percussion and groaning vocals) and repeating small portions of the song in a technique called 'chopping.'"[50] The rap song, "Pourin Up" (2006), with Houston's Pimp C, featuring Bun B and Mike Jones, later had several "chopped and screwed" mixes by various DJs.

Popular southern hardcore artists and styles received heavy hip-hop and commercial exposure, thanks to a number of events starting in the 1990s. New Orleans-born rapper-entrepreneur Master P moved his music business operation, No Limit Record Store, from Richmond, California, to Baton Rouge, Louisiana. He had successfully promoted his own music and that of family members, Silkk the Shocker, C-Murder, and eventually his own son, Lil' Romeo. His roster also included the West Coast's Snoop Dogg and New Orleans' Mystikal and helped bring exposure to the South as a legitimate center of hip-hop. He produced a business model based on self-reliance, diversification, and using one project to finance the next. Journalist Tariq Muhammad noted, "Rather than pay top dollar for sought after hip-hop producers who charge as much as $20,000 per track, No Limit uses mostly in-house producers and records in its own studios."[51] In 2002, Master P ranked eleventh as "America's 40 Richest Under 40" by *Fortune* magazine.[52] His additional ventures included clothing, real estate, film, and philanthropy.

In 1989, Atlanta-based producer Jermaine Dupri played a key role in establishing Atlanta, Georgia, as the epicenter of the Dirty South. While still a teenager, he became a successful producer, launching the teenaged pop-rap act Kris Kross and its hit album, *Totally Crossed Out* (1992).

Mixtape
Informal collection of songs, often assembled by a DJ, sometimes recorded with a unique sonic stamp.

Dawn M. Norfleet

Dupri later negotiated a lucrative deal with Columbia Records and launched other highly successful acts on his record label, So So Def. One of the artists on his roster included the highly successful female artist, Da Brat. Her pop-rap album, *Funkdafied* (1994), was the first by a female MC to sell over one million units.

Another commercially successful Atlanta artist is the eclectic act OutKast. Initially affiliated with the Goodie Mob, OutKast released its first album, *Southernplayalisticadillacmuzik* in 1994.[53] One of OutKast's biggest hits, "Hey Ya" (2003), was more similar stylistically to alternative rock than to hip-hop. It was sung nearly in its entirety and stood in brilliant contrast to the hardcore image of the previous decade. Another southern foray into the mainstream world was the collaboration between R&B superstar Usher and two Atlanta-based superstar rappers, Lil Jon and producer Ludacris. The result was Usher's huge hit, "Yeah" (2004), a crunk-infused R&B song that featured the two rappers.

Three 6 Mafia of Memphis gained national attention when their song, "It's Hard Out Here for a Pimp" in the hip-hop themed film *Hustle and Flow* won an Oscar in 2006 for "Best Original Song." In the group's acceptance speech, one of the members remarked, "We got an album out now . . . called *The Most Known Unknowns* [2005]. We named it that 'cause . . . we been rappin' for over sixteen years and nobody never knew who we were. Now, they know!"[54] Three 6 Mafia ("Sippin on Some Sizzurp," 2005) and other Dirty South hardcore artists also helped to expose the illicit drug of choice of the hardcore South: "purple drank" (also called "lean" or "syrup"), a potent mixture of cough syrup with codeine, sweetened soda, and hard candy. This concoction contributed to the deaths of DJ Screw and rapper Pimp C in 2000 and 2007, respectively.

Hit producer-rappers of Virginia Beach—Timbaland, Missy Elliott, and the Neptunes—represented eclecticism rather than a regional style branding of Virginia.[55] The Neptunes, comprised of Pharrell Williams and Chad Hugo, were a production team known for their innovative arrangements. A prime example of their unconventional but commercially viable production style was "Bouncin' Back (Bumpin' Me Against the Wall)," by the rapper Mystikal, in 2001. Rather than using "bounce" or East or West Coast styles for the New Orleans-based MC, the track referenced New Orleans through live and synthesized horn-lines reminiscent of second-line bands. Additionally, the drum "kick" (bass drum) rhythmically punctuated, rather than defined, the beat; this was unlike traditional hip-hop, where the kick starts the beat.[56] Without an easily predictable low end to ground the groove, the resulting effect was a kind of rhythmic suspension that was uncharacteristic of hip-hop beats, but perhaps closer to a highly altered "Big Four" New Orleans bass drum rhythm.[57] Pharrell Williams, also a rapper, produced a later hit for Snoop Dogg, "Drop It Like It's Hot" (2004), which featured percussion produced by sampled human mouth clicks. By 2010, the Dirty South had become a regional partner, arguably on equal ground with the East and West Coasts, complete with its own subgenres, and influence on the global hip-hop market.

OLD SCHOOL AND NEW SCHOOL

In the middle and late 1980s, a loose stylistic and temporal distinction, labeled "old" and "new" school, emerged as a way of distinguishing the party-oriented MCs of the pioneering hip-hop generation from the street-oriented MCs of the newer style. Old school corresponds to the period between 1972 and 1984 when rappers relied on live performance and word of mouth, rather than videos, to establish their reputation. The transition occurred around the same time as the emergence of the new sampling and video technology. In the latter part of the 1980s, MCs began to expand the timbre, rhythmic, thematic, and textual horizons of rap, ushering in the new school. By the early 1990s, the new school was in full gear.

Old School

Comparisons of **old school** and new school rap typically center on issues of poetic scheme, dress, rhythm, lyric themes, instrumental accompaniment, and use of technology. To some hip-hoppers, a major distinguishing mark of old-school rapping is its association with various types of live performance: graffiti writing, b-boying/girling, as well as DJ-ing and MC-ing (rapping). Crowd participation and call-and-response were essential elements of live performance, with such chants as "Throw your hands in the air / And wave them like you just don't care" being commonplace.

The poetic structure of old-school lyrics utilized an AABBCC rhyme scheme, whereby the rhymed words largely occurred in regular, predictable places. Sixteenth-note rhythms and simple syncopations were typical of old-school rap lyrics, as illustrated in "Spoonin' Rap: A Drive Down the Street/I was Spanking and Freaking" (1979) by Spoonie Gee (Figure 17.3; Track 40):[58]

> A1 I'm not conceited baby please don't take me for a **toy**
> A2 Just remember me-a Spoonie Gee the baddest lover **boy**
> B1 The Rhyme sayer girl player drink a lot of juice,
> B2 and what God gave me babe I'm gonna give it to **you.**
> C1 You go-a Fee fee fi, f-fo fo **fum,**
> C2 I smell the blood of an English**mun.**
> D1 Well if the people ain't dancing, they shouldn't be around.
> D2 So come on ev'rybody, let's all get **down** . . .

Stylistically and thematically, this song reflects its roots as recreational "party music." Spoonie Gee claims to be "the baddest lover boy," in keeping with the hip-hop tradition of boasting. Characteristic of the MC's initial role as the individual charged with keeping the patrons

Old-school rap
Early hip-hop that emerged during the 1970s, featuring DJs, a crew or posse of rappers, break dancers, and graffiti artists. Lyrics follow the AABB rhymed couplet format.

 40

"Spoonin' Rap: A Drive Down the Street/I was Spanking and Freaking."

Dawn M. Norfleet

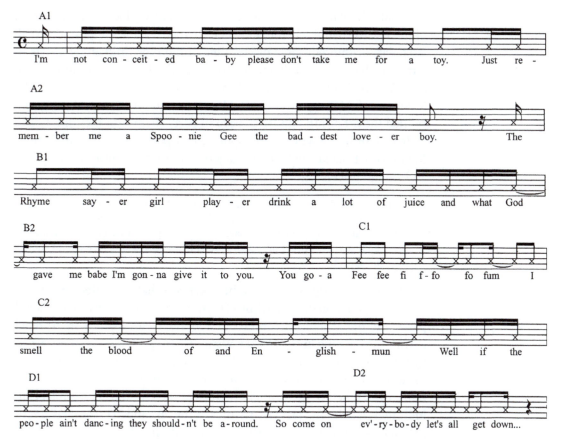

Figure 17.3

Transcription from "Spoonin' Rap: A Drive Down the Street/I Was Spanking and Freaking" (1979) by Spoonie Gee. Lyrics reprinted courtesy of Tuff City Music.

energized, the lyric contains references to "the people" dancing at their highest level.

From the 1970s to the mid-1980s, clothes were used to heighten the distinction between onstage performers and offstage audience members. Old-school performances tended to feature "dressing up," from the space fantasy outfits of Bambaataa—typical of African American and disco groups of the early 1970s—to displays of exaggerated wealth by the wearing of heavy gold jewelry and other expensive accessories. Early old-school recordings often featured live bands and/or congas and other Latin percussion, reflecting the large Puerto Rican presence and influence in the southern, Caribbean, and Latin American communities that produced hip-hop.

New School

New-school MCs expanded the rhyming and rhythmic possibilities of the party-rocking rapper, rather than completely rejecting and uprooting hip-hop traditions. **New-school rap** is more lyrically and stylistically diverse

> **New-school rap**
> Post-1985 technology-driven hip-hop that spotlights MCs whose raps are stylistically and lyrically diverse. The rhyme scheme departs somewhat from the AABB couplet format.

than old-school rap. It is characterized by a relatively looser interpretation of the AABB rhyme scheme, in which rhymed syllables appear at varied, irregular, or unpredictable places. One of the most influential artists in terms of rhythmic and thematic styles was the Long Island duo Eric B. and Rakim. With the album *Paid in Full* (1988), Rakim was at the forefront of MCs such as Kool Moe Dee and Big Daddy Kane, who refined the art of hip-hop lyrics beyond party rhymes in the mid- to late 1980s by infusing lyrics with sophisticated poetic devices and rhythm. Rakim constructed vivid street imagery with skillfully placed metaphors and rhyme placement:

> Rakim raised the bar for MC technique higher than it had ever been, helping to pioneer the use of internal rhymes—i.e., rhymes that occurred in the middle of lines, rather than just at the end ... Rakim was among the first to demonstrate the possibilities of ... writing intricately crafted lyrics packed with clever word choices and metaphors.[59]

By 1992, rap styles of the hip-hop pioneers that presented a relatively strict interpretation of the AABBCC rhyme scheme came to be considered passé and old school. In contrast to Spoonie Gee's literally interpreted rhyme, the opening lines of "They Want Efx" (1992; Figure 17.4), recorded by the Brooklyn rap artists Das Efx, characterize the trend toward more intricate rhymes that became commonplace in the 1990s. In the lyric transcription below, the primary rhymes of the "A" and "C" couplets are indicated in bold; the primary rhymes of the "B" and "D" couplets are in bold italics, while incidental rhymes are underlined:

(*Introduction*) **Bum** stickety **bum** stickety
A1   Bum **hon**, I got dat ol' pah **rum**-pum-pum **pum**, but I could
A2   Fee fi a *foe* diddly **fum**, here I **come**. So Peter
B1   Piper, I'm hyper than Pinocchio's *nose*, 'cause I'm a
B2   Super cali-fragi-listic tic tac *pro*. I gave my
C1   *Oop*-sy daisy, now you got the **crazy**
C2   **Drayz** with the *Books*,[60] googly *goo*, where's the **gravy**, so
D1   One *two*, un-buckle my um
D2   *Shoe*, yabba *do*, hibbity *hoo*, crack a *brew* ...

In this example, the rhythms are highly syncopated, giving the rap a swing feel (introduction, lines A1–2). In contrast, Spoonie Gee's rhymes, typical of the rhythm of old school rap artists, are characterized by regularly occurring rhythms largely made up of sixteenth-note syllables that are accented on the odd-numbered beats, which yield relatively predictable syncopations (see Figure 17.3, Spoonie Gee lines A1–2).

Distinctions between old school and new school are pliable rather than fixed. For example, in the 1990s many of the early new-school artists such as KRS-One and Run-D.M.C. were marketed as old school to promote radio and concert programming that featured hip-hop "classics." But in 2000, those same artists were referenced as old school, to distinguish them from newly emergent contemporary performance

    Dawn M. Norfleet

Figure 17.4
Transcription from "They Want Efx" (1992) by Das Efx. Words and music by Andre Weston and Willie Hines, © 1992 EMI April Music Inc., Sewer Slang Music, and Cellar to the Addict. All rights controlled and administered by EMI April Music Inc. All rights reserved, international copyright secured, used by permission. Contains elements of "Blind Men Can See It," by James Brown, Fred Wesley, and Charles Bobbit.

groups. The term "old school" became a hip-hop equivalent of the pop classics description, "oldies but goodies."

Groups that emerged in the mid- to late 1980s, such as Run-D.M.C. ("Jam Master Jay," 1984),[61] characterized both old and new schools, since the groups' careers began in the transitional period of the mid-1980s. Despite their explosive, percussive vocals and tough image that characterized the new school, their rhyme structure did not significantly differ from that of the old school. The rhyme scheme used by storytelling MCs such as Slick Rick and Dana Dane in the mid-1980s was similar to that of old-school artists such as Kurtis Blow and Melle Mel.

In spite of the numerous changes that took place in the 1980s, new-school artists still maintained certain elements of the old-school hip-hop tradition, thematically as well as structurally. Like the earlier rap of Spoonie Gee (see Figure 17.3, lines A2, D2), the Das Efx text also utilizes hip-hop poetic norms such as party-rocking boasting (Figure 17.4, line B1), nursery rhymes, and alliteration (Spoonie Gee, lines C1–2; Das Efx line A2). Later artists, including OutKast and Eminem (Eminem featuring Dido, "Stan," 2000), continued to push the structural and thematic envelope even further.

The first artists of the new school (c.1985–90) preferred programmable percussion, such as the electronic beat box and other synthesized instruments, refraining from live instruments nearly altogether. They and other new-school artists later used sampled material from popular and obscure 1960s and 1970s R&B, jazz, and rock recordings as the foundation for new songs. Producers with sampling units and programmable drum machines became vital components of rap production. Toward 2000, however, many artists began to reincorporate live instruments in their recordings and live performances. Despite this re-emergence of live musical instruments, new-school recordings nevertheless de-emphasized acoustic percussion. As a result, the Latin percussion influence so prominent in early rap music recordings all but disappeared as hip-hop became electronic.

HIP-HOP DANCE MUSIC

Hip-hop dance is an individual expression, rather than a coupled activity (compared to salsa or "the bump" of the 1970s, for instance). As with the music, its central characters have been largely male, although females do participate. The dance is arguably aimed at impressing one's peers at least as much, if not more than, the opposite sex. From its inception, hip-hop music provided the soundtrack to various dances. "Locking" and the "Robot" gave way to loose-limbed b-boying/girling, which was supplanted by "poplocking" and the "electric boogie"—dances with largely instrumental music marked by quick, intricate, abrupt, angular movements of limbs and joints. However, all of these were considered passé by the 1990s, as was instrumental hip-hop.

By 2002, intricate, limber-legged dances took over, known as the "Harlem shuffle" and the "crip-walk." Because of feared gang affiliations, the "crip-walk" was euphemized as "clown walk," or simply the "C-walk."[62] By 2009, "jerking"—and its associated moves: the "pin drop," "stanky leg," "reject," "dipping," and "Dougie"—was a kind of California-generated dances that were highly popular among youth wearing "skinny jeans." The dance craze spread by dance-rap crews, such as the New Boyz and the R3jectz (pronounced "rejects"), and exposure and tutorials via YouTube, such as those posted by the duo, Audio Push. "Twerking," a highly suggestive dance originating from the 1990s New Orleans "bounce" scene, was thrust into worldwide pop culture some twenty years later. At the 2013 MTV Video Music Awards, White pop stars Miley Cyrus and Robin Thicke imitated twerking during their performance.

UNDERGROUND, ALTERNATIVE, AND SPOKEN WORD

In response to—or in spite of—hip-hop's commercialization, loose alliances of artists and artistic outlets known as the "underground" flourished in the early 1990s and beyond. Depending on context, "underground" can refer to an event, musical style, or place that operates beneath the commercial radar and widespread public view.[63] According to Q-Tip (a.k.a. Kamaal Fareed), former frontman of A Tribe Called Quest, the underground "is real important, because that's where your new [material] comes from . . . Underground is like [stuff] that you wouldn't normally hear every day."[64]

The underground sound rose in the early 1990s as networks of small local venues, independent radio or programs, promoters, events, and artists devoted themselves to nurturing emerging local hip-hop artists. With the prevalence of gangsta rap and public fears of violence by Black youth, it became difficult to book popular rap acts beginning in the mid-1980s and difficult for emerging artists to find places to perform.[65] Consequently, young entrepreneurs self-produced events largely independent of the commercial industry.

In the underground, new hip-hop artists could perform, experiment, hone stage skills, and gain a following. In a deliberate attempt to maintain a connection to hip-hop's early tradition of live performance, popularity in the underground was measured by an MC's performance skills, as well as lyrical content and the ability to verbally improvise.[66] An artist also could acquire and sharpen improvisational skills known as "freestyling" in small, informal groupings of MCs known by the mid-1990s as "ciphers." Here, MCs traded rhymes one at a time, often with the accompaniment of the vocal "beat box," or oral percussion sounds that emulate electronic or acoustic drums.

An underground aesthetic grew in the 1990s as hip-hop diversified. In contrast to the well-produced sounds of classic hip-hop, the Wu-Tang Clan's debut album *Enter the Wu-Tang (36 Chambers)* (1992) popularized a sound often referred to as "underground." In this case, underground is an adjective for the often raw production sound that characterized emerging rap artists who usually used low-budget and home recording studios, and had little professional training in music recording.

The raw sound was achieved in part by using a nontraditional recording technique of speaking at high volume levels in very close proximity to the microphone. The resulting distorted sound, as exemplified in another hit song, "Method Man" (1993), came to be a desired trait for many in hip-hop during that decade. Hisses and pops from scratched records were intended to give desired old-school "flavor" or character to underground recordings. When digitally sampling, DJs and producers often chose worn records to achieve this specific effect.

Professionally aspiring artists identified positively with the gruff vocal timbres and rough sound. Wu-Tang Clan's signature sound featured dissonant chords and samples from 1960s soul music of the Stax catalog, creating a raw, unpolished timbre—despite the fact that the collective utilized pricey, top professional audio engineers. Their relatively low-tech minimalist sound contrasted with the complex, polyphonic, sampled layering of Public Enemy or the jazzy textures of A Tribe Called Quest, thus ushering in a new aesthetic of hip-hop of the 1990s: the gritty underground sound.

In addition to its reference to a specific hip-hop style, underground also referred to a network where MCs, DJs, and instrumentalists could experiment with like-minded rock, spoken word, jazz, and world music artists. "Alternative hip-hop" was a description applied to styles that had elements of traditional hip-hop rhyme structure, but often departed from the standard two- to four-bar sampled loop, in favor of a live band, guitars, or blended genres. Music videos by Digable Planets, ("Rebirth of Slick [Cool Like Dat]," 1993) and the Pharcyde ("She Keeps on Passin' Me By," 1992) vividly depict an eclectic realm that was distant from the rough-and-tumble world of hardcore rap videos.

Freestyling
The process used by MCs to improvise rhymes during hip-hop performance.

Freestyling was a valued skill in both underground hip-hop performance and jazz, so live and recorded collaboration was natural. MCs and DJs collaborated with jazz, R&B, and rock musicians in performance and on recordings. For example, Q-Tip, using his Islamic name, Kamaal Fareed, recorded an eclectic jazz/hip-hop fusion. The album, *Kamaal the Abstract*, was recorded in 2001 but was not released until 2009. One song, "Abstractionisms," featured jazz saxophonist Kenny Garrett.

In New York, seasoned jazz musicians Donald Byrd and Lou Donaldson and "free jazz" pianist Horace Tapscott of Los Angeles collaborated and recorded with hip-hop artists Guru and Jazzmatazz and Freestyle Fellowship, respectively. Many young jazz musicians in the 1990s listened to and were influenced by their their hip-hop contemporaries, and saw no conflict in expressing both streams of influence. Atlanta-based trumpet player, Russell Gunn, was a member of the very conservative Lincoln Center Jazz Orchestra in the mid-1990s. He eventually formed his own band, Ethnomusicology, and played a style he called "crunk jazz," which combined a southern style of hip-hop, traditional jazz, and R&B. Karriem Riggins was a respected drummer who played with jazz legend Betty Carter in the early 1990s; he eventually produced underground artists Talib Kweli and Slum Village, a group from his native Detroit. Brooklyn MC/actor Mos Def included versatile musicians from the Black rock group Living Color in his touring band. In New York and Los Angeles, the Nuyorican Poets Café and Fifth Street Dicks, respectively, were popular spots for hip-hop/live jazz collaborations. Although popularity in the underground networks did not guarantee success in the commercial industry, in the twenty-first century, some artists were able to develop and maintain a strong fan base through live performance and, increasingly, through iTunes and YouTube.

In the underground, there has been plenty of room for female rappers to thrive. Los Angeles-based MC Medusa was a prominent and respected MC, who had won battles against male MCs in the mid-1990s. As of 2010, she was still actively performing with her band, Feline Science. Pri the Honeydark has been a New York-based MC who, since the mid-1990s, has earned a strong reputation on the MC battle circuit and as a producer.

By the early 1990s, a spoken word scene was growing and sharing performance spaces and events with rappers. Many of the rappers and poets had similar backgrounds, and a cross-pollination of styles resulted. MCs such as Mos Def and Talib Kweli were also influenced by the relatively freer rhyme schemes and lyricism of underground poets. Similarly to rappers, underground poets often employed an aggressive verbal style, which they delivered over accompanying hip-hop-styled tracks.

Hip-hop spoken word artists typically expanded the rhyme and rhythmic schemes of the AABBCC form, or abandoned it almost entirely, while maintaining the poignant urban imagery and explosive delivery of hip-hop in their performances. Few of these artists received notable success in the commercial realm; instead, they earned a living through self-publishing or self-producing their recordings and/or books and through college and international tours, for which they lectured, acted, and performed in local venues. Poets/performance artists associated with the 1990s hip-hop underground included Jessica Care Moore, actor muMs da Schemer, and MC-activist Rha Goddess.

TWENTY-FIRST-CENTURY TECHNOLOGY

The rapid rate of communication technology breakthroughs in the latter part of the twentieth century resulted in the blurring of many boundaries in hip-hop: stylistic, demographic, and even philosophical. Toward the mid-2000s, commercial hip-hop incorporated a sound commonplace in mainstream pop music: the "**Auto-Tune**"—digital voice processing initially designed to correct a "pitchy" (out-of-tune) singer's voice. Similar to the vocoder of 1980s electro-funk, the Auto-Tune was also used to represent the voice as more "robotic" and less human, as was typical in mainstream dance and pop music, such as Cher's hit "Believe" (1998). Rap artists who commonly used the Auto-Tune included T-Pain ("Buy U a Drank," featuring Yung Joc, 2007), Lil Wayne ("Lollypop," featuring

Auto-Tune
A digital device used to manipulate vocal and instrumental pitch. The synthesized vocoder preceded the Auto-Tune.

Static, 2008) and Nicki Minaj ("Your Love," 2010). In the minds of some, the prevalence of the Auto-Tune in popular rap songs in 2009 helped blur the line between hip-hop and mainstream pop music in the first decade of the twenty-first century.[67]

The accessibility of professional recording and editing audio software and the expansion of the internet have had a major impact on the production, distribution, and marketing of hip-hop in the twenty-first century. High production costs of traditional studios were well beyond the reach of everyday music makers before the rise in small-scale, private, or home "project studios." In 2002, *Black Enterprise* noted, "[T]he average budget for recording a hip-hop album is upwards of $250,000 these days. Factor in pressing, distribution, and marketing, and a major label can easily spend more than $1 million before an album even hits the stores."[68]

While labels increased their investment in hip-hop, technological developments allowed emerging artists opportunities to produce themselves, with little or no financial backing. According to former West Coast rap producer DJ Slip, "Technology advanced farther and faster than the art form did. This allowed anyone access to the business."[69] Artists could eliminate the middle-man on several levels, and gain skills as do-it-yourself business people:

- The number of home recording studios built in artists' basements, bedrooms, and garages grew rapidly. User-friendly, computer-based, professional software and affordable equipment cut out professional audio engineers and studios, which could charge as much as one hundred dollars per hour.[70]
- The internet permitted artists to do their own promotion on their own websites, cutting out promoters, postage, and "street teams," who would post flyers around the city advertising an artist.
- The internet also facilitated artists based in different regions or even countries to collaborate and record with each other by e-mailing audio files, eliminating transportation and postage costs.
- Social networking sites allowed artists to attract and build audiences free of charge, eliminating promoters.[71]
- Cyberspace song commerce and music "sharing" via sites or "burning"/"ripping" one's own preferred music made the purchase, distribution, and exchange of music convenient, and diminished the need for record companies to market and distribute products.

The technological advancements, for some professional artists, came as a double-edged sword. DJ Slip continues:

> This [technological innovation] gave access to individuals that had no desire to create art, or push the creative envelope. This brought in a "fast food," lowbrow type of mentality that was about making a quick buck and creating artists with less shelf life than ever.[72]

Hip-hop careers were notoriously short with a plethora of one- and two-hit "wonders." The former producer of MC Eiht and Compton's Most Wanted feared that the new media would accelerate the rate of short careers, presumably due to music being perceived as a disposable commodity like an outdated cellular phone.

Indeed, with the rapid advances in digitally facilitated networking—i.e., Myspace (2003), Facebook (2004), and YouTube (2005)—in the first decade of the twenty-first century, even diligent middle-schoolers could now become music producers and collaborate with their rapping friends.[73] They could produce and record their songs on home computers, sell them on iTunes, gain a following on Facebook, and advertise their talent by posting home-produced videos on YouTube, for free. By conducting a simple internet search in 2009, anyone could find out "How to Make a Dirty South Beat," "How to Make Crunk Southern Beats," and "How to Make Creole Mashed Potatoes for Thanksgiving," within three mouse clicks of each other on eHow.com (September 10, 2009). With no pressure to produce a body of work in an album form to be purchased as a unit, young amateurs could produce singles that their fans could download on mp3 players or burn to CDs on home computers, eliminating the practical need for large music outlets. Indeed, large music chains such as Tower Records and Virgin Megastores closed in 2006 and 2009, respectively—collateral damage of the explosive growth of online stores, music streaming services, and illegal downloading.

HIP-HOP IN THE MAINSTREAM (2000–10)

Aside from the overall decline of the recording industry since 2000, hip-hop continued to infiltrate and dominate American mainstream popular culture. Russell Simmons's venture, *Def Poetry Jam*, hosted by eclectic MC Mos Def, aired on HBO from 2002 to 2007 and featured spoken word artists. A staged, Broadway version of *Def Poetry Jam* won a Tony Award in 2003 and in 2010. Will Smith joined fellow hip-hop icon Jay-Z as a producer of the Broadway musical production, *Fela!* (2010), which celebrated the late Nigerian musician-activist, Fela Anikulapo Kuti. The production won several Tony Awards.

Hip-hop also made inroads into the African American religious arena. "Stomp" (1997), a multiplatinum hit by contemporary gospel artist Kirk Franklin, featured Cheryl "Salt" James of the 1980s hip-hop group, Salt-N-Pepa. Using high-tech video production atypical of gospel artists at the time, Franklin's hip-hop–gospel fusion was consciously directed toward a non-church-based youth market.[74] Kanye West pushed the sacred–secular envelope even further with "Jesus Walks" (2004). The Grammy Award-winning song's storyline juxtaposes spiritual struggle with the vagaries of the street life; but unlike Franklin's gospel "Stomp," West used explicit language uncharacteristic of the religious arena.

Whether against "the power," sexism, or "sucka MCs," struggle has defined hip-hop since its inception. The irony of its ever-shifting and blurring lines of what defines the boundaries, and what lies within or outside of them, is not lost on its practitioners. MC, activist, and former Zulu Nation leader Rha Goddess reflects, "Within our society, there is a romanticization of this idea of struggle . . . It's the mythology of transformations—the ugly duckling becomes the beautiful swan . . . What happens when the struggle doesn't lead to triumph?"[75] But real life is not as easily marketable as a catchy slogan. "Keepin' it real" was the hip-hop's mantra for at least a decade and provided the fuel for hip-hoppers to constantly prove their fidelity to the community. The struggle to keep up with the demands of hardcore realness proved lucrative for some artists and devastating for others. Yet, another category of hip-hop artists successfully managed their public persona and savvy business practices and enjoyed sustained acceptance in both hip-hop and mainstream societies.

Struggle and conflict seemed to define hip-hop in the 1980s and 1990s. Yet, hip-hop's first decade of the twenty-first century was arguably marked by little controversy. Perhaps little of shock value remained, since the hardcore aesthetic had been incorporated into the soundscape and visual images of mainstream popular culture. Moreover, hip-hop's professional rebels have grown older, with families to raise and mortgages to pay. While Snoop Dogg maintained his "smoked-out" street image by joking about drug use on talk shows into 2010, he also starred in a family-oriented reality show and founded a sports program for inner-city youth.

Meanwhile, hip-hop icons such as Master P, Jay-Z, and 50 Cent became moguls profiled in *Forbes Magazine*, and Lil Jon joined Donald Trump's cast of *Celebrity Apprentice* in 2011.[76] Beginning in 2000, Ice-T, once demonized for recording "Cop Killer" in 1992, has portrayed a New York City detective on the popular network television program *Law and Order: Special Victims Unit* (1999–). Referencing her birth name, Queen Latifah recorded *The Dana Owens Album* (2004), a collection of classic jazz and pop standards with lush string accompaniment that channeled Sinatra more than KRS-One. At the 2009 Oscars, she sang the classic song "I'll be Seeing You," which "Old Blue Eyes" had made famous. One year later, she hosted the BET Awards Show, where she proved she could still rock a crowd as a skilled MC. Queen Latifah, along with LL Cool J, Mos Def, and Will Smith, managed to expand their professional brands beyond their early rap star personas, and became widely recognizable American cultural symbols (if not icons) through their visibility in mainstream films and productions.[77]

Even the racial barrier, which traditionally barred White rappers from full acceptance into hip-hop, was seemingly broken in the twenty-first century. White rappers Paul Wall from Houston and Eminem from Detroit gained acceptance both in the hip-hop community and in the mainstream. By 2010, while maintaining his affiliation with Dr. Dre,

Eminem had become the top-selling recording artist of the first decade of the twenty-first century, with sales of 32.2 million albums.[78]

CONCLUSIONS

Hip-hop's history of transformation is a story of movement, friction, and conflict. In the post-Civil Rights era South Bronx, the narrative told of the desire for youth to create music by and for each other. It was Bambaataa's redirection of violent gang activities into b-boy battles. It was local, Black, underground music from Compton adopted as a symbol of rebellion for White America. It exposed societal issues and controversies of urban street culture once kept within the confines of the Black community, by which the outside world could be shocked and entertained. It saw women artists, producers, and writers devising ongoing strategies to remain viable and respected in a realm where they traditionally had been at the periphery. All in all, the transformation narrative of hip-hop symbolized the ongoing drama of the divergent, yet interconnected, human entities that made up late twentieth-century American society, and has kept audiences worldwide captivated by an ever-shifting narrative set to a danceable beat well into the new millenium.

KEY NAMES

Afrika Bambaataa	Marion "Suge" Knight
The Beastie Boys	Talib Kweli
Sean Combs	Kool DJ Herc
DJ Screw	LL Cool J
Dr. Dre	Ludacris
Eazy-E	Master P
Missy Elliott	MC Hammer
Eric B. and Rakim	Mos Def
50 Cent	Niggaz with Attitude (N.W.A)
Geto Boys	Notorious B.I.G. (a.k.a Biggie
Goodie Mob	Smalls)
Grandmaster Flash	OutKast
Grandmixer D.ST. (later, DXT)	Public Enemy
Grandwizard Theodore	Queen Latifah
Lauryn Hill	Rick Rubin
Ice-T	Run-D.M.C.
Jay-Z	Salt-N-Pepa
Jazzy Jeff and the Fresh Prince	Tupac Shakur
(Will Smith)	Roxanne Shante

Russell Simmons

Snoop Doggy Dogg (a.k.a Snoop Dogg)

Sugar Hill Gang

Three 6 Mafia

A Tribe Called Quest

Vanilla Ice

Kanye West

Wu-Tang Clan

QUESTIONS

1. What cultural and verbal traditions formed the basis for the development of rap music? Which of these traditions are still evident in current rap styles?

2. What is the role of the DJ in rap music? The role of the MC? What techniques do rap artists use to create new music?

3. What are the differences between hip-hop styles such as party, hardcore, gangsta, message, and pop-rap? How have geography and generation helped define distinctions within rap music?

4. Identify early and current controversies surrounding rap music.

PROJECTS

1. Create a plan for a compilation CD that traces the development of hip-hop and rap music. Identify at least ten tracks that you would include and write liner notes explaining your choices. Be specific about your overall vision for the album as well as your rationale for each selection. Address musical, technological, and stylistic elements; lyric form and content; and social, political, or historical significance. Also provide artist biographies.

2. Choose a specific event or issue that sparked public discussion of rap music (e.g., the backlash against Ice-T's "Cop Killer," the issue of "authenticity" vis-à-vis the criticism of Vanilla Ice, or the controversy over sampling and copyright). Research the people and issues involved and the different perspectives expressed, and then stage a live debate based on your findings.

3. Analyze and compare the careers of three different female rap artists, using such sources as recordings, videos, album sales data, chart success, media coverage, and published personal interviews. Consider how each woman has navigated issues of gender; made specific choices through her music and image; and engaged the public, the music industry, and other artists.

NOTES

Please see the discography for information on resources for further listening.

1. See Burns 1995. For further discussion of African retentions in hip-hop and its predecessors, see also Keyes 2002, 17–38.

Dawn M. Norfleet

2. Fernando Jr. 1994, 40.

3. Ibid., 34.

4. For further information on the influence of Jamaican musical practices on early hip-hop, see Fernando Jr. 1994, 34–47, and the documentary *Roots, Rock, Reggae: Inside the Jamaican Music Scene* (1977).

5. Burns 1995, 34. These films later influenced the direction of West Coast "gangsta" rap in the mid-1980s.

6. Chang 2006, 111, notes that several early graffiti artists did not associate graffiti with hip-hop, and preferred disco or rock music instead.

7. For further information on early hip-hop dance, see Schloss 2009.

8. DJ Herc used both "Herculords" and "Herculoids" to refer to his ensemble of dancers, MCs, and assistants. Chang 2006, 81.

9. Keyes 2002, 51–52, 58–59, 77.

10. Grandmaster Flash, interviewed in *The Source*, November 1993, 47.

11. See Schloss 2004, 32, for a discussion on the effects of musical break production on the early hip-hop aesthetic.

12. Afrika Bambaataa & the Soul Sonic Force, "Planet Rock" (1982).

13. Schloss 2004, 36

14. Fernando Jr. 1994, 10.

15. George 1998, 65–66.

16. Fernando Jr. 1994, 164.

17. Public Enemy, "Don't Believe the Hype" (1988).

18. Alternative rap typically draws from a wide range of genres, including funk, rock, jazz, soul, reggae, country, electronica, world music, and folk.

19. Treach from Naughty By Nature described his music as "classical hip-hop." Personally conducted interview, March 1, 1992.

20. Lauryn Hill, "Doo Wop (That Thing)" (1998).

21. The popularity of female artists seemed to have faded by 2000. Rapper/actor Eve lamented in the documentary, *My Mic Sounds Nice: A Truth about Women in Hip-Hop* (2010), that the Grammy Awards had eliminated the category for female rappers by that time, because so few were being nominated.

22. The harder sounds of songs of the mid-1980s, such as Run-D.M.C.'s "King of Rock" (1985) and "Proud to Be Black" (1986), were joined with visible images of machismo and power as a formidable marketing package for the new style, which became known as hardcore hip-hop. Artists of this decade included Philadelphia's Schoolly D ("Saturday Night," 1986) and New York's Just-Ice ("Gangster of Hip-Hop," 1986). Hardcore artists of the 1990s included: Kool G Rap and DJ Polo ("Talk Like Sex," 1990); Wu-Tang Clan, which put Staten Island on the hip-hop map of significance ("M.E.T.H.O.D. Man," 1993); and Junior M.A.F.I.A. ("Player's Anthem," 1995), which launched the solo rap careers of Notorious B.I.G. and female hardcore artist Lil' Kim.

23. Dyson 2001, 15.

24. The list of popular hip-hop personalities who were arrested and/or served jail time included: Tupac Shakur (1992), Snoop Dogg (1993), Old Dirty Bastard of the Wu-Tang Clan (1999), Mystikal (2002), and Lil Wayne (2010).

25. Quoted in Smith 1993, 66.

26. Eric B. and Rakim, "Follow the Leader" (1988). Norfleet 1997, 111–43, discusses key symbolic objects and places in the hip-hop cultural lexicon: the microphone, stage, cipher, battle, and show.

27. Taken from the title of a Boogie Down Productions song, "Stop the Violence" was a series of actions taken by notable rap artists of the time "to define the problem [of violence at hip-hop events] and defend themselves" in the face of mainstream condemnation of hip-hop (Nelson George, quoted in Chang 2005, 274). These actions included community outreach, activism, and collaborative recordings, such as "Self Destruction" (1989), which included diverse hip-hop luminaries: KRS-One, MC Lyte, and Doug E. Fresh; and California rappers, Tone-Lōc and Young MC (Keyes 2002, 164–66).

28. Pareles 1992.
29. Anderson 1990, 114, discusses how the power dynamic in African American street relationships is skewed toward young men, and that relationships can be combative, if not exploitative.
30. Norfleet 1997, 165–77, discusses the dynamics involving power hierarchy in male–female relationships found in the hardcore lifestyle.
31. "Chronic" is a street term for a type of very potent marijuana. *The Chronic* (1992) established Dr. Dre's reputation for characteristically slick production techniques and a strong bass sound; this recording also featured rap newcomer Snoop Doggy Dogg (later Snoop Dogg), also associated with gangsta rap.
32. Quoted in Phillips 1994.
33. Quoted in Cooper 1993, 17.
34. MC Lyte (spoken by KRS-One), "Intro" (1993).
35. Queen Latifah, "U.N.I.T.Y." (1993).
36. A discussion of the phrase "don't call me out [of] my name" is found in Benston 1982, 5.
37. Norfleet 1997, 138–39.
38. Early gangsta rap artist Ice-T references as an influence author and former pimp Iceberg Slim (Robert Beck), including his book *Pimp: The Story of My Life* (1969) and several other mini-books about his exploits in the street. Ice-T, born Tracy Marrow, explained that his professional name was a peer-created derivative of the author's name, because of his ability to recite passages from Slim's books as a youth. See Cross 1993, 182.
39. McDermott 2002, 16.
40. N.W.A., "F—— Tha Police" (1988).
41. Milt Ahlerich, assistant director of the FBI, quoted in McDermott 2002, 31.
42. N.W.A., "F—— Tha Police" (1988).
43. Quoted in Hilburn 2001, 80.
44. Generational rivalry also took place between "old-school" rapper Kool Moe Dee and "new-school"artist LL Cool J. The "battles" took place in "diss records" between the two between 1987 and 1991. (A "diss" is a harsh put-down.) Bronx-based Boogie Down Productions dissed then-popular groups from Queens and Long Island ("The Bridge is Over," 1987).
45. Keyes 2002, 168.
46. Because a musical artist had already recorded under the name "Biggie Smalls," Christopher Wallace used the name "The Notorious B.I.G." professionally. The hip-hop community and media still commonly referred to him as Biggie Smalls.
47. George 1998, 124.
48. Matt Miller 2008.
49. Bass's impact reached across the country. Another bass hit was "Baby Got Back" (1992) by Sir Mix-A-Lot, from Seattle, Washington. The multi-platinum-selling single poked fun at then-popular "waif" images of women, while humorously praising the stereotype of Black women's shapeliness.
50. Matt Miller 2008, 16.
51. Muhammad 1999, 79.
52. Boorstin, Freedman, and Tkaczyk 2002.
53. Suggested video: OutKast, "Ms. Jackson" (2000).
54. Three 6 Mafia members, interviewed by Harry Smith, cbsnews.com, March 10, 2006.
55. Matt Miller 2008, 30.
56. Traditionally, hip-hop percussion is modeled after the sonic layout of funk drumming. The drum kit terminology relating to low, medium, and high, unpitched percussion carried over into hip-hop. In a basic layout, the rhythmic "kick" (bass drum) marks all first and third beats, the first being of primary importance in funk. The snare drum sound, hand clap, finger snap, or rimshot occurs on the second and fourth beats. The high-hat, shaker, or (rarely) cowbell sound appear as eighth-notes. Rhythmic creativity occurs when the producer manipulates this standard formula, using syncopation, accents, and polyrhythm. In the Neptunes' arrangement, the kick occurs on the

expected "one," only once in a four-bar cycle, and on beat "three" of the fourth bar. The rest of the kicks occur as syncopated accents.

57. The "Big Four" is a central rhythm in second-line bands. For general information regarding traditional New Orleans jazz rhythms, see "New Orleans," in *Jazz for Young People Curriculum* (2002).

58. Spoonie Gee, "Spoonin' Rap: A Drive Down the Street/I was Spanking and Freaking" (1979).

59. Huey, "Rakim: Biography," www.allmusic.com.

60. From Das Efx, "They Want Efx" (1992). Drayz, pronounced "Dray-Zee," is one of the members of Das Efx. "Skoob" is the reverse spelling of "Books," the other member of the duo.

61. Run-D.M.C., "Jam Master Jay" (1984).

62. Hayasaki 2002.

63. Norfleet 1997, 98–102.

64. Quoted in Norfleet 1997, 107.

65. Rose 1994, 133.

66. Norfleet 1997, 238–76.

67. Superstar rapper-mogul Jay-Z recorded a diss and critique aimed at T-Pain and other hip-hop artists who used Auto-Tune, titled "D.O.A. [Death of Auto-Tune]," 2009.

68. Rhea 2002, 90.

69. Personal communication with DJ Slip, former producer of gangsta rap artists MC Eiht and Compton's Most Wanted.

70. Popular professional audio software included Logic, Pro Tools, and Reason. User-friendly amateur audio software, such as Garage Band, was also used by professional producers.

71. Myspace, ReverbNation, and Facebook music pages were among music commerce pages available in 2011, along with iTunes.

72. Personal communication with DJ Slip.

73. From 2006 to 2010, I mentored African American aspiring rappers, producers, and songwriters in the Los Angeles area. The students, grades 6–8, created their songs at school and at home, using the audio software Garage Band and Reason.

74. Kirk Franklin, acceptance speech at the 1998 Stellar Awards.

75. Goddess 2006, 341.

76. According to Forbes.com, Jay-Z and Sean "Diddy" Combs were the highest earners in hip-hop as of August 2010. In addition to their lucrative musical careers, both delved into clothing; Jay-Z also became part owner of the New Jersey Nets, and Combs (perhaps the first mogul-rapper) had been involved in restaurant ownership, vodka and cologne sales, and a reality show. Additional hip-hop impresarios Lil Jon and Dr. Dre capitalized on their "brand" to push energy drinks and headphones, respectively (Forbes.com, accessed August 16, 2010).

77. With starring roles in hit sitcoms and films since 1985, LL Cool J has perhaps successfully navigated the borderline between commercial success and hip-hop acceptance for the longest time period; his biggest role at the time of publication was co-star Navy crime investigator in the syndicated drama, *NCIS: Los Angeles* (2009–). Mos Def was cast among respected mainstream actors in *The Italian Job* (2003), and his band performed at LA's Hollywood Bowl in 2005. Will Smith branched out well beyond his comedic role as "The Fresh Prince" on the successful television sit-com *The Fresh Prince of Bel-Air* (1990–96) and gained critical acclaim as a dramatic actor when he portrayed a gay, troubled young man in the independent film, *Six Degrees of Separation* (1993). Will Smith was named "the most powerful actor in Hollywood" by Sean Smith of *Newsweek* (April 15, 2007).

78. According to Forbes.com (August 16, 2010), Eminem's record sales of $32 million surpassed those of the Beatles.

Glossary

12-inch single
An extended-play 45-rpm record that accommodated remixed and rearranged versions of hit songs, permitting longer, uninterrupted dancing, especially for disco audiences.

Acculturation
The process of change that occurs when two different cultural groups come into prolonged contact.

After-hours clubs
Small, non-alcoholic venues where patrons gathered after the curfew of those licensed to sell alcoholic beverages.

Alternative rap
Hip-hop music that does not conform to commercial forms of rap, such as gangsta, hardcore, and pop-rap. Instead, alternative rap freely draws from other genres, uses a loose interpretation of the rhymed couplet tradition, and/or includes themes that are more blatantly political than those of commercial rap.

Antebellum period
The period before the Civil War, when slavery was still the law of the land.

Arpeggiated chord
A chord in which the notes are played in sequence or succession rather than simultaneously.

Arranged/concert spiritual
The post-Civil War form of spirituals in a fixed, non-improvised form, which evolved in schools created to educate emancipated slaves.

Artists and Repertoire (A&R)
The individual who scouts talent and oversees the artistic development of recording artists. Includes songwriters, arrangers, and/or producers.

Auto-Tune
A digital device used to manipulate vocal and instrumental pitch. The synthesized vocoder preceded the Auto-Tune.

Banjo
Instrument of African origin, originally with one to six strings and a neck running parallel to a gourd body.

Barrelhouse
A wooden structure on logging and turpentine camps in forest areas of the rural South where laborers gathered to drink and gamble. Pianists played ragtime and blues. Term "barrelhouse" references the storage of alcohol in barrels.

Bebop
Combo jazz improvised style that evolved from big band swing in the 1940s, characterized by exceedingly fast tempos, with improvisational lines based on the harmonic structure rather than on the melody.

Bend
An instrumental technique used to slightly raise or lower pitch. For example, on guitar, the player pushes the string sideways against the fret.

Big band jazz
A form that evolved from New Orleans-styled combos in the late 1920s, characterized by the use of written arrangements and featuring the brass and reed sections trading melodic phrases in a call–response style.

Blackface *see* **Burnt-cork/blackface makeup.**

Black Power Movement
A movement of the late 1960s and early 1970s that emphasized Black unity, Black pride, and self-determination.

"Blaxploitation" film
1970s film genre that featured stereotypical images of Black urban life.

Blue note
A note, sounded or suggested, that falls between two adjacent notes in the standard Western division of the octave, most often the third or seventh degrees in a scale.

Blues scale
The incorporation of the flat third, flat fifth, and flat seventh degrees in a scale.

Bohemian
A person who lives and acts without regard for conventional rules and practices.

Boogie-woogie
Piano style popularized in the 1930s and 1940s that features repeated bass figures (riffs) against a syncopated improvised melody.

Break dancing
Often acrobatic, early hip-hop dance, initially performed during the percussive "break" of a song, when the DJ performed extended instrumental sections suited to dancing. The dancers were known as "b-boys/girls."

Burnt-cork/blackface makeup
Makeup used by minstrel performers to blacken their faces in caricature of African Americans.

Cabaret
In Detroit, a type of social gathering usually associated with a community of unionized workers or other socially specific group. DJs perform at these gatherings, and attendees dress in formal clothing, dance, eat, and drink.

Cadenza
An extended, sometimes improvised section in a vocal or instrumental performance, usually occurring at the end.

Cakewalk
A dance that parodies White upper-class behavior, originally performed by African American slaves; the best performance was awarded a prize, usually a cake, from which the dance takes its name.

Call–response
A song form that characterized many of the earliest documented spirituals; a song structure or performance practice in which a singer or instrumentalist makes a musical statement that is answered by another soloist, instrumentalist, or group. The statement and answer sometimes overlap. Also called antiphony and call-and-response.

Civil Rights Movement *see* **Modern Civil Rights Movement.**

Classic ragtime
Notated or written compositions for piano, in four sections; associated with Scott Joplin and his contemporaries.

Classic rap
Rap with elements of hardcore and pop-rap affirmed by the core hip-hop audience and the mainstream.

Clavinet
An electronic version of the clavichord, a medieval keyboard instrument.

Club music
Music produced for and promoted at dance clubs during and after the disco era. DJs typically play a broad range of music, assembling material from various musical styles.

Common meter
4/4 time; sometimes superimposed over 12/8 meter or triplet background.

Concept album
A collection of songs based on a theme that is reflected in the album's cover design and graphics.

Contemporary gospel music
Post-1970 gospel that embraces elements of R&B, rock, funk, jazz, and other popular styles, usually performed by a small ensemble.

Cool jazz
1950s jazz style often associated with the West Coast, characterized by a relaxed feeling and light tone color and texture.

Coon song
Popular song style of the late nineteenth and early twentieth centuries that presented a stereotyped view of African Americans, often performed by White singers in blackface.

Cover record
A recording made by a White artist that attempted to replicate or approximate the sound, arrangement, and content of an earlier Black hit, aimed at selling to the White teen market.

Creole
In southwest Louisiana, historically a person of mixed French and African ancestry.

Crossover
The process by which a recording released in a secondary market achieves hit status in the mainstream market.

Crossover aesthetic
Highly lyrical vocals with limited ornamentation, supported by lush orchestral arrangement and simple rhythmic foundation. Often strophic with hook line or verse–refrain structures.

Crossover quartet
A group that switched from the performance of sacred repertoire to secular.

Cutting contest
Informal competition among musicians, intended to identify the artist with the greatest creativity and skill.

"Dancing the slaves"
Method used on slave ships to exercise human cargo to reduce the rate of mortality during the Middle Passage.

Disco
Genre of 1970s dance music, derived from the abbreviation of discothèque, the main venue of consumption.

DJ
Short for "disc jockey"; a person who plays records in a dance club or on radio. In hip-hop, one who uses turntables to accompany rappers and break dancers or to perform as featured instrumentalist.

Doo-wop
Typically, a cappella vocal harmony groups that emphasized the rhythmic delivery of phrases consisting of vocables (syllables without lexical meaning) such as "doo-wop."

Double entendre
Song text with double meanings.

Double time
A section in which the rhythmic pulse of a piece is doubled for dramatic effect (although the actual length of the measure remains the same).

Dub
Jamaican-derived concept of creating instrumental versions of popular songs, over which DJs rap to audiences.

Emancipation Proclamation
The official 1863 proclamation by President Lincoln, which freed slaves below the Mason-Dixon line.

Fiddlesticks
Devices such as straws, sticks, or knitting needles used to tap out rhythms on the strings of a fiddle.

Field holler or cry
Short, florid, improvised melody sung by an individual working in the fields.

Fifth lead
Baritone singer who can double as falsetto lead in a gospel quartet.

Folk spiritual
The earliest form of indigenous a cappella religious music created by African Americans during slavery.

Free jazz
Style that began in the late 1950s and abandoned the practice of utilizing fixed harmonic and rhythmic patterns as the basis for improvisation.

Freestyling
The process used by MCs to improvise rhymes during hip-hop performance.

Fusion
1970s jazz style that incorporated rhythms, harmonies, and melodic motives from popular forms, especially funk and rock.

Gangsta rap
A hardcore style popularized on the West Coast, beginning in the late 1980s, with street-oriented lyrics and delivery associated with gang culture.

Gospel music
Religious music of African Americans that emerged in urban centers during the early decades of the twentieth century.

Gospel musical
A play with a theme loosely derived from biblical stories, featuring music that either imitated or was directly drawn from African American gospel traditions.

Gospel quartet
Male or female ensemble of four to six voices singing close vocal harmonies, featuring melismatic lead singers and instrumental accompaniment of drums, guitar, and bass.

Gospel-styled vocals
A melismatic vocal style that employs various timbres. Melodies incorporate slides, bends, moans, shouts, and other indicators of strong emotions.

Grace note
A short ornamental note performed as an embellishment before the principal pitch.

Great Awakening
Period of religious revival that swept the American colonies in the mid-eighteenth century.

Great Migration
The mass movement of southern African Americans to urban cities during the period surrounding World Wars I and II.

Griot
West African music specialist of a social caste who serves as a custodian of cultural history.

Groove
Syncopated and repetitive rhythmic foundation established by the bass and drum.

Hambone
A form of rhythmic body percussion that involves slapping the hands against the thigh and hip bones.

Hard bop
A combo jazz style of the 1950s that incorporated the phrasings and harmonies of blues, rhythm and blues, and gospel music.

Hardcore rap
A controversial hip-hop style characterized by hypermasculine images, exaggerated street themes, aggressive delivery, and often explicit language.

Harlem Renaissance
A period of literary and artistic flowering by African American intellectuals based in Harlem during the 1920s.

Heterophony
The simultaneous rendering of slightly different versions of the same melody by two or more performers.

Hocket
Interlocking patterns shared by two or more voices or instruments that produce a single melody.

House music
A style of electronic music originating in gay Black clubs in Chicago in the 1980s.

Human beat box
A form of vocal percussion that mimics instrumental rhythmic patterns and timbres.

Hymn
Metrical compositions in strophic form, typically eight bars of rhyming couplets, loosely based on biblical scripture.

Invisible church
Sites where slaves worshipped in secret, often in defiance of laws that prohibited their assembly without White supervision.

Jim Crow laws
Laws limiting African American freedoms and rights in US society, named for the minstrel character "Jim Crow."

Jubilee
Nineteenth-century genre with sacred or secular narrative texts, sung in moderate or fast tempo.

Jubilee quartet
Male or female a cappella ensemble of four to six voices that performs formal arrangements of spirituals and jubilee songs in close four-part harmony, with emphasis on a percussive and rhythmic style of singing.

Juke joint
A small rural drinking establishment that features music and dance.

Jump blues
An up-tempo blues style of the 1940s and 1950s characterized by boogie-woogie bass lines, shuffle rhythms, and prominent brass and reed sounds.

Jungle sound
Term referencing Africa, associated with unique instrumental timbres typical of Duke Ellington arrangements in the 1920s and 1930s.

Kpelle
A people who live in Liberia, West Africa.

Krautrock
Electronic music played by European groups of the 1980s, particularly German groups such as Kraftwerk, which featured heavy use of drum machines.

La calinda
African dance performed in the French West Indies and Louisiana in the eighteenth century.

Leslie speaker
An amplifier that produces special sound effects via rotating sound waves in the speakers. Primarily associated with the Hammond organ.

Life cycle
Major events in life, such as birth, puberty, marriage, and death.

Lined hymn
A style of hymn singing in which each line of text is sung or chanted first by the song leader and then echoed by the congregation.

Loop
A short recorded phrase programmed to repeat indefinitely or for a designated length of time.

Mbira
An African melodic instrument with varying numbers of plucked keys made of either metal or wood.

MC
Also spelled "emcee" (abbreviated from "master of ceremonies"); a rapper who performs in a hip-hop context (typically, to accompaniment by a DJ, an instrumental track, vocal percussion known as a "beat box," or a cappella).

Mechanics of delivery
The manipulation of variables of time, text, and pitch in African American performance practice.

Melisma
A single syllable sung over several pitches.

MIDI (Musical Instrument Digital Interface)
A digital interface developed in the early 1980s, which allowed computers, synthesizers, samplers, and other electronic equipment to communicate with each other.

Minstrel show
Full-length theatrical entertainment featuring performers in blackface who performed songs, dances, and comic skits based on parodies and stereotypes of African American life and customs.

Mix (disco and house)
(1) Verb: The recording studio term for combining and balancing instruments, vocals, and special effects in a sound recording. (2) Noun: A seamless progression of pre-recorded songs.

Mix (hip-hop and rap)
(1) Verb: To collage several songs, with the goal of maintaining a consistent, danceable rhythm. (2) Noun: A "new" song that the DJ (or producer) assembles from brief sections of current hits.

Mixtape
Informal collection of songs, often assembled by a DJ, sometimes recorded with a unique sonic stamp.

Modal jazz
Music based on the repetition of one or two chords, or music based on modes (scales) instead of chord progressions.

Modern Civil Rights Movement
A movement beginning in the late 1940s and blossoming in the late 1950s to mid-1960s that pushed for equal rights for African Americans.

Motown
Record label created by Berry Gordy, named for its original location in Detroit, a.k.a. "Motor Town."

Musical comedy
A play with humorous content featuring songs that advance the storyline.

Musical processes
The way music is created, performed, and experienced.

Neo-soul
A marketing term used to promote soul music created by the second generation of soul singers.

New-school rap
Post-1985 technology-driven hip-hop that spotlights MCs whose raps are stylistically and lyrically diverse. The rhyme scheme departs somewhat from the AABB couplet format.

New Traditionalists *see* Young Lions.

Old-school rap
Early hip-hop that emerged during the 1970s, featuring DJs, a crew or posse of rappers, break dancers, and graffiti artists. Lyrics follow the AABB rhymed couplet format.

Patting (pattin') juba
Rhythmic body percussion used by slaves to accompany singing or dancing.

P-Funk
Short for "pure funk," a style pioneered by George Clinton, whose lyrics promoted Black self-determination and liberation.

Play-party
A celebration for children and young adults that features games, singing, and dancing without instrumental accompaniment.

Polyrhythm
Several contrasting rhythms played or sung simultaneously.

Pop production formula
Highly lyrical vocals without ornamentation, supported by lush orchestral arrangement and a simple rhythmic foundation; lyrics are often strophic with hook line or verse–refrain structures.

Pop-rap
Rap characterized by humorous, catchy, and upbeat lyrics with little controversial subject matter, which targets a mainstream audience.

Quartet
In Western music, a musical composition or ensemble of four voices or instruments.

Race records
Music industry term used from the 1920s through the 1940s to designate recordings produced by and marketed to African Americans.

Race series
Special series of recordings issued between the 1920s and 1940s performed exclusively by African Americans and directed to an African American market.

R&B rap
Hip-hop/R&B hybrid considered middle ground between hardcore and pop-rap; characterized by rapped verses, sung refrains, and harmonized choruses.

Rag or ragging
The term applied to syncopated or embellished melodies during the ragtime era.

Ragtime
Style of African American music popular at the turn of the twentieth century, characterized by a syncopated melody placed against a steady bass line.

Rap
A popular African American dance musical style usually featuring an MC, who recites rhymed verses over an accompaniment created by a DJ or pre-recorded tracks.

Rave
A large-scale, all-night party featuring electronic dance music, primarily house and techno.

Remix
Typically, a popular song that has been reassembled by a turntablist DJ or producer, which is then recorded or presented during a DJ's performance. The

vocals or recordings are recorded or played over an entirely different track from the original, to achieve a contrasting groove and/or to extend the shelf life of a hit song.

Revue
A series of brief skits mixed with songs and dances.

Rhythm and blues (R&B)
A form of Black dance music that evolved during the World War II era and the two decades that followed as a fusion of blues, big band swing, gospel, and pop elements.

Riff
A short, recurrent melodic-rhythmic phrase.

Ring shout
A form of folk spiritual characterized by leader–chorus antiphonal singing, hand clapping, and other percussion, which incorporates highly stylized religious dance as participants move in a counterclockwise circle.

Rock and roll
1950s derivative of rhythm and blues, characterized by Black gospel and pop influences; created for consumption by Black and White teenagers.

Royalties
Payment made by a music publisher to a composer based on the number of printed or recorded copies sold. Also, payments made by record labels to artists and song publishers based on the number of records sold.

Sampler
An electronic unit that records sound digitally, allowing for the recording of a phrase that can be "looped," or programmed to repeat for a designated length of time.

Santería (also **Lucumí**)
African-derived syncretic religion that originated in Cuba.

Scratching
Technique used by hip-hop DJs to create a percussive sound, produced by moving a very short section of a record back and forth under the record needle.

Second Great Migration
The period between 1940 and 1970 during which five million Black southerners moved to the North and West.

Shout
An ecstatic expression of worship through demonstrative behavior, often reflecting an altered state of being. Not to be confused with the "ring shout."

Shout chorus
In swing music, a climactic section usually occurring near the end of the arrangement.

Shout songs
Emotionally charged gospel songs performed with heightened vocal delivery.

Slide or bottleneck
A playing technique in which a guitar player slides a metal bar or glass neck from a bottle across the strings to alter the timbre.

Soul music
Gospel-influenced African American popular music style that began to emerge in the late 1950s and became popular during the 1960s.

Speaking in tongues
Uttering words or phrases in charismatic worship, which are spoken in a language intelligible only through spiritual discernment. Also known as "glossolalia."

Spiritual
Religious music of African Americans during slavery.

Spoken word style
Sung with the rhythmic flow of the spoken word.

Stono Rebellion
An eighteenth-century slave revolt, during which slaves danced and beat drums.

Storefront church
A retail business structure that has been converted into a worship site.

Strophic
Song form in which a single melody is repeated with a different set of lyrics for each stanza.

Structural characteristics
The form as well as rhythmic, melodic, and harmonic organization of music.

Style of delivery
The physical mode of presentation—how performers engage the body in movement and adornment during performance.

Swing
Big band jazz style developed in the 1930s that emphasized horn riffs and a rhythmic drive derived from the boogie-woogie bass line.

Switch/swing/double lead
Alternation of verses or phrases in a single song between two lead singers.

Syncopation
The shifting of accent from standard Western stressed beats to atypical stress points in the measure.

Syncretism
Process of hybridization that occurs when different cultures come into sustained contact.

Synthesizer
Any electronic musical instrument that creates its sounds through digital means, allowing the performer to vary pitch, timbre, attack, decay, and other basic sound elements.

Techno
A form of dance music that emerged in Detroit in the early to mid-1980s that primarily features electronic instruments, including drum machines, multi-track mixers, computers, and samplers.

Territory jazz bands
Jazz bands based in smaller cities, primarily in the Midwest and Southwest.

Texture
The interaction among the vocal and instrumental lines in an ensemble.

Third Stream
Style that combines jazz improvisation with instrumentation and compositional forms associated with classical music.

Timbre
The quality of sound that distinguishes different voices or instruments from one another.

Tin Pan Alley
Composed styles of popular music reflecting the musical values of middle-class White America; published between 1880 and 1950, primarily by New York-based firms.

Toast (African American)
Long verbal narrative, performed from memory and passed orally from generation to generation, that celebrated the feats of such cultural heroes as Staggolee and Signifying Monkey.

Toast (Jamaican)
A DJ rap that praised dancers and addressed topical concerns over an instrumental track.

TONTO
The Original New Timbral Orchestra; a large multitimbral polyphonic analog synthesizer.

Traditional gospel music
Black religious music that emerged in urban contexts during the 1930s; pervasive in present-day African American worship.

Transcription
The process of notating musical performance.

Transitional gospel music
Forms of African American religious music that represent the bridge between the spiritual and its twentieth-century counterpart of traditional gospel music.

Twelve-bar blues
A stanza of three lines (AAB) of four measures each, the lines beginning respectively in the I, IV, and V chords and resolving in the I chord.

Uncle Tom
A derogatory term for a Black person seen as supporting rather than challenging the racist power structure. The term is based on the empathetic title character of Harriet Beecher Stowe's 1852 novel, *Uncle Tom's Cabin.*

Urban contemporary
A term coined in the mid-1970s to identify radio stations located in cities with sizable African American populations that played contemporary Black music, including rhythm and blues and electronic dance music, and, in later decades, early hip-hop and hybrid styles. These stations were known as rhythm and blues radio in the 1950s and soul radio in the mid-1960s through the early 1970s.

Vaudeville
Theatrical form consisting of a variety of unrelated performing acts, including actors, singers, dancers, acrobats, comedians, magicians, trained animals, and other specialty acts.

Vocoder/voice box
An electronic device that is used to distort natural vocal sounds.

Walking/pumping bass
Stepwise (walking) or intervallic (pumping) percussive, rhythmic foundation provided by bass singers in jubilee and gospel quartets.

Young Lions/New Traditionalists
1980s movement led by Wynton Marsalis, designed to highlight the traditional jazz styles of the pre-1950s era.

Bibliography

Abbott, Lynn. "The Humming Four and the Hawks." *Whiskey, Women and . . .* 11 (June 1983a): n. p.

———. *The Soproco Spiritual Singers: New Orleans Quartet Family Tree.* Monograph. New Orleans: Jean Lafitte National Historical Park, 1983b.

———. "'Play That Barber Shop Chord': A Case for the African American Origin of Barbershop Harmony." *American Music* 10(3) (Fall 1992): 289–325.

Albiez, Sean. "Post Soul Futurama: African American Cultural Politics and Early Detroit Techno." *European Journal of American Culture* 24(2) (August 2005): 131–52.

Allen, Ray. *Singing in the Spirit: African American Sacred Quartets in New York City.* Philadelphia: University of Pennsylvania Press, 1991.

Allen, William Francis, Charles Pickard Ware, and Lucy McKim Garrison, eds. *Slave Songs of the United States.* 1867. Reprint, Mineola, NY: Dover, 1995. E-text available at www.docsouth.unc.edu/church/allen/allen.html.

Anderson, Elijah. *Streetwise: Race, Class, and Change in an Urban Community.* Chicago: University of Chicago Press, 1990.

Anderson, Tammy. *Rave Culture: The Alteration and Decline of a Philadelphia Music Scene.* Philadelphia: Temple University Press, 2009.

Arbus, Doon. "James Brown is Out of Sight." *The New York Herald Tribune*, March 20, 1966. Reprint in *The James Brown Reader: 50 Years of Writing about the Godfather of Soul*, edited by Nelson George and Alan Leeds, 18–34. New York: A Plum Book/Penguin Press, 2008.

Argyle, Ray. *Scott Joplin and the Age of Ragtime.* Jefferson, NC: McFarland & Company, 2009.

Arnold, Jacob. "Chicago House Roots: Italo." *Gridface* (webzine), September 13, 2009. Accessed June 10, 2012, www.gridface.com/features/chicago_house_italo.html.

Arthur, Sylvia. "The Brilliance of Badu." *Clutch Magazine* (online), February 1, 2008. Accessed August 9, 2010, www.clutchmagonline.com/2008/02/the-brilliance-of-badu/.

Arvey, Verna. *Studies of Contemporary American Composers: William Grant Still.* New York: J. Fischer & Bro., 1939.

———. *In One Lifetime.* Fayetteville: University of Arkansas Press, 1984.

Aswell, Tom. *Louisiana Rocks! The True Genesis of Rock & Roll.* Gretna, LA: Pelican, 2009.

"At a Glance: College of Arts and Media." University of Colorado Denver website, n.d. Accessed August 11, 2012, www.catalog.ucdenver.edu/content.php?catoid=6&navoid=573.

Averill, Gage. *Four Parts No Waiting: A Social History of American Barbershop Harmony.* New York: Oxford University Press, 2003.

Badger, Reid. *A Life in Ragtime: A Biography of James Reese Europe.* New York: Oxford University Press, 1995.

Baker, David N., Linda M. Belt, and H.C. Hudson, eds. *The Black Composer Speaks.* Metuchen, NJ: Scarecrow Press, 1978.

Baker, Houston A. *Long Black Song: Essays in Black American Literature and Culture.* Charlottesville: The University of Virginia Press, 1972.

Bane, Michael. *White Boy Singin' the Blues.* New York: Da Capo Press, 1992.

Baraka, Amiri (LeRoi Jones). *Blues People: Negro Music in White America.* New York: Morrow, 1963. Reprint, New York: HarperCollins, 1999.

Barker, Danny. *Buddy Bolden and the Last Days of Storyville.* New York: Cassell, 1998.

Barlow, William. *Voice Over: The Making of Black Radio.* Philadelphia: Temple University Press, 1999.

Barton, William E. "Recent Negro Melodies." 1899. Reprint in *The Negro and His Folklore in Nineteenth-Century Periodicals, Vol. 18,* edited by Bruce Jackson, 302–26. Austin: The University of Texas Press, 1967.

Basie, Count (as told to Albert Murray). *Good Morning Blues: The Autobiography of Count Basie.* London: Paladin, 1987.

Beams of Heaven: Hymns of Charles Albert Tindley. New York: General Board of Global Ministries, The United Methodist Church, 2006.

Bebey, Francis. *African Music: A People's Art.* Westport, CT: Lawrence Hill, 1975.

Benston, Kimberly W. "'I Yam What I Am': Naming and Unnaming in Afro-American Literature." *Black American Literature Forum* 16(1) (Spring 1982): 3–11.

Berlin, Edward A. *Ragtime: A Musical and Cultural History.* Berkeley: University of California Press, 1980.

———. "Joplin, Scott." In *New Grove Dictionary of Music and Musicians,* edited by Stanley Sadie and John Tyrrell. New York: Macmillan, 2001.

———. *King of Ragtime: Scott Joplin and His Era.* New York: Oxford University Press, 1994. Reprint, Lincoln, NE: iUniverse, 2002.

Berliner, Paul F. *Thinking in Jazz: The Infinite Art of Improvisation.* Chicago: University of Chicago Press, 1994.

Berry, Jason, Jonathan Foose, and Tad Jones. *Up From the Cradle of Jazz: New Orleans Music Since World War II.* Lafayette: University of Louisiana at Lafayette Press, 2009.

"Billboard Adopts 'R&B' as New Name for 2 Charts." *Billboard,* October 27, 1990.

"Billboard Top 100 Songs of 2010—Year End Charts." bobborst.com. Accessed December 22, 2013, www.bobborst.com/popculture/top-100-songs-of-the-year/?year=2010.

Biography and Genealogy Master Index. Farmington Hills, MI: Gale, Cengage Learning, 1980–2014.

Black, Donald Fisher. "The Life and Work of Eva Jessye and Her Contributions to American Music." PhD diss., University of Michigan, 1986.

Blesh, Rudi, and Harriet Janis. *They All Played Ragtime: The True Story of an American Music.* 4th ed., New York: Oak, 1971.

Bogle, Donald. *Toms, Coons, Mulattoes, Mammies, and Bucks: An Interpretive History of Blacks in American Film.* 3rd ed., New York: Continuum, 1994.

Bohlman, Phillip. *Music in American Religious Experience.* New York: Oxford, 2006.

Bontemps, Arna. "Rock, Church, Rock!" *Common Ground* 3 (Autumn 1942): 75–80. Reprint in *The Book of Negro Folklore,* edited by Langston Hughes and Arna Bontemps, 313–20. New York: Dodd, Mead, 1958.

———, and Jack Conroy. *Anyplace But Here.* New York: Hill and Wang, 1966. Originally published in 1945 as *They Seek A City.*

Boorstin Julia, Jonah Freedman, and Christopher Tkaczyk. "America's 40 Richest Under 40: Easy come, easy go. We envied them once—okay, we still do. (A net worth of more than $100 million isn't exactly chicken feed.) But many of them have taken an even bigger shellacking in the market this year than we have." *Fortune,* September 16, 2002. Accessed 9 November 2012, http://money.cnn.com/magazines/fortune/fortune_archive/2002/09/16/328569/index.htm.

Bordman, Gerald. *American Musical Theatre: A Chronicle*. New York: Oxford University Press, 1978.

Borzillo, Carrie. "Franklin, Family Cross Lines: Gospo Centric Act Multichart Success." *Billboard*, February 25, 1995, 22–23.

Bowman, Robert M.J. *Soulsville, U.S.A.: The Story of Stax Records*. New York: Schirmer Books, 1997.

———. Liner notes to *Sing and Make Melody Unto the Lord*. Performed by Harps of Melody. Compact disc. HMG 6510, 1998.

Boyer, Horace. "Thomas Dorsey: An Analysis of his Contributions." *Black World* 23(9) (July 1974): 20–28.

———. "A Comparative Analysis of Traditional and Contemporary Gospel Music." In *More Than Dancing*, edited by Irene V. Jackson, 127–45. Westport, CT: Greenwood Press, 1985.

———. "Charles Albert Tindley: Progenitor of African American Gospel Music." In *We'll Understand It Better By and By*, edited by Bernice Johnson Reagon, 53–78. Washington, DC: Smithsonian Institution Press, 1992a.

———. "Gospel Blues: Origin and History." In *New Perspectives on Music*, edited by Josephine Wright and Samuel A. Floyd Jr., 119–47. Detroit, MI: Harmonie Park Press, 1992b.

———. "Roberta Martin: Innovator of Modern Gospel Music." In *We'll Understand It Better By and By*, edited by Bernice Johnson Reagon, 275–86. Washington, DC: Smithsonian Institution Press, 1992c.

———. *How Sweet the Sound: The Golden Age of Gospel*. Washington, DC: Elliott & Clark, 1995.

Boykin, Keith. *One More River to Cross: Black & Gay in America*. New York: Anchor Books, Doubleday, 1996.

Brackett, David. "(In Search of) Musical Meaning: Genres, Categories and Crossover." In *Popular Music Studies*, edited by David Hesmondhalgh and Keith Negus, 65–84. New York: Oxford University Press, 2002.

Braithwaite, J. Roland "Introduction." *A Collection of Hymns and Spiritual Songs*, by Richard Allen, 1801. Reprint with new introduction. Philadelphia: Mother Bethel African Methodist Episcopal Church, 1987.

Braunstein, Peter. "The Last Days of Gay Disco: The Current Disco Revival Conceals Its Homo Soul." *Village Voice*, June 30, 1998, 54–55, 58.

Breda, Malcolm Joseph. "Hale Smith: A Biographical and Analytical Study of the Man and His Music." PhD diss., University of Southern Mississippi, 1975.

Bremer, Fredrika. "The Homes of the New World: Impressions of America." 1853. Reprint in *Readings in the Music of Black Americans*, edited by Eileen Southern, 103–15. New York: W.W. Norton, 1983.

Broughton, Viv. *Black Gospel: An Illustrated History of the Gospel Sound*. Poole, Dorset: Blandford Press, 1985.

Broven, John. *Rhythm and Blues in New Orleans*. 1974. Reprint, Gretna, LA: Pelican, 1978.

Brown, Ernest D. "Children Are the Wisdom of the Nation: The Significance of Children's Music in Afro-American Cultures." *The Black Perspective in Music* 5(2) (Autumn 1977): 137–45.

———. "Drums of Life: Royal Music and Social Life in Western Zambia." PhD diss., University of Washington, 1984.

———. "Something from Nothing and More from Something: The Making and Playing of Music Instruments in African-American Cultures." *Selected Reports in Ethnomusicology* 8 (1990a): 275–91.

———. "Carnival, Calypso, and Steelband in Trinidad." *The Black Perspective in Music* 18(1/2) (1990b): 81–100.

Brown, James, with Bruce Tucker. *James Brown: The Godfather of Soul*. New York: Collier Macmillan, 1986.

Brown, John Mason. "Songs of the Slave." 1868. Reprint in *The Negro and His Folklore in Nineteenth-Century Periodicals, Vol. 18*, edited by Bruce Jackson, 109–19. Austin: The University of Texas Press, 1967.

Brown, Rae Linda. "Selected Orchestral Music of Florence B. Price (1888–1953)." PhD diss., Yale University, 1987.

Brubach, Holly. "Ruin with a View." *New York Times Magazine*, April 9, 2010. Accessed May 10, 2011, www.nytimes.com/2010/04/11/t-magazine/11talk-brubach-t.html.

Büchmann-Møller, Frank. *You Just Fight for Your Life: The Story of Lester Young*. New York: Praeger, 1990.

Burnim, Mellonee V. "The Black Gospel Music Tradition: A Complex of Ideology, Aesthetic, and Behavior." In *More Than Dancing: Essays on Afro-American Music and Musicians*, edited by Irene V. Jackson, 147–67. Westport, CT: Greenwood, 1985.

———. "Religious Music." In *The Garland Encyclopedia of World Music, Vol. 3*, edited by Ellen Koskoff, 624–36, New York: Garland, 2001.

———. "Women in Gospel." In *African American Music: An Introduction*, edited by Mellonee V. Burnim and Portia K. Maultsby, 493–507. New York: Routledge, 2006.

———, and Portia K. Maultsby. "From Backwoods to City Streets: The Afro-American Musical Journey." In *Expressively Black: The Cultural Basis of Ethnic Identity*, edited by Geneva Gay and Willie L. Baber, 109–36. New York: Praeger, 1987.

Burns, Kephra. "Word from the Motherland: Rap, the Dozens, and African Griots." In *Rap on Rap: Straight-Up Talk on Hip-Hop Culture*, edited by Adam Sexton, 30–38. New York: Delta Books, 1995.

"The Cake Walk in Vienna." *The New York Times*, February 1, 1903, 5.

Cantwell, Robert. *Bluegrass Breakdown: The Making of the Old Southern Sound*. 1984. Reprint, New York: Da Capo Press, 1992.

Carroll, Jack. *Around Stonewall*. Online resource, 1994. Accessed September 7, 2002, www.jessecc.com/index3.html. Site discontinued.

Carter, Marva Griffin. "Hall Johnson: Preserver of the Old Negro Spiritual." MA thesis, Boston University, 1975.

Chang, Jeff. *Can't Stop, Won't Stop: A History of the Hip-Hop Generation*. New York: St. Martin's Press, 2005.

———, ed. *Total Chaos: The Art and Aesthetics of Hip-Hop*. New York: Basic Civitas Books, 2006.

Chapple, Steve, and Reebee Garofalo. *Rock 'n' Roll Is Here to Pay: The History and Politics of the Music Industry*. Chicago: Nelson-Hall, 1977.

Charpié, Stephen K. "Johnson, Francis ('Frank')." In *International Dictionary of Black Composers*, edited by Samuel A. Floyd Jr. Chicago: Fitzroy Dearborn, 1999.

Charters, Ann. *Nobody: The Story of Bert Williams*. New York: Macmillan, 1970.

Charters, Samuel B., and Leonard Kunstadt. *Jazz: A History of the New York Scene*. 1962. Reprint, New York: Da Capo Press, 1984.

Chernoff, John Miller. *African Rhythm and African Sensibility: Aesthetics and Social Action in African Musical Idioms*. Chicago: Chicago University Press, 1979.

Chin, Brian. "In the Beat of the Night." Liner notes to *The Disco Box*. Rhino Records 75595, 1999.

Clarke, Mary Olmsted. "Song Games of Negro Children." *The Journal of American Folklore* 3 (1890): 288–90.

Clemenson, Barbara. "Justin Holland: Black Guitarist in the Western Reserve." Paper presented at Western Reserve Studies Symposium, Cleveland, OH, November 10–12, 1989. Symposium paper. Accessed June 21, 2010, http://hdl.handle.net/2186/ksl: clejus00/clejus00.pdf.

Clendinen, Dudley, and Adam Nagourney. *Out for Good: The Struggle to Build a Gay Rights Movement in America*. New York: Simon & Schuster, 1999.

Cobb, Buell. *The Sacred Harp: A Tradition and Its Music*. Athens: University of Georgia Press, 1978.

Cockrell, Dale. *Demons of Disorder: Early Blackface Minstrels and Their World*. Cambridge: Cambridge University Press, 1997.

Cole, Malcolm S. "'Afrika Singt': Austro-German Echoes of the Harlem Renaissance." *Journal of the American Musicological Society* 30(1) (Spring 1977): 72–95.

Collier, James Lincoln. *Louis Armstrong: An American Genius*. New York: Oxford University Press, 1983.

———. *Benny Goodman and the Swing Era.* New York: Oxford University Press, 1989.

Collins, Lisa. "Making a Difference: Vicki Mack Lataillade." *Score* (July/August 1994): 27.

Collins, Philip. "Homegrown Sounds: The San Jose Symphony Focuses on American Composers." *Metroactive*, January 16–22, 1997. Online resource. Accessed August 19, 2009, www.metroactive.com/papers/metro/01.16.97/symphony-9703.html.

Collins, Willie R. "California Rhythm and Blues Recordings, 1942–1972: A Diversity of Styles." In *California Soul: Music of African Americans in the West*, edited by Jacqueline Cogdell DjeDje and Eddie S. Meadows, 213–43. Berkeley: University of California Press, 1998.

Complete Catalogue of Sheet Music and Musical Works, 1870. Issued by the Board of Music Trade of the United States of America, 1871. Reprinted with introduction by Dena Epstein, New York: Da Capo Press, 1973.

Conroy, Frank. "Stop Nitpicking a Genius." *New York Times Magazine*, June 25, 1995, 28–31+.

Cooper, Carol. "According to Conventional Wisdom, Women Rappers Don't Sell." *Net Magazine*, July 1993, 17.

Cosgrove, Stuart. "Seventh City Techno." In *The Faber Book of Pop*, edited by Hanif Kureishi and Jon Savage, 677–81. London: Faber and Faber, 1995.

Countryman, Matthew J. *Up South: Civil Rights and Black Power in Philadelphia.* Philadelphia: University of Pennsylvania Press, 2006.

Courlander, Harold. *Negro Folk Music, U.S.A.* New York: Columbia University Press, 1963.

Crawford, George W. "Jazzin' God." *The Crisis* 36(2) (1929): 45.

Cross, Brian. *It's Not About a Salary: Rap, Race, and Resistance in Los Angeles.* New York: Verso, 1993.

Crouch, Stanley. "Wynton Marsalis: 1987." *Down Beat* 54(11) (1987): 16–19+.

Cunningham, Phillip Lamarr. "'There's Nothing Really New under the Sun': The Fallacy of the Neo-Soul Genre." *Journal of Popular Music Studies* 22(3) (2010): 240–58.

Curtis, Susan. *Dancing to a Black Man's Tune: A Life of Scott Joplin.* Columbia: University of Missouri Press, 1994.

Cusic, Don. *The Sound of Light: A History of Gospel Music.* Bowling Green, OH: Bowling Green State University Popular Press, 1990.

Daniels, Douglas Henry. *Lester Leaps In: The Life and Times of Lester "Pres" Young.* Boston: Beacon Press, 2002.

Davidson, Basil. *The African Past: Chronicles From Antiquity to Modern Times.* Boston: Little, Brown and Company, 1964.

Davidson, Celia Elizabeth. "Operas by Afro-American Composers: A Critical Survey and Analysis of Selected Works." PhD diss., Catholic University of America, 1980.

Davin, Tom. "Conversations with James P. Johnson." In *Ragtime: Its History, Composers, and Music*, edited by John Edward Hasse, 166–77. London: Macmillan, 1985.

Davis, Carl H., Sr. *The Man Behind the Music: The Legendary Carl Davis.* Matteson, IL: Life To Legacy, 2009.

Davis, George, and Glegg Watson. *Black Life in Corporate America.* Garden City, NY: Anchor Press, 1982.

Davis, Miles, with Quincy Troupe. *Miles: The Autobiography.* New York: Simon and Schuster, 1989.

Dery, Mark. "Now Turning the Tables . . . The DJ as Star." *The New York Times*, April 14, 1991, H-28, H-30.

DeVeaux, Scott. *The Birth of Bebop: A Social and Musical History.* Berkeley: University of California Press, 1997.

Devereux, George, and Edwin Loeb. "Antagonistic Acculturation." *American Sociological Review* 8(2) (1943): 133–47.

Dixon, Robert M.W., John Godrich, and Howard Rye. *Blues and Gospel Records, 1890–1943.* 4th ed., Oxford: Clarendon Press, 1997.

DjeDje, Jacqueline Cogdell. "West Africa: An Introduction." In *The Garland Handbook of African Music*, 2nd ed., edited by Ruth M. Stone, 166–97. New York: Routledge, 2008.

Dodge, Timothy. *The School Of Arizona Dranes: Gospel Music Pioneer*. Lanham, MD: Lexington Books, 2013.

Dorsey, Thomas A. "Gospel Music." In *Reflections on Afro-American Music*, edited by Dominique-René de Lerma, 189–95. Kent, OH: Kent State University Press, 1973.

Drake, St. Clair, and Horace R. Cayton. *Black Metropolis: A Study of Negro Life in a Northern City*. 1945. New York: Harper Torchbooks, 1962. Revised and enlarged ed., Chicago: University of Chicago Press, 1993.

Duckett, Alfred. "An Interview with Thomas Dorsey." *Black World* 23(9) (July 1974): 4–18.

Dyson, Michael E. *Holler If You Hear Me: Searching for Tupac Shakur*. New York: Basic Civitas Books, 2001.

Early, Gerald Lyn. *One Nation Under a Groove: Motown and American Culture*. Hopewell, NJ: Ecco Press, 1995.

Eastman, Ralph. "'Pitchin' Up a Boogie': African-American Musicians, Nightlife, and Music Venues in Los Angeles, 1930–1945." In *California Soul: Music of African Americans in the West*, edited by Jacqueline Cogdell DjeDje and Eddie Meadows, 79–103. Berkeley: University of California Press, 1998.

Edwards, Paul. *How to Rap: The Art and Science of the Hip-Hop MC*. Chicago: Review Press, 2009.

"The Edwin Hawkins Singers, 'Oh Happy Day.'" *Sepia* 19(8) (August 1969): 66–68.

Elliot, Lawrence. *George Washington Carver: The Man Who Overcame*. Englewood Cliffs, NJ: Prentice Hall, 1966.

Ellison, Ralph. *Shadow and Act*. New York: Vintage, 1964. Reprint, New York: Quality Paperback, 1994.

Emery, Lynne Fauley. *Black Dance in the United States from 1619 to 1970*. Palo Alto, CA: National Press Books, 1972.

Encyclopédie, or Dictionnaire Raisonné Des Sciences, Des Arts Et Des Métiers. Paris: Briasson, 1751–65.

Ennett, Dorothy. "An Analysis and Comparison of Selected Piano Sonatas by Three Contemporary Black Composers: George Walker, Howard Swanson, and Roque Cordero." PhD diss., New York University, 1973.

Epstein, Daniel Mark. *Nat King Cole*. New York: Farrar, Straus and Giroux, 1999.

Epstein, Dena J. "The Folk Banjo: A Documentary History." *Ethnomusicology* 19(3) (1975): 347–71.

———. *Sinful Tunes and Spirituals: Black Folk Music to the Civil War*. 1977. Reprint with additional preface, Urbana: University of Illinois Press, 2003.

———. "A White Origin for the Black Spiritual? An Invalid Theory and How It Grew." *American Music* 1(2) (1983): 53–59.

Eshun, Kodwo. *More Brilliant Than the Sun: Adventures in Sonic Fiction*. London: Quartet Books, 1998.

Europe, James Reese. "A Negro Explains 'Jazz.'" 1919. Reprint in *Keeping Time: Readings in Jazz History*, edited by Robert Walser, 12–14. New York: Oxford University Press, 1999.

Evans, David. *Big Road Blues: Tradition and Creativity in the Folk Blues*. Berkeley: University of California Press, 1982.

———, ed. *Ramblin' on My Mind: New Perspectives on the Blues*. Urbana and Chicago: University of Illinois Press, 2008.

Fabbri, Franco. "Theory of Musical Genres: Two Applications." In *Popular Music Perspectives*, edited by D. Horn and P. Tagg, 52–81. Göteborg, Sweden: International Association for the Study of Popular Music, 1982.

Fancourt, Les, and Bob McGrath. *The Blues Discography, 1943–1970*. Vancouver, BC: Eyeball Productions, 2006.

Feagins, Joe R., and Melvin P. Sikes. *Living with Racism: The Black Middle-Class Experience*. Boston: Beacon Press, 1994.

Fernando, S.H. Jr. *The New Beats: Exploring the Music, Culture, and Attitudes of Hip-Hop*. New York: Anchor Books/Doubleday, 1994.

Fine, Sidney. *Violence in the Model City: The Cavanagh Administration, Race Relations, and the Detroit Riot of 1967*. Ann Arbor: University of Michigan Press, 1989.

Fisher, Mark. "Mike Banks Interview." *The Wire: Adventures in Modern Music*, no. 285 (November 2007). Accessed February 28, 2011, www.thewire.co.uk/articles/271/.

Fletcher, Tom. *The Tom Fletcher Story: 100 Years of the Negro in Show Business*. New York: Burdge, 1954.

Floyd, Samuel A. Jr. *The Power of Black Music: Interpreting Its History from Africa to the United States*. New York: Oxford University Press, 1995.

———, ed. *International Dictionary of Black Composers*. Chicago: Fitzroy Dearborn, 1999.

———, and Marsha J. Reisser. "Social Dance Music of Black Composers in the Nineteenth Century and the Emergence of Classic Ragtime." *Black Perspective in Music* 8(2) (Autumn 1980): 161–93.

Ford, Robert. *A Blues Bibliography*. 2nd ed., New York and London: Routledge, 2007.

Fox, Jon Harley. *King of the Queen City: The Story of King Records*. Urbana: University of Illinois Press, 2009.

Fox, Ted. *In the Groove: The People Behind the Music*. New York: St. Martin's Press, 1986.

Franklin, Kirk, with Jim Nelson Black. *Church Boy: My Music and My Life*. Nashville, TN: Word, 1998.

Frew, Tim. *Scott Joplin and the Age of Ragtime*. New York: Friedman/Fairfax, 1996.

Frith, Simon. *Sound Effects: Youth, Leisure, and the Politics of Rock 'n' Roll*. New York: Pantheon Books, 1981.

"Fromm Music Foundation at Harvard Announces 2000 Commissions." *NewMusicBox: The Web Magazine from the American Music Center* (February 2001). Online resource. Formerly available at www.newmusicbox.org/news/feb01/22nw04.html.

Funk, Ray. "The Imperial Quintet." *Blues and Rhythm—The Gospel Truth*, 9 (1985): 24.

———. "Atlanta Gospel." Liner notes to *Atlanta Gospel*. Heritage HT 312, 1987.

Garelick, Jon. "Donal Fox." *Boston Phoenix*, April 2002.

Garofalo, Reebee. *Rockin' Out: Popular Music in the USA*. 2nd ed., Englewood Cliffs, NJ: Prentice Hall, 2002.

Gart, Galen, and Roy C. Ames. *Duke/Peacock Records: An Illustrated History with Discography*. Milford, NH: Big Nickel, 1990.

Gellman, David N. "Festivals." In *Encyclopedia of African American History 1619–1895: From the Colonial to the Age of Frederick Douglass, Vol. 2*, edited by Paul Finkelman, 2–6. New York: Oxford University Press, 2006.

George, Nelson. *The Death of Rhythm and Blues*. New York: Plume/Penguin Books, 1988.

———. *Buppies, B-Boys, Baps, and Bohos: Notes on Post-Soul Black Culture*. New York: HarperCollins, 1992.

———. "Hip-Hop's Founding Fathers Speak the Truth." *The Source* (November 1993): 44–50.

———. *Hip-Hop America*. New York: Viking, 1998.

Georgia Writers' Project. *Drums and Shadows: Survival Studies among the Georgia Coastal Negroes*. Athens: University of Georgia Press, 1940.

Giddens, Gary. *Celebrating Bird: The Triumph of Charlie Parker*. New York: Beech Tree Books, 1987.

Gill, Gerald. *Meanness Mania: The Changed Mood*. Washington, DC: Howard University Press, 1980.

Gillespie, Dizzy, with Al Fraser. *To Be or Not . . . to Bop: Memoirs*. New York: Da Capo, 1979.

Gillett, Charlie. *Making Tracks: Atlantic Records and the Growth of a Multi-Billion-Dollar Industry*. New York: E.P. Dutton, 1974.

Gilroy, Paul. "Between Afro-Centrism and Euro-Centrism: Youth Culture and the Problem of Hybridity." *YOUNG: Nordic Journal of Youth Research* 1(2) (1993): 2–12. doi: 10.1177/110330889300100201.

Gioia, Ted. *West Coast Jazz*. New York: Oxford University Press, 1992.

Goddess, Rha. "Scarcity and Exploitation: The Myth and Reality of the Struggling Hip-Hop Artist." In *Total Chaos: The Art and Aesthetics of Hip-Hop*, edited by Jeff Chang, 340–48. New York: Basic Civitas Books, 2006.

Goff, James R. Jr., *Close Harmony: A History of Southern Gospel*. Chapel Hill: University of North Carolina Press, 2002.

Goldman, Albert. *Disco*. New York: Hawthorn, 1978.

Goosman, Stuart L. *Group Harmony: The Black Urban Roots of Rhythm and Blues*. Philadelphia: University of Pennsylvania Press, 2005.

Gordy, Berry. *To Be Loved: The Music, the Magic, the Memories of Motown*. New York: Warner Books, 1994.

Goreau, Laurraine. *Just Mahalia, Baby*. Waco, TX: Word Books, 1975.

Gourse, Leslie. *Madame Jazz: Contemporary Women Instrumentalists*. New York and Oxford: Oxford University Press, 1995.

———. *Straight No Chaser: The Life and Genius of Thelonious Monk*. New York: Schirmer, 1997.

Grandmaster Blaster. *All You Need to Know about Rappin'! from Grandmaster Blaster*. Chicago: Contemporary Books, 1984.

Graziano, John. "The Early Life and Career of the 'Black Patti': The Odyssey of an African American Singer in the Late Nineteenth Century." *Journal of the American Musicological Society* 53(3) (2000): 543–96.

Green, Jared. *DJ, Dance, and Rave Culture*. Detroit, MI: Greenhaven Press, 2005.

Green, Mildred Denby. *Black Women Composers: A Genesis*. Boston: Twayne, 1983.

Gridley, Mark C. *Jazz Styles; History and Analysis*. 10th ed., Upper Saddle River, NJ: Pearson, 2009.

Guralnick, Peter. *Dream Boogie: The Triumph of Sam Cooke*. New York: Little, Brown, 2005.

Haas, Robert Bartlett, ed. *William Grant Still and the Fusion of Cultures in American Music*. Santa Barbara, CA: Black Sparrow Press, 1972.

Haden-Guest, Anthony. *The Last Party: Studio 54, Disco, and the Culture of the Night*. New York: William Morrow, 1997.

Hadley, Richard. "The Published Choral Music of Ulysses Kay, 1943–1968." PhD diss., University of Iowa, 1972.

Hajdu, David. "Wynton's Blues." *Atlantic Monthly*, March 2003, 43–58.

Hall, Fred. *It's About Time: The Dave Brubeck Story*. Fayetteville: University of Arkansas Press, 1996.

Hammer, Bob. Liner notes to *1984: Yusef Lateef*. Released 1965. Impulse! AS 84, 1972.

Handy, D. Antoinette. *Black Conductors*. Lanham, MD: Scarecrow Press, 1995.

———. *Black Women in American Bands and Orchestras*. 2nd ed., Metuchen, NJ: Scarecrow Press, 1998.

Handy, W.C. *Father of the Blues: An Autobiography*. New York: Macmillan, 1941.

Hannerz, Ulf. *Soulside: Inquiries into Ghetto Culture and Community*. New York: Columbia University Press, 1969.

Hannusch, Jeff. *The Soul of New Orleans: A Legacy of Rhythm and Blues*. Ville Platte, LA: Swallow, 2001.

Haralambos, Michael. *Soul Music: The Birth of a Sound in Black America*. 1974. Reprint, New York: Da Capo, 1985.

Harding, Vincent. *There Is a River: The Black Struggle for Freedom in America*. 1981. Reprint, New York: Vintage Books, 1983.

Harer, Ingeborg. "'Lustige Neger.' Verbreitung und Nachahmung der Musik der Afro-Amerikaner in Österreich um 1900." *Jazzforschung/Jazzresearch* 30 (1998a): 181–96.

———. "'Was ist Cakewalk?' Zum Stellenwert der Amerikanischen Unterhaltungsmusik im Grazer Kulturleben der Jahrhundertwende." *Historisches Jahrbuch der Stadt Graz* 27/28 (1998b): 641–58.

———. "'Dieses böse etwas, der Jazz.' Varianten der Jazz Rezeption in Österreich von der Jahrhundertwende bis zu den 1920er Jahren." In *Fremdheit in der Moderne, Studien zur Moderne 3*, edited by Rudolf Flotzinger, 139–71. Wien: Passagen Verlag, 1999.

————. "Zwischen zwei Welten—Ragtime als Ergebnis von Spielpraxis (Between two worlds—ragtime as performance practice)." *Akkulturation im Jazz: Jazzforschung/ Jazzresearch* 38 (2006): 87–102.

————. "Afrikanisierungs- oder Europäisierungstendenzen? Quellen zur Frühgeschichte des Ragtime" (Africanizing or Europeanizing tendencies? Sources on the early history of Ragtime). *Festschrift Franz Kerschbaumer zum 60. Geburtstag: Jazzforschung/ Jazzresearch* 39 (2007): 171–84.

Harris, Michael W. *The Rise of Gospel Blues: The Music of Thomas Andrew Dorsey in the Urban Church.* New York: Oxford University Press, 1992.

Haskins, James, and Kathleen Benson. *Scott Joplin.* Garden City, NY: Doubleday, 1978.

Hasse, John Edward. *Beyond Category: The Life and Genius of Duke Ellington.* New York: Simon and Schuster, 1993.

Hay, Samuel A. *African American Theater: A Historical and Critical Analysis.* Cambridge: Cambridge University Press, 1994.

Hayasaki, Erika. "Some Principals Ban Dance with Gang Ties." *Los Angeles Times,* June 5, 2002.

Hayes, Cedric J. *A Discography of Gospel Records, 1937–1971.* Copenhagen, Denmark: Karl Emil Knudsen, 1973.

————, and Robert Laughton. *Gospel Records, 1943–1969: A Black Music Discography.* London: Record Information Services, 1992.

Hayes, Laurence. "The Music of Ulysses Kay, 1939–1963." PhD diss., University of Wisconsin, 1971.

Heavenly Light Quartet. *The Heavenly Light Quartet,* compact disc and liner notes. Marguerite Productions HLQ CD GN13/MRA, 1996.

Heilbut, Tony. *The Gospel Sound: Good News and Bad Times.* 1971. Reprint, New York: Anchor, 1975.

Helm, MacKinley. *Angel Mo' and Her Son, Roland Hayes.* Boston: Little, Brown, 1942.

Henderson, Clara E. "Dance and Gender as Contested Sites in Southern Malawian Presbyterian Churches." In *The Garland Handbook of African Music,* 2nd ed., edited by Ruth M. Stone, 429–48. New York: Routledge, 2008.

————. "Dance Discourse in the Music and Lives of Presbyterian Myano Women in Southern Malawi." PhD diss., Indiana University, 2009.

Henry, Jim. "The Historical Roots of Barbershop Harmony." *The Harmonizer* 61(4) (July/August 2001): 13-17.

Hentoff, Nat. "The Hawk Talks: Coleman Discusses Individuality and Some Young Musicians." *Downbeat* 23 (1956): 13, 50.

Herron, Jerry. *AfterCulture: Detroit and the Humiliation of History.* Detroit, MI: Wayne State University Press, 1993.

Herskovits, Melville J. *The Myth of the Negro Past.* Boston: Beacon Press, 1941.

————. "The Role of Culture-Pattern in the African Acculturative Experience." 1960. Reprint in *Cultural Relativism: Perspectives in Cultural Pluralism,* edited by Melville J. Herskovits, 173–84. New York: Random House, 1972.

Higginson, Thomas Wentworth. *Army Life in a Black Regiment.* 1869. Reprint, Boston: Beacon Press, 1962.

Hilburn, Robert. "Rap History Lessons." *Los Angeles Times Calendar,* December 9, 2001, 80.

Hine, Darlene Clark, and Kathleen Thompson, eds. *Facts on File Encyclopedia of Black Women in America.* New York: Facts on File, 1997.

————, William C. Hine, and Stanley Harrold. *African Americans: A Concise History.* Combined volume. Upper Saddle River, NJ: Pearson Education, 2004.

Hirshey, Gerri. *Nowhere to Run: The Story of Soul Music.* New York: Times Books, 1984.

Hodeir, André. *Jazz: Its Evolution and Essence.* Translated by David Noakes, 1956. Reprint, New York: Grove Press, 1979.

Hodges, Michael. "Detroit's Ruins Bring Visitors, but Rankle Critics Within the City." *The Detroit News,* July 1, 2010.

Hogan, Steve, and Lee Hudson. *Completely Queer: The Gay and Lesbian Encyclopedia.* New York: Henry Holt, 1998.

Holloway, Joseph E., ed. *Africanisms in American Culture*. 2nd ed., Bloomington, IN: Indiana University Press, 2005.

Holt, Fabian. *Genre in Popular Music*. Chicago: University of Chicago Press, 2007.

Horn, Martin E. *Innervisions: The Music of Stevie Wonder*. Bloomington, IN: 1st Book Library, 2000.

Horne, Gerald. *Race Woman: The Lives of Shirley Graham DuBois*. New York: New York University Press, 2000.

Horton, James Oliver, and Lois E. Horton. *Hard Road to Freedom: The Story of African America*. New Brunswick, NJ: Rutgers University Press, 2001.

Huey, Steve. "Rakim: Biography." Accessed August 31, 2012, www.allmusic.com/artist/rakim-mn0000389137.

Hughes, Rupert. "A Eulogy of Ragtime." *The Musical Record* 447 (April 1899): 157–59.

Hughes, Timothy. "Groove and Flow: Six Analytical Essays on the Music of Stevie Wonder." PhD diss., University of Washington, 2003.

Hughes, Walter. "In the Empire of the Beat: Discipline and Disco." In *Microphone Fiends: Youth Music & Youth Culture*, edited by Andrew Ross and Tricia Rose, 147–57. New York: Routledge, 1994.

Hulse, Nora, and Nan Bostick. "Ragtime's Women Composers: An Annotated Lexicon." *The Rag Time Ephemeralist* 3 (2002): 106–35.

Hunkemöller, Jürgen. "Ragtime." In *Die Musik in Geschichte und Gegenwart, Sachteil 8*, edited by Ludwig Finscher, 58–68. Kassel: Bärenreiter, 1998.

Hurston, Zora Neale. "Sometimes in the Mind." In *Book of Negro Folklore*, edited by Langston Hughes and Arna Bontemps. New York: Dodd, Mead, 1958.

Illustrierte Zeitung Leipzig, Nr. 3110, February 5, 1903, 202–04.

"An Introduction to Soul." *Esquire* 69 (April 1968): 79–90.

Jackson, Barbara Garvey. "Florence Price, Composer." *Black Perspective in Music* 5(1) (1977): 30–43.

Jackson, Bruce, ed. *The Negro and His Folklore in Nineteenth-Century Periodicals, Vol. 18*. Austin: The University of Texas Press, 1967.

Jackson, John A. *Big Beat Heat: Alan Freed and the Early Years of Rock & Roll*. New York: Schirmer Books, 1991.

Jackson, Joyce Marie. "The Performing Black Sacred Quartet: An Expression of Cultural Values and Aesthetics." PhD diss., Indiana University, 1988.

———. "The Cultural Evolution of the African American Sacred Quartet." In *Saints and Sinners: Religion, Blues and (D)evil in African-American Music and Literature*, edited by Robert Sacre, 97–112. Liége, Belgium: Société Liégeoise de Musicologie, 1996.

———. "Working Both Sides of the Fence: The African American Sacred Quartets Enter Realm of Popular Culture." In *Bridging Southern Cultures: An Interdisciplinary Approach*, edited by John Lowe, 154–71. Baton Rouge: Louisiana State University Press, 2004.

Jackson, Judge. *The Colored Sacred Harp, For Singing Class, Singing School, Convention and General Use in Christian Work and Worship*. 1934. 3rd revised ed., Montgomery, AL: Brown Printing, 1992.

Jackson, Mahalia, with Evan McLeod Wylie. *Movin' On Up*. New York: Hawthorn, 1966.

Jackson, Raymond. "The Piano Music of Twentieth-Century Black Americans as Illustrated Mainly in the Works of Three Composers [Dett, Swanson, and Walker]." PhD diss., Juilliard School of Music, 1973.

Jasen, David A. *Ragtime: An Encyclopedia, Discography, and Sheetography*. New York: Routledge, 2007.

———, and Gene Jones. *Spreadin' Rhythm Around: Black Popular Songwriters, 1880–1930*. New York: Schirmer Books, 1998.

———, and ———. *That American Rag: The Story of Ragtime from Coast to Coast*. New York: Schirmer Books, 2000.

———, and ———. *Black Bottom Stomp: Eight Masters of Ragtime and Early Jazz*. New York and London: Routledge, 2002.

———, and Trebor Jay Tichenor. *Rags and Ragtime: A Musical History*. New York: The Seabury Press, 1978.

Joe, Radcliffe A. *This Business of Disco*. New York: Billboard Books, 1980.

"John Coltrane: Dealer in Discord." *Muhammad Speaks* 2(9) (1963): 21.

Johnson, E. Patrick. "Performing Blackness Down Under: The Café of the Gate of Salvation." *Text and Performance Quarterly* 22(2) (April 2002): 99–119.

Jones, A.M. "African Music." *Africa: Journal of the International African Institute* 24(1) (January 1954): 26–47.

Jones, Bessie and Bess Lomax Hawes. *Step It Down: Games, Plays, Songs, and Stories from the Afro-American Heritage*. Athens: University of Georgia Press, 1972.

Jones, Faustine Childress. *The Changing Mood in America: Eroding Commitment?* Reprint, Classic Editions Library Series, Washington, DC: Howard University Press, 1977.

Jones, Lisa C. "Kirk Franklin: New Gospel Sensation." *Ebony* 50(12) (October 1995): 64–67.

Jones, Marcus E. *Black Migration in the United States with Emphasis on Selected Central Cities*. Saratoga, CA: Century Twenty One, 1980.

Jones, Ralph. *Charles Albert Tindley: Prince of Preachers*. Nashville, TN: Abingdon, 1982.

Jost, Ekkehard. *Free Jazz*. New York: Da Capo Press, 1994.

Kahn, Ashley. *Kind of Blue*. New York: Da Capo Press, 2000.

Katz, Bernard, ed. *Social Implications of Early Negro Music in the United States*. New York: Arno Press, 1969.

Keepnews, Peter. "Why Big Record Companies Let Jazz Down." *Jazz* 4(1) (Winter 1979): 60–64.

——. "Jazz Since 1968." In *The Oxford Companion to Jazz*, edited by Bill Kirchner, 488–501. Oxford: Oxford University Press, 2000.

Keil, Charles. *Urban Blues*. Chicago: University of Chicago Press, 1966.

Keiler, Allan. *Marian Anderson: A Singer's Journey*. Urbana: University of Illinois Press, 2002.

Kelly, Kate. *Election Day: An American Holiday, an American History*. New York: Facts of File, 1991.

Kenney, William H. *Chicago Jazz: A Cultural History, 1904–1930*. New York: Oxford University Press, 1993.

Kent, Don. "An Interview with Rev. F.W. McGee." In *The American Folk Music Occasional*, edited by Chris Strachwitz and Pete Welding, 49–52. New York: Oak, 1970.

Kernfeld, Barry Dean. *What to Listen for in Jazz*. New Haven, CT: Yale University Press, 1995.

Keyes, Cheryl L. *Rap Music and Street Consciousness*. Urbana: University of Illinois Press, 2002.

Kilham, Elizabeth. "Sketches in Color: IV." 1870. Reprint in *The Negro and His Folklore in Nineteenth-Century Periodicals, Vol. 18*, edited by Bruce Jackson, 120–33. Austin: The University of Texas Press, 1967.

Kimball, Robert, and William Bolcom. *Reminiscing with Noble Sissle and Eubie Blake*. New York: Cooper Square Press, 2000. Originally published as *Reminiscing with Sissle and Blake*. New York: Viking Press, 1973.

Kisliuk, Michelle. "Musical Life in the Central African Republic." In *The Garland Handbook of African Music*, 2nd ed., edited by Ruth M. Stone, 362–77. New York: Routledge, 2008.

Kmen, Henry. *Music in New Orleans: The Formative Years, 1791–1841*. Baton Rouge: Louisiana State University Press, 1966.

Kofsky, Frank. *Black Nationalism and the Revolution in Music*. New York: Pathfinder Press, 1970.

Komara, Edward, ed. *Encyclopedia of the Blues*, 2 vols. New York and London: Routledge, 2006.

Koskoff, Ellen, ed. *The Garland Encyclopedia of World Music, Vol. 3: The United States and Canada*. New York: Garland, 2001.

Krasnow, Carolyn. "Fear and Loathing in the 1970s: Race, Sexuality, and Disco." *Stanford Humanities Review* 3(2) (1993): 37–45.

Kubik, Gerhard. "Intra-African Streams of Influences." In *The Garland Encyclopedia of World Music, Vol. 1*, edited by Ruth M. Stone, 293–326. New York: Garland, 1998.

Kwakwa, Patience A. "Dance in Communal Life." In *The Garland Handbook of African Music*, 2nd ed., edited by Ruth M. Stone, 54–62. New York: Routledge, 2008.

"Lady Soul Singing It Like It Is." *Time*, June 28, 1968, 62–66.

Landau, Jon. "A Whiter Shade of Black." In *The Age of Rock: Sounds of the American Cultural Revolution; A Reader*, edited by Jonathan Eisen, 298–306. New York: Random House, 1969.

"Largest U.S. Cities by Population, 1850–2010." US Census Bureau. In *World Almanac and Book of Facts 2012*, edited by Sarah Janssen, 613. New York: World Almanac Books, 2012.

"Largest U.S. Metropolitan Areas by Population, 1990–2010." US Census Bureau. In *World Almanac and Book of Facts 2012*, edited by Sarah Janssen, 612. New York: World Almanac Books, 2012.

Lee, Vera. *The Black and White of American Popular Music: From Slavery to World War II*. Preface by Ellis Marsalis. 2nd revised ed., Bloomington, IN: Xlibris Corporation, 2010.

Lehár, Franz. *Rastelbinder—Cake Walk*. Vienna: Josef Weinberger, n.d.

Lemann, Nicholas. *The Promised Land: The Great Black Migration and How It Changed America*. New York: Alfred A. Knopf, 1991.

Levine, Lawrence W. *Black Culture and Black Consciousness: Afro-American Folk Thought from Slavery to Freedom*. New York: Oxford University Press, 1977.

Lewis, Cary B. "William Marion Cook." *The Chicago Defender*, May 1, 1915.

Lewis, George E. "Improvised Music after 1950: Afrological and Eurological Perspectives." *Black Music Research Journal* 16(1) (1996): 91–122.

———. "Singing Omar's Song: A (Re)Construction of Great Black Music." *Lenox Avenue* 4 (1998): 69–92.

Lichtenstein, Grace, and Laura Dankner. *Musical Gumbo: The Music of New Orleans*. New York: W.W. Norton, 1993.

Lincoln, C. Eric, and Lawrence H. Mamiya, eds. *The Black Church in the African American Experience*. Durham, NC: Duke University Press, 1990.

Lindemann, Carolynn A., comp. and introd. *Women Composers of Ragtime: A Collection of Six Selected Rags by Women Composers. Reprinted from the Original Sheet Music*. Bryn Mawr, PA: Theodore Presser Company, 1985.

———, and Virginia Eskin. Liner notes to *Fluffy Ruffle Girls: Women in Ragtime*. Northeastern 9603-CD, 1992.

Litweiler, John. *The Freedom Principle: Jazz after 1958*. New York: Da Capo, 1984.

Logan, Wendell. "Notes on a Musical Setting of Robert Hayden's 'Runagate, Runagate.'" *Field Magazine* 47 (Fall 1992): 41–46.

Lomax, Alan. *Land Where the Blues Began*. 1993. Reprint, New York: DeltaBooks/Dell, 1995.

Lornell, Kip. Liner notes to *Happy in the Service of the Lord: Memphis Gospel Quartet Heritage—The 1980s*. Documentary booklet and 12" LP. High Water 1002, 1983.

———. *"Happy in the Service of the Lord": Afro-American Sacred Vocal Harmony Quartets in Memphis*. 2nd ed., Urbana: University of Illinois Press, 1995.

———, and Charles C. Stephenson Jr. *The Beat! Go-Go Music from Washington, D.C.* Jackson: University Press of Mississippi, 2009.

Lott, Eric. *Love and Theft: Blackface Minstrelsy and the American Working Class*. New York: Oxford University Press, 1993.

Lotz, Rainer. "Foolishness Rag: Ragtime in Europa—Neue Gedanken zu alten Tonträgern." *Jazzforschung/Jazzresearch* 21 (1989): 114–35.

———. *Black People: Entertainers of African Descent in Europe and Germany*. Bonn, Germany: Bigit Lotz, 1997.

———. *Deutsche Hot-Discographie: Cake Walk, Ragtime, Hot Dance & Jazz—ein Handbuch*. Bonn: Birgit Lotz Verlag, 2006.

Lovell, John. *Black Song: The Forge and the Flame*. New York: Macmillan, 1972.

Lucas, Gary. Liner notes to *Rhythm Come Forward: A Reggae Anthology*. CBS FC 39472, 1984.

Lundy, Ann. "Conversations with Three Conductors: Dennis Decoteau, Tania León, Jon Robinson." *Black Perspective in Music* 16(2) (1988): 218–19.

Magee, Jeffrey. "Ragtime and Early Jazz." In *The Cambridge History of American Music*, edited by David Nicholls, 388–417. Cambridge: Cambridge University Press, 1998.

Mahar, William J. *Behind the Burnt Cork Mask: Early Blackface Minstrelsy and Antebellum American Popular Culture*. Urbana and Chicago: University of Illinois Press, 1999.

Major, Clarence, ed. *Juba to Jive: A Dictionary of African-American Slang*. New York: Penguin Books, 1994.

Malone, Jacqui. Steppin' on the Blues: *The Visible Rhythms of African American Dance*. Urbana and Chicago: University of Illinois Press, 1996.

Marable, Manning. *Race, Reform, and Rebellion: The Second Reconstruction in Black America, 1945–2000*. 3rd revised ed., Jackson: University Press of Mississippi, 2007.

Marcus, Greil. *Mystery Train: Images of America in Rock 'n' Roll Music*. New York: Faber and Faber, 1975.

Marquis, Donald M. *In Search of Buddy Bolden: First Man of Jazz*. Revised ed., Baton Rouge: Louisiana State University, 2005.

Marschall, Fritz. "The Country Gospel Artists." *Storyville* 16 (April/May 1968): 8–10.

Marsh, J.B.T. *The Story of the Jubilee Singers: With Their Songs*. London: Hodder and Stoughton, 1876. Reprint, Boston: Houghton Mifflin, 1971.

Marshall, Bertie. "The Bertie Marshall Story: Pan is Mih Gyul." *Tapia* 2/3 (1972): 11.

Mason, Elsie W. "Bishop C.H. Mason, Church of God in Christ." In *Afro-American Religious History: A Documentary Witness*, edited by Milton Sernett, 285–95. Durham: Duke University Press, 1985.

Maultsby, Portia K. "Music of the Northern Independent Black Churches During the Antebellum Period." *Ethnomusicology* 19(3) (1975): 401–20.

———. "Gospel Quartets: A Source for Rhythm and Blues Styles." Paper presented at the Black American Quartet Traditions colloquium, sponsored by the Program in Black American Culture, Smithsonian Institution, Washington, DC, November 21, 1981.

———. "The Impact of Gospel Music on the Secular Music Industry." In *We'll Understand It Better By and By*, edited by Bernice Johnson Reagon, 19–33. Washington, DC: Smithsonian Institution Press, 1992.

———. "R&B and Soul." In *The Garland Encyclopedia of World Music, Vol. 3*, edited by Ellen Koskoff, 667–79, New York: Garland, 2001.

———. "Africanisms in African-American Music." In *Africanisms in American Culture*, 2nd ed., edited by Joseph E. Holloway, 326–55. Bloomington: Indiana University Press, 2005.

McCall, John. "The Representation of African Music in Early Documents." In *The Garland Encyclopedia of World Music, Vol. 1*, edited by Ruth M. Stone, 74–99. New York: Garland, 1998.

McDermott, Terry. "N.W.A. and the Album That Changed the World." *Los Angeles Times Magazine*, April 14, 2002, 12–17, 30–33.

McDonough, John. "Coleman Hawkins: Biography and Notes on the Music." Liner notes to *Coleman Hawkins. Giants of Jazz series*. Time Life records P14783–5, 1979.

McGregory, Jerrilyn. *Downhome Gospel: African American Spiritual Activism in Wiregrass Country*. Jackson: University of Mississippi Press, 2010.

McIntyre, Dianne. *EAR Magazine of New Music* 12(8) (1987): 5.

McKim, J[ames Miller]. "Negro Songs." 1862. Reprint in *The Negro and His Folklore in Nineteenth-Century Periodicals, Vol. 18*, edited by Bruce Jackson, 57–93. Austin: The University of Texas Press, 1967.

Merz, Karl. "Obituary for Justin Holland." *Brainard's Musical World* 24(282) (1887): 204.

Miller, Matt. "Dirty Decade: Rap Music and the US South, 1997–2007." *Southern Spaces*, June 10, 2008. Accessed August 21, 2011, www.southernspaces.org/2008/dirty-decade-rap-music-and-us-south-1997%E2%80%932007.

Monson, Ingrid. *Saying Something: Jazz Improvisation and Interaction*. Chicago: University of Chicago Press, 1996.

———. "Oh Freedom: George Russell, John Coltrane, and Modal Jazz." In *In the Course of Performance: Studies in the World of Musical Improvisation*, edited by Bruno Nettl and Melinda Russell, 149–68. Chicago: University of Chicago Press, 1998.

———. *Freedom Sounds: Jazz, Civil Rights, and Africa, 1950–1967*. New York: Oxford University Press, 2007.

Moodymann. "Red Bull Music Academy, Video Archive." London, 2010. Accessed November 4, 2010, www.redbullmusicacademy.com/video-archive/lectures/moodymann_henny_and_kenny.

Moore, William Jr., and Lonnie H. Wagstaff. *Black Educators in White Colleges*. San Francisco: Jossey-Bass, 1974.

Morath, Max. "May Aufderheide and the Ragtime Women." In *Ragtime: Its History, Composers, and Music*, edited by John Edward Hasse, 154–65. London: Macmillan, 1985.

Moreau de Saint-Méry, Médéric. *Déscription Topographique, Physique, Civile, Politique et Historique de l'isle Saint-Dominigue* . . . Philadelphia: Chez l'auteur, and Paris: Chez Dupont, 1797.

Morgan, Thomas L., and William Barlow. *From Cakewalks to Concert Halls: An Illustrated History of African American Popular Music from 1895 to 1930*. Washington, DC: Elliott and Clark, 1992.

Muhammad, Tariq K. "Hip-Hop Moguls: Beyond the Hype." *Black Enterprise* 30(5) (December 1999): 78–84.

Muir, Peter. *Long Lost Blues: Popular Blues in America, 1850–1920*. Urbana and Chicago: University of Illinois Press, 2010.

Murphy, Jeanette. "The Survival of African Music in America." *Popular Science* 55 (1899): 660–72. Reprint in *The Negro and His Folklore in Nineteenth-Century Periodicals, Vol. 18*, edited by Bruce Jackson, 327–29. Austin: The University of Texas Press, 1967.

Murphy, Joseph. *Santería: African Spirits in America*. Boston: Beacon Press, 1993.

———. *Working the Spirit: Ceremonies of the African Diaspora*. Boston: Beacon Press, 1994.

Neal, Mark Anthony. *Soul Babies: Black Popular Culture and the Post-Soul Aesthetic*. New York: Routledge, 2002.

———. *Songs in the Key of Black Life: A Rhythm and Blues Nation*. New York: Routledge, 2003.

Negus, Keith. *Music Genres and Corporate Cultures*. London: Routledge, 1999.

Nicholson, Stuart. *Billie Holiday*. Boston: Northeastern University Press, 1995.

Nisenson, Eric. *Ascension: John Coltrane and His Quest*. New York: St. Martin's Press, 1993.

Nketia, J.H. Kwabena. *African Music in Ghana*. Evanston, IL: Northwestern Press, 1963a.

———. *Drumming in Akan Communities of Ghana*. London: Thomas Nelson and Sons, 1963b.

———. "The Study of African and Afro-American Music." *Black Perspective in Music* 1(1) (Spring 1973): 7–15.

———. *The Music of Africa*. New York: Norton, 1974.

———. "African Roots of Music in the Americas: An African View." In *Ethnomusicology and African Music: Collected Papers. Vol. 1: Modes of Inquiry and Interpretation*, 318–36. Accra, Ghana: Afram, 2005. Originally published in *Report of the 12th Congress*, edited by Daniel Heartz and Bonnie C. Wade, 82–88. Berkeley, CA: American Musicological Society, 1977.

———. "The Scholarly Study of African Music: A Historical Review." In *The Garland Encyclopedia of World Music, Vol. 1*, edited by Ruth M. Stone, 13–73. New York: Garland, 1998.

Norfleet, Dawn. "'Hip-Hop Culture' in New York City: The Role of Verbal Musical Performance in Defining a Community." PhD diss., Columbia University, 1997.

———, and Monique R. Brown. "A Sound Investment: Here's a Step-By-Step Guide to Building Your Own Home Studio and Tips on Turning a Profit." *Black Enterprise Magazine*, December 1999, 107–16.

Northup, Solomon. *Twelve Years a Slave: The Narrative of Solomon Northup, A Citizen of New York, Kidnapped in Washington City in 1841 and Rescued in 1853, from a Cotton Plantation near the Red River in Louisiana.* Auburn, NY: Derby and Miller, 1853.

Nunez, Jessica. "Movement Festival 2010 Sees Highest Paid Attendance in History." *MLive.com*, June 1, 2010. Accessed February 21, 2011, www.mlive.com/entertainment/detroit/index.ssf/2010/06/movement_festival_2010_sees_hi.html.

Oja, Carol. "New Music Notes." *Institute for Studies in American Music Newsletter* 31(2) (2002): 6, 14.

Oliver, Paul. *Savannah Syncopators: African Retentions in the Blues.* New York: Stein and Day, 1970.

———. *Songsters & Saints: Vocal Traditions on Race Records.* Cambridge: Cambridge University Press, 1984.

Olmsted, Frederick Law. *A Journey in the Seaboard Slave States in the Years 1853–1854, with Remarks on the Economy.* 1856. Reprint, New York: G.P. Putnam's, 1904.

O'Meally, Robert. *Lady Day: The Many Faces of Billie Holiday.* New York: Arcade, 1991.

O'Neal, Jim, and Amy O'Neal. "Georgia Tom Dorsey." *Living Blues* 20 (March/April 1975): 17–34.

Osumare, Halifu. *The Africanist Aesthetic in Global Hip-Hop.* New York: St. Martin's Press, 2009.

Oteri, Frank J. "In the First Person [Interview with Tania León]." *New Music Box* 4 (August 1999). Online resource. Formerly available at www.newmusicbox.org/first-person/aug99/interview2.html.

Otis, Johnny. *Upside Your Head! Rhythm and Blues on Central Avenue.* Hanover, NH: University Press of New England, 1993.

Owen, Frank. "Hip Hop Bebop." *Spin* 4(7) (October 1988): 60–1, 73.

Owens, Thomas. *Bebop: The Music and Its Players.* New York: Oxford University Press, 1995.

Pareles, Jon. "On Rap, Symbolism, and Fear." *The New York Times*, February 2, 1992, sec. 2.

Patricola, Vincent. "The Electrifying Mojo: Part 1, The Mission." *Detroit Electronic Quarterly*, 3 (2005): 44-51.

Pavlow, Al. *Big Al Pavlow's The R&B Book: A Disc-History of Rhythm and Blues.* Providence, RI: Music House, 1983.

Payne, Daniel Alexander. *Recollections of Seventy Years.* 1888. Reprint in *Readings in Black American Music*, 2nd ed., edited by Eileen Southern, 65–70. New York: W.W. Norton, 1983.

Peretti, Burton W. *The Creation of Jazz: Music, Race and Culture in Urban America.* Urbana: University of Illinois Press, 1992.

Perkins, Kathy A. "The Unknown Career of Shirley Graham." *Freedomways* 25(1) (1985): 6–17.

Peterson, Bernard L. Jr. *A Century of Musicals in Black and White.* Westport, CT: Garland Press, 1993.

Phillips, Chuck. "Rap Finds a Supporter in Rep. Maxine Waters." *Los Angeles Times*, February 15, 1994.

Pickering, Michael. *Blackface Minstrelsy in Britain.* Aldershot, UK: Ashgate, 2008.

"Point of Contact: Discussion." *Down Beat, Music '66: 11th Yearbook* (1966): 19–31, 110–11.

Porter, Clara Womack. "A Study of Selected Art Songs of Howard Swanson." DMA diss., University of Kentucky, 1983.

Porter, Lewis, and Michael Ullman. *Jazz: From Its Origins to the Present.* Englewood Cliffs, NJ: Prentice Hall, 1993.

Puckett, Newbell N. *Folk Beliefs of the Southern Negro.* Chapel Hill: University of North Carolina Press, 1926.

Raboteau, Albert. *Slave Religion.* 1978. Reprint, New York: Oxford University Press, 1980.

Radano, Ronald M. "Jazzin' the Classics: The AACM's Challenge to Mainstream Aesthetics." *Black Music Research Journal* 12(1) (1992): 79–95.

———. *New Musical Figurations: Anthony Braxton's Cultural Critique.* Chicago: University of Chicago Press, 1993.

Randel, Don Michael, ed. *The Harvard Concise Dictionary of Music and Musicians.* Cambridge, MA: The Belknap Press of Harvard University Press, 1999.

Rascher, Sigurd. "Once More—The Saxophone." *The Etude Music Magazine* 60 (1940): 95–96, 132.

Raynor, Henry. *Music & Society.* New York: Taplinger, 1978.

Reagon, Bernice Johnson. "Let the Church Sing 'Freedom.'" *Black Music Research Journal* 7 (1987): 105–18.

———, ed. *We'll Understand It Better By and By: Pioneering African American Gospel Composers.* Washington, DC: Smithsonian Institution Press, 1992a.

———. "Kenneth Morris: I'll Be a Servant for the Lord." In *We'll Understand It Better By and By*, edited by Bernice Johnson Reagon, 329–41. Washington, DC: Smithsonian Institution Press, 1992b.

———. "Searching for Tindley." In *We'll Understand It Better By and By*, edited by Bernice Johnson Reagon, 37–52. Washington, DC: Smithsonian Institution Press, 1992c.

Reidy, Joseph P. "'Negro Election Day' and Black Community Life in New England, 1750–1860." *Marxist Perspectives* (Fall 1978): 102–17.

Reiterer, Ernst. *Cake-Walk aus der Operette Frühlingsluft nach Motiven von Josef Strauss.* Vienna: Ludwig Doblinger, n.d.

Reynolds, Simon. *Generation Ecstasy: Into the World of Techno and Rave Culture.* New York: Routledge, 1999.

Rhea, Shawn E. "Music Masters [Hip-Hop Economy, Part 3 in a Series]." *Black Enterprise* 33(1) (August 2002): 90.

Richardson, Joe M. *A History of Fisk University, 1865–1946.* 1980. Reprint, Tuscaloosa: University of Alabama, 2002.

Ricks, George Robinson. *Some Aspects of the Religious Music of the United States Negro.* 1960. Reprint, New York: Arno Press, 1977.

Riis, Thomas L. *Just Before Jazz: Black Musical Theater in New York, 1890–1915.* Washington, DC: Smithsonian Institution Press, 1989.

———. *More Than Just Minstrel Shows.* Brooklyn, NY: Institute for Studies in American Music, 1992a.

———. "Pink Morton's Theater, Black Vaudeville, and the TOBA: Recovering the History, 1910–30." In *New Perspectives on Music*, edited by Josephine Wright and Samuel A. Floyd Jr., 229–73. Detroit, MI: Harmonie Park Press, 1992b.

Ritzel, Fred. "Negerständchen—Über amerikanische Einflüsse auf die Tanz—Und Unterhaltungsmusik der Wilhelminischen Ära." In *Studien zur Instrumentalmusik: Lothar Hoffman-Erbrecht zum 60. Geburtstag*, edited by Anke Bingmann, Klaus Hortschansky, and Winfried Kirsch, 497–508. Tutzing, Germany: H. Schneider, 1988.

Roberts, John Storm. *Black Music of Two Worlds: African, Caribbean, Latin, and African-American Traditions.* 2nd revised ed. New York: Schirmer Books, 1998.

Robeson, Susan. *The Whole World in His Hands: A Pictorial Biography of Paul Robeson.* New York: Citadel Press, 1981.

Robinson, Danielle. "Performing American: Ragtime Dancing as Participatory Minstrelsy." *Dance Chronicle* 32 (2009): 89–126.

Roots of Techno: Black DJs and the Detroit Scene. A mini conference presented by the Archives of African American Music and Culture, Indiana University, Bloomington, IN, October 21, 2006.

Rose, Cynthia. *Living in America: The Soul Saga of James Brown.* London: Serpent's Tail, 1990.

Rose, Tricia. *Black Noise: Rap Music and Black Culture in Contemporary America.* Hanover, NH: Wesleyan University Press/University Press of New England, 1994.

Rosenbaum, Art. *Shout Because You're Free: The African American Ring Shout Tradition in Coastal Georgia.* Athens: University of Georgia Press, 1998.

Rosenthal, David H. *Hard Bop: Jazz and Black Music, 1955–1965.* New York: Oxford University Press, 1992.

Rubman, Kerill. "From 'Jubilee' to 'Gospel' in Black Male Quartet Singing." Master's thesis, University of North Carolina at Chapel Hill, 1980.

Russell, Henry. *Cheer! Boys, Cheer!: Memories of Men and Music.* London: J. Macqueen, 1895.

Russell, Tony and Chris Smith. *The Penguin Guide to Blues Recordings.* London: Penguin, 2006.

Ryan, Robin. "Dream N. The Hood for Rapper and Orchestra—Gregory T.S. Walker." *Counterpoint*, February 1997, 14–21.

Sacks, Howard, and Judith R. Sacks. *Way Up North in Dixie: A Black Family's Claim to the Confederate Anthem.* Washington, DC: Smithsonian Institution Press, 1993.

Sadie, Stanley, and John Tyrrell, eds. *The New Grove Dictionary of Music and Musicians.* 2nd ed., London: Macmillan, 2001.

Sanders, Charles. "Aretha." *Ebony* 27(2) (December 1971): 124–34.

Sandmel, Ben. *Ernie K-Doe: The R&B Emperor of New Orleans.* New Orleans: The Historic New Orleans Collection, 2012.

Saulny, Susan. "Razing the City to Save the City." *New York Times*, June 20, 2010. Accessed March 13, 2012, www.nytimes.com/2010/06/21/us/21detroit.html.

Savannah Rhythms: Music of Upper Volta. Liner notes by Kathleen Johnson. Electra/Asylum/Nonesuch Records, Nonesuch Explorer Series H-72087, 1981.

Sawyer, Charles. *The Arrival of B.B. King.* New York: Da Capo Press, 1980.

Sayce, Katherine, ed. *Tabex Encyclopedia Zimbabwe.* Harare, Zimbabwe: Quest, 1987.

Sayers, W.C. Berwick. *Samuel Coleridge-Taylor, Musician: His Life and Letters.* London: Cassell, 1915.

Schafer, William J., and Johannes Riedel. *The Art of Ragtime: Form and Meaning of an Original Black American Art.* Baton Rouge: Louisiana State University Press, 1973.

Schloss, Joseph G. *Making Beats: The Art of Sample-Based Hip-Hop.* Middletown, CT: Wesleyan University Press, 2004.

———. *B-boys, B-girls and Hip-Hop Culture in New York.* New York: Oxford University Press, 2009.

Schuller, Gunther. *Early Jazz: Its Roots and Musical Development.* 1968. Reprint, New York: Oxford University Press, 1986a.

———. *Musings: The Musical World of Gunther Schuller: A Collection of His Writings.* New York: Oxford University Press, 1986b.

———. *The Swing Era: The Development of Jazz, 1930–1945.* New York: Oxford University Press, 1989.

Schwerin, Jules. *Got to Tell It: Mahalia Jackson, Queen of Gospel.* New York: Oxford University Press, 1992.

Segal, Ronald. *The Black Diaspora: Five Centuries of the Black Experience.* New York: Noonday Press, 1995.

Self, Geoffrey. *The Hiawatha Man: The Life and Work of Samuel Coleridge-Taylor.* Aldershot, UK: Scholar Press, 1995.

Seroff, Doug. *Black Religious Quartet Singing.* Washington DC: Smithsonian Performing Arts, Program in Black American Culture, 1981.

———. "The Continuity of the Black Gospel Quartet Tradition." Paper presented at the conference on Sacred Music in the Black Church, National Baptist Convention Sunday School Publishing Board, Nashville, TN, December 9, 1982.

———. "One Hundred Years of Black Religious Quartet Singing." Unpublished paper presented at the ARSC Convention, 1983.

Shapiro, Peter. *Modulations: A History of Electronic Music: Throbbing Words on Sound.* New York: Caipirinha Productions, 2000.

Shaw, Arnold. *The World of Soul: Black America's Contribution to the Pop Music Scene.* New York: Cowles Book Company, 1970.

———. *Honkers and Shouters: The Golden Years of Rhythm and Blues.* New York: Macmillan, 1978.

Shepp, Archie. "An Artist Speaks Bluntly." *Down Beat* 32(26) (1965): 11, 42.

Shipton, Alyn. *Groovin' High: The Life of Dizzy Gillespie.* New York: Oxford University Press, 1999.

Sicko, Dan. *Techno Rebels: The Renegades of Electronic Funk.* 2nd ed., New York: Watson-Guptill, 2010.

Silveri, Louis. "The Singing Tours of the Fisk Jubilee Singers: 1871–1874." In *Feel the Spirit: Studies in Nineteenth-Century Afro-American Music*, edited by George R. Keck and Sherrill V. Martin, 105–16. Westport, CT: Greenwood Press, 1988.

Simond, Ike. *Old Slack's Reminiscence and Pocket History of the Colored Profession from 1865 to 1891*. 1891. Reprint, Bowling Green, OH: Bowling Green University Popular Press, 1974.

Smallwood, Lawrence. "African Cultural Dimensions in Cuba." *Journal of Black Studies* 6(2) (1975): 191–99.

Smith, Charles. "New Orleans and Traditions in Jazz." In *Jazz: New Perspectives on the History of Jazz by Twelve of the World's Foremost Jazz Critics and Scholars*, edited by Nat Hentoff and Albert McCarthy. New York: Da Capo Press, 1975.

Smith, James Lindsay. *Autobiography . . . Including Also Reminiscences of Slave Life, Recollections of the War, Education of Freedom, Causes of the Exodus, etc.* Norwich, UK: Press of the Bulletin, 1881.

Smith, R.J. "T-ing Off: This Time It's Personal." *Village Voice*, April 13, 1993, 66.

Smith, Suzanne E. *Dancing in the Street: Motown and the Cultural Politics of Detroit*. Cambridge, MA: Harvard University Press, 1999.

Southall, Geneva Handy. *Blind Tom: The Post-Emancipation Reenslavement of a Black Musical Genius*. Minneapolis, MN: Challenge Productions, 1979.

———. *Continuing "Enslavement" of Blind Tom, the Black Pianist-Composer, 1865–1887*. Minneapolis: Challenge Productions, 1983.

Southern, Eileen. "The Religious Occasion." In *The Black Experience in Religion*, edited by C. Eric Lincoln, 52–63. New York: Anchor, 1974.

———. "Frank Johnson and His Promenade Concerts." *Black Perspective in Music* 5(2) (1977): 3–29.

———. *Biographical Dictionary of Afro-American and African Musicians*. Westport, CT: Greenwood Press, 1982.

———, ed. *Readings in Black American Music*. 2nd ed., New York: W.W. Norton, 1983.

———, ed. *African-American Theater: Out of Bondage (1876) and Peculiar Sam; or the Underground Railroad (1879), Vol. 9: Nineteenth-Century American Musical Theater*, edited by Deane Root. New York and London: Garland Press, 1994. Vocal score with libretti.

———. *The Music of Black Americans: A History*. 1971. 3rd ed., New York: W.W. Norton, 1997.

Spellman, A.B. *Four Lives in the Bebop Business*. New York: Limelight Editions, 1985.

Spencer, Jon Michael. "R. Nathaniel Dett's Views on the Preservation of Black Music." *The Black Perspective in Music* 10(2) (Autumn 1982): 132–48.

———. "The R. Nathaniel Dett Reader: Essays on Black Sacred Music." Special issue of *Black Sacred Music: A Journal of Theomusicology* 5(2) (1991).

Springer, Robert, ed. *Nobody Knows Where the Blues Come From: Lyrics and History*. Jackson: University Press of Mississippi, 2006.

Steel, David Warren, with Richard H. Hulan. *The Makers of the Sacred Harp*. Urbana, Chicago, and Springfield: University of Illinois Press, 2010.

Stewart, Alexander. "'Funky Drummer': New Orleans, James Brown, and the Rhythmic Transformation of American Popular Music." *Popular Music* 19(3) (2000): 293–318.

Still, Judith Anne. *William Grant Still: An Oral History*. Fullerton: California State University, Fullerton, 1984.

———, Michael J. Dabrishus, and Carolyn L. Quin, eds. *William Grant Still: A Bio-Bibliography*. Westport, CT: Greenwood Press, 1996.

Still, William Grant. "A Composer's Viewpoint." In *William Grant Still and the Fusion of Cultures in American Music*, edited by Robert Bartlett Hass. Los Angeles: Black Sparrow, 1975. Reprinted in *Black Sacred Music: A Journal of Theomusicology* 6(2) (1992): 215–31.

St. John, Graham. *Technomad: Global Raving Countercultures*. Oakville, CT: Equinox, 2009.

Stone, Angie. Liner notes to *Black Diamond*. Arista 07822-19092-2, 1999.

Stone, Ruth M. "African Music Performed." In *Africa*, 2nd ed., edited by Phyllis M. Martin and Patrick O'Meara, 233–48. Bloomington: Indiana University Press, 1986.

———, ed. *The Garland Encyclopedia of World Music, Vol. 1: Africa*. New York: Garland, 1998.

———. *Music in West Africa: Experiencing Music, Expressing Culture*. New York: Oxford University Press, 2005.

———, ed. *The Garland Handbook of African Music*. 2nd ed., New York: Routledge, 2008a.

———. "Exploring African Music." In *The Garland Handbook of African Music*, 2nd ed., edited by Ruth M. Stone, 13–21. New York: Routledge, 2008b.

Stowe, David W. *Swing Changes: Big Band Jazz in New Deal America*. Cambridge: Harvard University Press, 1994.

Straw, William. "Popular Music as Cultural Commodity: The American Recorded Music Industries, 1976–1985." PhD diss., McGill University, 1990.

Strayhorn, Billy. "The Ellington Effect." In *The Duke Ellington Reader*, edited by Mark Tucker, 269–70. New York: Oxford University Press, 1993.

Strobert, Nelson T. "Daniel Alexander Payne: Venerable Preceptor for the African Methodist Episcopal Church." In *Witness at the Crossroads: Gettysburg Lutheran Seminary Servants in the Public Life*, edited by Frederick Wentz, 27–39. Gettysburg, PA: The Lutheran Theological Seminary of Gettysburg, 2001. E-text available at www.ltsg.edu/Alumni/files/Daniel_A_Payne-bio. Accessed July 23, 2013.

Stuckey, Sterling. *Slave Culture: Nationalist Theory and the Foundations of Black America*. New York: Oxford University Press, 1987.

Sugrue, Thomas J. *The Origins of the Urban Crisis: Race and Inequality in Postwar Detroit*. Princeton, NJ: Princeton University Press, 1996.

Sukenick, Ronald. *Down and In: Life in the Underground*. New York: Collier Books, Macmillan, 1987.

Sutton, Allan. *Cakewalks, Rags, and Novelties: The International Ragtime Discography (1894–1930)*. Highlands Ranch, CO: Mainspring Press, 2003.

"Syd Nathan's King Records," DK Peneny. Accessed April 25, 2014, www.history-of-rock.com/king_records.htm.

Sykes, Charles. "Profiles of Record Labels: Motown." In *African American Music: An Introduction*, edited by Mellonee V. Burnim and Portia K. Maultsby, 431–52. New York: Routledge, 2006.

Sylvan, Robin. *Trance Formation: The Spiritual and Religious Dimensions of Global Rave Culture*. New York: Routledge, 2005.

Szwed, John F. *Space Is the Place: The Life and Times of Sun Ra*. New York: Pantheon Books, 1997.

———. *So What: The Life of Miles Davis*. New York: Simon and Schuster, 2002.

Tallmadge, William H. "The Responsorial and Antiphonal Practices in Gospel Song." *Ethnomusicology* 12(2) (1968): 219–38.

———. "Jubilee to Gospel: A Selection of Commercially Recorded Black Religious Music, 1921–1953." Documentary booklet to *Jubilee to Gospel*. JEMF Records 108, 1981.

———. "Ben Harney: The Middlesborough Years, 1890–93." *American Music*, 13(2) (Summer 1995): 167–94.

Tanner, Paul, Maurice Gerow, and David W. Megill. *Jazz*. 11th ed. Boston: McGraw Hill, 2008.

Tarradell, Mario. "Leela James Talks about Soulful Lyrics, Versatility." *The Dallas Morning News* website, October 18, 2010. Accessed August 9, 2012, www.dallasnews.com/entertainment/columnists/mario-tarradell/20101016-Leela-James-talks-soulful-lyrics-6641.ece.

Teachout, Terry. "The Color of Jazz." *Commentary*, September 1995, 50–53.

Tetzeli, Rick. "5 Thoughts about 'The Detroit Story.'" *TIME.com*, March 22, 2010. Accessed April 25, 2012, http://detroit.blogs.time.com/2010/03/22/5-thoughts-about-the-detroit-story/.

"Texas Tommy." Sonny Watson's StreetSwing.com, updated January 10, 2010. Accessed October 15, 2013, www.streetswing.com/histmain/z3tex1.htm.

Thomas, Anthony. "The House the Kids Built: The Gay Imprint on American Dance Music." In *Out in Culture: Gay, Lesbian, and Queer Essays on Popular Culture*, edited by Corey K. Creekmur and Alexander Doty, 437–48. Durham, NC: Duke University Press, 1995.

Thompson, Jewel Taylor. *Samuel Coleridge-Taylor: The Development of His Compositional Style*. Metuchen, NJ: Scarecrow Press, 1994.

Thornton, John K. *Warfare in Atlantic Africa, 1500–1800*. London: Routledge, 1999a.

———. "African Dimensions of the Stono Rebellion." In *A Question of Manhood: A Reader in U.S. Black Men's History and Masculinity*, edited by Darlene Clark Hine and Earnestine Jenkins, 115–29. Bloomington: Indiana University Press, 1999b.

Thornton, Sarah. *Club Cultures: Music, Media, and Subcultural Capital*. Hanover, NH: Wesleyan University Press, 1996.

Tibbetts, John C., ed. *Dvořák in America, 1892–1895*. Portland, OR: Amadeus Press, 1993.

Toll, Robert. *Blacking Up: The Minstrel Show in Nineteenth-Century America*. New York: Oxford University Press, 1974.

"Top Gospel Albums." *Billboard, One Hundredth Anniversary Issue, 1894–1994*, 106 (November 1994): 246.

Triandis, Harry C., ed. *Variations in Black and White Perceptions of the Social Environment*. Urbana: University of Illinois Press, 1976.

Trotter, James Monroe. *Music and Some Highly Musical People*. 1878. Reprint, New York: Johnson, 1968.

Trotter, Joe William Jr. "Blacks in the Urban North: The 'Underclass' Question in Historical Perspective." In *The Underclass: Views from History*, edited by Michael B. Katz, 55–81. Princeton, NJ: Princeton University Press, 1993.

———. *River Jordan: African American Urban Life in the Ohio Valley*. Lexington: University Press of Kentucky, 1998.

Tucker, Ken. "The Seventies and Beyond." In *Rock of Ages: The Rolling Stone History of Rock 'n' Roll*, edited by Ed Ward, Geoffrey Stokes, and Ken Tucker, 467–624. New York: Summit, 1986.

Tucker, Mark. *Ellington: The Early Years*. Urbana: University of Illinois Press, 1989.

———. *The Duke Ellington Reader*. New York: Oxford University Press, 1993.

———. "In Search of Will Vodery." *Black Music Research Journal* 16 (1996): 123–82.

Tucker, Sherrie. *Swing Shift: "All-Girl" Bands of the 1940s*. Durham, NC: Duke University Press, 2000.

Ture, Kwame, and Charles V. Hamilton. *Black Power: The Politics of Liberation*. 1967. Reprint, New York: Vintage Books, 1992.

Underwood, Lee. "Boy Wonder Grows Up." *Downbeat* 41(15) (1974): 14–15, 42.

US Bureau of the Census. Series B48-71. Washington, DC: US Government Printing Office, 1949.

US Census Bureau. *QuickFacts*. Detroit, MI: US Census Bureau. Accessed July 8, 2010, http://quickfacts.census.gov/qfd/states/26/2622000.html.

US Census Bureau. *World Almanac and Book of Facts 2012*, edited by Sarah Janssen. New York: World Almanac Books, 2012.

Van Deburg, William L. *New Day in Babylon: The Black Power Movement and American Culture, 1965–1975*. Chicago: University of Chicago Press, 1992.

Vangilder, Marvin. "James S. Scott." *The Ragtimer* (Sept./Oct. 1976): 15–19.

Vecchiola, Carla. "Detroit's Rhythmic Resistance: Electronic Music and Community Pride." PhD diss., University of Michigan, 2006.

Vincent, Rickey. *Funk: The Music, the People, and the Rhythm of the One*. New York: St. Martin's Griffin, 1996.

Waldo, Terry. *This Is Ragtime*. New York: Hawthorn Books, 1976. Reprint, New York: Jazz at Lincoln Center Library Editions, 2009.

Walker-Hill, Helen, ed. *Black Women Composers: A Century of Piano Music, 1893–1900*. Bryn Mawr, PA: Hildegard Press, 1992.

———. *From Spirituals to Symphonies: African-American Women Composers and Their Music*. Westport, CT: Greenwood Press, 2002.

Ward, Andrew. *Dark Midnight When I Rise: The Story of the Fisk Jubilee Singers*. New York: Farrar, Straus, and Giroux, 2000.

Ward, Brian. *Just My Soul Responding: Rhythm and Blues, Black Consciousness, and Race Relations*. Berkeley: University of California Press, 1998.

Wardlow, Gayle Dean. "Rev. D.C. Rice—Gospel Singer." *Storyville* 23 (June/July 1969): 164–67.

Ward-Royster, Willa. *How I Got Over: Clara Ward and the World-Famous Ward Singers*. Philadelphia: Temple University Press, 1997.

Watson, John F. *Methodist Error*. 1819. Reprint in *Readings in Black American Music*, 2nd ed., edited by Eileen Southern, 62–64. New York: W.W. Norton, 1983.

Werner, Craig. *Higher Ground: Stevie Wonder, Aretha Franklin, Curtis Mayfield, and the Rise and Fall of American Soul*. New York: Crown, 2004.

Wesley, Charles. *Richard Allen: Apostle of Freedom*. 1935. Reprint, Washington, DC: Associated Publishers, 1969.

Wesley, Fred Jr. *Hit Me, Fred: Recollections of a Sideman*. Durham, NC: Duke University Press, 2002.

West Coast Ragtime Society. Accessed February 6, 2014, www.westcoastragtime.com.

White, Cliff. "After 21 Years, Still Refusing To Lose . . .." *Black Music* (April 1, 1977). Reprint in *The James Brown Reader: 50 Years of Writing about the Godfather of Soul*, edited by Nelson George and Alan Leeds, 124–44. New York: Plume/Penguin Group, 2008.

White, H. Loring. *Ragging It: Getting Ragtime into History (And Some History into Ragtime)*. Lincoln, NE: iUniverse, 2005.

White, Shane. "It Was a Proud Day: African-American Festivals and Parades in the North, 1741–1834." *Journal of American History* 81(1) (1994): 13–50.

Williams, John Bileebob. "1217." *Famzine.com*, July 2, 2010. Accessed August 10, 2010, http://famzine.com/blog/?page_id=6.

Williams-Jones, Pearl. "Afro-American Gospel Music: A Brief Historical and Analytical Survey (1930–1970)." In *Development Materials for a One-Year Course in African Music for the General Undergraduate Student*, edited by Vada E. Butcher, 201–19. Washington, DC: US Department of Health, Education, and Welfare, 1970.

———. "Afro-American Gospel Music: A Crystallization of the Black Aesthetic." *Ethnomusicology* 19(3) (September 1975): 373–85.

———. "Roberta Martin: Spirit of an Era." In *We'll Understand It Better By and By*, edited by Bernice Johnson Reagon, 255–74. Washington, DC: Smithsonian Institution Press, 1992.

Wilson, Doris Louise Jones. "Eva Jessye: Afro-American Choral Director." EdD diss., Washington University, 1989.

Wilson, Mary. *Dreamgirl: My Life as a Supreme*. New York: St. Martin's Press, 1986.

Wilson, Olly. "The Heterogeneous Sound Ideal in African-American Music." 1981. Reprint in *New Perspectives on Music*, edited by Josephine Wright and Samuel A. Floyd Jr., 327–38. Detroit, MI: Harmonie Park Press, 1992.

Wolff, Daniel, with S.R. Crain, Clifton White, and G. David Tenenbaum. *You Send Me: The Life and Times of Sam Cooke*. New York: Quill, 1995.

Woll, Allen. *Black Musical Theater: From Coontown to Dreamgirls*. Baton Rouge: Louisiana State University Press, 1989.

Wood, Peter H. "Stono Rebellion." In *Encyclopedia of African-American Culture and History*, Vol. 5, edited by Jack Salzman, David Lionel Smith, and Cornel West, 1818–1907. New York: Macmillan Library Reference USA, 1996.

Work, John. *American Negro Songs and Spirituals*. New York: Bonanza Books, 1940.

"Works and First Performances." Jeffrey Mumford's official website. Accessed August 11, 2012, www.jeffreymumford.com.

Wright, Josephine. "Early African Musicians in Britain." In *Under the Imperial Carpet: Essays in Black History, 1780–1950*, edited by Rainer Lotz, 14–24. Crawley, UK: Rabbit, 1986.

———, and Samuel A. Floyd Jr., eds. *New Perspectives on Music: Essays in Honor of Eileen Southern*. Detroit, MI: Harmonie Park Press, 1992a.

———. "Black Women in Classical Music in Boston During the Late Nineteenth Century: Profiles of Leadership." In *New Perspectives on Music*, edited by Josephine Wright and Samuel A. Floyd Jr., 373–404. Detroit, MI: Harmonie Park Press, 1992b.

Yetman, Norman, ed. *Voices from Slavery*. New York: Holt, Rinehart and Winston, 1970.

Young, Alan. *The Pilgrim Jubilee*. Jackson: University Press of Mississippi, 2001.

Zolten, Jerry. *Great God A' Mighty! The Dixie Hummingbirds: Celebrating the Rise of Soul Gospel Music*. New York: Oxford University Press, 2003.

Discography

THE TRANSLATED AFRICAN CULTURAL AND MUSICAL PAST

Arom, Simha. *République Centrafricaine: Banda Polyphony*. UNESCO/Auvidis D 8043, 1992. CD.

Baker, Anita. *Rapture*. Atlantic 60444-2, 1997. CD.

Been in the Storm So Long: A Collection of Spirituals, Folk Tales and Children's Games from Johns Island, South Carolina. Smithsonian Folkways/Rounder Records CD SFW 40031, 1990. CD.

Best Of Delta Blues. X5 Music Group, 2013. MP3.

Big Jay McNeely. *Nervous*. Big Jay McNeely Masters, 2009. MP3.

Boyz II Men. *Cooleyhighharmony*. Motown/Polygram Records 314 530 231-2, 1993. CD.

Dehoux, Vincent. *Centrafrique: Musique Gbáyá—Chants a penser*, Paris: OCORA C 580008, 1992. CD.

Drums of Burundi. ARC Music Productions EUCD 2053, 2007. CD.

Duke Ellington. *Blues in Orbit*. Columbia/Legacy CK 87041, 2004. CD.

—— and His Famous Orchestra. *Happy-Go-Lucky Local*. Musicraft Records MVSCD-52, 1992. CD.

Ewe Drumming from Ghana: The Soup Which Is Sweet Draws the Chairs in Closer. Topic Records TSCD 924, 2004. CD.

Franklin, Aretha. *Amazing Grace (with James Cleveland and the Southern California Community Choir)*. Rhino 7567813242, 1987. CD.

Franklin, Kirk. *Hello Fear*. GospoCentric 77917, 2011. CD.

Graham Central Station. *Release Yourself*. Warner Bros. Records 9 2814-2, 1997. CD.

Hancock, Herbie. *Head Hunters*. Columbia/Legacy CK 65123, 1997.

——. *Secrets*. Columbia CK 34280, 1988.

Hawkins, Walter. *The Very Best of Walter Hawkins and the Hawkins Family*. Artemis Gospel 51753, 2005. 2-CD set.

Jazz Odyssey, Vol. 1: The Sound of New Orleans (1917–1947). Columbia C3L 30, 1964. LP.

The JBs. *Funky Good Time: The Anthology*. Polydor D208152D2, 1995.

Keys, Alicia. *Songs in A Minor*. J Records 80813-20002-2, 2001. CD.

Kisliuk, Michelle. *Mbuti Pygmies of the Ituri Rain Forest*. Recordings by Colin Turnbull and Frances S. Chapman. Smithsonian/Folkways CDSF 40401, 1992. CD.

Mitchell, Vashawn. *Triumphant*. EMI Gospel 5099960660121, 2010. CD.

Muddy Waters. *The Complete Plantation Recordings: The Historic 1941–42 Library of Congress Field Recordings 1941–1942.* Chess/MCA CHD-9344, 1993. CD.

Negro Religious Field Recordings, Vol. 1: From Louisiana, Mississippi, Tennessee (1934–1942). Wien Document Records DOCD-5312, 1994, CD.

Parliament. *Parliament's Greatest Hits.* Casablanca/Polygram 822 637 2, 1984. CD.

Por Por: Honk Horn Music of Ghana. Smithsonian Folkways Records SFW CD 40541, 2007. CD.

The Rough Guide to West African Gold. World Music Network RGNET 1173, 2006. CD.

Tracey, Hugh, and John Storm Roberts. *From the Copperbelt: Zambian Miners' Songs.* Original Music OMCD 004, 1989. CD.

AFRICAN AMERICAN INSTRUMENT CONSTRUCTION AND MUSIC MAKING

Armstrong, Louis. *Hello Dolly: The Essential Louis Armstrong.* Air 002, 2005. CD.

Biz Markie. *Diabolical: The Biz's Greatest Hits.* Cold Chillin'/Traffic TEG 78310, 2009. CD.

Brown, James. *20 All-Time Greatest Hits!* Polydor 314 511 326-2, 1991. CD.

Dett, R. Nathaniel. *R. Nathaniel Dett: Piano Works.* New World Records NW 367-2, 1988. CD.

Doug E. Fresh. *The Greatest Hits.* JTC Atlantic Partners, 2011. CD.

Europe, James Reese. *Lieut. Jim Europe's 369th U.S. Infantry "Hell Fighters"Band: The Complete Recordings.* Memphis Archives 7020, 1996. CD.

The Fat Boys. *Fat Boys,* 1984. Reissue, Tin Pan Alley TPA-101, 2012. CD.

Hawkins, Coleman. *Body and Soul.* RCA/Bluebird ND 85717, 1986. CD.

Henderson, Fletcher. *1924–1938.* Giants of Jazz Recordings 53179, 1998. CD.

Little Walter. *The Best of Little Walter.* Chess CHD-9192, 1986. CD.

Missy Mist. *Gettin' Bass.* Dead Line, 1991. 45-rpm.

Muddy Waters. *You Shook Me: The Chess Masters, Vol 3, 1958 to 1963.* Geffen 3716465, 2012. CD.

Rahzel. *Make the Music 2000.* MCA E1119382, 1999. CD.

Sweet Honey in the Rock. *All For Freedom.* 1989. Reissue, Music for Little People/Warner Bros. 42505, 1992. CD.

Thomas, Henry. *Texas Worried Blues: Complete Recorded Works, 1927–1929.* Yazoo 1080/1, 1989.

Turner, Tina. *Simply the Best.* Capitol Records CDP 7 97152 2, 1991. CD.

Wonder, Stevie. *Talking Book.* 1972. Motown 012 157 354-2, 2000. CD.

SECULAR FOLK MUSIC

Afro-American Blues and Game Songs. Recorded by John and Alan Lomax, 1933–39. Rounder Select CD 1513, 1999. CD.

Afro-American Spirituals, Work Songs, and Ballads. 1942. Reissue, Rounder CD 1510, 1998. CD.

Been in the Storm So Long: A Collection of Spirituals, Folk Tales and Children's Games from Johns Island, South Carolina. Smithsonian Folkways/Rounder Records CD SF 40031, 1990. CD.

Black Banjo Songsters of North Carolina and Virginia. Smithsonian Folkway Recordings SFW40079, 1998. CD.

Music Down Home: An Introduction to Negro Folk Music, U.S.A. Folkways Records FW02691, 1965.

Negro Blues and Hollers. The Library of Congress/Rounder CD 1501, 1996. CD.

Negro Folk Music of Alabama, Vol. 1: Secular Music. Folkways Records FW04417, 1951.

Negro Work Songs and Calls. Recorded by Herbert Halpert. 1943. Rounder CD 1517, 1999. CD.

Ring Games: Line Games and Play Party Songs of Alabama. Folkways Records FW07004, 1953.

Roots of Black Music in America. Folkways Records FW02694, 1972.

Roots of the Blues. 1977. Reissue, New World Records 80252-2, 1991. CD.

Slave Shout Songs from the Coast of Georgia. The McIntosh County Shouters. Folkways Records FW-04344, 1984.

SPIRITUALS

The Battle of Jericho: Moses Hogan Conducts 15 Choral Arrangements, Vol. II. MGH Records 0505CD, 1995. CD.

Been in the Storm So Long: A Collection of Spirituals, Folk Tales and Children's Games from Johns Island, South Carolina. Smithsonian Folkways/Rounder Records CD SF 40031, 1990. CD.

The Fisk Jubilee Singers. *The Fisk Jubilee Singers.* Directed by John W. Work. Folkways Records FA2372, 1955. LP.

———. *The Fisk Jubilee Singers: In Bright Mansions.* Curb Records D2-78762, 2003. CD.

———. *Fisk University Jubilee Singers, in Chronological Order, Vol. 1: 1909–1911.* Vienna, Austria: Document Records DOCD-5533, 1997. CD.

Negro Religious Music, Vol. 1: The Sanctified Singers. Blues Classic BC-17, 1968. LP.

Religious Music: Congregational and Ceremonial. 1976. On *Folk Music in America, Vol. 1*, edited by Richard K. Spottswood. Library of Congress LBC 1, 1980. LP.

Robeson, Paul. *Paul Robeson in Live Performance.* New York: Columbia M30424, 1971. LP.

Spirituals: Tuskegee Institute Choir. Directed by William Dawson. Westminster Gold Series WGM-8154, 1968. LP.

Tuskegee Institute Singers/Quartet. *Complete Recorded Works in Chronological Order, 1914–1927.* Document Records DOCD-5549, 1997. CD.

Wade in the Water: African American Sacred Music Traditions, Vols 1–4. Smithsonian Folkways Recordings SF 40076, 1996. CD.

Wilmington Chester Mass Choir. *Victory Shall Be Mine.* Sweet Rain SR 115, 1990. Cassette.

QUARTETS

A Cappella Gospel Singing. Folklyric Records 9045, 1986. LP.

Atlanta Gospel. Heritage HT 312, 1986. LP.

Birmingham Jubilee Quartet. *Birmingham Quartet Anthology.* Clanka Lanka CL 144.001/002, 1980. 2-disc LP set.

———. *Jubilee to Gospel: A Selection of Commercially Recorded Black Religious Music, 1921–1953.* JEMF 108, 1996. Cassette.

Black Vocal Groups: Complete Recorded Works in Chronological Order, Vol. 8: 1926–1935. Booklet notes by Jerry Zolten. Document Records DOCD-5556, 1997. CD.

The Christianaires. *Saints Hold On.* Booklet notes by Paul Porter. CGI Records 5141612132, 1997. CD.

———. *The Vision Becomes Clearer . . .* Liner notes by James Chambers. CGI Records 5141650002, 1993. CD.

The Delta Rhythm Boys. *Dry Bones.* Collectors ed. Liner notes by Greg Gormick. Magnum America MCCD 028, 1996. CD.

Detroit Gospel. Heritage HT 311, 1986. LP.

Dixieaires. *Let Me Fly.* Heritage HT 317, 1987. LP.

The Dixie Hummingbirds. *The Best of the Dixie Hummingbirds.* MCA Special Products MCAD-22043, 1991. CD.

———. *The Good Health.* Liner notes by The Dixie Hummingbirds. Atlanta International AIR 10184, 1993. CD.

———. *Looking Back (A Retrospective).* DCC Compact Classics/3X Platinum Records TXP-10001, 1998. CD.

———. *Music in the Air: All Star Tribute: 70th Anniversary Celebration.* Platinum Entertainment 5141614612, 1999. CD.

———. *Thank You for One More Day: The 70th Anniversary of the Dixie Hummingbirds*. Liner notes by Marilyn A. Batcher and Jerry Zolten. MCA Records 11882, 1998. CD.

The Earliest Negro Vocal Quartets: 1894–1928. Document Records DOCD-5061, 1991. CD.

The Fairfield Four. *The Bells are Tolling*. Liner notes by Opal Louis Nations. ACE Records CDCHM 771, 2000. CD.

First Revolution: A Cappella Gospel Singers. Laser Light Digital 12 864, 1997. CD.

Five Blind Boys of Alabama. *Five Blind Boys of Alabama*. Heritage HT 315, 1987. LP.

———. *Oh Lord—Stand By Me/Marching Up To Zion*. Liner notes by Barret Hansen. Specialty Records SPCD-7203-2, 1991. CD.

Five Blind Boys of Mississippi. *Best of the Blind Boys*. MCA Special Products MCAD-22047, 1991. CD.

The Golden Age of Gospel Singing. Folklyric Records 9046, 1986. LP.

The Golden Gate Quartet. *Negro Spirituals, Vol. 1: My Walking Stick*. Music of the World CD 12537, 1996. CD.

———. *Negro Spirituals, Vol. 2: When the Saints Go Marching Home*. A World of Music. CD 12541, 1996. CD.

———. *Swing Down, Chariot*. Liner notes by Peter A. Grendysa. Columbia/Legacy CK 47131, 1991. CD.

———. *Travelin' Shoes*. Booklet notes by Billy Altman. BMG Music 07863 66063 2, 1992. CD.

———. *The Very Best of the Golden Gate Quartet*. World Pacific CDP 7243 8 54659 2 5, 1997. CD.

Gospel Hummingbirds. *Steppin' Out*. Liner notes by Lee Hildebrand. Blind Pig Records, Whole Hog BP74691, 1991. CD.

Harps of Melody. *Sing and Make Melody Unto the Lord*. Booklet notes by Rob Bowman. Hightone Music Group/Horizon HMG 6510, 1998. CD.

Heavenly Gospel Singers. *Dip Your Fingers in the Water/Beautiful City*. Bluebird 6073, 1935. 78-rpm.

Heavenly Light Quartet. *The Heavenly Light Quartet*. Marguerite Productions HLQ CD GN13/MRA, 1996. CD.

I Hear Music in the Air: A Treasury of Gospel Music. Booklet notes by Billy Altman. RCA 2099-2-R, 1990. CD.

Mighty Chariots of Fire. *Let's Praise Him*. We Have a Dream WHD30001, 2003. CD.

The Paschall Brothers. *On the Right Road Now*. Booklet notes by Joyce Marie Jackson. Smithsonian Folkways Recordings, SFW CD 40176, 2007. CD.

The Pilgrim Travelers. *The Best of the Pilgrim Travelers, Vols 1–2*. Booklet notes by Barret Hansen. Specialty Records SPCD-7204-2, 1991. CD.

———. *Better Than That*. Liner notes by Ray Funk. Specialty Records SPCD-7053-2, 1994. CD.

———. *Walking Rhythm*. Liner notes by Anthony Heilbut. Specialty Records SPCD-7030-2, 1992. CD.

Quartet Gospel. CGI Platinum 5341, 1999. CD.

Sam Cooke with the Soul Stirrers. Booklet notes by Lee Hildebrand. Specialty Records SPCD-7009-2, 1991. CD.

The Sensational Nightingales. *Stay on the Boat: Acts 27:31*. Malaco MCD 4453, 1992. CD.

The Skylarks. *The Best of the Skylarks*. Booklet notes by Opal L. Nations. Nashboro Records NASH4005, 1995. CD.

The Southern Sons: Deep South Gospel. Booklet notes by Ray Funk. Alligator Records & Artist Mgmt ALCD 2802, 1993. CD.

Swan Silvertones. *My Rock/Love Lifted Me*. Liner notes by Barret Hansen. Specialty Records SPCD-7202-2, 1991. CD.

———. *Only Believe*. HOB Records HBD 3517, 1992. CD.

Vocal Quartets, Vol. 4: K/L/M 1927–1943. Booklet notes by Ken Romanowski. Document Records DOCD-5540, 1997. CD.

A Warrior of the Battlefield: A cappella Trail Blazers: 1920's-1940's. Booklet notes by Kip Lornell and Dick Spottswood. Rounder Records CD 1137, 1997. CD.

Zion Harmonizers. *New Orleans Gospel Glory!* Mardi Gras Records MG 1042, 1998. CD.

RAGTIME

Century of Ragtime, 1897–1997. Various pianists. American Ragtime Company VC-0167,
    1997. 2-CD set.
Fluffy Ruffle Girls: Women in Ragtime. Virginia Eskin (pianist). Northeastern NR 9003-CD,
    1987. Reissued Koch International Classics B00000IYNJ, 1999.
Joplin, Scott. *Classic Ragtime from Rare Piano Rolls.* Micro Werks B003JA5MFQ, 2010.
    3-CD set.
Real Ragtime: Disc Recordings from Its Heyday. Produced and remastered by Richard Martin.
    Originally released 1998, originally recorded 1898–1917. Archeophone Records 1001A,
    2005. CD.

BLUES

And This Is Maxwell Street, Vols 1 and 2. Produced by Ian Talcroft. Rooster Blues Records
    R2641, 2000. CD.
The Blues. Smithsonian/Sony RD 101, 1993. 4-CD set.
The Blues Is Alright, Vol. 1. Malaco Records MCD 7430, 1993. CD.
Don't Say That I Ain't Your Man!—Essential Blues: 1964–1969. Columbia/Legacy CK 57631,
    1994. CD.
The Great Women Blues Singers. Deluxe Gold Edition. Fine Tune 2223-2, 2002. CD.
King, B.B. *B.B. King—Greatest Hits.* Geffen/MCA AAMCAD11746, 1998. CD.
Martin Scorsese Presents the Blues: A Musical Journey. Sony Music Distribution 5125782,
    2003. 5-CD set.
Mean Old World: The Blues from 1940 to 1994. Smithsonian Folkways 110, 1996. 4-CD
    set.
Muddy Waters. *Muddy Waters At Newport.* MCA/Chess CD 088 112 515-2, 2001. CD.
Smith, Bessie. *Bessie Smith: The Complete Recordings, Vols 1–5.* Columbia/Legacy C2K
    47091, C2K 47471, C2K 47474, C2T 52838, C2K 57546, 1991–96. Five 2-CD sets.
When the Sun Goes Down: The Secret History of Rock & Roll. Bluebird 09026-64006-2, 2002.
    4-CD set.

ART/CLASSICAL MUSIC

Adams, H. Leslie. *H. Leslie Adams: Love Rejoices.* Albany Records Troy 428, 2001.
    CD.
African Heritage Symphonic Series, Vol. 1. Music of Samuel Coleridge-Taylor, Fela Sowande,
    and William Grant Still. Chicago Sinfonietta, conducted by Paul Freeman. Cedille CDR
    90000 055, 2000. CD.
African Heritage Symphonic Series, Vol. 2. Music of Roque Cordero, Adolphus Hailstork,
    Ulysses Kay, Hale Smith, and George Walker. Chicago Sinfonietta, conducted by Paul
    Freeman. Cedille CDR 90000 061, 2001. CD.
African Heritage Symphonic Series, Vol. 3. Music of Michael Abels, David Baker, William
    Banfield, and Coleridge-Taylor Perkinson. Chicago Sinfonietta, conducted by Paul
    Freeman. Cedille CDR 90000 066, 2002. CD.
Alston, Lettie B. *Lettie Beckon Alston: Keyboard Maniac.* Albany Records Troy 439, 2001.
    CD.
Amen! African-American Composers of the 20th Century. Includes works by Harry T. Burleigh,
    Avery Robinson, R. Nathaniel Dett, Francis Hall Johnson, William Grant Still, John
    Wesley Work III, Margaret Bonds, Florence Price, Betty Jackson King, Robert Owens,
    Uzee Brown Jr., and Jester Hairston. Oral Moses, bass-baritone; George Morrison
    Bailey, piano. Albany Records Troy 459, 2001. CD.
Anderson, Marian. *Marian Anderson: Spirituals.* RCA Victor LM-2032, 1956. LP.
Baker, David. *Starker Plays Baker.* Janos Starker, cello; George Gaber, percussion; Alain
    Planes, piano. Laurel Record LR 817, 1981. LP.

————. *Through the Prism of the Black Experience.* Liscio Recording LAS-11972, 1997. CD.

Bang on a Can Live, Vol. 2. Music of Shelley Hirsch, Lois V. Vierk, Jeffrey Brooks, Elizabeth Brown, David Lang, Jeffrey Mumford, and Phil Kline. CRI CD 646, 1993. CD.

Bethune, Thomas Green Wiggins "Blind Tom." *John Davis Plays Blind Tom, The Eighth Wonder.* Newport Classics NPD 85660, 2000. CD.

The Black Composers Series. 1974. Works by 16 composers. Reissue, The College Music Society CBS Special Products P19425-P19433, 1986. 9-LP set.

Black Diamonds: Althea Waites Plays Music by African-American Composers. Music of Florence Price, William Grant Still, Margaret Bonds, Ed Bland. Althea Waites, piano. Cambria Master Recordings CD-1097, 1993. CD.

Briscoe, James R., ed. *Historical Anthology of Music by Women.* Bloomington: Indiana University Press, 1997. Accompanying CD.

Burleigh, Harry T. *Deep River: Songs and Spirituals of Harry T. Burleigh.* Oral Moses, baritone; Ann Sears, piano. Albany Records Troy 332, 1999. CD.

Character Sketches: Solo Piano Works by 7 American Women. Music of Victoria Bond, Tania León, Jane Brockman, Ruth Schonthal, Gwyneth Walker, Marga Richter, and Jeanne Zaidel Rudolph. Nanette Kaplan Solomon, piano. Leonarda Records LE 334, 1994. CD.

Dark Fires: 20th Century Music for Piano. Music by Delores White, Lettie Beckon Alston, Tania León, Hale Smith, Roget Dickerson, Jeffrey Mumford, and Adolphus Hailstork. Albany Troy 266, 1997. CD.

Dark Fires, Vol. 2. Music of Ellis Marsalis, David Baker, Alvin Elliot Singleton, Adolphus Hailstork, and Coleridge-Taylor Perkinson. Karen Walwyn, piano. Albany Troy 384, 2000. CD.

Davis, Anthony. *X: The Life and Times of Malcolm X: An Opera in Three Acts.* Gramavision Records R2-79470, 1992. CD.

————. *Tania.* Koch International Classics 3-7467-2 HI, 2001. CD.

Dédé, Edmond. *American Classics: Edmond Dédé.* Hot Springs Music Festival Orchestra, conducted by Richard Rosenberg. Naxos 8.559038, 2000. CD.

Dett, R. Nathaniel. *Dett: Magnolia Suite/In the Bottoms/Eight Bible Vignettes.* Denver Oldham. New World Records 80367, 1992. CD.

Electronic Music, Vol. 4. Includes music of Olly Wilson, Pril Smiley, and Will Hellermann. Various artists. Turnabout TV 34301, 1968. LP.

Frederick Moyer, Pianist: Reger, Walker, Ravel, Liszt/Busoni. GM Recordings GM 2016 CD, 1986. CD.

Hail to the Chief! Includes works by William Appo, A.J.R. Connor, and Frank Johnson. Sony 62485, 1996. CD.

The Incredible Flutist: American Orchestral Works by Still, Kay, Coolidge, Mason, Piston. Westphalian Symphony Orchestra, conducted by Paul Freeman. Vox Box CDX 5157, 1996. CD.

Jackson, Ernie, ed. *The Music of Justin Holland.* Port Chester, NY: Cherry Lane Music, 1995. Accompanying CD.

Jubal Songs. Music of Don Freund, Leslie Bassett, Harvey Sollberger, Tania León, and Eric Stokes. The Jubal Trio. CRI CD 738, 1997. CD.

Kaleidoscope: Music by African-American Women. Includes works for piano by Margaret Bonds, Valerie Capers, Rachel Eubanks, Nora Douglas Holt, Lena Johnson McLin, Undine Smith Moore, Julia Perry, and Florence Price. Helen Walker-Hill. Leonarda Productions LE 339, 1995. CD.

A La Par: Music of David Baker, Tania León, Wendell Logan, Coleridge-Taylor Perkinson. CRI CD 823, 1999. CD.

Lambert, Charles Lucien, Sr., and Lucién-Léon Guillaume Lambert Jr. *American Classics: Charles Lucien Lambert Sr. & Lucién-Léon Guillaume Lambert Jr.* Hot Springs Music Festival Orchestra, conducted by Richard Rosenberg. Naxos 8.559037, 2000. CD.

León, Tania. *Tania León: Indígena.* Continuum, The Western Wind, conducted by Tania León. CRI CD 662, 1994. CD.

Mumford, Jeffrey. *The Focus of Blue Light*. CRI CD 650, 1993. CD.

The Music of Francis Johnson & His Contemporaries: Early 19th-Century Black Composers. Music of Francis Johnson, A.J.R. Connor, Isaac Hazzard, Edward Roland, and James Hemmenway. The Chestnut Brass Company and Friends. Musicmasters MMD6 0236, 1990. CD.

The Negro Speaks of Rivers and Other Art Songs by African-American Composers. Music of Leslie Adams, Margaret Bonds, Charles Brown, Cecil Cohen, Undine Moore, Robert Owens, Coleridge-Taylor Perkinson, Florence Price, Howard Swanson, George Walker, and John W. Work Jr. Odekhiren Amaize, bass-baritone; David Korevaar, piano. Musicians Showcase Recordings MS 1011, 1999. CD.

The New American Scene II: 5 Distinguished African American Composers. Performed by the Cleveland Chamber Symphony. Music by Wendell Logan, T.J. Anderson, Leroy Jenkins, Dolores White, and David Baker. Albany Records Troy 303, 1998. CD.

Paul Freeman Introduces . . . Williams, Rendleman, Logan, Yardumian, Saltzman. Music of James Kimo Williams, Richard J. Rendleman, Wendell Logan, Richard Yardumian, and Peter Saltzman. Czech National Symphony Orchestra. Albany Records Troy 312, 1998. CD.

Piano Music by African-American Composers. 1970. Music of R. Nathaniel Dett, Thomas Kerr, William Grant Still, John W. Work III, George Walker, Arthur Cunningham, Talib Rasul Hakim, Hale Smith, and Olly Wilson. Natalie Hinderas, piano. Reissue, CRI CD 629, 1993. CD.

Piano Music of Black Composers. Music of William Grant Still, Howard Swanson, R. Nathaniel Dett, Ulysses Kay, Henry Clay Work, Oscar (Emmanuel) Peterson, Edward "Duke" Ellington, and Samuel Coleridge-Taylor. Monica Gaylord, piano. Music and Arts Program 737, 1992. CD.

Price, Florence. *Florence Price: The Oak/Mississippi River Suite/Symphony No. 3*. The Women's Philharmonic. Koch 7518, 2001. CD.

Robeson, Paul. *Spirituals and a Robeson Recital of Popular Favorites*. Columbia Masterworks, ML-4105, 1948. LP.

Roumain, Daniel Bernard. *I, Composer*. DBR Music, 2001. CD.

———. *String Quartets*. DBR Music, 2001. CD.

Sence You Went Away: Contemporary African American Art Songs & Spirituals. Music of Leslie Adams, Valerie Capers, Adolphus Hailstork, Cedric Dent, Eugene Hancock, John Carter, and Wendell Whalum. Various artists. Albany Records Troy 387, 2000. CD.

Shades of Blue: Symphonic Works by African American Composers. Music of David Baker, H. Leslie Adams, and Stephen Michael Newby. Prague Radio Symphony and Washington Symphony, conducted by Julius P. Williams. Visionary Records/Albany Records Troy 431, 2000. CD.

Singleton, Alvin. *Alvin Singleton: Extension of a Dream*. Various performers. Albany Records Troy 527, 2002. CD.

———. *Alvin Singleton: Shadows/After Fallen Crumbs/A Yellow Rose Petal*. Atlanta Symphony Orchestra. Elektra/Nonesuch 9 79231-2, 1989. CD.

———. *Alvin Singleton: Somehow We Can*. Various performers. Tzadik 7075, 2002. CD.

Still/Dawson/Ellington: Symphony No. 2/Negro Folk Symphony/Harlem. Music by William Grant Still, William Levi Dawson, and Edward "Duke" Ellington. Chandos 9226, 1993. CD.

Still, William Grant. *Works by William Grant Still*. Videmus. New World Records 80399-2, 1990. CD.

Symphonic Brotherhood: The Music of African-American Composers. Music of Adolphus Hailstork, Harry T. Burleigh, Julius P. Williams, Gary Powell Nash, and David Baker. Bohuslav Martinu Philharmonic. Albany Records Troy 104, 1993. CD.

Thomas, Augusta Read, and Tania León. *Augusta Read Thomas: Triple Concerto/Wind Dance, Tania León: Batá/Carabali*. First Edition Recordings, Louisville Orchestra LCD 010, 1995. CD.

Tillis, Frederick. *Freedom*. Various performers. New World Records 80455-2, 1996. CD.

———. *Music of Frederick Tillis, Vol. 1*. Serenus SR 12087, 1979. LP.

Voces Americanas: Voices of Change. Music of Robert Rodriguez, Mario Lavista, Roberto Sierra, Mario Davidovsky, and Tania León. Various performers. CRI 773, 1998. CD.

Walker, George. *George Walker: Chamber Music.* Various performers. Albany Records Troy 154, 1995. CD.

———. *George Walker in Recital.* Albany Records Troy 117, 1994. CD.

———. *Lilacs for Voice and Orchestra: The Music of George Walker.* Faye Robinson, soprano, Arizona State University Symphony Orchestra. Summit Records DCD 274, 2000. CD.

———. *The Music of George Walker.* George Walker, piano. CRI CD 719, 1997. CD.

Watch and Pray: Spirituals and Art Songs by African-American Women Composers. Music of Betty Jackson King, Margaret Bonds, Undine Smith Moore, Florence Price, and Julia Perry. Videmus. Koch International Classics Koch 3-7247-2H1, 1994. CD.

William Grant Still, Nathaniel Dett: Piano Music. Denver Oldham, piano. Altarus 9013, 1995. CD.

William Grant Still: Symphony No. 1 (Afro-American), Duke Ellington: Suite from The River. Detroit Symphony Orchestra. Chandos 9154, 1993. CD.

Wilson, Olly. *Music for Chamber Ensemble.* The Boston Musica Viva. Neuma Records 450–79, 1992. CD.

———. *Sinfonia.* Boston Symphony Orchestra, conducted by Seiji Ozawa. New World Records, 80331-2, 1985. CD.

Works by T.J. Anderson, David Baker, Donal Fox, Olly Wilson. New World Records 80423-2, 1992. CD.

The World So Wide. Music of Aaron Copland, John Adams, Leonard Bernstein, Tania León, Douglas S. Moore, Kurt Weill, Samuel Barber, and Carlisle Floyd. Dawn Upshaw, soprano. Nonesuch 79458, 1998. CD.

JAZZ

Armstrong, Louis. *The Best of Louis Armstrong: The Hot Five and Seven Recordings.* Columbia 86539, 2002. 4-CD set.

Big Band Jazz: From the Beginnings to the Fifties. Smithsonian Collection of Recordings, DMC4-0610, 1991. 4-CD set.

Big Band Jazz: The Jubilee Sessions, 1943–1946. Hindsight Records HBCD-504 (HBCD504-1–HBCD-504-3), 1996. 3-CD set.

Coltrane, John. *My Favorite Things.* Reissue of Atlantic 1361-2, 1960. Atlantic 8122-75350-2, 1998. CD.

Jazz: The Smithsonian Anthology. Washington, DC: Smithsonian Folkways SFW CD 40820, 2010. 6-CD set.

Morgan, Lee. *The Rumproller.* Remastered by Rudy Van Gelder, originally released as Blue Note 46428, 1965. Blue Note, 2004. MP3 download.

———. *Search for the New Land.* Remastered reissue of Blue Note 84169, 1964. Blue Note Records, 2003. CD or MP3 download.

———. *The Sidewinder.* Remastered by Rudy Van Gelder. Originally released as Blue Note 84197, 1963. Blue Note Records, 2007. MP3 download.

The Smithsonian Collection of Classic Jazz. CBS/Smithsonian RD 033, 1987. 5-CD set.

GOSPEL

Arizona Dranes: Complete Recorded Works in Chronological Order; 1926–1929. Document Records DOCD-5186, 1993. CD.

Beams of Heaven: Hymns of Charles Albert Tindley. GBG Musik, General Board of Global Ministries CD 1-025, 2006. CD.

The Edwin Hawkins Singers. *The Edwin Hawkins Singers: Let Us Go Into the House of the Lord.* Buddah Collector's Classics. BMG Direct 75517-49515-2, 1996. CD.

Franklin, Aretha. *Amazing Grace (with James Cleveland and the Southern California Community Choir).* Rhino 7567813242, 1987. CD.

Franklin, Kirk. *God's Property: From Kirk Franklin's Nu Nation*. B-Rite Music INTD-90093, 1997. CD.

——. *Kirk Franklin and the Family*. GospoCentric GCD2119, 1993. CD.

Jackson, Mahalia. *Mahalia Jackson Sings the Best-Loved Hymns of Dr. M.L. King*. Columbia CS 9686, 1968. LP.

——. *21 Greatest Hits*. Kenwood KW-20510, 1979. LP.

James Cleveland and the Salem Inspirational Choir. *I Don't Feel Noways Tired*. Savoy 1981.

Johnson, Blind Willie. *The Complete Blind Willie Johnson*. Columbia/Legacy C2K 52835, 1993. CD.

McClurkin, Donnie. *Live in London and More*. Verity Records 01241-43150-2, 2000. CD.

Precious Lord: Recordings of the Great Gospel Songs of Thomas A. Dorsey. Liner notes by Tony Heilbut. Columbia/Legacy CK 57164, 1994. CD.

Say Amen, Somebody. Music from the original soundtrack. DRG Records SB2L 12584, 1983. 2-LP set.

Spreading the Word: Early Gospel Recordings. JSP Records JSP 7733, 2004. 4-CD set.

Take 6. *Greatest Hits*. Reprise Records 9 47375-2, 1999. CD.

Wow Gospel 2005: 30 of the Year's Top Gospel Artists and Songs. Zomba 82676-65244-2R. 2-CD set.

MUSICAL THEATER

Don't Give the Name a Bad Place: Types and Stereotypes in American Musical Theater, 1870–1900. New World 80265, 1996. CD.

The Early Minstrel Show. New World 80338, 1998. CD.

Europe, James Reese. *Lieut. Jim Europe's 369th U.S. Infantry "Hell Fighters" Band: The Complete Recordings*. Memphis Archives 7020, 1996. CD.

Lost Sounds: Blacks and the Birth of the Recording Industry, 1891–1922. St. Joseph, IL: Archeophone Records Arch 1005, 2005. 2-CD set.

Williams, Bert. *Bert Williams: The Remaining Titles, 1915–1921*. Document 5661, 2000. CD.

RHYTHM AND BLUES/R&B

Atlantic Records. *Atlantic Rhythm and Blues, 1947–1974*. Atlantic 7 82305-2, 1991. 8-CD set.

After 7. *Reflections*. Virgin Records 7243 40547 2, 1995. CD.

Baker, Anita. *Rapture*. Atlantic 60444-2, 1997. CD.

Berry, Chuck. *The Best of Chuck Berry*. ATF Media, 2013. MP3.

Beyoncé. *Dangerously in Love*. Columbia CK 86386, 2003. CD.

Blige, Mary J. *What's the 411?* Uptown/MCA D130845, 1992. CD.

——. *Stronger With Each Tear*. Geffen B0013722-02 , 2009. CD.

Bo Diddley. *Bo Diddley: The Chess Box*. Chess/MCA CHD2-19502, 1990. CD.

Boyz II Men. *Legacy: The Greatest Hit Collection*. Universal Records 440 016 083-2, 2001. CD.

Brown, Bobby. *Don't Be Cruel*. MCA Records MCAD-42185, 1988. CD.

Brown, Charles. *Driftin' Blues: The Best of Charles Brown*. Collectables Records COL-CD-5631, 1995. CD.

Brown, Chris. *Exclusive—The Forever Edition*. Jive/Zomba 88697-12049-2, 2008. CD.

——. *F.A.M.E. (Deluxe Version)*. Jive 88697-86070-2, 2011. CD.

Brown, James. *Live at the Apollo (1962)*. Remastered and expanded, Polydor/Universal B0001715-02, 2004. CD.

——. *Live at the Apollo, Vol. II*. 1968. Polydor 823 001-2, 1990. CD.

——. *Star Time*. Polygram 849108-2–849111-2, 1991. 4-CD set.

Carey, Mariah. *The Emancipation of Mimi*. Island Def Jam B0003943-02, 2005. CD.

Charles, Ray. *The Best of Ray Charles: The Atlantic Years*. Rhino/Atlantic R2 71722, 1994. CD.

Cole, Nat King. *The Best of the Nat King Cole Trio: The Vocal Classics (1942–46)*. Capitol Jazz CDP 7243 8 33571 2 3, 1995. CD.

The Complete Stax/Volt Singles, 1959–1968, Vol. 1. Atlantic Group 7 82218-2, 1991. CD.

Daddy, Puff. *Forever*. Bad Boy Records 78612-73033-2, 1999. CD.

D'Angelo. *Brown Sugar*. EMI Records 724383262922, 1995. CD.

Destiny's Child. *The Writing's on the Wall*. Columbia Records CK 69870, 1999. CD.

The Doo Wop Box. Rhino R2 71463, 1994. 4-CD set.

The Doo Wop Box, Vol. 2. Rhino R2 72507, 1996. 4-CD set.

En Vogue. *Born to Sing*. Atlantic 82084-2, 1990. CD.

Fats Domino. *The Fat Man: 25 Classic Performances*. EMI 7243 8 52326 2 6, 1996. CD.

Franklin, Aretha. *Greatest Hits (1980–1994)*. Arista 18722, 1994. CD.

From Where I Stand: The Black Experience in Country Music. Produced by the Country Music Foundation. Warner Bros. Records 9 46248-2, 1998. 3-CD set.

Guy. *Guy*. MCA Records MCAD 42176, 1988. CD.

Hayes, Isaac. *Hot Buttered Soul*. Fantasy/Stax 7231458, 2009. CD.

———. *The Isaac Hayes Movement*. Fantasy/Stax 1010, 2004. CD.

———. *Shaft*. Stax 4015, 2007. CD.

Houston, Whitney. *Whitney Houston*. Arista ARCD8212, 1985. CD.

The Isley Brothers. *Groove With You: The Collection*. Sony MEG2 4846, 2003. CD.

Jackson, Freddie. *The Greatest Hits of Freddie Jackson*. Capitol Records D125323, 1993. CD.

Jackson, Janet. *Control*. A&M 95025, 2005. CD.

———. *Janet Jackson's Rhythm Nation 1814*. A&M 3939202, 1993. CD.

Jackson, Michael. *The Essential Michael Jackson*. Epic/Legacy E2K 94287, 2005. CD.

———. *Thriller (25th Anniversary Deluxe Edition)*. Legacy 88697220962, 2008. CD.

Jagged Edge. *The Hits*. Sony Urban Music/Columbia 88697023712, 2006. CD.

Jodeci. *Forever My Lady*. MCA Records MCAD-10198, 1991. CD.

Johnny Otis. *The Greatest Johnny Otis Show*. Ace CDCHD 673, 1998. CD.

Jordan, Louis. *Let The Good Times Roll: The Anthology, 1938–1953*. MCA/Decca MCAD2-11907, 1999. 2-CD set.

R. Kelly. *Love Letter*. Jive Records 88697808742, 2010. CD.

———. *The R. in R&B Collection, Vol. 1*. Jive 82876-53706-2, 2003. CD.

Keys, Alicia. *Girl on Fire*. RCA 88697-94182-2, 2012. CD.

———. *Songs in A Minor*. J Records 80813-20002-2, 2001. CD.

The King R&B Box Set. King 7002, 1996. 4-CD set.

Labelle, Patti. *The Essential Patti*. Sony BMG Music Entertainment 88697 21092, 2008. CD.

Liggins, Joe. *Joe Liggins & the Honeydrippers*. Speciality SPCD 7006, 1989. CD.

Little Richard. *The Essential Little Richard*. Fantasy/Specialty Records 21542, 1996. CD.

Martha & the Vandellas. *20th Century Masters: The Millennium Collection; Best of Martha Reeves & The Vandellas*. Motown/Uptown/Universal AA121533992, 1999. CD.

Maze Featuring Frankie Beverly. *Maze Featuring Frankie Beverly: Greatest Hits*. Capital/Right Stuff, 72435-79856-2-8, 2004. CD.

Mint Condition. *The Best of Mint Condition: 20th Century Masters; The Millennium Collection*. HIP-O/A&M/Universe B0006881-02, 2006. CD.

The Moonglows. *Blue Velvet: The Ultimate Collection*. Chess CHD2-9345, 1993. CD.

New Edition. *Candy Girl*. Streetwise/Warlock WARCD-8701, 1990. CD.

New Orleans. *The Best of New Orleans Rhythm and Blues, Vol. 1*. Rhino R2 75765, 1988. CD.

———. *The Best of New Orleans Rhythm and Blues, Vol. 2*. Rhino R2 75766, 1988. CD.

———. *The New Orleans Sound*. Time-Life Music 2RNR-39, 1991. CD.

Notorious B.I.G. *Life After Death*. Bad Boy Records 78612-73011-2, 1997. 2-CD set.

Motown Records. *Hitsville USA: The Motown Singles Collection 1959–1971*. Motown 3746363122, 1992. 4-CD set.

———. *Hitsville USA, Vol. II: The Motown Singles Collection 1959–1971*. Motown 37463 6358 2, 1993. 4-CD set.

Prince. *1999*. Warner Brothers 9 23720-2, 1982. CD.

———. *Ultimate*. Rhino R2 73381, 2006. 2-CD set.

Richie, Lionel. *The Definitive Collection*. Motown 440 068 140-2, 2003. CD.

Rihanna. *Talk That Talk*. Def Jam Records 2790454, 2011. CD.

Sledge, Percy. *The Best of Percy Sledge*. Atlantic 8210-2, 2009. CD.

Songz, Trey. *Ready [Deluxe]*. Atlantic 518794-2, 2009. CD.

Stax Records. *Top of the Stax: Twenty Greatest Hits*. Stax Records SCD-88005-2, 1988. CD.

———. *Wattstax: Music from the Wattstax Festival and Film*. Stax Records STX-330315, 2007. 3-CD set.

SWV. *It's About Time*. RCA 66074-2, 1992. CD.

TLC. *CrazySexyCool*. Laface Records 26009-2, 1994. CD.

———. *Oooooohhh . . . On the TLC Tip*. LaFace Records 26003-2, 1992. CD.

Turner, Joe. *Joe Turner: Flip, Flop & Fly*. Original Jazz Classics 10532, 2001. CD.

Usher. *Confessions*. Arista 82876-52141-2, 2004. CD.

Vandross, Luther. *The Essential Luther Vandross*. Epic/Legacy E2K 89167, 2003. CD.

Wilson, Charlie. *Just Charlie*. Jive 88697-81696-2, 2010. CD.

———. *Uncle Charlie*. Zomba 88697-23389-2, 2009. CD.

Wilson, Jackie. *The Jackie Wilson Story*. Epic EGK 38623, 1983. CD.

Xscape. *Hummin' Comin' at 'Cha*. Columbia/Sony Music Entertainment CK57107, 1993. CD.

———. *Off the Hook*. So So Def CSK 7214, 1995. CD.

SOUL

Badu, Erykah. *Baduizm*. Universal Records UD-53027, 1997. CD.

———. *Mama's Gun*. Motown 012153 259-2, 1997. CD.

Benét, Eric. *A Day in the Life*. Warner Bros. 9 47072-2, 1999. CD.

Brown, James. *The Singles, Vol. 6: 1969–1970*. Hip-O/Hip-O Select 1787359, 2009. 2-CD set.

———. *The Singles, Vol. 7: 1970–1972*. Hip-O Select/Polydor 2700161, 2009. 2-CD set.

Charles, Ray. *The Best of Ray Charles: The Atlantic Years*. Rhino/Atlantic R2 71722, 1994. CD.

Cooke, Sam. *The Late & Great Sam Cooke*. RCA 1080, 1969. LP.

D'Angelo. *Brown Sugar*. EMI Records 724383262922, 1995. CD.

Franklin, Aretha. *Aretha Franklin: 30 Greatest Hits*. Atlantic 81668-2, 2000. CD.

———. *Aretha Live At Fillmore West*. 1971. Reissue, Rhino R2 71526, 1993. CD.

Hayes, Isaac. *Shaft*. Stax 4015, 2007. CD.

Maxwell. *Maxwell's Urban Hang Suite*. Columbia CK 66434, 1996. CD.

Mayfield, Curtis. *Curtis Live!* Rhino R2 79933, 2000. CD.

———. *People Get Ready: The Curtis Mayfield Story*. Rhino/Warner Bros. 9 45 143-2, 1996. 3-CD set.

NdegéOcello, Me'Shell. *Plantation Lullabies*. Maverick/Sire/Reprise 9 45333-2, 1993. CD.

The R&B Box Set: 30 Years of Rhythm and Blues. Rhino R2 71806, 1994. 6-CD set.

Scott, Jill. *Who Is Jill Scott? Words and Sounds, Vol. 1*. Beach Recordings EK 62137, 2000. CD.

Staple Singers. *The Best of the Staple Singers*. Stax Records/Fantasy FCD-60-007, 1986. CD.

Stone, Angie. *Black Diamond*. Arista 07822-19092-2, 1999. CD.

Wonder, Stevie. *Innervisions*. 1973. Reissue, Motown 157355, 2000. CD.

———. *Talking Book*. 1972. Reissue, Universal/Motown 012 157 354-2, 2000. CD.

FUNK

Bar-Kays. *The Best of Bar-Kays*. Mercury/Polygram 314 514 823-2, 1993. CD.

Brothers Johnson. *Look Out for #1*. Originally released 1976. A&M Records 75021 3142 2, 1996. CD.

Cameo. *The Best of Cameo*. Mercury/Polygram 314 514 824-2, 1993. CD.

Collins, William "Bootsy." *Bootsy? Player of the Year*. Originally released 1978. Warner Bros. 3093, 1998. CD.

Commodores. *The Ultimate Collection*. Motown 530501, 1997. CD.

Con Funk Shun. *The Best of Con Funk Shun*. Mercury/Polygram 510275, 1993. CD.

Dayton. *Dayton*. Originally released 1980. EMI Music 072435711722, 2004. CD.

———. *Hot Fun*. Originally released 1982. EMI Music 5789002, 2004. CD.

Earth, Wind & Fire. *The Eternal Dance*. Originally released 1972. Reissue, Columbia/Legacy 52439, 1992. 3-CD set.

Funkadelic. *Let's Take It to the Stage*. Originally released 1975. Westbound 215, 1992. CD.

———. *One Nation Under a Groove*. Priority 72435-39378-2-9, 2002. CD.

Gap Band. *The Best of Gap Band*. Mercury/Polygram 314 522 457-2, 1994. CD.

Graham Central Station. *Release Yourself*. Warner Bros. Records 9 2814-2, 1997. CD.

Heatwave. *Too Hot to Handle*. Originally released 1976. Epic EK-34761, 1989. CD.

The Isley Brothers. *Groove with You: The Collection*. Sony MEG2 4846, 2003. CD.

James, Rick. *Street Songs*. Originally released 1981. Motown 37463-5405-2, n.d. CD.

Kool & the Gang. *The Best of Kool & the Gang, 1969–1976*. Mercury/Polygram 314 514822-2, 1993. CD.

Lakeside. *Galactic Grooves: The Best of Lakeside*. Capitol 96935, 1998. CD.

Midnight Star. *No Parking on the Dance Floor*. Originally released 1983. ZYX Music 7117, 2003. CD.

Ohio Players. *Funk on Fire: The Mercury Anthology*. Mercury/Polygram 314 528 102-2, 1995. CD.

Parliament. *Parliament's Greatest Hits*. Casablanca/Polygram 822 637 2, 1984. CD.

Prince. *The Hits 1*. Paisley Park 9 45431-2, 1993. CD.

———. *The Hits 2*. Paisley Park 9 45435-2, 1993. CD.

Slave. *Stellar Fungk: The Best of Slave*. Rhino/Atlantic 71592, 1994. CD.

Sly & the Family Stone. *The Essential Sly & the Family Stone*. Epic/Legacy E2K86867, 2002. CD.

———. *There's A Riot Goin' On*. Originally released 1971. Epic/Legacy 726953, 2008. CD.

The Time. *The Time*. Originally released 1981. Warner Bros. 2-3598, 1987. CD.

———. *What Time Is It?* Originally released 1982. Warner Bros. 23701, 1987. CD.

War. *The Best of War and More*. Originally released 1987. Priority Records 894672, 1990. CD.

Zapp & Roger. *All the Greatest Hits*. Reprise 9 45143-2, 1993. CD.

DISCO AND HOUSE

The Casablanca Records Story. Casablanca/Polygram/Chronicles 314516917-2, 1994. 4-CD set.

David Mancuso Presents The Loft, Vol. 1. Nuphonic 136, 1999. 2-CD set.

David Mancuso Presents The Loft, Vol. 2. Nuphonic 154, 2000. 2-CD set.

Disco Italia: Essential Italo Disco Classics, 1977–1985. Strut STRUTCD 036, 2008. CD.

Larry Levan Live at the Paradise Garage. Strut/Westend STRUTCD 006, 2000. 2-CD set.

Louie Vega Choice: A Collection of Classics. Compiled and mixed by Louie Vega. Azuli Records AZCD27, 2004. CD.

Manuel Göttsching. *E2-E4*. Originally released 1984. MG Art 304, 2007. CD.

MFSB. *Love Is The Message: The Best of MFSB*. Legacy 66689, 1995. CD.

Nicky Siano's The Gallery: The Original New York Disco, 1973–77. Soul Jazz SJRCD 100, 2004. CD.

Nu Groove Records Classics, Vol. 1. Essential Media EM 942311483-2, 2009. CD and MP3.

Nu Groove Records Classics, Vol. 2. Essential Media EM 942311484-2, 2009. CD and MP3.

The Original Chicago House Classics. MCI MCCD485, 2002. CD.

The Original Salsoul Classics: The 20th Anniversary. Salsoul 1000, 1992. 2-CD set.

Saturday Night Fever: The Original Movie Soundtrack. Polydor/UMGD 825389, 1996. CD or MP3.

DETROIT TECHNO

Atkins, Juan. *20 Years Metroplex: 1985–2005*. Tresor 216, 2005. 2-CD set.

Baxter, Blake. *Dream Sequence*. Remastered reissue of Tresor 2. Recorded 1991. Tresor 149, 2000. CD.

Craig, Carl. *From the Vault: Planet E Classics Collection, Vol. 1*. Planet E PEJPCD-001, 2006. CD.

Drexciya. *Neptune's Lair*. Tresor 129, 1999. CD.

Hand, K. *On a Journey*. LP originally released 1996. Studio/!K7 K7R001CD, 1998. CD.

Mills, Jeff. *Metropolis*. Tresor 155CD, 2000. CD.

Moodymann. *Moodymann Collection*. Mahogani Music MM-18, 2006. CD.

Reynolds, Kevin. *Built For Athletic Response*. Todhchai Records, 2005. CDr format.

Shakir, Anthony "Shake." *Frictionalism 1994–2009*. Rush Hour Recordings RH 110, 2009. 3-CD set.

Techno! The New Dance Sound of Detroit. Ten Records DIXCD 75, 1988. CD.

X-102. *Rediscovers the Rings of Saturn*. Tresor 234, 2008. CD.

HIP-HOP AND RAP

Afrika Bambaataa & the Soul Sonic Force. *Street Jams: Electric Funk, Part 1*. Originally released 1982. Rhino Records/Skanless Records R270575, 1992. CD.

Das Efx. *Dead Serious*. EastWest Records America 91827-2, 1992. CD.

Hill, Lauryn. *The Miseducation of Lauryn Hill*. Ruffhouse Records/Sony Records SRCS 8788, 1998. CD.

MC Lyte. *Ain't No Other*. First Priority Records 7922302, 1993. CD.

N.W.A. *Straight Outta Compton*. Island Records 260 286, 1988. CD.

Public Enemy. *It Takes a Nation of Millions to Hold Us Back*. Originally released 1988. Def Jam Recordings 314 542 423-2, 2000. CD.

Queen Latifah. *Black Reign*. Motown Records 374636370-2, 1993. CD.

Run-D.M.C. *Playlist: The Very Best of Run-D.M.C.* Originally released 1984. Arista 88697 41345 2, 2009. CD.

———. *Raising Hell*. Originally released 1986. Arista 07822-16408-2, 1999. CD.

———. *Run-D.M.C.* Originally released 1984. Profile/Arista 07822-16406-2, 1999. CD.

Spoonie Gee. *Godfather of Hip-Hop*. Originally released 1979. Ol' Skool Flava OSF CD 4014, 2004. CD.

Videography

Afro-Punk. Written, produced, and directed by James Spooner. Originally issued as a motion picture by Afro-Punk Films, 2003. Chatsworth, CA: Image Entertainment, 2006. DVD.

Amandla! A Revolution in Four Part Harmony. Directed by Lee Hirsch (South Africa/USA). Available from Facets Multi-Media. Santa Monica, CA: Artisan Home Entertainment, 2002. DVD.

Battle Sounds. 1997 Whitney Biennial Cut. Directed by John Carluccio. New York: Battle Sounds, 2000. VHS.

The Best of Funk: Brothers Johnson. ABC Entertainment/Voiceprint, 2009.

The Best of Funk: Dazz Band. [United Kingdom]: ABC Entertainment/Voiceprint, 2009.

Better Living Through Circuitry: A Digital Odyssey into the Electronic Dance Underground. Directed by John Reiss. Mvd Visual, 2000.

Blind Boys of Alabama: Go Tell It On the Mountain; Live in New York. Recorded at the Beacon Theater, New York City, December 2003. Broadcast on PBS, December 2004. [United States]: Eagle Eye Media, 2005. DVD.

The Blues Accordin' to "Lightnin'" Hopkins. Directed by Les Blank and Skip Gerson. Original release 1968. El Cerrito, CA: Flower Films, 2004. DVD.

Breath Control: The History of the Human Beat Box. Film by Joey Garfield. Filet 'O' Fresh Productions, 2001. VHS.

Canton Spirituals: Live Experience 1999. Directed by Ron Yeager. New York: Zomba, 1999. VHS.

Chicago Blues. Directed by Harley Cokliss. Narrated by Dick Gregory. Originally filmed 1972. Cambridge, MA: Vestapol Productions, distributed by Rounder Records, 2004. DVD.

Chuck D's Hip-Hop Hall of Fame. Produced by Lathan Hodge. Oaks, PA: Music Video Distributors, 2003. DVD.

Cycles of the Mental Machine. Directed by Jacqueline Caux. Paris: La Huit, 2008.

Deep Blues. Directed by Robert Mugge. Los Angeles: Shout Factory, 1991.

Devil Got My Woman: Blues at Newport 1956. Directed by Alan Lomax. Cambridge, MA: Vestapol Productions, distributed by Rounder Records, 2001.

The Drive Home: The Story of the Detroit Electronic Music Festival. Directed by Rita Sayegh and Scott Stephanoff. Detroit, IL: Pilot Pictures and Hogpath, 2010.

Drums of Africa: Talking Drums of Techiman. Directed by Christopher D. Roy (USA/Ghana). Distributed by CustomFlix, 2004. DVD.

Dub Echoes. Directed by Bruno Natal. [London]: Soul Jazz Records, 101 Distribution, 2009.

Earth, Wind & Fire: Live. Image Entertainment, 1995.

Freestyle: The Art of Rhyme. Directed by Kevin Fitzgerald. Produced by Henry Alex Rubin. Organic Films, 2002.

The Freshest Kids. Produced and directed by Israel. Los Angeles: QD3 Entertainment, 2002.

The Godfather Chronicles: The Ghetto Tech Sound of Detroit. Directed by Amil Khan, Baseball Music, 2004.

Graffiti Rock (and Other Hip-Hop Delights). Directed by Clark Santee. Oaks, PA: Music Video Distributors, 2002.

G(raffiti)V(erite)5: The Sacred Elements of Hip-Hop. Directed by Bob Bryan. Los Angeles: Bryan World Productions, 2003.

Heroes of Latin Hip-Hop. Directed by Joe Ritter. Oaks, PA: Music Video Distributors, 2002. DVD.

High Tech Soul: The Creation of Techno Music. Directed by Gary Bredlow. [New York]: Plexifilm, 2006.

Hip-Hop: Beyond Beats and Rhymes. Written, produced, and directed by Byron Hurt. Northampton, MA: Media Education Foundation, 2006.

Hip-Hop: A Culture of Influence. Directed by Torrance York and Steven Goodman. New York: Educational Video Center, 1999.

Hip-Hop Story: Tha Movie. Directed by Sal Martino. Edgewater Entertainment, 2003. DVD.

Hip-Hop Story 2: Dirty South. Directed by Jeffrey "Smoot" Huntley. Thousand Oaks, CA: Urban Works Entertainment, 2003.

Hip-Hop Story 3: Coast to Coast. Directed by Jeffrey "Smoot" Huntely. Thousand Oaks, CA: RapRock Records, 2004. DVD.

Hitmakers: The Teens Who Stole Pop Music. Written, directed, and produced by Morgan Neville. Produced by Peter Jones Productions for A&E Network. [United States]: A&E Home Video, distributed by New Video, 2001. VHS.

The Human Hambone. Directed by Mark Morgan. Brooklyn, NY: First Run/Icarus Films, 2005. DVD.

I'm Rick James: The Definitive DVD. Hip-O Records/Historic Music, 2009.

Jazz for Young People Curriculum. Disc 1. New York: Jazz at Lincoln Center, 2002. 10-CD set and VHS.

Juju Music! Produced and directed by Jacques Holender. New York: Rhapsody Films, 1991. VHS.

Kraftwerk and the Electronic Revolution. Produced by Rob Johnstone, Video Music, 2008.

Lee Williams and the Spiritual QCs: Fall on Me. Produced and directed by Deborah Walker. Alpharetta, GA: MCG Records, 2009. DVD.

Lee Williams and the Spiritual QCs: Good Time; Live in Memphis. 2000. Alpharetta, GA: MCG Records, distributed by the Malaco Music Group, 2004. DVD.

Le Festival au desert/Festival in the Desert. Directed by Lionel Brouet (Mali/France). Distributed by World Village, 2004. DVD.

Legends of Country Blues Guitar, Vols 1-3. Cambridge, MA: Vestapol Productions, distributed by Rounder Records, 2001.

Listen to the Silence: Rhythm in African Music. Directed by Peter Bischof. New York: Filmakers Library, 2003. DVD.

Living Legends of Gospel, Vol. 1: The Quartets. 1998. Produced and directed by Robert Swope. New York: Good Times Entertainment, 2004. DVD.

Lyricist Lounge: Dirty States of America—The Untold Story of Southern Hip-Hop. Directed by FLX. MIC Media, 2004. DVD.

Maestro. Directed and produced by Josell Ramos. Originally released as a motion picture, 2003. ARTrution, Sanctuary Records Group, 2005. 2 DVDs.

Mande Music and Dance. Performed by Mandinka musicians of The Gambia in the late twentieth century. Directed by Roderic Knight (The Gambia/USA). New York: Lyrichord Discs; Montpelier, VT: Multicultural Media, 2005. DVD.

Masters of the Country Blues: Rev. Gary Davis and Sonny Terry. Produced by John S. Ullman. Directed by Donald Ciro. Newton, NJ: YaZoo Video, 2001. DVD.

Material Witness: Race, Identity, and the Politics of Gangsta Rap, with Michael Eric Dyson. Directed by Sut Jhalley. Northampton, MA: The Media Education Foundation, 1995.

Modulations: Cinema for the Ear. Produced by George Gund, directed by Iara Lee. New York: Caipirinha Productions, 1998.

Moog. Directed by Hans Fjellestad, Brooklyn, NY: Plexifilm, 2005.

The Mothership Connection. George Clinton, Parliament Funkadelic. Gravity/Pioneer Artists, 1998.

Movin' On Up: The Music and Message of Curtis Mayfield and The Impressions. Directed by David Peck, Phillip Galloway, and Tom Gulotta. Santa Monica, CA: Reelin' In the Years Productions, 2008. DVD.

My Mic Sounds Nice: A Truth about Women in Hip-Hop. Directed and produced by Ava DuVernay. [United States]: Forward Movement, 2010.

Ohm+: The Early Gurus of Electronic Music. Produced by Thomas Ziegler, Jason Gross, and Russell Charno. Roslyn, NY: Ellipsis Arts, 2006.

On the Battlefield: Gospel Quartets in Jefferson County, Alabama. Directed by Geoffrey Haydon and Dennis Marks. 1984. Princeton, NJ: Films for the Humanities & Sciences, 2003. DVD.

Pass the Mic! Written, directed, and edited by Richard Montes. Chatsworth, CA: Image Entertainment, 2002. DVD.

Piano Players Rarely Ever Play Together. Directed by Stevenson Palfi. Original 76-minute version. New Orleans, LA: Stevenson Productions, 1982.

Prince: Purple Rain. 20th Anniversary. Two-disc special edition. Purple Films, 1984, 2004.

Rap: Looking for the Perfect Beat. Directed by Susan Shaw. Princeton, NJ: Films for the Humanities, 2000.

Record Row: The Cradle of Rhythm and Blues. Written and produced by Michael D. McAlpin. Original broadcast on PBS, February 20, 1997.

Rhyme & Reason. Directed by Peter Spirer. Burbank, CA: Buena Vista Home Entertainment, 2000.

Rhythm of Resistance: Black South African Music. Part of the 14-volume *Beats of the Heart* series. Produced and directed by Jeremy Marre (UK). Newton, NJ: Shanachie, 1979. DVD.

Rock and Roll: The Early Days. Produced and directed by Patrick Montgomery. [United States]: Archive Film Productions, 1985.

Roots, Rock, Reggae: Inside the Jamaican Music Scene. Produced and directed by Jeremy Marre. Newton, NJ: Shanachie Entertainment, 1977.

Say Amen, Somebody. Directed by George T. Nierenberg. Santa Monica, CA: Xenon Pictures, 2000 (1982). DVD.

Scratch. Directed and edited by Doug Pray; produced by Brad Blondheim and Ernest Meza. New York: Palm Pictures, 2002. 2 DVDs.

A Singing Stream: A Black Family Chronicle. 1986. Produced by Tom Davenport of Davenport Films, Dan Patterson, and Allen Tullos of University of North Carolina at Chapel Hill Curriculum in Folklore. Delaplane, VA: Davenport Films, 1989. VHS.

Speaking In Code. Directed by Amy Grill. [United States]: sQuare Productions, 2009.

St. Louis Blues. Directed by Dudley Martin. W.C. Handy, music director. Originally produced at Gramercy Studio and presented by RKO Radio Pictures, 1929. National Film Preservation Foundation, 2006.

Straight from the Streets. Directed by Robert Corsini and Keith O'Derek. Burbank, CA: UpFront Productions, 1999.

Style Wars. Directed by Tony Silver. Originally released in 1983. Los Angeles: Public Arts Films, 2004. DVD.

T.D. Jakes—Still Friends? Camarillo, CA: Goldhil Entertainment, 2006. DVD.

Tha Westside. Directed by Todd Williams. Niche Entertainment, 2002. DVD.

The Unusual Suspects: Once Upon a Time in House Music. Presented by Chip Eberhart and Kimmie D. Chicago: Chicken Lunch Productions, 2005.

War: Loose Grooves, Funkin' Live in England, 1980. RPM Films/Cherry Red Records, 2007.

A Well Spent Life. Directed by Les Blank and Skip Gerson. Originally a motion picture, 1971. El Cerrito, CA: Flower Films, 2004.

Wild Combination: A Portrait of Arthur Russell. Directed by Matt Wolf. Brooklyn, NY: Plexifilm, 2008.

Wild Style. Directed, produced & written by Charlie Ahearn. Originally produced by Wild Style Productions as a motion picture in 1982. Distributed by Rhino Home Video, 2002. DVD.

Word: A Film of the Underground Hip-Hop Scene. Directed and produced by Tony Greer. Los Angeles, CA: HIQI Media, 2002.

Editors and Contributors

MELLONEE V. BURNIM is Professor of Ethnomusicology in the Department of Folklore and Ethnomusicology, Adjunct Professor of African American and African Diaspora Studies, and Director of the Archives of African American Music and Culture at Indiana University. She is a Distinguished Alumnus of the University of North Texas and was selected as the first Distinguished Faculty Fellow in Ethnomusicology and Ritual Studies at the Yale Institute for Sacred Music in 2004. As a performer-scholar, Burnim has done fieldwork and led workshops on African American religious music across the United States, as well as in Cuba, Liberia, and Malawi. Her writings on African American religious music and theoretical issues in ethnomusicology appear in various edited volumes and journals, including *Ethnomusicology*, *The Western Journal of Black Studies*, and *The Music Educator's Journal*, among others.

PORTIA K. MAULTSBY is Laura Boulton Professor Emerita of Ethnomusicology in the Department of Folklore and Ethnomusicology, and Adjunct Professor Emerita of African American and African Diaspora Studies at Indiana University. In the spring of 1998, she was the Belle van Zuylen Professor of African American Music in the Department of Musicology at Utrecht University, the Netherlands. Maultsby's writings on African American religious and popular music appear in various journals and edited volumes, including *Ethnomusicology*, *The Black Perspective in Music*, *Journal of Popular Culture*, *The Western Journal of Black Studies*, *Bulgarian Musicology*, *The Harvard Guide to African-American History* (Harvard University Press, 2001), and *Ashgate Research Companion to Popular Musicology* (Ashgate, 2009). In addition to her scholarly work, she is a keyboard player and the founding director of the IU Soul Revue, a touring ensemble specializing in the performance of African American popular music. Her current project examines issues of transnationalism, focusing on Euro-Dutch choirs in the Netherlands specializing in Black gospel music as a case study.

CONTRIBUTORS

ERNEST D. BROWN Jr. (1947–2012) was professor of music (ethnomusicology) at Williams College from 1988 until he retired in 2011. A specialist in the musics of Africa and the African diaspora, he conducted research in Zambia, Zimbabwe, Ghana, Trinidad, and Cuba, and published on these traditions in various journals and edited volumes. Building on his research in Africa, Brown explored the relationships between African and African American musics. In 1990, he published his initial findings on this topic in the article "Something from Nothing and More from Something" in *Selected Reports in Ethnomusicology*. An accomplished performer of African traditions, Brown studied Zimbabwean marimba and mbira music with Dumisani Maraire and Ephat Mujuru, and Ghanaian drumming with master drummer Obo Addy. At Williams College, he founded and directed the Zambezi Marimba Band (1991–2012) and in 1990 co-founded and co-directed Kusika ("to create" in Shona), an African music and dance ensemble for students and community members.

DENISE DALPHOND is the vice president of the Detroit Sound Conservancy and an ethnomusicologist specializing in Detroit electronic music. She has written a dissertation on the legacy of electronic music in African American culture and its important place in Detroit's musical history, highlighting rich diversity among musicians, performers, and fans, and the related eclecticism of musical influences and styles represented in Detroit. Dalphond co-founded the Detroit Sound Conservancy to help preserve Detroit's musical heritage of all genres and historical periods. With this organization, she has hosted a Detroit music conference, conducted oral history preservation projects with musicians, and organized public educational events in Detroit. Her work has been featured on *Afropop Worldwide*, Swedish Television, and the online music magazine *Little White Earbuds*. She has maintained a blog about Detroit music since 2008 and currently writes at schoolcraftwax.com.

DENA J. EPSTEIN (1916–2013) received a BA from the University of Chicago and BS and MA degrees in library science from the University of Illinois. After a career in music librarianship, she retired from the University of Chicago as curator of recordings and assistant music librarian in 1986. She received a citation for distinguished service to music librarianship from the Music Library Association in 1986 and a Lifetime Achievement Award from the Society for American Music in

2005. Her prize-winning book, *Sinful Tunes and Spirituals: Black Folk Music to the Civil War* (University of Illinois Press, 1977, reissued 2003 with a new preface), is a pathbreaking and definitive study of slave music based on twenty years of research.

DAVID EVANS is professor of music at the University of Memphis and director of its ethnomusicology PhD program. He began fieldwork in African American folk music in 1965 and received his PhD from UCLA in 1976. He is the author of *Tommy Johnson* (Studio Vista, 1971), *Big Road Blues: Tradition and Creativity in the Folk Blues* (University of California Press, 1982), and *The NPR Curious Listener's Guide to Blues* (Perigee Books, 2005), as well as many articles and chapters on blues and related types of African American folk and popular music. He has produced over forty albums of blues and folk music, and compiled and annotated many others. In 2003, he received a Grammy Award for his notes to *Screamin' and Hollerin' the Blues: The Worlds of Charley Patton*. Evans performs country blues (vocal and guitar) and has appeared in concerts and festivals throughout the United States, Europe, and South America.

KAI FIKENTSCHER is a performer-scholar with a background in jazz performance and ethnomusicology. His research into the links between music, dance, technology, and culture has been published in several languages, in various edited volumes and journals, and in his award-winning book, *You Better Work! Underground Dance Music in New York City* (Wesleyan University Press, 2000). After obtaining degrees in music from Berklee College of Music and Manhattan School of Music, and in ethnomusicology from Columbia University, he taught at his alma mater as well as at New York University, Tufts University, Rhode Island School of Design, and Ramapo College of New Jersey. As a guitarist and a disc jockey, he has recorded and performed both in the United States and in Europe.

INGEBORG HARER is an associate professor in the Institute of Early Music and Performance Practice at the University of Music and Performing Arts Graz, Austria. As a scholar, Harer has concentrated on general performance issues concerning music of various genres, including popular music of North America as well as Europe, Baroque music, and European music of the late eighteenth and nineteenth centuries. Since 2001 she has repeatedly combined "historically informed performance practice" with "gender studies," a focus that can be traced in her teaching responsibilities as well as many of her publications. Harer's work also shows an emphasis on African American music. Her writings on ragtime and the reception of early jazz in Europe have appeared in various journals and encyclopedia, such as *Musik in Geschichte und Gegenwart*, *Österreichisches Musiklexikon*, *Studien zur Moderne*, and *Jazz Research*.

JOYCE MARIE JACKSON, an ethnomusicologist, is associate professor in the Department of Geography and Anthropology and director of African and African American Studies at Louisiana State University. From 2002 to 2006, she directed the university's Sénégambia Study Abroad Program. Jackson, a specialist in African American music and musics of the African diaspora, has conducted research in the southern United States, Sénégal, Ghana, Bahamas, and Trinidad. Her publications on African American quartets and New Orleans Black Mardi Gras Indians appear in journals, edited volumes, and encyclopedias, including *American Anthropologist, African American Review*, and *The New Encyclopedia of Southern Culture* (University of North Carolina Press, 2009). Jackson also works as a public folklorist/ethnomusicologist, contributing to projects of the Smithsonian Folk Life Center and the broader Smithsonian Institution. In 2006, Jackson, with Nash Porter, co-curated the exhibition "New Orleans Black Mardi Gras Indians: Exploring a Community Tradition from an Insider's View" at the Smithsonian Anacostia Community Museum. Jackson also wrote the liner note booklet for *The Paschall Brothers: On the Right Road Now* (Smithsonian Folkways Recordings, 2007).

INGRID MONSON is Quincy Jones Professor of African American Music at Harvard University. Her books include the award-winning *Saying Something: Jazz Improvisation and Interaction* (University of Chicago Press, 1996) and *Freedom Sounds: Jazz, Civil Rights, and Africa, 1950–1967* (Oxford University Press, 2007). She is the editor of *The African Diaspora: A Musical Perspective* (Garland, 2000), and her articles have been published in *Ethnomusicology, Critical Inquiry, World of Music*, the *Journal of the American Musicological Society, Women and Music*, and the *Black Music Research Journal*. In addition to her work in jazz, African American music, and music of the African diaspora, Monson is also a trumpet player and an original member of the nationally known Klezmer Conservatory Band.

DAWN M. NORFLEET is a professional jazz flutist, vocalist, and award-winning composer, and has made live and televised appearances as a bandleader and side musician, having recorded for Eddie Murphy and soul stars Joe, Karyn White, and Monica. She completed her PhD in music (ethnomusicology) at Columbia University, where she focused on the "MC" (rapper) and the underground hip-hop music scene of New York City. She has taught and/or given concert-lectures at California State Polytechnic University, Pomona; Wellesley College; University of California, San Diego; and University of Virginia, and was a scholar in residence at Grinnell College. Norfleet's writings have appeared in *The Garland Encyclopedia of World Music* and *Black Enterprise* magazine.

THOMAS L. RIIS has taught at the University of Colorado as the Joseph Negler Professor of Musicology since 2002 and has directed its American

Music Research Center since 1992. A specialist in musical theater and nineteenth-century African American popular music, he lectures and writes on a variety of topics. His book *Just Before Jazz* (Smithsonian Institution Press, 1989), devoted to African American Broadway shows from 1890 to 1915, received an ASCAP Deems Taylor Award in 1995. His other interests include medieval lyrics, historical performance practice, and the songs of Frank Loesser and Paul Robeson.

ROSITA M. SANDS is professor of music/associate chair in the Music Department of Columbia College Chicago. She joined Columbia in 2000 as associate director of the Center for Black Music Research and served for four years as the CBMR's executive director. During this tenure, she led the research efforts of the CBMR's former remote research site, the Alton Augustus Adams Music Research Institute in St. Thomas, Virgin Islands, and began her ongoing work with the Caribbean Music Repatriation Project of the Alan Lomax Archives and the Association for Cultural Equity. Dr. Sands formerly served on the faculties of the University of Massachusetts Lowell; California State University, Long Beach; and Berea College. She is a contributor to *Critical Essays in Music Education* (Ashgate, 2012) and *Multicultural Perspectives in Music* (Rowman & Littlefield Education, 2010) and is also published in the *Journal of Music Teacher Education, The Black Perspective in Music,* and the *Black Music Research Journal.*

JOSEPHINE R.B. WRIGHT is a professor of music, the Josephine Lincoln Morris Professor of Africana Studies, and the chair of Africana Studies at the College of Wooster. She served as former editor of the Society of American Music's journal, *American Music,* and was an adviser for the revised *Grove Dictionary of American Music* (Oxford University Press, 2013). She has published articles and reviews in numerous journals. Wright is the co-editor of *New Perspectives in Music: Essays in Honor of Eileen Southern* (with Samuel A. Floyd Jr., Harmonie Park Press, 1992), and she is the co-author (with Eileen Southern) of *African American Traditions in Song, Sermon, Tale, and Dance, 1600s–1920* (Greenwood Press, 1990) and *Images: Iconography of Music in African-American Culture (1770s–1920s)* (Garland, 2000).

Audio Credits

Listed in order of first appearance

Track 1:   "Hammer, Ring" (Traditional). Jesse Bradley. Courtesy of Alan Lomax Archive and American Folklife Center, Library of Congress.

Track 2:   "Who Are the Greatest?" Johns Island children from the recording entitled. *Johns Island, South Carolina: Its People and Songs*, FW03840. Courtesy of Smithsonian Folkways Recordings. ℗ © 1973. Used by permission.

Track 3:   "Edom Sasraku." Praise poetry by Asantehene (Asante King's) Ntahera-Royal Trumpet group. Recorded by Kwasi Ampene at Manhyia Palace-Kumasi, Ghana, 2009. Used by permission. Courtesy of Kwasi Ampene.

Track 4:   "Inanga Bongerera." Whispered song by Joseph Torobeka, *inanga* (trough zither) and voice. Recorded by Cornelia Fales in Bujumbura, Burundi, August 19, 1986. Courtesy of Cornelia Fales.

Track 5:   "Dekuor" from *Bernard Woma: Guba Gyil, Vol. 2*, self-released CD. Religious song of the Dagara people in northern Ghana. Performed by Bernard Woma and members of the Saakumu Dance Troupe. Recorded by Bernard Woma in Accra, Ghana, 2008. Courtesy of Bernard Woma.

Track 6:   "Talking 'Bout a Good Time" (Traditional). The Moving Star Hall Singers, from the recording entitled *Been in the Storm So Long— Spirituals & Shouts, Children's Game Songs, and Folktales*, FW03842. Courtesy of Smithsonian Folkways Recordings. ℗ © 1967. Used by permission.

Track 7:   "Arwhoolie (Traditional—Cornfield Holler)" by Thomas J. Marshall. Courtesy of Alan Lomax Archive and American Folklife Center, Library of Congress.

Track 8:   "Viola Lee Blues" by Noah Lewis/Gus Cannon. Cannon's Jug Stompers, USBB10200466. Originally recorded 1928. All rights reserved by RCA Records, a division of Sony Music Entertainment. Under license from

Sony Music Commercial Music Group, a division of Sony Music Entertainment.

Track 9: "Potato Head Blues" by Louis Armstrong. Louis Armstrong and His Hot Seven, USSM10003884. Originally released 1927. All rights reserved by Sony Music Entertainment. Under license from Sony Music Commercial Music Group, a division of Sony Music Entertainment.

Track 10: "Strings of Life" by Derrick May and Michael James. Rhythim Is Rhythim (a.k.a. Derrick May). Transmat: Relics. DFC 57711D, 1992. Published by EMI (previously Zomba Music). Copyright Transmat Mayday Music, Ltd. 1987. Used by permission.

Track 11: "God Moves on the Water" written and performed by W. Johnson/ Blind Willie Johnson, USSM12900054. Originally released 1930. All rights reserved by Sony Music Entertainment. Under license from Sony Music Commercial Music Group, a division of Sony Music Entertainment.

Track 12: "Flash Light" by George S. Clinton, Bernard Worrell, and William Earl Collins. Parliament, 0:05:46, USPR37700065. Published by Bridgeport Music, Inc./Universal–Songs Of Polygram International Publishing Inc. Produced and arranged by George S. Clinton. ℗ 1977 The Island Def Jam Music Group. Courtesy of The Island Def Jam Music Group under license from Universal Music Enterprises, a division of UMG Recordings, Inc.

Track 13: "Christian's Automobile" by Jessie Archie. The Dixie Hummingbirds, 0:02:16, USMC17355316. ℗ 1973 Motown Records, a division of UMG Recordings, Inc. Courtesy of Motown Records under license from Universal Music Enterprises, a division of UMG Recordings, Inc.

Track 14: "Maple Leaf Rag" written and performed by Scott Joplin. Recording from 1916 piano roll.

Track 15: Kpatsa (social or recreational song of the Ga people of the greater Accra region of Ghana). Bernard Woma and the African drum ensemble at SUNY State-Fredonia. 2005. Recorded by Bernard Woma in Fredonia, New York, 2008. Courtesy of Bernard Woma.

Track 16: "So Ruff, So Tuff" by Roger Troutman. Zapp and Roger, ℗ 1993 Reprise Records 2, a label of Warner Bros. Records. Produced under license from Warner Bros. Records, Inc.

Track 17: "Take My Hand, Precious Lord" by T. A. Dorsey. Mahalia Jackson, *Mahalia Jackson Sings the Best-Loved Hymns of Dr. M. L. King.* Columbia CS 9686, 1968. USSM19802089. Originally released 1963. All rights reserved by Sony Music Entertainment. Under license from Sony Music Commercial Music Group, a division of Sony Music Entertainment.

Track 18: "Sincerely" (Single Version) by Alan Freed and Harvey Fuqua. The Moonglows, USMC15420004. Published by Irving Music, Inc./Liaison Two Publishing, Inc. Produced by Phil Chess and Leonard Chess. Originally released 1954. Courtesy of Geffen Records under license from Universal Music Enterprises, a division of UMG Recordings, Inc.

Track 19: "Ezekiel Saw De Wheel" (Traditional). The Tuskegee Institute Choir, 0:02:23, USMC10412390. Arranged by William L. Dawson. Originally released 1971 Geffen Records. Courtesy of Geffen Records under license from Universal Music Enterprises, a division of UMG Recordings, Inc.

Track 20: "Juba" by Bessie Jones. Sweet Honey in the Rock. *All for Freedom*. 1989. Reissued, Music for Little People/Warner Bros. 42505, 1992. Copyright SHEROCKS 5, Inc. All rights reserved. Used by permission.

Track 21: "New Railroad" (Traditional). Lucius Smith, and recorded by David and Cheryl Evans in Mississippi, 1971. *Afro-American Folk Music from Tate and Panola Counties, Mississippi*. Library of Congress AFS L67, 1978. Reissued, Rounder Records 18964–1515–2, 2000. Used by permission.

Track 22: "Jesus Knows All About My Troubles." Wesley Methodist Church (Johns Island, S.C.). Excerpt from the recording entitled *Johns Island, South Carolina: Its People and Songs*, FW03840, courtesy of Smithsonian Folkways Recordings. ℗ © 1973. Used by permission.

Track 23: "Deep River" (Traditional). Paul Robeson. Used by permission of Vanguard Records, a Welk Music Group Company, 1991.

Track 24: "Let the Church Roll On" (Traditional). Southern University Quartet, *Black Vocal Groups*: Vol. 8. Used by permission of Document Records.

Track 25: "Dusty Rag" by May Frances Aufderheide. "Perfessor" Bill Edwards, ragtime pianist and musicologist, 2014, ragpiano.com, Ashburn, Virginia.

Track 26: "Crazy Blues" by Perry Bradford. Mamie Smith and Her Jazz Hounds, USSM12000005. Originally released 1920. All rights reserved by Sony Music Entertainment. Under license from Sony Music Commercial Music Group, a division of Sony Music Entertainment.

Track 27: "Leave It There" by Rev. Charles Albert Tindley. Pace Jubilee Singers, *Pace Jubilee Singers Volume 2*. Used by permission of Document Records.

Track 28: "Oh Happy Day" by Edwin R. Hawkins. The Edwin Hawkins Singers, USBR16900001. Originally recorded 1969. All rights reserved by RCA Records, a division of Sony Music Entertainment. Under license from Sony Music Commercial Music Group, a division of Sony Music Entertainment.

Track 29: "I Don't Feel Noways Tired" by Curtis Burrell. James Cleveland, Keith Pringle, soloist. Peermusic III, Ltd/Savgos Music, Inc., admin. by Peermusic III, Ltd. (BMI), used by permission.

Track 30: "Saturday Night Fish Fry" by Louis Jordan and Ellis Walsh. Louis Jordan and His Tympany Five, USGR10201451. Published by Cherio Music Publ. Corp./Ocheri Publishing Corp. Originally released 1957. Courtesy of The Verve Music Group, a division of UMG Recordings, Inc. under license from Universal Music Enterprises, a division of UMG Recordings, Inc.

Track 31: "Shake, Rattle & Roll" by Charles Calhoun (Jessie Stone). Joe Turner, produced under license from Atlantic Recording Corp.

Track 32: "Tutti Frutti" by Little Richard and Dorothy LaBostrie. Little Richard, *Here's Little Richard*, SPC-33300. Used by permission of Concord Music Group, Inc.

Track 33: "My Baby Loves Me" (Single Version) by Ivy Joe Hunter, Sylvia Rose Moy, William "Mickey" Stevenson. Martha Reeves & the Vandellas, USMO16600462. Produced by William "Mickey" Stevenson and Ivy

Joe Hunter. Preliminary Publisher Information: Sylvia Moy, William "Mickey" Stevenson, Ivy Jo Hunter; Jobete Music Co., Inc. (admin. by EMI April Music, Inc.) (ASCAP); Stone Agate Music (A division of Jobete Music Co., Inc.); admin. by EMI Blackwood Music, Inc. (BMI). Originally released 1966. Courtesy of Motown Records, a division of UMG Recordings, Inc. under license from Universal Music Enterprises, a division of UMG Recordings, Inc.

Track 34: "We're a Winner" (Single Version) by Curtis Mayfield. The Impressions, 0:02:22, USMC16742831. Published by Warner-Tamerlane Publishing Corp. Produced by Curtis Mayfield. Originally released 1968. Courtesy of Geffen Records under license from Universal Music Enterprises, a division of UMG Recordings, Inc.

Track 35: "Dr. Feelgood (Love is a Serious Business)" by Aretha Franklin and Ted White. Aretha Franklin. Produced under license from Atlantic Recording Corp.

Track 36: "Stand!" by Sylvester Stewart. Sly and the Family Stone, USSM19901648. Originally recorded 1968. All rights reserved by Sony Music Entertainment. Under license from Sony Music Commercial Music Group, a division of Sony Music Entertainment.

Track 37: "T.S.O.P." by Kenneth Gamble and Leon Huff. MFSB, USSM10210295. ℗ 1973 Sony Music Entertainment. Under license from Sony Music Commercial Music Group, a division of Sony Music Entertainment. Used by permission.

Track 38: "Move Your Body" by Marshall Jefferson. Casablanca Media Songs LLC. Used by permission of Demon Music Group, Ltd.

Track 39: "Roaming" by Anthony "Shake" Shakir, from *Frictionalism 1994–2009*. Used by permission of Rush Hour Recordings.

Track 40: "Spoonin' Rap: A Drive Down the Street," written and performed by Gabriel Jackson p/k/a "Spoonie Gee." Licensed by Tufamerica.

Index

Page numbers in *italics* denotes an illustration.

Baker, David 152
Ball, Charles 6
Bambaataa, Afrika 312, 329, 357–58, 359;
    "Planet Rock" 359, 359
Bandana Land 225, 226
banjo 34, 35, 36
Banks, Mike 343, 349
Bar-Kays 262, 279, 305, 306, 307, 311
Baraka, Amiri 180
barbershop community quartets 81
barrelhouse 131
Barrelhouse Tom see Thomas Dorsey
Bartholomew, Dave 249, 249
Basie, Count: "Set for You Yesterday" 171,
    172, 173
Battle, Kathleen 66
Beastie Boys 361
beat box 358
Bebey, Francis 8, 10
bebop 173–76, 181, 240, 355; and blues
    136; definition of 173; hard bop
    176–77; musical innovations of 174;
    phrasings 174; subcultural qualities of
    174–75
Bell, Al 261, 262
bend 126
Benét, Eric 292–93
Benson, Al 252
Berger, Shelly 258, 259
Berlin, Edward 99
Berry, Chuck 251
Bethune, Thomas Green Wiggins (Blind
    Tom) 142
Beyoncé 267–68
Bibb, Henry 26
big band jazz 168–69, 171, 173, 241, 242
Big Maybelle (Mabel Louise Smith) 133
Billboard 208, 222, 239, 243, 254, 265,
    279, 327–28
"bird" groups 247
Black Artists Group (BAG) 179
Black Patti (Sissieretta Jones) 221, 222
Black pop 263
Black Power Movement 181, 261, 277, 303;
    and funk 303, 316; impact on musical
    theater 232–33; and soul 256, 278–79,
    281–85
black revues 221–22, 228; comedic
    dialogue of 222–23; definition 222;
    Duke Ellington and 232; speciality acts
    222, 228; theme of 222, 228; Ziegfeld
    Follies 226, 228
blackface makeup 215, 216, 217;
    authenticity 217; and Booker T.
    Washington 226; definition of 215;
    stage message 215, 217; see also
    minstrel show

Blackmon, Larry 313
Blackwell, Bumps 250
Blake, Eubie 227
Blakey, Art 176, 178
Bland, Bobby "Blue" 17
Bland, James 218
blaxploitation films 355–56
Blige, Mary J. 265–66
Blind Tom see Thomas Green Wiggins
    Bethune
Blondie 358
blue notes 79, 125–27, 126–27
blues 11, 119–37; and boogie-woogie 133;
    contexts for performance of 122–24;
    distinctive characteristics of 124–29;
    early forms that influenced 121–22;
    and electric guitar 134; European and
    African elements 120–21; expansion
    of the audience of 135; forms of
    127–28; and gospel music 136, 190;
    and griots 121; historical background
    and content 119–22; and jazz 136;
    jump 132, 242; locations for
    performing of 123; lyrics 124–25;
    perception of 123–24; popularization
    of 130–34; and ragtime 136; and rap
    136; recordings 130–33; and riff 128;
    role of in American popular music
    136; role of instruments 28, 125, 132;
    scale 126; soul 134; twelve-bar 127, 127;
    urban 242
boat songs see work songs
Boatner, Edward 146
Bogel, Alan 346–47
Bohannon, Hamilton 305
Bolden, Buddy 165–66
boogie-woogie 133, 245
Booker T. & the MGs 260, 260, 261
Bosman, William 8
Bowie, Howard 85, 87
Boyz II Men 267, 268
Bradford, Perry 130
Brady, William 141
Braxton, Anthony 182
break dancing 356
Bremer, Fredrika 16
Brewster, William Herbert 82, 203, 205
Bring in da Noise/Bring in da Funk 235
Brown, Anthony 184
Brown Buddies 230
Brown, Charles 241
Brown, James 17, 279–80, 283–84, 284,
    285, 288, 289–90, 302, 304, 308, 316;
    "Please, Please, Please" 279–80; "Say
    It Loud" 283
Bronzeville see Chicago
Brubeck, Dave 177

cultural memory 55
cutting contest 107
Cybotron 336–37

D

Da Brat 373
Dagara people 14
dance music: hip-hop 378–79
dance(s)/dancing 17, 41; *la calinda* 39; and disco 321–23; popular 39; and ragtime 164; role of in ring shout 55–57; separation of jazz from 181; in seventeenth/eighteenth centuries 36–38
D'Angelo 292; *Brown Sugar* 291–92, 295
Darktown Follies 223
Das Efx 378; "They Want Efx" 376, *377*
Davies, Samuel 52
Davis, Anthony 154
Davis, Rev. Gary 199
Davis, Miles 175, 176, 178, 181–82, 183; *Bitches Brew* 181
Dayton 310
Debussy, Claude 115
Dédé, Edmund 143
Deep Space 336
Def Jam Records 361–62
Delos Mars, Louisa Melvin 221
Delta Rhythm Boys 91
Detroit 342, 350; electronic music in *see* Detroit Techno
Detroit Electronic Music Festival 339, 350
Detroit Techno 9, 10, 335–53; and 1217 Griswold 346–47; black culture and musical institutions in 342–45; characteristics of 335–36; definition 339–42; and disco 336, 337, 339, 343, 344; history 336–37; masks and invisibility 347–50; corporate connection 349; and radio 343–44; and rave scene 337, 339, 345–47
Dett, R. Nathaniel 26, 146–47
DeVeaux, Scott 173
Diddley, Bo 136, 248, 251
Dilla, J. (Jay Dee) 371
Dilworth, Thomas 215
Dinwiddie Colored Quartet 80–89
"Dip Your Finger in the Water" 79
Direct Drive 336
disco 263, 289, 296, 310, 320–30, 333: African American roots 325, 333; backlash 328–29; beat 326; blending 325; and club music 329–30; and dance 321–23; definition 289; and DJs 320, 323–25, 326–27; emergence of 320, 321; experimenting with by soul artists 290; fusion with funk 310–12;

and gays 322–23; and house 330–32; industry 327–28; role of television 327; and 12-inch single 325, 328; and *Saturday Night Fever* 328; sound of 326–27; venues 321–22
Dixie Hummingbirds 82
Dixon Jr, Kenny 338, 339, 347–49
Dixon, Willie 87
DJ Screw 372
DJ Slip 382–83
DJs 30, 252, 267, 278, 282, 295, 312, 315, 322, 328, 329, 330, 355; and Detroit techno 337, 340, 343, 344, 345, 346; and disco 320, 323–25, 326–27; hip-hop 357–58, 360; and house 332; and the "mix" 359; mobile 354–55, 357; and old school rap 374; rap 30, 355, 357; and underground 380
Domino, Fats 249, 254
doo-wop 251, *251*
Dorsey, Thomas A. 136, 189, 190, 194–95, *194*, 197, 202–03, 207; "Precious Lord, Take My Hand" 201
double entendre 54
double time 168
Douglass, Frederick 6, 34
Dozier, Lamont 290
Dr. Dre 295, 316, 365, 371, 384
drama shout 56
Dranes, Arizona 193
Drifters, The 248, 256
drug use 175; and funk 307
drums/drumming 6, 8, 14, 24, 25, 27, 35, 55; and art/classical music 155, 156; African instrument 4, 5; body as substitute 25; in Congo Square 39; *deba* 5; and Detroit techno 335, 345, 346; and disco 326; drum machine 10, 312, 327, 331, 345, 368, 378; and funk 302, 307; and gospel 193; and hip-hop/rap 359, 360, 373, 378; and jazz 166, 167, 168, 173, 174, 179; and *la calinda* 39; and quartets 86; and rhythm and blues (R&B) 248, 259; in seventeenth/eighteenth centuries 36–38; and slaves 6, 25, 27; and soul 293, 294; talking 10
dub 355; definition of 355
Dunn, Johnny 11
Dupri, Jermaine 372–73
Dvořák, Antonin 144

E

Earth, Wind & Fire 306, 313, *313*, 314
Eazy-E 369
ecstatic worship 54
Edmonds, Kenny "Babyface" 265

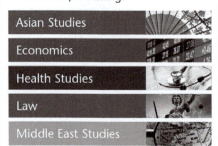

#0582 - 240616 - C0 - 254/178/26 - PB - 9780415881814